D1035001

The Biographical Bible

The Biographical *Bible*

Exploring the Biblical Narrative *from* Adam and Eve *to* John of Patmos

Ruth A. Tucker

BakerBooks
a division of Baker Publishing Group
Grand Rapids, Michigan

Published by Baker Books
a division of Baker Publishing Group
P.O. Box 6287, Grand Rapids, MI 49516-6287
www.bakerbooks.com

Printed in the United States of America

Library of Congress Cataloging-in-Publication Data is on file at the Library of Congress, Washington, DC.

ISBN 978-0-8010-1481-9 (pbk.)

13 14 15 16 17 18 19 7 6 5 4 3 2 1

In keeping with biblical principles of creation stewardship, Baker Publishing Group advocates the responsible use of our natural resources. As a member of the Green Press Initiative, our company uses recycled paper when possible. The text paper of this book is composed in part of post-consumer waste.

To four extraordinary
and delightful grandchildren

Kayla Tucker
and
Mitch, Ashley, and Zach Bylsma

CONTENTS

ACKNOWLEDGMENTS

I wish to thank the many individuals at Baker Books for their confidence and enthusiasm in publishing this volume. From beginning to end I have benefited from an unswerving professionalism and a very accommodating spirit. Thanks to Michael Cook, Heather Brewer, and Ruth Anderson for their expertise and collaboration with me in matters of design and publicity. Special appreciation goes to Executive Editor Robert Hosack for his confidence in my work over the years and in this book specifically. To my editor James Korsmo I owe a debt of gratitude for going above and beyond the call of duty in working though the manuscript. He is an avid reader and scholar, and his editorial proficiency has served this volume well. I also thank my friend and colleague Jean-Paul Heldt for his careful reading and hunt for errors. To the extent that there are any errors remaining, I take sole responsibility.

Without my husband John Worst, I cannot imagine how I would have brought this book to completion. He read through and edited the entire manuscript four times. And not just that. He pored over it as though it were his own. Our lively interaction and arguments over points of interpretation and presentation are lurking behind virtually every page. To him I express my profound gratitude and abiding love.

MAPS

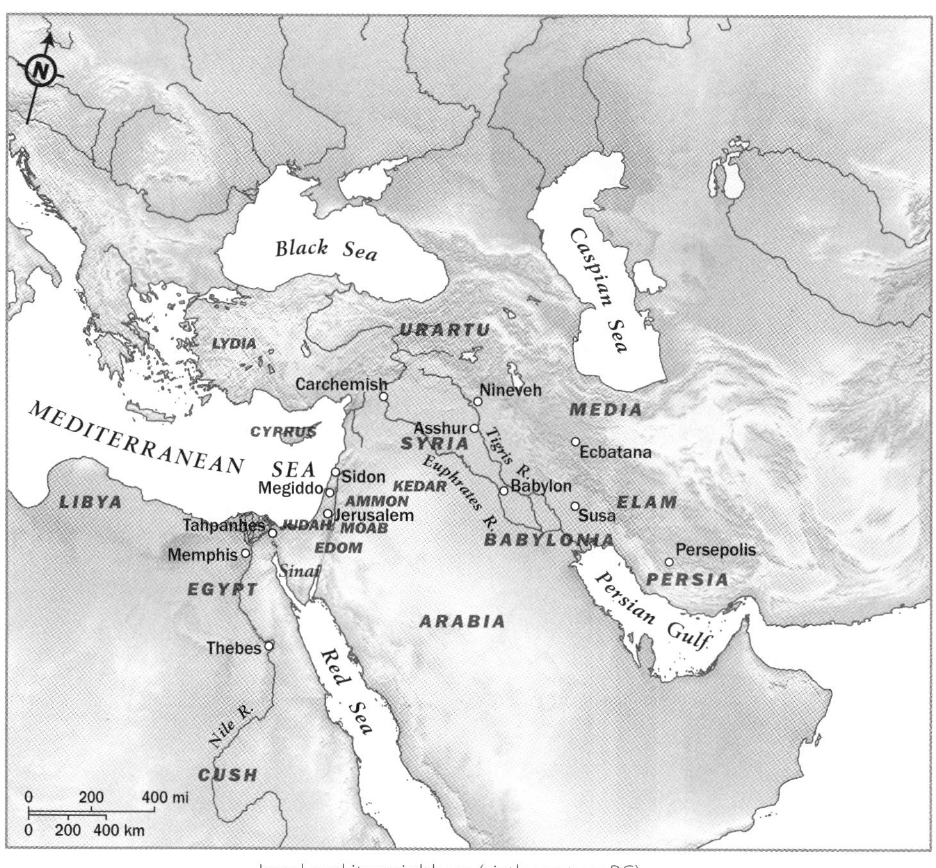

Israel and its neighbors (sixth century BC)

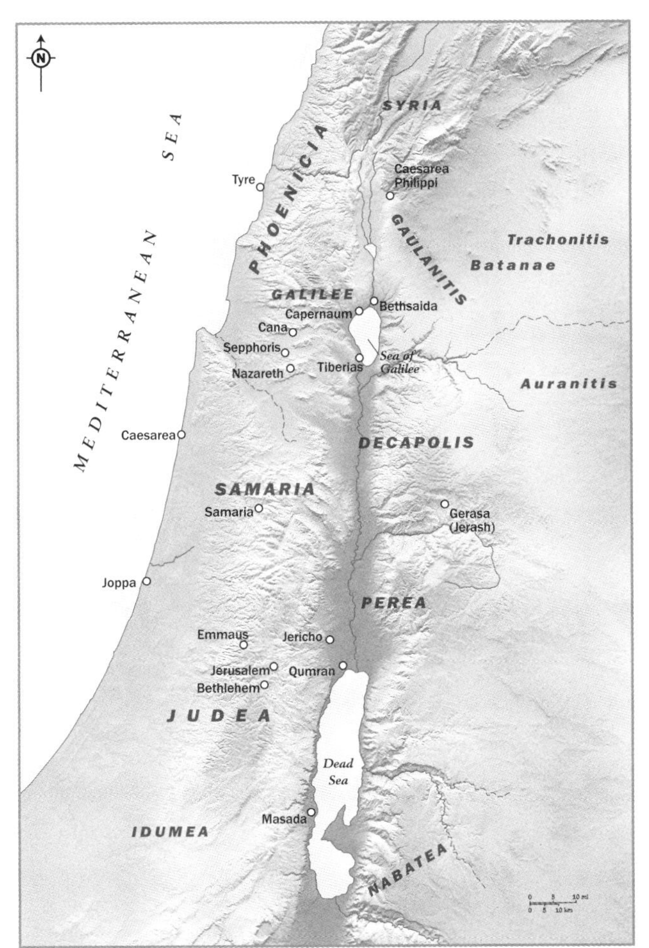

Palestine in the time of Jesus

Major locations of the New Testament

INTRODUCTION

When King Hezekiah learns from the prophet Isaiah that he is terminally ill (with a boil) and that he ought to set his house in order, he breaks down and weeps, pleading with God to heal him. Isaiah departs and is hardly out of earshot when the Lord speaks, telling him to inform Hezekiah not to worry—more precisely, that he has heard Hezekiah's prayer and seen his tears and will reward him with fifteen more years of prosperous rule. With a lump of figs, per Isaiah's instructions, the boil is healed. But how will Hezekiah know for certain that God really means what he says? He is apprehensive. He needs a guarantee. (Does he have a fifteen-year planner with appointments already scheduled?) He tells Isaiah he wants a sign. Isaiah gives him a choice. The sundial can go either forward ten degrees or backward the same distance. Hezekiah, desperate for peace of mind, is determined to put God to the hardest test. He opts for backward. Isaiah cries out to the Lord, and the sundial goes backward.

Generations earlier the prophet Balaam has a short and rather routine conversation with his ass, leaving the reader with the distinct impression that the prophet and the ass may have conversed before. Later on Elisha is traveling with his students to establish a satellite campus near the Jordan River. As they are felling trees to frame out the student center, an ax head flies off the handle and lands in the river. Elisha tosses a stick into the water and the ax head swims to meet it, and the felling of trees continues.

The prophet Hosea is ordered by the Lord to marry a prostitute. Jonah, swallowed by a big fish, lives in its innards for three days and is spewed out no worse for wear. Paul is caught up to the third heaven, where he experiences such indescribable wonders that he is dumbstruck. John of Patmos tops that when he becomes more than a spectator in the most spectacular apocalyptic live production of all times.

The Bible is the most fantastic book to fall into the hands of humankind. Its characters are alive, authentic, and utterly unpredictable. They work miracles and serve the needy as often as they succumb to Satan's wiles; they murder and rape; they marry, mourn, and manipulate; they confess sordid sins and worship God in ways that would today gross us out. Every predicament and emotion and enchantment found in the twenty-first century is somewhere lurking in the pages of Scripture.

Yet for many publishers and preachers and ordinary people, the Bible is largely a manual of propositions. The colorful personalities pushing their way out of its pages are seen as secondary—if that. But any attempt to turn this incredible chronicle into a theological dissertation destroys the very essence of its message. We learn how to live and how to die by putting ourselves into the narrative. Indeed, we recognize these characters by looking in the mirror.

By getting to know biblical characters we also find role models whose actions and words are as contemporary today as they were in ancient times. Who would have thought that stodgy old Nehemiah would rise out of the Old Testament demanding fairness in civic life? He rails at those who are grasping for wealth on the backs of workers: "What you're doing is wrong. Is there no fear of God left in you? . . . Give them back their foreclosed fields, vineyards, olive groves, and homes right now. And forgive your claims on their money, grain, new wine, and olive oil."[1]

My perspective on the Bible as I present these fascinating characters is not one of a textual critic. Nor do I seek to *harmonize* passages that appear to be in conflict. It is not my purpose to interact with the scholarly literature over such matters as the location of geographical sites or the authorship of biblical books. Rather, this volume is a serious endeavor to offer a very basic biographical overview of the Bible without any attempt to explain what sometimes appear to be historical or geographical inaccuracies or contradictions. Here we see the Bible unvarnished in its natural beauty with all its knots and rough edges. I make no effort to sand it down and smooth it over.

Indeed, we often do a great disservice to the Bible when we expend our energy in forcing the characters and events into logical formulas that fit our rational twenty-first-century minds. There is a place for simply letting the Bible be the Bible without assuming it needs our scholarly elucidation. At the same time, to maintain the flow of the narrative, I make judgments regarding such matters as geography, chronology, and familial relationship when the text is less than clear.

Like the Bible itself, this volume is at times repetitive. The account of Moses naturally overlaps with that of Joshua. So also Saul and David, Jesus and Peter. Yet it is my goal to give each individual featured his or her own story. When Abigail seems entirely glossed over in the section on David, the reader must wait for Abigail's own story. The same is true for Joseph. He is often appended to Mary in a way that does not allow him to stand alone.

I purposely avoid controversial biblical debates such as whether and how the sun stood still, and the time frame of the six days of creation. In the seventeenth century Irish Archbishop James Ussher calculated that the earth was created in six days, beginning October 23, 4004 BC. For the purposes of this volume that date works as well as any other, far better, indeed, than the 13.7 billion-year span since the Big Bang.

The Bible comes with ready-made partitions: Old and New Testaments and sixty-six books. In this volume there are twenty-four chapters collected in three eight-chapter parts. Part 1, "From Paradise to the Land of Promise," begins with Adam and ends with the conquest of Canaan. Land is a key theme. Part 2, "Kings and Prophets Guide God's People," begins with the story of Ruth that leads to the line of David and successive kings with prophets close at hand. Governance is a key theme. Part 3, "A Messiah and His Mission," begins with a young virgin who gives birth to the *Son of the living God* and ends with an astonishing Revelation. Following Jesus is the central theme.

By allowing the structure of the Bible to serve as an outline, a less-than-precise chronological account, combined with a topical layout, emerges. For example, in part 3, on the New Testament, Jesus' lesser-known disciples and his women followers are grouped together in separate chapters. In the Old Testament the so-called Major Prophets precede the Minor Prophets, and are often out of chronological order. Likewise Job, whose story is told in what is often thought to be the oldest book of the Bible, follows Esther. For the student interested in chronology, biblical time lines are readily available elsewhere.

An acquaintance recently asked if I would be including a section on the reliability of the biblical texts. I told him, much to his chagrin, that I would not. I intentionally avoid such matters as inerrancy, inspiration, poetic license, apologetics, and theological debates. Nor do I seek to present the Bible as a grand narrative. There are biblical scholars and theologians who are far better equipped to handle these areas of study than I am. My aim is to present figures in Scripture as the Bible portrays them—nothing more, nothing less.

It is true that many readers of the Bible challenge its reliability, though not always so lightheartedly as George Gershwin envisioned in *Porgy and Bess.* "The things that you're liable to read in the Bible," sings Sportin' Life, "ain't necessarily so." This volume, however, is not for believers only. The Bible is universally hailed as a singularly great collection of ancient literature. Biblical stories and quotations have become embedded in our language. The Bible is the best seller of all time. Publication, circulation, and translation statistics are mind-boggling. Yet biblical literacy even among devout Christians is shockingly low. The Beloit College "Mindset List" for the class of 2016 supports this conclusion: "The Biblical sources of terms such as 'Forbidden Fruit,' 'The writing on the wall,' 'Good Samaritan,' and 'The Promised Land' are unknown to most of them."[2]

Hopefully this book will serve to enlarge the illustrious world of the Bible for believers and skeptics alike.

But even believers struggle with believing the Bible. So it was with Billy Graham.

Early in his ministry he was wracked with doubts and at a turning point, not knowing which way to go. He later recalled being alone on a moonlit night at a mountain retreat center in San Bernardino, California. He gripped his Bible and prayed a prayer that would define his life: "Father I am going to accept this as Thy Word—by *faith*. I'm going to allow faith to go beyond my intellectual questions and doubts, and I will believe this to be your inspired Word."

Intellectual questions and doubts naturally arise when we read Bible stories because to our rational minds they often seem so utterly unbelievable. Perhaps we need a new frame of reference. When we open the Bible we should enter its pages with an attitude of *Bring it on!* Only then will we see the power of this incredible book.

Bible people are part of my earliest memories. As a child they effortlessly inhabited my psyche. I looked forward each summer to vacation *Bible* school. Then on graduating from high school, I enrolled in a *Bible* college, transferring later to a liberal arts college where I graduated with a *Bible* minor with four semesters of biblical Greek under my belt. I have been a member of three different *Bible* churches and have for some three decades taught in *Bible* colleges and seminaries. I have truly been immersed in the Bible my entire life. In writing this volume, however, I have come to love the Bible as never before. For the first time ever I have been able to relax and allow the Bible to simply speak for itself, without fighting to make it suit contemporary mores and my own tastes. It is my hope that readers will come to love the Bible as I do.

PART 1

FROM *Paradise* TO THE LAND OF *Promise*

1

ADAM, EVE, AND THE BOYS

From Eden to the Tower of Babel

The Bible begins with biography. The opening summary of creation quickly zeros in on Adam and Eve. The astronomer, the geologist, the botanist, or the zoologist looking for specialized facts finds the record wanting. But the biographer fares far better.

Perhaps the most striking feature of Adam and Eve is that they have no history. They have no conversations that begin with *Remember when . . .* Nor do they have a context apart from the unpopulated haven in which they live. They name animals and eat from fruit stands in the Garden, but there is no chitchat about neighbors or the weather. Nor do they have aches and pains to discuss—no bickering or boasting in that perfect paradise. Life might seem mundane to a modern observer, but they know nothing else.

Before they die, however, when they are centenarians many times over (Adam, navigating his tenth century), they have a shared history. They have memories of joys and sorrows. Life has been anything but a free ride in Paradise. They have children and grandchildren (perhaps to twenty generations) and neighbors.

Noah, too, has a history—an entire half millennium before his life's calling begins. He has ancestors and neighbors, and he worries about the weather. Life is anything but mundane.

After the flood, Noah's family of eight starts all over again. It is an opportunity for a new beginning. But hardly are they back on dry land when the sinning resumes, this time without the aid of a serpent. How different, in comparison to the Garden, is the mucky land and all its post-flood wreckage. This is surely no paradise for Noah's family. But they soldier on and populate the earth and build cities and a magnificent Tower until once again God is pushed to the limit.

The introductory chapters of Genesis present God as personally proactive with humankind. God walks in the Garden in the cool of the evening and indeed gets up close and personal when Adam and Eve disobey. God is also in the thick of it when Cain kills his brother. In fact, there are five times prior to the call to Abraham when God's judgment, with far-reaching consequences, falls on human beings: on Adam and Eve and the serpent, on Cain, on the whole earth at the time of Noah, on Canaan (Ham's son), and on the earth's inhabitants when the Tower was built.

Nothing, however, bears consequences comparable to the first sin in the Garden. That Adam and Eve disobeyed God would appear on the surface to be less than noteworthy. Turn on the evening news; sin is featured in almost every story. In comparison, the sin in the Garden appears petty. But their succumbing to temptation is anything but trivial. It upended their world. Indeed, their story of disobedience will be told to the end of time as a deterrent to all those who would defy God.

This story of sin, however, is much more than a morality tale. The kicker in God's punishment (as it was in the initial warning) is death. Adam and Eve will return to the dust of the ground. Bad enough. But it would be left to the apostle Paul to reveal the cosmic repercussions. Paul

Saint Augustine and Adam and Eve

Augustine believed that Adam and Eve's choice to disobey God had led to disobedience within their own bodies. Sexual desire, because it operates independently of the human mind and will, became for Augustine a privileged symptom of the sinful human attempt to assert autonomy against God. The result of the original sin, Augustine argued, was that human beings lost control even over themselves. . . . From the very beginning, Augustine argues, God intended human community to be knit together by the closest possible bond, that of blood relationship. Therefore, God determined that sexual reproduction should be the natural means of producing individuals who were, quite literally, born for friendship in community. This, Augustine says, was the significance of God's taking of Eve from Adam's side. It signified the powerful union of two people who walk side by side, with their eyes fixed ahead of them, focused on the same goal.

David G. Hunter, "Sex, Sin and Salvation: What Augustine Really Said" proclaims point-blank: "By one man sin entered into the world."[1] Because of their colossal—and *original*—sin, neither Adam nor Eve has fared well since Paul's writing.

It is interesting to note that the story of Adam and Eve is never again mentioned in Scripture, except by Paul in passing. He states in 1 Timothy 2 that Eve was the one who was deceived and became the sinner (while Adam apparently sinned knowing full well what he was doing). Elsewhere he states that "just as Eve was deceived by the serpent's cunning," all Christians are vulnerable to being "led astray from . . . sincere and pure devotion to Christ."[2]

Nor, for all its significance to the antediluvian world, is the story of Noah and the flood mentioned again in the Old Testament.[3] In the New Testament Jesus compares the end times to "the days of Noah," and Peter refers to Noah in both of his epistles and the writer of Hebrews champions him for his faith.[4]

Adam and Eve, not surprisingly, merit no mention in Hebrews or elsewhere for any admirable traits. A closer look at this first couple, however, should challenge us to rethink our preconceptions of them. Hitler, Stalin, and Osama bin Laden are rightly identified by their sins. Not Adam and Eve. They are *us*—in the mirror and in God's image. We see our own reflections in them more than in any other male/female partnership in the Bible.

Adam and Eve No Fairy Tale

But so far as this account is concerned, what, I ask you, could sound more like a fairy tale if you were to follow your reason? Would anyone believe this account about the creation of Eve if it were not so clearly told? This is a reversal of the pattern of the entire creation. Whatever is born alive, is born of the male and the female in such a manner that it is brought forth into the world by the female. Here the woman herself is created from the man by a creation no less wonderful than that of Adam, who was made out of a clod of earth into a living soul. This is extravagant fiction and the silliest kind of nonsense if you set aside the authority of Scripture and follow the judgment of reason.

Martin Luther, *Lectures on Genesis 1–5*, 123

Adam and Eve: Paradise Lost

The story of Adam and Eve is the culmination of the creation account told in the first chapters of Genesis—the world created in six days, humankind being the capstone. There are two versions of this fashioning of man and woman. In the first account, found in chapter 1, the human being—male and female—is created in God's own image and charged with the responsibility of being fruitful in populating the earth as well as caring for it. There is not yet any mention of the Garden or of sin lurking just around the corner. All is good—so good that on the seventh day the Lord rests from his six days of labor.

The second creation story, as told in chapter 2 of Genesis, makes reference to the lack of vegetation and then jumps directly to the more personalized creation of the male Adam. This is the most familiar account—no doubt because it is such a mesmerizing story.

The Creator forms the man out of dirt and then breathes life into him. In the twinkling of God's eye, Adam is alive and aware of his luxuriant surroundings.

This lush oasis is all Adam knows. He has no idea that there is another whole world outside the Garden, a wild rocky arid range where loneliness and perils abound. Here in the Garden there is abundance—a verdant arboretum overflowing with shade trees and palms and vines and ferns and moss and berry bushes and hanging fruit and fragrant flowers. Here he is soothed by the sounds of rippling brooks and waterfalls and songbirds, and the sight of newborn speckled fawns. Here in the Garden the man enjoys his very own paradise.

Adam has no boyhood. No nursing at a mother's breast, no toddling from bench to bench, no climbing trees or building forts. His consciousness begins as a fully formed man. His first recollections are of God taking him and putting him to work in a glorious botanical garden with a river running through it. *Work* is his first activity. He is the groundskeeper.

With work comes hunger. He hears God's voice telling him that the plump, ripe fruit hanging from the trees is there for his nourishment. He can eat anything he likes except the fruit from the Tree-of-Knowledge-of-Good-and-Evil. It stands in the middle of the Garden in plain sight. If he eats from it, he will die. Adam might have responded with the most-often-asked child's question, *why?* Or he might have asked God what he meant by the word *die*. But maybe he simply shrugs *whatever* and goes back to his work.

Eve tempts Adam with forbidden fruit

The next time Adam encounters God, he is watching what seems like the equivalent of a circus parade. Unbeknownst to Adam, God has decided that he is not complete without a mate. So God lines up the living creatures and parades them in front of Adam. Life is now getting a lot more interesting as he studies them, comprehending for the first time that these creatures and he have common characteristics: eyes, ears, mouth, legs. Adam does what comes naturally. He forms a word for each and every animal he sees. He names the birds as well.

As Adam names the creatures he is also unconsciously sizing up each one as a potential mate. Nothing he sees is remotely suitable. So, interesting as this parade has been, he is left with a hollow feeling inside. He's not sure what he wants, but whatever it is, he has not as yet laid eyes on it. In the midst of his contemplation, he falls asleep. In his deep slumber, God performs surgery, fashioning Eve from one of his ribs.

The next thing he knows he's shaking his head and blinking his eyes in the recovery room—actually the spot on the ground where he dozed off. But this was something more historic than a nap or night's rest. He reaches for his side and pulls away, wondering what's happened to his rib cage. What's going on? At that moment, she is standing before him in all her naked beauty. Wow! He immediately recognizes her as bone of his bone, and flesh of his flesh. She is *woman* because she is part of him.

Even though they have never met before and are both stark naked, neither one reaches for a fern or a giant tropical hibiscus for covering. They have no shame, and with no rings, no veil, no tux, they become husband and wife.

Whether or not there is conversation between them is not disclosed. But sometime later Eve finds herself talking with a serpent. That a snake would talk does not appear to surprise her. Why not? She barely comprehends the particulars of God's incredible creation. The snake asks her a question that to her seems innocuous.

A Lonely Woman in the Garden

SATURDAY.—I am almost a whole day old, now. I arrived yesterday. . . .

NEXT WEEK SUNDAY.—All the week I tagged around after him and tried to get acquainted. I had to do the talking, because he was shy, but I didn't mind it. . . .

WEDNESDAY.—We are getting along very well indeed, now, and getting better and better acquainted. He does not try to avoid me any more, which is a good sign, and shows that he likes to have me with him. . . . During the last day or two I have taken all the work of naming things off his hands, and this has been a great relief to him, for he has no gift in that line. . . . Whenever a new creature comes along I name it before he has time to expose himself by an awkward silence. . . . I have no defect like this. The minute I set eyes on an animal I know what it is.

THURSDAY.—My first sorrow. Yesterday he avoided me and seemed to wish I would not talk to him. . . . But when night came I could not bear the lonesomeness, and went to the new shelter which he has built, to ask him what I had done that was wrong and how I could mend it and get back his kindness again; but he put me out in the rain, and it was my first sorrow.

SUNDAY.—It is pleasant again, now, and I am happy; but those were heavy days; I do not think of them when I can help it. . . . He talks very little. Perhaps it is because he is not bright, and is sensitive about it and wishes to conceal it. . . .

TUESDAY.—All the morning I was at work improving the estate; and I purposely kept away from him in the hope that he would get lonely and come. But he did not.

Mark Twain, *Eve's Diary*

She does not know that the serpent is more crafty than his speech reveals. Indeed, he appears to be no more than curious. "Do I understand," he casually asks, "that God told you not to eat from any tree in the garden?"[5]

The woman responds by telling the serpent that his understanding is wrong. They, in fact, are permitted to eat from any and all of the fruit trees in the Garden, with the exception of the tree growing right in the middle, which she does not identify by its full seven-word name. That one, she tells him, they dare not eat or even touch, or they will die. Why did she add the *touching* restriction? Had Adam embellished the rule for her just to add weight to God's words?

The snake, clever as he is, tells the woman with all the calm confidence he can muster: "You won't die. God knows that the moment you eat from that tree, you'll see what's really going on. You'll be just like God, knowing everything, ranging all the way from good to evil."[6] He is pitting her against the Creator. *God has his selfish reasons*, he is telling her, *but they do not coincide with your own best interests*.

Knowledge is not Eve's (nor Adam's) strong suit. As a fully formed woman, she does not have the advantage of twenty years of living and learning. There are so many facts and figures and philosophical conundrums that she no doubt would love to have at her fingertips. If the serpent is right, the fruit on this tree just might be the key to wisdom. And the name—Knowledge of Good and Evil—surely does make the tree alluring.

So she succumbs to the serpent's wiles. She takes the fruit in her hand. Nothing happens when she touches it, as she had been led to believe. So far, so good. Then she takes a bite and gives some to Adam, who also eats it. He apparently has been standing right there all the while, making no protest.

At that moment something happens—something both psychological and spiritual. Neither one could have articulated exactly what transpired, but they now see themselves for who they are. They are suddenly ashamed of their nakedness—so ashamed they tie together fig leaves so as to cover their private parts. No sooner have they done that than they hear God rustling the branches as he moves through the Garden.

The breezy sound is something they had no doubt heard before and easily took for granted. This time, however, they are afraid and try to conceal themselves from God. Then they hear his voice. This, they quickly realize, is no game of hide and seek. God is dead serious. He calls them up short by simply asking, *Where are you?*

They know immediately they're in trouble. Adam admits that he had heard God in the Garden but that he was too fearful

Adam Acting Stupidly

Just as Adam stupidly began to flee, so he answers most stupidly; so thoroughly had sin deprived him of all discernment and good sense. He wants to inform God that he is naked—God, who created him naked.

Martin Luther, *Lectures on Genesis 1–5*, 174

to respond because he was naked. So God asks him straight up who had informed him he was naked. How did he even come up with the concept of nudity? (Did his eating the fruit give him this insight?) Then God goes directly to the heart of the matter: "Did you eat from that tree I told you not to eat from?"[7]

A straightforward answer would have been *yes*. But Adam blames "the Woman you put here with me."[8] She was the one who took the fruit, ate it, and then handed it to him. So God asks the Woman what this is all about. She blames the serpent, insisting he deceived—or seduced—her.

At this point Adam talks no more. He only listens as God pronounces curses, first to the serpent, who had apparently come back around in the cool of the evening when God was having his less-than-pleasant conversation with Adam and Eve. Adam and Eve hear God say to the serpent that he will be the most cursed of the creatures, slithering on his belly and eating dirt.

In all the circumference of Expression, those guileless words of Adam and Eve never were surpassed, "I was ashamed and hid myself."

Emily Dickinson, cited in Kathleen Norris, *Cloister Walk*

Then it is the Woman's turn to hear her penalty for disobedience. She will now have pain in childbearing, as she apparently otherwise would not have had. And she will now be under the rule of her husband. Even though she wants to please him, he will seek to dominate her.

Finally they hear God pronounce Adam's portion of the curse. Because he did not obey God and refuse to eat the fruit his wife offered him, the ground will be cursed, bringing forth thorns and thistles and weeds of all sorts. He will sweat and toil all day long just to get a decent harvest. He will endure long years of arduous labor in the process of providing sustenance for his family. But at the end of his life, he as well as the Woman will die and return to the earth: "You started out as dirt, you'll end up dirt."[9]

They had eaten from that tree, and they now have a vast sense of understanding that they would not have otherwise had. Did the Woman imagine she would have babies painlessly, or did she not even know there was such an experience as childbirth until this time? Does she dread the idea of Adam's ruling over her—indeed, *lording* it over her? What does Adam think when he hears he will be attempting to dominate her? And can he even imagine the kind of work God is assigning him? Until now he has enjoyed all the sustenance he needs without undue hardship in tilling the hardscrabble soil.

And death? Had he even known he had been molded from the dust of the ground? Having apparently assumed that he and the Woman would live forever, he now hears that he will die and end up as dirt. And does he now realize how much pain and sickness they will endure?

What they were thinking is pure conjecture, but they take the penalties in silence—no complaints, no excuses. Instead Adam turns to the Woman and gives her a name:

The Good Old Days in the Garden

Around the fire and smoke on damp, chill evenings Adam and Eve would rest and tell Abel and Cain about how life used to be in the garden. They made no secret to their children of their disobedience. For centuries, by word of mouth, the record of their trespass was to be passed down through elders to children, until with the invention of writing the whole story could be put down on dried sheepskin and so preserved. But in the beginning, the tale was recounted to Abel and Cain by its two human actors, told under the stars, in the warmth of the blazing cedar boughs and the pungent incense of smoke.

Fulton Oursler, *The Greatest Book Ever Written*, 10

Eve. He now realizes the incredible role she will play as *the mother of all the living*.

Things appear to be happening quickly. Eve, now with her new name, suddenly has a new wardrobe, as does Adam—fashioned in leather by God. A nice gift. But before they have time to look at themselves in the river's reflection, they are on a forced march. Unbeknownst to them, God has been concerned about their trying to take advantage of him—perhaps even with the serpent's help. Musing to himself, God says: "The Man has become like one of us, capable of knowing everything, ranging from good to evil. What if he now should reach out and take fruit from the Tree-of-Life and eat, and live forever? Never—this cannot happen!"[10]

Cain killed Abel, and the blood cried out from the ground—a story so sad that even God took notice of it.

Marilynne Robinson, *Housekeeping*

Adam and Eve are banished from the Garden of Eden. They will meet with fierce opposition if they attempt to return. At the east entrance is stationed an angel waving a fiery sword. As for them, the unspoken message is: *Get to work. You made your bed, now lie in it.*

Cain and Abel: The Blood Cries Out

So Adam and Eve relocate outside the Garden, perhaps constructing a makeshift dwelling before tilling the soil. The hunting and gathering and homemaking roles are agreed upon as they struggle to make ends meet. In the course of coming to terms with their new life, they have sexual relations—even as they may have enjoyed in Eden. Eve becomes pregnant and bears a son. She sees him for the first time and thinks of her husband: "I've gotten a man." She is, however, quick to add—"with GOD's help."[11] They name him Cain.

Her second child, also a *man*, they name Abel. The boys grow up, and Cain's interests lie in planting and harvesting. He tills the soil by the sweat of his brow. Abel is into animal husbandry. Perhaps they work together, one growing the crops and the other tending the herds.

One day, with no apparent prompting, Cain comes to God with an offering. He harvests some of his produce and offers it to God. Abel also brings an offering—his being the choicest of the firstborn in the herd. God is pleased with the meat offering of Abel's but is displeased with Cain's offering of vegetables and grain. Cain becomes very upset. God is not impressed. "Why this tantrum?" he asks. "Why the sulking? If you do well, won't you be accepted? And if you don't do well, sin is lying in wait for you, ready to pounce; it's out to get you, you've got to master it."[12]

Cain's anger is directed not only at God but also at Abel. They are out in the field together when Cain unloads his fury on his brother. How Abel might have reacted is not revealed, but one thing leads to another, and in the end Abel is dead, Cain the killer.

Everyday *Life*

Sheepherding and Truck Farming

Cain—minus the truck—was the first truck farmer: a horticulturalist who raises grain and vegetables primarily for market. Neither Cain nor Abel appears to have been a subsistence farmer, each with a small garden and few sheep. Rather they specialized, and perhaps traded their produce and flocks with each other and on a wider scale, Cain trucking his produce to market with a donkey.

> *In ancient times, donkeys were the trucks and tractors, performing myriad agricultural and mercantile tasks, essential to commerce and daily life.*
>
> Jon Katz, *The Dogs of Bedlam Farm*, 81

"The Stone Age people of the Middle East were becoming farmers—the first farmers in the world," writes Jared Diamond in *Guns, Germs, and Steel*. "Without realizing it, these new farmers were changing the very nature of the crops around them. With every round of planting and harvesting, they'd favor ears of wheat and barley whose seeds were the biggest, tastiest or easiest to harvest."

The account of Cain and Abel does not fit the hunter/gatherer description of life that still exists in remote areas of the world today. "The transition to farming was clearly a decisive turning point in human history," continues Diamond. "People who remained hunter/gatherers couldn't produce anywhere near as much food as farmers, and also couldn't produce much food that could be stored" (*Guns, Germs, and Steel*, "Episode 1: Out of Eden," http://www.pbs.org/gunsgermssteel/show/transcript1.html).

Sheepherding, beginning in Asia Minor some four thousand years before Christ, is also a very old vocation. Because the animals needed large grazing lands, herdsmen were typically nomadic. As now, the wool provided clothing, and the meat, nourishment; also important, however, was their milk and their favored use for religious sacrificial rites.

When flocks increased in size, hired hands were employed to tend the sheep. These lowly shepherds lived solitary lives, sleeping in the open under the stars or in tents—the very sort of humble laborers who would welcome the arrival of Jesus in Bethlehem.

Cain angered by Abel's sacrifice

Cain departs in a fury, leaving Abel behind with no apparent effort to revive him. What will he tell his folks? But before he has opportunity to make up a lie for them, he is approached by God: "Where is your brother Abel?" Cain, still mad at God, snaps back: "I don't know. Am I my brother's keeper?"[13]

God, of course, knowing exactly where Abel is, tells Cain that his brother's blood is crying out to him from the ground. Then God pronounces a curse on Cain. He is driven away from the ground he once tilled and will get no more than curses from the soil he tries to work. He will continue to plant crops, but they will not thrive. More than that, God tells him he will be a restless drifter without a home.

Cain does not tell God he is sorry for the horrible crime he has just committed. Rather, he is concerned about himself. He cries out to God that his penalty is too harsh. What will he do with no fields to till and harvest? Worse than that, he fears he himself will be killed—a fear common to homeless people. God, however, is not

John Calvin and the First Brothers

Whether both the brothers had married wives, and each had a separate home, Moses does not relate. This, therefore, remains to us in uncertainty, although it is probable that Cain was married before he slew his brother; since Moses soon after adds, that he knew his wife, and begot children: and no mention is there made of his marriage. Both followed a kind of life in itself holy and laudable. For the cultivation of the earth was commanded by God; and the labor of feeding sheep was not less honorable than useful; in short, the whole of rustic life was innocent and simple, and most of all accommodated to the true order of nature. This, therefore, is to be maintained in the first place, that both exercised themselves in labors approved by God, and necessary to the common use of human life. Whence it is inferred, that they had been well instructed by their father. The rite of sacrificing more fully confirms this; because it proves that they had been accustomed to the worship of God. The life of Cain, therefore, was, in appearance, very well regulated. . . . [But] it is not to be doubted, that Cain conducted himself as hypocrites are accustomed to do; namely, that he wished to appease God, as one discharging a debt, by external sacrifices, without the least intention of dedicating himself to God.

John Calvin, *Commentary on Genesis*, Vol. 1, Gen. 4:3–5

about to end Cain's line. He promises that if he is murdered, the guilty one will suffer seven times over. For protection, God puts a mark on him to ward off any attacks.

So Cain goes off to a desolate area east of Eden where he is no longer in the presence of God. Adam and Eve are surely heartbroken when they learn what has happened.

Through intercourse with her companion the woman conceived and bore two sons. But when God received the sacrifice of the one with honor, the other was inflamed with envy; he rushed on his brother, overcame and killed him, becoming the first parricide by shedding a brother's blood. Then the whole race rushed into accursed crime, except the just Enoch, who walked in the ways of God.

Gregory of Tours, *History of the Franks* (AD 594)

Their sons had somehow compensated for the pain and toil they encountered outside Eden. Now they have lost both of them. The sorrow seems almost too much to bear, though they may have had other children who brought comfort. And then joy comes back into their lives when Eve becomes pregnant again. Adam is 130 when she gives birth to Seth, who grows up and at age 105 gives them a grandson, Enosh, and later on more grandchildren of both sexes.

The marriage of Adam and Eve is a long one by any standard, and they have more children, daughters as well as sons. Adam lives on to be 930. Eve's death is not recorded.

In the meantime, Cain finds a wife, and she gives birth to a son, whom they name Enoch (not to be confused with Enoch in Seth's line). After a time they have a grandson, Irad, and in their old age a great-grandson, Mehujael, whose grandson Jubal took to making and playing musical instruments, particularly the flute and the lyre.

Noah: Shipbuilder for God

Noah's ancestors go back eight generations to Seth and then to Adam and Eve. When he was born his father Lamech, then 182, made a pronouncement: "He will comfort us in the labor and painful toil of our hands caused by the ground the LORD has cursed."[14] At age 500, Noah has three sons: Shem, Ham, and Japheth.

Noah is perhaps the only household name to be associated almost entirely with an object. His name is inextricably linked to the ark. Moses is associated with the burning bush, Jonah with a whale (or big

Think of all the squabbles Adam and Eve must have had in the course of their 900 years. Eve would say, "You ate the apple," and Adam would retort, "You gave it to me."

Martin Luther, *Table Talk*

fish), but only as one aspect of their stories. For Noah, the ark is essentially what defines his life.

Taken at face value, the story of the flood is horrific. It is a tsunami of historic proportions. There are no survivors apart from Noah's immediate family. The aunts and uncles and cousins—and even grandparents—die in this deluge.

Noah is the first biblical prophet, identified in the New Testament as "a preacher of righteousness."[15] Like most prophets, he no doubt appears to his neighbors and kinfolk to be more than slightly deranged. He not only calls his hapless (and wicked) neighbors to repent and warns of dire consequences if they do not, but he also demonstrates that he believes his own prophecy. He devotes all his resources, time, and energy to carrying out God's instructions.

Sons of God and Daughters of Men

That ancient figment, concerning the intercourse of angels with women, is abundantly refuted by its own absurdity; and it is surprising that learned men should formerly have been fascinated by ravings so gross and prodigious. The opinion also of the Chaldean paraphrast is frigid; namely, that promiscuous marriages between the sons of nobles, and the daughters of plebeians, is [*sic*] condemned. Moses, then, does not distinguish the sons of God from the daughters of men, because they were of dissimilar nature, or of different origin; but because they were the sons of God by adoption, whom he had set apart for himself; while the rest remained in their original condition.

John Calvin, *Commentary on Genesis*, Vol. 1, Gen. 6:1–2

Although Lamech made an optimistic prediction about his son, there is no evidence that Noah made farming any easier for his contemporaries. Lamech would live on nearly six hundred years (dying only five years before the flood), and during that time he would witness the world becoming more evil every century. It seemed everyone was in on it—people trying to outdo each other in contriving ways to act out the most disgusting and immoral behaviors possible.

And the evil does not involve humans only. Life is most strange during this era. Creatures known as Sons of God are looking down on the increasing numbers of sexually alluring girls coming to maturity. So they come down and have sexual intercourse with them, and the offspring turn out to be giants—"the mighty men of ancient lore."[16] (Perhaps mighty women as well.) As mighty as these men were, they were anything but impressive in the eyes of God:

> When human beings began to increase in number on the earth and daughters were born to them, the sons of God saw that the daughters of humans were beautiful, and they married any of them they chose. Then the Lord said, "My Spirit will not contend with humans forever, for they are mortal; their days will be a hundred and twenty years."[17]

This evil and intermingling is simply not what God had intended. Initially he cuts back the human life span. Then he becomes so disgusted that he regrets the whole creation thing altogether and says:

"I will wipe from the face of the earth the human race I have created—and with them the animals, the birds and the creatures that move along the ground—for I regret that I have made them."[18] Everyone is evil. There is simply no hope for a revival. There is not one righteous man—except for Noah.

Noah wants no part of the cesspool of sin engulfing every town and hamlet. He is basically a decent man. He does not lie, cheat, brawl, and carouse around like his neighbors do. He worships God, and God takes note of that. In fact, the two of them commune together. Noah is aware of how dire moral conditions are, but as yet he is not aware that God has come to his wits' end and plans to make a clean sweep of his creation.

The clean sweep God is talking about is a flood that will cover the entire earth—destroying absolutely everything. Before Noah has a chance to respond in horror, God tells him that he is making a covenant with him. Noah and his wife, his three sons, and his daughters-in-law will be spared.

Then God tells him to construct a huge boat that will be a refuge for not only his immediate family but also every living creature, both male and female—"two of every species of bird, mammal, and reptile."[19] The scope of this project is surely daunting. What on earth is God thinking? Indeed, Noah may have envied those who would be carried away in the clean sweep.

Noah is a farmer, and there is no indication that he had ever actually been a general contractor or builder of any kind. Nor is there any report of him being a wealthy man. How could he possibly be responsible for such a massive undertaking? God gives him guidelines, but nothing resembling a detailed blueprint.

The size of the ship alone must have made Noah dizzy. It is to be 450 feet long—the length of a football field and half again. The width is to be 75 feet, and the height 45 feet—the height of a four-story house, though the boat is to have only three stories, or decks. This gigantic structure must have a roof, a window, and a door, as well as an unspecified number of rooms. The materials list alone would have stopped anyone but Noah dead in his tracks. He must secure enough teakwood for the entire skin of his watercraft, perhaps the frame also. And the immense amount of sealer seems astronomical. It is to be coated both inside and out with pitch.

But Noah apparently doesn't blink. He simply does what he is told to do. It is hard to imagine, however, that he didn't have

An Apparent Crazy Man

Imagine that Noah knocked his house apart and used the planks to build an ark, while his neighbors looked on, full of doubt. A house, he must have told them, should be daubed with pitch and built to float cloud high, if need be. A lettuce patch was of no use at all, and a good foundation was worse than useless. The neighbors would have put their hands in their pockets and chewed their lips and strolled home to houses they now found wanting in ways they could not understand.

Marilynne Robinson, *Housekeeping*, 184

doubts. Did he ever wonder if the voice of God had been no more than a figment of his imagination? The Euphrates River certainly was known for flooding, and in his five hundred years he would not have been oblivious to such floods. But the flood of which God has warned is no mere flowing over the banks. This one would be cosmic in proportions.

There is no further communication until the work is fully accomplished. Then God tells Noah to get on board with his family and with the animals. If Noah had thought it an impossible task to corral two of every kind of creature, he now learns that the two-of-a-kind requirement refers only to unclean animals. He is to make room in his boat for seven pairs of clean animals as well as birds. But the animals seem to cooperate in this embarkation, moving up the ramp in pairs with apparently little prodding.

> *It's easy to understand the fame of the Euphrates. More than seventeen hundred miles long, it is one of the longest rivers in the world. In the spring, the melting snow from the Armenian mountains can cause it to flood twelve feet over its banks.*
>
> Charlotte Gordon, *The Woman Who Named God: Abraham's Dilemma and the Birth of Three Faiths*

Remembering the Mothers Who Drowned

Let God purge this wicked sadness away with a flood, and let the waters recede to pools and ponds and ditches, and let every one of them mirror heaven. Still, they taste a bit of blood and hair. One cannot cup one's hand and drink from the rim of any lake without remembering that mothers have drowned in it.

Marilynne Robinson, *Housekeeping*, 193

The time frame God gives him for collecting the animals seems utterly inadequate—a measly seven days. He had upwards of one hundred years to build the boat, but gets only one week to gather together the creatures. Working day and night, he gets the job done. Then the eight of them get on board. The waters begin surging from below even as the heavens open up with rain pouring down from above.

Soon the boat is afloat. Noah and his family are safe and sound inside. But surely he must be desperately trying not to think about all the kinfolk and neighbors outside caught up in the floodwaters. What a life it has been. He's less than a year shy of his six hundredth birthday. The rain and the groundwater eruptions continue for forty days and nights straight. This is the mother of all floods. Even the peaks of the tallest mountains are covered.

Then everything becomes calm and the huge ship simply drifts on the water. Month after month the flood recedes. Finally the waters evaporate to the point that the bottom of the ship stabilizes on land—turns out, however, that it is caught on a mountain in the Ararat range. Noah repeatedly scans the horizon, and at last, after some nine months, he is able to see the peaks of the range. Then some weeks later he lets loose a raven, later a dove, but neither can find a landing perch. A week goes by and he sends out the dove again,

Noah's Disgrace and Ham's Depravity

The holy patriarch, though he had hitherto been a rare example of frugality and temperance, losing all self-possession, did, in a base and shameful manner, prostrate himself naked on the ground, so as to become a laughing-stock to all. . . . God brands him with an eternal mark of disgrace. . . . Ham, by reproachfully laughing at his father, betrays his own depraved and malignant disposition. . . . He not only took pleasure in his father's shame, but wished to expose him to his brethren.

John Calvin, *Commentary on Genesis*, Vol. 1, Gen. 9:22–25

and it returns with a twig from an olive tree. The next time he sends out the dove, good news. It does not return.

When the earth is at last dried up, Noah and his family get off the boat, followed by the parade of animals. How they accomplished this while perched on a mountain range is not revealed. But the ordeal is finally over. The first thing Noah does is to make an animal offering to God. God is pleased and promises never again to destroy everything on the face of the earth. In fact, God promises to never again send a flood of such biblical proportions. That promise is sealed with a sign: "I have set my rainbow in the clouds, and it will be the sign of the covenant between me and the earth."[20]

After properly worshiping God, Noah gets down to business and back to his day job of farming. He plants a vineyard. After the vines have grown, he harvests the grapes and enjoys his first taste of wine in years. One sip leads to another until he is out cold, naked, and drunk.

Noah's son Ham goes into the tent to check on his father and sees him stark naked. He tells his brothers; they're mortified. So they together walk backward into the tent, and without accidentally stepping on their father, they cover his naked body with a blanket. The next day when Noah sobers up, he learns that Ham had seen him exposed and he curses him, or rather Ham's son Canaan. Shem and Japheth receive a blessing, but Canaan is cursed to be a slave.

As for Noah, despite the stress he has endured, he lives on for more than three hundred years, dying at the age of 950.

Top Ten Supercentenarians

A supercentenarian is someone who lives beyond 110. The book of Genesis features such individuals, whose ages are truly numbered in biblical proportions. And those are men only. Accounting for a woman's longer life span, we can speculate that members of the *second sex* lived beyond a thousand. Abraham, Isaac, and Jacob died relatively young in comparison (175, 180, 147 respectively). The top-ten countdown begins in Genesis 5, Enoch being a special case in that "he walked faithfully with God; then he was no more, because God took him away" (Gen. 5:24 NIV).

10. Enoch, 365
9. Lamech, 777
8. Mahalalel, 895
7. Enosh, 905
6. Kenan, 910
5. Seth, 912
4. Adam, 930
3. Noah, 950
2. Jared, 962
1. Methuselah, 969

Medieval depiction of the Tower of Babel

Nimrod: A Mighty Hunter

In the generations after the flood, there is a population explosion among Noah's descendants. But the world is anything but a paradise. Amid warring factions, a singular individual elbows his way to the top of the heap. Before Nimrod, there were no powerful leaders. Certainly not Adam or Cain—or Noah. Noah obeyed God, but he failed, if indeed he tried, to rally others (besides his small family) to his cause. But Nimrod comes along and is described as a mighty warrior and hunter, or perhaps better rendered "a mighty *despot*."

His realm is massive, eventually encompassing not only Babel but also several other population centers in Shinar and far beyond into Assyria, where he ruled over several more cities, including Nineveh. The Genesis text reveals nothing more of Nimrod, but according to various traditions, Nimrod was the force behind the building of the Tower of Babel. It is not a stretch to make that assumption, because the account of the Tower of Babel follows soon after the mention of Nimrod.

The Tower is one of the most fascinating little stories to find its way into the pages of Scripture. People are moving east onto the vast plain of Shinar. At that point in time everyone on the face of

Wicked Nimrod

Late one October evening, I flew into Urfa, the city believed by Turkish Muslims to be the Ur of the Chaldeans, the birthplace of the prophet Abraham. . . . Tens of thousands of people come here every year to visit a cave where Abraham may have been born and a fishpond marking the site of the pyre where he was almost burned up by Nimrod, except that God transformed the fire into water and the coals into fish. According to another local legend, God sent a swarm of mosquitoes to torment Nimrod, and a mosquito flew up Nimrod's nose and started chewing on his brain. Nimrod ordered his men to beat his head with wooden mallets, shouting "Vur ha, vur ha!" ("Hit me, hit me!"), and that's how his city came to be called Urfa.

Elif Batuman, "The Sanctuary: The World's Oldest Temple and the Dawn of Civilization," 72 the earth is speaking the same language and apparently sharing the same cultural traditions (perhaps under the tight rule of Nimrod). So they spread the word, perhaps at the prompting of their leader, that they should all come together in a bond of unity to build a great city. But more than that, they are determined to build the highest skyscraper ever known to humanity—a tower that touches the very edge of heaven. "Let's make ourselves famous," was the rationale, "so we won't be scattered here and there across the Earth."[21]

But then God comes down and checks things out. The people are up to no good. One thing leads to another, and who knows what will come of it? So God garbles their speech. Their words sound more like babbling than ordinary language. The structure becomes known as the Tower of Babel. The people are unable to carry on with further building projects, and they are all scattered, speaking different languages.

The scrambling of speech and the scattering of the people are the last recorded acts of God before he calls Abraham to leave his country and move to a new land. The span of time between Adam and Abraham as laid out in the genealogies covers some two thousand years, nearly half the time span of the entire Bible.

Concluding Observations

Incredible things happen in the eleven-chapter whirlwind introduction to the Bible. Adam and Eve inhabit the Garden; they fall into sin; one son murders another; things go from bad to worse until the whole of humankind, but for Noah and his wife and children, are wiped out in a flood. When it's all over, Noah gets drunk and a son is cursed. The creation begins anew, only to be scrambled and scattered by God.

Here in the brief biblical brochure, God creates, destroys, re-creates, and jumbles languages. In fact, no other eleven chapters of the Bible cover so much time and have made such an indelible impact on Western culture—and world culture, for that matter. The names and events are easily recognized in art, music, theater, literature, and pop culture. Who doesn't know about Adam and Eve, Cain and Abel, Noah and the ark, and the Tower of Babel?

For the reader, the two thousand years between the *In the beginning* of the first verse of the Bible and the call of Abraham in Genesis 12 fly by quickly. But for the participants the years must have dragged on. Life is incredibly hard in this era. A life span of more than nine hundred years—in an age before memory-foam mattresses, antibiotics, thermal socks, shuffleboard, and early-bird specials—can feel like forever.

Life had begun, however, in paradise. The Garden has all the comforts of home and more—no need or desire to travel. But on the outside, Adam and Eve and all their descendants will never feel fully at home again. From the Garden Adam and Eve are banished to make their dwelling east of Eden, Cain in the land of Nod. Noah floats higher on water than any human being before or since. The Tower generation is scattered. But it will be left to Abraham to journey far beyond his homeland. That journey will continue through the pages of Scripture, and from there around the globe until it ends one day in the garden along the crystal river of the New Jerusalem in John's Revelation.

Further Reading

Cassuto, Umberto. *From Adam to Noah: A Commentary on the Book of Genesis*. Jerusalem: Hebrew University, 1961.

Mathews, Kenneth A. *The New American Commentary: Genesis 1–11:26*. Nashville: Holman, 1996.

Thompson, John L. *Genesis 1–11: Reformation Commentary on Scripture*. Downers Grove, IL: InterVarsity, 2012.

2

ABRAHAM AND SARAH

Joys and Tribulations of Old Age

The literary leap from Noah and Nimrod to Abraham is far greater than two mere chapters in Genesis. Noah's personal story is thin, Nimrod's thinner yet. Noah's wife and daughters-in-law are nameless; Nimrod's are not mentioned at all. Neither one is fleshed out as a personality, apart from Noah's obedience to God and his rage at his son Ham and grandson Canaan following his drunken stupor.

Abraham, on the other hand, merits one of the most complete biographies in the entire Bible. His story begins at the end of Genesis 11 and extends to his death in chapter 25. Second only to Moses, he is the most frequently mentioned Old Testament character in the New Testament—no less than seventy-four times. His wife is named and is a personality in her own right; so also his concubine. His travel, his wealth, his network of relatives and acquaintances, his shortcomings and virtues are dished up for the biographer's buffet, though admittedly in meager portions in some instances.

As the *father* of three faiths—Judaism, Christianity, and Islam—Abraham has received considerable attention in recent years. How can the followers of these three religions live in peace? How can they work together for a better world? Is the kinship they have in Abraham a starting point? It would seem that Abraham ought to be a key that

Father of Three Faiths

The great patriarch of the Hebrew Bible is also the spiritual forefather of the New Testament and the grand holy architect of the Koran. Abraham is the shared ancestor of Judaism, Christianity, and Islam. He is the linchpin of the Arab-Israeli conflict. He is the centerpiece of the battle between the West and Islamic extremists. He is the father—in many cases, the purported biological father—of 12 million Jews, 2 billion Christians, and 1 billion Muslims around the world. He is history's first monotheist.

Bruce Feiler, *Abraham: A Journey to the Heart of Three Faiths*, 9

would unlock the door to harmonious coexistence and leave behind the millennia of rivalry and outright religious warfare. Abraham, after all, is a man who strives for peace with his neighbors. He likewise longs for peace in the family—between Sarah and Hagar, between Ishmael and Isaac.

But Abraham may be perceived as more than a peacemaker. In recent decades he has also been cited as the starting point for world evangelism—the missionary task of making disciples of all nations. "It is essential," writes John R. W. Stott, "for Christians to understand the grounds on which the Christian mission rests. Only then shall we be able to persevere in the missionary task, with courage and humility." He then points to Genesis and the call of Abraham in Genesis 12 and the accompanying promises of making him a great nation through whom all families on earth would be blessed. Stott sees Abraham as, in essence, the first missionary sent out by God: "God chose one man and his family in order, through them, to bless all the families on the earth."[1]

That the reader should find support for religious harmony and world evangelism in the life of Abraham may seem less obvious to some. Indeed, Abraham's settling in Canaan sets the stage for biblical warfare. Land and water will be the source of conflict for generations to follow and up to the present time. Warring over West Bank settlements has its origins with Abraham.

Abraham surely does not stand alone on the threshold of this early biblical narrative. His nephew Lot also plays a significant role, as does his wife Sarah and his concubine Hagar. His children and grandchildren will rise in prominence and claim the Land of Promise in the centuries that follow.

Pitying Abraham

He's childless. He's aging. He's stuck in Harran. Abraham has lived nearly half of his life . . . seventy-five years old before anything happens to him. The only thing we're told is that he comes from a long family line (the text traces his father back to Noah) and can't father children of his own. For Genesis, a narrative consumed with men, lineage, and power, the diminishing effect of this debility on Abraham is staggering. Our chief reaction upon meeting him is not admiration; it's indifference or pity. He's the ultimate blank slate: childless and childhood-less.

Bruce Feiler, *Abraham: A Journey to the Heart of Three Faiths*, 22

Abram aka Abraham: A Call to the Promised Land

In less than a dozen generations after the flood, the descendants of Noah have dispersed throughout the eastern Mediterranean world. One of those descendants is Terah, who traces his lineage back to Noah's son Shem. Like Noah, he has three sons, Abram (whose name is later changed

Everyday *Life*

High Culture in Ancient Times

Abraham was a man on the go. He is the first traveling man of the Bible. Called out of Ur of the Chaldeans, he moves to Haran, then on to the Promised Land, down to Egypt, and back again.

On leaving Ur, Terah, Abraham, and company were leaving anything but a backwater encampment. Indeed, Ur was a bustling commercial center of some one hundred thousand inhabitants—and much more: "a place of beauty, graced with towers, palaces, temples, law courts, market squares, statues, shrines, gardens, mosaics, friezes, reliefs and monuments. It was divided into rectangular blocks by paved streets lined with two-story houses. It had its own seaport and man-made canal."

It would seem to be a wonderful place to raise a family—but for its infatuation with false gods. "And so, one fine day, when the winter rains were almost over, they [Terah's household] packed all their goods and chattels onto a few dozen four-wheeled carts drawn by oxen" (Martin, "Footsteps of Abraham"). Far from being a danger-filled trek through the wild west, the route they followed was a well-patrolled, busy trade thoroughfare.

Apart from dust storms, the journey might have seemed like a summer vacation. They were on the "royal highway"—along the way encountering people "who enjoyed music and painting and sculpture and a written literature of plays, poems, epics, songs and novels" (Martin, "Footsteps of Abraham"). Upon leaving what is present-day Iraq, however, the travel would become more arduous and the culture less colorful—until later when they would encounter the glories of Egypt.

Ur in the Iraqi Desert

Today, Ur is a desert scrubland with miserable ruins jutting from terrain of sand and mud . . . in the country we now call Iraq. Unlikely or not, however, very nearly 40 centuries ago, here began a journey that transcended history, and whose arc etched a crescent of hope and faith so indelibly that it determined the motive and course of events for centuries down to this day and far beyond the borders of the nations that were in its path—places we know as Iraq, Turkey, Syria, Lebanon, Israel, Egypt, Jordan. . . . From Ur, Abraham traveled 700 miles to the borders of present-day Iraq, another 700 miles into Syria, another 800 down to Egypt by the inland road, and then back into Canaan—what is now Israel.

Malachi Martin, "Footsteps of Abraham"

to Abraham), Nahor, and Haran. Haran dies, leaving behind a son and daughter, Lot and Milcah.

Born when his father is seventy, Abraham grows up with his brothers in the bustling metropolis of Ur of the Chaldeans. The Bible gives no hint of Abraham's childhood or youth, not even a glimpse of his mother. He marries his half sister Sarah, who will hold the dubious distinction of being the first barren woman of the Bible. They are among those in Terah's large extended and intermarried family who pull up stakes and set out on an arduous journey to Canaan.

The most likely route they traversed from southern Mesopotamia (present-day Iraq) is along the western bank of the Euphrates River. They would have passed through population centers, though the caravan no doubt skirted such regions in favor of the open desert. If they had kept a steady pace they could have made the nearly seven-hundred-mile trek to Haran in a matter of months.

Where Is Ur?

Scholars disagree whether the Ur of the Chaldeans mentioned in Genesis is identical with the Sumerian city of Ur that flourished in southern Mesopotamia in the third millennium BCE. Some scholars have attempted to locate Ur in northern Mesopotamia, near the city of Haran. . . . The majority of scholars today, however, still accept the ancient Sumerian city of Ur, located on the southern bank of the Euphrates, as the place referred to in the patriarchal narratives. They also accept the biblical tradition which affirms that the ancestors of Abraham came from southern Mesopotamia.

Claude Mariottini, "Ur and Abraham"

Canaan is the final destination, but by the time they reach Haran, the northernmost point of their journey, they decide to settle down. Exhausted by the daily grind of travel, they need a rest, as do their herds and flocks. The trip may have taken a particularly hard toll on Terah, who had now passed his two hundredth birthday. During their prolonged stay, he dies at age 205.

If Abraham, now the head of the household, had intended to remain in Haran, his plans suddenly change. From seemingly out of nowhere, he hears God's voice telling him to leave his country, his kinfolk, and, more specifically, his father's household. That he would hear the voice of Yahweh in the midst of a culture of idol worship is astonishing—not entirely different from Paul hearing the voice of Jesus some two millennia later while traveling on the road to Damascus. Unlike Jesus' voice on that occasion, however, the voice Abraham hears pronounces no censure. Not a critical word about his idol-worshiping heritage. Rather, a promise:

> I will make you into a great nation,
>   and I will bless you;
> I will make your name great,
>   and you will be a blessing.
> I will bless those who bless you,
>   and whoever curses you I will
>   curse;
> and all peoples on earth
>   will be blessed through you.[2]

Abraham does not question God. In fact, he does not even reveal a normal sense of curiosity. He does not ask how he and his barren wife could possibly become a nation, much less a great one. Nor does he question God about how he could gain such a great name whereby all the inhabitants of the world would be blessed. Most notably, he does not ask, as does Paul, whose voice he is hearing. Is he already acquainted with Yahweh? Has he perhaps heard the voice of God before? Indeed, elsewhere in Scripture Abraham is said to have been called out of Ur of the Chaldeans—perhaps at the very time his father decided to leave that city.

With no further instructions or directions, Abraham begins packing for this momentous move. Everything must go—or be disposed of in a giant yard sale. He has already endured a lengthy road trip, but this time he, not his father, is calling the shots. At seventy-five he sets out for Canaan with Sarah, his nephew Lot, and a caravan that includes perhaps hundreds of kin and servants, plus a train of donkey carts, cattle, and flocks. They pass through remote terrain as well as populated regions, where the locals must surely have gaped at the gypsy tribe passing by.

As they travel they see mountains in the distance and a pass that permits them to ascend and peer down at the valley below. Here is a fertile basin bordering the Mediterranean Sea—a land like none other: barley fields, olive and fruit trees, sheep and cattle. It truly is a land flowing with milk and honey. Abraham may have asked, *Are we there yet?* But he hears no word from God.

From Haran to Canaan

This trek was like moving a small town. . . . To take all of their belongings—tents, flocks, camels, food and herds of animals—was a great undertaking.

PicturesofSilver.com, "Abraham—Father of Believing"

When he reaches Shechem, however, God appears to him, indicating that this indeed is the Promised Land. Like Noah, who acknowledged God after his safe landing centuries earlier, Abraham keeps his priorities straight. He collects stones and fashions an altar and settles down for a time. From there, the party moves on toward Bethel (near Jerusalem), and again Abraham pitches his tents and builds an altar of stones.

The Bible emphasizes Abraham's faith. That he travels with a large party of people and animals while not knowing where he is going is surely an example of faith. That he should end up settling in Canaan makes his faith even more impressive. Canaan is not a land waiting to be inhabited. Besides well-cultivated farmland and orchards, there are prosperous towns with a thriving cultural climate. Archaeological sites show well-built homes and an impressive sense of design in jewelry, furniture, and pottery.

The Canaanites, unlike Abraham and most of his kin, are literate, many of them multilingual. They, too, build altars and worship gods on special occasions. They fear their enemies; thus the heavily walled towns. Does Abraham wonder how he and his wife—with no children—along with his small band of followers and servants could ever take over this well-fortified land and populate it with countless descendants?

If the superior civilization and apparent military capabilities of the Canaanites do not shake Abraham's faith, famine does. He has hardly entered the region when the lush landscape begins to wilt. Crops and orchards dry up. How can this really be the Promised Land? So Abraham and his followers pack up and begin a long and difficult journey to Egypt through the Negev desert, the most desolate land they have yet traversed.

Egypt is an ancient civilization that towers over that of Canaan, even more so over Abraham's homeland. Stories of the glories of the successive dynasties had circulated throughout the known world. Slaves propped up the economy. It was no secret that the famed Pharaohs and their royal entourages were not necessarily friendly to outsiders. Their rule was autocratic. Indeed, Pharaohs were considered gods.

Abraham needs respite for himself and his followers, but at what price? He has heard stories of misfortune in Egypt, and he fears for his life—particularly as it relates to his drop-dead gorgeous wife. Though in her seventies, she is still a smashing lady to behold. Word will quickly spread to the Pharaoh's chambers, Abraham reasons, and she will be snatched as another concubine, though not before he is disposed of. Even the Pharaoh could not rightfully take another man's wife—a widow, yes.

So Abraham comes up with a scheme and spells it out very clearly to Sarah. In fact, his connivance constitutes the first recorded words of Abraham in the Bible: "Look. We both know that you're a beautiful woman. When the Egyptians see you they're going to say, 'Aha! That's his wife!' and kill me. But they'll let you live. Do me a favor: tell them you're my sister. Because of you, they'll welcome me and let me live."[3] Sarah is, in fact, Abraham's half sister, so he may have rationalized that this was merely a white lie. But it was deceit that would have serious consequences, particularly for Sarah.

A Long-Suffering Pharaoh

It's hard to be sympathetic to a biblical character with the name of Pharaoh, but there are certain few pharaohs who have done okay by the Jews. . . . In any case, our Pharaoh is the victim of circumstances, and a circumstance of Abraham's making. Pharaoh protests, "What have you done to me?! Why didn't you tell me she was your wife?" . . . He is clearly upset, affronted. He cannot imagine the type of person who might put another man at risk of committing adultery, to say the least of someone pimping his own wife. Pharaoh is outraged, upset, he doesn't know what to do first, he's so befuddled. He certainly pays Abraham off, loads of silver and gold as hush money. But unlike the triumphal march I imagined as a child, Pharaoh sets armed guards on Abraham, declares him persona non grata, and boots him out of the country: "'Now, here's your wife. Take her and go!' Pharaoh set a guard upon him and exiled him and his wife and all that was his."

Burton L. Visotzky, *The Genesis of Ethics*, 33–34

The account leaves little to the imagination: "When Abram arrived in Egypt, the Egyptians took one look and saw that his wife was stunningly beautiful. Pharaoh's princes raved over her to Pharaoh. She was taken to live with Pharaoh."[4]

Abraham milks the relationship between the Pharaoh and Sarah for all it is worth. He is pampered as a privileged guest among the royals, and in the process amasses a fortune in flocks and herds as well as servants. But God is anything but amused. He strikes down the royal household with a most dreadful plague.

> *England's Queen Victoria declared on her deathbed that she did not expect to see Abraham in heaven after his betrayal of Sarah.*
>
> Charlotte Gordon, *The Woman Who Named God: Abraham's Dilemma and the Birth of Three Faiths*

The Pharaoh immediately perceives the cause. He is furious. He rises from his sickbed, summons Abraham, and takes him to the woodshed, demanding to know what he has done. Already having no doubt heard by the grapevine that he has been duped, the Pharaoh rails at the fraudulent foreigner: "Why did you say, 'She's my sister' so that I'd take her as my wife? Here's your wife back—take her and get out!"[5]

Abraham and Lot separate

So Abraham and his household make their way out of Egypt. Indeed, quite safely. No mighty armies in their wake. How different it will be generations later when Moses and his followers depart Egypt.

Back in Canaan, the famine is over. Abraham arrives this time as a very rich man, bringing with him the luxuries of Egypt. In fact, he and his nephew Lot have accumulated so much wealth in livestock that the land cannot support them both. Tempers flare among the hired hands on both sides. Uncle Abraham wants no part of it. In a moment of magnanimity, he gives Lot first choice. He can go west or east, the former appearing to be little more than an arid wasteland. For Lot it's a no-brainer. He chooses the land to the east—"the whole plain of the Jordan spread out, well watered . . . like GOD's garden."[6] But God's garden it is not. Lot locates near Sodom, a cesspool of immorality and evil, while Abraham settles in Hebron near the great oak forest of Mamre.

Lot's trouble is just beginning. He has hardly settled in when tribal warfare explodes. Chieftains (or *kings*) join ranks to fight other chieftains and their allies. In the midst of the combat, the kings of Sodom and Gomorrah fall into tar pits, while their allies flee to the mountains as the two infamous cities are being raided and their citizens ravaged. King Kedorlaomer and his allies prevail. Lot is hauled away as a hostage, his possessions plundered.

Melchizedek according to Hebrews 7

Melchizedek was king of Salem and priest of the Highest God. He met Abraham, who was returning from "the royal massacre," and gave him his blessing. Abraham in turn gave him a tenth of the spoils. . . . Melchizedek towers out of the past—without record of family ties, no account of beginning or end. In this way he is like the Son of God, one huge priestly presence dominating the landscape always.

You realize just how great Melchizedek is when you see that Father Abraham gave him a tenth of the captured treasure. . . . This man, a complete outsider, collected tithes from Abraham and blessed him, the one to whom the promises had been given. In acts of blessing, the lesser is blessed by the greater.

Or look at it this way: We pay our tithes to priests who die, but Abraham paid tithes to a priest who, the Scripture says, "lives." . . . The Melchizedek story provides a perfect analogy: Jesus, a priest like Melchizedek, not by genealogical descent but by the sheer force of resurrection life—he lives!—"priest forever in the royal order of Melchizedek."

Heb. 7:1–17

When word reaches Uncle Abraham, he wastes no time taking action. He has no standing army, but he has 318 rough-and-ready male servants. With these ragtag farmhands, trained to do battle, Abraham sets forth a simple strategy: split the men into small militias and attack during the dark of night. He and his men chase the enemy nearly to Damascus, where they defeat Kedorlaomer and his allies. Lot and all his people and possessions are rescued.

Abraham returns to Sodom in triumph—all but a ticker-tape parade. The king of Sodom (apparently having been rescued from the tar pit) comes out to greet him, as does the king of Salem, none other than Melchizedek, priest of the High God. He blesses Abraham and *his* "High God," who has given him victory.

Abraham bows before Melchizedek and gives him a tenth of the possessions he brought back home—presumably belonging to Lot and other captives. Moreover, he recovers for the king of Sodom everything that had belonged to him. He also gives his hired hands a bonus, but will not accept so much as a piece of thread or a shoelace for himself.

No sooner has Abraham returned from battle than he receives another visionary message from God, telling him not to be afraid. More than that, God tells him he will be richly rewarded. Abraham, however, is not buying it. He has all the riches he could ever want. His concern is his failure to have a child. With no son, his chief servant, Eliezer, will inherit everything, and Abraham's own lineage will die.

God has a quick retort: "Don't worry, he won't be your heir. . . . Look at the sky. Count the stars. Can you do it? Count your descendants! You're going to have a big family, Abram!"[7] With those words the relationship between Abraham and God is sealed. But there are hard times ahead. In a dream Abraham receives the ominous prophecy that his descendants will suffer maltreatment and indignities for four hundred years before they live peacefully in the land. Only then does God clearly map out the land deal. Without signatures or survey or title or quitclaim deed, his descendants will become the world's largest landowners: "from the Nile River in Egypt to the River Euphrates in Assyria—the country of the Kenites, Kenizzites, Kadmonites, Hittites, Perizzites, Rephaim, Amorites, Canaanites, Girgashites, and Jebusites."[8]

But how can this possibly come true? At this late date it seems inconceivable that Sarah will conceive. Her biological clock has been running down for decades. So she concocts a scheme. At her bidding Abraham takes her maidservant to bed, and nine months later he hears the midwife proclaim *It's a boy*. But not Sarah's boy, as she had schemed. As she grows older and baby Ishmael grows up, domestic turmoil permeates the household.

Thirteen years later, when Abram is ninety-nine, God again renews his covenant with him, this time with a name change (from Abram to Abraham), plus an utterly shocking stipulation: "Circumcise every male. Circumcise by cutting off the foreskin of the penis; it will be the sign of the covenant between us."[9] *O my God!* Abraham must have gasped. But now with his new name that comes with the renewed covenant, God tells him to change his wife's name (Sarai to Sarah) and promises that she in her old age will indeed give birth to a son. Abraham laughs at this absurdity. He's one hundred; Sarah's ninety. But he immediately gathers all the men and boys in his household, both slave and free, and performs the painful surgery.

The next incident in Abraham's life is equally momentous. He is sitting out in the heat of the day in the shade of the Oaks of Mamre. From a distance he sees three visitors approaching. He hurries to greet them and invites them to rest—to take water and wash their feet while Sarah prepares bread and a servant roasts the best calf in the herd. After they have eaten, God, who is disguised as one of the men, tells Abraham that God will return in a year to see the baby boy that will be born to Sarah.

Abraham accompanies the men as they leave, and God, still speaking through one of the men, again confirms his covenant. He also tells Abraham he has heard of the wickedness of Sodom and Gomorrah

God's Thirteen Years of Silence

Thirteen years elapsed between the events of chapter 16 and those of chapter 17, and we can well suspect they were years of unhappiness and unrest in Abram's household. The presence of Ishmael in the home created endless contempt, bitterness, envy, jealousy, weariness of spirit, and rebellion. These thirteen years were designed by God to teach Abram the folly of acting on his own. . . . After thirteen years of silence, God appears to Abram in a new revelation and with a new name—God Almighty. In the Hebrew it is *El Shaddai*, which essentially means "the God who is sufficient," "the all-competent God," "the adequate God, who knows what he is doing and how to do it." . . . In this new light from God came a new demand from God: "Walk before me and be blameless."

Ray C. Stedman, *Man of Faith: Learning from the Life of Abraham*, 112–13 and is headed there to check things out. Abraham panics. Lot and family live in Sodom. Is God going to punish the city and in the process rain down vengeance on his kin as well? Thus begins Abraham's legendary bargaining with God. He begs God to spare the city if there are even fifty righteous ones there. God makes the concession. *What about forty-five? Forty? Thirty? Twenty? Ten?* God concedes all the way down to ten. Abraham, relieved, heads home.

But there are not even ten righteous people in Sodom and Gomorrah. So God rains down fire and brimstone, allowing Lot to escape in the nick of time. Perhaps fearing what might happen next, Abraham decides to pull up stakes and head south.

What Abraham does next is inexplicable apart from his colossal character flaws. He sets up his tents in Gerar and spreads the word, as he had done previously, that Sarah is his sister. King Abimelech promptly takes her into his harem, but before he can defile her God comes to him in a dream and tells him she is married. God also strikes Abimelech with a deadly disease and brings barrenness on his wife and female servants. In dread fear of God, Abimelech returns Sarah and for good measure throws in flocks and herds and servants and silver. If that is not enough, he permits Abraham and his household to live wherever they please in his realm. Only then does Abraham pray to God to heal the king and lift the baby ban, but Abimelech is wary of the devious Abraham, convinced that God is on his side.

And that's the story: When God destroyed the Cities of the Plain, he was mindful of Abraham and first got Lot out of there before he blasted those cities off the face of the Earth.

Genesis 19:29

In the meantime Abraham, at the age of one hundred, receives from God his promised son Isaac by the once-barren Sarah. But the family tension does not diminish. Sarah demands that Abraham send Hagar and Ishmael away. Despite his anguish, he does so.

Abraham has not had an easy life. He is a man of wealth, much of it gained through

The Silence of God

It was such a shock for Abraham to hear God's familiar voice telling him to set Isaac on fire. . . . There was no word from the Lord as Abraham rose the next morning to chop firewood in the dark, burying his ax in the grain again and again. God was silent as Abraham saddled his donkey and went to wake his servants and his child. God was silent as the small party set out, and silent for the three days. . . . Never in the history of the world, I think, had there been such a silence. No one said a word. Not Abraham. Not Isaac. Not God. It was the knife's turn to speak, until an angel cleared its throat: "Abraham," it said. . . . And Abraham said, "Here I am." It was the word he had been waiting for. His son was spared. He had passed the test, but Abraham never talked to God again.

Barbara Brown Taylor, *When God Is Silent*, 60–61

How Can God . . . Command This Cold-Blooded Cruelty?

The defining event in the way of Abraham takes place on Mount Moriah: the Binding of Isaac, the *Akedah* (the term the rabbis use for this story, after the Hebrew word for "binding"), Abraham binding Isaac and offering him as a sacrifice on the altar that he has just built expressly for this purpose. This story has absorbed the imagination of the people of God and plunged generation after generation of us into facing and dealing with the fundamental mystery that is God: There is so much here that we cannot comprehend, so much that violates our pious sensibilities, so much that refuses to conform to our expectations. How can God command a murder? And not just murder in general but the murder of a beloved son? How can God go back on the miracle-promise fulfilled in the birth of Isaac? How can God, who our parents and pastors have taught us loves us from eternity, command this cold-blooded cruelty? How can God, who Jesus tells us has such a tender heart that he is moved even by the death of sparrows, command a father to kill his son, without so much as a hint of explanation?

We can't handle this. When we try to imagine ourselves as either Isaac submitting to the binding or Abraham lifting the knife to slit his throat, we cannot do it. It is too terrible to admit into our consciousness, especially a consciousness that includes a good and sovereign God.

Eugene Peterson, *The Jesus Way*, 42

cowardly conniving. But despite his riches, he lives in smelly, sun-baked tents, travels through parched deserts, and endures famine, family drama, warfare, circumcision, and the destruction of the cities of the plain. Now more than a centenarian, he longs for tranquility. Instead, he faces the ultimate test.

Again he hears God's voice—that unmistakable resonance. The words leave no room for misunderstanding. God is plainly telling him to take his son Isaac, now a youth, to the land of Moriah and sacrifice him as a burnt offering. Abraham neither argues nor talks back. Indeed, he is so certain that this astonishing command is from God—not a figment of his imagination—that he saddles his donkey and sets out with his son and two servants for Moriah.

As they approach the mountain on the third day, Abraham tells the servants to remain back with the donkey while he and Isaac take the wood for the burnt offering. But there is no ewe or ram to be sacrificed. Bewildered, Isaac questions his father. His father brushes him off, saying the Lord will provide. When they get to the designated spot, Abraham builds the altar while Isaac presumably stands by watching, still utterly confused. After Abraham lays the wood out, he binds up Isaac and places him on the wood. Here is one of the most stunning scenes in the whole Bible. But there are no details. Does Isaac struggle? Does he scream for help? Does he weep? Does he faint? And what is Abraham's state of mind? All we know is that he raises the knife to kill Isaac. Then an angel stops him.

That a father could take his son of promise on a three-day journey for the purpose of killing him as a sacrifice to God is

Abraham Weeping over Isaac

Come, all ye tender hearted parents, who know what it is to look over a dying child: fancy that you saw the altar erected before you, and the wood laid in order, and the beloved Isaac bound upon it: fancy that you saw the aged parent standing by weeping. . . . I see the tears trickle down the Patriarch Abraham's cheeks. . . . I see Isaac at the same time meekly resigning himself into his heavenly Father's hands, and praying to the most High to strengthen his earthly parent to strike the stroke. But why do I attempt to describe what either son or father felt? It is impossible: we may indeed form some faint idea of, but shall never fully comprehend it, till we come and sit down with them in the kingdom of heaven, and hear them tell the pleasing story over again.

George Whitefield, "Abraham's Offering Up His Son Isaac"

mind-boggling. But it speaks to Abraham's growing understanding of God—his faith, his love, and his fear. God had clearly spoken before and had fulfilled his promises as well as carried out threats, as in the case of Sodom and Gomorrah. Heart-wrenching as it is, Abraham has no other choice but to obey God.

What was God thinking? How could he have ordered Abraham to commit murder? The Bible states elsewhere that the Almighty is a jealous God. Did God suspect that Abraham worshiped his son of promise more than God himself? Abraham is alone when he comes down from the mountain. There is no record that he ever spoke to Isaac again—or Ishmael or Sarah or Hagar. He might have had misgivings about his treatment of them. His unqualified devotion is to God alone.

Abraham and Sarah are not together when she dies in Hebron at age 127. He comes to bury her alone; neither Isaac nor Ishmael is present. And there is no eulogy, no account of deep sadness—only that he mourns and weeps. He conducts protracted negotiations with his Hittite neighbors to purchase, with a valid deed, a cave that Ephron, the owner, prefers to give him at no charge. This is no mere cemetery plot. It is *land*, the first land that Abraham rightfully owns in Canaan.

After his period of mourning, he directs a servant to go back to his homeland and fetch a wife for Isaac, who is now approaching forty. After that plan is set in motion,

Mount Moriah from a Jewish Perspective

Terrifying in content, it has become a source of consolation to those who, in retelling it, make it part of their own experience. Here is a story that contains Jewish destiny in its totality. . . . In passing, we should mention the role played by this scene in Christianity: the threat hanging over Isaac is seen as a prefiguration of the crucifixion. Except that on Mount Moriah the act was *not* consummated: the father did *not* abandon his son. Such is the distance between Moriah and Golgotha. In Jewish tradition man cannot use death as a means of glorifying God. Every man is an end unto himself, a living eternity; no man has the right to sacrifice another, not even to God. Had he killed his son, Abraham would have become the forefather of a people—but not the Jewish people.

Elie Wiesel, *Messengers of God*, 69, 76

Abraham acquires a wife for himself. Keturah bears him six sons. Isaac's place, however, is not threatened by his younger half brothers. He is *the* son of promise. Abraham gives gifts to his other children, but Isaac inherits everything. That is how Sarah would have wanted it.

> *Not only does Isaac not come down the mountain with Abraham, but we're never shown another conversation between them. The next time you see them together, Isaac is burying his father—which, in some way, speaks of the horror the son has undergone at the hands of his father.*
>
> Burton L. Visotzky, quoted in Bill Moyers, *Genesis: A Living Conversation*

One full century after God had called him to leave his country and kin and journey to the Promised Land, Abraham dies at 175 in that very land. What a journey it had been. His two sons Ishmael and Isaac reunite to bury his body in the Cave of Machpelah, next to his wife Sarah.

Lot: A Controversial—and *Righteous*—Man

Lot first appears in Genesis as an adult. His father Haran is Abraham's brother. After Haran dies, Lot looks to Abraham as a father figure and moves with him from Ur of the Chaldeans and resettles in Haran. Later he follows Abraham and his household to Canaan and on to Egypt and then back into the land of Canaan. Here Lot's less-than-appealing traits are first noted. By this time he is a very wealthy man whose cattle and herds have vastly increased. His herders are fussing and fighting with Abraham's herders over the best grazing land, so nephew and uncle split.

Lot moves his herds east into the well-watered "garden" on the plain of the Jordan,

Two Men and the Land of Promise

Abraham and Lot stood together on the heights of Bethel. The Land of Promise spread out before them as a map. On three sides at least there was not much to attract a shepherd's gaze. The eye wandered over the outlines of the hills which hid from view the fertile valleys nestling within their embrace. There was, however, an exception in this monotony of hill, toward the southeast, where the waters of the Jordan spread out in a broad valley, before they entered the Sea of the Plain.

Even from the distance the two men could discern the rich luxuriance. This specially struck the eye of Lot; he was eager to do the best for himself, and determined to make the fullest use of the opportunity which the unexpected magnanimity of his uncle had thrown in his way.

But the time would come when he would bitterly rue his choice, and owe everything to the man of whom he was now prepared to take advantage.

F. B. Meyer, *Great Men of the Bible*, 1:23

leaving the poor grazing land to the west for his uncle. True, Abraham, his uncle and father-figure, has graciously offered him first choice, but he seems all too eager to put wealth above family honor. In choosing the good grazing land, however, Lot is not without neighbors. There are cities, including Sodom and Gomorrah. Among the inhabitants are warring tribes. Lot gets caught in the middle and is taken captive.

Abraham comes to the rescue, defeats the enemy, and returns with Lot, his servants, and all his property. But Lot stays on in the well-watered plain—amid the debauchery of Sodom and its sister city Gomorrah. One evening while he is sitting at the gate of the city, perhaps as one of the town elders or officials, he welcomes two men (angels in disguise) as he would any strangers and invites them to his house to spend the night.

They are reluctant, but at his insistence they agree to come with him, wash up, enjoy a hot meal, and stay until morning. Before they turn in for the night, however, there is a loud commotion outside. A mob has surrounded the house—utterly depraved men with the intent of gang-raping the guests. They demand that the visitors be sent outside for their own wicked designs.

Lot goes outside and pleads with the mob—indeed, to the point of offering to send out his own two virgin daughters to be gang-raped. The scoundrels will have none of it. Pushing past Lot, they go for the door, only to be held back by the angel-men, who pull Lot safely inside and bar the doors. The angels then inflict blindness on those attempting to batter their way inside.

The angels tell Lot to warn his family that the city will be destroyed. He does, but his soon-to-be sons-in-law scoff at the idea. In the morning the angels insist that Lot get out immediately with his wife and daughters. Lot fears going into the mountains and begs the angels to give him time to escape to the little town of Zoar. Hardly have they arrived when God rains down fire from above. Lot's wife ignores the warning not to look back. For her disobedience she is refashioned into a pillar of salt.

Her story has been passed down through countless generations—this nameless woman, both wife and mother, struck down by God in barely a nanosecond. Her *sin* seems so undeserving of death. Capital crimes are serious—murder, treason, rape—but turning back for a final look at one's hometown? The punishment, at least from a human perspective, is overkill. It simply does not fit the crime. Her daughters, in a premeditated act of seduction, would rape their own drunken father and live. Her penalty is death.

Lot and his daughters are apparently not welcome in Zoar and fear for their lives. So they depart to live in a cave in the mountains. Here they are exiles living on whatever they can forage from the land. Holed up in a cave, life apparently becomes unbearably grim. The daughters imagine they will never escape to find husbands in order to continue the family line. The older sister concocts a scheme to get their father drunk and have sex with him to carry on their progeny. They do just that on successive nights, and both become pregnant.

These pregnancies will have significant future consequences. The older daughter's son, named Moab (meaning "from my father"), will give rise to the Moabites (a bloodline that will be carried through to Jesus by way of Ruth, a Moabite, and her husband Boaz). The younger daughter's son, Ben-Ammi (meaning "son of my kinsman"), will become the father of the Ammonites.

Sarah: Beautiful and Barren Wife

Throughout her lengthy marriage to Abraham, until she is ninety years old, the beautiful Sarah is labeled *barren*. Indeed, that fact is the first piece of information the Bible records about her. Her *barrenness* defines her and her relationships. Year after year, decade upon decade, she lives with the anguish of having no children. Her association with Hagar is surely strained by that fact, but also, no doubt, her relationship with other women who live in the camp, be they relatives or servants. Baby showers and the scurrying of midwives can hardly bring her any pleasure.

Sarah and Abraham are siblings, growing up in the household of Terah in Ur of the Chaldeans. Abraham's mother had presumably died, and Sarah, some ten years younger than Abraham, is the daughter of another wife. Why Terah would have arranged a marriage between half brother and sister is not divulged. Their marriage appears to be unique in the scriptural record.

There are no hints in the biblical text that Sarah and Abraham have a happy marriage. When Adam sees Eve for the first time, he exults: "Bone of my bone, flesh of my flesh!" The text goes on to say that they then become one flesh. Isaac takes Rebekah as his wife and loves her. Jacob is in love with Rachel and agrees to work seven years (and more) for her. Ruth and Boaz come together in love. Elkanah and Hannah have a loving relationship despite her barrenness.

To the contrary, the relationship between Sarah and Abraham seems to be fraught with tension. Sarah is beautiful—absolutely gorgeous even in her old age. One might think that such an asset would endear her to her husband and that he would defend her to the point of death. Rather, he uses her beauty to save his own skin. In fact, he explains to Abimelech that he had plotted the deception with her when they left Haran: "This is how you can show your love to me: Everywhere we go, say of me, 'He is my brother.'"[10] How must Sarah have felt when she was given such instructions—in the name of love, no less?

Later, when Sarah suggests Abraham have a child by Hagar, he does not object. He simply acquiesces. When he does get Hagar pregnant, Sarah is furious with him. Even then there is no expression of his love for her. Still another time, however, he pawns her off as his sister.

When Sarah finally overhears from an angel (disguised as a man) that she will become pregnant, she is more than a little dubious. Eavesdropping from inside her own tent, she apparently imagines this to be no more than a cruel joke. She laughs

Faith and Barren Women

God wanted faith, the Bible says, and that is the lesson Abraham finally learned. He learned to believe when there was no reason left to believe. And although he did not live to see the Hebrews fill the land as stars fill the sky, Abraham did live to see Sarah bear one child—just one—a boy, who forever preserved the memory of absurd faith, for his name, Isaac, meant "laughter."

And the pattern continued: Isaac married a barren woman, as did his son Jacob. The esteemed matriarchs of the covenant—Sarah, Rebekah, Rachel—all spent their best child-bearing years slender and in despair. They too experienced the blaze of revelation, followed by dark and lonely times of waiting that nothing but faith would fill.

A gambler would say God stacked the odds against himself. A cynic would say God taunted the creatures he was supposed to love. The Bible simply uses the cryptic phrase "by faith" to describe what they went through. Somehow, that "faith" was what God valued, and it soon became clear that faith was the best way for humans to express a love for God.

Philip Yancey, *Disappointment with God,* 70–71

(or sneers) under her breath. God picks up on it immediately and asks why she has laughed. She denies it. God insists she did. This is the only time God's words are directed specifically to her, and they are words of reproof.

God's rebuke, however, is a small price to pay for promise of pregnancy. But even this joyful announcement does not appear to bring this elderly couple mutual joy. Sarah has endured more than a dozen years of resenting Hagar and her son Ishmael. Now at last she is vindicated, but there is no dancing in the desert with Abraham. True, she laughs. The thought of giving birth at her age is wholly absurd. But she is not laughing with Abraham. Even at this moment of sheer wonderment and bliss there is no indication that their pleasure is shared.

Sarah's interaction with Abraham comes to the fore most clearly as she defends her turf in the threesome that involves Hagar. Here, unlike the situation with the Pharaoh, her pent-up rage and vulnerability emerge. Her frustration is unleashed on Hagar.

Hagar (and Sarah Continued . . .)

The Genesis account of Hagar and Sarah is a fascinating story of interpersonal struggles that are systemic in every culture and all generations. These two women present a timeless case study of familial relationships. Their story is irresistible. Even the apostle Paul draws on them for illustrative material, though not primarily on the theme of family struggles. For him, Hagar represents the slavery of being bound by the law—from Mount Sinai. Sarah represents freedom from the law.

Paul concludes with no hint of empathy for Hagar. He is making an argument, and the Genesis story illustrates his point: "But what does Scripture say? 'Get rid of the slave woman and her son, for the slave woman's son will never share in the inheritance with the free woman's son.'"[11] It is probable that Hagar, Sarah's Egyptian house slave, was much younger than Sarah herself. She may have been a young girl when she came into the household, and perhaps not out of her teens when she suddenly becomes the center of attention for this elderly couple always on the move. As such, she had not likely clashed with her mistress before. But now she has become a baby maker for a barren woman. Hagar has no choice in the matter. But in no time she conceives and seemingly cannot conceal the glow of her pregnancy. Surrogacy in any era often goes awry; biological bonds of motherhood are not easily broken. Hagar is with child, and her relationship with Sarah seriously sours.

Sarah reports to Abraham that Hagar despises her, thus giving her cause to abuse her young charge. Sarah, whose idea it was for Hagar to conceive by Abraham, turns the tables and blames him: "You are responsible for the wrong I am suffering. I put my slave in your arms, and now that she knows she is pregnant, she despises me." Then she adds a final taunt to establish his guilt and her innocence: "May the LORD judge between you and me."[12]

That Sarah imagines the Lord would take her side harks back to the blame game Adam and Eve played in the Garden. In this instance, Sarah may have devised the surrogacy scheme in order to shift the blame for barrenness away from herself. Wasn't Abraham, at nearly one hundred years, too old to father a child?

What Sarah alleges to be hatred on Hagar's part may be no more than maternal instinct for the mother-to-be. Hagar is fully aware of Sarah's intentions—that this baby she is carrying will be Sarah's child; she will be expected to give up the newborn infant to another woman, albeit her mistress. How can she possibly do this—relinquish her own offspring, her very own flesh? Thus, she despises, she disdains, she disparages, she resents, she fears this old woman who has power over her.

She knows Abraham all too well as a man of personal flaws and weaknesses. He is a mighty warrior who can chase after and defeat an enemy army, but he does not stand up like a man and protect his own wife in the face of Pharaoh. He's out to save his own skin. But now, it must seem to Hagar that he is giving in to every one of Sarah's whims. Will he take pity on her and recognize her need to be the mother of her own child? Will he stand up to Sarah on her behalf? Of course not. Hagar is a mere slave, with no more rights than a pregnant ewe among her master's flocks.

For people who have encountered abuse, it is natural to take the side of Hagar in this battle of wills. She did not come up with the idea of having sex with the old man. Besides, she is a mere slave girl. But maybe not. She may have been part of the loot that Pharaoh gave Abraham for having taken Sarah into his harem—part of the loot just to get him and his entourage out of Egypt. Indeed, Pharaoh is very generous with Abraham, and if he wants to make nice to Sarah as well, the gift of a choice slave girl would have been culturally appropriate.

Patriarchal Oppression

This story—the story of Sarah and Hagar—is a story of terror for those who are marginalized or oppressed. . . . The two women are caught in a downward spiral of patriarchal oppression. They are linked by the process of male succession, yet are not able to see this nor are they able to resist the barriers it places between them. Sarah, depressed, suppressed and repressed, takes out her own terror on the one she can oppress.

Letty Russell, "Women Quilting a Biblical Pattern"

If that were the case, Hagar may have been serving in the royal household with all its luxuries. Being sent away to serve an old woman who lives in tents and is always on the move is a humiliating cultural demotion. In Egypt, even as a slave, she no doubt had friends and family. In Canaan there is no one to whom she can pour out her heart.

Unhappiness tinged with resentment festers and is not easily concealed. It is a hopeless situation for Hagar. She is essentially doomed for a lifetime—that is, until she becomes pregnant. Suddenly her status changes. Though surely not Sarah's equal, she is comparable perhaps to a concubine or second wife. Her biological clock has not begun to wind down. She is on a roll. Why should she serve Sarah when she herself needs a nursemaid? Will she have more babies with Abraham, and will she soon be overseeing her own servants? It would be easy for her to imagine that her days as a lowly slave are now over.

With such a mind-set, why should she respect this old nomadic woman? What could Sarah do to harm her? Isn't she—Hagar—carrying the son of promise? Without a son, Abraham would go to the grave with no progeny, a truly agonizing outlook. She is the solution to his predicament. She's smug—and safe.

But not in Sarah's eyes. Sarah has already suffered the indignity of being pawned off to the Pharaoh in Egypt and, besides that, has daily mourned her barrenness. Will she now be snubbed by a mere slave? Hardly. Indeed, Sarah's ill treatment of Hagar becomes so intolerable that the pregnant Hagar runs away. Egypt only is on her mind. *Good riddance* is likely Sarah's unspoken response.

But heading to Egypt is a treacherous undertaking. She sets out on a trade route through the Wilderness of Shur, where, after a long, arduous journey, she finds respite by a spring of water. Here she might encounter other weary travelers. But surely not an angel of the Lord—or God himself? Strange. The conversation, however, begins routinely except for the familiarity: "Hagar, slave of Sarai, where have you come from, and where are you going?"[13]

Hagar does not act shocked and ask, *Who are you?* Rather, she responds as though talking with angels is a normal activity: "I am running away from my mistress Sarai." The angel of the Lord instructs her, "Go back to your mistress and submit to her. . . . I will increase your descendants so much that they will be too numerous to count."[14] She is to name the son she is carrying Ishmael (meaning "God hears"). And he will not be just an ordinary son:

> He will be a wild donkey of a man;
> his hand will be against everyone
> and everyone's hand against him,
> and he will live in hostility
> toward all his brothers.[15]

Hagar's response is interesting. She interacts with God almost as an equal. God has named the son she will bear, and now she names God—an unusual act and the first such instance in Scripture. "You are the God who sees me," and not only that, but "I have now seen the One who sees me."[16] Then, without argument, she returns to Sarah's household. Soon after, she gives birth to Ishmael. Then she disappears again for a lengthy time—at least from the pages of Scripture.

The relationship between Hagar and Sarah for the next sixteen or so years is not recorded in the Bible, nor are there any hints about Ishmael's early years. He is fourteen years older than his half brother Isaac, Sarah's son. When little Isaac is weaned as a toddler, Abraham throws a big party. In the midst of the festivities, Sarah notices that Ishmael is mocking Isaac. She is quick on the draw. To Abraham she rails: *Get rid of that slave woman and her son*. Sarah wants them out—*now*. Never will she allow *that boy* to share in the inheritance.

This incident indicates that Hagar has not had an easy time over the past years rearing her son while trying to avoid Sarah's wrath. Sarah surely realizes that Abraham loves Ishmael, but she has been biding her time. Her husband is now in a moment of weakness, doting over the baby of the family amid all the celebrants. She catches the adolescent scoffer in the act and demands that Abraham get him out of the house.

Abraham is caught between Sarah on the one side and Ishmael and Hagar on the other. How can he so cruelly throw them out? But God intervenes, telling him not to be distressed: "Listen to whatever Sarah tells you."[17] God reminds him that his descendants will come through Isaac. Ishmael, however, will not be forgotten. His offspring will also become a nation.

Abraham goes to bed, gets up early, and sends Hagar and Ishmael away into the desert with "some food and a skin of water."[18] After wandering in this arid, desolate no-man's-land, they run out of water and any hope of survival. Hagar has Ishmael lie down in the shade of a bush, and she goes some distance away so that he will not hear her sobs and she will not have to watch him die.

Hagar's Descendants

Hagar hasn't seen the end yet. After she and her son drank from God's well in the wilderness four thousand years ago, they went on and prospered. The boy grew and became a strong warrior. Hagar got him a wife from Egypt, and he had sons and daughters. And some of these sons are mentioned in Isaiah 60 where we read about the peoples of the earth coming to the throne to give God homage at the end of time. We read about Nabaioth, Hagar's first grandson, and Kedar, another grandson, coming in that great procession and bringing sacrifices that will be acceptable upon God's altar.

Miriam Adeney, *A Time for Risking: Priorities for Women*, 84

When God hears the boy crying, an angel is dispatched to deal with Hagar, telling her not to fear. God has had pity on the boy. She is told to help Ishmael up and take him by the hand. As she does so, God opens her eyes and she sees a well of water. They drink; their thirst is quenched; that is all they need; life goes on. Hagar does not take her son to Egypt, that land of wealth and glamour. Rather, they live in the desert, a vast, treacherous wasteland where twice Hagar has encountered God. Ishmael spends long hours in target practice and becomes a recognized archer. Hagar, the dutiful mother, arranges for him to marry a young woman from Egypt. All the while, God is watching over him.

The biblical record of Hagar ends with her in the desert. Some rabbis and other scholars have speculated that Keturah, whom Abraham marries after Sarah dies, is actually Hagar. They argue that Keturah is not a Hebrew name and that its meaning ("spice") is associated with Egypt. If true, it would be a *happily ever after* ending to the story: a man long separated from the one he sent away—the woman he loved—now reunited again and busily making babies.

For Sarah there is no scenario with a happy ending. She dies sometime after Abraham takes Isaac to be sacrificed on Mount Moriah. Some have speculated that she may have learned what he was up to and that she died of a broken heart—a fitting ending for a weary woman whose life was filled with decades of discontent.

Concluding Observations

Abraham is the leading character in the book of Genesis. Sarah, Hagar, and Lot are key people in his life, but primarily as they relate to him. His son Isaac, grandson Jacob, and great-grandson Joseph will all play important roles in succeeding generations, but none will rise to the stature of Father Abraham. He is an all-around decent man who intends no harm to anyone. He is generous with Lot in land division and pleads with God to spare the wicked cities on the plain. He recognizes Sarah's struggle in dealing with Hagar but is anguished when Hagar and Ishmael are sent away. Though cowardly, he is not mean-spirited.

If Abraham at 174 had reminisced on his long life, he might have pondered his good fortune. Despite the hardships of crossing deserts and doing battle with enemies, he always comes out on top—wealthier than before. He might have been killed and his servants and cattle captured at any given time as his caravan trespassed through Canaan. The same is true later on as he wiggles out of a most unpleasant situation involving the Egyptian Pharaoh—still later with Abimelech. But he always prevails. More important than wealth, however, is progeny. He fathers sons in his old age and passes God's tests with both of them.

He might have also reminisced about his friendship with God. Indeed, Abraham, perhaps more than anyone else in the history of humankind, has a *personal* relationship with the Lord. God and angels come in person to deliver the news of his fathering a son by Sarah, and God repeatedly intervenes with instructions or information. And Abraham talks back.

His relationship with God, more than anything else, illustrates what is meant by *faith*. In the *hall of faith* chapter (Heb. 11), Abraham is the prime example. By faith "from this one man," the writer declares, "came descendants as numerous as the stars in the sky and as countless as the sand on the seashore."[19]

Amazingly, Lot fares well in the biblical record. Despite his disagreeable traits, he is described by Peter as a righteous man. Jesus also references Lot. Speaking of the last days, when "the Son of man is revealed," he warns that life will seem normal, as "in the days of Lot." People will be eating, drinking, buying, selling, planting, and building. But suddenly fire and brimstone will rain down from heaven. Run. Do not look back. Jesus concludes with the memorable words: "Remember Lot's wife!"[20]

Sarah has stood the test of time as the greatest of all the patriarchal wives, though in recent decades Hagar has come to the fore. Their combined story represents in many ways the struggles women—both rich and poor—have endured through the ages.

Further Reading

Boice, James Montgomery. *Ordinary Men Called by God: A Study of Abraham, Moses, and David.* Grand Rapids: Kregel, 1998.

Dennis, Trevor. *Sarah Laughed: Women's Voices in the Old Testament.* London: SPCK, 2010.

Feiler, Bruce. *Abraham: A Journey to the Heart of Three Faiths.* New York: William Morrow, 2002.

Getz, Gene A. *Men of Character: Abraham; Holding Fast to the Will of God.* B&H Books, 1996.

Gordon, Charlotte. *The Woman Who Named God: Abraham's Dilemma and the Birth of Three Faiths.* New York: Little, Brown, 2009.

Gossai, Hemchand. *Barrenness and Blessing: Abraham, Sarah, and the Journey of Faith.* Eugene, OR: Cascade Books, 2008.

Hunt, Steven A., ed. *Perspectives on Our Father Abraham: Essays in Honor of Marvin R. Wilson.* Grand Rapids: Eerdmans, 2010.

3

ISAAC AND REBEKAH

Marital Missteps and Misery

As is true with many sons of celebrated fathers, Isaac simply cannot compete. Abraham is larger than life, a fascinating figure whose flaws and failures are easily ignored while his heroism is commemorated. Indeed, Father Abraham possesses a universal quality that few biblical characters can match. *Father Abraham*, the children sing in worship, *Many sons had Father Abraham; I am one of them and so are you—So let's all praise the Lord*. Would such laudatory lyrics ever be sung to Isaac? Surely not.

The twists and turns in Abraham's life are played out on the world stage, from Ur to Haran and Canaan and Egypt, and back to Canaan. Isaac's story takes place on a much smaller scale, and even then he is often overshadowed by his father (as on the hike to Moriah) or mimicking his father's behavior in saying Rebekah is his sister. For travel and adventure, Abraham's colorful story has few equals in Scripture. Alongside of this, Isaac's story almost seems drab.

The setting for the account of Isaac is primarily the home front. The domestic tension that permeated Abraham's household is repeated in his son's. Indeed, for those fascinated by family dysfunction, Isaac's story surpasses that of his father.

From the moment she is introduced in the text, Isaac's wife Rebekah is a commanding presence. As a young woman she exudes poise and hospitality. She is strong willed and a force to be reckoned with. Isaac is no match. When she enters the room, all eyes are on her. She steals the show with her dynamic personality. But she is also a master manipulator, who easily outsmarts her husband.

Like Abraham, Isaac demonstrates no real emotional attachment toward his sons. His favoritism for Esau seems to be associated more with the tasty meals he prepares from wild game than with love for the boy himself. Absent is the passion that Rebekah displays for Jacob or that Jacob has for his son Joseph.

Even Isaac's relationship with his half brother Ishmael demonstrates no real emotion or passion. It does not rise to the standard of biblical drama—drama of bitter sibling rivalry. The enmity they are supposed to harbor against each other is less theirs than it is their mothers'. In fact, there is virtually no interaction between the two of them.

The Pentateuch often pairs brothers: Cain and Abel, Ishmael and Isaac, Esau and Jacob, Moses and Aaron. More often than not they are at odds, in part because God reverses tradition and selects for special honor the younger brother. So it is with Ishmael and Isaac. Ishmael is Abraham's firstborn dear son. But he is passed over when his baby half brother joins the family. From this point on Isaac almost seems to be a pawn in the fulfillment of God's promise. He is acted upon more than he acts.

Second-Rate Treatment of Firstborns

Given God's apparent preference for firstborns, why is it that Genesis seems to afford them such second-rate treatment? Cain murders his younger brother Abel, and is cursed to be a fugitive wanderer. Esau, cheated of his birthright by his younger twin, Jacob, is banished to live outside the promised Land. Jacob's firstborn, Reuben, commits incest, joins in selling Joseph into slavery, and is later toppled by his father. The fate of these firstborns is remarkably similar to the fate of Abraham's first issue, Ishmael, who is also exiled into the desert.

Bruce Feiler, *Abraham: A Journey to the Heart of Three Faiths*, 67

It is noteworthy that Ishmael fares far better in the hands of God than he does in the hands of Jewish and Christian interpreters. But why should he be neglected—and arrogantly dismissed? He is, after all, the son of Abraham, which alone should make the reader sit up and take notice. He is the son of Hagar who also receives God's blessing. But even in the text Ishmael is an outsider making a life of his own—ever on the fringe. His influence will prove to be enormous, however, as the head of a warring people who will be a thorn in Israel's side for generations to come.

Ishmael: Shoved-Aside Son

The nativity of Ishmael is noteworthy. Apart from the annunciation of the birth of Jesus to Mary, there is no more startling and descriptive birth prophecy in Scripture.

From this pregnancy, you'll get a
son: Name him Ishmael;
for God heard you, God answered you.
He'll be a bucking bronco of a man,
a real fighter, fighting and being fought,
Always stirring up trouble,
always at odds with his family.[1]

There is no question about the paternity of the child—eighty-six-year-old Abraham. But his mother? Who was she? Servant girl Hagar is a surrogate mother. Sarah, according to her own scheme, is to be the baby's mother. But it does not work out that way, as is often the case with such setups. So some thirteen years later Isaac, the *real* son of promise, is born to Abraham and Sarah.

But Ishmael is also a son of promise. God's promise to Hagar is virtually identical to the one given to Abraham. In the desert these are the first words she hears the angel of the Lord say: "I will increase your descendants so much that they will be too numerous to count."[2] If the message she receives is not enough to confirm Ishmael as a son of promise, a second message is even stronger, in this case given to Abraham.

When Abraham is ninety-nine and hears from God that he will father a son by Sarah, he thinks he has misunderstood and begs God to keep Ishmael safe and spare his life. God explains that he truly means that Abraham will have a second son, this one Sarah's biological child. But Ishmael will not be forgotten. God says to Abraham: "I heard your prayer for him. I'll also bless him; I'll make sure he has plenty of children—a huge family. He'll father twelve princes; I'll make him a great nation."[3]

There is an interesting contrast between the promise the slave girl alone in the desert receives from God and the one the wealthy herdsman receives. She hears God speak of a mighty fighter at odds with his family. It is no doubt reassuring to Hagar that her son will be the protector she needs against the family—the power of Sarah and her household. But the message Abraham hears highlights Ishmael as the father of princes and a great nation. In neither case should this extraordinary son of promise be sidelined.

Ishmael grows up in the shadow of the great patriarch Father Abraham and two mothers: Sarah, a beautiful old woman, and Hagar, the fetching servant girl. Does he feel the intense rivalry between them? Does his fighting spirit and tendency to stir up trouble begin as he sees the old one abuse the younger?

At thirteen Ishmael is circumcised. Why the long delay? Because it is only then when God gives the command. It is mass circumcision that includes ninety-nine-year-old Abraham himself and all the other males in the household. For the boy just coming of age this experience must surely have been no less than traumatic.

The next episode involving Ishmael occurs when Abraham is throwing a party to celebrate the weaning of little Isaac. Ishmael is stirring up trouble, as adolescents are prone to do, apparently poking fun of Isaac. Ever accusatory, his *mother* Sarah

Firstborn and Marginalized

The biblical narrative dealing with the figure of Ishmael is a story of marginalization par excellence. He is Abraham's firstborn, circumcised with Abraham, yet he is not the son of the covenant. He is part of the family, yet he is excluded. His presence is felt, yet his actions are few. He is spoken about, yet never speaks. God hears his voice, but the reader hears silence. He will be a great nation, but "his hand will be against everyone, and everyone's hand against him." He is loved, and although expelled from Abraham's house, he is not rejected.

Carol Bakhos, *Ishmael on the Border*, 14

catches him and explodes. She orders both him and his biological mother out of her house. She makes it very clear that she is no *mother* of this wicked boy.

Abraham is devastated. How can he send Hagar and his son Ishmael out into the desert to die? But God makes it clear that this is part of the plan: "Regarding your maid's son, be assured that I'll also develop a great nation from him—he's your son, too."[4] Here, for the third time, is a message that clearly identifies Ishmael as a son of promise.

Ishmael must have wondered how his father could allow such a dreadful thing to happen to him. He heard no voice from God, and had his father told him of the voice he had heard, it would have only added insult to injury. So he is sent on what seems to be a death march with his mother into the arid desert. There he is left alone under a shrub because his mother does not want to watch him die. What a pitiful scene. Ishmael is in the desert dying alone. Hagar, because of her own neediness, does not even stay with him. He has been abandoned three times over: by his surrogate mother Sarah, by his aged father, and now his birth mother. What does he do? He weeps.

But there is a sudden turn for the better when God hears his cries and sends an angel, who speaks to Hagar (with perhaps more concern for the boy than for her, the mother who had given up). The angel says: "God has heard the boy and knows the fix he's in. Up now; go get the boy. Hold him tight. I'm going to make of him a great nation."[5] This is now the fourth time his status as son of promise is confirmed.

At that moment Hagar spots a well of water. She goes immediately to fill her jug and brings a drink to her crying son. Ishmael had been abandoned by everyone

A Bedouin shepherd boy today

except God. The descendants of Ishmael will be a thorn in the side of the Israelites for ages to come, leaving the reader to realize once again that God's ways and purposes are very intentional, though not easily understood.

As for Ishmael himself, the text is very clear: "God was on the boy's side as he grew up. He lived out in the desert and became a skilled archer. He lived in the Paran wilderness. And his mother got him a wife from Egypt."[6] He died at age 137, having seen his twelve sons grow up. Though not as familiar as Isaac's sons, their names are all recorded in Scripture: "Nebaioth the firstborn of Ishmael, Kedar, Adbeel, Mibsam, Mishma, Dumah, Massa, Hadad, Tema, Jetur, Naphish and Kedemah."[7]

Isaac

Isaac's name, not Ishmael's, will forever be linked with Abraham's as father and son. *Abraham, Isaac and Jacob*, a legendary trio embedded deep in the soil of Scripture. Isaac is *the* son of promise. No other recorded birth in the Bible, apart from that of Jesus, is so significant—and so extraordinary. Though not a virgin birth, it seems equally implausible. Sarah is ninety years old, long past menopause. Abraham is one hundred. How could she possibly get pregnant? But angels pay a visit and make a prophecy. The following year a son is born. Isaac means "laughter flowing from gladness." How appropriate. At his birth, both Abraham and Sarah must have laughed for sheer delight. Then eight days later he is circumcised.

The next big event in Isaac's life is his weaning, which Abraham celebrates with an extravagant party. Sarah notices that Ishmael is poking fun of his little brother and goes ballistic. She may very well have been looking for an excuse to evict Ishmael and his mother Hagar from the house. And she succeeds.

More than a dozen years after this, when Isaac is an adolescent or perhaps a young adult, he is on a three-day hike with his father, two servants, a donkey, and a load of wood for a burnt offering. To any passing stranger nothing would have appeared notably peculiar as the four trek on to Mount Moriah.

There is no record of any conversation along the way. Without warning the little party comes to a stop. Abraham tells the servants to stay with the donkey while he and Isaac continue on with the wood, a knife, and burning embers. Isaac trudges along with the pile of wood hoisted on his

Isaac's Ambiguous Blessing

It is interesting to note that Abraham never explicitly gives Isaac his blessing, Isaac is never commanded to "go" (*lech*) and he never leaves the land. He never sees clearly, never laughs (despite his name) does not find a wife and does not find the "right" son to bless. Isaac's role is to be Abraham's son. He is the weak son of a strong father and the weak father of two strong twin sons. To be a strong father or strong husband is too demanding for his passive status. He receives the blessing from God not for himself but "for the sake of Abraham" (Gen. 26:24).

Moshe Reiss, "Rebekah and Isaac and Their Children"

back, bewildered by the turn of events. He is not used to challenging the good sense or authority of his father, but he screws up enough courage to ask where the lamb is for the offering. He has no doubt witnessed many such offerings—perhaps cringing at the killing of the lamb—and knows very well something is missing.

His father is evasive, saying God will provide the lamb, while knowing full well that Isaac himself is the one to be sacrificed. They continue walking in silence until they reach a spot where the father tells the son he can relieve himself of the bundle of wood. The father goes about building an altar and places the wood on it. Then, instead of God providing a lamb, as Isaac had imagined would happen, the father grabs ropes—perhaps those holding the wood or their robes together—and begins binding up the astonished son. Far worse is the sight of his father grabbing the knife.

Abraham and Isaac on Mount Moriah

A Man of Weak Character

The Bible does not spare Isaac; in no way does it seek to give us an enhanced impression of him. Indeed it takes care not to pass over or minimize certain traits which emphasize the weakness of his character. . . . Some episodes related in Genesis seem to show Isaac as of only medium intelligence, to say the least. . . . Time and again he gives us the impression of being a man of weak character and indeed inconsistent. There is none of the superhuman greatness and the energetic, forceful activity evinced on occasion by Abraham. There is none of the subtlety, adroitness, and flexible diplomacy of Jacob.

Henri Gaubert, *Isaac and Jacob: God's Chosen Ones*, 8–9

Is he nuts? Isaac surely must have wondered. *Has he lost all sense of reality in his old age?* His mind is racing; his heart is pounding. But there is no indication that he even struggles to escape. As a youth, he could have decked the old man and been done with it. He does not. A patriarchal father is to be feared and respected. The son submits. Just before the knife slices his throat, however, his father cocks his head as though hearing voices. Then Isaac is set free.

There are no consoling words from the father. No *I'm so sorry; I didn't want to. God made me do it*. Nothing. He simply walks over to where he sees a ram in the thicket, catches it by its horns, kills it, and places it on the altar prepared for Isaac. God speaks again to the father, and after that Abraham heads back to where he left the servants. The whereabouts of the traumatized Isaac are unknown.

Did Isaac ever hear *the rest of the story*? There is no evidence that he did. It is entirely possible that all he knew was that his father was about to kill him and then changed his mind.

How Isaac spent his life for the next decades in not recorded. He is apparently not present when his mother dies and when his father purchases a burial plot for her. But he grieves. Indeed, his grief is not assuaged until he takes Rebekah into his mother's tent and loves her.

Isaac is not involved in any way in his

Everyday *Life*

Arranged Marriages

Arranged marriages were the norm in the ancient world, that of Isaac and Rebekah being an intriguing example. It was not uncommon that a potential bride would be given an opportunity to reject a proposal, as was true with Rebekah. Indeed, she had far more say in the matter than did her intended husband.

In many instances the bride and groom were in the same clan or otherwise related, though they may have never had an opportunity to meet. A marriage partner was often chosen sight unseen.

The bride-price, however, was out in the open, often determined at the end of hard-nosed negotiations. In some cases, the wealthy family of the groom could so impress the bride's family that there would be no cause for wrangling. So it was with Rebekah. The gifts for her and her family were extravagant by any standard.

The dowry was different from the bride-price. It was given to the bride by her family and consisted of gifts of clothing and jewelry and items for her new home as well as servants. This was given in lieu of an inheritance. Such valuables protected her in the case of widowhood or abandonment and would be passed on to sons—never to fall in the hands of her husband's family.

When all such gift giving and negotiations were completed, the bride was officially betrothed to the groom. They were married. No further promises or ceremonies or rites were necessary. A celebratory feast, however, was in order, and after that the marriage would be consummated.

Marriage Gain and Loss

The newly married man usually did not found a new home for himself, but occupied a nook in his father's house. The family of the groom gained, and the family of the bride lost, a valuable member who helped . . . with all household tasks. It was reasonable, therefore, that the father of the groom should pay the father of the bride the equivalent of her value as a useful member of the family.

Hayyim Schauss, *The Lifetime of a Jew throughout the Ages of Jewish History*, 128 father's arranging to secure a wife for him. At forty he's still a bachelor, perhaps wondering if the right woman will ever come along. Older brother Ishmael is probably a grandfather by now. Isaac does not know that his father has been working behind the scenes. Indeed, Abraham feels compelled to demand of his servant (who swears an oath) that he will not get a Canaanite wife for Isaac, but will travel to his home country and arrange for a wife from among his kin. Abraham is adamant that Isaac must remain at home. So the servant sets out with ten camels loaded down with gifts for the prospective bride's family.

Isaac was an unbuttered bagel kind of a guy. Plain. That's why we have the old saying: "An Abraham is usually followed by an Isaac."

Stephen M. Miller, *Who's Who and Where's Where in the Bible*

One day when Isaac is out in a field meditating, he hears sounds in the distance. And then, from seemingly out of nowhere, a loaded caravan arrives, headed by Eliezer, his father's most trusted servant. Abraham's servant now tells Isaac the whole story. But Isaac, unlike the servant, is not a talker. Rather, he does what is expected of him or what he is prodded to do. He takes the veiled stranger into his mother's tent and seals the deal; they consummate their marriage.

Now as husband and wife they see each other for the first time, and he falls in love with her. Strong-willed and stunningly beautiful, she no doubt reminds him of the one for whom he grieves. Indeed, it is only now that he finally finds some solace over the death of his dear mother.

For Isaac, Rebekah is everything he could want in a wife, but for her barrenness. Apart from consoling her, what can he possibly do about this unfortunate situation? He prays for her. God answers the prayer twice over, and Isaac becomes the father of twin boys—an incredible gift from God. But even as the boys are growing up, they become a source of tension between the parents. Isaac favors Esau, the one who loves the outdoors, over Jacob, who hangs around the house with his mother.

One of the most perplexing episodes in Isaac's marriage and his occupation as a wealthy nomadic herdsman is his encounter with King Abimelech during a time of famine in Canaan. In a déjà vu scenario that harks back to Abraham, he tells Abimelech that Rebekah is his sister. It is a bald-faced lie. She is not his sister. A relative, yes, but not sister.

Abimelech believes him, but when he sees Isaac being intimate with Rebekah he knows he has been duped. He asks Isaac why he has lied to him. That is a good question. Did Isaac tell Abimelech his wife was his sister simply because that is exactly what his father had done? He uses the same excuse his father had used—that he feared he would be killed.

Abimelech allows Isaac and his household to settle on the same land utilized by Father Abraham, but Isaac ends up having serious conflicts over water rights. He has the advantage of using the very wells his father had dug, indeed, becoming so prosperous that fierce resentment flares up. The locals, having been pushed aside, vent their fury by filling the wells with dirt. Abimelech then orders Isaac and company out of the area.

Isaac moves on and his servants rejuvenate old wells Abraham had dug decades earlier. When the servants discover a spring of fresh water, the local shepherds are furious, insisting the water is theirs. So his servants move on and dig another well, but that water is contested also. Finally Isaac moves on to an area where his men can graze the livestock and dig for water without conflict. It is named Rehoboth, meaning "wide-open spaces." From there he goes to Beersheba, where God appears to him and repeats the blessing he has already given to Father Abraham. Isaac builds an altar and prays, referencing God by name. And again he digs a well.

No sooner has he settled down than Abimelech and his army show up. Isaac is startled by this show of force, because he had obediently moved on when Abimelech ordered him out of the territory. But Abimelech suspects God is on Isaac's side, and he wants to secure peace. So dinner it is: Isaac as host, a toast, a treaty of friendship the next morning.

But there are serious conflicts on the distant horizon. When we meet Isaac again he is a blind old man, and he thinks he is about to die. But he wants one final tasty meal and he wants to bestow his blessing on his elder son. So he sends for Esau and makes a request that his son is most obliged to carry out. His appetite is not for leg of lamb or prime rib. He wants wild game that is hunted down and delectably prepared by his sportsman son.

Isaac: Not Half the Man Abraham Was

One generation of founding has barely been achieved, and the question for this generation is: Can the new way that was begun with Abraham survive another generation, especially when the father of the second generation is not even half the man his father was? There are all kinds of indications of the weakness of Isaac before this story. But in this story, Isaac appears to have a dubious reason for preferring his firstborn son. He loves Esau because he loves the game Esau provides for him to eat.

Leon R. Kass, quoted in Bill Moyers, ed., *Genesis: A Living Conversation*, 257

While Esau sets off on his safari, Isaac sits back and waits, knowing it will be a long time before Esau returns home. But hardly have a few hours ticked by when his son shows up with the meal—already prepared, no less. Blind old Isaac is confused, asking which son he is. Prodded by his mother, Jacob confounds the old man into giving him the blessing, thinking he is Esau.

Soon thereafter Esau arrives with a hearty dish he himself has prepared from wild game. Only then does the old man realize he has been tricked by Jacob. He begins to tremble, shaking violently. In confusion, he cries out to Esau, asking who it was that just brought him a meal—who it was that received his blessing.

Whether Isaac ever learns that Esau had earlier traded his birthright for a bowl of stew is not recorded. Rebekah no doubt finds out, but Isaac seems often out of the loop. Although he had thought he was near

A Strange Marriage

When Rebekah arrives, Isaac, coming from Be'er Lahai Ro'i—the well of seeing—sees the camel but not Rebekah. Rebekah, however, sees Isaac (Gen. 24:63–64). How does Rebekah react? She came to marry her rich uncle, she was far removed from her family of origin, where she was considered an independent woman. However immediately upon seeing her husband she realizes he is damaged. But even so she could not have understood the complex family relations she had entered. The text tells us of no ceremony and gives us no exchange of words that they spoke to each other. Rebekah and Isaac do not appear to engage in communication. And this is a prelude to the tragic lack of communication between her, Isaac and their twin children.

Moshe Reiss, "Rebekah and Isaac and Their Children"

death when he sent his son out to hunt game for his final meal, Isaac lives on for many years, becoming a grandfather many times over. He dies at age 180. Together Esau and Jacob bury him in the family plot, the Cave of Machpelah.

Rebekah: Strong, Confident—and Manipulative

Rebekah, like the mother-in-law she never met, is a looker—a striking young woman who, on top of that, takes seriously her purity ring. She's a virgin. She is also competent, gracious, and strong, with an altogether impressive demeanor. She draws buckets from the well for ten thirsty camels, each of which is capable of a massive intake of water. Abraham's servant is truly awed.

She also comes with an amazing pedigree: the daughter of Bethuel, son of Milkah, wife of Nahor. This stellar lineage is repeated three times in the story because of its significance. Since Rebekah's mother is not closely related to Abraham, she is not mentioned. Her grandparents on her father's side, however, are Abraham's close relatives—Nahor, his brother, and Milkah, his sister-in-law.

After showing exceptional hospitality to Abraham's servant, she returns home to bring the news to her family. Brother Laban hurries out to represent the family in welcoming Uncle Abraham's emissary. Such a visitor bringing news from faraway places is a refreshing interruption to everyday life—all the more so because he has arrived with gifts.

It is significant that Rebekah is brought into the conversation about an arranged marriage. Typically a daughter would not be party to such negotiations, even if she did have some right of refusal. But Rebekah is not one to be ignored. Nevertheless,

Rebekah gives water to Eliezer

she is not in control of her own destiny. Abraham's servant asks Laban and Bethuel (brother and father) if Rebekah can return home with him, explaining how God had answered his prayer by sending her to the well to give him and the camels water. They immediately respond in the affirmative, though insisting the matter is out of their hands—not, however, because the decision is Rebekah's. Rather, they insist, it is God's: "This is totally from GOD. We have no say in the matter, either yes or no. Rebekah is yours: Take her and go; let her be the wife of your master's son, as GOD has made plain."[8] Whether they would have seen the clear hand of God in the matter without the expensive gifts is doubtful. Laban would later show himself to be a most devious wheeler-dealer.

Though Rebekah's fate is determined by God, through Laban and Bethuel as mediators, she does hold the authority as to when she would leave. Both Laban and her mother want her to wait ten days before leaving, but she informs them she is prepared to go immediately.

As she departs with Abraham's servant, Rebekah knows she will never see her family again. But she is determined to carry on the family line in obedience to God. So she and her servants journey by camel to meet the forty-year-old groom. When they arrive, they see him at a distance; he is out in a field. When he sees the camel caravan and begins walking to meet them, Rebekah covers herself with a veil and soon after that enters the tent with Isaac.

What happens next is not offered in the text. Sure, Isaac *knew* his wife. But before that did they share their hopes and dreams for the future? Did she tell tales of her childhood growing up on the farm? Was there any chitchat about the weather or the dust storms she encountered along the way? Or did they simply get down to business? What happens behind closed doors of a marriage is often kept secret—especially when two decades pass with no children. How do they pass the time? Does he ever tell her about his father, who was about to make a human sacrifice out of him? Does she even meet her father-in-law?

Unfortunately, the newlyweds soon discover that, like Isaac's mother, Rebekah is barren. She has come into all the wealth she could want, but for the next twenty years she counts down the weeks, not missing a menstrual period. Then God answers Isaac's prayer and she conceives. But the pregnancy is anything but routine. The cramps and kicking of one fetus can be painful enough; turns out she is carrying twins. And no ordinary twins. They are kicking and punching to the point that death would be sweet relief. She pleads with God for an explanation. This dreadful discomfort is not simply her imagination. God knows exactly what is ailing her:

> Two nations are in your womb,
> two peoples butting heads while
> still in your body.
> One people will overpower the
> other,
> and the older will serve the
> younger.[9]

This diagnosis would have hardly brought her joy, but at least she knows why she is having such a painful pregnancy. When the time comes for her to deliver, she and her midwives are prepared for a difficult childbirth. And so it is—one right after the other. The first is born as a baby should be, head first. But the second is coming through the birth canal arm first, and not only that but clutching the heel of the first. Truly an abnormal birth. But both mother and babies survive.

The young boys grow up heading in very different directions and under the care of parents who play favorites. Esau, the rough-and-tumble, burly boy who loves to be outdoors, is his father's favorite. Jacob, the more thoughtful boy, who hangs around the house, is his mother's pet. They are rivals, and they know how to jerk each other around—particularly when Esau sells his birthright for a pot of porridge.

The next we hear of Rebekah is when she, Isaac, and the entire household are sojourning among the Philistines due to a famine in Canaan. Isaac is introducing her to King Abimelech as his sister. She is his cousin but surely not his sister. She may have feared being taken into his harem and may have staged a public show of affection for her husband. At any rate, Abimelech looks out his window and sees them making out—or at least Isaac fondling Rebecca with no apparent objection from her. Brother and sister? He's no fool. He's onto Isaac and orders him to get out of his kingdom.

The years fly by and the boys are approaching middle age. Esau leaves home at forty and marries two Hittite women. Rebekah is furious, and she never gets over it, commenting to Jacob that she is absolutely fed up with these *Hittite women*.

Many years later, when the feeble Isaac has perhaps passed his 120th birthday, Rebekah overhears him telling Esau to prepare for his blessing. She's heard decades earlier that Jacob is to be his father's successor, and now she's determined to take matters into her own hands. So while Esau is out hunting, she prepares a stew—and the reluctant Jacob—for the blessing. With skins on his arms and a tasty bowl of food, they pull it off, only to face Esau's fury when he returns.

Rebekah obtains the blessing for her son, but she loses her son in the process. She sends him off to live with her brother Laban, where he will work and marry and father children who will never know their grandmother. The time of her death is not mentioned in the text, but it is presumed to be many years before the death of her husband. She is buried in the family plot in the Cave of Machpelah.

Rebekah and the Blessing

Rebekah, perhaps the least recognized . . . is in fact the most powerful and significant of the matriarchs. She is the recipient of Abraham's blessing rather than her husband and she is told by God that the promised blessing from Abraham will go to her younger child Jacob. In Biblical terms it is virtually unheard of for a woman to be granted the blessing to carry forward and the mission to choose the next recipient.

Moshe Reiss, "Rebekah and Isaac and Their Children"

John Calvin Comparing Sarah and Rebekah

Here, however, a question might be raised as to the view to be taken of Sarah and Rebekah, both of whom, impelled as it would seem by zeal for the faith, went beyond the limits of the word. Sarah in her eager desire for the promised seed, gave her maid to her husband. That she sinned in many respects is not to be denied; but the only fault to which I now refer is her being carried away by zeal, and not confining herself within the limits prescribed by the Word. It is certain, however, that her desire proceeded from faith. Rebekah, again, divinely informed of the election of her son Jacob, procures the blessing for him by a wicked stratagem; deceives her husband, who was a witness and minister of divine grace; forces her son to lie; by various frauds and impostures corrupts divine truth; in fine, by exposing his [God's] promise to scorn, does what in her lies to make it of no effect. And yet this conduct, however vicious and reprehensible, was not devoid of faith. . . . In the same way we cannot say that the holy patriarch Isaac was altogether void of faith, in that, after he had been similarly informed of the honor transferred to the younger son, he still continues his predilection in favor of his first-born, Esau.

John Calvin, *Institutes of the Christian Religion*, bk. 1, 375–76

Concluding Observations

Rebekah's character is easily painted in bold strokes. She is out there for everyone to see and hear—as well as criticize and admire. So also Ishmael, though he merits far less coverage in the Bible than does Rebekah.

But who is Isaac? Because the Bible offers so few details about this patriarch sandwiched between Abraham and Jacob, scholars are tempted to speculate. We can only imagine how deeply traumatized he was as a youngster on Mount Moriah, no doubt seriously questioning his father's love. Indeed, the reader might question Abraham's love for him. Why did Abraham argue so adamantly with God to spare the cities on the plain but not his own son? Might Isaac have been what Abraham considered a *defective* child? Is that why Ishmael poked fun of him? Did Abraham favor Ishmael and fear that Isaac would not marry and carry on the family line? Why was he so insistent that a servant go alone to secure Isaac a wife? Why did Isaac as a wealthy adult live in his mother's tent rather than having a tent of his own?

Why did he not immediately recognize that Jacob was pulling a fast one on him when he gave Jacob Esau's blessing? Is it possible he was mentally impaired?

Isaac was born to parents, half brother and sister, at a time when his mother was well past childbearing age—both factors considered to be serious issues for normal births. Is it possible that Isaac was afflicted with Down syndrome? Such a scenario does not require a massive stretch of the imagination.

Some might argue that an individual with such an impairment could not have maintained herds and flocks and dug wells and contracted business deals. Isaac did that and more, but such activities are not beyond the ability of someone with Down syndrome, especially someone pushed to succeed by his determined mother. Likewise, he learned by working with his father, who had herdsmen and personal servants to carry out his wishes.

Might Isaac have carried an extra chromosome 21? If so, how appropriate it is that a biblical patriarch would serve as a model for all those who have been marginalized by this condition.

Further Reading

Bakhos, Carol. *Ishmael on the Border*. Albany, NY: SUNY Press, 2006.

Gaubert, Henri. *Isaac and Jacob: God's Chosen Ones*. Translated by Lancelot Sheppard. New York: Hastings House, 1969.

Moyers, Bill, ed. *Genesis: A Living Conversation*. New York: Doubleday, 1996.

4

JACOB AND ESAU

Feuding, Brooding Brothers

I will kill my brother. Such malice has not been expressed since Cain killed Abel. But Esau's fury is uncontained. Fortunately for Jacob, Esau waits, not wanting the sin of murder to desecrate the period of mourning his father, who he assumes is near death. By that time, Jacob has the good sense to get out of town.

Jacob have I loved, Esau have I hated.[1] The apostle Paul, speaking for God, writes these harsh words. But the Genesis account is far more gentle in its telling. Indeed, there is no indication at all that God hates Isaac's dear son Esau. But Rebekah, not Isaac, is the one who will maneuver events for the benefit of her favorite son—and God's chosen one. Esau will sow his wild oats with trashy Hittite women, while Jacob will be sent away to wrangle with his wily uncle Laban, a man who has all the cunning of his sister Rebekah and more.

About all Jacob has in common with his father Isaac is that he also is God's chosen younger son. Jacob is his mother's boy and with her prodding will prove to be fully as clever and manipulative as she is. But there is another side of Jacob that will emerge—his deeply spiritual side as he wrestles with God. Indeed, the good and bad will war inside

Esau and Unitarian Pottage

Jacob, like David, rides high in the popular imagination. Children in Sunday school still sing the story of his dream, "We are climbing Jacob's ladder," even as they sing, "Only a boy named David, but five little stones he took." Esau is not the hero and is cast in the popular imagination as the bad one of the twins. (Children do not sing choruses about him.) Contemporary assessment of him is drawn mainly from his foolish business deal. A blogger uses it to lament how easily some scholars abandon historic Christian beliefs: justification by faith, the atonement, the Trinity, and others. "For a Christian," he asserts, "this amounts to giving up one's birthright for a mess of Unitarian pottage" (John Hobbins, "Breathing New Life into the Doctrine of Inerrancy").

him and will play out publicly even as it will generations later with David, who also wrestles with God.

Both Jacob and David, with multiple wives, are less than admirable in their family relationships. They would be accused of having significant baggage if they were running for office today. Yet both are uniquely blessed by God and stand head and shoulders above others in the lineage of God's chosen people. Jacob is named *Israel*, and David is ever associated with the *city* from where the *Son of David* will appear.

The book of Genesis and Paul's letter to the Romans are not the only books of the Bible that make reference to Jacob and Esau and their descendants. Obadiah begins his prophecy with words directed toward Edom and the Edomites, the descendants of Esau. God is calling for all the nations, the "godless" included, to declare war on Edom. In fact, he speaks very directly to Esau himself. Thieves will "take Esau apart, piece by piece, empty his purse and pockets." God does not quickly forget sins of the past: "Because of the murderous history compiled against your brother Jacob, You will be looked down on by everyone. You'll lose your place in history. . . . Esau will go up in flames, nothing left of Esau but a pile of ashes."[2]

The writer of Hebrews also refers to Esau and Jacob, first in chapter 11, crediting Isaac for blessing both of them, but then in the following chapter calling Esau up short. Readers are warned: "Watch out for the Esau syndrome: trading away God's lifelong gift in order to satisfy a short-term appetite. You well know how Esau later regretted that impulsive act and wanted God's blessing—but by then it was too late, tears or no tears."[3]

But it is Paul (paraphrasing Malachi) who, in speaking for God, lets the ax fall: "Jacob have I loved, but Esau have I hated."[4] Seen in another light, this passage is not so severe. Paul is speaking of God's election and is illustrating the doctrine by calling to mind the Old Testament story. In reference to Malachi, he says: "Later that was turned into a stark epigram: 'I loved Jacob; I hated Esau.'"[5] As such, Paul is not saying *God* hated Esau, but this was a common witticism.

In life, Esau actually fares better than is typically presumed. A key question is, did Jacob actually steal the birthright? He is forced to flee and earn his wealth by hard labor. When he returns home two decades later, he gives gifts to Esau, who has prospered with his family inheritance and has presumably looked after his parents in old age—the benefits and responsibilities of an older son. So who really held the birthright?

Like Jacob and Esau, Rachel is referenced outside Genesis. In the context of the Jewish exiles in Babylon, Jeremiah speaks of her as weeping for her children. In the Gospel of Matthew, her weeping becomes a metaphor for the sorrow felt when Herod decrees the murder of all the baby boys in Bethlehem: "Rachel weeping for her children, Rachel refusing all solace, Her children gone, dead and buried."[6]

Leah, in the popular imagination, has not fared as well as Rachel. Her honor is derived through her descendants. Most notably, her son Judah is progenitor of the tribe from which Jesus is born.

Jacob: Clever, Crafty, and Destined for Greatness

In the biblical drama involving Jacob and Esau, there is no question that Jacob has the starring role. Esau is certainly a significant supporting actor, but he competes with the likes of Uncle Laban and Jacob's wives for stage time.

Though the younger of the twins, Jacob is destined at birth to inherit the patriarchal line from his father and grandfather. This is a matter of far more significance than merely inheriting wealth. It is a monumental turn in the religious realm. Amid all the gods in the ancient world, the true God would often be identified as *The God of Abraham, Isaac, and Jacob*—not Esau. Indeed, if God had been playing by the so-called *rules*, he might have been referred to as the God of Abraham, Ishmael, and Esau. But the Bible often presents God coloring outside the lines. Thus he colored when fashioning Jacob.

God, however, does not pass the mantle on to Jacob as a matter of wholly divine course. Jacob, with his mother's scheming, acts on his own and often does so in a less than admirable way. As a fetus he fights his brother, struggling to establish preeminence in birth order. So ferociously do they fight in the womb that their mother contemplates death as a better option than carrying them to term. But God settles her nerves by explaining what is going on. The twins represent two future nations, the younger ruling over the older.

Jacob is tenacious from the start, grasping his brother's heel for a free ride through the birth canal, though in actuality trying to pull him back so that he could win that all-important birth race. They are anything but identical twins. Unlike his vigorous outdoorsman brother, Jacob is more sedate and settled, preferring a domestic life in the family compound. As such, he is his mother's favorite. It is under her tutelage that he no doubt learns to cook—and connive.

One day Esau comes in from the field, exhausted from working in the blazing sun. Whom should he encounter but Jacob, leisurely cooking up one of his culinary delights—red meat stew. Esau asks for a bowl. He is starving, or at least he says he is. If Esau is toiling in the field, why should his brother not share the stew with him? It's the least he could do. But the wily Jacob recognizes in an instant that he has his brother in a vulnerable position. Esau is independent—has probably never needed a thing from his *little brother* until now.

So Jacob goads him. *I'll make a deal with you. You get the stew; I get the rights as firstborn.* The proposal is so ludicrous that Esau blows him off. *I'm totally famished—starving to death. What's the use of the birthright if I'm dead?* Jacob had never

Everyday *Life*

Birthright and Blessings

Jacob, the second-born twin, cunningly appropriated both the birthright and blessing from his older brother Esau. The birthright is the larger inheritance the older son receives, while the blessing is the father's entreaty to God for the son's success and well-being. Inheritance traditions, however, were anything but rigid in ancient Israel. Indeed, time and again the younger son was favored over the older. Isaac, Jacob, Joseph, and David are prime examples. Even God, in establishing the covenant line, often passed over the oldest son, sometimes with the support of a strong woman, as in the case of Rebekah.

Yet the status of the firstborn held great significance among the Israelites and other cultures. And among sons, being the oldest generally carried a significant advantage. He was first in line for the role of head of the family, should his father die prematurely. His entitlement upon his father's death was a double share of the estate. Along with that, however, came the obligation to care for his mother should she survive his father. A further responsibility was seeking husbands for unmarried sisters.

Such inheritance customs were necessary—and complicated—in the case of polygamous fathers. Jealousy among brothers arises in every generation. Family rivalry, in fact, is one of the prominent themes of the Old Testament. Few are the accounts of deep brotherly love—unless between an unrelated David and Jonathan.

For a bowl of stew, Esau traded his birthright, an incident that seems to be a necessary prelude to Jacob's receiving the blessing from his father.

The End of Israelite Primogeniture

We may next observe that from this point, the law of primogeniture seems to have been annulled and never restored again in its full form and force as it existed before. When Jacob came to die, he called together all his sons and gave them all his blessing. They all alike seem to have become partakers of the promises. The birthright seemed to diffuse itself over the whole family. Together they became a nation of God's people, heirs in common of most of those blessings which came down to Isaac and to Jacob in the narrow line of the birthright.

Charles G. Finney, "Forfeiting Birth-right Blessings"

imagined it would be so easy. He makes Esau swear an oath before he agrees to give his brother any food.

After that the household is facing famine, and the twins travel with their parents to sojourn in the land of Gerar, in the land of the Philistines. This journey is in many ways a metaphor for their lives. They are always on the move, facing problems wherever they go. From their parents comes a continual flow of mixed messages: hospitality on the one hand, deception on the other.

The years pass and Isaac grows old as the twins are approaching middle age. Jacob, ever aware that the birthright is now his, also wants the blessing. So when his mother, now old herself, concocts a scheme to outsmart her husband, Jacob's only objection is that he fears it won't work. But he acquiesces when his mother offers to take the curse upon herself if it doesn't pan out. Curses and blessings are critical elements in the ancient world.

So Jacob, arms bound in goatskins and wearing Esau's clothes, brings his father a tasty meal his mother has prepared. When he is questioned about his identity, he holds out his hairy arms and lies, telling his father he is Esau. He sounds like Jacob but he smells like Esau. So he gets the blessing.

When Esau learns what has happened, he is furious. Jacob has tricked him before, but this is identity theft, pure and simple. It's a malicious crime, and he is not about to let the liar get away with it. He will terminate the trickster once and for all. But Mother Rebekah gets a tip from an insider and insists Jacob get out of town in a hurry. As usual, she has a plan. He can escape to the safety of her brother Laban—at least until Esau has calmed down.

Before Jacob leaves, his father, echoing his mother, tells him not to take a local wife, rather to arrange with Uncle Laban to marry one of his daughters. Then Isaac bestows another blessing on him.

While he is traveling to Paddan Aram to Uncle Laban's spread, Jacob stops for the night. It is after sundown, he's on the run, traveling light with no apparent camping gear. So he lies down on the ground, using a stone for a pillow. Strange. But what is about to happen is stranger yet. He has a dream and sees a stairway reaching from the ground all the way up to heaven, angels passing each other as they climb up and down. Suddenly God appears right in front of him, identifying himself as the God of Grandfather Abraham and Father Isaac. God then bestows on him the surrounding land, promising protection and blessings and descendants as numerous as the dust of the earth.

Jacob wakes up and realizes that for the first time he has encountered God. He is both awestruck and terrified. God is in this place, the very gates of heaven. To mark this holy ground he props up the stone pillow, anoints it with oil, and names the spot Bethel, meaning "God's house."

But Jacob is still not prepared to make a complete commitment. He brazenly formulates a conditional vow: "If God stands by me and protects me on this journey on which I'm setting out, keeps me in food and clothing, and brings me back in one piece to my father's house, *this* God will

A Horizontal Man

It is ironic, but Jacob is now leaving the promised land which was part of his blessing. It ought to be obvious to Jacob that there is something wrong with this picture. It ought to indicate that the way Jacob got the blessing was not what God would have planned. However, we see that in spite of Jacob's deceitful way of obtaining the blessing, God is going to honor it. . . . God has just promised that He will bless Jacob, but Jacob doesn't really believe Him. He is trying to cut a deal. . . . he is focused on physical blessings. He is a very horizontal man.

Hampton Keathley IV, "Jacob"

be my God."[7] Then and only then will he truly worship God. He further pledges to give back a tenth of what this God gives to him—a most favorable business transaction, since he is running for his life and appears to have taken nothing with him. Indeed, his hijacking God for 90 percent of the take tops his brazen trading of the stew for a birthright.

Jacob continues his journey and arrives at a well, where he finds three shepherds with their flocks. He wonders why they are not watering their sheep and returning to graze. They explain that they have to wait for other shepherds to help them remove the rock needed to keep intruders away. He also learns they are from Haran and know his uncle Laban. In fact, Laban's daughter appears with her father's sheep, right on cue as Jacob is single-handedly rolling away the huge boulder. (Where does a homeboy obtain this kind of strength? one might ask.) He waters her sheep, kisses her, breaks down weeping, and explains that he is her cousin. She runs back and relates the news to her father, who hurries to meet Jacob, kisses him, and brings him home.

Jacob gives Uncle Laban the details of all that has happened back home. The reader can only wonder about those messy details that wily Jacob leaves out. Did he tell his uncle about how his mother connived to fake his identity in order to get the blessing from his father? Did he tell how he had traded stew for the birthright? Actually, if he had, his cunning uncle might have been impressed. Indeed, the two would have been a match for each other, but Jacob has become almost immobilized. He has fallen helplessly in love with a beautiful girl.

After Jacob has stayed on for a month, Laban offers to pay him for his work. He asks him what a fair wage would be, no doubt surmising what his nephew really wants. So smitten by love is Jacob that he offers seven years of hard labor for the beautiful Rachel. The girls here in Haran are high priced. Indeed, Jacob's mother was *sold* for gifts that weighed down ten camels. Jacob is broke; all he can give his uncle is his time.

The seven years fly by quickly as he keeps his eye ever on the gorgeous girl. But Jacob does not want to work any longer than he has to. He keeps track. "Give me my wife," he boldly says to Laban when the seven years are up. "I'm ready to consummate my marriage."[8]

So Laban throws a big party, the guests eating, drinking, and making merry. Then he presents the veiled bride to the starry-eyed groom, and the couple make a quick exit, Jacob bringing her to his bed. But Jacob has been had. Not until morning does he realize that Leah, Rachel's older sister, is in bed with him. He is seething. Laban is a lying weasel—a sleazy, shifty-eyed, smooth-talking cheat. (Jacob should know.) And dear Leah? Nice girl though nothing to look at, but she's not his heart-throb Rachel. Jacob's mother Rebekah had used animal skins to deceive; her brother Laban uses a veil.

When the furious nephew (now son-in-law) confronts him, Laban plays it cool. Indeed, he seems to almost blame Jacob, the hick from Canaan, for his ignorance regarding proper etiquette: "We don't do it that way in our country," he chides. "We don't marry off the younger daughter before the older. Enjoy your week of honeymoon, and then we'll give you the other one also. But it will cost you another seven years of work."[9]

What can Jacob do but accept the outcome? He grudgingly spends the first week with Leah, and then with no fanfare Laban gives him Rachel. So now Jacob has two wives, each with a maid, Zilpah serving Leah and Bilhah serving Rachel. And Jacob is himself a *maid*, serving Laban for seven more years.

Jacob and the flocks of Laban

With Leah, the wife he does not love, Jacob has four sons. But he is unsuccessful in getting Rachel pregnant. She blames him. He retorts that he is not the God of babies. But at her suggestion, he takes her maid Bilhah to his bed, and she gives birth to Dan first and later Naphtali.

Then Leah gets back into the competition and sends her maid Zilpah to bed with Jacob. Gad is the first to be born of this union, then Asher. But then he is back with Leah, and she gives birth to Issachar, and not long after to Zebulun, and finally a daughter, Dinah.

After carrying out his term of service for Laban—and after giving Rachel a much-longed-for son, Joseph, Jacob wants out. He confronts his father-in-law: "Let me go back home. Give me my wives and children

Beloved Scoundrel

Jacob is one of the more beloved scoundrels of the Bible, perhaps because he exemplifies the mercy of the God who draws great works out of very flawed men. Jacob was a liar, a cheat, a confidence man, and perhaps at times even an idolater; yet he became a patriarch of Judaism so important that for millennia thereafter God would be known as the God of Abraham, Isaac, and Jacob.

Richard R. Losch, *All the People in the Bible*, 177–78

for whom I've served you. You know how hard I've worked for you."[10]

Laban responds by asking Jacob to tell him what he is owed. Jacob points out that under his supervision Laban's wealth has greatly increased. Again, Laban asks Jacob how much he owes him. So Jacob proposes that he cull out all the spotted and speckled sheep and goats from Laban's flocks and keep them for himself.

Laban readily agrees. But Laban is Laban. He is a lying cheat. It's part of his DNA. Before Jacob can carry out the agreement, Laban does his own culling, separating out all the animals that should have been Jacob's and sending them off to pasture with his sons. Jacob remains calm; he continues to tend the flock, minus the spotted and speckled ones.

I confess I have no idea just what it is that Jacob does in his specialized program of animal husbandry. I do not know how peeled saplings of any trees . . . influence the genetic pool of the herds.

Burton L. Visotzky, *The Genesis of Ethics*

He has no need to protest because he has a magical formula up his sleeve and a clever plot in mind that he carries out with God's blessing. He peels part of the bark off tree branches so as to make white stripes on them. Then he places them in front of the watering tanks. When the sheep and goats mate near the striped branches they produce striped and speckled offspring. And Jacob makes sure that only the healthiest of the flock mate in front of the striped sticks. It appears on the surface to be a crazy scheme, but it works. His flocks and herds increase in number, as do his donkeys and camels.

No surprise that Laban and his sons are upset. Their stock is tanking while Jacob is multiplying his wealth through insider trading. Tensions are rising. Should Jacob stay in the market and continue to see his profits soar, or should he get out before it's too late? God has the answer. He tells Jacob to go home, promising him protection.

Jacob sends word to Rachel and Leah to get things ready for the move. He explains how their father has repeatedly cheated him and how he has nevertheless prospered under God's provision. In fact, God speaks through an angel in a dream and confirms that he had been the one behind the mating of the flocks that gave Jacob such an abundance of wealth.

If Jacob is concerned that he will have a hard sell with Laban's daughters, he is pleasantly surprised. Both Rachel and Leah testify that they too have been treated badly by their father and that they stand to receive nothing from his estate. They both readily cast their lot with their husband. So the three of them bide their time, and when Laban is away shearing sheep, they make their break, but not before Rachel steals the family idols.

They are on the road to Canaan, moving as fast as the cumbersome caravan can go. They are three full days out, across the Euphrates and into Gilead, before Laban learns of what has happened. Laban for once has been outsmarted, and he is not about to let his son-in-law get away with it. He rounds up his best men, and they are off in hot pursuit.

A Consultation with Two Wives

It is also quite striking here that Jacob invites both Rachel and Leah into the field to talk, to discuss leaving Laban. Jacob could have thought in that situation, "Now's my big chance—I can dump the wife I don't love, and be with the one I do." But this is not what he does.

Nora Gold, "Rachel and Leah: A Jewish Model of Sisterhood," 96–105

After seven days they catch up with the caravan and set up tents nearby. But before Laban can confront Jacob, God comes to him in a dream, warning him not to provoke Jacob. So Laban calms down, determined to do nothing rash. He approaches Jacob with questions rather than brute force. *Why did you sneak away? Why did you trick me? What was your point—not even letting me kiss my daughters and grandkids "good-bye"?* He implies that Jacob has affronted him for no good reason. Why would a father not want the best for his daughters and grandchildren? Why, he wonders, didn't Jacob inform him so that he could have sent them all off with a grand farewell party?

Then comes the threat. He tells his son-in-law that if he had wanted to, he could have decimated Jacob and his entourage on the spot. But God came to him in a dream, and he now understands why Jacob would want to go back home to Canaan. Okay, he can let bygones be bygones. But there's a bigger issue. *What about the household gods? Why did you steal them?* Jacob is taken aback. He knows nothing about the theft. He surely didn't steal any gods. In fact, if Laban finds out that someone in his camp did it, that person will be put to death. For that matter, Laban can take anything he finds that actually belongs to him.

So Laban begins the search through the tents. He finally comes to Rachel's tent. She has hidden the gods inside a cushion on which she rests while her father searches. "Rachel said to her father, 'Don't think I'm being disrespectful, my master, that I can't stand before you, but I'm having my period.' So even though he turned the place upside down in his search, he didn't find the household gods."[11]

Now Jacob has the upper hand. Apparently Laban himself or one of his sons has misplaced the household gods. Jacob and company are innocent. But more than that, Jacob has worked his heart out for twenty years, and what thanks does he get? He lashes out in anger: "I was out in all kinds of weather, from torrid heat to freezing cold, putting in many a sleepless night. . . . I slaved away fourteen years for your two daughters and another six years for your flock and you changed my wages ten times. . . . You would have sent me off penniless."[12]

But Laban comes back at Jacob and insists everything Jacob possesses is actually his—daughters, grandchildren, flocks, everything. But he relents and agrees to settle things with a covenant and let Jacob and his household (with all his possessions) go in peace. Jacob and his children build a monument of stones to serve as a witness to this covenant. Then Laban offers a blessing that includes a warning for Jacob not to mistreat his wives or to trespass into

Laban's territory. With the conclusion of the blessing, Jacob offers a sacrifice and worships God, and they all have a meal together. In the morning Laban heads for home after kissing and blessing his daughters and grandchildren.

Jacob and his entourage also break camp and continue their journey to Canaan. On the way he meets angels and once again marks the spot. But with every hour that they move closer to home he becomes more agitated about Esau. He fears he is still on his brother's *most wanted* list and knows that he and his household and all his livestock can hardly sneak back home unnoticed. So he sends a servant ahead to break the news. On Jacob's instructions the servant is to tell Esau essentially that after staying with Laban all these years he has acquired wealth. Such a message would not necessarily have endeared him to Esau. But he ends the message by begging for Esau's approval, calling him *my master.*

Really. Does Jacob truly regard Esau as master? Jacob is clever—and is shaking in his boots. He knows all too well that he and his servants are no match for the hardened hairy hunter and all his men.

The servant returns. The news is grim. Esau is on his way with four hundred men. That's a small army. It's too late to rush back to Laban. Esau would overtake him in a day. So he devises a plan. He separates his entire household into two groups, each headed in different directions. If Esau strikes at one, the other has a chance of escaping. That is the best strategy he can muster, but he still has an ace up his sleeve: God. For Jacob, scheming often trumps spirituality. This time, however, he prays, begging for mercy while at the same time reminding God of his promises of protection.

After a restless night he comes up with an addendum to his plan. He sends gifts ahead for his brother, his *master*. And not merely a bouquet of flowers and a box of chocolates. Esau will be impressed with the hundreds of goats and sheep, dozens of cows, camels, and donkeys. All this wealth, Esau will learn, is a gift from his *servant* Jacob.

Jacob assumes Esau holds a major grudge and that the gifts will assuage his anger. That night he sends his whole household ahead, while he stays behind alone. He is so fearful of Esau that he may be thinking that his wives and children are safer without him. But alone in the dark night of the desert he has an unforgettable encounter. Indeed, it is one of the strangest episodes in Scripture.

Lying down in preparation for a night's sleep, he realizes that someone has snuck up on him. A man begins wrestling with him—a struggle that continues until dawn. But Jacob seems to have the upper hand, even after the man purposely throws his hip out of joint. By daybreak, the man is begging for mercy, but Jacob refuses to let him go until he blesses him. The man asks his name and then changes it from Jacob to Israel (meaning God-Wrestler). Only then does he bless him. Jacob lets him go and names the spot Peniel because that is where he saw the face of God.

The next morning Jacob leaves with a limp, catches up with the rest of his

Jacob Wrestling Himself

But there is more here than guilt. The adversary is not simply Jacob's internalized Esau but has become the representation of Jacob's own shadow as well. It is not merely the voice of Esau that condemns him, but also something in himself, of himself, condemns him. He wrestles with his fear of the advancing Esau, but he wrestles as well with his own neglected shadow side . . . that defrauded Esau and until now has lived by manipulating fate through conning, deceit, and trickery. Hence the timing. It is just here and just now that the "man" attacks him, for at last here and now Jacob can no longer avoid coming to terms within himself with the objective situation created by treachery.

Walter Wink, "Wrestling with God: Psychological Insights in Bible Study," 11

household, and sees in the distance Esau coming toward him with four hundred men. He quickly makes some readjustments by moving to the head of the caravan with the maid servants directly behind him, next Leah and her children, with Rachel and Joseph pulling up the rear. He bows in obeisance before Esau, but Esau will have none of it. He runs to give his long-lost brother a bear hug. He kisses him, and they both break down weeping.

Esau asks about all the people with Jacob, and Jacob begins the introductions, all of them bowing before Esau. Esau says he cannot accept the gifts—that he has wealth of his own. But Jacob insists, and he agrees. Esau offers to lead the way home, but Jacob wants to take his time, for his exhausted family and livestock.

The next major incident in Jacob's life involves his daughter Dinah, and once again we see him in a less-than-admirable light. He does not take charge of the situation when she is violated, nor does he prevent the carnage that follows.

Later God tells him to go to Bethel, the spot where he dreamed of a ladder ascending to heaven. Jacob gathers his family to make the journey, and only then does he tell them to throw away all their idols—and to bathe and put on clean garments. Jacob takes their idols and charms and buries them, and then the whole company sets off for Bethel. On the way he observes an unusual sense of foreboding among the locals. In fact, in every village they pass the people regard him with such

Jacob's Strength in Weakness

The presents mean little to Esau who could soon take all which Jacob possessed. Esau becomes disarmed when he finally sees Jacob, dragging himself forward, bowing down to the ground seven times, behind him a crowd of women and children. This limping, defeated man, hobbling forward with difficulty is hardly the same Jacob who had once been so agile, against whom he had trained his warriors. God saved Jacob by making him weaker and thus defeats Esau's purpose. He feels himself vanquished by seeing a vanquished man before him.

Benno Jacob, quoted in Walter Wink, "Wrestling with God," 19 dread that they dare not even inquire of his plans or pursue him as an enemy.

When they arrive at Bethel, Jacob builds yet another altar, and God confirms his new name of *Israel* and once again blesses him. They have begun their journey of departure when Jacob's world is turned upside down in sorrow. His beloved Rachel dies in childbirth. Baby Benjamin, however, lives. After this Jacob returns to Mamre, where his aged father is residing. When he dies, Jacob and Esau meet for the burial rituals.

Like his parents, who each gave preferential treatment to a favorite son, Jacob loves his son Joseph more than any of his many other sons—and daughter. Nor does he attempt to conceal his blatant favoritism. He bestows on Joseph a richly colored garment, a most envied fashion statement. Why would Jacob do this? It would only incite envy in his other sons. It's unconscionable. He would end up paying dearly for his actions.

At one point Jacob scolds Joseph, particularly when Joseph interprets a dream foretelling that even Jacob himself will bow before him. Dreams are not to be ignored, however, and Jacob broods over what his son has said. Even though his older brothers are seething over Joseph's self-aggrandizement, Jacob sends the boy to check up on them where they are tending the flocks. The next news Jacob hears is that his son is dead, and there is proof. His beautiful coat has been bloodied and torn to pieces. Jacob is inconsolable, certain that he will grieve for his son until the day he dies.

The years go by, Jacob still grieving over Joseph. Then in one of its usual cycles, famine strikes the land—no food anywhere except in the storehouses of Egypt. Jacob sends his ten sons for food, all but Benjamin, the youngest. Only nine sons return with food; they show their father the grain they have brought home but report that a leading Egyptian official has jailed Simeon until they return with Benjamin. Jacob adamantly refuses. But the famine worsens. Finally he relents and lets Benjamin return to Egypt with his brothers.

The next thing he hears from his sons is almost impossible to comprehend: Joseph is alive and well and a ruler in Egypt. How can this be? But then he sees all the wagons that Joseph has sent for the household's relocation. With God's specific directive, Jacob's family caravan makes its way

Jacob's Callousness and Suffering

Here we have another example of Jacob's callousness toward other human beings. Leah is caught in a tragic web no less than Esau, and Jacob, while not the weaver of either, is very much involved in heightening the pain of their respective tragedies. In the end, each is somewhat compensated by God; Esau becomes wealthy and powerful in his own right (Chapter 36), Leah (and her concubine) provide most of Jacob's sons, and Jacob loses Rachel (Chapter 35), lives for years in the belief that Joseph, his favorite son, is dead (Chapter 37), and finally is forced to end his days in Egypt (Chapter 46). It is through Jacob's tempering by life that he is transformed to become Israel.

Daniel J. Elazar, "Jacob and Esau and the Emergence of the Jewish People" south. Joseph goes out to meet the wagons. When he sees his father, they hug and weep. Joseph takes him to meet Pharaoh, who inquires of the patriarch's age—130—and gives him the best land available for grazing.

Jacob spends the next seventeen years in Egypt with his entire household. Knowing his time on earth is running low, he asks Joseph to take an oath promising to bury him back in Canaan. Before he dies he blesses Joseph's two sons, the younger Ephraim with a greater blessing than the older Manasseh.

On his deathbed Jacob gives a final acknowledgment and blessing to each of his sons and then dies sometime after his 147th birthday. His body is embalmed in Egypt and returned to Canaan, accompanied by his entire family and a large contingent of Egyptian officials. There his body is laid to rest on the very plot that Abraham had purchased for Sarah's burial. Was Esau among the mourners? There is no biblical record, but if he were still living and in good health, he no doubt would have wanted to pay his respects to his twin brother.

Esau: Losing a Birthright and Blessing

Esau was an odd infant, perhaps appearing to resemble a furry animal as much as a human baby. He was covered in a blanket of hair, not just his head but his whole body. Whether his mother Rebekah rejected him from infancy or whether that came later is not recorded, but it is clear that as he was growing up she loved his twin Jacob far more than she loved him. To grow up rejected by a mother can have serious psychological consequences. Esau's grandmother Sarah had loved Isaac and spurned Ishmael, but Ishmael had his own doting mother Hagar. In this case there is only one mother to cling to, and she is turning away to gush over his brother.

While it is true that Father Isaac favors Esau, there is no reason to believe that the two of them were close. Esau is a sportsman, and Isaac approves of him because he has a taste for the wild game Esau hunts and brings home.

The incident Esau is most remembered for may have involved one of his hunting expeditions. He has been far out in the country and, famished, comes home, where he finds Jacob cooking up some pottage. Despite his hunger, his twin will not share. He will sell the stew, however, for Esau's birthright. One might wonder why this incident did not turn violent. Esau, the rough, hairy, ruddy-faced hunter, might have pushed Jacob aside and cleaned up the whole pot in a dozen gulps. But he gives in and gives up his birthright, perhaps fearing the consequences of laying a hand on Mama's boy.

When hard times come to Canaan, the household moves down to Gerar in the land of the Philistines. Here Isaac and Rebekah are involved in a deceptive scheme with King Abimelech, and the servants play an important role involving water rights and well digging, but Esau and Jacob seem to be sidelined during this period of their lives.

At age forty, however, Esau makes a major decision that will alienate him from his parents. He goes a-courting and ends up marrying two Hittite women—Judith and Basemath—women who cause Isaac and Rebekah endless grief.

The next big episode for Esau is when his father calls him in to receive the blessing. Isaac, thinking he is near death, asks Esau to get his gear, go out game hunting into the country, and return and prepare for him a tasty meal. They will eat together, and the meal will be followed by the blessing. Such an assignment is right up Esau's alley. He goes out, stalks and waits for the kill, and comes home with meat ready for the fire. He has gone through this ritual before, and he knows exactly how his father likes the food prepared. With the bowl in hand he goes to the old man's tent.

> *For although Esau, with his posterity, took precedence over Jacob in his lifetime, his status, like a bubble, burst as soon as he died. . . . The splendor attributed to Esau was like a vanishing vapor and all of his pomp disappeared like the closing of a scene onstage.*
>
> John Calvin, *Genesis*

Esau is stunned to hear his father ask who he is. *Has he lost his mind?* Seeing his father virtually go into a convulsion is more shocking, especially when Isaac bursts out with the news that he has already blessed the son who has just brought him a meal. Jacob has received the blessing, and there is no taking it back. Amid his howls of anguish, Esau begs his father to at least bless him as well. But his father holds firm, and makes the situation sound worse than it actually is. The earth's bounty and heaven's mercy will be lavished on Jacob, and he will rule over Esau.

Amid his weeping, Esau keeps begging his father to bless him. So Isaac offers up what might be termed a reverse blessing: "You'll live far from Earth's bounty, remote from Heaven's dew. You'll live by your sword, hand-to-mouth, and you'll serve your brother." But he continues, adding a final qualifier: "But when you can't take it any more you'll break loose and run free."[13] Hardly enough to restrain the rage. The tears have turned into venom. Esau is livid. He walks out, and under his breath he is spewing hatred: *I will kill the bastard. The old man will die within days, and Jacob will be dead meat.*

Warned by a servant who overhears Esau's rage, Rebekah sends her favorite son packing. Esau remains with his parents on the home place. His rage restrained, he sets out to get another wife. He's now the only son left, and in an effort to please his parents he marries his cousin Mahalath, daughter of Ishmael. His life is not nearly so grim as his father had foretold. Indeed, while his brother slaves away for Uncle Laban, Esau is accumulating wealth. Perhaps he often wonders about his brother—whether he's alive or dead.

When Jacob returns after twenty years of hard labor, Esau appears to have long gotten over the birthright-and-blessing fraud. He welcomes his brother with open arms, albeit after a parade of livestock has been sent ahead as a peace offering. Jacob has missed some of the most critical events of a son's life, including the death and burial of his mother. The greetings and introductions surely must have included reminiscences and details of her passing.

Like his twin brother Jacob, Esau has been given another name: Edom. And like Jacob, he has multiple wives—including Canaanite women and two daughters of Ishmael—and many children. He likewise has prospered, even more so after Jacob returns and gives him huge gifts of livestock. But like Abraham and his nephew Lot, the brothers are forced to separate because the land simply cannot support so many herds and flocks. Esau moves to the hilly region of Seir and becomes the father of the people known as Edomites.

For Esau and Jacob, at least in regard to their mended relationship, this seems to be a *happily ever after* story. Whether Esau became aware of Jacob's grief over the presumed loss of Joseph and the family's flight to Egypt due to famine is not recorded, but there is no reason to doubt that he would have cared deeply. The reconciliation and goodwill they have shown to each other, however, will not be passed down to succeeding generations.

Esau the Good Brother

Take the story of Jacob and Esau. I thought Esau was the bad brother and Jacob was the good brother, and no! Jacob is this kind of con-artist sleazeball who is a lot smarter than Esau, and Esau is the one who is forgiving, just, and good. Why do we cherish the one brother and not the other?

David Plotz, "Blogging the Bible"

Leah: Unwanted Wife

Leah in the eyes of Jacob is simply Rachel's sister. He is not attracted to her sexually or emotionally. She is not beautiful like her sister; she has weak eyes—an unspecified eye blemish that detracts from her physical appearance. Though she is his first wife, he makes no pretense of loving her. God is not pleased. He takes Leah's side and opens her womb. She gives birth to a son and names him Reuben. Leah sees this as an endorsement from God and a positive step in her marriage—a hopeful sign that her husband might now love her. What more can Jacob want? She has given him a son.

But Jacob still does not love her. So God opens her womb again, and Simeon is born. Yet again she gives birth to a son, Levi. Exasperated, she thinks that now, after she has given him three sons, Jacob will surely love her. But despite her longing, she is perceptive enough to see there is still no sparkle in his eye. Again she becomes pregnant and she gives birth to Judah. She will have to wait, however, before she gets another son. Jacob, perhaps at Rachel's prodding, is no longer intimate with her.

Leah's loneliness and depression are not easily disguised. Indeed, the names of her first three babies relate to her misery and lack of love from Jacob. Her oldest son Reuben is troubled. What can he do to cheer her up? He knows she wants another baby, always thinking that just one more will capture the heart of his father. So while he is out working the wheat harvest,

No Sisterly Reconciliation

Just before the Rachel-Leah story, we read of the tumultuous relationship between Jacob and Esau, and in the generation that follows Rachel and Leah, we have the story of Joseph and his brothers. The Rachel-Leah story is "sandwiched" in between these two brother stories, and it has similarities to them thematically. But there are also several important differences. . . . Unlike Jacob, Rachel never gets the chance to be transformed. . . . There is never any explicit reconciliation between Rachel and Leah. Jacob's inner transformation after struggling with the angel is inextricably bound up with his capacity to reconcile with his brother.

Nora Gold, "Rachel and Leah"

he comes across some mandrakes, plants thought to have magical potency—properties that were thought to spur pregnancy in otherwise barren women.

Reuben dutifully brings them to his mother. Barren Aunt Rachel, nearby, begs Leah to have some. What! How dare she? Leah lets loose the pent-up emotions she has stifled for years: "Wasn't it enough that you got my husband away from me? And now you also want my son's mandrakes?"[14] She's furious. But Rachel will not be cowed. She makes a deal: husband for mandrakes. She will *let* Jacob sleep with Leah if she gives up the mandrakes. Rachel has power over Jacob, and she knows it. Leah is forced into a humiliating situation. She might have thrown a left hook at her snide younger sister, but instead she hands over the mandrakes in exchange for having a night with her own husband.

Rachel: Adored Wife with False Gods

Rachel is a shepherd out in the country overseeing a large flock of sheep in a rough-and-tumble man's world. Other shepherds waiting at the well acknowledge her routine arrival with neither catcalls nor surprise. Jacob, the stranger at the well, sees her for the first time. Here Rachel emerges from the biblical text in all her feminine glory. Laban's daughter and Leah's younger sister, she is drop-dead gorgeous like her aunt Rebekah (who would also become her absentee mother-in-law) and her great aunt Sarah. So stricken by her is the stranger that he goes into an adrenalin high and rolls a huge boulder away from covering the well. Then, without missing a beat, hormones still racing, he sets his sights on her. She is no doubt surprised and taken aback when the stranger begins kissing her—and weeping. Only then does he disclose that he is her cousin. She runs. What else can she do? Back home, she tells her father, and he goes to the well to offer an official welcome.

How much Rachel knows about her upcoming marriage arranged by Jacob and her father is not recorded. Nor is there any mention of friendship between them during the seven years he is laboring for her. Does she understand the custom that the oldest daughter must marry first? When her father throws the marriage feast, does she imagine it is for her as Jacob does? There is no indication that either sister plays any part in the decision-making process, as did Rebekah when she decided on

Love at First Sight

Jacob is outstanding among male lovers in the Bible for the true, romantic, abiding love he bore for Rachel. Whether such a deep and ardent love was reciprocated we are not told. The Bible has no reference to Rachel's love for Jacob.

Herbert Lockyer, *All the Women of the Bible*, 128

her own to leave immediately with Abraham's servant to marry Isaac.

Rachel's name is added to a long list of barren women of the Bible. She watches Leah and her maid getting pregnant and envies them to the point of despair. It cannot be her husband's fault. He's virile enough to make babies with Leah and her maid. But to Jacob she wails, *Give me sons or I will die*. Jacob snaps back, *It's not my fault. I'm not God*. Here we see Rachel's fury, not unlike the rage Sarah vented at Abraham over Hagar. Rachel's retort is to push a surrogate at Jacob—Bilhah her maid. Other barren women have done that very thing, but never with happy results.

When Bilhah becomes pregnant and bears a son, and becomes pregnant again, Rachel now thinks she has bested her sister. But she hasn't. Though she has Jacob wrapped around her little finger, she's still barren. Soon Leah has two more sons and a daughter. Finally, after years of discontent and bickering and family turmoil, God remembers Rachel and *opens her womb*. She is ecstatic when Joseph is born. Her humiliation is lifted, and her whole attitude seems to change.

When Jacob is conspiring to flee from Laban, he consults with the sisters and they actually agree with each other. They respond as one in their commitment to leave their father's household and run away with him to Canaan. And so they pack up their belongings and prepare themselves for the arduous journey.

That Rachel has been depressed by her barrenness and that she has burned with jealousy toward Leah are normal reactions. The reader is not surprised. But when she steals and conceals the household gods before escaping with Jacob, her behavior is not easily explained. She acknowledges that God speaks with her husband, but she apparently cannot trust in God herself.

When her father and his men catch up with the fleeing party, he demands the household gods be returned. She panics—especially when she hears Jacob say that whoever has taken them will be put to death. Quick thinking. She hides them in a cushion and sits on it, telling her father she is sick with menstrual cramps. Later, after the entire party has arrived in Canaan, Jacob tells his family—especially Rachel—to get rid of their false gods and wash themselves and put on clean clothes.

Not long after this Rachel becomes pregnant with her second son. Things are not going well. The entire company has been traveling under the scorching sun on the dry, dusty roads. When her time comes, it's a very difficult labor. Baby Benjamin is born healthy, but Rachel will not make it. She dies, and her body is buried on the road to Bethlehem, with a

Women in Genesis

Even when you pay very close attention, they can just vanish right before your eyes. I'm referring here to the women of Genesis, who play an increasingly diminished role as the book moves along. In the beginning, man and woman got equal billing, both created in the image and likeness of their Creator. From that point onward, women seemed to get a shorter and shorter end of the stick. By now we have seen strong matriarchs, women who talk with God, women who get their own promises. We've seen active women who are willing to beat and banish others. We've seen women who are not afraid to pull a fast one to ensure that the covenant will pass on to the right member of the family. But by the time we come to Jacob, father of the people of Israel, there are more and more women who play less and less a role in the fate of the nation.

It is almost as though the crowded stage of Jacob's tent, with four different women coming and going, demands that their speaking roles are accordingly attenuated. Sarah and Hagar each managed to occupy the entire stage when it was their turn to speak. . . . Rebecca basked in the limelight—with no women to share the stage. . . . But when Rachel, Leah, Bilhah, and Zilpah all have to vie for Jacob's attention, each simply gets less airtime. . . . It comes as little surprise, then, that by the time we get to Jacob's daughter she vanishes. And she does so in a way that is especially demeaning. [Dinah is one of Jacob's thirteen children when the family crosses the river, but she is not counted.]

Burton L. Visotzky, *The Genesis of Ethics*, 193–94

stone marking her grave. She is the first woman recorded in the Bible to have died in childbirth.

Concluding Observations

The legacy of dishonesty and manipulation left by Isaac and Rebekah is passed down most notably to Jacob. Both twins grow up learning to play the game for their own advantage, but Jacob excels as the premier trickster, second only to Uncle Laban. Jacob is arrogant and treats Leah badly. Only in old age does he mellow—and that comes through suffering. Esau, by patriarchal standards, seems in many ways to be a remarkably decent man. He forgives and forgets and welcomes Jacob home.

As wives in a polygamous marriage, Leah and Rachel play their parts. Jealousy and bickering mar their legacies. All in all, the dysfunction in the household in which Jacob grew up and the one he himself is head of is striking—far beyond the reach of routine family therapy.

It is most significant that the dead and the living are closely bound together. Indeed, Scripture tells us that when Jacob "breathed his last," he "was gathered to his people." Just before he dies, he gives Joseph and his other sons instructions that establish the deep and lasting connection from one generation to another long after death:

> I am about to be gathered to my people. Bury me with my fathers in the cave in

> the field of Ephron the Hittite, the cave in the field of Machpelah, near Mamre in Canaan, which Abraham bought along with the field as a burial place from Ephron the Hittite. There Abraham and his wife Sarah were buried, there Isaac and his wife Rebekah were buried, and there I buried Leah. The field and the cave in it were bought from the Hittites.[15]

Here is Jacob at age 147, dying, surrounded by his loved ones. There is a little phrase that profoundly captures his final moments. He draws his feet up into the bed—perhaps in a fetal position. Was this recapitulating his birth? He came into the world from the womb, his arm grasping his brother's heel, his feet no doubt kicking in a struggle to overtake his twin. Now, however, his feet are drawn up, and he is leaving the world to join the old ones who have gone before, never to struggle again.

Further Reading

Buechner, Frederick. *Son of Laughter*. San Francisco: HarperOne, 1994.

Garland, David E., and Diana R. Garland. *Flawed Families of the Bible: How God's Grace Works through Imperfect Relationships*. Grand Rapids: Baker, 2007.

Klitsner, Shmuel. *Wrestling Jacob: Deception, Identity, and Freudian Slips in Genesis*. Teaneck, NJ: Ben Yehuda Press, 2006.

Zakovitch, Yair. *Jacob: Unexpected Patriarch*. New Haven, CT: Yale University Press, 2012.

5

JOSEPH AND HIS SIBLINGS

Playing King of the Hill

Joseph is the first modern man of the Bible. He moves seamlessly from his role as spoiled son of a wealthy herdsman to hostage to second in command of Pharaoh's household. No other individual in Genesis has held such a high position, and in a foreign court at that. There are obstacles along the way, but he swaggers through the setbacks with smugness and self-confidence.

Joseph is the star of his own show. No one else in his colorful cabaret plays more than a minor role. Unlike the three great patriarchs before him, who dance with partners—such luminaries as Lot, Sarah, Hagar, Ishmael, Rebekah, Esau, Rachel, Leah, and Laban—Joseph essentially dances alone on the stage. Indeed, he's a pro who makes his moves look easy. Even his parents are in the background in his story. None of his brothers or his sister rise above a bit part, nor do Potiphar and his wife. Indeed, his own wife is barely mentioned, nor are the births of his children. No one competes with him for attention, either in Genesis or in subsequent accounts. Joseph steals the show.

And dance he does—around his brothers, showing off his good fortune and telling them his dreams. He dances to the delight of Potiphar, picking up the tempo to escape Potiphar's wife. He's even dancing in prison as he interprets dreams and later when he toys with his famine-fleeing brothers. And he dances all the way to the twenty-first century, starring in the long-running musical *Joseph and the Amazing Technicolor Dreamcoat*. (As part of this production, he is accorded an official internet site. The web surfer first finds a greeting: "With a crash of drums and a flash of light we welcome you to the official Joseph website!") Here he shines in virtual reality like no other biblical figure.

Yet apart from Stephen's fiery sermon before the Sanhedrin in Acts 7, Joseph is barely mentioned in the New Testament. Here Stephen recounts the story of the Hebrews and their centuries-long quest to settle in the Promised Land. Abraham and Moses are the bookends of the sermon, both given lengthy coverage. The stories of Isaac and Jacob are barely fleshed out, while Joseph again seems to steal the show, though no mention is made of his Technicolor coat.

Joseph as a Modern Business Manager

Although the Joseph story can be viewed through the lens of the great man and charismatic leadership theories . . . the Joseph story best illustrates the servant leadership approach. . . . Joseph [develops] from a self-centered brother to a servant leader in several different contexts: as slave, as prisoner, and as the highest-ranking official in Pharaonic Egypt. . . . Joseph's story illustrates that servant leadership stems, in large part, from the development of stewardship, foresight, empathy and healing. The biblical account of Joseph contributes to business management scholarship.

Toby H. Birnbaum and Paul J. Herskovitz, "The Biblical Story of Joseph: Lessons in Servant Leadership," 158

In comparison, the faith chapter Hebrews 11 seems almost to slight him: "By faith Joseph, when his end was near, spoke about the exodus of the Israelites from Egypt and gave instructions concerning the burial of his bones."[1]

Joseph's is a great story but not one of biblical proportions comparable to that of his great-grandfather Abraham, nor that of Moses, Joshua, or David.

Nevertheless, Joseph is abundantly blessed in his posterity. The tribes bearing the names of his two sons (Ephraim and Manasseh) are among the most populous and prosperous of the twelve tribes. Thus Joseph in effect is given the double portion accorded the firstborn son. But for all his father's favoritism, he will be excluded from Jesus' genealogy. That distinction will belong to his brother Judah.

Joseph: Favored Son of Jacob

After years of depressing infertility, Rachel finally gives birth to a boy. But such great news does not necessarily bring joy to everyone in Jacob's large, dysfunctional household. Aunt Leah, it is safe to assume, is not knitting blankets and booties for baby Joseph. The baby-bearing rivalry between his mother and his aunt is palpable. Tension reverberates through every nook and cranny of the household. In this setting little Joseph grows up much doted on by his parents. His mother dies when he is a young boy, and he is quickly

Excruciating Pitch of Family Problems

Situations that were problematical for Abraham and Sarah worsened in the family of their son Isaac and his wife, Rebekah, where there was strife between the two; between their twin sons, Esau and Jacob; between wives Rachel and Leah; between Uncle Laban and nephew Jacob; and between God and the would-be-partner, Jacob. Now, in the last story of Genesis, family confusions and hurts are brought to their most excruciating pitch. It's the familiar problem of making a name for oneself at the expense of others, among a family of twelve brothers and between the brothers and their father Jacob.

Paul Borgman, *Genesis: The Story We Haven't Heard,* 176

designated Papa's pet, playing the role of spoiled brat.

Indeed, it is no secret that Jacob loves Joseph more than any of his other sons—and blatantly so. The brothers hate Joseph, not least because, at their father's instructions, he snitches. He goes out in the field with them, all too eager to bring back a bad report to his father. On one such occasion when he is seventeen, he adds salt to their wounds by strutting before them in a handsomely designed multicolored outer garment. It is a fashion statement like none they had ever seen. They know exactly where it came from. Their father had never lavished anything so nice on any of them.

Being the pet, however, is not always an easy role to play. He's a motherless child confronting a gang of jealous brothers. But Joseph is anything but a pitiable character. In this patriarchal society a father's favor goes a long way—even more so, God's.

Before fully enjoying his status as first son, however, Joseph will run the gauntlet in more ways than one. His brothers loathe his arrogance. Not only does Joseph act the dandy and flaunt his duds; he flaunts his dreams. And in an era when dreams are deemed highly significant, he relates them with flair. In one such dream he and his brothers are out in a field gathering bundles of grain. Suddenly his bundle stands straight and tall, as all the other bundles bow down before him. His brothers are incredulous. How could a mere callow youth rule over them? None of them believe what his dream is suggesting, but they hate him even more.

This coat indicated more than preference; it symbolized preeminence and superiority of rank. . . . In the context of our passage I believe that Joseph's coat was considered to be symbolic of his authority in the same manner as stripes on the sleeve of a military uniform. Joseph's brothers hated this garment and what it symbolized, for their first act of violence was to strip his coat from him.

Bob Deffinbaugh, "Jacob, Joseph, Jealousy, and a Journey to Egypt"

Does Joseph not realize he is alienating his brothers? Of course he does, and that seems to be the point. He boasts of another dream that carries the same message. In this instance the sun, moon, and eleven stars bow down to him. Now he commands even his father's attention. This truly is a case of the *spoiled child syndrome.* His father is irritated and scolds him for the outrageous assumption that even he will be under Joseph's rule.

Still Joseph remains the favorite and the one his father expects to bring back reports on the others. Indeed, his father sends him off alone to check on his brothers, who are herding their flocks near Shechem. As he

Everyday *Life*

Men's and Women's Apparel

Clearly Joseph's coat of many colors was more than casual-Friday attire. Donned in his striking garment, he stood out in a crowd—and in his family. No doubt fashioned out of fine linen and colored with expensive dyes, his was the robe of wealth and royalty or perhaps the priesthood. Typical dress for ordinary citizens, whether at work or travel, would have been coarser and would have featured earth tones. Linen and wool were the fabrics of choice. Leather thongs served as shoes, and some form of turban was the typical head covering.

Women's garments, like the outer robes of the men, were long and flowing. But their gender-specific fashion was never to be mistaken for that of the other sex. The Mosaic law forbade cross-dressing: "A woman must not wear men's clothing, nor a man wear women's clothing, for the Lord your God detests anyone who does this" (Deut. 22:5 NIV).

Both men and women wore girdles, a wide sash that kept the garment closed and tight—sometimes folded and used as a pocket for money. Like men's fashions, women's wear was designed for travel and work, whether gleaning in a field or baking over a fire. Women were typically veiled or wore a scarf with their face showing. A veil covering the face was appropriate before a wedding ceremony, but not otherwise. The beauty of women—like Sarah or Rebekah or Rachel—was widely heralded.

A woman's jewelry and makeup distinguished her attire from a man's. Jewelry was a status symbol and worn especially for festive occasions.

Unlike in the modern era, fashions in biblical times changed little over the course of generations.

A Poor Man's Cloak

Most peoples' clothes were homespun, loose fitting, in one of the soft colors of natural dyes—a dark red, brown or yellow, perhaps striped. . . . A poor man's cloak was so important to him that if it was handed over to guarantee repayment of a debt, it had to be returned to him at sunset.

Elizabeth Fletcher, "Clothes"

searches for them, the open land seems to rise endlessly from the horizon, but there is no sign of his brothers. Finally he meets a man who tells him they have moved on to Dothan. So Joseph continues his search. They see him coming from a distance, and before he approaches, they hatch a scheme to do away with him, disposing of his body in a dry cistern. But Reuben is alarmed and warns them: *Whatever you do, don't injure him.*

Joseph crosses the field toward them, sporting his extravagant coat. He is prepared to exchange the usual greeting rituals, maybe electrify them with the details of another dream, and make mental notes of their deficiencies to report back to Father Jacob.

But something is wrong. He senses it. Then, without a second's warning, they grab him, yank off his coat, throw him down a dry well, and go off to have their dinner. What is he thinking at that point? Is he screaming out for mercy? Is he even within earshot of them while they are eating? Is he wishing he had not strutted around in this colorful coat and bragged about his dreams? He knows his brothers, and at this point he's probably thinking he will be left to suffer a slow, agonizing death.

But then he hears a commotion—a distant caravan on the trade route heading south. And suddenly he's being pulled out of the cistern as roughly as he was thrown in. Have his brothers had a change of heart? Did Reuben quash the plot to kill him? He quickly realizes that Reuben is nowhere to be seen and his other brothers are forcibly packing him with the caravan headed for Egypt. This, he surely surmises, is no tourist package to visit the pyramids. There is only one reason these traders would want him: to sell him as a slave.

Joseph Sold into Slavery

They then sold him for the price of a slave, stripped him of his coat, and sent him naked, they knew not, and they cared not, whither, so long as he might be out of their way, and no longer provoke their envy and their anger. Oh! the agonies he felt—parted from his father, losing his brethren, without a friend, dragged away by cruel man-sellers, chained upon a camel it may be, with fetters on his hands.

C. H. Spurgeon, "Joseph Attacked by the Archers"

Upon arrival in Egypt, Joseph is quickly recognized as more than a dim-witted field hand. He is so quick and clever and capable that he is soon sent to serve Potiphar, a high official, the captain of Pharaoh's palace guards. So now Joseph is living in luxury, albeit as a servant. Potiphar senses that there is something different about this young man—that he has some sort of pipeline to God, who bestows blessings on him. In fact, as time passes, Potiphar's affection for him grows, and he turns over the management of his personal affairs to Joseph. With that move, God prospers Potiphar to the point that he can simply sit back and enjoy the good life.

Like his mother Rachel, Joseph is easy on the eyes. His confidence and good looks are a striking combination that does not go unnoticed by Potiphar's wife, who is smitten by the handsome young man, albeit a mere servant. She's a powerful woman possessed of shocking boldness. So she says to Joseph one day, *Come to bed with me.*

Had he been sending her the wrong signals? Whatever the case, he adamantly refuses to get involved, not because she is not appealing to him. He is more chivalrous than that. Rather, he goes straight to the matter of his loyalty to her husband, explaining that Potiphar treats him with great respect and as an equal, giving him supervision over everything except, of course, his wife. Joseph insists, therefore, that he could not even entertain the thought of betraying him.

Used to getting what she wants, she will not be put off. She keeps trying to seduce him, perhaps thinking he is playing hard to get. Later he is in the house when no one is around. Again she approaches him. They're alone. No one will find out. *Come on*, she teases. Then she grabs hold of him; he pulls away, and in the process she yanks his coat off as he escapes.

She is furious and is left holding the coat. How dare the servant say his master treats him as an equal and then haughtily pull away from her advances? This probably isn't the first time. She may very well have had her way with servants before. She immediately moves into action, running outside screaming hysterically that the Hebrew slave tried to rape her. She has proof; he left his coat behind. The servants are wide eyed. They will quickly spread the news, embellished with every retelling.

That is just the prelude. Next comes the clincher. When Potiphar returns home, she is ready, coat in hand. She repeats the story.

Joseph flees Potiphar's wife

The Hebrew slave—*the one* you *brought into this household*—would have raped her but for her screaming. She plays the part well. He doesn't doubt her word and is outraged at Joseph. This too-good-to-be-true servant he had been treating like one of the family has now double-crossed him. That wretched gigolo!

Potiphar might have called in the executioners, but instead he throws Joseph in jail. As a slave, Joseph has no recourse, no such luck as to be merely fired, downsized, terminated; he's sent straightaway to a dungeon where the other criminals are housed. His life takes a rapid downward turn.

But through it all God is with him. In fact, God opens the way for him to sidle up to the head jailer. Joseph is a charmer, and soon the top official at the jail puts Joseph in charge of all the others, allowing him to move about freely. Those incarcerated are mainly nondescript royal servants. But then one day rumors are flying as two high officials are brought in: Pharaoh's head cupbearer and his chief baker. Joseph is in charge of them. Coincidentally, soon after they arrive they both have portentous dreams, on the same night no less.

The next morning Joseph notices they are acting unusually solemn. He inquires. They tell him they are distraught because there is no dream interpreter in jail. *Why would they need an interpreter?* he asks. *Isn't God the one who interprets dreams?* Perhaps they have already gotten wind of his reputation for being close to God, so, without so much as a *Huh?* they tell him their dreams. The cupbearer dreamed that a vine with three branches was blooming and ripening with bunches of grapes; he squeezed the grapes into grape juice and gave a cup to Pharaoh. That's it. There's no punch line. But Joseph is unfazed.

The three branches represent three days. Pharaoh will release him in three days, and he will go back to serving him cups of wine. There is no charge for the favorable interpretation, but Joseph reminds the cupbearer to speak well of him when he is back in his official position.

Now, it's the head baker's turn. In his dream he saw three baskets on his head, the top one filled with baked goods. Birds were having a heyday pecking at the pastries. Once again Joseph is on-the-spot ready with an interpretation. The baskets are days. In three days Pharaoh will decapitate the baker, and vultures will devour him like roadkill.

Three days later Pharaoh throws a birthday party for himself. Both the cupbearer and baker are designated to sit at the head table. He toasts the cupbearer, giving him back his position of honor. But his toast to the baker falls flat. He is sent away and beheaded. The cupbearer is ecstatic. He returns to serve the king but forgets entirely about Joseph, still incarcerated within the prison walls.

The weeks and months drag into years—two long years. Then it's Pharaoh's turn to have dreams. The first involves cattle. Seven well-fed cows emerge from the Nile, followed by seven gaunt cows. The thin cows eat the fat ones. In the second dream seven withered heads of grain devour seven full heads. These are bizarre dreams, and he calls in the interpreters—the best sages and magicians in the land.

But they are at a loss. They all say they don't have a clue what the dreams mean. At this point, they are well aware that interpreting Pharaoh's dreams can be risky business. The cupbearer remembers Joseph and recommends him. Joseph comes forth and promises the Pharaoh that God will wipe away his worries. Turns out that the second dream confirms the first. There will be seven years of plenty followed by seven years of famine.

The upshot of all of this, Joseph continues, is that the Pharaoh needs to take immediate action by appointing someone to be in charge of storing up grain for the famine to come. It makes perfect sense to follow this course, and the right man seems obvious:

> So Pharaoh commissioned Joseph: "I'm putting you in charge of the entire country of Egypt." Then Pharaoh removed his

> signet ring from his finger and slipped it on Joseph's hand. He outfitted him in robes of the best linen and put a gold chain around his neck. He put the second-in-command chariot at his disposal, and as he rode people shouted "Bravo!"[2]

If that is not enough, Pharaoh emphasizes that no major decision will be made without Joseph's approval. Moreover, Pharaoh gives him a new Egyptian name and an Egyptian wife, Asenath, the daughter of a royal priest. Never before has a follower of Yahweh held such a high position, and he's only thirty. Abraham is one hundred by the time Sarah gives birth to the son of promise. Joseph's grandfather Isaac is forty when his father procures a wife. Father Jacob spends his best years slaving for a sleazy uncle. But Joseph is young, vigorous, immensely popular—and virile. His wife bears him two sons, Manasseh and Ephraim.

Pharaoh's dreams come true: seven years of plenty, seven years of famine—famine that spreads far beyond Egypt. Joseph oversees everything with earnest efficiency. People from all over the known world come to purchase grain from Egypt's massive storage facilities.

Then in the midst of his hectic schedule one day he does a double take. There in the front of the line of people waiting to purchase grain are his own brothers. He plays it cool, treats them like strangers—no pleasantries or signs of recognition. They bow before him with no thought that he might be Joseph. He asks the standard questions, and then, out of the blue, accuses them of being spies, persisting in his allegations amid their adamant denials. They insist they are all brothers and tell him about their aged father and the youngest son left back home, but he will have none of it. He throws all ten of them in jail.

After three days, Joseph relents and releases nine of them to return home with food. Simeon is kept as a hostage until they come back with the youngest brother. He makes sure all their money has been surreptitiously returned to them hidden in their bags—no doubt knowing this will only increase their dread.

Time passes; the famine continues, and they return for more grain. Joseph sees his brothers arriving with Benjamin. He calls the steward to bring his brothers into the palace. Nice gesture, but they are edgy, fearing the worst—not knowing that a feast is being prepared for them. They think that they are going to be accused of stealing the money that had been put in their sacks of grain. The steward puts them at ease and then brings out Simeon. Joseph arrives, accepts their gifts, inquires of their father, is introduced to Benjamin, and makes a quick exit before they catch him weeping.

Joseph returns and they all sit down to eat, though he dines alone at his own table. In the spirit of his father, he shows obvious favoritism, ordering the chef to give Benjamin a double helping—Benjamin, who is no doubt used to being doted on by his father.

Before the brothers return to Canaan the following morning, Joseph has seen to it that once again their money has been returned in the sacks of grain; his own silver chalice is placed in Benjamin's sack of food. So they depart, but no sooner have they set off for home than the steward catches up with them. He accuses them of stealing the chalice; they deny it, swearing death upon any one of them should it be found among their possessions. Benjamin is the guilty one, and he must return to become a slave.

What appalling pranks Joseph plays. He's toying with them, getting even with them for selling him into slavery. But his father? How can he put his father through such agony? The brothers are beside themselves. They are innocent. They tear their clothes in grief and return to Joseph, throwing themselves before him, pleading for mercy. They say that they will all become his slaves, but, for God's sake, spare Benjamin. Judah becomes the spokesman and pleads for Benjamin, insisting their father will die.

By faith Jacob, when he was dying, blessed each of Joseph's sons, and worshiped as he leaned on the top of his staff.
Hebrews 11:21 (NIV)

With that Joseph loses it. He breaks down, wailing so loudly that servants rush to tell the Pharaoh. The brothers are stunned at his weeping, even more so when he reveals who he is. They are both happy and horrified at the same time. After all, they sold him into slavery. But he reassures them—essentially saying: *All things work together for good to those who love God.*[3] Thus, their selling him paved the way for him to save the whole family from famine.

He tells them to hurry home to their father with the good news. Joseph promises good land for the entire household and all their flocks. The Pharaoh even gets in on the act and sends wagons of provisions from Egypt and everything needed to bring all their possessions south. The brothers are sent away with Benjamin receiving a bonus of hundreds of pieces of silver and several new garments—without a word of grumbling from the older brothers.

When his father's entire household arrives in Egypt, Joseph helps them settle into the best land. But the famine continues year after year. Land dries up in Egypt and the surrounding regions. Joseph takes good care of his extended family, but the Egyptians have no one to look after them. They trade their cattle for food; then the next year, with no possessions to trade, they give up their farms and agree to become slaves just to eat. "Joseph reduced the people to slavery from one end of Egypt to the other."[4] But there is a caveat. They can become sharecroppers on their own land, working for the Pharaoh. They can plant with the seed they are allotted and must return one-fifth of their harvest as payment.

The final episodes in Joseph's life involve his dying father. He brings his sons into his father's presence, and Jacob continues a generations-long practice of giving the younger son the primary blessing. So despite Joseph's objections, Jacob blesses Ephraim with his right hand and Manasseh with his left.

Sometime after this, Jacob gives all his sons blessings or curses, as the case may be. His first and favorite son by Rachel surely hears his father's words with pleasure. His focus has been on worldly wealth, and he will receive a material blessing, but it will be an older brother who receives the real spiritual blessing—one that will have profound consequences. Speaking of Joseph, Jacob begins with words that hark back to a description of his uncle Ishmael:

> Joseph is a wild donkey,
> a wild donkey by a spring,
> spirited donkeys on a hill.
> The archers with malice attacked,
> shooting their hate-tipped arrows;
> But he held steady under fire,
> his bow firm, his arms limber,
> With the backing of the Champion of Jacob,
> the Shepherd, the Rock of Israel.
> The God of your father—may he help you![5]

Soon after that, Jacob dies. Joseph throws himself on his father, weeping and kissing him. Then he takes charge of the burial, but only after obtaining permission from the Pharaoh to return to his homeland of Canaan.

After the burial Joseph and his brothers return to Egypt. But the brothers are still very insecure and fearful now that their father is dead. Joseph assures them that he will care for them and their children; they have nothing to fear. He also reminds them that one day they will return to Canaan. When they do, he specifies that his bones be returned to the Land of Promise. He dies at age 110, his body embalmed and laid in a coffin in Egypt.

Parallel Stories of Joseph and Moses

Frequently, the Bible presents characters whose personalities and roles confront those of other characters in order to make its point. This part of the biblical message reaches its apogee in the parallel cases of Joseph and Moses who are presented as binary opposites, Joseph because of his assimilation into Egypt and his unrestrained service to the pharaoh in subordinating the Egyptians and bringing his brother Israelites down to Egypt, is not counted among the patriarchs and indeed represents the end of the patriarchal line, while Moses, who represents the new leadership that inherits the mantle of the patriarchs, liberates his people not only from Egypt but, insofar as possible, from Egyptian culture, after starting at the very heart of that culture in the pharaoh's palace and family.

Daniel J. Elazar, "Jacob and Esau and the Emergence of the Jewish People"

Dinah: Misadventure in Shechem

Wives of the patriarchs and other important Old Testament figures are often accorded significant space in the text. Daughters and sisters, however, are typically neglected—unless men grab the headlines. So it is with Dinah, whose brutal brothers steal her story.

The account of Dinah, daughter of Leah and Jacob, is a one-episode story, a painful one to recount. She goes off to the nearby town of Shechem—perhaps bored out of her mind—to spend time with some of the women there. The chief, whose name is Shechem, spots her and seduces or rapes her. Whether she may have shown interest in him and given him some sort of signal

Dinah, Young and Daring

Dinah's love for sightseeing sets off a train of tragic consequences. Young and daring, and curious to know something of the world outside, she stole away one day from the drab tents of her father, to see how the girls in their gorgeous Oriental trappings fared in nearby Shechem. Roaming around, the eyes of Prince Shechem, son of Hamor, lighted upon her. . . . Although Dinah's vanity was flattered at Shechem's attention so that she went to his palace, she never meant to go so far.

Herbert Lockyer, *All the Women of the Bible*, 45

is pure speculation, but her brothers will later suggest that she was being used as a prostitute, not a mere victim. At any rate Shechem falls head over heels in love and speaks tenderly to her, desiring her for his wife. He arranges for his father to meet with Jacob to ask her hand in marriage.

In the meantime, Dinah's brothers get news of what has happened, and they are livid. But they listen to the father's proposal—that the two tribal groups intermarry and that Jacob and his sons settle down nearby and live with them in peace. Then Shechem himself speaks up: "Please, say yes. I'll pay anything. Set the bridal price as high as you will—the sky's the limit! Only give me this girl for my wife."[6]

Jacob's sons might have pummeled Shechem on the spot, but like Jacob himself, they possess a cruel cunning that will one day come to haunt their father. Rather than show their honest outrage, they pretend the only matter separating their household from Shechem's is circumcision. If Shechem and his household will become circumcised, then they will intermarry and live together as one extended family. Shechem will do anything for Dinah; he and his father agree for themselves and all the men in the tribe.

Three days after the surgery, the men are still very weak and sore and may have been in an alcohol-induced stupor. It is then that Simeon and Levi take advantage of them, going through the town and murdering every one of them. Then the other brothers arrive and steal the livestock. If that is not enough, they go through the houses, snatching everything of value they can find, taking captive the women and children, bringing Dinah home with them.

Dinah had not been consulted. Indeed, she may have been pleased to become the wife of the adoring Shechem. One can only imagine how traumatized she is by the slaughter. Jacob, too, is traumatized—as much for fear as regret. If the neighboring tribes should unite, they could annihilate his entire household. The sons are unmoved: "Nobody is going to treat our sister like a whore and get by with it."[7]

Reuben: Oldest Son of Jacob

Reared in an utterly dysfunctional family, he might have broken loose and stood head and shoulders above his brothers, but Reuben, the oldest, does not. His mother is Leah, who desperately longs for his father's love. Reuben no doubt senses a lack of love himself, especially when his father shows such obvious favoritism for his much younger half brother Joseph, Rachel's son.

Reuben and Gad ask for land

Yet as the sons of Jacob go, he possesses more redeeming qualities than most of the rest.

Though the firstborn son of Jacob, Reuben is not a prominent biblical figure, at least in the ranking of the firstborn in previous generations—Ishmael and Esau. He first emerges as a character in his own right when he is working out in the wheat field and finds some mandrakes and brings them to his mother. A mandrake is a plant with leaves, flowers, and a large bulbous root, all of which are potentially poisonous and may have hallucinogenic qualities. In ancient times the mandrake was thought to make an effective aphrodisiac, a love potion—even to the extent of bringing fertility to an otherwise barren woman. Whether or not Reuben knows why the plant is so valued is not divulged; he is simply gratifying his mother.

Reuben's name appears in the narrative later on in a rather offhand manner. The text simply states that after Rachel died Jacob moved on and set up camp. While he "was living in that region, Reuben went and slept with his father's concubine, Bilhah. And [Jacob] heard of what he did."[8] The reader is left wondering about Reuben's motive and Jacob's reaction.

The longest narrative relating to Reuben involves his response to his brothers, who are plotting to get revenge on Joseph. When he learns of the conspiracy, he intervenes—in a less-than-forceful way: *Whatever you do, don't injure him.* Thinking he could sneak back later and rescue his little brother, he agrees that they can throw him into the cistern. Then he leaves, perhaps imagining that his absence erases his guilt. While he is away, the brothers yank Joseph out of the cistern, dust him off, do some hard bargaining with traders, and send him off to Egypt for twenty pieces of silver.

As the caravan continues on its way and Reuben returns, he walks over, peers down into the cistern, and howls in despair. He's beside himself. Joseph is gone. As the oldest of the brothers, he must answer to his father. But the brothers have concocted a plan. They kill a goat and smear the blood all over the multicolored coat, making it look like Joseph has been attacked. Then they all head home and inform their father that they have found a coat and ask him if he thinks it looks like the one he gave to Joseph. He recognizes it immediately and begins to wail. The scheme has worked.

Later, when the brothers go to Egypt for grain, Joseph, whom they do not recognize, accuses them of being spies. He demands Simeon stay behind while the others return home and bring back Benjamin. In a flash, Reuben is flooded with memories of that awful day when Joseph was sold into slavery. To his brothers he hisses: "Didn't I tell you not to sin against the boy? But you wouldn't listen! Now we must give an accounting for his blood."[9]

His brothers were scoundrels, and he knew it. They had most viciously avenged Dinah's rape by Shechem, a gory mass murder in which he apparently was not involved. Why he would have trusted them enough to walk away, leaving Joseph in their hands, is inexplicable.

Before he dies, Jacob gives his final blessing to Reuben. There is nothing subtle about his words, words that clearly reveal his pent-up resentment. But not because Reuben was less than an upstanding oldest brother who reined in the wickedness of his younger siblings. Rather, Jacob's words go back to one incident—an incident he took as a grievous personal affront.

> Reuben, you're my firstborn,
> my strength, first proof of my manhood,
> at the top in honor and at the top in power,
> But like a bucket of water spilled,
> you'll be at the top no more,
> Because you climbed into your father's marriage bed,
> mounting that couch, and you defiled it.[10]

Simeon and Levi: Two of a Kind

To suggest Simeon (as well as his brother Levi) is a hothead who explodes with anger when their sister Dinah is seduced—or raped—by Shechem is missing the point. When he conspires to kill all the men in the town after they have in good faith agreed to be circumcised, he is nothing short of a cruel, calculating, vicious murderer. With his younger brother Levi, he slaughters the men of Shechem, wives and children crying out in anguish. They show no apparent remorse. When Father Jacob lashes out at his sons, the brothers defend their actions, saying essentially, *They deserved what they got.*

When the brothers are in Egypt to purchase grain, unknowingly dealing with Joseph, it is Simeon who is selected to stay behind. It is Simeon who is tied up and held as a hostage. He is released when the brothers return with Benjamin. Later Simeon marries a Canaanite woman, who bears him six sons.

Father Jacob, when he offers his benediction before his death, tells it like it is, actually cursing their sins and not sparing them with the consequences.

> Simeon and Levi are two of a kind,
> ready to fight at the drop of a hat.
> I don't want anything to do with their vendettas,
> want no part in their bitter feuds;
> They kill men in fits of temper,
> slash oxen on a whim.
> A curse on their uncontrolled anger,
> on their indiscriminate wrath.
> I'll throw them out with the trash;
> I'll shred and scatter them like confetti throughout Israel.[11]

Ironically, Levi, who lived to be 137, would have the distinction of heading the priestly tribe of Levites, with honorable descendants that include the likes of

Moses, Samuel, Ezekiel, Ezra, John the Baptist, Matthew, Mark, and Barnabas.

Judah: Leaving Behind a Formidable Legacy

"Jacob had Judah and his brothers."[12] These startling words pop out of the genealogy of Jesus (through his stepfather Joseph). Judah follows in the line that begins with Abraham and continues with Isaac and Jacob. The student of the Bible is used to the phrase *Joseph and his brothers*, but here Judah is heralded as the primary son of Jacob. And indeed he is. In fact, if there were a fourth patriarch following Abraham, Isaac, and Jacob, it might well be Judah.

From the sons of Jacob come the twelve tribes of Israel, the tribe of Judah holding the distinction of carrying on the line that includes Jesus. Judah is Jacob's fourth son by Leah and one who holds his own in the biblical text, though not necessarily with a flattering portrait. He does defy his brothers when they plot to kill Joseph. He's the one who insists they sell him as a slave.

The more lengthy account of Judah relates to his son Onan. Soon after falsely claiming to their father that Joseph is dead, Judah splits from the family and marries a Canaanite woman, the daughter of Shua. They have three sons, Er, Onan, and Shelah. When the boys come of age, Judah arranges for Er to marry Tamar, a local lass. Er does something so bad that God takes his life. What terrible deed he might have committed is left to the reader's imagination.

Judah then orders second son Onan to have sexual intercourse with Tamar, as was apparently the custom, thus giving his deceased brother progeny. Onan, however, does not wish to father a child that is technically not his. So when he sleeps with Tamar, he *spills his semen* on the ground. God is not pleased. So Onan goes the way of Er. Now Judah is nervous. God has given the death penalty to his two older sons, and Shelah is still a kid. So he asks Tamar to return home as a widow to reside with her father. There she is to wait for Shelah to grow up—unless of course God puts him to death first.

Widow Tamar returns to her father's house, and sometime later Judah himself is widowed. He is in Tamar's neighborhood one day shearing sheep, and Tamar gets wind of it. She suddenly gets an idea. She wants a baby and she wants to carry on her husband's line. Things have not worked out with Shelah. Now is her chance. So she tosses aside her widow's garments and dons a veil, disguising herself as a prostitute, and sits by the road. Sure enough, Judah comes along and requests her services. He quickly discovers she's not an easy mark, so they negotiate a kid goat in payment. But how can she be sure he will actually return with the goat? So she insists on his "personal seal-and-cord" and his staff.

From this business deal she becomes pregnant—exactly as she had hoped. When Judah's friend returns to deliver the goat, however, she is nowhere to be found. Some three months later, Judah hears by the grapevine that Tamar had sold herself as

Judah propositioning Tamar

a prostitute. Judah is furious. *Burn her at the stake*, he fumes. But before they can do that, she sends word to Judah that the father of her unborn child is the man who owns the seal and staff. So Judah admits he is in the wrong for not allowing her to have a child by Shelah, and he lets her live.

Several months later, though there is no indication he has taken Tamar as a wife or even lives with her, Judah becomes the father of twins. Tamar experiences an unusual—and no doubt difficult—childbirth. The first baby is coming through the birth canal and is so close to delivery that one hand is sticking out. So the midwife ties a red thread around it. Then the baby pulls his hand back and the other twin, Perez, moves ahead of him and is actually born before Zerah, who wears the red string bracelet.

When his father is dying, Judah receives from him an unusually positive blessing, at least in comparison with the unpleasant words rained down on his brothers:

> You, Judah, your brothers will
> praise you:
> Your fingers on your enemies'
> throat,
> while your brothers honor you.
> You're a lion's cub, Judah,
> home fresh from the kill, my son.
> Look at him, crouched like a lion,
> king of beasts;
> who dares mess with him?
> The scepter shall not leave Judah;
> he'll keep a firm grip on the command staff
> Until the ultimate ruler comes
> and the nations obey him.[13]

Concluding Observations

Everyone knows and loves the story of Joseph, the crafty younger brother who goes through one ordeal after another and emerges king of the hill. Like the three patriarchs of generations past, he is flawed. But God raised Joseph to a worldly position that none other had ever achieved. Abraham, Isaac, and Jacob all reach their pinnacle among other sheep and cattle barons in Canaan. But Joseph finds his place managing the wealth of Egypt, and in that capacity saves his entire family and their posterity.

Of the twelve sons, he is from the beginning his father's favorite, God's favorite, and our favorite. Bible stories are built around his life—far less so the life of Reuben, Judah, Levi, or Benjamin, who also has a favored status, but not enough to make a good story.

Two fascinating side stories in the broader account of Joseph relate to Dinah and Tamar. Here we are introduced to shocking behavior that includes murder and prostitution as almost part of the course of everyday life.

What is perhaps most striking about the story of Joseph and its ending is that this most favored son of Jacob—and God—will be denied a place in the genealogy of Jesus. That honored spot goes to Judah, a most unlikely candidate. He and his tribe will be prominently featured in the remainder of the Old Testament. Judah is the tribe out of which King David springs, and it becomes the Southern Kingdom after the split from the Northern Kingdom of Israel.

Further Reading

Butler, John G. *Joseph: The Patriarch of Character*. Bible Biography Series 1. Clinton, IA: LBC Publications, 1993.

Getz, Gene A. *Joseph: Overcoming Obstacles through Faithfulness*. Nashville: Broadman & Holman, 1996.

Swindoll, Charles. *Joseph: A Man of Integrity and Forgiveness*. Nashville: Word, 1998.

6

MOSES

From Water's Edge to Wilderness

Moses' name appears no less than eight hundred times in the Bible, second only to the names of Jesus and King David. In the Qur'an he is named 136 times, more than any other individual. No Old Testament figure ranks higher than he does in Jewish understanding. His roller-coaster ride through a life of highs and lows not only makes for interesting reading but also serves as a case study in human development. His story can be summed up in a sentence: Inexperienced and insecure, he begs God to look elsewhere for leadership and then goes on to become a commanding leader.

Moses lives today not only in the Bible but also on the bookshelves of libraries and bookstores. His name is on the cover of leadership books as well. Indeed, his stock value has not depreciated nor his luster dimmed in the millennia since his earthly demise.

After Joseph and his siblings die, the grandchildren and great-grandchildren and their descendants—the *children of Israel*—continue to multiply in their new homeland of Egypt. In fact, there is a population explosion. Egypt is overrun with Hebrews. The new Pharaoh does not know about Joseph, that brilliant *Hebrew* administrator who decades before had saved Egypt from the brink of disaster. He is now alarmed

Surprising Symbol of America

On a trip to visit my sister in Philadelphia, we went to see the Liberty Bell. The quotation on its face is from Leviticus 25, which God gave to Moses on Mount Sinai. . . . In coming weeks I found a similar story over and over again. Columbus comparing himself to Moses when he sailed in 1492. George Whitefield quoting Moses as he traveled the colonies in the 1730s forging the Great Awakening. Thomas Paine, in *Common Sense,* comparing King George to the pharaoh. Benjamin Franklin, Thomas Jefferson and John Adams, in the summer of 1776, proposing that Moses be on the seal of the United States. And the references didn't stop. Harriet Tubman adopting Moses' name on the Underground Railroad. Abraham Lincoln being eulogized as Moses' incarnation. The Statue of Liberty being molded in Moses' honor. Woodrow Wilson, Franklin Roosevelt, and Lyndon Johnson tapping into Moses during wartime. . . . Martin Luther King, Jr., likening himself to Moses on the night before he was killed. . . . For four hundred years, one figure stands out as the surprising symbol of America.

Bruce Feiler, *America's Prophet: Moses and the American Story*, 4

with this turn of events. The Hebrews are expanding and taking over the land and—who knows?—may someday stage a coup and become the rulers of Egypt. More realistically, they might take the side of the enemy if a neighboring army were to attack.

This is the conundrum that Egypt confronts. Even if this large foreign ethnic population were to simply pick up and leave, it would cause great upheaval to the economy.

From his point of view, the Pharaoh is simply being proactive when he brings in his counselors and seeks to establish an agenda for the future. The twin concerns are security and prosperity. His government still has a firm grip on law enforcement within its borders, so, before it is too late, steps are taken to initiate a policy of compulsory work teams. It doesn't happen overnight, but within a short time the descendants of Jacob are being treated as slaves. The Egyptian taskmasters are brutish and virtually work them around the clock.

Still the population is exploding, and the Pharaoh is nervous. These Hebrews will not remain passive slaves forever; they will rise up and overthrow his own regime if he is not on top of things. Drastic action is required. So he pulls aside two prominent Hebrew midwives, perhaps suggesting some favorable treatment if they will carry out a little assignment for him. All they need do is make sure none of the boy babies they deliver will survive. He offers no specific plans or potions. *Just get the job done.*

Time passes and the Hebrews are still throwing baby showers for their infant boys. Pharaoh is more than a little agitated. He orders the midwives to appear before him. *What's going on*, he demands. *Why have you blatantly ignored my order?* They have a ready excuse. Turns out Hebrew women give birth so fast the midwives can't make it to the house before the baby is bundled up and nursing.

His surreptitious plan foiled, Pharaoh now goes for the jugular. Forget the midwives, he'll take care of the matter himself. He puts out a decree to his own people that every Hebrew male infant shall be drowned in the Nile River. What a horrific declaration. Nursing mothers, pregnant mothers, and whole families are simply beside themselves.

This ever-increasing enslavement and persecution and outright murder is the backdrop for the life of Moses. He is a heralded leader whose story has been passed down through the ages in art, literature, music, and film. Like his forebears, he is anything but a supersaint. Indeed, his temper is terrifying. But he is the man God uses to carry out his demand to the Pharaoh: *Let my people go!* Moses in some respects is the most privileged of men. He is snatched as an infant from a floating basket to live in Pharaoh's palace. A defiant rich kid, he runs away. Then after forty years of herding sheep and finding himself—and God—he is back in Pharaoh's court. And God comes with him.

Moses is a mighty leader. Or is he? He is not a military strategist, nor is he a visionary who captures the hearts and minds of the people. His spectacular successes are engineered by God alone; his failures are his own. But he's not a lone ranger. His biography is incomplete without adequate mention of his brother and sister, Aaron and Miriam. They serve as both his supporters and rivals in this electrifying story of both suspense and certitude.

Moses: Mighty Leader, Lawgiver, and More

It is interesting that Moses, the great hero of the faith, comes from the tribe of Levi on both sides of the family. Levi, after all, along with his brother Simeon, was given a very negative "blessing" from his father Jacob, who actually cursed the violent tempers of these two brothers and prophesied that their descendants would be scattered. This scattering comes true most specifically when Moses later appoints Levites as priests, who would be dispersed throughout the tribes, with no designated territory of their own.

Moses' birth story is filled with drama and suspense. Baby boys are on Pharaoh's hit list. His parents, Amram and Jochebed, are terrified. For the first three months he is hidden in the family dwelling, but they worry that he will be discovered. So his mother makes a floating basket and tucks him in, placing it amid the reeds presumably so that he won't be discovered. His sister Miriam, avoiding any appearance of suspicion, watches nearby.

Moses and the Bulrushers

After supper [Widow Douglas] got out her book and learned me about Moses and the Bulrushers, and I was in a sweat to find out all about him; but by and by she let it out that Moses had been dead a considerable long time; so then I didn't care no more about him, because I don't take no stock in dead people.

Mark Twain, *The Adventures of Huckleberry Finn*, chap. 1

But why would Jochebed leave her infant son at the bank of the very river where the Pharaoh drowns the baby boys? It's the last place one would want to hide a child. On the surface it seems absurd. Is it possible, however, that she hopes he will be discovered? Has she noticed that the Pharaoh's daughter, with her attendants, often comes to bathe at that very spot? Does she know she cannot hide her child indefinitely, and does she hope that this young woman's maternal instincts will kick in?

When Pharaoh's daughter does come down to the water's edge, Baby Moses melts her heart. Was he cooing? Did he light up with a smile when she peered into the basket? All we know is that Miriam does not panic. She doesn't race home to fetch her mother. Rather, she calmly does what her mother has instructed her to do. She confidently approaches the grand princess and asks if she would like her to fetch a Hebrew nursing mother who can serve as a nursemaid. If the princess thinks it is odd that a little girl jumps out of the bushes with a plan, she doesn't say so.

Indeed, Pharaoh's daughter readily agrees, with no further questions or hint of suspicion. Surely she must have realized this was a setup. She appears most eager, however, to save a baby from the vicious decree of her father. When Jochebed arrives, Pharaoh's daughter hands over the baby and agrees to pay her for the trouble. What a deal.

The downside, however, is that Jochebed must give him back to his adoptive mother after he is weaned. Pharaoh's daughter names him Moses (meaning "pulled out") because she pulled him out of the water. He grows up in the luxury of the palace, perhaps arranging surreptitious meetings with his family by sneaking out at night or during the day when he is off by himself. Or perhaps he quickly forgets his family amid the palace riches. But he does not altogether forget his heritage. How could he? Unlike Egyptian boys and men, he is circumcised.

As he is coming into adulthood, he begins to notice the ill treatment of the Hebrew slaves. His adoptive mother may have emphasized to him how fortunate he was to have been saved from slavery. But now he is realizing what is happening to his own people. They are working long hours under ruthless conditions. Then he sees an Egyptian overseer hit one of the slaves. He's the son of the Pharaoh's daughter, after all, and might be able to influence the court. But he has no such self-control. His rage is uncontained. His is like the uncontrolled anger of Levi before him—anger *cursed* by Jacob when he was handing out blessings to his sons. Moses murders the Egyptian.

Thinking no one has seen him, he quickly buries the man in the desert sand. But his sin has not been covered up. The next day when he tries to intervene between two Hebrew men who are quarreling, one of them snarls: "Who do you think you are, telling us what to do? Are you going to kill me the way you killed that Egyptian?"[1] He has been found out. And he learns quickly that defending his people is not appreciated. Worse yet, the Pharaoh has learned of the murder and now has a price on his head. Moses flees to Midian.

Herding Sheep on the Front Yard of Hades

For Moses, there was no escaping the desolation. . . .

Can you believe it? A man with advanced knowledge in hieroglyphics, science, literature, and military tactics was now eking out his existence on the backside of the desert, living with his father-in-law, raising a couple of boys, and watching over little flocks of sheep. . . .

. . . He entered the desert at forty and didn't leave until he was eighty. So during those years—considered by many the most productive years of a person's life—Moses herded sheep on what might well have been the front yard of Hades.

Charles Swindoll, *Moses: A Man of Selfless Dedication*, 81, 85

Alone and dejected, Moses sits down by a well to contemplate his situation. He once had a good life in Egypt, living in the court and enjoying all the perks of royalty. Now he is in the middle of nowhere, running for his life. Just then he looks up and sees seven young women coming to the well to water their sheep. But at the same time he sees some surly shepherds pushing their way ahead of the girls, preventing them from carrying out their task. Moses to the rescue. He steps up, takes control, and draws the water for the girls' sheep. The girls go back home but soon return, at their father's bidding, to invite this *Egyptian* stranger to their home.

Turns out, the father of the girls is Jethro, the priest of Midian, a descendant of Abraham and his second wife Keturah. He is impressed with this mannerly man who defended his daughters, and he invites him to settle down. Indeed, he goes a step further. He offers his daughter Zipporah in marriage. Soon the newlyweds are the proud parents of a baby boy, Gershom. He's now a family man—and a shepherd. His is a classic case of downward mobility.

The years and decades pass uneventfully. Then one day Moses is tending Jethro's sheep in a remote wilderness near Mount Horeb. It's an ordinary day, one hour dragging after another. All of a sudden a nearby bush bursts into flame. Hot—really hot—sun, maybe? But it doesn't burn up. Moses is incredulous. How can sagebrush be on fire and not burn up? Then he hears a voice calling his name. His response is most interesting: "Yes? I'm right here!"[2] as though he has heard a parent calling a child. And truly that is the case.

God is calling Moses, telling him to stand back and remove his sandals because the ground he is standing on is holy. Then God identifies himself as the God of Abraham, Isaac, and Jacob. Does Moses even know of this God and the patriarchs who worshiped him? After all, he had been raised in the royal pagan court of Egypt. Nevertheless, Moses is duly humbled; he hides his face, afraid to even look up at God.

Then God speaks. He tells Moses that he has heard the generations-long cries of his people for deliverance and he is going to free them from Egypt's tyranny. He will bring them out of Egypt and into a land of milk and honey. God truly cares for his people. So far Moses understands and agrees. But suddenly the generalities

Moses and Holy Ground

A man named Moses is tending his sheep in the land of Midian when he comes upon a burning bush. He moves closer to see more and hears the voice of God speaking to him about his people and their need to be delivered from the land of Egypt. God tells Moses to take off his sandals, for the ground he is standing on is holy. Moses has been tending sheep in this region for forty years. How many times has he passed by this spot? How many times has he stood in this exact place? And now God tells him the ground is holy?

Has the ground been holy the whole time and Moses is just becoming aware of it for the first time?

Do you and I walk on holy ground all the time, but we are moving so fast and returning so many calls and writing so many emails and having such long lists to get done that we miss it?

Rob Bell, *Velvet Elvis: Repainting the Christian Faith*, 91

slide into specifics: "It's time for you to go back: I'm sending you to Pharaoh to bring my people, the People of Israel, out of Egypt."[3]

Now the stunned Moses speaks. *Why me?* he pleads. How can a simple shepherd possibly rattle the chain of a Pharaoh? God promises to be with him, but Moses is not convinced. He is not even sure to *whom* he is talking. So he asks, though not directly. Rather, he lays out a scenario: *Just suppose I do what you say, and the people ask what your name is, what name should I give?* God answers: "I AM WHO I AM. This is what you are to say to the Israelites: 'I AM has sent me to you.'"[4]

God instructs Moses to go back to Egypt, rally the leaders of Israel, and then go to the Pharaoh and tell him to let everyone go into the wilderness for three days to worship. He warns Moses that freeing the slaves in Egypt will not be easy—that the Pharaoh will not simply submit to Moses' demands. He "won't let you go unless forced to, so I'll intervene and hit Egypt where it hurts."[5]

Part of the hurting, God promises, will entail booty. He assures Moses that the people will leave with the treasures of Egypt: "Each woman will ask her neighbor and any guests in her house for objects of silver and gold, for jewelry and extra clothes; you'll put them on your sons and daughters. Oh, you'll clean the Egyptians out!"[6]

But Moses is not convinced. He's lived in Egypt. He knows firsthand the cultural and political conditions. Indeed, he might have started a revolt years earlier when he killed the Egyptian, but he was rebuffed by the very Hebrew slave he sought to help. There is no way they will listen to him now. God, however, is having none of his excuses. He decides to put Moses to the test. He tells him to identify what he's holding in his hand. It's an ordinary staff. So God tells him to throw it on the ground. It miraculously turns into a snake—so menacing that Moses jumps back. God now tells him to pick it up by the tail. When Moses does so, it reconstitutes itself into a staff. Wow! There's no doubt that he is dealing with the true God.

But God knows human nature all too well. So he demonstrates his power with another miraculous sign, this time letting Moses physically realize the consequences of disobedience. God tells him to slide his hand inside his garment. When Moses pulls his hand back out as God instructs, he is horrified to see he has leprosy. It's incurable—a slow and painful death. But when he obeys God's command to put his hand back under his garment, he's instantly cured. God promises Moses similar miracles in dealing with Pharaoh.

Still Moses protests. Obviously this *I-AM* God is right for the job, but he, Moses, is not. He has no speaking capabilities. Worse than that, he stutters. He's a shepherd wandering around in a remote wilderness on the backside of a mountain. There's no way he could ever

Everyday *Life*

Slavery in Ancient Israel

Slavery was common throughout the ancient Near East and was practiced in the families of the patriarchs. The account of Sarah's mistreatment of her slave girl Hagar illustrates the evils of that institution. Abraham, on the other hand, treated his slave Eliezer almost as a son, and designated him as his heir before the birth of his own son. He was a trusted friend who sought out a wife for Isaac.

In subsequent generations the Hebrew people themselves would endure harsh enslavement during their lengthy sojourn in Egypt. They languished under the callous taskmasters, enduring long hours of forced labor, poor living conditions, and heavy taxes.

Such treatment might have motivated the Hebrew people to later abolish slavery themselves. It did not. But under the Mosaic law, some of the harshest evils of slavery were minimized. A six-year limitation for holding a slave, for example, made the Hebrew system much less severe than that of neighboring cultures. A master who killed a slave faced the death penalty. Equally amazing was the protection of runaway slaves: "If a slave has taken refuge with you, do not hand them over to their master. Let them live among you wherever they like and in whatever town they choose. Do not oppress them" (Deut. 23:15–16 NIV).

A Consciousness of Slavery

The reason for this placement of slavery laws in primary position [in the Torah], and for the relatively beneficent treatment of slaves in Israel, is clear. Israel's national experience had been one of slavery. Indeed, the people had emerged as a unified nation during the period of slavery in Egypt. This experience was so central to Israel's consciousness that it never forgot its roots. It permeates the Bible, and thus explains both the position and the particulars of the laws of slavery in the Torah.

Gary A. Rendsburg, "The Fate of Slaves in Ancient Israel"

possibly confront the Pharaoh and be a spokesman for all the Hebrew slaves. He begs God to pick on someone else.

By this time God is angry, though he does relent, if ever so slightly. God points to Moses' brother Aaron. He is a smooth talker, as God reminds Moses. Aaron has a way with words, and he will help out. And it just so happens that he is right now on his way to meet Moses. Moses leaves the wilderness, returns to Jethro, and begs permission to go back to Egypt. With Jethro's blessing he takes his wife and sons and heads home.

During this journey there are two visitations from God. The first one is a stern reminder to do exactly what the Lord has told him to do. The second is the strangest and most shocking of all. Moses is obeying God's directive and is no longer remonstrating. He has given in. He is headed in the right direction. The family sets up camp for the night. And it is here that God meets Moses "and would have killed him but Zipporah took a flint knife and cut off her son's foreskin, and touched Moses' member with it. She said, 'Oh! You're a bridegroom of blood to me!' Then God let him go. She used the phrase 'bridegroom of blood' because of the circumcision."[7]

They continue on their journey, and whom should they meet but Aaron, sent by God's prompting. Together the brothers return to Egypt, where they gather the Hebrew leaders, who are ready and eager to carry out the plan Aaron and Moses present to them. Pharaoh, however, is not. He is insulted by the demands for time off. In fact, he makes life much harder for the Hebrew slaves, giving the overseers explicit instructions to intensify their misery so as to get their minds off their god.

So awful is the lot of the slaves that they cry out to Pharaoh for relief, to no avail. In anger, they turn on Moses and Aaron. Moses blames God. This is exactly what he feared would happen—exactly. Why would God put him through this? God reminds him of who he is and tells him to go back to the Hebrews and tell them, but Moses is not persuaded. He reiterates his inability to persuade either the Israelites or the Pharaoh. And besides that, he stutters.

Moses Haunted and Haunting

Moses is the most haunted and haunting figure in all the Bible. To be sure, he is often portrayed as strong, sure, and heroic, but he is also timid and tortured with self-doubt at key moments in his life. He is a shepherd, mild and meek, but he is also a ruthless warrior who is capable of blood-shaking acts of violence, a gentle teacher who is also a magician and a wonder-worker, a lawgiver whose code of justice is merciful except when it comes to purging and punishing those who disagree with him, an emancipator who rules his people with unforgiving authority . . . [known] to act in timid and even cowardly ways, throw temper tantrums, dabble in magic, carry out purges and inquisitions, conduct wars of extermination, and talk back to God.

Jonathan Kirsch, *Moses: A Life*, 2

God reminds Moses again what he is capable of doing, so Moses relents and, with Aaron, appears before Pharaoh. The two old men, eighty and eighty-three, are hardly an impressive duo. But they have God on their side. Before Pharaoh, they demonstrate their prowess. God has told them to prove themselves by throwing down a staff that turns into a snake. Problem is, Pharaoh's sorcerers can do the same trick. But then Aaron's staff consumes those of the sorcerers.

With that Pharaoh should have realized that Aaron and Moses—and God—are more powerful than his team, but he is stubborn. What follows is a series of plagues, and before each one the Pharaoh does receive fair warning. First, all bodies of water, including the Nile River, are turned to blood. Then a plague of frogs, followed by gnats, swarms of flies, sickness and death of livestock, boils, hail, locusts, darkness, and finally the threat of death to every firstborn creature, animal and human. That should have been the final straw, but God hardens Pharaoh's heart.

At this point God instructs Moses and Aaron to tell the Israelites to make a sacrifice of a lamb, one for each household, and to smear the blood over the doorposts. That will prepare the way for God to go throughout Egypt after nightfall and strike dead the firstborn of every family except for the families whose houses had blood on their doorposts. When God sees the blood, he will pass over the household—thus the institution of the Jewish Passover, a day to celebrate God's salvation down through the ages.

The next morning, after God had passed over all the Jewish households, the Egyptians are wailing in grief—even in the court of Pharaoh. At last Pharaoh has had enough. He calls in Moses and Aaron and orders them and all their people and cattle out of the land. So exactly 430 years after Jacob and his sons arrived at the invitation of Joseph, the *children of Israel* are on their way out. On their departure they take from the Egyptian people valuables—gold, silver, and fine garments. Besides the confiscated loot, they take with them Joseph's bones, Moses fulfilling a four-hundred-year-old promise to bury his remains in Canaan.

In addition to the death of all the firstborn, the population of Egypt has suddenly taken a sharp downward turn—six hundred thousand men and their families, plus "a crowd of riffraff tagging along, not to mention the large flocks and herds of livestock."[8] What an incredible scene: more than a million people marching out of Egypt.

They are headed back to the Promised Land of Canaan. So why on earth would God be leading them by a pillar of cloud by day and a pillar of fire by night in a southeasterly direction toward the Red Sea? There are at least two much shorter routes to take. But God does not lead them through the land of the warring Philistines to the north, lest they become afraid and turn back.

While it is true that Pharaoh has finally given them permission to leave, Moses and Aaron and all the rest of the Israelites know that his word is anything but reliable.

They are obviously nervous. So when God tells Moses to turn back in the direction they came from and camp by the Red Sea, it seems on the surface no less than ludicrous. But God knows what he's doing as he explains to Moses. If they turn back, the Pharaoh will assume the Israelites have gotten lost. He will send his troops after them, giving God an opportunity to again show his glory.

No surprise here. The Egyptian army pursues the Israelites, who appear to be trapped. The Israelites are petrified—and furious. *Weren't there gravesites enough in Egypt*, they demand of Moses. *Why bring us all here to die!* By now Moses has found his voice. With God's help he has come into his own. His speech carries the weight of authority: "God will fight the battle for you. And you? You keep your mouths shut!"[9]

Then on God's orders Moses holds his staff out toward the sea and marches his people forward. Aided by a strong east wind, the waters part, and the people walk across on dry land, a wall of water on either side of them. The Egyptian army, in hot pursuit, drowns—but only after God jams the chariot wheels and, at Moses' command, lets loose the walls of water. Safely on dry land, Moses leads a mass choir singing songs of victory and celebration.

This truly is a grand occasion, but the problems for the Israelites are not over. No sooner are they on the other side of the Red Sea in the Wilderness of Shur than their water supply runs out. They arrive in Marah only to discover the water is bitter. They will all die of thirst—until Moses, on God's command, throws a stick into the water and it becomes sweet. But life continues to be difficult, and the people complain that they are no longer enjoying hearty stew and bread. So God causes manna to fall from heaven for the people to gather every morning, and quail to fly in every evening. The manna keeps coming during their forty-year sojourn in the wilderness; the quail do not.

At Horeb when there is no water and the people complain, God tells Moses to strike a rock—and water gushes out. There will be even more spectacular miracles to follow. Indeed, Moses directs armed warfare against the Amalekites by simply raising and lowering his hands. When his hands are raised, his people prevail. At the end of the day the army of Israel, commanded by Joshua, defeats the enemy.

While he is out in the wilderness, Moses receives word from his father-in-law Jethro, priest of Midian. Moses had sent his wife and sons home to her family, and now Jethro is returning to Moses with them. It is more than just a joyful reunion. Moses tells him all that God has done for him and the Israelites, and Jethro in turn blesses God, who is "greater than all other gods."[10]

On a more personal level, Jethro's visit proves to be life changing for Moses. Moses does not understand the principles of leadership. He has no concept of a pyramid organizational chart. He is spending his entire days judging matters when conflicts arise between individuals as they form long lines waiting for their cases to be heard. Jethro tells him, "This is no way to go about it. You'll burn out."[11] Jethro cuts to the chase and wisely suggests Moses appoint trusted individuals as his lieutenants and others beneath them to handle routine cases.

Still there are difficulties. There are no legal standards. Cases are judged by individual merit, and decisions are often subjective. Three months have passed since they have left Egypt. They have arrived at the Desert of Sinai and are still without a uniform code of conduct. Moses, eighty years old, trudges up Mount Sinai with the expectation that God has an important message for him. Indeed, he actually goes up the mountain to meet God. This is no burning-bush experience when God unexpectedly seems to come from out of nowhere.

It is here on the mountain, Mount Sinai, that the Israelites receive the defining set of laws and codes that will place them apart as a nation beloved of God, a "treasured possession" who have been carried out of Egypt on "eagles' wings."[12] But not for nothing. As God's people, they must keep his covenant. When Moses comes down the mountain and conveys the message to the people, their response is unanimous. *Of course, we will do all the Lord commands.*

Moses makes the hike up and down the mountain (more than a mile high) at least five times as liaison between God and the people. On one of his returns down the mountain, he instructs them to wash themselves in preparation for God's presence and warns them to stand clear of the mountain lest they die.

Moses and His African Wife

Miriam and Aaron . . . "spoke against Moses because of the Cushite woman whom he had married" (Num. 12:1). The Book of Exodus makes it clear that Moses marries a Midianite woman named Zipporah, but the Book of Numbers suggests that he also has a Cushite (that is Ethiopian) wife. One rabbinical tradition suggests that Moses traveled to Ethiopia before he showed up at Jethro's house in Midian and was already married to a "woman of color" when he met Zipporah.

Jonathan Kirsch, *The Harlot by the Side of the Road*, 168

Tensions are high. And the spectacular show of force begins. The mountain smokes. God thunders. Lightning flashes. Moses appears transfigured. The people are terrified. Out of all this drama come the Ten Commandments and a host of other laws that cover a wide range of topics, including laws that are not always favorable to women. For example, "When a man sells his daughter to be a handmaid, she doesn't go free after six years like the men." Both genders, however, receive the severest penalty for disrespect: "If someone curses father or mother, the penalty is death."[13]

If at times the law seems harsh, it also has a tender side: "Don't abuse or take advantage of strangers; you, remember, were once strangers in Egypt." And, "Don't mistreat widows or orphans."[14] God continues on and on and on with law giving—dozens of laws, ceremonial and communal. Moses, with his photographic memory, goes to the people and tells them everything God has said, and they agree in unison that they will abide by them. Then he writes everything down.

Now Moses again climbs to the top of the mountain, where over a forty-day period he receives the stone tablets inscribed with the Ten Commandments and very detailed instructions on how to make everything for the tabernacle, from tables to vestments. All seems to be going well until the most devastating incident in the life of this emerging nation of former slaves occurs. God is furious. There is trouble down below, and he vows to destroy every one of them.

Moses hurries down the mountain and, much to his utter disgust, finds the people engaging in an orgy of wild dancing around a golden calf. He smashes the stone tablets on the ground, melts down the calf, grinds the remains into powder, scatters the powder on the water, and forces the people to drink. Then he orders the Levites to slaughter people left and right. They obey and kill three thousand.

The next day Moses goes back up the mountain and earnestly beseeches God to forgive his chosen people and spare their lives. But God does not relent. He sends a plague on them. From this point on, because of God's anger with the people, he no longer will lead them in person. Rather, an angel will guide them. Moses is concerned, however, about losing God's presence. He begs to see God's glory. But God won't let him see his face—only his back. At God's command, Moses chisels two more stone tablets with the Commandments engraved on them and remains on the mountain forty days, during which

Moses breaking the stone tablets

time God renews his covenant with him, promises victory over the heathen Canaanites, and gives Moses additional laws and restrictions.

In the days that follow, the people begin constructing all the items God has commanded them to make for the tabernacle: tapestries, chest, table, lampstand, altars, washbasin, courtyard, and vestments. When they are done, Moses blesses them. He goes through the Tabernacle rituals as God has commanded. The Tabernacle and all it contains are covered by a cloud that periodically lifts, signaling to Moses and the people that they should move on in their journey to the Promised Land.

Moses conducts a major census, numbering every tribe and clan and individual.

The books of Leviticus and Numbers contain more religious rules, dress codes, food restrictions, and other behavioral and cultural guidelines. Deuteronomy is essentially Moses' grand farewell address, but embedded in the text are significant events.

Complaining in the camp has been routine, but sometimes these complaints erupt. The people are sick and tired of manna—day after day, year after year. They long for the meat and vegetables of Egypt, and they grumble at Moses. God overhears and blasts Moses for it. Moses is taken aback: "Why are you treating me this way? What did I ever do to you to deserve this? Did I conceive them? Was I their mother? So why dump the responsibility of this people on me? . . . I've had enough. Let me out of here."[15]

God feels Moses' pain and makes an unusual offer. He will take some of the Spirit that is on Moses and distribute it among seventy of the most trustworthy Israelite leaders. That will take some of the weight off Moses' shoulders. Moses is further mollified when God provides meat by sending winds that blow massive flocks of quail in from the sea. So eager are the people to eat something other than manna that they eat themselves sick and die by the thousands.

When the Israelites had initially crossed the Red Sea to safety, Moses had expected to set out for Canaan and conquer the land. He did not, however, want to make hasty decisions that he would later regret. So now, more than a year later, he sends out twelve spies, one from each tribe. Returning after forty days, ten of them foretell dire consequences for Israel if they try to conquer the land. Only Caleb and Joshua present an optimistic report. The people are so upset by the negative news that they grumble against God.

From God's perspective, this is a blatant betrayal. The death penalty is in order. Moses intervenes, pleading with God to spare his people. Nevertheless the punishment is severe. They are sentenced to wander in the wilderness for forty long years.

During the forty years of wandering in the wilderness, Moses continues to speak to the people, specifying God's laws for everything from ritual cleanliness to punishment for sin. Yet there continues to be discontent and rebellion. In particular, three trouble-makers, Korah, Dathan, and Abiram, with two hundred followers claim there should be some sort of a democracy rather than a dictatorship run by Moses. After all, God is in the whole community, not just one man. Moses, after throwing himself flat on the ground, gets up and calmly tells Korah that God will decide in

The Exodus Tells Our Story

The Exodus tells our story. Each of us has a personal journey to make, from our own Egypt to our promised land. We have left something behind in order to make this journey. We have had to break free from our former lives in order to begin afresh. *We* were in Egypt. *We* were delivered from bondage. *We* are in the wilderness, on our way to the promised land. The story of the exodus *involves* us—because it is *about* us.

Alister McGrath, *The Journey: A Pilgrim in the Lands of the Spirit*, 23 the morning who governs Israel. He and his people are to return and bring incense to offer to God. Aaron must do the same.

The next day the glory of God shines as Korah, his cohorts, and all their people arrive. God tells Moses and Aaron to separate themselves and all the rest of the Israelites from those who have rebelled. Moses speaks to the people, telling them that God will decide who leads them—whether it is he or the rebels. No sooner does he finish speaking than the earth opens up and swallows these three rebels, their families, their cattle, and their belongings; and fire from heaven consumes their followers.

Now Moses was a very humble man, more humble than anyone else on the face of the earth.

Numbers 12:3 (NIV)

In spite of that incredible demonstration of God's power, some of the people continue to mutter against the leadership of Moses and Aaron. God sends a plague as punishment, and 14,700 die as a result. Despite the loss of life, the rebellions against Moses and God just don't end. Sometime after this, the Israelites set up their tents in Shittim near where Moabites have settled. Moabite women begin inviting Israelite men to join them in ritual meals and the worship of their god, Baal of Peor. The men might have ignored the request but for the fact that the worship involves sexual rites. So they readily join in.

God is enraged and tells Moses to hang them all. Word gets out and the people are beside themselves, crying out and begging forgiveness. Amid all this weeping, Zimri comes along and flaunts his immoral behavior. In fact, he brings a Midianite woman straight into a tent and has sexual relations with her. One of Aaron's grandsons goes in after them and stabs his spear through both their bodies. This ends the religious sex rites, but not before twenty-four thousand more either are executed or die of the plague.

Early on in Moses' career, the Israelites had run out of water, and God told Moses to strike a rock and the water would come forth. Nearly four decades later this same problem develops again. The people are complaining not only about the detested manna but also about the lack of water. This time Moses and Aaron throw themselves before God, and God tells Moses to *speak* to the rock that stands in front of them.

But Moses doesn't follow directions. He remembers the situation from before, and he doesn't want to be made a fool of in front of the whole congregation. So he strikes—angrily strikes—the rock with his staff, not once but twice. Water does come forth, but God is irate. For their disobedience, Moses and Aaron will never set foot in the Promised Land.

The most recurring themes of the forty-year trek in the wilderness are disappointment with God and disillusionment with Moses. Things have not gone well, and they blame Moses for dragging them out to die in the godforsaken desert. It's a miserable life, tedious, day after day the same. Not even a change of diet. They are sick of manna and the lack of good fresh spring water.

But every time they turn against God, like clockwork, they are punished. On one occasion they are on the road along the Red Sea when God has had all he can take of their complaining. So he sends snakes—countless poisonous serpents. People are dying right and left from the venomous bites. They cry out to Moses in repentance, pleading with him to pray to God to rid them of this awful infestation. Moses prays and God instructs him to fashion a copper serpent and hoist it up on a pole. "Whoever is bitten and looks at it," God declares, "will live."[16]

After so many years of their infidelities and subsequent punishments, God finally gives the Israelites a morale booster: victory over the Amorites and other tribes who threaten them.

When that journey is nearly over and Aaron has died on Mount Hor and has been "gathered to his people,"[17] God shows Moses the Promised Land from Mount Nebo in the land of Moab and tells him that this is where his descendants will live, but that he will not be able to enter it himself. Though well over one hundred, he still has good eyesight and walks with a brisk gait. He dies at age 120 and God buries him. Everyone weeps and mourns his passing.

His legacy is large. No Old Testament prophet equals Moses.

> Since then, no prophet has risen in Israel like Moses, whom the LORD knew face to face, who did all those signs and wonders the LORD sent him to do in Egypt—to Pharaoh and to all his officials and to his whole land. For no one has ever shown the mighty power or performed the awesome deeds that Moses did in the sight of all Israel.[18]

Balaam: An Improbable Prophet

He lives along the bank of the Euphrates River in the town of Pethor—perhaps a shingle hanging from his house that reads "Prophet: No Appointment Necessary." He's a non-Israelite seer. But his reputation has gone before him into bordering lands. So it is that some officials arrive at his house one day. They know before they knock that he is Balaam, son of Beor, credited with working wonders through his god.

The officials are from Moab, commissioned by their king, Balak, to bring Balaam back with them. It seems the massive Israelite army is assembling on their border, and the Moabites will be slaughtered unless there is supernatural intervention. Balaam is the man for the job. The emissaries have a wad of money in their pockets and are prepared to pay Balaam well. He insists, however, that they stay the night with him to allow him time to make the decision.

That night God speaks to Balaam and asks about the visitors. Balaam relates the story, telling God that they want him to go with them and curse the Israelites. God makes it clear to Balaam that he should not go because the Israelites have his blessing. The next morning Balaam declines the offer from Balak's officials. When they return to Balak, he sends them back with his highest emissaries and an even larger purse. In fact, Balak sends word that he'll give Balaam anything he wants if only he will put a curse on the Israelites.

But Balaam is now on God's side. To the officials he declares: "Even if Balak gave me his house stuffed with silver and gold, I wouldn't be able to defy the orders of my God to do anything, whether big or little."[19] But then he keeps the door open a crack by inviting them to stay the night so that he can once again consult with God.

The next morning, following God's instructions, he agrees to follow behind them to Moab with his two servants. Along the way, his donkey suddenly veers into the ditch. Balaam hits the donkey so hard that she scrambles back on the road. But shortly thereafter, as they are going through a vineyard, the donkey jumps off the road again, slamming Balaam's foot against a stone wall. Balaam is furious and strikes the donkey repeatedly.

Still again a short distance farther, at a narrow passage between two walls, the donkey stops dead in her tracks and lies down. This time Balaam loses his temper. He beats the donkey with his walking stick.

The donkey asks Balaam why he is beating her like this. Rather than being bowled over by a talking donkey, Balaam simply explains to her that she certainly deserved what she got and worse. In fact, if he had brought his sword along he would have killed her. "Am I not your trusty donkey," the creature pleads. "Have I ever done anything like this to you before? Have I?"[20] Balaam concedes she has not.

Only then does God allow Balaam to see the light—more specifically, the angel that has been blocking his donkey's path. Indeed, the angel is threatening him with a sword. Balaam falls on his face before the angel, who demands to know why he has been beating his loyal donkey. Balaam

God "Opened the Mouth of the Ass"

And the Lord opened the mouth of the ass. Skeptical persons criticize this passage, and ridicule it, as if Moses related an incredible fable. And, indeed, their scoff appears to be plausible, when they object that there is a great difference between the bray of an ass and all articulate voice. . . . God "opened the mouth of the ass." For whence would men possess the faculty of speech, unless God had opened their mouth at the first creation of the world? Whence comes it that magpies and parrots imitate the human voice, unless it were the will of God to manifest in them a specimen of a certain extraordinary power? Who is there, then, who shall now impose a law upon the Maker of the world, to prevent Him from adapting the mouth of a beast to the utterance of words? Unless perhaps they would suppose Him to be bound irrevocably, because He has once appointed a certain order in nature, to abstain from displaying His power by miracles. If the ass had been changed into a man, we should have been bound to reverence this proof of God's incomprehensible power; now, when we are told that merely a few words were drawn from it without intelligence or judgment, as if a sound of any kind were diffused through the air, shall the miracle be regarded as a fable?

• John Calvin, commentary on Numbers 22:28

now knows he has sinned against God. The angel tells him to keep on going but not to say another word unless it comes from God.

King Balak, having gone out to meet Balaam, scolds him for his tardiness. Balaam tells him straight up that he is bound to speak only the words God gives him. So together they go into town, where Balak sets up a huge altar and sacrifices livestock. The next morning the two of them hike up to the highest point in the area to look down over the valley. Then Balaam instructs Balak to build seven more altars and sacrifice more animals. Balaam then leaves, hoping to get a message from God.

When he returns, he gives a message to Balak, essentially saying, "How can I curse whom God has not cursed? How can I damn whom God has not damned?"[21] Balak is not pleased with the message. He asks Balaam to come to another high point to get a better view, and there Balaam agrees to sacrifice more animals. This time after Balaam returns to Balak, he tells him that God brought him to this place to bless the Israelites, and he can do nothing other than that.

Still Balak doesn't give up. He begs Balaam to do anything but bless the Israelites. So Balaam tells him to build still more altars and sacrifice more animals. This time when Balaam goes off by himself, he fully understands that God wants him to bless the Israelites—and that he's not to work magic as he tried to do earlier. Then the Spirit of God comes upon him, and God makes it absolutely clear to Balaam that he must bless the Israelites, which Balaam does with startling clarity and vigor.

The Other Side of Balaam

The books of Deuteronomy, Joshua, and Nehemiah put a different cast on the story. They tell of Balaam cursing the Israelites but God reversing the curse and turning it into a blessing.

In the New Testament, Balaam is said to have "loved the wages of wickedness" (2 Pet. 2:15), and the book of Revelation says that he "taught Balak to entice the Israelites to sin by eating food sacrificed to idols and by committing sexual immorality" (Rev. 2:14).

Richard R. Losch, *All the People in the Bible*, 55

Balak is furious and tells Balaam to get out and go home—that he's not getting one penny for his services. Balaam calmly reminds him that he would not have taken money anyway—that he is bound to obey God. Then after prophesying doom and gloom for Moab, Balaam heads for home.

The story does not end here, however. The next we learn of Balaam is that he has been killed with a sword during a battle with the Midianites, after which he is accused of having "enticed the Israelites to be unfaithful to the LORD."[22]

Aaron: A Much-Appreciated Older Brother

Being the high priest, whose duty is to supervise all the religious rites and rituals for the Israelites, Aaron assumes a critical role in the development of the nation. But he always plays second fiddle to Moses. *Moses and Aaron* is the turn of phrase that most commonly bears his name.

Unlike his younger brother Moses, whose résumé includes accounts of a floating basket and burning bush, murder and marriage in between, Aaron appears out of nowhere. He is middle aged and on his way to Midian to see Moses, unaware that God has called his younger brother to lead the Israelites out of Egypt. Nor does he know that he himself will be the public voice for his stuttering sibling. When they meet each other, coming from opposite directions, Aaron embraces and kisses his long-lost brother. Does Moses even know that Aaron is married to Elisheba and has four sons, Nadab and Abihu, Eleazar and Ithamar?

Aaron and Moses

So they met and embraced. . . . This is the first time I read that Moses was able to tell anyone else about the burning bush. . . . He said, "Aaron, listen to this. You won't believe it. There I was, out with the sheep one day, just like a thousand other days before. And all of a sudden—whoosh!—this bush caught fire, and it wouldn't stop burning. So I stopped and stared. And as I got closer—Aaron, listen to this, man—*God* was speaking from that bush. . . ." If Aaron doubted a single word of the account, Scripture never mentions. In fact, he was already prepared to believe every word Moses told him. Hadn't God called him out of Egypt to meet his younger brother in the desert?

Charles Swindoll, *Moses: A Man of Selfless Dedication*, 145

When Aaron and Moses arrive in Egypt, Aaron plays a key role in dealing with Pharaoh and the Israelite people. Indeed, without him, it is difficult to imagine that either side would have taken Moses seriously. Contact is made in person. Crisp communication is a must. Indeed, Aaron is one of the most effective communicators in the Bible, though many of his messages are opposed or ignored by his listeners.

Superior speaking skills, however, would have been utterly insufficient for the task Aaron is assigned. He needs God's support, and he gets it. When it is time to show Pharaoh that Aaron's speech is supported by supernatural power, Aaron turns his rod into a snake. When the Egyptian magicians duplicate the performance, his serpent swallows all of theirs. Then as plagues strike Egypt, Aaron continues to serve as the chief liaison between Pharaoh and God.

After the people escape Egypt, Aaron communicates with them, as when he announces God's plan to send manna down from heaven. He and Moses confer on virtually every issue that arises, major and minor. He ascends the mountain with Moses prior to the giving of the Ten Commandments. Then after the covenant is ratified, he and two of his sons, as well as seventy elders, accompany Moses up the mountain. An interesting slight, however, occurs on their way up. He is left behind while Joshua alone accompanies Moses the rest of the way. What has happened? *Moses and Aaron* have been the ultimate partnership. Now it is *Moses and Joshua*, though Joshua does not enter the cloud to converse with God.

Moses alone receives God's instructions relating to Aaron. Aaron is to be consecrated as the high priest of Israel (his sons as lesser priests). Indeed, the priesthood is to be the Aaronic priesthood that entails a very precise ordination ceremony and a wide range of duties, including making sacrifices and keeping lamps burning, as well as wearing special vestments.

God is communicating all these details regarding Aaron's ministry while Aaron himself is having second thoughts. He goes back down the mountain and finds the people very anxious. Where is Moses? He's been gone way too long. So the people acknowledge the smooth-talking Aaron as their leader. They insist that he *do something*, urging him to fashion gods who will lead them straightaway through this awful wilderness to the Promised Land. Moses has abandoned them. What else can they do?

So Aaron, sidekick of Moses, simply complies. Not one word about how terrible it would be to worship false gods. Rather, he tells the people to remove their rings and bring them to him. Then he melts down the gold and forms it into the likeness of a calf. The people are excited. After that he builds an altar in front of the image, announcing that the next day they will have a grand feast.

They arrive on the morrow and begin eating and drinking and dancing and having a regular wild time of it—that is, until Moses shows up. He's furious with Aaron. Aaron acts sorry and shifts the blame to the people. In fact, Aaron, who fashioned the calf with his own hands, has the gall to add that he simply threw their jewelry into the fire and—voilà—out comes a calf. Disingenuous, to be sure.

Moses, directed by God, orders the Levites to kill three thousand people, and then God sends a plague. But Aaron? Amazingly he comes through this ordeal virtually unscathed. Not so long after this, Moses ceremonially washes him and dresses him in a special sashed tunic, a robe, a breastpiece, and a turban featuring a gold plate with the words "Holy to the Lord."

Aaron's sons, now also priests, are likewise dressed for the celebration. The sacrificial rites and rituals and ceremonies are detailed and complicated, but Aaron and his sons follow instructions from God, through Moses, and they manage to get everything right—except for a glitch involving sons Nadab and Abihu. Whether they were rebellious or careless, the text does not specify. But they clearly do something that offends God by offering an inappropriate kind of fire and incense. Perhaps they had taken a page from the rituals to pagan gods. But for that they are struck down by God and die on the spot.

Moses explains that God's sudden anger relates to his holiness. Aaron doesn't say a word. He remains silent. Then Moses orders the bodies hauled away and turns to Aaron and his surviving sons, Eleazar and Ithamar. He knows they are numb with grief, but he issues an order that on the surface appears unduly cruel: *If they dare mourn, they too will die.*

Soon after this, the surviving sons fail to make a proper sacrifice. This time Aaron comes to their aid immediately, pointing out that it is an honest mistake. These sons, unlike their brothers, are spared.

Because of what must have seemed like arbitrary power-grabbing by Moses, Aaron and sister Miriam are upset, though their issues relate to matters besides that of Moses' apparently high-handed control. For one thing, they do not like Moses' Cushite wife. But more than that, they believe they ought to wield more authority than they do. For their grumbling, Miriam is punished with leprosy. Aaron appears to get off scot-free.

After the rebellion and death-by-sinkhole of Korah and his cohorts, the people are once again complaining. Many are wondering why Aaron should wield so much power, second only to Moses himself. So God proffers a test. All the leaders of the tribes are to leave their staffs in the Tent of Meeting for the night. In the morning, it is obvious that Aaron's high position of authority is authorized by God. His staff handle not only buds and blossoms, but is producing almonds.

Despite such recognition, Aaron, along with Moses, is punished by God and not allowed to enter the Promised Land. The two of them hike to the top of Mount Hor to take a look, but that is as close as they get. They are accompanied by Eleazar, Aaron's son, and it is there that Moses gives Eleazar Aaron's garments, thus symbolizing Eleazar's succession as high priest. With that ceremony over, Aaron dies. He never makes it down from the mountain. His death is followed by thirty days of mourning in the Israelite camp.

Miriam: Prophet, Leader, and Leper

She is the older sister of Moses, no doubt the sister who was given the responsibility of watching the basket floating in the Nile with her baby brother inside. The next time we hear of her, she has left Egypt with all the children of Israel. There is nothing recorded of her reunion with Moses when he returns to Egypt with brother Aaron, who has gone out to meet him. But she crosses safely over the Red Sea with the Israelites, and she takes the lead as soon as it is learned that the Egyptian army has perished when God rolls back the water.

Miriam's dance

She is identified as a prophetess, and in that role she grabs her tambourine and begins to dance and sing. So contagious is her act that all the women in the camp follow her lead—tambourines and dancing. She makes up the song on the spot—four short lines, catchy and easy to memorize:

> Sing to God—
> what a Victory!
> He pitched horse and rider
> into the sea![23]

But even a prophet is vulnerable to life's normal ups and downs, temptations and sins. So it is with Miriam and Aaron, who with all the Israelites are camped at Hazeroth. They are criticizing Moses and especially their sister-in-law, his Cushite wife. But it is more than an in-law issue. There is the matter of Moses running the show. He has a pipeline to God. They are left out of the communications and conversations. It's not fair.

God overhears their backbiting and summons all three of them for an appointment in the meeting tent. They arrive as God is coming down in a cloud. Then God approaches the opening of the tent and calls out Miriam and Aaron. He angrily reminds them that he speaks to prophets (as they rightly are) through visions and dreams. But he goes on to say that with Moses it is entirely different. He speaks to him in plain language as one person talks with another.

God leaves in the same cloud in which he had come. Aaron and Miriam are numb. They have just been berated by none other than God himself. But if that is not bad enough, Miriam suddenly realizes that her skin is all white with leprosy. Aaron is stunned to see his sister now a leper—afflicted with this terrible disease and an outcast forever.

Aaron begs brother Moses to undo this terrible misfortune. Moses prays for God to heal her. God responds by pointing out that if her own father had spit in her face—as God himself had essentially done—she would be sent out of the camp for seven days. So will it be with Miriam. She will be banished from the community—sent outside the camp and shunned for a week.

God would later warn the Israelites to remember what happened to Miriam—that she was quarantined, as all lepers should be. Miriam's punishment and disease were not to be forgotten—nor was her leadership of the Israelites. Miriam dies and is buried in the parched Desert of Zin shortly before Aaron dies on the Mountain of Hor.

Much later, long after she and Aaron and Moses are dead, the prophet Micah, speaking for the Lord, remembers her along with her brothers:

> I brought you up out of Egypt
> and redeemed you from the land
> of slavery.
> I sent Moses to lead you,
> also Aaron and Miriam.[24]

Concluding Observations

Three siblings. The two older are natural leaders, Aaron a smooth talker, Miriam a charismatic leader whose dancing sparks a revival. They seem to have the qualities necessary to influence people and get things done. The youngest possesses no such traits. But God chooses him for the critical task that will have a profound influence and cast a spotlight on God's people down to the present day.

Indeed, throughout history, to be a great leader is to be a *Moses*. Harriet Tubman, of Underground Railroad fame, is referred to as the *Moses* of her people. Brigham Young, who led his Mormon followers to Utah, is called the American *Moses*. Abraham Lincoln was a *Moses*. In recent times even the evil Kony, a rebel leader in Uganda, has identified himself as a *Moses*, ruthlessly demanding that the Ten Commandments be the law of the land.

There were certainly rebels who challenged Moses in his day, but their names have largely been lost in history's scrap heap of failures. Balaam, pagan prophet who stood by Moses, might well be forgotten, but for his talking donkey.

Moses himself is a role model in part because, despite his deficiencies, he rises to the occasion and becomes one of the most heralded leaders in all history. He is endearing because he is the last person anyone could imagine capable of the job.

What was his secret?

> By faith Moses, when he had grown up, refused to be known as the son of Pharaoh's daughter. He chose to be mistreated along with the people of God rather than to enjoy the fleeting pleasures of sin. He regarded disgrace for the sake of Christ as of greater value than the treasures of Egypt, because he was looking ahead to his reward. By faith he left Egypt, not fearing the king's anger; he persevered because he saw him who is invisible.[25]

Further Reading

Feiler, Bruce. *America's Prophet: Moses and the American Story*. New York: William Morrow, 2009.

Kirsch, Jonathan. *Moses: A Life*. New York: Random House Ballantine, 1998.

Swindoll, Charles. *Moses: A Man of Selfless Dedication*. Nashville: Nelson, 1999.

7

JOSHUA AND CALEB

Gangsters for God

And the walls came a-tumblin' down. The lyrics of this lively spiritual say it all. The stronghold of Jericho is taken by Joshua, his small fighting force—and God. Indeed, Joshua is the recipient of more military miracles than any other warrior in the Bible. The first real military strategist and commander, he courageously leads his men into battle. Abraham led no more than a small militia, and Moses was not directly involved in warfare at all.

Joshua had grown up a slave in Egypt with no apparent preparation in the art of warfare, though he may have observed the highly trained professional Egyptian army. Like Moses, those who lead the way into the Promised Land and carry out God's plans appear to be a most unlikely and hapless lot. They sometimes possess remarkable courage and faith, but little more. They appear on the surface to be the least probable candidates for greatness.

Caleb is also a key player in this drama, but he is eighty-five when he begins his undercover career. None of the other spies except Joshua are worth their salt. Rahab will lend her support, but she's a harlot. What is God thinking? Where are the lean, muscular, disciplined young men?

Where is the taut, handsome specimen of humanity like Alexander the Great?

And from a strategic perspective, the timing seems off. Wandering in a wilderness eating manna for forty years does not equate with normal preparedness for major military campaigns. The incredible defeat of the Egyptians would seem to have served as a much better launching pad for conquest than decades of complaining, defying, rebelling, and the consequent harsh punishments meted out by God.

But God's timing does not necessarily correlate with humanity's, nor does his choice of leaders. Indeed, the underlying theme relating to great heroes of the faith like Joshua and Caleb is, yes, they have courage, but God is the one pulling the strings. God gets things done and oversees the entry into the Promised Land.

The occupiers—or enemies—in Canaan are not a cohesive population that is easily differentiated from those followers of Moses and Yahweh. The term *Hebrews* was a term of derision, often referring to social outcasts; it sometimes included the Canaanites themselves, and of course it included those entering the land with Joshua. Later the term would be associated almost exclusively with the people of Israel. But the Israelites would intermarry, and among them would be many *outsiders*, including Rahab, a Canaanite, and Caleb, a Kenizzite (a Canaanite people partially absorbed by the tribe of Judah).

Notwithstanding all of Joshua's victories, vast numbers of those who had occupied the land would remain and cause problems in the generations to follow. In fact, some three hundred years later King Solomon would force large numbers of non-Israelites into slave labor.

> There were still people left from the Hittites, Amorites, Perizzites, Hivites and Jebusites (these people were not Israelites). Solomon conscripted the descendants of all these people remaining in the land—whom the Israelites had not destroyed—to serve as slave labor, as it is to this day.[1]

Joshua: Successor to Moses

It is the first skirmish of his military career. He's in a valley at Rephidim in the heat of battle. The enemy is ferocious. These Amalekites, a warring nomadic tribe, have ambushed the Israelites from the rear. But Joshua and his fierce fighting men have the upper hand. Then, in the blink of an eye, with no obvious explanation,

Joshua's Preparation

Another thing is clearly seen in God's preparation of Joshua: Joshua was reminded of the interplay between the seen and the unseen worlds. There is no vast chasm between them; the unseen world is right here. The unseen world is always immediately present, not far off. Above everything and overshadowing everything is the reality of God in his glory. It undoubtedly stood Joshua in good stead many times for him to understand that God was close at hand, that he is the god who exists and who is "here."

Francis A. Schaeffer, *Joshua and the Flow of Biblical History*, 18 the Amalekites are crushing them. What's happening? What did he do wrong? How did they so quickly gain the advantage? But suddenly, again for no apparent reason, the tide turns and his men are triumphing over these vicious warriors in hand-to-hand combat. But it doesn't last. Soon the enemy is again prevailing, and it goes back and forth until his men finally gain the advantage and hold it through the afternoon. By nightfall they have thoroughly trounced the enemy.

Unbeknownst to Joshua, when Moses raises his hands, his men prevail, but when Moses tires and lowers his hands the Amalekites are winning. Only with the assistance of Aaron and Hur is Moses able to hold up his hands until sundown. A strange military strategy, but it works.

This account introduces the military leader who fights his way into the Promised Land. Joshua, son of Nun, had worked closely with Moses since he was a young man—so close and faithful to the master that he becomes his successor. To Moses, he is loyal to a fault. On one occasion when two men are prophesying in what he perceives to be an unauthorized manner, he runs to his boss: "Moses, master! Stop them!" Moses gently reproves him: "Are you jealous for me? Would that all GOD's people were prophets."[2]

Joshua goes with Moses, Aaron, Aaron's two sons, and seventy elders up to Mount Sinai after the covenant had been ratified. But only Moses and Joshua continue up the mountain. Why was Joshua alone afforded this privilege? Was he Moses' personal attendant, or was he simply his most faithful lieutenant? While Moses is in the cloud for forty days, Joshua waits. Together they descend the mountain, and Joshua reports to Moses that he hears a noise like the sound of war, which turns out to be the celebration of the golden calf. Joshua is stunned by the brazen display of idolatry.

Before he dies, Moses gives Joshua a charge from God: "Be strong and of a good courage: for thou shalt bring the children of Israel into the land which I sware unto them: and I will be with thee."[3]

Now Joshua is hearing directly from God, who commissions him to cross the Jordan River and enter the Promised Land. God does not beat around the bush: "Get going. Cross this Jordan River, you and all the people. . . . I'm giving you every square inch of the land you set your foot on—just as I promised Moses."[4]

Joshua wastes no time. He sends his captains throughout the camp with an

Joshua's Sobering Experience

Imagine how the young man Joshua felt. Moses had left him and gone beyond. There had been thunder and lightning. Moses came down and had stone tablets in his hands, and on these tablets were words that could be read, words that had been placed there by God himself. Imagine the emotion! Yet when the two men came back into the camp, the people were in total rebellion. Here Joshua learned another truth: the terribleness of sin, especially among the people of God. This was sobering, and Joshua never forgot it.

Francis A. Schaeffer, *Joshua and the Flow of Biblical History*, 20 order to pack up belongings and begin the crossing in three days. The people promise to follow the command of Joshua *to the letter*—even as they did Moses (which can hardly reassure him).

The first military operation Joshua carries out as leader of the Israelites in his own right is to send two spies to Jericho. They arrive at the walled city in broad daylight, appearing like any other travelers, and ask around for lodging and the services of a prostitute. They are referred to Rahab. Working undercover, they avoid raising eyebrows. But someone is alert, concerned about homeland security. A report comes to the king, who sends word to the prostitute that she must bring these strangers to him. Instead, she hides them and engineers their escape under cover of darkness.

The spies hide in the hills for three days and then return to Joshua, giving him the news he wants to hear. They report that the inhabitants are afraid of the Israelites and are beginning to panic. The next day Joshua prepares the entire company to cross over the Jordan River. From God he receives confirmation of his leadership: "This very day I will begin to make you great in the eyes of all Israel. They'll see for themselves that I'm with you in the same way that I was with Moses."[5]

As confirmation of his leadership, Joshua witnesses a miracle fully as spectacular as the parting of the Red Sea. The priests, toting the Chest of the Covenant, dip their toes in the water, and the river stops flowing. It simply "piled up in a heap" until all the people pass through on dry land.[6]

After crossing the Jordan, Joshua, following God's instructions, chooses one man from each of the twelve tribes. Each of them is to take a large stone from the dry riverbed and carry it to the bank where the camp will be set up for the night. There they will build an altar of memorial stones. Why? "When your children ask you, 'What are these stones to you?' you'll say, 'The flow of the Jordan was stopped in front of the Chest of the Covenant of God as it crossed the Jordan—stopped in its tracks. These stones are a permanent memorial for the People of Israel.'"[7]

Piling up stones is easy. The next event for the Israelites will not be. Under God's direction, Joshua makes stone knives and then circumcises all the males who had left Egypt and had not been present for the previous mass circumcision ceremony. The men should not have been surprised, since the account of the previous event had no doubt been told and retold. They might have complained loudly, but they have just

The Dark Cloud of Moses

Imagine trying to fill the shoes of someone as legendary as Moses! This was the task Joshua faced. You will notice that the name Moses pops up many times in the book of Joshua. At times Joshua must have felt that the memory of Moses hung over him like a dark cloud. Now that it was his turn to lead, Joshua needed to know if the people would follow him as they had Moses. More importantly, he needed to know if God intended to help him as he had Moses.

Donald Baker, *Joshua: The Power of God's Promises*, 9–10

witnessed Joshua's access to the power of God. They submit to the surgery, and the place is called Foreskins Hill—another memorial to God.

Having crossed the Jordan, Joshua and some two million Israelites settle down, now eating produce from fields rather than manna from heaven. Then one day, while Joshua is out gazing toward Jericho, he comes face-to-face with his own *burning bush*—in this instance an angel appearing as a man wielding a sword. Joshua boldly demands whose side he is on—the side of the Israelites or the enemies? The answer is astounding. The angel declares neutrality. He's on neither side. Rather, he commands God's army. He might have added: *God doesn't take sides with people; rather, people are compelled to take sides with God.*

Joshua's response is instantaneous. He falls on the ground and worships, and only then inquires what he should do. The angel, in words eerily reminiscent of God's words to Moses from the burning bush, tells Joshua to take off his sandals because he is standing on holy ground.

Now Joshua is ready to face Jericho head-on. With God's detailed plan, he orders seven priests with trumpets and all his soldiers to march around the walled city. On the surface this is hardly a sound military strategy. But they follow God's orders and march around the city one time each day for six days. On the seventh day they march seven times. As they march, the priests blast their ram's horns. On the final march on the last day, all the armed men, on command, scream at the top of their lungs. With that, the walls collapse and the soldiers rush in and kill everything alive, both humans and animals.

Joshua then orders the city to be burned, but not before looting all the precious metals they could find as well as rescuing Rahab and her family. This incredible victory over Jericho brings Joshua widespread fame as an army general to be feared.

But there is sin in the camp. Achan and others appropriate valuable items from Jericho for themselves, thinking they will not be discovered. But when the Israelites attack Ai, the army is soundly defeated.

So beside himself is Joshua that he tears his clothes and flings himself on the ground, throwing dirt on his head, a ritual imitated by others as well. He cries out to God in anguish over the decision to cross the Jordan and settle in hostile territory. God is not moved by his groveling. Israel

The destruction of the walls of Jericho

deserves the defeat. Play by God's rules or suffer the consequences.

On orders from God, Joshua then calls each tribe, clan by clan and family by family, to appear before him for inspection. Everyone is searched. Anyone found with pilfered goods is to be burned to death along with the valuables. When Achan is called up, he admits his wrongdoing, confessing he had stolen a priceless robe along with silver and gold, all of which he has buried in his tent. The punishment is severe. Joshua takes the valuables and then orders him and his family and all their livestock and possessions to be removed to the Valley of Achor. There he and his family are stoned to death.

With the punishment over, Joshua, again under the command of God, sends thousands of soldiers to sneak back toward Ai

Everyday *Life*

Warfare and Weapons

Joshua is the first great Israelite warrior and military commander of the Bible. His career profile is filled with war stories and victories—victories engineered by God. Indeed, the Hebrew people, after hundreds of years of slavery in Egypt, were no match for their enemies, many of whom employed iron weapons. The Philistines in particular manufactured weapons that were far more advanced than anything Joshua and his men would have had access to.

The armies of ancient Israel often fought in hand-to-hand combat against their enemies. The commanders or kings might be in the midst of battle on a horse or in a chariot, but foot soldiers made up the ranks of the fighting force. Their weapons were sometimes no more than farming implements. On the other hand, a well-supplied militia would go to battle with swords, spears, javelins, slingshots, and bows and arrows. Defensive gear consisted of everything from shields, breastplates, and helmets to full body armor—sometimes carried by an armor bearer. In later years David for a time served as one of Saul's armor bearers.

War, War, War

Though the history of war is not the history of the Old Testament, we cannot understand the Old Testament without reference to war. It may be too much to claim that one can find war and conflict on every page of the Hebrew Bible, but not by much. War was almost a daily part of ancient Israelite life, primarily because of that nation's size and location. Here was a nation no larger than the state of Vermont located in the strategic Syria-Palestinian corridor—and all the surrounding nations coveted it. Egypt in the south and various Mesopotamian empires in the north-northeast saw that territory as a buffer zone to protect themselves from encroaching armies bent on conquest and pillage.

John A. Wood, "War in the Old Testament," 11–12

to lie in wait for an ambush. Joshua arrives in the light of day ready for battle. The whole city comes out for the fight. But he and his men make a hasty retreat before the battle can even begin. As the enemy army chases after them, the hidden army ambushes the empty city and sets it on fire. When Joshua and his men see the flames, they turn around to face the enemy, with the remainder of the army attacking from the rear.

Joshua, with his javelin held high, commands the day-long attack. The twelve thousand inhabitants of the city are slaughtered, including the king, who is taken alive but later hanged. With that accomplished, Joshua builds an altar and worships God.

Though a capable military leader, Joshua uncharacteristically allows himself to be deceived by the Gibeonites. They convince him they have recently moved close by and want only to live in peace. So he makes a treaty with them. He discovers too late, however, that they are up to no good. In the end it is decided that they can be a part of the people of Israel, but must be servants to them—haulers of water and hewers of wood.

Joshua burns the town of Ai

Such treaties terrify neighboring tribes. They form a league to do battle against Joshua and his army, but they don't stand a chance. "God pitched huge stones on them out of the sky." Indeed, "More died from the hailstones than the People of Israel killed with the sword."[8]

But another incident during this battle is more spectacular yet. "The sun stopped in its tracks in mid sky; just sat there all day"[9] until the battle is over and Joshua defeats the enemy. Even those who are on the run are eventually killed or captured, including five tribal chieftains. Joshua himself has the grisly pleasure of hanging each of them on his own tree. More battles will follow, and by the time Joshua is done, his conquest includes virtually the entire southern region.

His work is not over, however. The tribes in the northern mountains and elsewhere are joining together to put an end to Joshua and his army once and for all. But through battle after battle, the region is conquered with the defeat of a total of thirty-one kings. The land now belongs to the Israelites, and Joshua begins assigning a region to each of the tribes.

This is a major undertaking. The road to land division is rocky and there are many

John Calvin and the Sun Standing Still

Joshua bids it [the sun] stay and rest there, in other words, remain above what is called the horizon. In short, the sun, which was already declining to the west, is kept from setting. I do not give myself any great anxiety as to the number of the hours; because it is enough for me that the day was continued through the whole night. Were histories of that period extant, they would doubtless celebrate this great miracle; lest its credibility, however, should be questioned, the writer of this book mentions that an account of it was given elsewhere, though the work which he quotes has been lost.

John Calvin, *Commentary on Joshua*

potholes along the way. But eventually the allotments are doled out, and Joshua, who is now very old, begins to turn over leadership to tribal elders. When the apportionment is completed he calls the Israelites together and gives his farewell address: "I'm an old man. I've lived a long time. You have seen everything that God has done to these nations because of you. . . . Now, stay strong and steady. Obediently do everything written in the *Book of The Revelation of Moses*."[10]

Joshua's final message also contains a history lesson from God, beginning with Abraham, who, with his father and brother, worshiped false gods. But then God called Abraham to leave that behind and to journey to Canaan. The narrative moves on to Isaac, Jacob, Esau—nothing about Joseph—and on to Moses and Aaron, where the account becomes much more detailed, as various battles are recalled.

The sermon ends with a challenge. Recognizing that these often-wayward Israelites had many options, he boldly lays the choice before them: "Choose you this day whom ye will serve; . . . but as for me and my house, we will serve the Lord."[11] The people have a choice, but Joshua's history lesson makes it very clear that if they do not serve the Lord, there will be hell to pay. God had not dealt kindly with those who had strayed off to worship other gods. He is a jealous God, who does not take sin lightly. The people in unison commit themselves to obeying and worshiping God.

Joshua leaves nothing to chance. He lays out a detailed covenant for all the people gathered at Shechem. It is an official set of guidelines they must follow that he designates as the "Book of The Revelation of God."[12] To mark the occasion, he places a large rock at the base of an oak tree. This, he tells the people, is a reminder should they be tempted to sin against God.

Soon after this, Joshua dies at the age of 110. He has carried out his duties well. He was a warrior and a leader of the people, though not a lawgiver. From beginning to end he has held fast to the law of his master and mentor Moses.

Caleb: Spy with Strong Convictions

He is introduced as a spy. And although he is far more than that—a soldier and Joshua's most trusted lieutenant—he will always be remembered primarily as a spy. Soon after Moses leads the children of Israel across the Red Sea, he sends out spies to scout out Canaan. It is Moses' hope that, once the spies return with a positive report, the conquering of Canaan will be the next step.

Twelve spies are selected from each of the tribes, among them Caleb from the tribe of Judah and Joshua from Ephraim. Moses instructs them to essentially *exegete* the land. They are to examine every angle and gather all pertinent information on encampments, cities, countryside, military might, population statistics, farming trends, produce samples, and anything else that could aid in his plans to conquer the region.

After forty days of investigation, they return. Standing before Moses and Aaron, they give their report. The good news: "It *does* flow with milk and honey! Just look at this fruit!" The bad news: "The people who live there are fierce, their cities are huge and well fortified. Worse yet, we saw descendants of the giant Anak."[13]

Whether true or not, this is the majority report. The people are groaning. Here they are in the wilderness, only to learn that the Promised Land is occupied by giants and dotted by militarized cities. But then Caleb interrupts and demands the people shush. He presents the minority report, introduced with a fight song: "Let's go up and take the land—now. We can do it."[14]

But the majority takes the floor, insisting there is no way this land can be conquered. Indeed, the giants in the land are so huge the spies seem in comparison no more than grasshoppers. The people take seriously the majority report and begin to weep and wail, and keep it up all night long. How can they trust Moses? He has led them into the wilderness, and now they have no place to go. They demand a new leader.

Now everything is falling to pieces: the people in an uproar, Moses and Aaron flat on their faces in front of them, Joshua and Caleb tearing their clothes in despair. Joshua and Caleb feel utterly betrayed by the other ten and plead with the vast crowd to consider the fact that God is on their side, which makes all the difference. Besides, they emphasize, the might of the enemy has been grossly exaggerated.

But the people are not convinced. They are scared silly and cannot get the majority report out of their heads. So furious are they with Caleb and Joshua that they begin hurling rocks at them. In the midst of the mayhem the glory of God shines forth. God is livid and says to Moses: "How long will these people treat me like dirt? . . . I've had enough—I'm going to hit them with a plague and kill them."[15]

Moses tries to reason with God, pointing out that killing them would be a bad testimony to the Egyptians. God relents, and the Israelites are condemned to wander in the wilderness for forty years.

After the debacle of the spying expedition and report, Caleb seems to disappear for forty-five years until he is appointed by Moses to assist with the distribution of the land to the various tribes. While performing this task, he and other leaders of his tribe come to Joshua's headquarters at Gilgal. Caleb is the spokesman. He reminds Joshua of what God told Moses regarding the two of them forty-five years earlier. He was just forty years old at that time when he was commissioned to spy out the land. He recalls how he had brought back an honest assessment (making no mention of Joshua himself), while the other returning spies insisted the enemy was too fierce. Moses had promised him land, so now he is asking Joshua for the hill country around Hebron—the whole mountain, for that matter.

It is true that he was promised the land, but not without his having to put up a fight for it. Populated by fortified cities of the Anakim, Caleb has battles ahead of him. But with God's help, Caleb promises to conquer the cities and drive the people out of the land. Joshua blesses him and gives the land to him as his rightful inheritance. And Caleb fulfills that promise by conquering the resident population of the hill country that is to become Judah, and he takes over their cities.

What is perhaps most interesting about this encounter between Caleb and Joshua after forty-five years is Caleb's testimony regarding his own health. He is remarkably fit for eighty-five: "I'm as strong as I was the day Moses sent me out. I'm as strong as ever in battle, whether coming or going."[16]

Rahab: Prostitute Who Hid Spies

She is a harlot working in the *world's oldest profession*, a career considered shameful not just among the Israelites but even in the ancient pagan world. Although prostitutes sometimes gained prestige by being associated with cults, they nevertheless often found themselves on the lowest rung of society and were regarded as morally deficient. Such a stigma was attached to Rahab. She lives in a condo on the massive wall of Jericho, referred to as the "city of palms." She is not married herself but has family—parents and siblings (no mention of children)—in town. She makes a living by offering sexual services and overnight accommodations. Life is anything but boring.

Strangers coming through town seek her out, and she is not surprised when two undercover agents show up at her door. What transpires after that is not told, but

Caleb, the Grand Old Man

How the mothers would hold up their little children in their arms to look at Caleb as he walked down the street! . . . Caleb had the distinguished reward of being *put upon the hardest service.* That is always the lot of the most faithful servant of God. There were three huge warriors in Mount Hebron; no one will undertake to kill them, except it be our good old friend Caleb. These Anakims, with their six toes on each foot, and their six fingers on each hand, are to be upset and driven out. Who is to do it? If nobody else will offer himself, here is Caleb. Nay, he does not merely allow himself to be sent upon the service, but he craves permission to be allowed to take the place, the reason being because it was the worst task of the war, and he panted to have the honor of it. Grand old man!

C. H. Spurgeon, "Caleb—The Man for the Times"

when she learns that the king wants the men turned in, she hides them on the roof under a pile of flax. Not only that; she sends word back to the king that the men had stayed with her but have already left town. She further spins her story: "I have no idea where they went. Hurry up! Chase them—you can still catch them!"[17] All of this after being told they are foreign spies up to no good.

Why would Rahab betray her own city? Had she been treated so badly by the townspeople that she wanted to get back at them? Or is she only seeking to protect herself and her family? That night she goes to the roof and tells the men she knows exactly what they are up to: "I know that God has given you the land. We're all afraid. Everyone in the country feels hopeless. We heard how God dried up the waters of the Red Sea" and much more.[18]

She is in a panic and ready to bargain. She is saving their lives and expects them to save hers and that of her father, mother, brothers, and sisters. They agree. If she saves their lives, they will remember her

Rahab concealing the spies

A Jericho Harlot

Rahab indulged in venal wantonness as traveling merchants came her way and were housed in her ill-famed abode. Evidently Rahab had her own house and lived apart from her parents and family. Although she never lost her concern for her dear ones, perhaps she was treated as a moral leper. . . . So, high-spirited and independent she left her parents, set up her own apartment with dire consequences. Frequently women like Rahab are more often sinned against than sinners. Man's lust for the unlawful is responsible for harlotry.

Herbert Lockyer, *All the Women of the Bible*, 131

when the army of Israel attacks. So she lets them down from her upper-story dwelling. They crawl out the window and down a rope in the dead of night. She advises them to run directly to the hills and hide for three days before getting on the road back to the Israelite encampment.

Before leaving, the men give her a red string and instruct her to hang it as a pledge of their agreement. They tell her to prepare for their return. She must gather her family inside her house. When the day of attack comes, they will be safe as long as they display the scarlet cord.

True to their word, the spies, on orders of Joshua, rescue Rahab and her family before the final destruction of Jericho. The story of Rahab does not end here. She marries Salmon, an Israelite (one of the spies, according to rabbinic tradition), and bears a son. This child is none other than Boaz, who as an adult marries Ruth. Rahab's grandson is Obed, and her great-grandson is Jesse, the father of David.

Spies and a Prostitute

The obvious question that the story raises is why would the Israelite spies be consorting with a prostitute? Perhaps they hoped to overhear the talk of the town at the brothel. At such a place, strangers would not be particularly conspicuous or suspicious. Perhaps they might have thought a harlot would be more open to outsiders than other citizens of Jericho.

Alice Ogden Bellis, *Helpmates, Harlots, and Heroes: Women's Stories in the Hebrew Bible*, 113

Thus Rahab the harlot finds her way into the genealogy of Jesus. Indeed, she is so heralded that she is not only honored for her faith in the Epistle of James, but also in Hebrews 11, among such great figures as Noah, Abraham, Isaac, Jacob, Joseph, and Moses. There she is mentioned by name; Joshua is not.

Concluding Observations

Although Joshua is not mentioned by name in the Hebrews *Hall of Faith*, he clearly plays the lead role in the conquering of Canaan. His preparation for carrying out this assignment begins with his sending spies to Jericho, even before the crossing of the Jordan River. Here the spies and Rahab steal the story. The next hurdle Joshua confronts is the crossing of the Jordan, no easy feat with a seemingly endless line of households and all their possessions. But for a mighty miracle, he would have been at his wit's end. God intervenes and paves the crossing with dry ground.

Following the crossing, Joshua is confronted with a mission far beyond the ability of any mere military commander. But with more miracles he conquers the land. Jericho, in retrospect, looked easy. March around the city, blow horns, and the walls fall down, almost like Humpty Dumpty. From this point on—if not earlier—Joshua surely knows who the real military commander is. Miracles pile upon miracles, and the sun stands still.

In a sense, the hardest work for Joshua is dividing up and assigning the land. No military miracles in this stage of the game. The focus is back on the mundane work of governing an unruly people. In the process, Joshua's star seems to dim.

Caleb plays a critical role as a spy, as does Rahab in her own way. She alone among those in the initial conquering of the Promised Land will find her way into New Testament genealogy.

Further Reading

Baker, Donald. *Joshua: The Power of God's Promises*. Carol Stream, IL: InterVarsity, 1999.

May, Roy M. *Joshua and the Promised Land*. New York: United Methodist Global Board of Ministries, 1997.

Schaeffer, Francis A. *Joshua and the Flow of Biblical History*. Wheaton: Crossway, 1975.

8

DEBORAH, GIDEON, AND SAMSON

Disputations and Decision Making

All rise. Court is now in session. The setting is solemn as the robed magistrate enters the courtroom, walks to the raised bench, and brings down the gavel. Such a scenario should not be mistaken for the ancient practice of *judging* in the book of Judges. In fact, this book focuses more on the continuation of conquest than on matters of law and arbitration.

Joshua has now passed from the scene. It is a time in biblical history when God is not quite so generous with spectacular military miracles. Tribes such as Judah and Simeon join forces to fight for their promised inheritance, and the Lord gives "the land into their hands."[1] But with every step forward Israel seems to take two steps back.

What was supposed to have been a conquest has taken a different turn. In many cases the inhabitants remain in their own towns, sometimes under the thumb of the Israelites. In other instances, however, the Israelites make covenants with their pagan neighbors rather than driving them wholesale out of the land as God had commanded. They intermarry and worship other gods, often utterly forsaking the God of Joshua and Moses. Wickedness pervades the land.

Judges with Weapons

It is frequently pointed out that the word "judge" is a poor name for the book of Judges and an inaccurate description of its major characters. The term "judges" . . . suggests to most people some sort of legal functionary—a black-robed person sitting behind a bench, holding a gavel, and making decisions on points of law. With the apparent exception of Deborah, who held court under the palm tree known by her name (Judg. 4:5), the judges do not seem to have been legal interpreters. . . . Indeed, it can be argued that the primary activity of the judges was leading the Israelites (or at least some of the Israelite tribes) against their oppressive enemies.

J. Clinton McCann, *Judges: A Bible Commentary for Teaching and Preaching*, 3

Indeed, with Joshua gone, the moral fabric of the Israelites deteriorates rapidly as idolatry and infidelity run rampant. God is more than displeased and gives them over to their enemies to be harassed, plundered, and enslaved. But when they plead with God and repent of their evil ways, he mercifully raises up judges who save them from their enemies. After each such intervention, the people of Israel follow the precepts of God, but when a good judge dies, they again return to their evil ways. And "every man did that which was right in his own eyes."[2]

One of the first judges is Othniel, Caleb's nephew, to whom Caleb had earlier given his daughter in marriage for having captured a key city. He now comes to the rescue after eight years of Israel's servitude to the Syrians. Filled with the Spirit of God, he rallies the people and leads the Israelite army into battle against their oppressors. He defeats them soundly and ushers in four decades of peace.

But after Othniel dies, the Israelites go right back to their wicked ways. So God punishes them by setting King Eglon and his Moabite forces against them. Through an alliance with the Ammonites and Amalekites, he marshals enough troops to make a major strike and subdue Israel. It is a mighty blow that decimates the army. The result is fourteen years of slavery, Eglon as master tyrant.

Not surprisingly, the people are now crying out to God, begging for release. God hears their pleas and raises up Ehud from the tribe of Benjamin. He is a left-handed and clever fellow. He fashions a short-handled, two-sided sword that can be strapped to his right thigh and hidden under his garment. The Israelites send word to the king that they would like to pay him tribute. The morbidly obese King Eglon welcomes Ehud as their envoy. Ehud presents the tribute, brought in by his aides, and then departs. But then Ehud turns around and asks if he can speak privately with the king.

Suspecting nothing, King Eglon orders his servants to depart. Ehud tells the king he has a message from God. With proper respect, the king stands up. Ehud then raises no suspicion when he reaches across with his left hand. But in an instant he has his sword in his hand and he thrusts it into the king's stomach. Indeed the whole sword sinks so far into his belly that "the fat closed in over it so he couldn't pull it out."[3] Ehud gets out in a hurry, locking the door behind him and slipping away, eluding the guards.

With that dark deed accomplished, Ehud rallies the Israelite army and attacks and subdues the Moabites. Eighty years of peace follow this stunning victory.

Israel's enemies, however, are ever present. The Philistines in particular are more than a bothersome threat. And now Shamgar comes to the rescue. He goes on the offensive, and with a cattle prod single-handedly kills six hundred of the pesky Philistine enemy. But, not surprisingly, the people return to their evil ways. God, true to his nature, punishes them by selling them over to the Canaanite king Jabin, who, along with fierce army commander Sisera, oppresses them for twenty years. And, of course, once again, the Israelites cry out to God for relief.

Enter Deborah, prophet and judge.

Deborah: Judge and Military Leader

A few strong, independent women preceded her, but she alone courageously leads the Israelites in her own right. Her husband is Lappidoth, of whom nothing more is known. She is the first female leader mentioned in Scripture, though nothing at all is made of her gender. The people seem to take it in stride, and there is no apparent opposition on that count. People travel from great distances to bring their matters before her court at Deborah's Palm, located in the hill country of Ephraim.

Judging cases is her day job, but Deborah is also a prophet. In this capacity, she

Deborah, judge and prophetess

sends a message from God to military commander Barak, telling him to make ready ten companies of soldiers and head for Mount Tabor in preparation for war. She adds a postscript: "I will lead Sisera, the commander of Jabin's army, with his chariots and troops to the Kishon River and give him into your hands."[4]

Barak is a military man, but he recognizes the spiritual and temporal authority of Deborah. He agrees under one condition: "If you go with me, I'll go. But if you don't go with me, I won't go." She has a quick retort: "Of course I'll go with

The Remarkable Women of Judges

In Genesis, the women characters all assume essentially the same role, as they seek to ensure the continuation of Abraham's patriarchal line. . . . Judges' women stand in striking contrast. . . . Deborah, Jael, and the woman of Thebez, for example, are all noteworthy for the actions they take within the traditionally male domain of battle, and Deborah is also described as a religious functionary (a prophet) and as one of Israel's political leaders (a judge). Elsewhere in biblical tradition, these offices are occupied almost exclusively by men.

Susan Ackerman, *Warrior, Dancer, Seductress, Queen: Women in Judges and Biblical Israel*, 5 you. But understand that with an attitude like that, there'll be no glory in it for you."[5] Rather, it will be a woman, she prophesies, who will do Sisera in. On the surface this scenario appears to be a display of woman power, but God is truly behind it all.

Deborah meets Barak, who then marshals together ten companies of soldiers from the tribes of Zebulun and Naphtali. Word gets out to Sisera that Barak and his men are heading for Mount Tabor. So Sisera brings his big guns—nine hundred chariots of iron—and all his soldiers to fight the battle. Barak's troops position themselves on Mount Tabor, where Deborah orders Barak and the ten companies of soldiers to make what would appear to be a foolhardy frontal attack down the hill against the incredibly well-armed

Everyday *Life*

Justice in God's Court of Law

Deborah, among other things, served as an arbitrator in her informal court under a palm tree. In ancient Israel at the time of the book of Judges there were no courthouses where attorneys came before an official to adjudicate a case. Rather, a wise individual became a judge solely on the basis of reputation. Such a person offered counsel when disputes arose among neighbors.

Long before the time of Deborah, the legal system involving judges was introduced by Moses after his father-in-law Jethro had noted how inefficiently judicial matters were being handled. And the system continued far beyond the end of the book of Judges. Kings and prophets would come and go, while judges continued to administer legal affairs.

Most such adjudicators were older men who sat at the gates of the city. Job, by his own testimony, is an example: "For I assisted the poor in their need and the orphans who required help. I helped those without hope, and they blessed me. And I caused the widows' hearts to sing for joy" (Job 29:12–13 NLT). His involvement as an elder at the gates goes to the heart of Old Testament justice—summed up in God's word to Amos: "I hate all your show and pretense. . . . Instead, I want to see a mighty flood of justice" (Amos 5:21, 24 NLT)—justice directed particularly at the enslaved, the innocent, the poor, and the widows.

Sitting at the Gate

The gate was the center of city life in biblical times. Originally designed to defend a city against attack, this massive structure soon became a combination of community center, city hall, and marketplace. People paid their taxes in the city gate, and officials settled legal matters there. . . . In the gate, Boaz established his legal right to marry Ruth.

Ray Vander Laan, *That the World May Know*, Teacher's Guide, 14

A Woman Judge

How difficult was it for Deborah to fulfill her role as a judge? It is possible that in ancient Israel women sought advice from other women, but there is nothing in the biblical text to indicate that Deborah's work as a judge was limited only to women. As a woman who functioned as God's spokesperson, the people of Israel would evaluate Deborah's wisdom and the conviction of her call as a validation of her work as a judge. Because of her God-given abilities, the people would accept her work and follow her leadership.

Claude Mariottini, "Deborah: A Judge in Israel"

Canaanites. But God is right in the thick of it. In the end, Sisera's entire army is slaughtered.

Only Sisera survives. He heads for the hills on foot and comes to a tent belonging to Jael, whose husband, Heber the Kennite, is a friend of the Canaanite king. Jael invites him into her tent and offers him protection from the Israelite army. She covers him with a blanket, and then brings him milk to quench his thirst. She agrees, at his request, to stand at the door of the tent and to tell anyone who might inquire that no one is inside. Exhausted, he falls asleep.

As Deborah has prophesied, it is a woman who puts an end to this brutal warrior. Jael simply takes a peg from the tent, walks over to the almost comatose Sisera, and drives it through his head, one thundering hammer blow after another. Soon thereafter Barak comes along looking for Sisera. Jael invites him in to see the corpse with a tent peg through its head. Through the work of God, carried out by two women, King Jabin is beaten back until his kingdom is demolished.

The victory celebration includes a long, elaborate song sung by both Deborah and Barak. One of the lines explains that they are singing and making music to God. But the song goes on to recall Deborah's part in the victory.

> Warriors became fat and sloppy,
> no fight left in them.
> Then you, Deborah, rose up;
> you got up, a mother in Israel.
> God chose new leaders,
> who then fought at the gates.[6]

Another verse praises Jael, telling the story with a certain amount of poetic license. In the song she is giving him milk in a bowl and hardly waiting a second before she grabs the peg and hammer, driving it through his temple while he slumps at her feet, dead.

After they sing this victory cantata, peace reigns over the land for forty years.

Unforgettable Females in the Book of Judges

Some of the most unforgettable females of the Hebrew Bible make their appearances in the book of Judges. . . . When we realize that eleven full differentiated females take part in various narrative segments . . . we recognize that an unusual density and variety of women appear in these pages.

Lillian R. Klein, *Deborah to Esther: Sexual Politics in the Hebrew Bible*, 9

Gideon: Successful Soldier and Father of Seventy Sons

The era of peace after Deborah's victory comes to an end because of sin. Exasperated by the Israelites' evil ways, God puts them under the thumb of Midian for seven years. The people take shelter in mountain caves, sneaking down to plant crops. But the forces of Midian, as well as Amalek, charge in from the east with their armies of camels and, like an invasion of locusts, steal cattle and destroy crops. Running for their lives and utterly impoverished, the people again cry out to God. It's like a broken record. Will these fickle people ever learn?

God sends a prophet with a reminder of how he had delivered them from Egypt and much more, but still they flirt with false gods. And they misbehave in every way imaginable. Is it any wonder that they are eating dirt and living in caves?

But they are God's people, and he does have compassion on them. He sends an angel, who finds a cool resting place under an oak tree that belongs to Gideon's father Joash. Gideon's ingenuity has allowed him to escape the notice of the Midianites as he threshes wheat in a hidden winepress. The angel spots him and comes over, declaring that he is a mighty warrior and that God is with him. Gideon looks around as if to say *Who, me?* He's stunned, but he also has a quick retort. *If that's true, why are we under the thumb of the Midianites? Where is the God of miracles who led the people out of Egypt?*

Now it is God himself who looks him straight in the eye and orders him to go in his own strength and save Israel. But, like Moses before him, Gideon is not convinced. He is a farmer, not a military officer. He rightly asks how he could ever become a mighty warrior. Moreover, he's from the weakest clan in the tribe of Manasseh. And Gideon himself? "I'm the runt of the litter."[7]

God is not put off. In fact, he almost seems to enjoy this encounter. He assures Gideon he is the man who will prevail over Midian. Fully conscious of his shortcomings, Gideon wonders if he's hearing things, perhaps hallucinating. He will make a fool of himself—and no doubt die—if he goes off to battle. So he asks God for a sign. But first he asks God to wait around for a while, giving him time to come back with a gift. Gideon returns with an offering of roasted goat, bread, and broth.

The angel of God, waiting under the oak, takes charge of the meal and tells Gideon how to properly prepare it. Gideon follows instructions precisely, placing the meat and bread on a rock and pouring the broth over the top. No sooner is that accomplished than the angel stretches out a stick and fire consumes Gideon's food. With that the angel disappears. Gideon, having already interacted with God and the angel, panics on seeing the fireworks. But God assures him he will be safe.

A sense of peace falls upon this "runt of the litter," and he builds an altar, naming it Peace of God. That night God comes to him again and tells him to make a sacrifice by confiscating the best of his father's bulls. He is to build an altar on the very spot where his father has erected an altar to Baal, next to a sacred pole for Asherah, goddess of fertility. To accomplish this he must destroy all reminders of his father's false gods. He does so, but under cover of darkness.

The crime does not go unnoticed. The townspeople are up in arms. Who's behind all this vandalism? Rumors fly. Word leaks out that it is the son of Joash. The neighbors are furious. They order Joash to send his son out of the house. The mob will give him his due. But Joash is quick witted and defies the multitude. He shouts above the rabble, *If Baal's a real god, let him go after my son. Let Baal defend himself. Death to anyone defending Baal.*

The townspeople back down and come to recognize Gideon as their leader. But the Midianites and Amalekites continue to breathe down their necks. So Gideon blows his horn, sending word out to all of Manasseh and surrounding tribes that they should take up arms and prepare to fight. Still Gideon is second-guessing himself. The enemy is fierce. He fears there will be a bloodbath, and that he will be held responsible.

Gideon pleads with God for a sign. He tells God that he's going to set out a wool fleece on the floor of the winepress. If God is really going to do what he has said, Gideon wants to see dew in the morning on the fleece only, not on the floor. The next morning he gets up and finds the fleece so wet with dew that he's able to wring out a full bowl of water. God must be behind this risky military venture. But maybe not. Gideon's nerves are on edge. He can't get it out of his head that he's a farmer, not an army general. So back to God. Once more with the fleece challenge—this time the fleece dry and the floor wet. The next morning he wades through a puddle on the floor and picks up the fleece—not even a hint of dampness.

The following day he marches forward, with thirty-two companies of men in lockstep behind him. By this time he has acquired a sense of confidence. But then he hears the voice of God. It is the last thing he wants to hear. God directs him to send back home all those who are questioning this military operation. Gideon makes the announcement, and twenty-two entire companies depart.

But God tells Gideon there are still too many men. This time God will divide the men from the boys. The whole army is to go to a nearby stream and drink. Those who cup their hands full of water and lap it up with their tongues like a dog are to be separated from those who slurp it up with face in the water. The dogs win the prize; they get to go forward into battle. The bad news is there are only three hundred of them.

Gideon and the fleece

To Fight or to Go Home?

God looked at Gideon's army of 32,000 and knew that somehow, even though they were vastly outnumbered, the people would still find some way to take the glory. So God shrank the army. He told Gideon to tell any of the men who were afraid, to go on home; their services would no longer be needed. I often wonder if I had been part of the original 32,000, had looked down into the valley, and saw 135,000 armed forces of the enemy, if I would have stayed to fight or gone home. I think we need to be somewhat careful reading too much into those who were considered scared or were considered brave. . . . The argument could be made that God looks for courageous men who are willing to follow orders at all costs. I am not sure you can automatically draw that assumption from this text.

Chad Keck, *Ordinarily Faithful: Life Lessons from the Judges*, 57–58

Below Gideon and his men are the Midianites, stretched out across the valley as far as the eye can see—vast swarms of them. God tells Gideon to take his armor bearer, sneak up near the guard post, and listen in on the conversation, for what he hears will indeed give him courage. And Gideon does overhear a soldier telling his comrade about a strange dream he's just had. A big barley loaf rolls into the valley and smashes the tent. The comrade interprets the dream to mean that Gideon and his men will overwhelm the whole Midianite encampment.

Now the reluctant Gideon is ready to do battle. He is finally convinced that God will give him the victory. He divides his men into three companies, each man with a ram's horn and a jar with a torch in it. The soldiers are to watch him and do exactly what he does. They arrive at the valley camp in the middle of the night. In unison, the men break the jars and blow their horns. Then one grand rallying cry: "A sword for GOD and for Gideon!"[8] So convinced are the Midianites that thousands of Gideon's men are swarming around them that they in their sleepy confusion begin killing each other.

But most of the Midianites are on the run. Gideon sends word to the adjoining tribes to join in the battle. The Ephraimites respond and capture two Midianite kings, but jealousies flare and they resent Gideon's leadership. Gideon, however, manages to smooth things over. Then he and his band of three hundred continue beyond the Jordan in hot pursuit of some of the still surviving Midianite kings.

Desperately hungry on arrival in Succoth, their plea for food is denied. Gideon warns the men of Succoth of the consequences of their inhospitable behavior and moves on to the town of Peniel, where again he is denied rations. Without food but vowing revenge, he moves on and defeats Midianite forces five times his size. On his return trip, he brings back two hostage kings to prove he had indeed been on a legitimate military mission. His troops thrash the men of Succoth and destroy the tower in Peniel, killing the men of the town.

Gideon learns from the two Midianite kings that they had massacred his brothers in an earlier battle. He immediately orders them killed. Jether, his oldest son, is to do the job. Still a boy, Jether freezes. These are kings after all. He just can't do it. The kings taunt Gideon, questioning his manhood because he won't do it himself. He answers their taunts by putting them to the sword.

After such incredible triumphs, the Israelites beg Gideon to be their ruler, with his son and grandson to succeed him. Gideon emphatically declines. Only God will be their king; he will rule over them.

Gideon's last hurrah is most strange. He asks his soldiers for gold earrings they have taken from the Midianite enemies they have killed. They eagerly comply, donating more than forty pounds. He melts them down and makes the gold into a sacred object—an ephod—and sets it up in his hometown. Here Israelites come and kneel before it—even Gideon and his family. "All Israel prostituted themselves by worshiping it there, and it became a snare to Gideon and his family."[9] Do the Israelites return to the actual worship of God? All that is revealed is that there follow forty years of peace.

Gideon's claim to fame was his victorious military career. But another significant aspect of his life related to family matters. He took polygamy seriously and acquired many wives, who bore him seventy sons. Actually he fathered at least seventy-one sons. But because Abimelech was the son not of a wife but of a concubine from Shechem, he did not have the status of the other sons, a matter that would tarnish Gideon's legacy. Gideon himself lived to be an old man, ever a hero among his people.

Abimelech: Gideon's Son by a Concubine

Gideon's funeral is hardly over when the Israelites resume their wicked ways, particularly in their worship of Baal. Amid this evil, Abimelech goes back to his mother's hometown and asks his relatives if they would rather see Gideon's seventy sons in authority over them or him alone. The answer is easy. After all, he is one of them. With him as ruler, they reason, things will go better for them.

So they give him seventy pieces of silver, which he uses to hire a band of thugs. Arriving at his late father's home, he proceeds to kill all his half brothers except for the youngest, Jotham, who manages to escape, but not before pronouncing a curse on the wicked Abimelech. The slaughter over, Abimelech heads back to Shechem, where he is crowned king and rules over Israel for the next three years.

But he is not universally loved, even in his hometown. Plots are hatched against him, and hired assassins are brought to overthrow him. Tipped off, Abimelech takes his men and lies in wait outside Shechem, preparing to ambush the enemy. A battle ensues, and Abimelech's men prevail. He eventually captures the city, massacres the inhabitants, and demolishes the town.

Meanwhile the locals who had plotted against him are taking refuge with their families in the fortified city tower. Abimelech and his men arrive with armloads of kindling and set the tower ablaze, burning alive some one thousand people. From there he moves on to Thebez, where again the townspeople are holed up in a tower. Just as Abimelech is starting to torch the door, a woman from above drops a millstone on his head. He is fatally wounded, but has the presence of mind to make one final demand of his youthful aide. He asks him to kill him with his sword so it could never be said that he was killed by a woman. His aide does as he is told, and Abimelech dies.

In the decades that follow there are times of peace when judges arise and rule Israel effectively. However, the vicious cycle continues: the people of Israel fall into idolatry, God allows enemy tribes to attack and oppress them, and, like clockwork, the people cry to God for relief. But God is sick and tired of their broken promises to repent of their infidelities. Finally, after spiritual and moral renewal, the Israelites do get rid of their foreign gods, and God does take their issues seriously—though the cycle surely does not end.

Jephthah: Son of a Prostitute

He is the black sheep of the family, the son of Gilead. His brothers run him out of town because his mother is a prostitute. They do not want him claiming any of their father's inheritance. So Jephthah travels to the region of Tob, where he hangs around with a tough crowd. There he eludes the plots against him from his brothers. He is a fighter who forges a reputation as a mighty warrior.

Some years later, when the Israelites are struggling to fend off attacks from the Ammonites, the leaders in Gilead send for Jephthah. He is skeptical. Why should he fight their battles when they had run him out of town? On his insistence, they take an oath before God to live under his military rule.

Now as army general, Jephthah sends a message to the Ammonite king, asking why he is attacking Israel. The response is straightforward: *You took our land. If you give it back we won't bother you.* Jephthah sends back a lengthy message—a history lesson essentially saying that the land on which the Ammonites are settled is not theirs to begin with. In fact, when the Israelites came out of Egypt, they were forced to detour around Ammonite land to avoid any trouble. Besides, the Israelites have never pushed anyone off the land. God has, but not Israel.

The Ammonites pay him no heed, so Jephthah marshals his troops and prepares for battle. But the enemy is strong, and Jephthah knows he needs God's help. He calls on God, as had his predecessors, for victory over the enemy. Then he makes a vow to God—a strange vow that will have dire consequences. Should God allow him to return home in triumph, he promises to sacrifice on an altar whatever emerges first from his doorway. What is he thinking! True, a lamb or goat or calf might be in the house and wander out, but typically a family member would most likely enter and exit from the same door. It's a foolish vow, and he lives to regret it.

Jephthah is victorious. He and his army slaughter the Ammonites. Word of the triumph arrives home before he does. As he nears his home, his daughter—his darling daughter, an only child—does what is most

Jephthah and his daughter

natural. She runs out of the house to greet her beloved father. And not only that; she grabs her tambourine and dances in celebration. She is thrilled to know her father has survived the battle.

Jephthah is beside himself. He tears his clothes and cries out in anguish: "Ah, dearest daughter—I'm dirt. I'm despicable. My heart is torn to shreds."[10] Then he reveals his vow. Amazingly, she doesn't cut and run. She acquiesces. But only perhaps because he has reneged on his original vow, spinning a more-than-minor revision. His claim to her appears to have been that he vowed virginity, not sacrifice, of the first one coming through the door.

She is willing to fulfill a vow of virginity, though not without great sorrow. With her father's permission, she goes off to the hill country with her friends for a two-month period of lament. Then she returns to officially fulfill the vow and never marry, perhaps meaning that she will remain behind closed doors. Or, is she indeed sacrificed as a virgin by her father? The text is less than clear.

As her story is passed down through the generations, it takes on significant meaning for young women who are saddened by it. In fact, it soon becomes a tradition for young Israelite women to take a four-day retreat, lamenting the grim circumstances of Jephthah's unnamed daughter.

Did Jephthah Kill His Daughter?

In the story of Jephthah and his daughter, the Bible is strangely silent on what happened. Furthermore, if Jephthah did indeed have his daughter killed, why isn't the punishment mentioned? And this isn't the last time Jephthah is mentioned in Scripture. He is mentioned in 1 Samuel 12 as a deliverer that God sent and, even more confusingly, Jephthah is mentioned in Hebrews 11:32 as a man of faith. Can God proclaim Jephthah as a man of faith if he killed his own daughter? The more one examines the questions in this narrative, the more convincing it becomes that Jephthah did not promise to offer a human sacrifice to the Lord and did not kill his own child.

Robert Booth, "Did Jephthah Kill His Daughter? An Examination of Judges 11:29–40," 10

Jephthah's battles, however, are not over. He is the military hero, but not everyone in Israel is happy about his leadership, particularly considering his mother's shameful status. The Ephraimites show up one day in Jephthah's hometown of Gilead, accusing him of going off to war without them to fight the Ammonites, their archenemies. They threaten to torch his house. He claims that he had asked for their help but that they had ignored his request. They are not satisfied with his answer and refuse to back down. They say he and all Gileadites are simply renegades and mongrels from Ephraim and Manasseh.

Stung by the insult, Jephthah summons his troops for action. When the civil war is over, he is the victor. Indeed, in one battle alone forty-two divisions from Ephraim are wiped out. After that Jephthah serves as judge over Israel for six years, until his death.

Judges Ibzan, Elon, and Abdon follow after Jephthah, none of them known for military prowess as their predecessors had been. Ibzan and Abdon, however, are prolific fathers. Ibzan sires thirty sons and thirty daughters, and Abdon forty sons. Times are good, but after the death of Abdon the cycle of evil resumes. God's punishment this time is to allow the Philistines to put a forty-year stranglehold over the people of Israel.

Samson and Delilah

Samson has a remarkable birth story. An angel appears to his long-barren mother, telling her that she is going to bear a son and she is not to drink beer or wine during her pregnancy. He will be a Nazirite, dedicated to abstinence and various other ritual observances. Moreover, this boy will grow up to deliver the Israelites from the tyranny of the Philistines. When the angel leaves, the startled woman tells her husband Manoah about the visitation.

Manoah is anxious and prays to God for operating instructions—how to raise this extraordinary child. The angel—the man of God—appears again to the woman while she is alone in the field. She immediately runs for Manoah, who follows her to the field, where the man of God repeats, for Manoah's benefit, the instructions he had given to his wife. Manoah then invites the *man* to dinner, not knowing he is an angel. The angel declines but suggests he sacrifice a goat, which Manoah does, along with a grain offering.

There is nothing recorded about Samson's actual birth and childhood. But as a young man he travels to Timnah, where he sees a beautiful young woman, a Philistine. He returns home and tells his parents about her and asks them to arrange a marriage. They're mortified. Why can't he find a pretty girl among the Israelites? But Samson is used to getting his own way. He doesn't take no for an answer.

His parents relent and go with him to Timnah to ask for the young woman. As they approach vineyards at the edge of town, he strays away from them—just long enough to tear to shreds an approaching lion. How is this possible? The Spirit of God comes upon him. He then rejoins his folks without saying a word. He finds the young woman and apparently gets her consent, because a few days later they all return to fetch her. This time he leaves his parents again to check on the lion and finds bees making honey in the carcass. He reaches in for the honey and brings some back for his parents to eat, not telling them he had taken it from roadkill.

In no time Samson and his folks are making wedding plans. He arranges his own feast, but locals are fearful of him—his strength and hot temper. So they make sure that plenty of security is on hand—thirty *companions* to take control if things go awry. Samson throws out a riddle at them with a bet. If they can come up with the answer, they get thirty sets of expensive clothes; if they can't figure it out, he gets the entire wardrobe. He lays out the riddle:

> From the eater came something to eat,
> From the strong came something sweet.[11]

They know nothing about his encounter with the lion—and its carcass. For three days they are at their wit's end. Then they secretly threaten the bride to weasel the answer out of him, or else—or else they will burn down her and her father's entire household. There's no way they can afford thirty outfits for Samson, linen undergarments and all. So she begs and pleads and cries for seven days until he finally relents and tells her the riddle.

The men, as if they are contestants on *Jeopardy*, call out the answer:

> What is sweeter than honey?
> What is stronger than a lion?[12]

Samson surely suspects his bride of spilling the beans and accuses them of *plowing with his heifer*. But then the Spirit of God comes upon him again, and he goes to a nearby town, kills thirty Philistine men, takes their clothes, returns, and gives them to the security detail. He leaves the wedding party in a fury. The startled father of the bride, not knowing what else to do, gives her to the best man.

Sometime later Samson shows up at the bride's house and learns she's married to another. He goes out into the bush, catches three hundred jackals, ties them together by the tails, attaches a torch onto their tails, and lets them into the Philistine grain fields as well as their orchards and vineyards, destroying the year's harvest. They get even by setting a torch to his would-be bride and her father. Now it is Samson's turn. He goes after the guilty by tearing their arms and legs off and slaughtering them as he had the lion. But he's still in a rage.

The Philistines set out to attack the tribe of Judah. The tribe is upset with Samson because his deeds are ruining their lives. So they tie him up and are in the process of turning him over to the enemy when he breaks loose, grabs a jawbone of an ass and with his Spirit-given strength kills the entire company of Philistine soldiers. With that victory, he settles down as a judge for the next two decades.

But all the while he's up to his old antics. He goes to Gaza and spots a prostitute. While he is spending the night with her, the townspeople plot to kill him first thing in the morning. He arises at midnight to leave, but not without making his mark. He tears down the locked town gate, posts and all, hauling the wreckage on his shoulders out of town.

As judge, Samson could have had almost any Israelite virgin he desired, but for some reason he is enticed by trashy Philistine women. So again he heads off into Philistine territory, and this time falls in love with Delilah. Again the Philistines plot against him; they go to Delilah behind his back and convince her to sweet-talk him out of the secret of his incredible strength so that they can overpower him. Three times he tells her, but each time she discovers he is toying with her, making her look ridiculous among her own people.

She is tenacious and begs him day after day to reveal his secret. He so desperately desires her love that he finally breaks down and tells her it is his hair. Because he is a Nazirite, he cannot cut his hair or his strength will depart. He falls asleep in her arms, and she promptly cuts his hair. In an instant his strength is gone, and the Philistines pounce on him. They poke out his eyes, shackle his legs, and compel him to grind at the wheel all day long like a yoked team of oxen.

His capture is cause for celebration among the Philistines. They prepare a grand feast and a stage show featuring Samson. They will laugh and scorn and mock this shackled, blind Israelite. They pack the temple while he is paraded before them, not realizing that his hair is growing back. Amid their jeers, he prays to God for his strength to return, vowing to die with the three thousand spectators. He asks his guards to let him lean against the pillars for a short rest. Again he prays, this time pushing against each of the two central support pillars, which crack and crumble as the temple crashes in a cloud of dust, killing everyone.

Delilah cutting Samson's hair

He dies with the spectators—as presumably does Delilah. His brothers and other kin retrieve his body and bury it in the family tomb.

Micah, Two Levites, and the Benjamites

In many ways Micah is simply an ordinary Israelite of his day, from the hill country of Ephraim—no patriarch or warrior or judge. Actually he is a common thief—worse than that, he steals from his own mother. And no small amount: eleven hundred pieces of silver. He fears what will happen to him because he has overheard his mother utter a curse on whoever stole her money. He returns the money, and she promptly gives a portion of the silver to a sculptor, who melts it down and fashions a little idol for her.

Micah then has a small temple built for the god, adds some other images, and starts a cult, conscripting his own son to serve as priest. Like so many other Israelites, he worships his images and pays little heed to God. Then one day a young Levite from Bethlehem happens by. Micah convinces him to serve as another priest, giving him room and board, clothing, and ten pieces of silver for his yearly salary. Micah assumes that having a real Levite priest in his household will bring him success in life and favor with God.

In the meantime, five warriors from the tribe of Dan wander through the countryside, looking for a suitable place on which the tribe can settle. They stop by Micah's home and immediately demand to know how he has acquired a Levite priest. The men want the priest to serve as their personal prophet—to let them know if they will have success in their endeavor. The priest gives them a good word, and they leave and travel on to a remote area near the town of Laish, where they discover a group of unsuspecting people living peacefully, without any military aspirations.

The five men return to their home in Zorah and stir up a fighting force of six hundred to go and attack this community. On the way they stop again at Micah's home, steal his goods and his gods, and take the Levite priest with them. When Micah realizes that his whole cult has collapsed, he and his neighbors head out after the thieves, their courage fading when they realize the strength of the enemy.

When the fighting force arrives at the quiet community of Laish, they slaughter the inhabitants and burn down the buildings. They rebuild the town, rename it Dan, and set up Micah's gods for worship.

Sometime later a Levite (not Micah's former priest) living in the backwoods of Ephraim sets out seeking a concubine. He travels to Judah and makes arrangements with a young woman's father to take her with him. She refuses, argues with him, and returns to her father's house. The Levite follows her and tries to win her back. Her father welcomes him, feeds him, and presses to delay his departure. But finally, after much eating and drinking, the Levite, his servant, and his reluctant concubine begin their journey back home. On the way the Levite stops off in Gibeah, a town in the tribe of Benjamin. He is refused lodging until a kindly old man invites them to his house. That night evil men in the town come to the house and demand the Levite come outside for sex. The old man offers his own virgin daughter and the Levite's concubine. In the end the Levite pushes his concubine out the door, where she is gang-raped and left for dead. Indeed, the next morning the Levite finds her dead on the doorstep.

What then does he do? He hefts her onto his donkey and heads home. There he cuts her body into twelve pieces and sends one chunk to each tribe, carried by a messenger with the ominous words: "Has such a thing as this ever happened from the time the Israelites came up from the land of Egypt until now? Think about it! Talk it over. Do something!"[13]

This truly is a heinous crime, and the Israelites are enraged, vowing revenge on the Benjamites. But first they demand that the tribe of Benjamin hand over the guilty men. When the Benjamites refuse, the rest of the Israelite armies descend on Benjamin, though they are hesitant to fight one of their own tribes. As it happens, even with God's permission the Benjamites initially prevail, not once but twice. At last, however, God promises victory over them. In the end the entire Benjamite army is wiped out, the towns are burned, and their inhabitants slaughtered, but for six hundred men who manage to escape.

So disgusted are the Israelites with the tribe of Benjamin that they vow their daughters will never marry any of the survivors. But that would mean that one of the twelve tribes would disappear altogether. So to rectify the situation, the Israelites send warriors to Jabesh Gilead to kill everyone—except four hundred virgins who live there. They are spared so that they can become wives of the surviving men of Benjamin. Why Jabesh Gilead? Because they had not sent a single soldier to participate in the campaign against Benjamin.

But there are still two hundred Benjamite men without wives, so the Israelite elders encourage them to go to a festival in Shiloh and hide in the vineyards. When they see young girls take the dance floor, they are to race out and grab them as wives for themselves. The tribe fathered by Benjamin, the youngest son of Jacob and Rachel, is spared, but at such a price.

These drawn-out narratives in Israel's history, beginning with Micah's theft, are strange stories that almost appear to have no redeeming purpose in the biblical text.

Micah's initial sorry, idolatrous mess is followed by terrifying episodes: rape, slaughter, more rape and slaughter, often of innocent people. And the two Levites? Anything but role models of priestly behavior.

Concluding Observations

It is difficult to read the book of Judges without cringing. Regular folks seem to be carrying out so much needless carnage. And apart from Deborah, no one stands tall to the very end. Gideon dies an idolater; Abimelech is a ruthless killer; Jephthah is a fool and a liar; Micah is a thief and an idolater. And the Benjamites? More than any other tribe, they deserved to be wiped out, but they are spared for the sake of familial loyalty. Nevertheless, God is ever present and participates by giving and withholding support for the armies of Israel. He punishes severely at times, while on other occasions he does not intervene and almost seems to let the sin be swept under the carpet.

That women play a significant role in the book of Judges does not mitigate the carnage. Indeed, they are sometimes as likely as their male counterparts to carry out conspiracies and bloodthirsty acts of violence.

One can only wonder what Moses would have thought. He left behind an uneventful life of herding sheep on the backside of a mountain for these rebellious and often utterly wicked people. Had he been on a fool's errand? Or what would Noah have thought? But for the promise sealed in a rainbow, he might have expected God to send the rains—this time without an ark.

Further Reading

Ackerman, Susan. *Warrior, Dancer, Seductress, Queen: Women in Judges and Biblical Israel.* New York: Doubleday, 1998.

Keck, Chad. *Ordinarily Faithful: Life Lessons from the Judges.* Bloomington, IN: LifeWay, 2011.

Klein, Lillian R. *Deborah to Esther: Sexual Politics in the Hebrew Bible.* Minneapolis: Fortress, 2003.

McCann, J. Clinton. *Judges: A Bible Commentary for Teaching and Preaching.* Louisville: Westminster John Knox, 2011.

PART 2

Kings AND *Prophets* GUIDE *God's People*

9

NAOMI, RUTH, AND HANNAH

Seasons of Motherhood

Journey is an appropriate metaphor for the lives of Naomi, Ruth, and Hannah. Naomi journeys to Moab; Ruth joins her on the return trip to Judah. But more than a geographical journey, theirs is a spiritual journey. Naomi makes a journey into faith as surely as Ruth does. For Hannah, the longest journey of her life is the twenty-five miles between Ramathaim and Shiloh, taking her young son Samuel to the temple to be left with old Eli—some might say, *abandoned*. For Hannah, however, this is first and foremost a spiritual journey.

The book of Judges concludes with a horrific story of a concubine whose dead body, after she had been gang-raped, was cut into twelve parts, one part sent to each of the twelve tribes of Israel. Her torturous death was avenged by more bloodthirsty killing, and women from pagan tribes are kidnapped as wives for the guilty men. *Texts of terror* are what these biblical passages have been called. Women here are unfortunately seen as expendable.

But with the turn of a page the scene suddenly changes. Women are the lead characters. The pastoral setting in which Naomi and Ruth find themselves is vastly different from the battlefields of the Judges.

Naomi and Ruth as well as Hannah are all featured in the private realm, as opposed to the public realm of Deborah, Gideon, Samson, and other judges. Their issues are personal, familial, and relational. The pain is that of widowhood and barrenness, not military defeats. The pace has slowed down, and the reader is able to catch a breath and empathize with the difficulties these women are facing.

Throughout the history of ancient Israel, there is a mingling with the so-called enemy tribes. The Israelites make war with them, to be sure. But they also interact and intermarry with apparent ease. There is no effort to apologize for Naomi and her husband taking their sons to Moab, where they marry local women. If times are hard in Judah, why not move to Moab? It is a mobile society. Relocation offers better opportunities.

In many respects Naomi and Elimelech have much in common with Hannah and Elkanah. Like so many of their nameless neighbors, they are ordinary folks who are facing difficult circumstances. Neither family commands wealth or power or influence like the great patriarchal families of Genesis. Nor are the two wives imposing women as Sarah and Rebekah had been. Their stories, rather, represent the *silent majority*, whose legacies will nevertheless have historic consequences.

The writing of history is most often focused on great leaders and events, as in Judges. But the Bible also gives a prominent place to the private side of life, as in the accounts of Naomi, Ruth, and Hannah.

Celebrating Female Friendship

Ruth's story is unique among ancient literature in celebrating female friendship. . . . The power of the story lies largely in the hands of female characters. Elimelech, his wife, and sons commence the story, but the males soon die. Thereafter, Ruth and Naomi are the main characters, with Boaz being given third place. In a sense, his is a supporting role, and the heroine receives the larger role, highlighted by the fact that it is Ruth, not Boaz, who proposes marriage. . . . The story of Ruth is a reminder of how much women with chutzpah can achieve even in a society that restricts their roles.

Murray D. Gow, "Ruth," 108

Naomi: Much-Loved Mother-in-Law

As wife and mother she surely must have discussed a major relocation with her husband. The crops are burning up in the field. All of Judah is facing a famine with no end in sight. In the marketplace, stalls are bare except for a few high-priced bags of grain. How can a husband and wife survive, to say nothing of two growing sons, in an economy like this? So they face the most difficult decision of their lives. Bethlehem is the only home they have known. But they pack up their belongings, bid farewell to their neighbors and kin, leave their parched land, and set off on the road to Moab.

Moab would certainly not have been their first option. There is grain aplenty there, but it is an altogether pagan land. However, they have to make a choice: famine, or false gods and food. They opt for the latter. So Naomi settles down among the strange gods and heathen temples with her husband Elimelech and her sons Mahlon and Kilion. They would stay true to God and perhaps return home soon. But the plans go awry when Elimelech dies.

Now widowed, Naomi has all she can do to keep her family afloat. After a time the sons each marry Moabite women, Orpah and Ruth. Life is getting back to an even keel. But in the decade that follows, even greater affliction befalls the household. Both sons also die. She has barely progressed through the stages of grief when they start all over again. Life is utterly grim—but for her dear daughters-in-law.

Initially Naomi is so prostrated by grief that she barely functions. But as she begins to take charge of her life again, she contemplates returning to Bethlehem. That is her hometown. Perhaps a change of scenery will lift the pall that covers her days. She has no means of livelihood in Moab and no blood relatives. Maybe kinfolk will take her in if she goes back home. Her decision is clinched by the news trickling back to her from Judah that God has now broken the stranglehold of the famine.

She informs Orpah and Ruth that she will be heading home to Bethlehem. They are troubled. How can they stand by and allow her to make this journey alone? They will go with her. After all, she is the family matriarch, and, outside of their own memories, she is the only link they have to their late husbands. It is the proper thing to do.

They haven't traveled far, however, when she stops and informs them that they must not accompany her. She wants the best for these women who have become like daughters to her: "Go back. Go home and live with your mothers. And may God treat you as graciously as you treated your deceased husbands and me. May God give each of you a new home and a new husband!"[1]

Here is a woman who, it seems, has known only grief: grief over the loss of home and kinfolk and country, grief over the loss of beloved husband Elimelech and sons Mahlon and Kilion. Now she is voluntarily losing her dear daughters-in-law. She can hardly get the words out amidst their weeping. But she has to do it. She kisses them farewell, knowing she would never see them again.

They both insist that they will not return home. Rather, they will go with her and live in Bethlehem. Their bond with her is unusually strong. She had told them to return to live with their mothers, which suggests that their fathers may also have died. Their own mothers, Moabites themselves and perhaps with other children

Naomi, Ruth, and Orpah

close by, would not have been as vulnerable as Naomi, alone on the road with an uncertain future in Judah.

But Naomi is serious. This is no game that she is playing. These are her *dear daughters*, and she wants what is best for them. There is simply no future for them back in Judah, living in a foreign country with no network of friends or support system of any kind. It will be hard enough for the widowed Naomi to find lodging for herself. *Go back home*, she insists. And then she resorts to sarcasm.

Even if she should find a husband right now in her old age, and even if she should get pregnant immediately, and even if she should bear two sons, would Orpah and Ruth want to wait until they are grown to marry them? She might have added: *Would the sons want to marry these two much older Moabite women?* The whole idea is preposterous. It would be silly for them to return to Bethlehem with her.

A Spiritual Journey

Elements of Naomi's faith and Ruth's commitment echo Moses' faith and the Exodus story, although the female figures stand in shocking contrast in their courage and simplicity; Naomi and Ruth had no burning bush, no manna in the desert, no pillar of flame and no promise of final security, yet they undertook a desert journey toward the promised land. . . . If Moses led a people to external freedom and identity, Naomi and Ruth led us to an internal promised land of spiritual wholeness and integration.

Marjory Zoet Bankson, *Seasons of Friendship: Naomi and Ruth as a Pattern*, xiii

Orpah relents. She kisses her beloved mother-in-law farewell and in a flood of tears turns around and heads back home. But Ruth, also weeping, will not let go of Naomi. Naomi is persistent. She has not been fooling: "Look, your sister-in-law is going back home to live with her own people and gods; go with her."[2] Ruth persists, and Naomi finally backs down, no doubt grateful to be accompanied by her daughter-in-law on the road to Bethlehem.

They arrive in town right at the beginning of the annual barley harvest. The marketplace is suddenly caught up in the news that Naomi, gone so long, has now returned—without husband and sons. She pours out her story. Indeed, Naomi is not shy about her miserable circumstances and who is to blame. She lays the responsibility squarely on God—God, who has ruined her. They should not even call her Naomi. Rather, *Bitter*, because she is so bitter about her terrible losses. She owns nothing besides the clothes she is wearing.

Here she is going on and on about her utter poverty and having nothing at all to be thankful for, as though her devoted daughter-in-law is not even there. What must Ruth be thinking?

In the days that follow, Naomi settles into the routine of village life, staying with kinfolk or an old neighbor until she and Ruth can find permanent lodging. When Ruth offers to go out into the barley fields and pick up what is left by the harvesters, Naomi is relieved. Any shame associated with such work is balanced by the necessity of eating. When Ruth returns late in the day with a big bag of barley, Naomi is incredulous. Sure, Ruth is competent enough, but gleaners typically don't find that much grain left in the field after a harvest.

Naomi inquires where Ruth had been working, only to learn that she had been gleaning in the field of Boaz, a relative of her late husband. God perhaps isn't so stingy after all. Naomi explains that Boaz is not merely a close relative, but part of the inner circle who would want to help in time of need, a "kinsman-redeemer." Naomi ponders all of this in her heart, and each day she welcomes Ruth home with her sack of barley.

Toward the end of the harvest, Naomi comes up with a plan. She has been contemplating the good fortune of Ruth's having become acquainted with Boaz and how he seems to have taken a special interest in her. Is this perhaps a way out of their poverty? Might there be a light at the end of this tunnel? Naomi has taken matters into her own hands by returning to Bethlehem. She surely has chutzpah and the wherewithal to further nudge the future in a favorable direction.

She has her ear to the ground and knows what is going on in the neighborhood. So she lays out her strategy to Ruth, first pointing out that it's time for her to arrange for Ruth to have a home of her own. Ruth has become more than a dear daughter to her. She is the one who, hopefully, will care for Naomi in her old age—and the only one who can bring her the joy of grandchildren. She reminds Ruth that Boaz is a close kinsman and suggests that now might be just the right time to *grab the bull by the horns*, so to speak.

Taking this motherly advice, Ruth makes her move, going in the dark of night to see Boaz. When she returns, Naomi wants to know exactly what has happened. Naomi listens with optimism. She is convinced that Boaz will work things out. Indeed, he does just that, in a manner that would bring her great benefit.

Boaz makes the deal, by going to the town square and waiting for a certain close relative of Naomi's late husband—closer than Boaz himself—to walk by. Boaz, with ten of the town's leading men standing by, informs the relative that Naomi is selling property and that he, the closest kinsman, has first option to buy. The kinsman says he would like to purchase it. Only then does Boaz tell him that marriage to the widowed Moabite Ruth would come with the deal. The kinsman immediately backs out, not wanting to take on any legal liabilities that might jeopardize his own estate. He gives up his right to the property—and Ruth—and Boaz buys it and acquires Ruth in the deal. The kinsman seals the transaction by removing a sandal as proof of his honor.

Naomi's life has turned around. She's back home and no longer bitter. The women around town are all talking about how God has blessed her. She has family: a beloved daughter and son-in-law, and soon a grandson. Indeed, she is such a doting grandmother—"cuddling him, cooing over him, waiting on him hand and foot"—that the women call him "Naomi's baby boy!"[3] Life is good.

Ruth: A Love Story with a Lasting Legacy

She hails from Moab, a plateau region on the eastern shore of the Dead Sea. Here people worship false gods and sometimes even sacrifice their own children. But for Ruth this is the only land she has ever known. She apparently has had a good upbringing, or she might not have grown into the stalwart adult she became.

As a young woman she marries a foreigner, with his own foreign God. Did she meet him on the street and fall in love, or

Everyday *Life*

Harvest Work and Celebration

The story of Ruth and Boaz brings together two significant aspects of everyday life in biblical times: harvest and care for the poor. Concern for those who were marginalized in society was embedded in Old Testament law. The poor—particularly widows and orphans—were an integral part of communities, and their well-being was not to be neglected. This was particularly true during harvest seasons, when gleaners worked alongside paid workers and landowners.

Gleaning was respectable work, and kindly landowners like Boaz acknowledged the presence of these workers and included them in the noon meal. Indeed, during this season there was often a celebratory spirit in the air in anticipation of the feasting and festivities that marked the end of the harvest.

The barley harvest came in first, then wheat, followed by the harvesting of grapes. The threshing floor—a flat clay surface—was where the threshing and winnowing of the barley and wheat was done. Workers used heavy sticks to beat the stalks of grain to open the ripened kernels. Then the stalks were shaken with the chaff flying away in the breeze while the kernels fell to the floor.

After the Midianites had stolen some of the grain stored on the threshing floor, Gideon (in Judg. 6) hides the rest of the harvest in the winepress, the last place they would look for it. Unlike the threshing floor, the winepress was made of stone. Grapes were stomped on the stone floor, and the juice collected and fermented for wine.

A Carnival-Like Atmosphere

The Feast of Harvest, also called the Feast of Weeks, Shevuoth, coincided with the wheat harvest and was celebrated some seven weeks after the beginning of the spring harvest season. The Feast of Ingathering, or Feast of Booths, Sukkoth, was observed in the autumn at the completion of the agricultural year (grapes and olives were gathered in the fall). It was also a New Year celebration . . . the commencement of a new agricultural year . . . an occasion of great celebration, a vintage festival, with a carnival-like atmosphere.

John Haralson Hayes, *Introduction to the Bible*, 94

Ruth's Simply Astonishing Commitment

Ruth's commitment to her destitute mother-in-law is simply astonishing. First, it means leaving her own family and land. Second, it means, as far as she knows, a life of widowhood and childlessness, because Naomi has no man to give, and if Ruth married a nonrelative, her commitment to Naomi's family would be lost. Third, it means going to an unknown land with a new people and new customs and new language. Fourth, it was a commitment even more radical than marriage: "Where you die I will die and there be buried" (v. 17). In other words, she will never return home, not even if Naomi dies.

But the most amazing commitment of all is this: "Your God will be my God" (v. 16). Naomi has just said in verse 13, "the hand of the Lord has gone forth against me." Naomi's experience of God was bitterness. But in spite of this, Ruth forsakes her religious heritage and makes the God of Israel her God.

John Piper, "Ruth: Sweet and Bitter Providence"

was there a more mundane reason for her relationship with this Jewish man? The Moabites and Israelites were enemies, though they interacted with each other on many levels.

The Bible does not mention her father—only her mother, perhaps a widow living in poverty. Her mother and Naomi may have been neighbors, and it might have seemed reasonable that their children marry. Ruth does marry Naomi's son Mahlon. But some ten years later both he and his brother (who is married to Orpah) die.

Naomi's decision to return to her homeland comes as a surprise to Ruth. Ruth has lost her husband, and now this. Why would Naomi return to Judah after all these years? Has Ruth failed to shower her mother-in-law with love and hospitality? But Ruth is adamant. If Naomi goes, Ruth will go with her. She and her sister-in-law Orpah both pack their bags and bid farewell to their families. Naomi is silent as they start down the road toward Bethlehem.

When Naomi stops and tells them both to go back to their own families, Ruth clings tenaciously to this Hebrew woman who has become a mother to her. Orpah sadly makes an about-face and heads home. But Ruth refuses. She pleads with Naomi and then makes a pledge of devotion that ranks among the greatest vows ever offered in the history of humankind: "Whither thou goest, I will go; and where thou lodgest, I will lodge: thy people shall be my people, and thy God my God: Where thou diest, will I die, and there will I be buried: the LORD do so to me, and more also, if ought but death part thee and me."[4]

When they arrive in Naomi's hometown, Ruth is clearly the *foreigner*. The whole community is abuzz about her. Ruth seems less concerned about fitting in than making herself useful. It's harvesttime, and she suggests to Naomi that she go out into the fields and glean the grain that has been left behind by the harvesters. She begins in a nearby field but then makes her way to a field belonging to Boaz.

Soon Boaz comes out to his field to check on his hired help and offer them the customary greetings. He notices Ruth gleaning and asks about her. The field supervisor

Ruth's Conversion Story

How am I to judge Ruth, that Old Testament saint for whom I was named? . . . In many respects this Moabite widow seems less than noble to me. Her decision to adopt the religion of the Hebrews placed her in the genealogical line of the Messiah, but the nature of that decision does not correspond with my concept of conversion. If I had fashioned her character, I would have brought her through a grueling ordeal of forsaking the decadent deities of Moab. . . . The Bible, however, offers no such portrait of Ruth. Indeed, her decision to follow the God of Israel could easily be missed by a speed-reader and seems altogether too anticlimactic for a modern-day evangelical. She is simply a loyal and faithful daughter-in-law who dutifully follows Naomi back to her homeland and seems to get religion as part of the package. . . . How did she arrive at [her] decision? Did the Lord "speak" to her? Did he "call" her? Did she pray about it? The Bible gives no indication of any input from God in Ruth's crucial decision—at a time in history when God was certainly on speaking terms with his people. Nevertheless, she stands as a remarkable example of the kind of spiritual choices that begin and sustain our Christian life.

Ruth A. Tucker, *Multiple Choices: Making Wise Decisions in a Complicated World*, 44

explains that she is the Moabite woman who recently returned with Naomi and that she has requested permission to glean. Not only that, but she is a hard worker: "She's been at it steady ever since, from early morning until now, without so much as a break."[5]

Boaz shows interest. He walks over to where Ruth is gleaning, kindly addressing her as "my daughter." He insists that she not glean on anyone else's fields, but rather should work on his field with the other young women who are harvesting. He will see to it that no one bothers her, and she is to drink from the same canteens that are used by the other workers.

Dropping down on her knees and bowing low, she offers a fitting response: "How does this happen that you should pick me out and treat me so kindly—*me*, a foreigner?"[6]

Boaz responds in kind, letting her know that he has heard about her compassion for Naomi and her willingness to leave her homeland and live as a stranger. Then he offers her a blessing: "GOD reward you well for what you've done—and with a generous bonus besides from GOD, to whom you've come seeking protection under his wings."[7]

Before he leaves, she again thanks him for his kindness. But it doesn't end there. At the noonday lunch break, he calls her over to join him and the other harvesters to eat some of his bread dipped in wine as well as all she wants of the baked grain. Then Boaz instructs the harvesters to leave plenty of grain behind for her.

When Ruth arrives home that evening, she shows her mother-in-law her heavy sack of barley and gives her some of the bread that she had saved from the noon meal. Naomi is pleased to learn about the generosity of Boaz. She insists Ruth stick with him and the women who are gleaning in his field. Both she and Ruth know,

Boaz and Human Trafficking

A family from Bethlehem went to Moab, where women were treated very poorly. Many of the low class women were taken into female prostitution centers, which were linked to the worship of fertility gods and goddesses. The narrative of Ruth tells us that at this place, the sons of Elimelech get sucked into the cultural view of women, and they "took the women of Moab." . . . The Hebrew phrase is meant to be seen as, "they forcibly took Moabite women," i.e., they raped them. The context suggests that they suffered the consequences of death because of their demeaning acts against the women of Moab. When one reads the narrative further, one discovers that the word used for Boaz marrying Ruth means to recreate. Boaz exclaims, "Ruth the Moabitess, the woman of Mahlon I have 'recreated' to be my woman to 'resurrect' the name of the dead . . . and the people at the gate and the elders said, "We witness. May the LORD make the woman coming into your house like Rachel and Leah, the two who built the house of Israel." . . . This is a great contrast to what the sons of Elimelech did. They engaged in human trafficking. Boaz, on the other hand, ordered his men to protect this woman, who was an alien and therefore trafficking material. Then he redeemed her, and gave her the place of highest honor, in front of the city gate, where historically the men and women of highest honor gathered—the lawns of the White House would be a modern analogy.

Rajkumar Boaz Johnson, "The Bible's Answer to Human Trafficking, Part 2"

however, the dangers that poor gleaning women face. With Boaz in charge, Naomi makes clear that she need not fear harassment of any kind.

With the harvest finished and the accompanying celebration at hand, Naomi hatches a plan and instructs Ruth in the proper protocol of courtship. Ruth takes her mother-in-law's advice and arranges a midnight rendezvous with Boaz. She bathes and dons her best clothes for the encounter. She waits in the shadows until he has finished eating and drinking—when everyone else has consumed plenty of wine as well. She sees him head off by himself, and she follows in the distance. He is going to the threshing floor to sleep there. When she knows he has settled down, she slips up to where he is sleeping next to a pile of barley and lies down at his feet. This will send him a clear signal—a signal that she wants to marry him.

Ruth gleaning in Boaz's field

She has rehearsed her words, so when he suddenly awakens before dawn not realizing who she is or what's going on, she explains that she is his relative and wants him to know she's available. He blesses her and compliments her, telling her that she is young and beautiful, but admits that she could have made a better choice for a husband than he.

Now wide awake, he explains that he's actually not the closest of kin, and that someone else might be waiting in the wings. But he's excited about the possibility and tells her to stay with him until morning. When she is getting ready to sneak back home before dawn, he stops her and asks her to spread out the outer garment she is wearing. He fills it full of barley to take home—perhaps thinking of it as an engagement gift.

Whatever the gift means, Ruth can feel no real sense of security. She is now fully aware that there is a nearer kin than Boaz. Who knows what kind of a man he is? She had her heart set on the kind and fatherly—and prosperous—Boaz. Israelite custom does not bow to a girl's fancies. Both land and woman are bartered as a business deal.

When the bargain between Boaz and the other relative is struck in the town square, it is witnessed by a crowd of people who had gathered. Not merely curiosity seekers, they are official witnesses who vow to stand behind the agreement. No doubt someone in the group cuts out early to divulge the outcome to Ruth and Naomi—or perhaps the women themselves are among the crowd.

That very day—or soon thereafter—Ruth and Boaz are married. Now Ruth is no longer a *stranger*. She has a husband and a home in her adopted land. Sometime later she bears a son, Obed. Through him she would become a grandmother to his son Jesse, and great-grandmother to David.

David would become the most celebrated hero and king of Israel and would stand in the genealogical line of Jesus of Nazareth. Ruth, a marginalized Moabite, a foreigner and stranger, is chosen by God to be forever enshrined in the bloodline of the Messiah.

Ruth and Hannah are separated by no more than a long day's journey. Ruth is probably old enough to be Hannah's mother. Did their paths ever cross? Elkanah, Hannah's husband, had lived previously in Bethlehem. Might Hannah and Samuel have returned to visit family and become acquainted with the beloved matriarch Ruth? An intriguing possibility.

Hannah: Giving a First-Born Son to God

Though Hannah may not have known of Ruth, she surely must have heard the stories of celebrated Israelite women of long ago. Some of their names were associated with the b-word. Sarah was barren; so were Rebekah and Rachel—until God opened their wombs. But they were famous wives of great patriarchs. Who was she that God should take notice of her anguish? Her husband was an ordinary Levite priest from the hill country of Ephraim.

Barrenness was bad enough, but when combined with the odious but socially accepted custom of polygamy, it was far worse. Malicious backbiting often permeated the household. The *other woman*, with her babies, knew that motherhood brought status. Hannah knows only the sting of infertility.

Like Rachel generations before her, Hannah is the more beloved of two wives. Her husband Elkanah is a religious man who comes from a long and distinguished line of the tribe of Levi. But he has no power to solve her problem. He dotes on her, however, giving her an extra helping of food during the annual time of worship and sacrifice in Shiloh. Second wife Peninnah makes a spectacle of trooping in with all her kids needing to be fed, always making a point that Hannah has no little ones trailing behind her. In fact, she taunts her to the point that Hannah breaks down weeping and cannot eat.

Elkanah tries to console her. They love each other deeply, and he thinks she should see the value of their relationship as worth more than children. Peninnah surely doesn't share that abiding love with him. So Hannah gets a grip on herself and eats a small portion of the meal, but then leaves unobtrusively while the celebration continues. She slips into the temple unnoticed. This is her opportunity to be alone and pour out her heart to God. But no sooner does she start to pray than the tears begin to flow. And not tears only; she is sobbing and heaving in utter anguish.

Amid her weeping, she begs God for a son. So desperate is she that she promises to give him back to God—to bring him to this very temple in holy service.

The priest on duty that day is Eli. Hannah surely knew him by reputation. Indeed, he is not merely a priest but a high priest and a judge for forty years in Israel. And surely she knows of the corruption going on under his oversight. In fact, perhaps her tears and pleas for a son have to do in part with the appalling vice associated with his sons' "ministry" and her deep longing to remedy the situation. At any rate she is weeping.

With no obvious training in pastoral care, Eli rebukes her. Here she is alone in the temple, silently praying and weeping, and he has no solace to offer. What he says is entirely out of order: "You're drunk! How long do you plan to keep this up? Sober up, woman!"[8] Drunk? What is he thinking? She might have stormed out, pushing the old man off his stool as she leaves. But she is most deferential, insisting she is not drunk: "I am a woman who is deeply troubled. I have not been drinking wine or beer; I was pouring out my soul to the Lord. Do not take your servant for a wicked woman; I have been praying here out of my great anguish and grief."[9]

The Grief of God's Disfavor

The Jews took to heart God's words about children being a blessing; thus they inferred that the lack of children could only be a sign of God's disfavor. Realizing that her ancestors had also known her pain might have offered Hannah great comfort. But these same stories could have just as easily added to her burden and grief. . . . Knowing her nation's history without seeing God answer her own pleas for a baby could well have been more discouraging than helpful.

Jennifer Saake, *Hannah's Hope: Seeking God's Heart in the Midst of Infertility*, 26

Eli bids her leave with a blessing that God will grant her request. She wants more than that. She asks him to pray for her, and then she returns to her unfinished dinner, her spirits lifted. She and Elkanah leave for home, and she soon discovers she is pregnant. Indeed, less than a year later she gives birth to baby Samuel.

When Elkanah makes his next trek to Shiloh for the annual worship celebration, Peninnah and her brood go along, but Hannah stays behind. She has promised she will give her baby back to God, but not too soon. He must first be weaned. After he is weaned—no more than four or five years old—Hannah then takes her little boy to the temple in Shiloh for the annual celebration. It is not enough that she brings her only child; she also brings sacrificial offerings: the best bull, as well as grain and wine.

Without even flinching, Hannah goes straight to Eli, reminds him of her prayer some years earlier, and hands over the child. To old Eli, of all people! It is a stunning act of faith. The once-weeping woman in the temple is back again, this time with no mention or evidence of tears. How could she do it? It would be impossible for most mothers. But not only does she hand him over without tears; she sings a wild song of praise to God in the process, beginning with these words:

Hannah presents Samuel to Eli

Hannah's Slender Space for Samuel

It requires a wise woman to train up a wise son, and therefore I regard Samuel's eminent character and career as largely the fruit of his mother's sorrow, and as a reward for her griefs. . . . She had slender space in which to educate her boy, or he left her early to wear the little robe, and minister before the Lord; but in that space her work was effectually done, for the child Samuel worshiped the very day she took him up to the temple.

Charles Haddon Spurgeon, "Hannah: A Woman of a Sorrowful Spirit," 68

> I'm bursting with God-news!
> I'm walking on air.
> I'm laughing at my rivals.
> I'm dancing my salvation.[10]

Following her song, Hannah and Elkanah return home. Each year Hannah makes the trip to Shiloh with Elkanah, heart pounding with excitement to see her son. She always has a gift—a garment that she has handcrafted especially for him. Each year Samuel would see more little brothers and sisters, five in all.

Hebrews 11 is known as the faith chapter that mentions one after another of the Old Testament saints whose faith was noteworthy. Why didn't the author of that book include Hannah? *By faith Hannah traveled to Shiloh to offer her only son Samuel to the aged and incompetent priest Eli, whose own adult sons were desecrating the place of worship. By faith she returned home, and God blessed her with more babies.*

Concluding Observations

Naomi, Ruth, and Hannah—weeping women whose circumstances change and whose hearts are made glad. In each case, they have trusted in God—simple faith. Their stories encompass the domestic sphere of life. There are no Red Seas, no Jordan Rivers to cross, no mighty armies to defeat, no sun stopping to help solve their personal plights. Yet their problems penetrate to the depths of their being. Their worlds revolve around the family, and it is in this realm where they fight their battles and in the end prevail.

These women serve more readily as role models than do the commanders of vast armies. Their issues are ours—and not women's only. They often feel like they have the weight of the world on their shoulders, but their problems are mostly personal or relational. They struggle not under the weight of global or national troubles, nor do they hold office or aspire to great prominence. Rather, they are ordinary individuals facing knotty issues not so different from those that people of every culture and social status have encountered in the millennia since.

Further Reading

Bankson, Marjory Zoet. *Seasons of Friendship: Naomi and Ruth as a Pattern*. Philadelphia: Innisfree Press, 1987.

Saake, Jennifer. *Hannah's Hope: Seeking God's Heart in the Midst of Infertility*. Colorado Springs: NavPress, 2005.

Sakenfeld, Katharine Doob. *Just Wives? Stories of Power and Survival in the Old Testament and Today*. Louisville: Westminster John Knox, 2003.

10

SAMUEL AND KING SAUL

Leadership of Different Stripes

Speak, Lord, for thy servant heareth. This response by the young Samuel sets the stage for his long and faithful ministry among the Israelites. It is difficult to imagine those same words in the mouth of Saul. Saul, the first king of Israel, is anointed by Samuel, an act of faith that would haunt Samuel in the years to come.

The book of 1 Samuel picks up where the book of Judges leaves off. Samuel is the last of the judges and the first great prophet among the Israelites. During this era Israel transitions from a loose association of tribes governed by judges to one nation—a united kingdom—governed by kings.

During much of the period of the judges, Israel is in a turmoil, with everyone *doing that which is right in his own eyes*. The people are rebellious and unwilling to live under God's law. That defiance continues in the following generations and is seen very explicitly in the early chapters of 1 Samuel. Here the sons of Eli, Hophni and Phinehas, disgrace the priestly profession by brazenly bringing prostitution and other vices into

Ritual Prostitution in God's House

The sons of Eli [Hophni and Phinehas] followed the example of Canaanite worship rather than the instruction of the Mosaic Law. Ritual prostitution was part of Canaanite worship, and Eli's sons seem to have adopted this custom. . . . Earlier in Israel's history another Phinehas, the godly son of another priest, Eleazar, had executed an Israelite named Zimri and a Moabite woman named Cozbi for practicing sexual immorality in the tabernacle (Num. 25). Now this Phinehas, a priest and the son of another priest, Eli, was practicing sexual immorality in the tabernacle. How far the priests had departed from the Lord during the approximately 300 years that separated these incidents!

Thomas L. Constable, "Notes on 1 Samuel," 15

the very house of God. Incredibly, there is no obvious negative influence on the young Samuel growing up under their noses in the midst of their priestly "ministry."

Despite such wickedness, properly ordained religious rituals continue, and it is in that setting that Samuel rises up as God's spokesman. The first major issue he will deal with is in some ways more political than religious. The Israelites are disgruntled. Their neighbors are ruled by kings, and the Israelites look on with envy. A king is exactly what they want.

Through Samuel, God warns them that a king will oppress them, but they pay no heed. So they are saddled with Saul as king. Samuel, the last judge, and Saul, the first king, are polar opposites. Indeed, Samuel is one of the few major figures in the Old Testament of whom nothing negative is reported, apart from his lack of control over his wicked sons.

Very few individuals in biblical times or since could reflect on their upright lives before a massive audience and not get heckled. Samuel was one of them. He was an honest man who had never exploited or stolen or taken advantage of anyone—never taken a bribe and always upheld the law. If anyone had ever lodged a complaint against him, he would have made it right. No one ever had.

Saul, on the other hand, is one of the more tragic figures in the Bible. Here is a man who had shown so much promise but ended up so badly. Early in his rule he wins major victories over both the Ammonites and the Amalekites. He takes all the credit himself. With his massive ego—as big as the monument he sets up in his own honor—he goes his own way, ignoring God's specific commands. He is rebuked by Samuel, who tells him God has rejected him. Saul pleads for another chance, insisting he has made a proper sacrifice. It is too late. He will be done in by the Philistines.

In the end he is spinning out of control and is utterly defeated. His life is a sad commentary on the consequences of arrogance, disobedience, infidelity. His voice rises out of the grave: *Turn your life around while yet there is time.* Samuel's final words to Saul carry a message of timeless truth:

> Does the Lord delight in burnt offerings and sacrifices
> As much as in obeying the LORD?
> To obey is better than sacrifice,
> and to heed is better than the fat of rams.[1]

Samuel: Judge and Prophet

He is a little boy on his first big trip away from home, perhaps running ahead of his parents and grabbing a pebble from the dusty road and tossing it up in the air. Has his mother attempted to explain to him that he will never come home again? Has she told him about the old man who will be his new *father*? If she had, how could he have possibly understood?

How would a mother prepare for such a separation? Would she push him out of the house and send him off to a cousin in another village to live for weeks on end? Or would she cling to him, knowing that their days together are numbered? There is no way to prepare a child for such an outcome, and little Samuel must have felt confused and utterly abandoned when his parents returned home without him. To complicate matters, he has just been weaned, a sometimes-stressful time for a child.

The little boy's reaction is not disclosed in the text—only the description of the environment in which he is left: the utterly dysfunctional family of the old priest Eli. His sons, Hophni and Phinehas, are *wicked* men. They make a sacrilege of the temple worship rites, demanding the best steaks before they're even offered as a sacrifice. Worse yet, they are making God's temple nothing less than a whorehouse, demanding sex from the female helpers. Eli begs them to reform their ways. They ignore him, and he is powerless to stop them. This is the atmosphere in which Samuel, a solemn little boy, is reared.

Young Samuel hearing God's call

But in the midst of this mess, God comes to Samuel in the dark of night. The boy is awakened by a voice calling his name. Thinking Eli needs something, he runs to help. But old Eli tells him he did not call and that Samuel should go back to bed. This happens again and still again, until it occurs to Eli that God may be calling Samuel. So he sends the boy back to bed and tells him to prepare to hear a message from God.

At dawn Samuel arises to do his usual temple duties, avoiding Eli. But Eli is on to him. He calls for him, asking precisely what the message from God was about. The words are not what Eli wants to hear. Samuel spills it out. God had informed him in the night that he is going to bring

Samuel's Words Repeated down the Centuries

When I was about fourteen . . . I began to suspect that I might be called to preach. . . . I knew the story of the boy Samuel, how he was called in the night by a voice speaking his name. I could imagine, so clearly that I could almost hear it, a voice calling out of the darkness: "J. Crow." And then I thought maybe the voice had called, and that I had almost but not quite heard it. One night I got out of bed and went to the window. The sky over the treetops was full of stars. Whispering so as not to waken my roommate, I said, "Speak, Lord; for thy servant heareth." And then, so help me, I heard the silence that stretched all the way from the ground underneath my window to the furthest stars. . . . Though I knew that actually I had heard no voice, I could not dismiss the possibility that it had spoken and I had failed to hear it because of some deficiency in me or something wrong that I had done. My fearful uncertainty lasted for months. . . . Finally I reasoned that in dealing with God you had better give Him the benefit of the doubt. I decided that I had better accept the call that had not come, just in case it had come and I had missed it.

Wendell Berry, *Jayber Crow*, 42–43

terrible judgment on Eli's family. Eli is not surprised. He had previously been warned by a prophet about his sons' evil ways.

In the ensuing years, Samuel's reputation as a man of God grows. Under his guidance Shiloh becomes a center of spiritual formation. People come from great distances to hear his prophetic words. The infidelities of Eli's household, however, had polluted all of Israel and would not go unpunished. Indeed, the Israelites suffer a great military defeat at the hands of the Philistines.

Rather than repenting and calling upon God for help, the Israelite leaders decide to transport the Ark of the Covenant from Shiloh to their encampment, thinking it will bring them victory. It is a most grievous mistake. Again the Philistines thoroughly trounce the Israelites. They seize the Ark and, as God had foretold, also kill Hophni and Phinehas.

When Eli, now ninety-eight years old and obese, hears the news, he falls off his chair, breaks his neck, and dies. He had led the Israelites as judge for forty years.

From this point on Samuel becomes a very effective leader of the Israelites, serving as prophet, priest, and judge. In fact, he functions as a circuit-riding magistrate, traveling to Bethel and on to Gilgal and Mizpah, and then returning to Ramah, the hometown of his parents, where he resides.

His first major address to the Israelites comes after the Ark of the Covenant has been returned. (It has brought terrible calamities upon the Philistines, and they are most eager to be rid of it.) He delivers a fiery sermon telling Israel to abandon their idols and serve God alone. Having witnessed supernatural judgments from God, the people are ready to take seriously Samuel's words. They are richly rewarded. When the Philistines are attacking, God launches explosions from heaven—blasts of thunder so deafening the enemy simply flees, with the Israelite army in hot pursuit and gaining a significant victory.

In thanksgiving to God, Samuel sets up a memorial pillar near Mizpah and names it Ebenezer: "Hitherto hath the LORD helped us."[2] The display of fireworks and the stone pillar mark the beginning of an extended time of peace between Israel and her pagan neighbors, especially the Philistines.

An unfortunate aspect of Samuel's leadership is his failure to guide his sons, Joel and Abijah, in the ways of the Lord. Samuel is following in the footsteps of his *father* Eli. Like Eli's sons, his own sons also turn away from God. Samuel, unlike his mentor, functions effectively as Israel's leader to the end of his life. But he is blind to the behavior of his sons and appoints them as judges. They are thoroughly corrupt, and the people are clamoring for another form of government.

Samuel strongly opposes the Israelites' desire to have a king as all their pagan neighbors have. The Israelites are a covenant people, who are to look to God alone

Everyday *Life*

Growing Up in Ancient Israel

The Bible makes reference to many young children, though never offering their own point of view. What, for example, was Isaac thinking when his father was about to sacrifice him on an altar? How did Ishmael feel when he was sent into the desert with his mother? And what was little Samuel thinking when his mother left him with an old priest and just walked away?

For Hannah, as painful as the parting must have been, her action was a fulfillment of a vow to God. Her sacrifice was her son. God was very personal and real to her, and she feared for her son—and for herself—if she reneged on her promise. Children were regarded as a gift from God, who both closed and opened women's wombs.

From the moment of birth infants were tenderly cared for—first by the midwife and then by the mother. The most complete description of such initial care comes from the prophet Ezekiel, who is actually describing what had not happened to Jerusalem: "on the day you were born your navel cord was not cut, nor were you washed in water to cleanse *you;* you were not rubbed with salt nor wrapped in swaddling cloths" (Ezek. 16:4 NKJV).

Before they were three, children were typically weaned, at which time there was a celebration. Samuel's weaning was perhaps delayed until he was presumably old enough to be left at the temple. Soon thereafter he was mature enough to hear the call of God, albeit with the prompting of Eli. Such religious maturity was not uncommon for children whose lives revolved around a culture of religious faith.

Childhood was short in the ancient world. Girls learned the duties of a homemaker from their mothers, while boys typically worked with their fathers in the fields or in a trade. By the time girls reached their teen years, they were eligible for marriage—childhood forever gone.

Israel without a King

The Israelites saw increasing corruption among the judges and when Samuel's own sons proved corrupt the Israelites had had enough and demanded to be ruled by a king instead of judges. Their argument (perhaps a valid one) was that a king could establish and maintain a standing national army to protect them from their enemies. The judges, on the other hand, had to muster a local militia and garner support from neighboring tribes every time a crisis erupted. . . . It is possible that if Samuel's sons had been righteous and wise judges, the history of Israel might have taken a very different path.

Richard R. Losch, *All the People in the Bible*, 6

as king and live by the law handed down by Moses. But despite Samuel's objections, God permits the people to have their own way—to have their own king. This even after Samuel lays out all the pitfalls and warns them of the inevitable tyrannies of kingly rule—forced labor, military conscription, burdensome taxation.

God becomes directly involved in the king-making process and sends Samuel to Saul, who is searching for donkeys and stops by Zuph, where Samuel has come to make a sacrifice and eat with the people. When they meet, Samuel invites Saul to join him for the feast. He first eases Saul's mind by telling him—before Saul has even inquired—that the donkeys have already been found. Then, without so much as a segue, he drops the bombshell: "At this moment, Israel's future is in your hands."[3]

Is Samuel for real? Saul is no ruler. He is out searching for runaway donkeys. He's never enrolled in even one seminar on leadership training, nor has he any administrative experience. To his credit, he protests. But Samuel piles it on, taking him into the private dining hall, where some thirty others are seated. There he requests the best steak and fixings to be served to the honored guest. Samuel then invites the by-now-giddy Saul to spend the night at his own house. The next day he anoints him king in a private ceremony. Samuel then sends him on the road toward home, where he is told he will notice very specific details of various people he will meet along the way—all signs confirming that his anointing is from God.

Sometime later Samuel calls the Israelites together at Mizpah and delivers a message from God, reminding them of how God delivered them from slavery in Egypt and how he has led them ever since. If they do not trust God to continue to lead them, well, then they can just have the king they are demanding. He lines up all the tribes as though he is searching for the right king. He narrows his search down to the tribe of Benjamin and finally picks Saul, the onlookers knowing nothing about the previous anointing. After a short delay, Samuel introduces Saul to the crowd. Before dismissing the tribes, he spells out the rules of this new system of government and puts it in writing as well.

In his old age, Samuel addresses the people again, this time seeking to assure them of his legitimate authority:

> I've led you faithfully from my youth until this very day. Look at me! Do you have any complaints to bring before God

> and his anointed? Have I ever stolen so much as an ox or a donkey? Have I ever taken advantage of you or exploited you? Have I ever taken a bribe or played fast and loose with the law? Bring your complaint and I'll make it right.[4]

The people insist that they have no complaints against him. Then he harangues them about the wrong they have done in demanding a king. This after Saul returns from the battlefield with his first great victory. The Israelites, Samuel insists, should have remembered their past and should have been willing to let God lead them as God led Moses and the patriarchs before him. It was simply wrong, he tells them, to demand a king. Indeed, to prove it God answers his prayer and sends a thunderstorm on that very day, long after the rainy season had ended.

In his old age Samuel might have hied himself away to a hermitage and stayed far from the battlefront. But one of his final acts is to meet Saul in Gilgal after Saul's decisive battle over the Amalekites. After informing Saul that his kingship is over, he orders the swaggering King Agag of the Amalekites be brought before him, and pronounces this sentence on him: "As your sword has made women childless, so will your mother be childless among women."[5] With those words, the old prophet takes out his sword and kills Agag.

Returning to his home in Ramah, Samuel has nothing more to do with Saul, though he can't stop grieving for him. Then one day God speaks to him out of the blue: "So, how long are you going to mope over Saul? You know I've rejected him as king over Israel. Fill your flask with anointing oil and get going. I'm sending you to Jesse of Bethlehem. I've spotted the very king I want among his sons."[6] As Samuel protests, fearing Saul will kill him, God continues his instructions and summons him forth.

Tomb and mosque of the prophet Samuel

Samuel travels to Bethlehem to make a sacrifice, inviting all the people, including Jesse and his sons, who are all brought before him. None of them suit God. Turns out Jesse had left his youngest son home to tend the flock. Samuel asks for him. Soon David is brought before Samuel, who anoints the boy with oil before returning to his home. When he dies sometime later, all the people of Israel come out for his funeral and bury him in his hometown of Ramah. They grieve the death of this beloved and righteous man.

Saul: A Wasted Life

The Israelites cry out, *Long live the king.* They now have what they want—a king to rule them just like their pagan neighbors have. Not everyone is excited about Saul, but he is the man God has chosen.

So how does he begin his rule as Israel's first king? Where is he when the enemy is threatening to gouge the eyes out of his people? Is he sitting on his throne consulting with his military advisors, ready to send his troops into action? Hardly. When messengers bring the news to the town folks in Gibeah, the people weep and wail. Saul is nowhere to be found. Then he's spotted heading home from the field where he has been plowing with his team of oxen.

Saul is a farmer, not a warrior. He is the son of Kish, who has a sterling pedigree from the line of Benjamin and is settled on a farm with his family and livestock. Saul had grown up a farm boy of no apparent distinction among his neighbors, apart from the fact that he is exceptionally handsome. Indeed, he's a stud who stands head and shoulders above the rest.

He might have simply settled down and farmed the land for the rest of his life had God not handpicked him as king. The backdrop for his royal appointment is most unusual. He is roaming the region with his servant, looking for stray donkeys. Three days on the trail, sweaty and dirty, he's ready to call it quits. But his servant suggests they go into the town of Zuph and consult a holy man who, by his reputation, might be able to help them.

They encounter some local girls at the town well and ask where they can find the *seer*. The girls tell them the seer just arrived to make a sacrifice. Almost immediately they meet Samuel, not knowing it is he, and ask him where the seer lives. Samuel responds: *I am that man*.

Samuel forthwith invites Saul to a feast and tells him his stray donkeys have been located and that he, Saul, will lead the Israelites. Saul is incredulous. He's out looking for lost donkeys, not a job—surely not the job of ruling Israel. Why him? He is from Benjamin, the least of the tribes, and the least of the clans in that tribe. Why on earth would this holy man be singling him out? Samuel ignores his protests and takes Saul to the dinner, where Saul is served up the best portion in front of all the guests.

Saul spends the night, and the next day Samuel privately anoints him king. Then he specifies three encounters with people that Saul will have on his way home. These encounters will serve as signs that God himself is behind this king-making business. Samuel leaves and Saul heads for home, meeting people along the way just as Samuel had prophesied. At the final encounter he meets an orchestra of prophets making music with their flutes, tambourines, harps, and drums. Here God's Spirit falls upon Saul, and he joins this parade of prophets and begins prophesying himself. Everyone is shocked that this farm boy has suddenly gotten the Spirit.

When he arrives home, Saul doesn't mention anything about being anointed king. Sometime later, however, his tribe, along with all the other tribes, is called before Samuel for the announcement of a king. When Samuel finally whittles the choice down to the correct tribe and clan and person, Saul is nowhere to be found. Turns out Saul, knowing what is coming,

Something within Saul Tragically Lacking

Israel's second king, David, will commit what looks like far greater wrong than anything done by God's first choice, King Saul. But David proves much the superior leader. Why might God have given up so quickly on Saul, and what does this intimate about God's reversal of choice in favor of David? Possible answers begin to emerge with the narrator's presentation of Saul's three anointings and paralleled wrongdoing, the latter sandwiching a picture of Jonathan, who is everything good that Saul isn't. With Saul we find an anatomy of failure that goes beyond mere wrongdoing. Something within Saul is tragically lacking, a flaw that will prove definitive as a contrast with David.

Paul Borgman, *David, Saul, and God: Rediscovering an Ancient Story*, 17

sneaks away from the crowd and hides under a pile of sacks. He is discovered, and the people hail him as king.

Saul's first act as ruler of the Israelites (after he is located back on the farm with his team of oxen) is to slaughter his oxen in a rage. He has just heard the news that makes his blood boil. The Ammonites, under King Nahash, have laid siege to Jabesh Gilead and are threatening to gouge out the right eyes of all the men and make them slaves. The besieged men send messengers to Saul explaining their dire straits.

Saul is irate. But will all the Israelites accept him as commander-in-chief? Maybe not. Some even despise him. Nevertheless, Saul acts boldly. As a sign of his leadership, he cuts the oxen into pieces and sends messengers with blood-soaked hunks of meat to distribute among all the people of Israel with this ominous message: "Anyone who refuses to join up with Saul and Samuel, let this be the fate of his oxen!"[7] The people respond in droves, and Saul takes command of an army numbering more than three hundred thousand, which soundly defeats the Ammonite enemy and rescues the city of Jabesh Gilead.

At this point Saul's loyal followers are prepared to take revenge on those who had earlier insisted he was not fit to rule. But Saul wants no part of it. Instead he and the troops go to Gilgal to renew his kingly status and worship God.

Unfortunately for Saul, such great victories do not continue. On one occasion when his army is far outnumbered by the Philistines and many of his soldiers have gone AWOL, he is overly anxious to attack. Samuel sends word that he should wait until he, Samuel, can arrive and make a sacrifice. Samuel is late in coming, so Saul sacrifices the burnt offering himself. Why not? It turns out to be a fatal mistake. Samuel tells him that this act has jeopardized his kingly reign.

From that point on things begin to fall apart. Nevertheless, Saul marches forward with his son Jonathan and six hundred soldiers, all of whom are armed only with sharpened farm tools. Despite being vastly outnumbered, he wins the battle, thanks to his son's unusual tactics. More victories follow. But then for no good reason he flagrantly disobeys God. Samuel had clearly set forth God's plan to totally destroy the Amalekites, including civilians and

David playing the harp for Saul

property, but Saul ignores the directive and keeps some of the best of the flocks and herds—for a sacrifice to God, he insists. Samuel castigates him for his disobedience and tells him he's fired. Saul begs God's forgiveness, but Samuel adamantly asserts God's word is final.

Unbeknownst to Saul, Samuel travels to Bethlehem to anoint David as king. At the very moment he does, Saul becomes seriously depressed. His aides suggest they can help bring him out of this depth of darkness by bringing in some good entertainment. They know just the musician, none other than David son of Jesse, who plays a harp. David is sent for and comes to live in Saul's house as court musician and assistant.

Saul continues to lead his troops, ever ready for action with the Philistines, who are now threatening Israel again, egging for a face-off. The armies are positioned on opposite hills with a valley below them. Before any actual fighting begins, however, a huge man, some nine feet tall, struts down into the valley from the Philistine side. He is covered from head to toe in heavy armor. This is certainly a strange turn of events.

As it turns out the man is Goliath, and he's taunting the Israelites. They cannot help gaping at him. They've never seen such a giant before. He wants to go one-on-one with an Israelite soldier. The Philistines are making a wager. *If any one of you can defeat him, we'll become your slaves*, and vice versa if he defeats his Israelite opponent. But this is no matchup at all. There is no one among Saul's men who can possibly take on this giant. Goliath continues his taunts for forty days.

Only then does David, who had returned home from serving Saul, appear on the scene. Saul is skeptical about the boy. But his own troops are scared silly,

If Saul Had Reflected on His Life

Although I know nothing of the details, I was later to find out that Samuel had snuck off to Bethlehem to anoint another king. He was literally going to follow through with the last detail as kingmaker. I honestly believe that his whole goal in life was to see me deposed before he died. . . . As I was to find out, on the very day that my replacement had been anointed something bizarre happened to me. It seemed that there was this evil spirit that harassed me until it drove me insane. It seemed that the only thing that helped was music. So we attempted to find somebody that was a skilled musician to soothe me when the foul air was upon me. As it would turn out, it was none other than David ben-Jesse—the very one Samuel had appointed to replace me. If only I'd known!

G. D. Vreeland, *The Darker Side of Samuel, Saul and David*, 178–79 and he has no other option. David takes down the giant with a slingshot and stone, and once again Israel is saved. After the deed is done, Saul calls David in and questions him, apparently not recognizing him. David is again invited to live in Saul's household.

But Saul is conflicted. On the one hand he needs David; on the other, he hates him and does whatever he can to be rid of this boy who has become a popular folk hero. He sends him into perilous battles, even promising David his daughter Michal in marriage if David risks his life against the Philistines. David prevails and becomes Saul's son-in-law. But still Saul goes after him, even going so far as to order his son Jonathan to murder him. Later he tries unsuccessfully to kill him himself. When he sends his guards to kill him, Michal warns him and he escapes.

Saul is making a crazy fool of himself in his desperate efforts to kill David. When he learns that David has gone to consult with Samuel, he sends his men after him. They find Samuel with a group of prophets all possessed of God's Spirit, prophesying up a storm. It is contagious. Before they know it, Saul's men have joined in. Saul gets the news and sends men again, and still again. All three times the men fall under the Spirit of prophecy. So Saul heads out to kill David himself, but what should happen when he arrives? "The Spirit of God was on him, too. . . . He was caught up in a babbling trance! He ripped off his clothes and lay there rambling gibberish before Samuel for a day and a night, stretched out naked. People are still talking about it: 'Saul among the prophets! Who would have guessed?'"[8]

But Saul will not give up his desperate efforts to kill David. When he hears that David has consulted with Abimelech, the priest, he orders Doeg, an Edomite, to kill not only Abimelech and more than eighty other priests but also everyone in the town. Saul has simply gone mad. Only one priest, Abiathar, survives the slaughter, and he joins with David and his men.

Still Saul will not give up. He is hot on David's trail, except when he must abandon the pursuit to fight off enemy troops from across the borders. On one occasion, after he has entered a cave to relieve himself, who should appear from deep inside the cave, but David himself. David bows before him, pledging his loyalty and pleading with him to stop his terrorizing pursuit. Saul, his bipolar personality disorder intact, begins to weep. "Can this be the voice of my son David?" he sobs. "You've heaped good on me; I've dumped evil on you."[9] He blesses David, for he knows for certain that David will be king, and begs him not to wipe out his family or erase his name from the record books.

Saul's sweet spirit, however, never lasts. He goes back and forth between repentance and rage. He will track David down and kill him one way or another. But Saul has real enemies to worry about as well. The Philistines are again on the attack. Their forces are frightening. What can he do but reach out to God for help? But God has deserted him. He makes no sound or sign, and Saul feels helpless. If only Samuel were still alive.

Then he has an idea. He sends one of his lackeys out to find a psychic—someone who can bring a spirit back from the grave. His men tell him about a witch living in Endor. So Saul, convinced this is his only hope, goes undercover and tells her he wants to talk with the deceased Samuel. When she brings back the spirit of Samuel, she immediately recognizes Saul and fears he will have her put to death as a witch. But he assures her he will do her no wrong, so she continues.

The witch, now in a trance, sees old Samuel in priestly robes. He is irritated that his final rest has been interrupted. Saul explains the danger he faces with the Philistines, pointing out that God is no longer responsive to his entreaties. Samuel reproves him and tells him what he certainly doesn't want to hear: *Israel will be soundly defeated by the Philistines.* But then comes the real bombshell: "Tomorrow you and your sons will be with me."[10] That means nothing other than death. Saul faints. The witch revives him. He hasn't eaten all day, but he still refuses her provisions. Finally, he is persuaded by his servants to take part in a feast she prepares—his final meal.

The next day Saul and his men are in full retreat, with the Philistine army breathing heavily down their necks. Saul is hit by an enemy arrow. Fatally wounded and fearing the enemy will come upon him and finish him off, he commands his armor bearer to kill him with his sword. The man refuses. In his final moments, Saul grabs for his sword and falls on it. With the enemy surrounding him, he commits suicide. But he is not the only one who dies that day—his three sons, including Jonathan, perish also at the hands of the uncircumcised Philistines. The men of Jabesh Gilead retrieve Saul's body and give him a proper burial.

So the downward spiral is complete. Death has visited the one who abandons God and whom God has abandoned.

Concluding Observations

The story of the boy Samuel is one of the most beloved children's Bible stories of all time. But if a child is listening closely, the seeming abandonment by his mother might bring more fear than comfort. In many respects, the accounts of Samuel and Saul raise more questions than they answer. Samuel brought back from the dead to speak to Saul? What a strange biblical episode that is. How is it that a witch is permitted to serve as medium, bringing God's message through Samuel? And what is going on with Samuel in his later years? Throughout his life Samuel appears to be a gentle man. He's a prophet, not a cold-blooded killer. So he surely must have surprised onlookers when in old age he pulls out his sword (who knew he even carried one?) and slays Agag.

Saul is another species altogether. He seems like such a normal kid, helping his father find the donkeys. He plows the fields with the family oxen—just a regular guy. So if God knows how this will turn out, someone might wonder, why does he choose Saul in the first place? Why doesn't he leave Saul alone to plow in his father's field? Saul surely didn't want the job. But God's ways are beyond our ways. So Saul becomes the crazy king. The story is just plain sad.

But if the reader fails to see humor in this account of Saul, there is a major disconnect between reader and text. Saul is sneaking away to hide under a pile of grain sacks at the very moment his royal status is being announced. Saul is running here and there after David as in a game of cat and mouse. Saul gets caught up in the Pentecostal praise meeting, speaking in tongues and getting naked. Saul goes into a cave because there is no outhouse nearby, and who should be inside and follow him out of the cave but David. If this is not knee-slapping hilarity, nothing is.

Further Reading

Barber, Cyril J. *The Books of Samuel: The Sovereignty of God Illustrated in the Lives of Samuel, Saul, and David*. Eugene, OR: Wipf & Stock, 2003.

Borgman, Paul. *David, Saul, and God: Rediscovering an Ancient Story*. New York: Oxford University Press, 2008.

Vreeland, G. D. *The Darker Side of Samuel, Saul and David*. Xulon Press, 2007.

11

KING DAVID

Colorful Friends and Bitter Enemies

How could he be anything less than a man after God's own heart? No one has ever praised God with more powerful and picturesque words than David. His Psalm 23 is the most memorable poem of the entire ancient world:

> The Lord is my shepherd;
> I shall not want. . . .
> He leadeth me beside the still waters.
> He restoreth my soul. . . .
> Yea, though I walk through the valley
> of the shadow of death,
> I will fear no evil:
> For thou art with me;
> thy rod and thy staff
> they comfort me.[1]

As a beloved Old Testament figure, no one ranks higher than David. He grabs the reader's attention from the moment he strides out of the text. Healthy, handsome, and charismatic, he will tear at the heartstrings of everyone he meets—down to the present day. He is the "*Israelite Idol*," attracting adoring fans wherever he goes.

He is anything but a perfect role model, however. His extravagant devotion to God is offset by his blatant shortcomings. In an era long before paparazzi and investigative journalism, his sins are almost flagrantly exposed. Indeed, no other biblical biography is so complete—a story that spans virtually his entire life, from boyhood to death. Complex relationships with both men and women, including Saul, Jonathan, Joab, Abigail, and Bathsheba are described in graphic detail.

> *Like everyone else, from Samuel, Saul, and Jonathan down to the present, Yahweh is charmed by David.*
>
> Harold Bloom, *The Book of J*

Apart from his personal life, David is remembered for his nation-building accomplishments more than anything else. After his encounter with Goliath, he is heralded as a hero, though a hero on the run from the insanely jealous Saul. After years as a guerrilla warrior, he ascends to the throne at a time when the future of the Israelites looks grim.

Looking back at this era, the historian knows that both Egypt and Assyria are in decline, allowing for expansion of the tiny Israelite kingdom. David, however, no doubt feels as hemmed in as did his predecessors. His immediate military ambition is to crush Israel's loathsome long-standing enemy, the Philistines. With that threat essentially out of the way, he goes after Jerusalem, a Canaanite stronghold.

The victory over the Jebusites paves the way for David to establish the capital in Jerusalem, a less-than-ideal site in many respects. No rivers or trade routes connected the city to other major commercial centers. But the region has religious significance to the Israelites—particularly a hill to the north of the city. Indeed, David makes a point of purchasing that hill in order to secure perpetual ownership.

David's deed of purchase for this sacred piece of real estate, however, would not survive the millennia. This much-fought-over piece of land has changed hands more than thirty times and today is the site of the Islamic Dome of the Rock.

Jerusalem now secure as the capital, David sends for the Ark of the Covenant, eager to give it a permanent home. A natural follow-up would be the building of the Temple. But the Temple is God's most holy dwelling on earth, and David, the fierce

David and the Divine Right of Kings

Even when we consider his military conquest, we see that the driving force behind them was his attachment to God. The hereditary bloodline of King David will become the only legitimate royal bloodline in Jewish history. From David will come all the future kings of Judah and ultimately, at the end of history, the Messiah. This idea of a God-ordained monarchy will be copied by many other nations throughout history and will serve as the basis for the concept of "the divine right of kings" in Medieval and Renaissance Europe.

Rabbi Ken Spiro, "David the King"

More about David than Jesus

We know more about [David] than anybody else in scripture, including Jesus, actually, because we have David's entire life, and we only have three years plus some snippets of Jesus's. Jesus is described as the son of David. There's an explicit connection made between their lives. David is an incredibly complex life in terms of the mixture of good and evil, faithfulness and adultery, loyalty and murder.

Eugene Peterson, Interview, 68

warrior, has blood on his hands. God will leave this enterprise to his son Solomon.

David: Charismatic and Culpable

The youngest of eight brothers, David, son of Jesse and great-grandson of Ruth, grows up in Naomi's hometown of Bethlehem. He may have heard stories about the famine of earlier times that prompted a hometown couple to journey to Moab. In the train of events that followed, his great-grandmother left Moab and settled in Bethlehem. Soon thereafter she gave birth to Obed, his grandfather. What if she had remained in her homeland? How different history would have been.

David's father, like many of the neighbors, raises sheep, and David and his brothers spend long days out on the hillsides tending the flocks. If sheepherding conjures up images of peaceful, pastoral, lackadaisical work, such is surely not the case for David. Dangerous wild animals are lurking in the forests and behind boulders and shrubs. In defending the flock he demonstrates incredible brute strength reminiscent of Samson. He later relates two feats of this sort to King Saul: "When a lion or a bear came and carried off a sheep from the flock, I went after it, struck it and rescued the sheep from its mouth. When it turned on me, I seized it by its hair, struck it and killed it."[2]

As with so many of God's chosen people, David (despite his ferocious defense of sheep) is an unlikely candidate for king. He alone is away from the household tending sheep when the prophet Samuel arrives to anoint him. After Samuel explains his mission and David is summoned (much to the incredulity of his family), Samuel pours the anointing oil over David's head. In an instant, God's Spirit descends upon him, empowering him for the remainder of his life.

Soon thereafter this Spirit-filled boy, whose harp playing has not gone unnoticed, is selected (upon recommendation from a royal servant) to serve as a music therapist for the bipolar King Saul. Saul is impressed by the boy's talent and soothed by his sweet melodies.

Bruce Springsteen from the Line of David?

A Springsteen show is a lot of things, and it's partly a religious experience. Maybe he comes from the line of David, a shepherd boy who could play beautiful music, so that the crazy become less crazy and Saul the king finally chills out.

Clarence Clemons Jake, quoted in David Remnick, "We Are Alive: Bruce Springsteen at Sixty-Two," 56

David continues part-time in Saul's service (as court musician and armor bearer), commuting from the family sheep ranch. Three of his brothers are off serving in Saul's army, fighting the Philistines some distance away. Concerned about the well-being of his sons, Jesse sends David to the front lines with provisions—roasted grain, bread, cheese.

Perhaps thinking he might see some action, David arrives amid a stalemate—and a great commotion. The Philistine giant Goliath is goading the Israelites to send out a man to fight him. And the Israelites are frightened beyond measure. David delivers the care packages to his brothers and begins inquiring about the reward for killing the giant. Overhearing the conversation, his older brother angrily rebukes him. Indeed, his bitterness and sarcasm bring to mind Joseph's brothers: "Why have you come down here? And with whom did you leave those few sheep in the wilderness? I know how conceited you are and how wicked your heart is; you came down only to watch the battle."[3] But David responds with his own bit of sarcasm and continues to mingle with the troops in an effort to get as much information as he can about the proposed matchup. Saul is informed of this upstart roaming the Israelite camp, so he summons the boy. David approaches Saul, who does not even recognize him, and tells him he wants to take on the giant. Saul is incredulous. Not a chance. But David persists. He tells the king that he once had fought a lion and a bear successfully and that he certainly can take out Goliath.

Saul, desperate for any ray of hope, brings out his armor and agrees to let David give it a try. But David rejects the armor, gathers five stones, and saunters out to meet the giant, his only weapon a slingshot. Goliath taunts and ridicules him until he's suddenly hit in the forehead with one of David's stones. He drops to the ground like a bag of cement. David grabs the giant's sword and slices off his head, and later presents it to Saul. In the meantime, Saul's army regains its courage, pursues the fleeing Philistines, and trounces them.

But serious problems lie ahead even as David goes on to enjoy one military success after another. David has become a hero, and Saul is not amused. Following the defeat of the Philistines, the women sing and dance in the streets:

> Saul kills by the thousand,
> David by the ten thousand![4]

David, having been befriended by Saul's son Jonathan, comes to live at court, where again he plays his harp to calm Saul's

David: Original Alpha Male

Something crucial in human history begins with the biblical figure of King David. He is the original alpha male, the kind of man whose virile ambition always drives him to the head of the pack. He is the first superstar, a figure so compelling that the Bible may have originated as his royal biography. He is an authentic sex symbol, a ruggedly handsome fellow who inspires passion in both men and women, a passion expressed sometimes as hero worship and sometimes as carnal longing.

Jonathan Kirsch, *King David: The Real Life of the Man Who Ruled Israel*, 1 demons. During this time David bonds with Jonathan to the point that they make a covenant of eternal friendship. Saul, in a jealous rage, twice tries to kill him, but David is invincible. God is with him. Saul then sends him to the front lines, hoping he might get rid of him once and for all. But his heroic stature only rises. Saul then arranges for David to marry his daughter Michal in exchange for the killing of one hundred Philistines, fully expecting David to die in the attempt.

The David of the Bible is a complex character. He is pious and faithful at times but is also capable of heinous crimes. He is a powerful and decisive man, except around his children whom he cannot control.

Steven L. McKenzie, *King David: A Biography*

Without so much as a wound, David and his men more than accomplish the task, depositing at Saul's feet a grand total of two hundred Philistine foreskins. That seals the deal, and David marries Michal, who is head over heels in love with him. But Saul is now even more angry and afraid, and his attempts to be rid of David are intensified. Every time, however, David outsmarts him. Through the intervention of Jonathan, David returns to the palace as court musician. But after Saul tries to spear him to the wall, David narrowly escapes. His new wife Michal connives against her father and engineers a clever deception that allows David to elude Saul's search party.

On one occasion, in an effort to escape the wrath of the king, David flees to Gath—of all places, Goliath's hometown. Not surprisingly, he is recognized and is trapped with no escape. So he feigns madness, beating his fists against his head, dribbling from the mouth, and scribbling in the dirt. When he is brought before King Achish, the king snorts his memorable one-liner: *Don't I already have enough lunatics around that you should bring me another!*

Soon thereafter David gathers around him a ragtag band of some four hundred loyal followers and hides out. His brothers are with him, and he has secured a safe haven for his parents in Moab, interestingly, the homeland of his father's grandmother Ruth. His first military skirmish with his militia is against the Philistines. He defeats them soundly. But Abiathar the priest warns David to get out of the walled city of Keilah, which they have just taken, because Saul's army is on the way. So David and his men are on the run, hiding out in the desert, ever on the lookout for King Saul.

Love between David and Jonathan

Now, I can imagine that Hollywood, the media, and the mood in which the media operates might want to make something evil out of the relationship between David and Jonathan. But so far as the Scriptures are concerned, it was truly the love of a man for a man. . . . [Jonathan] was the one person probably who had reason to be jealous of David in the greatest way because he was the son of Saul, and you might have thought that he might have succeeded his father as king in Israel, but . . . he was self-sacrificing because of his love for David.

S. Lewis Johnson Jr., "David and Jonathan"

Jonathan reports to David of his father's evil designs, and he and David renew their covenant.

In one instance when David is fleeing Saul's hot pursuit, he hides deep inside a cave. He and his men hear noise outside, and before they can make their escape, Saul comes in to use the cave as a toilet. While he's doing his business, David slips up near him and cuts a piece off his garment. David's men had whispered they wanted to kill Saul, but David will have no part in assassinating the king. When Saul takes his leave, David marshals forth his courage and, calling out to him, falls on the ground before him.

He informs the king that his own men had wanted to kill him, but he forbade them, for *King Saul is God's chosen ruler*. Then he shows Saul the piece of garment he had cut from his robe, proof enough that he would never lay a hand on God's anointed.

Saul repents and David promises he will never kill his family or forget the good Saul has done. But they go their separate ways. David never again returns to Saul's household.

David and his men live off the land and request food and necessities from local herdsmen in exchange for protection. This is the wild west of Canaan, and landowners are usually willing to barter for security. That is, all except Nabal. Nabal's name is well known in the region of Carmel. He farms on a massive spread with some four thousand sheep and goats.

It is shearing season, a big time of festivities and feasting. David sends word on ahead to Nabal, requesting in a courteous way that he share some of his provisions with his hungry foot soldiers. David reminds him that he and his militia had offered protection and did not harass his herders nor plunder any goods when they were camped nearby. All he is asking is food for his men.

Nabal's wealth and financial security, however, do not lead to generosity. He fumes. Who is David, and why should he share his food with him? Who is David! Really? Doesn't Nabal know he killed a

David's Specialty: Killing Philistines

David's refusal to kill King Saul catches and holds my attention . . . as completely uncharacteristic of David. David got his start by killing the Philistine giant Goliath. From that moment on, killing Philistines was a leitmotif in David's life. He made a specialty of killing Philistines: He killed a hundred as a bride-price to Saul for Michal's hand in marriage. . . . But not just Philistines—Geshurites, Girzites, Amalekites, Jerahmeelites, Kenites, Moabites, Aramaeans, Edomites, and Ammonites all contributed substantially to David's body count.

In the welter of all that killing, the thing that interests me most is the man he didn't kill. He didn't kill King Saul. And King Saul was the one man he had the most reason and motivation to kill. King Saul was obsessed with killing David.

Eugene Peterson, *The Jesus Way*, 84

giant and that the song of his *ten thousands* has been on everyone's lips? But Nabal has forgotten—either that or he couldn't care less. The answer is no. No food, not now or ever.

David is livid. He and his six hundred men did not have to ask for it in a nice way. They could have taken everything Nabal owned and more. So he's off with his troops, leaving two hundred behind to secure the camp. They head down into a ravine, approaching Nabal's settlement, when what should they meet? A train of pack animals loaded down with provisions, and behind them a beautiful woman astride her own donkey.

As the woman approaches, she dismounts and bows before David. What in heaven's name is going on? The woman rises, apologizes, blames herself for the trouble, and then blesses him. David responds in kind, blessing her and thanking

Everyday *Life*

Diet in a Land of Milk and Honey

The Bible has many references to festivals and feasts but virtually no descriptions of the various dishes and delectables that were served. One of the most detailed descriptions of foods that would have been consumed by rich and poor alike is that of the food Abigail furnished for the guerrilla warrior David and his army. When he threatened to take action against her husband, she spun into action, sending donkeys loaded down with "two hundred loaves of bread, two skins of wine, five sheep dressed out and ready for cooking, a bushel of roasted grain, a hundred raisin cakes, and two hundred fig cakes" (1 Sam. 25:18).

Most people, even those rich in land and cattle, ate a varied diet, though surely not a complex one. The Bible is anything but a recipe book, so we must guess how most dishes were prepared.

Beans, lentils, and cucumbers were available in season. Such vegetables were often added to a beef or mutton stew, flavored by garlic, onions, or leeks. Poultry and eggs were also part of the diet, as were olives and olive oil. Also part of the meal was a wide variety of fruit, including pomegranates, dates, and figs. No meal was complete without bread and for poor people barley bread was a staple and might serve as an entire meal, washed down with water or milk.

Wine, of course, was a key part of a complete meal and important for entertaining guests. Fertile soil and a temperate climate served very well for grape growing. Indeed, vineyards were an important part of a homestead, and most of the grapes were used for wine making.

No Obese Israelites

Although there is evidence that some of the ancient inhabitants of the region were not slim and trim, most of the available information suggests that most people were not overweight, due to their diet and the strenuous physical activities in which they were engaged.

Oded Borowski, *Agriculture in Ancient Israel*, 3

her for her compassion and for preventing him from murderous revenge. He and his men enjoy a hearty picnic, compliments of Abigail, Nabal's wife.

Saul again is hot on the trail. But David is wily. Somehow he manages to escape every time—sometimes right under Saul's nose. Indeed, he and one of his men sneak into Saul's camp late one night and find him and his soldiers all in a God-induced deep sleep. It's their opportunity to finish him off for good, but David refuses to even contemplate the idea. Instead he takes Saul's spear and canteen and sneaks away. At a distance, David calls out to Abner, Saul's general. He taunts him and shows him what he's holding in his hands. Saul awakens and comes out, and once again he's in a confessing, forgiving mood.

But David knows Saul all too well, so he moves across the border into Gath right in the midst of the Philistines, where he gets permission to settle down with his wives and soldiers and their households. They establish themselves in the small outlying town of Ziklag, where they spend the next sixteen months. From there he goes out raiding enemy villages, with the blessing of the Philistine king Achish.

Things get messy, however, when the Philistines make plans to attack Israel. David wants to join the offensive, but the Philistine captains won't have anything to do with him, fearing he will turn on them in the heat of battle. So David returns home, only to find his village raided by the Amalekites, the women and children taken prisoner—including his two wives, Ahinoam and Abigail—and his men on the verge of mutiny. Assured of success by Abiathar, David's loyal priest, David pursues and subdues the raiders, rescues the women and children, and reclaims all his and his soldiers' possessions, plus substantial plunder from the defeated Amalekites.

Soon after David and his men return to their village, a soldier in Saul's army shows up dirty and in disarray. He falls down before David, telling him he has just come from the Israelite camp, where he has witnessed great devastation by the Philistines. More than that, Saul and Jonathan are both dead. The soldier, an Amalekite, who thinks he's bringing David good news, claims that he was the one who put the wounded king out of his misery.

David is overwhelmed with sorrow. He and his troops all tear their clothes in mourning and weep the entire day. Later David questions the soldier further, and by that time his grief has turned to rage. This man—a foreigner—has killed the God-anointed king, a most treacherous deed and a capital offense. David orders one of his men to kill him on the spot.

After this David sings a lamentation for the ones he regarded as father and brother. Saul is the fearless warrior, but Jonathan, the loss of dear Jonathan is such deep sorrow as can be comprehended only by the anguish of his song:

> I grieve for you, Jonathan my
> brother;
> you were very dear to me.
> Your love for me was wonderful,
> more wonderful than that of
> women.[5]

After the time of mourning is passed, David, his family, and his militia move to Hebron in Judah. It is only then that the people of Judah make David their king. It is here that six sons are born to David (from six different women), and here that he begins to consolidate his power. The significance is that, unlike Saul, David is king of Judah only. Abner, Saul's military commander, sees to it that Saul's son Ish-Bosheth is made king of the other Israelite tribes. With that turn of events the armies on both sides begin to fight each other, both sides sustaining losses. Judah, under the command of Joab, however, loses fewer men than the Israelite forces fighting under Abner. But it is a bitter, protracted civil war.

Finally Abner, who has supported Ish-Bosheth, loses confidence in him and sends word to David that he is ready to make peace and bring all of Israel under David's rule. David jumps at the idea, with one condition: when they meet, Abner must bring with him David's wife Michal, Saul's daughter, whom Saul in one of his rages had married off to another man. Separately, David sends word to Ish-Bosheth demanding that he give him back his wife. The reader may be puzzled as to what would motivate Ish-Bosheth, who is being betrayed by Abner, to give orders to fulfill what David had demanded not of him but of his betrayer, Abner.

David wants her because she is a prize he won for bringing Saul two hundred Philistine foreskins. More than that, she is a political trophy. If he is going to rule the kingdom Saul once ruled, it doesn't hurt to be married to Saul's daughter. But does he love her? There is no evidence of that. There is evidence, however, that she is dearly loved by the man who is now her husband. But romantic love counts for little, and Ish-Bosheth orders that she be removed from the home of Paltiel, her husband. What follows is a tragic account of a man's love for a woman. Paltiel cannot let go. As she is taken away, he trails after her, wailing every step of the way until Abner orders him to return home.

The meeting between David and Abner sets the stage for peace between the two kingdoms, with David as king. But when Joab, David's commander, learns of this, he's outraged. Abner, Saul's commander, had killed his (Joab's) own brother in battle, and he's not about to let bygones be bygones. But Joab may have also worried that Abner would now outrank him in David's army.

Unbeknownst to David, Joab dispatches messengers to find Abner and bring him back. As soon as Abner returns with the messenger, Joab pulls out his sword and murders him. When David learns, he cries out in despair, calling for a season of mourning among his military and pronouncing a curse on Joab and his family.

The murder of Abner might have doomed the whole peace process, but David makes a very public display of his sincere sorrow. Indeed, instead of having a negative effect, this terrible incident brings the two sides together for a time of national mourning. But hardly is the period of mourning over when two men show up at David's door with Ish-Bosheth's head—proof that they had eliminated the rival king. David is irate and orders the men killed. His respect for God's anointed extends also to Saul's children, even to a rival claimant to the throne.

David's reign over Judah has lasted more than seven years. Had anyone else been at the helm, the rift among the descendants of Abraham might never have been healed. But through his political acumen and personal charisma—and God's guidance—he brings the warring sides together as one nation.

Now at thirty-seven, an age when many of his ancestors had remained unmarried and their careers far in the future, he already has lived what seems like more than a lifetime. He has come a long way from his days of herding sheep, with bears and lions his only enemies. With wives and children and all Israel's fighting men at his disposal, he is ready to begin a roller-coaster reign that will last more than three decades.

His top priority is to rid Jerusalem of the Jebusites. When this is handily accomplished, the fortress is named for him: *City of David*. King Hiram of Tyre provides builders and timber to construct a cedar palace. Here he will settle down with his family, his wives, concubines, and eventually eleven children, Solomon among them.

When the Philistines threaten to do serious damage to his kingdom, David and his men prevail. David dutifully acknowledges the one who brings victory. God is the one who carries off his enemies as in a flood of water. In the next battle, God gives David a specific winning military strategy. With that triumph behind him, he leads his best soldiers to Baalah to retrieve the Ark of the Covenant (containing the Ten Commandments on stone tablets) and relocate it in Jerusalem. On the return trip David and his men are parading in high spirits, singing loudly to the accompaniment of an entire orchestra of instruments.

Amid the festivity, the Ark of the Covenant is about to slide off the oxcart. One of the guards grabs it to prevent it from falling—a seemingly innocent, instinctive act. But God cuts him down on the spot. The Ark is sacred and must be handled with ritual care. David is furious, though also fearful of God's wrath. Indeed, so afraid is he of mishandling the Ark that he delays some months in bringing it to Jerusalem.

But when he learns the Ark has brought prosperity to the house of Obed-Edom, where it had been left, he travels with his aides to get it, making the round-trip a showy religious celebration. When they arrive back in Jerusalem, David is completely caught up in the moment, leaping and dancing half-naked in the streets. His wife Michal (forcibly separated from her husband Paltiel) sees the festivities from her window and with sharp sarcasm criticizes him for his unbecoming behavior when he returns home.

Knowing that she thinks her father King Saul would never have acted so undignified (though Saul himself had once danced naked with the prophets), David fires back that he'll dance for God as much as he pleases, and besides, God has chosen him over her father. If he looks the fool, so be it. He's *God's* fool. For her defiance of him, Michal is punished. He no longer has sexual intimacies with her, and she remains childless for the remainder of her life.

In the years that follow, David subdues his enemies (Moabites, Philistines, Ammonites, Arameans), killing tens of thousands, taking plunder, accumulating wealth and property, and establishing his reputation throughout the region. Amid the killing fields, David recalls his dearest friend Jonathan, wondering if any of his family are still alive. He discovers that Jonathan's son Mephibosheth is alive, though disabled—lame in both feet. David bestows on him all the properties that had belonged to Saul's household and requests that the young man from now on eat at the king's table.

During this time, while General Joab is off fighting the Ammonites, David himself remains at home in Jerusalem, administering affairs of state. The weight of the world sometimes lies heavily on his shoulders. He is ultimately responsible for an entire nation. In this mind-set he arises from a late afternoon nap and walks out on the palace rooftop balcony. He looks down and there she is—a perfectly gorgeous woman on her own rooftop next door taking her bath before dinner.

He should have turned around and gone back into the palace to flatter one of his own wives. Instead he inquires about the bathing beauty and learns she is Bathsheba, wife of Uriah, one of his own soldiers—a Hittite whose family had become assimilated into the Israelites. David sends for her. She spends the night. Soon she discovers she is pregnant. How can this be? Uriah has been out on the battlefront for months.

When Bathsheba sends word of her situation to David, he immediately recalls Uriah for a little vacation at home with his wife. But loyal soldier that he is, Uriah will not enjoy intimacies with his wife when his fellow soldiers are out on the battlefield, and he tells David as much. Frustrated, David might have sent one of his guards to put an end to this Hittite then and there. But word would get out, and the people would turn on him. Rather, he arranges to have Uriah murdered but to make the deed look like a war casualty.

So he sends a letter with Uriah to give to his field commander Joab. The orders

David: A Shakespearean Character

David, in a word, is human, fully, four-dimensionally, recognizably human. He grows, he learns, he travails, he triumphs, and he suffers immeasurable tragedy and loss. . . . David is almost, or perhaps more than, a Shakespearean character. Even at the height of his career, he is not a religious symbol, but the embodiment of worldly success. At the nadir of his fortunes, he embodies the fragility of achievement, the importance of the right life rather than a high station. But at almost all times, he is a *secular* icon—a character so extraordinary and yet so very human, so realistically fallible, that the innocent reader almost inevitably empathizes with him. His deeds are divorced from miracle, his relationships are with other people, whether friend or foe, rather than with his God.

Baruch Halpern, *David's Secret Demons: Messiah, Murderer, Traitor, King*, 6 are very specific. When the battle heats up, Joab is to send Uriah to the front and then immediately pull the other soldiers back, leaving him exposed. The plot plays out like clockwork, and the news comes back from the battlefield that Bathsheba is a widow. When her time of grieving is over, David sends for her, and soon thereafter she bears him a son.

David has gotten away with murder. Or has he? Prompted by God, Nathan the prophet pays him a visit. There is no small talk from Nathan. He tells David a story of a rich man and poor man living in the same town. A visitor stops by the rich man's house, but he is too miserly to roast a lamb from his own vast flock. Instead he takes the poor man's lamb, the only one he has—a family pet. As the poor man's family grieves, the rich man serves up lamb chops for his guests.

David hears the story and is outraged. *The rich man should be tracked down and hung from a limb.* He shouldn't get by with such awful behavior. Nathan looks him straight in the eye and, in chilling words of rebuke, says: *You are the man!*

Then Nathan speaks God's message to David, giving him a litany of his blessings, including the rule over both Judah and Israel. How then could David have committed such a crime? Because of his sin he will face terrible family problems. David confesses, and Nathan assures him that God forgives, but nevertheless he will suffer. The son born to Bathsheba and him will die.

The baby boy soon becomes deathly ill, and for six days David fasts and prays and weeps, hoping that God will change his mind and spare the child. But on day seven he dies. The servants expect David to completely fall apart, but he pulls himself together and begins to eat again. It's over; there is no need to continue fasting and praying. It's over. One day David will go to be with his son, but the son can never come back to him. David consoles Bathsheba, and sometime later she bears another son, whom they name Solomon.

Not long after this, Joab sends a message to David that he has just captured the water supply in the imperial city of the Ammonites. Loyal commander that he is, he requests David to come with reinforcements so that he will be credited with the victory. David and his men arrive in time to finish the job. They plunder the city, turn the citizens into an army of slaves, and return home to Jerusalem, David wearing the priceless crown of the Ammonite king.

David: A Man of Contradictions

From the beginning of the story to its choreographed resolution, the text invites its audience to explore specific tensions and possible contradictions about David, or within him: Apparently self-interested politician and pious worshiper; fierce warrior and accomplished musician; a king of justice and an adulterous murderer; an admitted sinner and self-proclaimed blameless one; brash, smooth-tongued talker and extraordinary listener; ruthless executioner and great weeper; fine administrator of people and terrible father (until finally he learns—and saves the nation).

Paul Borgman, *David, Saul, and God: Rediscovering an Ancient Story*, 9

The birth of a second son by Bathsheba and this grand military victory might have prompted David to think that his punishment is over and God is satisfied. But David's family problems continue, as Nathan had prophesied. There is incest among his own children. Amnon, David's oldest son, rapes his beautiful half sister Tamar. That is bad enough, but then he bitterly turns her out, instead of marrying her, as would have been expected in such an instance.

Her brother Absalom learns from the sobbing Tamar what has happened and is incensed. When David hears about the awful incident, he too is furious, but he metes out no discipline because Amnon is his beloved, firstborn, spoiled son; he gets off scot-free.

But anger and vengeance fester inside Absalom. The months pass. Two years after the rape he invites all his brothers for a festive sheepshearing party. Absalom has instructed his servants to wait until Amnon is drunk and then to pounce on him and kill him. They do just that, and the other brothers flee for their lives. David is beside himself when he learns of the murder. Absalom escapes across the border to Aram (Syria), where he finds safety in the court of the king of Geshur, his maternal grandfather.

Absalom returns some three years later through the clever intervention of Joab, and he lives in Jerusalem. But David will not see him until Joab once again intervenes. Nevertheless, Absalom behaves as though he is the crown prince, tooling around town in a chariot with fifty men in front hailing his arrival. He soon endears himself to the people, establishing his claim as a fair and honest judge—if only he were king. It does not hurt that he is strikingly handsome.

After some years of ingratiating himself with the people, Absalom, with his father's blessing, goes to Hebron, ostensibly to worship God and offer sacrifices. This is all part of a conspiracy to wrest the kingship away from his father. He is a popular leader, and he sends messengers throughout Israel to drum up support, particularly from one-time backers of King Saul. And so it is that in Hebron, where David first became king, Absalom declares himself king.

Finally the word comes to David: "The whole country has taken up with Absalom!" David's first words are: "Up and out of here! We've got to run for our lives or none of us will escape Absalom!"[6] Has David been living in a cave? Why has it taken him so long to figure out what is going on?

So King David is on the run from his own son, heading for a hideout in the wilderness, while Absalom and his men are setting up shop in Jerusalem. But David is not going to take this lying down. He sends back loyal followers, who tell Absalom that they have now joined his side, when in fact they are undercover agents for his father. With an inside track to Absalom, word gets back to David, and he now knows to move quickly to get a jump ahead of Absalom and his army.

David reorganizes his army with Joab as commander, and they march toward Jerusalem to meet the enemy, though David cautions his troops to treat Absalom with care. In fact, there is an incredible bloodbath, with some twenty thousand of Absalom's soldiers killed. Absalom, riding his mule, is fleeing from the carnage when he meets some of David's troops. He passes under a tree and is caught by the branches, while his mule runs away from under him. One of David's men reports back to Joab, who is furious that the soldier didn't kill him on the spot. So Joab, completely ignoring David's request, pulls out three knives and stabs Absalom in the heart. His armor bearers finish the job.

Such is fair punishment for the king's chief enemy. Nor does he deserve a decent burial. Joab and his bodyguards throw the corpse in a pit and cover it over with stones. When David receives the news, he is inconsolable. He cries out in anguish: "O my son Absalom, my son, my son Absalom! Would God I had died for thee, O Absalom, my son, my son!"[7] Nathan's curse continues to reverberate.

The victory won by David's forces turns into a time of national mourning. As the soldiers return to Jerusalem, they are disheartened, particularly as they pass by David, who just cannot stop wailing. Joab is anything but sympathetic. In fact, David's relationship with him and his two brothers—sons of Zeruiah—is contentious. They are courageous soldiers, but bloodthirsty. Joab himself is a very clever commander and is not afraid of standing up to the king. At this point he rails at David:

> Today you have humiliated all your men, who have just saved your life and the lives of your sons and daughters and the lives of your wives and concubines. You love those who hate you and hate those who love you. You have made it clear today that the commanders and their men mean nothing to you. I see that you would be pleased if Absalom were alive today and all of us were dead. Now go out and encourage your men. I swear by the Lord that if you don't go out, not a man will be left with you by nightfall. This will be worse for you than all the calamities that have come on you from your youth till now."[8]

David agrees to wipe his tears and to come out and review the troops. But David is not reigning in Jerusalem. He is still out across the Jordan in the wilderness. When he finally returns home, he encounters major rifts between the army of Judah, who claim him as their own, and the army of Israel, still with fond memories of Saul. Soon he has a revolt on his hands, when the army of Israel refuses to acknowledge David as king and they desert. David sends Joab's army after them, and their leader Sheba is killed.

Hard times follow, however, and there is no settled peace. David and his people endure a three-year famine as God's punishment for Saul's murderous betrayal of the Gibeonites. David makes things right with them, though his battles with the Philistines continue unabated. One of his final acts is a foolishly conducted census, which greatly displeases God and for which his people suffer a deadly plague as punishment.

By now his age is catching up with him, and he has little fight left. He has the chills, and no amount of bed coverings will warm him. His attendants bring in a beautiful young Shunammite woman to sleep with him in an effort to arouse him and heat up his body. But he remains cold and unresponsive.

With David at death's door, his son Adonijah clamors for attention. He is next in line for the crown, and he, like Absalom before him, parades around in a chariot and throws a feast in anticipation of his own coronation. But Nathan the prophet goes to Bathsheba, warning her to consult with David to remind him that he has vowed that Solomon, her son, will be the next king. As his final act, David issues an edict to have Solomon anointed king over Israel and Judah and to sit upon his very throne.

Sing the Man who Judah's Scepter bore,
In that right Hand which held the Crook before;
Who from best Poet, best of Kings did grow;
The two chief Gifts Heav'n could on Man bestow.

Abraham Cowley, *Davideis: A Sacred Poem*

Weak as he is, he finds the strength to give a final charge to his son: "I'm about to go the way of all the earth, but you—be strong; show what you're made of! Do what God tells you. Walk in the paths he shows you."[9]

Jonathan: Forever Best Friend

Is he insane or is he intoxicated with blind faith in God? The Philistine army is camped on the border, prepared to attack the crippled forces of the Israelites commanded by Saul. Jonathan sneaks away with his armor bearer and takes on the enemy in plain daylight. The two of them kill twenty armed men in a matter of minutes. The entire Philistine army falls into disarray and in the end is soundly defeated by Saul's forces. Thus begins Jonathan's career as a warrior, serving under his father Saul.

Yet on that very day, his father is prepared to have him put to death. Saul has made a stupid vow that none of his soldiers are to eat anything until the Philistines are defeated. Having slipped away from the rest of the troops, Jonathan doesn't hear the order. He dips his finger into a honeycomb for nourishment and doesn't give it a thought. Sometime later, Saul tries to consult with God about further battle plans but gets no response. He finds out there has been disobedience in the camp. When he learns Jonathan has eaten the honey against his orders, he is prepared to carry out the death penalty. But his men will have none of it and vow that no harm will come to him, for Jonathan is a brave warrior who has saved them from certain defeat.

When Jonathan sees David kill Goliath, he is in complete awe. The two of them soon commit themselves to each other as brothers, living together in Saul's household. Indeed, Jonathan makes a covenant with David, each vowing his eternal loyalty to the other. David in the meantime is serving Saul so effectively that he is given leadership over the military.

Jonathan at times seems caught between his father and David. Time after time, right in front of his nose, Saul tries to kill David. Yet Jonathan is unconvinced when David comes to him for help. He does in the end, however, warn David when his father accuses him of defending David and when Saul vows to kill David for sure.

Jonathan not only warns David but also renews his vow of undying love. They kiss and weep and bid each other farewell as David escapes with his life. While David is on the run, Jonathan meets up with him and again renews his friendship, promising fidelity and support when he becomes king. That will never happen. On the day Saul dies in battle, so also does Jonathan, leaving his dearest *brother* David grieving inconsolably.

Perhaps what stands out the most in the life of Jonathan is his utter lack of self-promotion and jealousy. As the oldest son of Saul, he is the natural successor to the throne. He is a most capable warrior and no doubt would have served Israel well. It would have been natural for him to resent the young upstart David. He does not. He is committed to him as a friend and convinced that God has chosen him to succeed his father. To that end he pledges his loyalty.

Abigail: Confident and Strong

Her name would not have been recorded in the biblical narrative but for her hot-headed husband Nabal, the Calebite. Abigail is a beautiful and articulate woman. More than that, she is a very competent and capable household manager. Unfortunately, she is married to Nabal, not only a fool but also a bully.

Abigail bringing sustenance to David

When she learns from a servant that Nabal had treated David and his militia inhospitably, she immediately goes into action. After preparing large quantities of foodstuffs and having them loaded on donkeys, she goes out to meet David. When they meet, she begs him to take all the provisions and to allow her to take the blame. What is she thinking? How is she to blame for the actions of her brutish husband? She offers David a lengthy blessing,

Smart Women, Foolish Choices

If Abigail were living today she might be considered a perfect candidate for a recovery group, perhaps Al-Anon or a support group for "women who love too much." Her profile also fits well with the women discussed in the best-selling book, *Smart Women, Foolish Choices.*

Ruth A. Tucker, *Multiple Choices: Making Wise Decisions in a Complicated World,* 111 one that acknowledges his God-anointed role as Israel's king. And she hopes he will one day remember her.

When she returns home, the shearing season celebration is in high gear. Nabal is feasting and drinking himself drunk. She stays clear of him until the next day. By this time he has slept off his hangover and is fully aware of what she is telling him. But now she is not taking the blame. He is responsible for what has happened, and he will face the consequences. It is a shock. He feels a sudden tightness in his chest—a heart attack and everything goes blank. For ten days he lies in a coma. Then he dies.

It is fair to say that Abigail is anything but numb with grief. She is better off without this surly brute, and she knows it. The word of his death soon reaches David, and he wastes no time in sending his servants with a message, asking for Abigail's hand in marriage.

Here she is, an intelligent, independent head of a household. Without Nabal, she now has the very peace David had requested in blessing her. Why would she agree to marry the leader of a wandering ragtag militia? She doesn't even know him. But David has charisma and charm, and she is brought under his spell. She leaves home riding her donkey, accompanied by five attendants, and marries a man on the run.

Unlike his relationship with Bathsheba, David's relationship with Abigail, now a widow, is scandal-free. And unlike Bathsheba, Abigail will suffer severely during her marriage to David. Shortly after they had pledged their vows and had established themselves in the small village of Ziklag, she and his other wife Ahinoam are kidnapped by the Amalekites. The two wives are eventually rescued, but Abigail is never heard from again except as the mother of David's son Kileab, born after the soon-to-be royal family moves to Hebron in Judah.

A Harebrained Girl?

The land, the orchards, the three thousand sheep, the thousand goats were forgotten as if she had been a harebrained girl, she joined the outlaw and shared the outlaw's life.

David Biale, *Eros and the Jews: From Biblical Israel to Contemporary America*, 220

Abigail on the Wild Side

As Abigail rode off behind the provision to meet David, did she feel a thrill and a pull at doing something a little on the wild side? Did she feel that doing this might be the magic she needed to give her life meaning? There is also the suspicion that she had an interest in making an acquaintance with David—such a famous and fascinating outlaw.

Sandra S. Williams, "David and Abigail: A Non-Traditional View"

Bathsheba: Bathing Beauty and Mother of Solomon

Because of her not-so-private bathing episode, Bathsheba has grabbed the headlines over the centuries—far more so than Abigail. Whether they ever met is doubtful. There is no reference to any interaction between the two of them, certainly not to the backbiting so characteristic of other polygamous situations in the Bible.

Before her encounter with David, Bathsheba is living in Jerusalem, her husband Uriah a soldier. She may have struggled with his deployments, as military wives so often do. Theirs was an intermarriage—an Israelite woman with a Hittite man. Such was not uncommon, and Uriah appears to be one of David's most faithful warriors, taking very seriously the military code of conduct.

It is often presumed that Bathsheba is the innocent victim, caught taking her monthly purification bath. She is a mere woman living in a rigidly patriarchal society. And he, after all, is the king, who summons her to his apartment. What choice does she have? But she may have been a more ambitious woman than would appear on the surface. (Later she would take an active role in her son's succession to the throne.)

Is it possible that Bathsheba knows very well she is in full view of the king's balcony? He surely wasn't living in the palace undercover. She has a body to die for, and she knows it. Is she purposely seeking to arouse sexual desire? Bathing, after all, can be a most erotic endeavor, and there surely must have been an option for her to shed her clothes behind closed doors.

But even if she were enticing him, David is the one who acts on the temptation that ends in one of the most notorious sex-and-murder scandals ever. When Bathsheba sends word to him that she is pregnant, there is no clue as to what is going on in her mind. What does she imagine David can do to solve the problem? David is clever, and he wants to pawn this pregnancy off on Uriah. So he graciously offers the soldier a little vacation with his wife.

Bathsheba preparing her bath

Faithful soldier that he is, however, Uriah will not enjoy sexual intimacies while his comrades are at war risking their lives. So David sends Uriah to the front lines to die.

Bathsheba apparently knows nothing about this evil plot, and she may not have ever learned. All she knows is that military officials are knocking at her door to tell her that her husband will be coming home in a body bag. Despite her adulterous relationship with David, she may have truly loved her husband and grieved deeply for him. After the period of mourning is over, she is again summoned by David—this time to marry him.

She is obviously *showing* as she walks down the aisle, and soon thereafter gives birth to a bouncing baby boy. However, the baby takes ill and dies. Both parents are heartbroken. David makes a special point

Power behind the Throne

If Bathsheba is portrayed as passive in her early relationship with David, she becomes strongly active toward the end of David's life in her successful attempt to ensure that her son Solomon will inherit the throne . . . plotting, along with the prophet Nathan and other supporters of Solomon, to convince David that he has promised the kingship to Solomon. David is by now a pathetic figure who had lost control over his sons long ago. The first three of David's sons have already died, and the succession will be decided between the fourth son, Adonijah, and the destined heir, Solomon. The operative familial relationship is the mother-son relationship, and it is emphasized in the way the narrator refers to the characters: "Adonijah, son of Haggith" (1 Kings 1:5), and "Bathsheba, Solomon's mother" (1 Kings 1:11). . . . Bathsheba plays an important role in the succession of Solomon to the throne.

Adele Berlin, "Bathsheba: Bible"

of consoling Bathsheba, and shortly afterward she is pregnant again. She gives birth to another boy, whom they name Solomon.

Because of David's grave sin, God punishes him—and Bathsheba also suffers. They are forced to flee Jerusalem due to internal strife. Her life is hardly that of a pampered queen. She knows all too well that there is always rivalry at court. Solomon's older brothers might at any time take action against him. Though Solomon is not next in line to the throne, the deaths of his three older brothers bring him closer.

By now David is old and essentially out of the loop. Bathsheba, in collusion with Nathan the prophet, takes action. In the end, she is the one to secure the throne for her son Solomon.

Concluding Observations

The telling of David's story has captivated Bible scholars, historians, novelists, and filmmakers through the centuries. He is a *boy wonder*, killing bears and lions while herding sheep. Anointed king by the great prophet Samuel, he goes on to kill a giant with one well-placed stone fired from a simple slingshot. Anyone who has ever tried her luck with a primitive slingshot knows this is a stunning feat.

David seems to take his sudden celebrity in stride. There is no parading around town in a chariot, as is later the case with Prince Adonijah. He welcomes the love of Jonathan, having been denied such love and attention back home with his brothers. But David's popularity extends far beyond his closest friendship. He is beloved by women and is able to marry two of the most beautiful women in the land, Abigail and Bathsheba. He is perhaps above all else a musician. He both plays and writes. So the David that captures the hearts of the people is not merely a boy with a good aim. He's a rock star. Without his incredible talent as a lyricist and harpist, David's story would still be mesmerizing. It has all the elements of good and evil in one fascinating character. But added to all the exploits and scandals are psalms that have never grown old. David above all else is God-intoxicated, and his spiritual sensitivities have never been surpassed.

> The earth is the LORD's, and the fulness thereof;
> the world, and they that dwell therein.
>
> For he hath founded it upon the seas,
> and established it upon the floods.
>
> Who shall ascend into the hill of the LORD?
> or who shall stand in his holy place?
>
> He that hath clean hands, and a pure heart;
> who hath not lifted up his soul unto vanity,
> nor sworn deceitfully.
>
> He shall receive the blessing from the LORD,
> and righteousness from the God of his salvation. . . .
>
> Lift up your heads, O ye gates;
> and be ye lift up, ye everlasting doors;
> and the King of glory shall come in.
>
> Who is this King of glory?
> The LORD strong and mighty,
> the LORD mighty in battle.
>
> Lift up your heads, O ye gates;
> even lift them up, ye everlasting doors;
> and the King of glory shall come in.
>
> Who is this King of glory?
> The LORD of hosts, he is the King of glory.[10]

Further Reading

Halpern, Baruch. *David's Secret Demons: Messiah, Murderer, Traitor, King*. Grand Rapids: Eerdmans, 2003.

MacDonald, Nathan. *What Did the Ancient Israelites Eat? Diet in Biblical Times*. Grand Rapids: Eerdmans, 2008.

McKenzie, Steven L. *King David: A Biography*. New York: Oxford University Press, 2002.

Meyers, Carol, ed. *Women in Scripture*. New York: Houghton Mifflin Harcourt, 2000.

Vamosh, Miriam Feinberg. *Food at the Time of the Bible*. Herzlia, Israel: Palphot, 2007.

12

SOLOMON AND A SUCCESSION OF KINGS

Reigns of Good and Bad

"Even Solomon in all his glory," Jesus said, in comparison to the lilies of the field, "was not arrayed like one of these." Jesus had it right. Wildflowers and the beauties of nature in general possess a glory far greater than that of material assets. Jesus also had it right in citing Solomon as the premier example of wealth. No one in ancient biblical times displayed such ostentatious affluence as did Solomon.

His riches, however, did come from God, who promised in a dream that Solomon would receive more than the wisdom he had asked for. "I will give you a wise and discerning heart, so that there will never have been anyone like you, nor will there ever be. Moreover, I will give you what you have not asked for—both wealth and honor—so that in your lifetime you will have no equal among kings."[1]

The wisest of men, Solomon presided as king for forty years over what has become known as Israel's Golden Age. It was an era of peace and prosperity, during which the Temple and the king's palace were built. Solomon would never surpass his father in personal charm and charismatic appeal, but like his father, he also would become a great

Parables, Poems, and Science

His fame spread through all the surrounding nations. He composed 3,000 parables, and 1,005 poems. He discoursed about trees, from the cedars of Lebanon to the hyssop that grows from the wall. He also discoursed about animals, birds, creeping things and fish. Men of all nations came to hear Solomon's wisdom, as did all the kings of the earth who had heard of his wisdom.

Rabbi Ken Spiro, "King Solomon"

poet—more than that, a philosopher and scientist.

Solomon dies before he celebrates his sixtieth birthday, though he is apparently old before his time—perhaps a result of far too many women to contend with. Like Saul and David before him, he does not end well. He does not go out with a bang—surely not in the eyes of God. "As Solomon grew old, his wives turned his heart after other gods."[2]

The book of Ecclesiastes, "the words of the Teacher, son of David, king in Jerusalem," speaks volumes, if indeed written by Solomon. What had all his wealth, women, and wisdom gotten him? In the end, nothing.

> "Meaningless! Meaningless!"
> says the Teacher.
> "Utterly meaningless!
> Everything is meaningless."[3]

Rehoboam, son of Solomon, stubborn and arrogant, succeeds his father, and the kingdom splits. His portion in the south becomes known simply as Judah, while rival King Jeroboam reigns in the north over Israel. This sets the stage for a most trying period in the divided nation's history, particularly in the north, where corrupt kings reign one after another. Among these corrupt kings is Ahab, married to the most corrupt queen of all, Jezebel. But there are also good kings during this era, including Joash, Hezekiah, and Josiah.

The era of the Hebrew kings is central to the biblical story. Beginning with Saul and David, who engaged in civil strife for their titles, it proceeds to Solomon, who reigns in power over twelve united tribes. After his death, kings will take a backseat in the biblical text to the great prophets of the era: Elijah, Elisha, Isaiah, Jeremiah, Amos, and Hosea. No kings will have name recognition equal to that of Saul, David, and Solomon.

Solomon: Reputation for Wealth and Wisdom

Raised in palace luxury, Solomon is the second son of Bathsheba and David. He is still a youth when he succeeds his father as king of Israel, and is no doubt overwhelmed. How can a child barely out of his teens reign over any kingdom, much less a nation of tribes as contentious as this one? Two great men have preceded him, and look what happened to them. The enormous undertaking weighs on him day and night until God comes to him in a dream, almost like a genie in the bottle. Solomon gets one wish. He is encouraged to ask for anything he desires. He asks for wisdom. His rationale for this request shows humility that is not often associated with Solomon: "I'm too young for this, a mere child! I don't know the ropes, hardly know the 'ins' and 'outs' of this job. And here I am, set down in the middle of the people you've chosen, a great people—far too many to ever count."[4]

God is pleased with Solomon's request—particularly because he has not asked for wealth, power, or longevity—so pleased that he gives him riches and splendor as perks. When Solomon awakens, he goes to Jerusalem to worship and throws a feast for his administrative staff and servants. It is in this setting that his wisdom first shines.

Two women who live together and make their livelihood as prostitutes come to him with their bitter dispute. Each in the space of three days has given birth to a baby boy. One of the infants has died, and each of the women is claiming the live baby as her own. Solomon hears their arguments and treats them with respect, with no snide remarks about their profession. But how is he to decide which one is the rightful mother? He has never before laid eyes on either one of them.

Solomon and the prostitutes

Luxury-Loving Leader Destroys a Golden Age

At various stages in his life, David is a ruthless leader, a greedy lover, a vacillating and sorrowful father. . . . In the same way, the biblical Solomon also reveals a darker, weaker side. Solomon eventually betrays his reputation as the pious founder of the Temple, succumbing to the lure of foreign women and gods. His vast harem of Moabite, Ammonite, Edomite, Sidonian, and Hittite wives introduces pagan worship into the holy city. God becomes angry. Once-defeated peoples rise up in rebellion. After Solomon's death, the ten northern tribes of Israel break free and establish a separate kingdom. It is a vivid lesson about how the religious faithlessness of a luxury-loving leader can destroy a golden age.

Israel Finkelstein and Neil Asher Silberman, *David and Solomon: In Search of the Bible's Sacred Kings*, 8–9

His advice to them is the classic illustration of his wisdom. He proposes settling the matter by simply cutting the baby in two parts and giving a half baby to each of them. One prostitute agrees, but the other cries out, begging the king not to kill the baby, but rather to give it to the other woman. Solomon, of course, knows in an instant who the real mother is, and she returns home with her baby boy. But Solomon's wisdom extends far beyond his quick-thinking solutions to everyday problems. People travel from great distances to consult with him and to benefit from his vast knowledge. Israel itself is secure; the people live in peace and contentment. Solomon's reign extends to the surrounding pagan nations, who pay him tribute.

Solomon: First Impressions

If the first impression a person makes is based on physical appearance, then Solomon never really makes a first impression because the Bible doesn't tell us what he looked like. This is in marked contrast to all of Israel's previous kings. Saul is said to have been a handsome young man who stood head and shoulders above everyone else. David is described as good looking, ruddy, and having beautiful eyes. Even Solomon's older brothers merit physical descriptions: no one was as beautiful as Absalom, with his striking long hair, and his younger brother Adonijah is also said to be handsome. . . . But of Solomon's appearance the text says nothing, as if his appearance was completely unremarkable.

Steven Weitzman, *Solomon: The Lure of Wisdom*, 1

Before God had come to him in a dream, Solomon had already made some very significant political decisions. He orders those he considers his greatest potential enemies killed, including his half brother Adonijah as well as Joab, David's army commander. Joab had not only supported Adonijah's succession as king, but he also had been responsible for killing Abner, a murder that must be avenged, even if punishment is delayed.

At the outset of Solomon's reign, Israel had been organized under twelve territorial governors, each of whom was required to collect a tax from his people. This supplied necessary provision for running the government, each region responsible for one month out of the year. In light of Solomon's lavish lifestyle, taxation was critical. Indeed, his reign is a classic example of the poor propping up the extravagant lifestyle of the rich and famous.

Solomon was known for hosting sumptuous banquets, and his household ate very well. Indeed, in a single day, his entire household regularly consumed hundreds of bushels of flour and meal, more than two dozen head of livestock, some one hundred sheep, and an assortment of wild game. The cost of maintaining his vast household and possessions added to the burden placed on the people. His chariot drivers alone numbered some twelve thousand, with tens of thousands of horses to be fed.

Additional costs mount as Solomon prepares to build a temple in Jerusalem. He has the good fortune of having a close friend of his father, Hiram of Tyre, who provides all the cedar necessary for the construction, as well as the artisans skilled in gold and bronze metalwork and sailors and ships for transport. Solomon agrees to pay fair wages for Hiram's lumbermen to cut the cedars and transport them to Jerusalem, but Hiram insists that all he will accept is provisions for his men. Solomon did build his own ships to import gold, silver, ivory, apes, peacocks, and other exotic animals.

When work on the Temple begins, Solomon conscripts ten thousand workers each month to travel to Lebanon to cut down timber, as well as tens of thousands of stonemasons and menial laborers: "Solomon conscripted the descendants of all these [Canaanite] peoples remaining in the land—whom the Israelites could not exterminate—to serve as slave labor."[5] The Temple is lavish, but by no means massive in size: only ninety feet long with a fifteen-foot porch, and thirty feet wide and three stories high—the size of a small church. To the exterior walls, smaller structures are attached.

But if the size is not overly impressive, the splendor of the structure, both interior and exterior, is a magnificent marvel like nothing seen before. The thirty-foot cube that houses the Ark of the Covenant, for example, is gold plated. Indeed, Solomon spares no expense. "Everywhere you looked there was pure gold: gold chains strung in front of the gold-plated Inner Sanctuary—gold everywhere—walls, ceiling, floor, and Altar. Dazzling!"[6]

Everyday *Life*

Wives, Wealth, and Power

Multiple wives were a sign of wealth and prestige in the ancient world, especially for kings who wanted to impress neighboring rulers. But polygamy was also practiced by those seeking to expand their private domain. Indeed, there are dozens of polygamists named in Scripture.

Abraham was convinced that he could not father descendants as numerous as the sands of the sea or the stars in the night sky if he had only a barren wife. So Hagar, a slave girl, became the mother of his first child. Jacob fathers twelve sons by multiple wives and concubines. Gideon, likewise, had many wives and through them seventy sons. David also had many wives and many sons.

But polygamy was surely not God's ideal plan of the husband cleaving to his wife, as outlined in Genesis 2. Time and again, the practice of bigamy or polygamy created serious family and spiritual problems. This is illustrated not only in the lives of Abraham and David and Solomon, but also with Elkanah and his two wives, Hannah and Peninnah. Yet, despite all the pitfalls, the practice continued far beyond the patriarchal era.

Solomon's Downfall

Solomon strengthened his kingdom through marital alliances. Less important kings would give Solomon their daughters in marriage for treaties to be signed, gifts of land, horses and other exchanges. The wives and concubines were no more than tokens of friendship. Even though he married them, many of them he was not personally acquainted with.

Solomon's downfall came because of his disobedience to God, his greed and his love for power and wealth. He had taken many foreign wives, whom he allowed to worship other gods. He even built shrines for the sacrifices of his foreign wives. . . . By the time Solomon had grown old, his heart had been completely changed from [serving] the one and only living God to the other gods of his wives and concubines.

Margaret Minnicks, "Why Solomon had 700 Wives and 300 Concubines"

Solomon's Wisdom—and Weakness

Solomon's image is the ideal convergence of wisdom, opulence, and power in the person of a king. Indeed, Solomon's rule in Jerusalem is a moment when the divine promise comes to its most tangible fulfillment; his reign is a golden age of prosperity, knowledge, and power for all the people of Israel. Forever after, Solomon's rule would be nostalgically recalled as a golden age of spiritual and material fulfillment that might, one day, be experienced again.

Finkelstein and Silberman, *David and Solomon*, 8

The Temple certainly does not rise up overnight. Three years pass before the foundation is fully laid, and it will take another four years before the last detail is finished. The seven years of construction on the Temple are followed by thirteen years of building Solomon's palatial residence, which also includes a public hall for judicial matters. When it is completed, the palace, like the Temple, is an architectural masterpiece. The furnishings and sculptures for both structures are the finest money can buy.

When everything is completed, Solomon sends for the Ark of the Covenant to be housed in the gold-plated inner sanctum, the Holy of Holies. All of Israel comes out for the great celebration, the culmination of which is the prayer of dedication led by King Solomon himself. The words form a powerful paean of praise, a series of requests for forgiveness, and a supplication that seeks God's blessing—and not only upon Israel. Solomon has many connections with people who live beyond his borders, and his prayer continues in a vein not typically associated with a leader of Israel:

> And don't forget the foreigner who is not a member of your people Israel but has come from a far country because of your reputation—people are going to be attracted here by your great reputation, your wonderworking power—and who come to pray to this Temple.
>
> Listen from your home in heaven
> and honor the prayers of the foreigner,
> So that people all over the world
> will know who you are and what you're like,
> And live in reverent obedience before you,
> just as your own people Israel do.[7]

Once the dedication is over, there are cost overruns to consider. Hiram, King of Tyre, had twenty years earlier told Solomon that his cedar for the Temple was being given at no charge. His only expectation was provisions for his men. But over the course of two decades, Hiram had gone far above and beyond the original agreement in his provision of all the cypress and gold needed for the palace, as well as the Temple. He expects to be fairly reimbursed, but Solomon is stingy, offering him only "twenty backwoods hick towns"[8] in Galilee. This in exchange for more than four tons of gold.

Although Solomon had remembered the foreigner in his dedicatory prayer, he treats badly those outside his borders—especially those who had been defeated in battle, conscripting them into forced-labor camps. The product of their labor further supports his sumptuous lifestyle.

Among those in the parade of dignitaries who make their way to the palace is the famed Queen of Sheba. She knows how to impress, and she makes a striking appearance as she enters the gates of Jerusalem with a train of camels loaded with gifts. Solomon is not hard to buy for; she knows exactly what he wants: gold, gems, spices, and more.

She also knows how to flatter, telling him that the acclamations of his wisdom had not been overstated and how fortunate the people are who work closely with him and have opportunity to benefit from his vast knowledge. In return Solomon lavishes gifts on her.

With his staggering assets, Solomon wallows in wealth. There is nothing his gold and silver and precious gems cannot buy. He is ostentatious in his tastes—gold-plated armor and gold dinnerware and almost anything else that could be fashioned from gold. He has a menagerie of exotic animals and an immense wardrobe of the most costly fabrics. His wealth allows him to have any woman he wants. But women will become his Achilles' heel.

His ancestors had multiple wives—three and four, sometimes more. But Solomon amasses trophy wives that rival his stables full of thoroughbreds. He rules over an exotic harem of a thousand: seven hundred wives, three hundred concubines, mostly foreign, who bring their idols with them. For his part, Solomon defies the clear command of God not to marry foreign women who bring their own gods into the household. But he sees himself as above the law. With all his wealth he can do what he pleases. As time passes, he actually begins worshiping many of the foreign gods, indeed, making shrines to them where sacrifices are offered. God is not pleased. Solomon's wealth has no sway with him. God lays out the grave consequences in no uncertain terms.

> Since this is the way it is with you, that you have no intention of keeping faith with me and doing what I have commanded, I'm going to rip the kingdom from you and hand it over to someone else. But out of respect for your father David I won't do it in your lifetime. It's your son who will pay—I'll rip it right out of his grasp. Even then I won't take it all; I'll leave him one tribe in honor of my servant David and out of respect for my chosen city Jerusalem.[9]

Dangerous Prosperity

From glory to vanity, Solomon's life has been an enigma. The king who began his reign in wisdom, love for God, obedience, and prosperity has finished his reign in foolishness, love for women, disobedience, and brokenness. The golden age of Israel serves as a model of the kingdom of God. . . . And the end of the golden age serves as a harsh reminder of how negligence and apathy toward God results in futility. For Solomon, prosperity—both the material and spiritual kind—was dangerous. For us, it's a blessing with a sharp edge.

Walk Thru the Bible, *A Walk Thru the Life of Solomon: Pursuing a Heart of Integrity*, 55

So while Solomon is relishing his riches and women and foreign gods, enemies are joining forces outside his borders, and plots are being hatched inside his kingdom—indeed, with God's blessing. After a forty-year reign, Solomon dies and is buried in Jerusalem, the City of David.

Jeroboam: King Who Made Israel to Sin

Jeroboam is a hard hat, working to shore up the fortified walls securing Solomon's capital city. He is highly competent and is soon promoted to foreman. He's loyal to the king. Then one day, as he is walking on a remote stretch of road outside Jerusalem, he meets the prophet Ahijah, who has a shocking prophecy, complete with an object lesson. Ahijah takes off his brand-new outer garment and tears it into ten pieces, which he hands over to Jeroboam.

These ten pieces of fabric represent the ten tribes—only ten, not twelve. The stunning punch line is that Jeroboam will rule over the ten tribes as king of Israel. If he is faithful to God alone, God promises him that his dynasty will be long and prosperous.

Jeroboam is the son of Nebat and his wife Zeredah. He hails from the tribe of Ephraim, with no close ties to the lines of either Saul or David. Word of the prophecy gets out, and Jeroboam is quickly placed on King Solomon's *most wanted* list. With a price on his head, he flees to Egypt, where he resides until he receives word that King Solomon is dead. Then he heads back to Israel, where he is hailed as king.

But Jeroboam is insecure now that Rehoboam has succeeded his father, and he fears his people will want to make pilgrimages to worship at the glorious Temple in Jerusalem. And once they start worshiping in Solomon's Temple, they will suppose his son is their rightful king. And then sure as summer follows spring, Jeroboam will be dead—murdered by his own people. A most dreadful scenario, but he nips it in the bud by fashioning two golden calves.

Golden calves? Has he forgotten the account of Aaron and the Israelites while Moses was on Mount Sinai? What is he thinking? Be that as it may, he tells the people they need not travel all the way to Jerusalem to worship. They now can go to either Bethel or Dan, where they can bow before an idol of gold.

In order to cover all his bases, Jeroboam constructs shrines and discharges the rightful Levite priests. He then appoints new priests, most of them utterly unqualified. He also declares a holiday to celebrate the New Year—a time of festivity and feasting to make the people feel as though they aren't missing anything by not worshiping in Jerusalem.

All the while God is biding his time until Jeroboam himself is making a sacrifice at the altar of the golden calf in Bethel. A prophet from Judah stops by and begins shouting at the altar, prophesying that a new king named Josiah will be born in the house of David who will destroy Jeroboam's altars, but not before the priests' bones are sacrificed on them. It all sounds crazy, but the holy man supports the message with a sign: this very altar will crack into two pieces, and the sacrifice on it will fall to the ground. And so it happens.

Jeroboam, embarrassed and outraged, reaches out to grab the man and have him arrested, only to suffer paralysis in his arm. When Jeroboam cries out for the holy man to pray for healing, his arm is restored. Returning to Judah, the holy man, having been deceived into disobedience to God, is killed by a lion. His burial site serves as a reminder to the people who pass by that this holy man's prophecy against Jeroboam will indeed come true.

Still Jeroboam continues in his wicked ways. Through the old prophet Ahijah, he learns of God's judgment on him, which will be manifested first in his son Abijah's death, but even more in his own death and those of his male descendants. In the years that follow, Jeroboam's forces suffer some half million casualties at the hands of Judah. After a twenty-two-year reign, Jeroboam's son Nadab succeeds him. Baasha, one of Nadab's own soldiers, assassinates him, declares himself king, and then assassinates Jeroboam's remaining male descendants, thus fulfilling the prophecy of Ahijah.

Jeroboam becomes the prototype of an evil king and is later repeatedly referred to as *Jeroboam, son of Nebat, who made Israel to sin*—anything but a flattering epitaph.

Wine Bottles and Kings

Some people, particularly those who do not consume significant quantities, may not realize that certain wine bottle sizes are named for biblical kings.

Name	Volume	Commonly used for
Jeroboam	3 liters	Bordeaux
Rehoboam	4.5 liters	Champagne and Burgundy
Solomon	20 liters	Champagne

Rehoboam: Successor to Solomon

Meanwhile, back in Judah, the political situation has deteriorated during the two decades of Jeroboam's reign in Israel. Rehoboam, son of Solomon, had taken the reins of government at age forty-one and continues as king until his late fifties. His mother, an Ammonite, is one of his father's seven hundred wives. Rehoboam therefore does not grow up in a God-fearing household, and he leads Judah down the wrong road. Indeed, under his rule, Judah, like Israel, is overrun with shrines dedicated to false gods, some of them featuring male prostitutes who combine idol worship with sex acts.

As Solomon's son and chosen successor, Rehoboam had traveled to Shechem after his father's death. There he had expected to be crowned king. But he ran into a snag—Jeroboam and the Israelites. They had been very dissatisfied with the rule of Solomon, whose wealth was derived largely from their hard labor. They agreed to pledge their loyalty to Rehoboam only if he eased up on them and lowered his expectations. He told them he needed time to consider.

After three days, he rejects the wise counsel of his father's closest advisors in favor of the foolish advice of the young fellows he hangs around with. He returns to the people and announces that he will have none of their bargaining. In fact, they should expect to work harder under him, with more severe punishment if they slack off. The people are in no mood to hear such a message, and they essentially run Rehoboam out of town. When he sends his father's administrator Adoniram to oversee the Israelite workers, they murder him.

The message to Rehoboam is loud and clear. The ten northern tribes that had been ruled by Saul and later David and Solomon are simply not going to buckle under the rule of the grandson of David. They have suffered too long, and now they are breaking free. Rehoboam, however, is not taking this lying down. He is back in the safety of Jerusalem in control of Judah, but is determined to bring the remaining ten tribes under his rule. He prepares for a holy battle with upwards of two hundred thousand men. But before his army even sets out for Israel, God, through the prophet Shemaiah, speaks to Rehoboam and stops the soldiers in their tracks. They are to go back to their homes and forgo any attack. So war between Judah and Israel is at least temporarily put on hold.

King Rehoboam

Rehoboam spends the next few years fortifying the border towns of Judah and fully secures his hold on the southern kingdom. But Judah has other enemies. Some years into Rehoboam's reign, Egypt attacks, pillaging Jerusalem, stealing the priceless treasures of Solomon, including the gold inlay and sculptures in the Temple. If this is not bad enough, war then breaks out with Israel and continues for most of his reign. He is succeeded by his son Abijah, who carries on with the wicked ways of his father, ruling for only three years, during which time his armies continually battle those of Jeroboam.

Asa: *Good* King Who Does Not Finish Well

Idol worship had been promoted by three successive kings—Solomon, Rehoboam, and Abijah—when Asa becomes king of Judah. His reign lasts more than forty years, during which time seven kings of Israel come and go. During the first decade of his reign Judah enjoys an era of peace, allowing Asa time to build up the kingdom's defenses. When he is attacked by the enemy, God gives him victory. Indeed the victory is so stunning that "many from Israel had left their homes and joined forces with Asa when they saw that God was on his side."[10]

Prompted by a message from the prophet Azariah, Asa is determined to rid the land of its foreign gods and shrines. He sets a date for a religious revival in Jerusalem and invites the people to come. They sacrifice thousands of animals and, amid the sound of joyful music, promise to be true to the God of their fathers.

No one is exempt from this housecleaning. Not even Maacah, the queen mother. Everything must go, including her sacred phallic pole. And with a royal decree, she loses her status as queen mother. Asa is determined to bring Judah back to God. The Temple in Jerusalem is refurbished and the gold and silver relics are restored. But not for long. The priceless treasures are used to fund the continual battles with Israel.

Throughout Asa's reign, however, Judah is relatively stable in comparison to Israel, with its continual succession of evil rulers. Asa is essentially a good king, but he fails to demolish all the pagan sex shrines, and he makes an unholy alliance with King Ben-Hadad of Syria against the king of Israel. The prophet Hanani brings God's word of reproach to Asa, telling him that he can expect continual war for the remainder of his reign. Rather than repenting, Asa arrests the prophet.

In his later years Asa suffers serious health problems, his feet swelling so much that he can hardly walk. Had he only turned to God in repentance instead of relying on the court physicians, such problems could have been averted. Nevertheless, he has gone down in history as a *good* king.

Ahab and Jezebel: Israel's Power Couple

When Asa is old and nearing the end of his reign, a change is also occurring in Israel.

Daring, Charming, Rich, and Evil

King Ahab was brilliant, daring, charming, and rich—everything but true. His Hebrew name suggests "God is a close relative," but his life belied his name. According to Israel's historian, he did more evil in the sight of the Lord than any other man . . . and he did so as the pawn of his shady lady, the infamous Jezebel.

David Roper, *Elijah: A Man like Us*, 13–14

King Omri dies after twelve years of defying God and fighting Judah. His son and successor Ahab will reign for twenty-two years and bring a certain amount of stability to Israel, though he will go down in history as the wickedest king of all.

Ahab's name does not stand alone. It is most often linked with that of his wife Jezebel. Like most of the kings before him, Ahab marries to strengthen political alliances. Jezebel is the daughter of King Ethbaal of Sidon, and through her, the worship of Baal becomes commonplace. But Baal is not a solitary god among the Israelites. Idols and shrines dot the towns and countryside. Though a worshiper of idols, King Ahab does not ignore ominous messages purporting to come from God. So when Elijah shows up talking famine, Ahab is upset and imagines that killing the messenger might annul the message. But Elijah, now with a price on his head, escapes Ahab's vengeance.

All of Israel suffers while Ahab sends out scouts looking for Elijah. The famine becomes so severe that Ahab summons his palace administrator Obadiah to go out and search for any spring and stream that may still have water. The king agrees to go in one direction while Obadiah goes another. While he is out hunting for water, Obadiah meets Elijah. With Elijah's prodding, Obadiah returns to Ahab with the message that Elijah is on his way.

After nearly three years of hunting for the prophet, Ahab is no doubt surprised that Elijah would risk his life to come and meet him. Ahab doesn't mince words when he sees Elijah: "So it's you, old troublemaker!"[11] It turns out Elijah is there to make a wager with Ahab: he and God will prevail over the prophets of Baal.

Ahab sends for his prophets to appear at Mount Carmel for a contest between Baal and God, between Ahab's 450 prophets of Baal and Elijah. Each side prepares an ox to be sacrificed on the altar. Each side prays the sacrifice will be burned up without their actually lighting a fire. God and Elijah prevail; the prophets of Baal are killed; the drought ends, and the rains descend in a torrent.

Rushing home to Jezebel, Ahab tells her what has transpired. She is furious. She immediately sends Elijah a message vowing to get even: within twenty-four hours, he will be as dead as the prophets of Baal. But her words are hollow.

Despite his detractors, Ahab is not a thoroughly evil man. He rules Israel effectively much of the time and is noted for the ivory palace he built and the frontier towns he fortified. On occasion he even takes heed of God's prophets. Therefore, he wins battles over his enemies. After defeating the army of King Ben-Hadad of Syria, he lets the king live, in blatant disobedience of God's orders. He even makes a covenant with him and regards him as a brother. But one of God's prophet's delivers a stinging message telling him that for letting Ben-Hadad live, Ahab will pay with his own life and the lives of his people.

Furious with both the prophet and God, Ahab arrives home only to confront another matter—seemingly minor in comparison to all he's been through. Naboth owns land adjacent to the palace. The king would like it for himself—and no doubt Jezebel would like it too. It's a great vineyard, but Ahab claims he wants to turn it into a vegetable garden. Ahab has money and tells Naboth he will give him a much better vineyard in trade. But Naboth likes his land, which has long been in the family, and he refuses the offer.

Ahab goes home upset—in such a funk that he refuses to eat. Jezebel wants to know what the problem is, and when he tells her, she belittles him. Why doesn't he, the king of Israel, *man up*? How dare Naboth think he can say *no* to the king? What happens next is reminiscent of King David's actions when he murders Uriah in order to marry Bathsheba, especially as his behavior is summed up by Nathan the prophet—a rich man taking a poor man's only lamb for his own feast. The difference in this case is that the evil offender is not the king, but the king's wife.

Jezebel tells Ahab to get a grip on himself and get out of his funk. She will handle the details of Naboth's vineyard. As it turns out, she devises a creative scheme. She sends messages that bear Ahab's royal seal and purport to be from his hand, ordering officials to throw a grand feast with Naboth seated as one of the dignitaries. Then, while he is enjoying the banquet, someone is to jump up in horror, accusing him of cursing both God and the king. The invited guests will have no choice but to ask him to step outside and be stoned to death. Thus it happens.

Then on Jezebel's orders, Ahab goes next door to put up a sign that the property is under new ownership. He lingers, plotting out how his workers will cultivate the ground and make new gardens—or maybe he'll just decide to maintain the wonderful vineyard as it is. Suddenly he's interrupted by his archenemy. Elijah has dared to enter *his* vineyard without an invitation. He might have called out his body guards and put an end to this nuisance once and for all, but he doesn't. He listens to the prophet's warnings of terrible doom to befall Ahab's household.

Indeed, influenced by Jezebel, Ahab had actually expanded his false-god collection and had become more involved in sexually explicit religious rituals. But now he tears his kingly robes in an act of repentance. He dresses in a pauper's attire and takes up fasting. In response, God seems to relent and does not bring down Ahab's kingdom in his lifetime.

Ahab would end up dying on the battlefield, though not gallantly in hand-to-hand combat. He forms an alliance with Jehoshaphat of Judah against the Arameans. He knows the enemy is out to get him, so he is in disguise, covered from head to toe in armor. By chance, a stray arrow penetrates a seam in the armor. He is mortally wounded, but he continues to fight until he bleeds to death just before sundown.

Jezebel, however, lives on, ruling through her sons Ahaziah and Joram. Ahaziah essentially continues the ways of his mother, while living a life of debauchery. Often drunk, he falls out of a window (perhaps prefiguring his mother's death) and dies sometime later of his injuries. Brother Joram succeeds him, and to his credit, he removes some of the shrines of Baal, but he worships idols, and under his rule the nation continues its idolatrous practices. He dies at the hand of Jehu, an army commander who becomes Israel's next king.

Jehu is the one who makes certain Jezebel is severely punished for her unspeakable wickedness. When he and his men lay siege to the town of Jezreel, Jezebel defies him openly. In fact, she stands in her palace window hurling insults down at him. Jehu commands her bodyguards to hurl her out the upper-story window. Her blood spatters on the palace walls, after which she is run over by horses. Jehu then strides inside his new palace and sits down for a feast. When he later orders his lieutenants to go outside and check on the queen mother, all that remain are her skull, hands, and feet. This is what Elijah had foretold—that wild dogs would feast on the body of Jezebel.

King Jehu: A Man of Action

A military officer anointed king of Israel by one of Elisha's student prophets, Jehu is charged with carrying out the curse against Ahab and his extended family. He is a man of action and wastes no time in disposing

Jehoshaphat, Jehoram, Ahaziah, and Athaliah

While Ahab rules over Israel, Jehoshaphat, son of Asa, is king of Judah. These two readily join forces to take back territory from their mutual enemies. But unlike Ahab, Jehoshaphat is a righteous king. He rules for a quarter century over Judah—one of the high points in that nation's history. He even attempts to construct a maritime fleet, and he reestablishes the system of judges, positioning one in each of the fortified cities of Judah. In fact, during his reign Judah and Israel make peace after decades of conflict. The alliance is reinforced by the marriage—though without God's approval—of Jehoshaphat's son Jehoram to Ahab's daughter Athaliah.

But this king of Judah is remembered most for his tearing down the altars of Baal and reinstituting the worship of God. Jehoram succeeds his father as King of Judah for eight years. To secure his position, his first act is to kill his six brothers and any officials who may be loyal to them. With his wife Athaliah, daughter of Ahab and Jezebel, he brings back Baal worship. For all of this and for killing his brothers, Judah is punished by a devastating plague and numerous attacks by enemies.

As for Jehoram, he suffers from a terrible disease, as Elijah had prophesied. His ailment is most likely colon cancer. He dies writhing in pain. So disgusted with him were the people that they did not inter him in a royal burial plot. Ahaziah, at age twenty-two, succeeds his father as king, with his evil mother Athaliah hovering in the wings. After he is chased down and murdered by Jehu, Athaliah seizes power and slaughters the whole royal family in order to secure her own status. Her bloody reign lasts six years, until her grandson Joash is brought out of hiding and crowned king. She is dragged out of the temple, where she had tried to interrupt the coronation, and is struck down near the palace stables.

of his rivals, including King Joram, whom he kills with an arrow as he seeks to escape in his chariot. He also kills Ahaziah king of Judah, one of Ahab's shirttail relations. An even more stunning deed is the decapitation of all seventy of Ahab's sons. Jehu, whose headquarters are in Jezreel, then has the heads piled up at the gate of the city. After that he tracks down and kills other relatives and associates of Ahab. But it doesn't stop there. Ahaziah's relatives are wiped out as well, and after that anyone in Samaria who had been associated with Ahab is slaughtered.

With all this accomplished, Jehu goes after the Baal priests and worshipers. He sets up a sting operation, sending out word that there will be a mass worship celebration at the temple of Baal. People come from all over, filling the temple to overflowing. Jehu carries out the rituals as his commandos wait for the signal. When he has finished, they attack and massacre everyone who has come, then demolish the temple and all its sacred relics.

For accomplishing the task of ridding Israel of all descendants and relatives of Ahab and all remnants of Baal worship, God promises Jehu that his sons will rule the nation for the next four generations. But Jehu himself does not steadfastly follow God's laws. He reigns over Israel for twenty-eight years, and when he dies he is buried in the family plot in Samaria.

Joash: Boy King Reigns Nearly a Half Century

Joash, the new king of Judah, will please God for most of his forty-year reign, although he does not destroy the pagan sex shrines. Only seven years old when he becomes king, Joash, with the tutelage of the priest Jehoiada, brings Israel back to the worship of God. With Jehoiada's help Joash collects a special tax to restore the Temple to its onetime grandeur. But after Jehoiada's death at age one hundred thirty, worship of God deteriorates as the Temple is desecrated and people go back to their false gods. Despite prophetic warnings, Joash does nothing to stop the evil—not even when Jehoiada's son Zechariah comes with a portentous message. In fact, Joash orders the stoning of Zechariah.

The following year Judah is attacked by Syrian forces, who destroy Joash's military and leave him severely wounded. While he is in bed hoping to recover, two of his servants, still angry over the stoning of Zechariah, kill him. He dies at age forty-seven, and is buried without the customary royal rituals. He is succeeded by his son Amaziah, who reigns twenty-nine years in Jerusalem. He lived a mostly righteous life, but in later years took to worshiping the gods of the neighboring Edomites. He did, however, avenge his father's murder by killing the two assassins.

King Hezekiah: A Deadly Boil and a Sundial

At twenty-five, Hezekiah succeeds his father Ahaz, king of Judah, who was an

Leprous King Uzziah

Uzziah could have been one of the greatest kings in Israel's history. He served for 52 years, more than half a century; that's longer than David or Solomon. He was a great military leader; he led the nation into a period of economic growth and security. He could have truly been the greatest king, and yet the Bible tells us in verse 16 [2 Chron.] that ". . . when he became strong, his heart was so proud that he acted corruptly, and he was unfaithful to the Lord his God." He had military and economic power, but that wasn't enough! All of that power went to his head, and he wanted more. He wanted the ability to serve in the temple. That was the one thing he could not do.

And so the Bible tells us that he "entered the temple of the Lord to burn incense on the altar of incense." The king knew he shouldn't be doing this. Everybody knew that only the priests were allowed in the temple. . . . God struck him with leprosy on the forehead. As far as I can tell, Uzziah became the first king of God's people to ever be struck with leprosy. The Bible tells us that King Uzziah was rushed out of the temple. Smitten by the Lord, King Uzziah lived the rest of his life in a separate house, completely cut off from the temple, and his son [Jotham] took over the daily responsibilities of the king. This one act of rebellion ruined his reputation as a good king, and he lived the rest of his life in quarantine, alone.

Baxter T. Exum, "King Uzziah"

idolatrous and wicked king who actually sacrificed one of his own sons in a pagan ritual. Hezekiah, who reigns for thirty years, does not follow in his father's footsteps. His first major initiative is the reconsecration of his subjects to the service of God, followed by a purification ceremony of the dissolute priesthood, a celebratory rededication of the Temple, and destruction of remaining pagan shrines.

Hezekiah then does what no king in Judah had ever done since the division following the reign of Solomon. He invites all the northern tribes to Jerusalem for a proper celebration of the Passover. These acts of spiritual renewal result in a sincere outpouring of gifts and tithes that strain the storage facilities of the Temple. And God is well pleased.

But danger lurks on the horizon. Hezekiah is able to drive the Philistines out of the land, but Judah is overwhelmed by the Assyrian king Sennacherib, who lays siege to Jerusalem. Hezekiah does lead a successful revolt against the occupying Assyrians, but can do little more against Assyria's massive military might. Amid his weakness, the king apologizes for the revolt and strips the Temple and shrines of gold and silver as a bribe to buy time and keep the Assyrian king from attacking.

Hezekiah shores up Jerusalem's fortifications and cuts off the water supply outside the city to foil enemy forces. He likewise builds up the store of arms and rallies the people so they will be prepared to defend their city.

But the Assyrian king's messengers make a public announcement to Hezekiah's subjects, telling them they will be far better off to peacefully submit to Assyrian rule than to trust the impotent king Hezekiah. When Hezekiah learns of the threats, he rips his clothes, dons sackcloth, goes to the Temple with his aides and priests, and forwards a message to the prophet Isaiah. Isaiah sends back good news. But the threats against Hezekiah and his kingdom keep coming.

Finally Hezekiah falls on his face before God and begs God to save Judah from the mighty Assyrian army. God answers and sends an angel, who slaughters nearly two hundred thousand Assyrian troops. Hezekiah is now free from the terrible threat that has been hanging over him. But his problems are not over.

Not long after this, Hezekiah falls ill from a very serious boil. He learns from the prophet Isaiah that he will not recover and that he should make preparations for dying. Isaiah leaves, and Hezekiah weeps and begs God for mercy. His prayer is barely over when Isaiah returns with a favorable report. In three days Hezekiah will be completely healed. Besides that, God is giving him fifteen more years to live.

On Isaiah's instructions, Hezekiah prepares a potion of figs for the healing. But he is insecure. How can he know for sure whether God is speaking or whether this is just some hocus-pocus? He asks for a sign. Isaiah gives him an option. God can make the sundial go either forward ten degrees or backward the same distance. His decision. Hezekiah considers it more difficult to make the instrument go backward, so that is his choice, and God makes it happen. Here is a miracle reminiscent of Joshua's battle when the sun stood still.

During his fifteen extra years, instead of becoming a more righteous king, he becomes haughty, no doubt exaggerating his own importance because God had turned the sundial backward just for him. God is upset by his attitude and takes it out on Jerusalem and all of Judah. Realizing his sin, Hezekiah repents, and God's wrath is appeased.

During the last decade of his life Hezekiah amasses great wealth, more, it would seem, than any other king apart from Solomon. And he's not shy about showing off his wealth. Among his treasures are not only gold, silver, and gems, but also livestock and land—and whole cities. There is apparently no resentment among the people because on his death, all Judah turns out to honor him. He is succeeded by his son Manasseh, who does evil in the sight of the Lord.

Josiah: Beloved King Who Follows God's Laws

Josiah is a mere boy—anointed king at eight years old. He reigns as king of Judah for thirty-one years, a reign that begins with his mother Jedidah as regent. As kings go, he ranks near the top, alongside his great-grandfather Hezekiah.

Josiah's birth was unique among all the kings. It had been part of a prophecy of judgment against King Jeroboam some three hundred years earlier that a son named Josiah would be born into David's family. This king, it was foretold, would demolish the altar at Bethel, dig up bones of evil priests, and burn them on the altar. That prophecy is fulfilled by Josiah, who initiates a wholesale cleansing of the land of all its false gods.

At age twenty-six, more than halfway through his reign, Josiah makes arrangements to have the Temple repaired. As the construction is moving forward, the high priest Hilkiah discovers the Book of the Law that had long been gathering dust. The book is brought to Josiah and he tears his clothes. He is horrified that this book has been left untended and unread. He fears that God's anger will explode, so he asks his spiritual advisors to pray to God for guidance on how to respond to the words written therein.

Hilkiah and the four others are at their wit's end. Who can help figure out exactly what God is saying in this book? Then it comes to them. There is a prophet living in Jerusalem. Her name is Huldah. All five go to consult with her. Bad news. She prophesies doom and gloom on Judah. God will judge his people because they have abandoned him and worshiped false gods.

But Josiah acts quickly. When he hears Huldah's prophecy, he appoints Hilkiah to be in charge of decontaminating the Temple by disposing of anything, dead or alive, that smacks of idol worship. Incense, relics, pagan priests, everything must go—and not in Jerusalem only. Throughout the country there is a thorough housecleaning. Only then is Josiah prepared to lead the people in a celebration of the Passover, which had not been commemorated since before the time of the judges.

During much of Josiah's reign, foreign powers are not pressing down on Judah's borders. With the Assyrian empire in decline, he is able to rule from Jerusalem without interference. He might have lived on and ruled longer than any other king, but he cannot resist leading his army in an attack against the Egyptian Pharaoh who is passing nearby with his mighty army. To his credit, the Pharaoh warns Josiah that he has no intention of harassing him or his people. In the name of God, he begs him to stay neutral. Josiah, however, refuses to listen to God, who warns not to attack. Josiah is wounded by an arrow and taken back to Jerusalem, where he dies.

He is a beloved king, and his funeral is a time of great sorrow for the people. Jeremiah offers the eulogy—a lament that would be sung by choirs for generations to come.

Concluding Observations

Who can possibly keep all these kings—since Saul and David—straight? Those who reign over Judah are easily confused with those many more who reign over Israel. Some are good; most are bad. But bad and good are categories that are easily blurred, especially when it comes to kingly behavior. Yet these kings are some of the most fascinating characters in the Bible.

Solomon, son of David, is of course the most famous of them all. His sin sets the stage for those who will follow. What if he had acted differently and followed in the ways of the Lord? Had he set a good example and trained his son Rehoboam to faithfully serve God, how different the history of the Israelites might have been. The kingdom might not have been divided, and wars upon wars might not have been fought. Solomon, though wealthy and wise, would never attain the timeless popularity or venerable reputation of his father King David. Yet Solomon's reputation has not dimmed even today, especially among certain Baptists. A Google search shows many results for King Solomon Baptist Church in cities across America: Memphis, Detroit, Abilene, Colorado Springs, Louisville, Little Rock, Jacksonville, and elsewhere.

Sandwiched in between both good and bad kings of Israel and Judah are fiery prophets of God. Among the most prominent are Elijah and his successor Elisha.

Further Reading

Finkelstein, Israel, and Neil Asher Silberman. *David and Solomon: In Search of the Bible's Sacred Kings*. New York: Simon and Schuster, 2006.

Knapp, C. *Kings of Judah*. Dubuque, IA: ECS Ministries, 2004.

Walk Thru the Bible. *A Walk Thru the Life of Solomon: Pursuing a Heart of Integrity*. Grand Rapids: Baker Books, 2009.

Weitzman, Steven. *Solomon: The Lure of Wisdom*. New Haven: Yale University Press, 2011.

13

ELIJAH AND ELISHA

Prophets with Power

Elijah and Elisha, twin prophets from Sunday-school days—one easily confused with the other. No other prophets are so tightly paired together. And for good reason. Elisha took up the mantle that Elijah had left behind as the chariot and fiery horses swung low in the midst of a whirlwind *comin' for to carry him home*. What an ending. What a way to go.

But for Elisha, this spectacular event was alarming. He did not even have a chance to say good-bye. He cried out in anguish, "My father, my father, the chariot of Israel, and the horsemen thereof."[1] Then he tore his clothes in grief. Now Elisha is on his own.

Both of these E-prophets pronounced the wrath of God on those who worshiped false gods, and both worked miracles. But as is so often true, the disciple does not surpass the master. In this case, the youthful successor can never quite reach the heroic stature of the elder statesman. Indeed, no prophet soars to such a lofty summit as does Elijah when he takes down the prophets of Baal. Ending his life in a chariot ride only enhances his legendary star power—star power so great that his anticipated return is heralded centuries later.

Indeed, the Old Testament ends with Malachi prophesying the coming of the Messiah. How will the people know the Messiah has come? God will send a forerunner: "See, I will send the prophet Elijah to you before that great and dreadful day of the LORD comes."[2] Some four hundred years later the angel Gabriel says of John the Baptist: "And he will go on before the Lord, in the spirit and power of Elijah."[3] He even looks like Elijah, a wild man of the desert.

Perhaps the most extraordinary event that would mark Elijah's high standing in Scripture is his appearance alongside Jesus and Moses on the Mount of Transfiguration. Peter, James, and John are stunned, and as they are walking back down the mountain with Jesus, they ask why teachers of the law have been saying that Elijah must return before the Messiah does. Jesus responds: "To be sure, Elijah comes and will restore all things. But I tell you, Elijah has already come, and they did not recognize him, but have done to him everything they wished. In the same way the Son of Man is going to suffer at their hands."[4]

Jesus is forewarning them of his own anguishing death on a cross, having just stood alongside the man who took a joyride to heaven, never having experienced death.

That Elijah's earthly life ends in such a dramatic fashion is not the only reason he far surpasses Elisha as a biblical character. Elijah is presented with a more well-developed personality. Religious seekers through the centuries have resonated with his bipolar tendencies. He's on the mountaintop of euphoria, only to sink into the valley of deep despair. The still small voice of God that whispers on the wind echoes through history in the lonely caverns of the soul.

A Standout among Peer Prophets

Others before him had uttered words of chastisement and calls to the straight path. Later prophets . . . would vigorously intervene in national life, warning of evils to come because of Northern Israel's sins. None appear in the pages of Scripture with more power than does Elijah, called by God to wrest the kingdom from worship of the Canaanite fertility god Baal. . . . The personal lives of other prophets active in the region were forgotten. . . . How different Elijah seems to be from his peers . . . his gestures, vocabulary, and people's specific reactions to him in striking anecdotes. . . . Elijah's personality . . . is also more vivid than that of other great biblical figures. . . . He always seems to have done, said, and dared more than others.

Jane Ackerman, *Elijah: Prophet of Carmel*, 2–3

Elisha will always play second fiddle to Elijah. Although his faithfulness to God and his record of miracles rank alongside or above those of his mentor, when it comes to biblical scholarship, biographical writings, music, art, and popular culture, Elijah wins hands down.

Elijah: From Tishbe to the Transfiguration

He is a bad-news prophet. Israel has had enough problems without him showing up and pitching a prophecy of doom and gloom. God has decreed a drought, not just for a single season but for seasons to follow. And not merely a drought with below-average rainfall. This will be a weather pattern so dry that not even dew will appear in the morning. Elijah leaves the message for king Ahab and hightails it away before the king has time to react.

Hailing from the town of Tishbe in Gilead, Elijah seems almost to appear from out of nowhere. His past is a blank slate. But God has beckoned, and he follows orders. Having delivered the prophecy, he flees east beyond the Jordan River to hide in a ravine where there is a stream of fresh water. God's directions had been clear: "Get thee hence, and turn thee eastward, and hide thyself by the brook Cherith, that is before Jordan."[5]

Is this the place where he will die of starvation? Surely not. God continues: "And it shall be, that thou shalt drink of the brook; and I have commanded the ravens to feed thee there."[6] But the water lasts only so long. Soon Elijah is sitting by a dry streambed. The land is parched. Now what? God instructs him to go to Zarephath in Sidon (ironically, the former home of Queen Jezebel), where he will find a generous widow who will take him in.

When he arrives in the town, he spots a woman picking up sticks for her fire. He asks her for a drink and a little something to eat. She tells him she has no food, not even a crust of bread. In fact, she is about to take the last bit of flour and oil and make a final meal for her son and herself. Her only option, she reasons, is to give up on life and die with her boy. Elijah instructs her to use the last bit of flour in the barrel and the last few drops of oil to prepare a meal for him and assures her that she will always have just enough left to feed herself and her son as long as the famine lasts.

So despite the terrible drought, the little household is fed. Sometime later the widow's son takes ill and eventually stops breathing. Since she had seen the miraculous power of God working through this visiting prophet, it would seem reasonable that the woman would plead with the prophet to heal her son. Instead she blames Elijah and his God: "Why did you ever show up here in the first place—a holy man barging in, exposing my sins, and killing my son?"[7]

Elijah orders her to bring her son's body to him, and he carries it to his upper-story guest quarters. He lays the boy down on the bed and stretches himself over the body, calling on God to restore him to life. Elijah prays, and the young lad comes back to life. His mother's grief is turned to joy; she now recognizes Elijah as a true prophet of God.

Later on, more than two years into the famine, God tells Elijah to appear before Ahab. Without protest or even evidence that he fears for his life, Elijah heads off to meet his archenemy. Along the way he meets Obadiah, a high official in King Ahab's court who happens to be a God-fearing man. Indeed, Obadiah is so faithful to God that he risked his own life to hide and feed one hundred prophets in caves when Jezebel had vowed to kill them. Elijah asks the very reluctant Obadiah to inform Ahab that he's on his way.

When Elijah confronts Ahab, he shows no sign of insecurity. He is following God's orders, and he is convinced God will not let him down. When Ahab accuses him of causing Israel's trouble, he turns the tables and accuses Ahab of abandoning God and worshiping Baal. Then he makes his bold proposal—a public showdown between God and Baal. He explains the rules and Ahab offers no objection. In fact, he rises to the occasion and calls not only the prophets of Baal but all of Israel to come out and watch the spectacle.

Everyday *Life*

Religious Syncretism in the Promised Land

Elijah's face-off with false prophets in a showdown between Yahweh and Baal was not an isolated confrontation. Indeed, the religion that competed most ardently for the hearts of the Israelites was Baal worship. The legends that formed this religion were diverse, and they differed somewhat from region to region. But they all focused primarily on nature and fertility. The farming seasons marked the religious year.

Marduk—the greatest of the pantheon of gods—is the creator god of the heavenly bodies as well as the earth. Lesser gods, particularly Tiamat, do battle with Marduk; thus the never-ending struggle with nature's malevolence—floods, winds, drought, pestilence, and infestations of all kinds. This cosmic war is fought every season of the year, with Marduk bringing new life each spring and Tiamat seeking to undermine the bounty.

Such beliefs proliferated in Canaan, and the Israelites flirted with this spiritual system that sometimes seemed more relevant to them than the worship of Yahweh. Whenever they observed their pagan neighbors prospering on the land, they were tempted to cover their bases and add Baal worship to their own religious customs. Yahweh was often seen as the god who had in the past defeated the Pharaoh and helped wage bloody battles. But for a farming culture, a nature religion was all too tempting. Syncretism, rather than wholesale conversion to another religion, was the greatest sin that beset the generations of Israelites who settled in the Promised Land.

Ba'al and Yahweh

While we have no surviving Canaanite religious texts, the accounts of Ba'al worship in the Old Testament correspond closely to the existing versions of the Ba'al myth and what we know of religious practices in surrounding areas. The influence of this religious system on Israel can hardly be overestimated. Contrary to how some statements in the biblical traditions are often understood, the problem that faced Israel through most of its history was not that the people totally abandoned Yahweh for the worship of Ba'al. Rather the problem was syncretism, the blending of Yahweh worship with Ba'al worship.

Dennis Bratcher, "Ba'al Worship in the Old Testament"

Soon there is a huge crowd gathered on Mount Carmel, including 450 prophets of Baal. Elijah addresses the crowd. He basically tells them to *fish or cut bait*. They must decide between God and Baal. Nobody in the crowd budges. Elijah goes on to introduce himself as the only faithful prophet remaining in Israel—making no mention of the one hundred prophets Obadiah had hid in caves. Then he specifies the rules of the match:

> Let the Baal prophets bring up two oxen; let them pick one, butcher it, and lay it out on an altar on firewood—but don't ignite it. I'll take the other ox, cut it up, and lay it on the wood. But neither will I light the fire. Then you pray to your gods and I'll pray to God. The god who answers with fire will prove to be, in fact, God.[8]

Thunder on His Brow and Tempest in His Voice

His eminence is seen both in the religious reformation which he wrought, and in the fact that the New Testament speaks of him more often than of any other Old Testament prophet. Moreover, it was he who was chosen to appear with Moses at our Lord's transfiguration. And further, it is from this point that the ministry of the *prophets* in the two Hebrew kingdoms becomes more prominently emphasized. One of Israel's most startling and romantic characters, he suddenly appears on the scene as the crisis-prophet, with thunder on his brow and tempest in his voice. He disappears just as suddenly, swept skywards in a chariot of fire. Between his first appearing and his final disappearing lies a succession of amazing miracles.

J. Sidlow Baxter, *Explore the Book*, 2:11

Elijah lets the prophets of Baal go first. They pray and wail and jump and dance and slash themselves until they are covered with blood. But there is not even a spark or a whiff of smoke on the altar. Hours into the ordeal, Elijah taunts the prophets by suggesting that Baal may be sleeping or off on a holiday. But the prophets don't calm down until Elijah tells them their time is up. Then he takes the stage, building an altar with twelve stones, one for each tribe of Israel. After that a trench for the water he will pour on the wood and the slaughtered ox. He turns the preparation into a performance culminating in a powerful prayer to God. Like clockwork (at the very hour of the afternoon sacrifice), fire falls from heaven onto the altar and incinerates it, not only the drenched pieces of oxen but also the wood, stones, dirt, and water.

With this spectacular miracle, the awestruck crowd—fickle as they are—falls down and worships God. This might have been a time for Elijah to sit back and celebrate, but his assignment is not over. He shouts to people in the crowd to seize the prophets of Baal before they escape. With their help, the prophets are rounded up and marched down to the stream where they are summarily slaughtered. That accomplished, Elijah turns to Ahab, who might have assumed he would be next in line for the death penalty. But Elijah's words to him are most unexpected. He tells Ahab to have a celebratory meal because the rain is coming.

So while Ahab dines, Elijah climbs Mount Carmel to thank God for answered prayer. God's marvel of sending fire to burn the sacrifice is only the prelude to the real miracle, however. What Israel needs is a downpour. Having already told Ahab that rain would be coming, Elijah is nervous. The land is parched. Will it really happen? He sends his servant to look at the sky. Nothing. Elijah sends him back, again and again. He checks six times. Nothing. Then he looks yet again the seventh time and sees a small cloud the size of his hand.

That's the signal. The storm is coming—wind and rain—a mighty show of God's power. Ahab is told to hitch up the chariot and be ready to move fast. He flies for home in Jezreel, getting ahead of the raging storm. Most amazing of all is Elijah. Not necessarily known as a world-class Olympic athlete, he pulls up his garment and races out ahead of the king's chariot all the way to Jezreel. Elijah is kicking up his heels for sheer joy.

But his ecstasy doesn't last long. Ahab tells Jezebel about the day's happenings. Baal is her primary god, and now all the prophets are dead. She is outraged and sends an ominous message—essentially that the jig is up for Elijah. This time he runs in terror, leaving his servant behind. He finally lies down under a bush exhausted. He can hardly think straight. Why is he racing to save his life, he wonders, when he'd be better off just giving up and dying? This whole prophet-thing is way too stressful. He'd rather be dead and done with it.

Cave of Elijah

Having fallen asleep, he is suddenly jerked awake. Is it Jezebel? He hears a voice telling him to rise and eat. It's an angel with provisions. He drinks the water and eats bread, hot-baked on the fire, and goes back to sleep. But not for long. The angel returns, telling him to eat enough for an extended trip. Then, on command, he hikes for forty days and forty nights to Mount Horeb, where he finds a cave for shelter. God asks why he's there.

Elijah unloads before God a litany of his troubles. Overcome with self-pity, he laments that he is the only true prophet left in Israel. God is unmoved. He tells Elijah to go up on the mountain to see what he is really like. Next thing Elijah knows, he is nearly blown away by a hurricane; after that comes an earthquake, and next fire, and finally a still small voice—a voice that asks again why he is there in the cave. Again Elijah explains. But God takes no account of it—rather he gives marching orders.

He is to anoint Hazael king of Aram, and Jehu king of Israel. Equally significant,

The Talk of the Nation

He steps onto the stage of biblical history at a low ebb in the history of Israel. . . . Feared by kings and false prophets, cheered and beloved by the young men he trained, he was the talk of the nation. He would suddenly appear, deliver a message from God, and then seemingly vanish into thin air for months at a time. He exploded onto the scene, grabbed center stage, came and went as he pleased, riled up the king and his evil wife, and called down fire from heaven. First he humiliated the false prophets, then he slaughtered them. And in the wake of his greatest victory, he ran away and prayed that God would take his life.

Ray Pritchard, *Fire and Rain: The Wild-Hearted Faith of Elijah*, 2–3

he is to name Elisha as his successor. God also reminds him that he is not the only one in Israel who serves and honors God. In fact, there are seven thousand people who have never worshiped Baal. Elijah goes straightaway to find Elisha.

Soon thereafter God tells Elijah to confront King Ahab about the murder of Naboth and the confiscation of his vineyard. The message Elijah is to bring is straightforward: "GOD's word: What's going on here? First murder, then theft?" Ahab will know God is onto him. Then he is to tell Ahab that "the very spot where the dogs lapped up Naboth's blood, they'll lap up your blood—that's right, *your* blood." But that's not all. "Dogs will fight over the flesh of Jezebel all over Jezreel."[9] Furthermore, those who were in cahoots with Ahab will be ravaged by dogs as well. And Elijah does exactly as God has instructed him.

After Ahab dies, Elijah takes it easy, until one day an angel tells him to get up and go out and meet some messengers from King Ahaziah (son of Ahab), who is severely injured after falling from a balcony. The messengers are seeking to consult with one of the Baal gods, but Elijah stops them and tells them to go back to the king and give him God's message: the king's injuries are fatal.

The king is suspicious. He wants to know more about this man with the message. They tell him he is unshaven, unkempt, wearing a leather belt. Ahaziah knows immediately that the man is Elijah the Tishbite. He sends a commander with fifty men. They find Elijah in plain daylight in a typical holy-man pose and setting: sitting on the top of a hill. The commander orders him to come down. Elijah responds by saying if he is actually a holy man, as the commander had addressed him, lightning will strike and kill him and all his men. Thus it happens. It occurs again with the same result when the king sends another squadron.

The third time, the commander appeals to Elijah to spare his life and come visit the king. At the angel's direction, Elijah accompanies him and takes a pronouncement of death directly to Ahaziah: *You have consulted a false god, and you will die.*

Soon after this, Elijah and Elisha are on the road to Gilgal. But they take detours along the way, each time because Elijah claims God has an errand for him, first in Bethel, then in Jericho, finally to the Jordan. Each time Elisha learns from the local school of prophets that this is Elijah's last day on earth, but Elisha doesn't want to

Elijah and Jesus

I have often thought of how closely [Elijah's] life resembled the Messiah, who was yet to come: the way he spent time alone; the courage he showed as he stood in the presence of his enemy and delivered God's message; the power he exhibited when it took a miracle to convince his audience that he was a man with a message from God—the one true God; the compassion he demonstrated when he cared about the widow's grief and brought her son back to life, even the anguish he felt in his own Gethsemane as he wrestled in his soul. And finally, how much like Christ was his departure. As others stood staring, he was taken up to the heaven out of their sight (Matt. 16:13–14).

Charles R. Swindoll, *Elijah: Man of Heroism and Humility*, 173

hear such talk. At the Jordan Elijah rolls up his outer garment and strikes the water so that they can walk across on dry land.

When they reach the other side, Elijah asks Elisha what he would like before he leaves. Elisha tells him he wants to be just like him, only doubly so. Elijah says *yes, but only if you carefully observe my departure*. As they are walking along, a chariot and horses come from seemingly out of nowhere and swoop Elijah up in the midst of a whirlwind, carrying him all the way to heaven. The startled Elisha now knows the prophetic mantle has indeed fallen upon him.

Elisha: In the Shadow of Elijah

He is a farm boy. His prosperous father Shaphat is getting ready for planting, having yoked up his twenty-four oxen. Elisha is among the sons and servants plowing the soil, each with a team. He is expected to put in a full day's work, but he looks up, and there in front of him is the great prophet Elijah. Before he knows it, Elijah has thrown his coat over his head.

Elisha knows what this means. He is supposed to follow after Elijah and serve God as a prophet himself. So he leaves the team in the field and goes with the master. But before taking leave he is granted a time to bid his father and mother farewell—and not just to kiss them good-bye. Rather, he makes a ritual feast out of his departure, slaughtering his team of oxen, starting a fire, and preparing steaks for the whole family. Only then does he join Elijah as his disciple.

Elisha is present, watching his mentor and dear friend fly away into heaven. He has asked Elijah for one parting gift—that Elijah's mantle might fall on him. And it does. He picks up Elijah's coat and strikes the water of the Jordan, and it separates so that he can walk back across, where prophets who had followed them are waiting. They witness the miracle and proclaim him as Elijah's successor, who has special access to God's power—in fact, a double portion of Elijah's spirit.

Almost immediately Elisha is called upon to work miracles. Elders in a nearby town come to him concerning a serious problem of water pollution. He adds some salted water to the spring, and the pollutants disappear.

In another instance, Elisha utilizes his power for revenge—revenge on children, no less. Indeed, there appears to be a whole playground full of them, ill-mannered youngsters emboldened by their numbers. They laugh and sneer and mock his baldness. Instead of just walking on and ignoring them, Elisha turns back and curses them in God's name. In an instant, before the children have a chance to escape, two ferocious bears emerge from the woods and attack forty-two of them, mauling and ripping their bodies to shreds.

Elisha simply walks on to Mount Carmel.

Sometime later, Elisha is confronted by three kings: from Judah, Israel, and Edom. They have joined forces and marshaled their armies to go on the attack against Moab. But they seem to have become lost in the wilderness and are out of water. Elisha has been summoned to solve their problem. Like his mentor, Elisha is bold and never at a loss for words. His contempt for Israel's king Joram, son of Ahab and Jezebel, is palpable: "What do you and I have in common? Go consult the puppet-prophets of your father and mother."[10]

But then Elisha turns and acknowledges Judah's king Jehoshaphat and agrees to consult God on his behalf. A minstrel is brought in and God's Spirit comes upon him, laying out a plan. They are to dig trenches throughout the parched valley. For what? God will miraculously fill the trenches with pure water for both man and animal. But more than that, their armies will soundly defeat Moab, and not just the Moabite army; they will also wreak havoc on Moabite cities, farms, and fields. And that is exactly what transpires.

Elisha is next called upon to perform a household miracle. A prophet colleague has died, and his wife calls on Elisha to save her from a creditor and her two children from slavery. All she has left is a small amount of oil. Following Elisha's instructions, she borrows jugs from everyone in town. Then she takes the tiny amount of oil in her own jug to fill all the jugs she has collected. The sale of the oil is enough to pay the creditor, and enough is left over to support the family.

As Elisha is traveling through the town of Shunem, a noted woman of the region asks him to stop by for dinner. She recognizes him as a holy man and invites him back again and again and finally convinces

Thugs Threatening Elisha

This was not a group of little boys; it was a gang of young trouble-makers. Remember, we know that 42 were injured. That means that the smallest number for this "gang" was 42, and there could have been others who were fortunate enough to escape from the bears. This could have been a very intimidating confrontation for Elisha. The "bad boys of Bethel" got what they deserved. Would they try to bully Elisha? Then let them face two mother bears and see what real intimidation feels like. . . . God's judgment was poured out on those who rebelled against God, who disobeyed His Word, and who mocked His servants, the prophets. If there was one lesson that the people of Bethel learned that day, it was that they must reverence God and His spokesmen.

Bob Deffinbaugh, "The Life and Times of Elisha the Prophet"

her husband to add a little bedroom upstairs, furnished for his needs. In appreciation for her hospitality he wants to give her a gift—anything she needs. But she has no needs. He has noticed, however, that she has no son, and her husband is old. He tells her that in a year she will be nursing her own infant son. She thinks he is kidding, but the following year she is coddling a baby in her arms.

Then tragedy strikes, and the baby dies. The woman leaves her infant at home, mounts her donkey, and rushes to Mount Carmel to find Elisha. She meets him and pours out her heart in distress. Elisha instructs his servant Gehazi to run on ahead and place his staff on the child's face, but Gehazi cannot restore the boy. When Elisha returns with the boy's mother, he goes into the room and stretches himself over the dead child. The baby sneezes and comes back to life, and the Shunammite woman is most grateful.

Elisha watching Elijah's ascension

Another life-saving miracle occurs when Elisha is in Gilgal, meeting with the local school of prophets. Times have been hard due to drought, but Elisha nevertheless wants to prepare a meal for the group. While Gehazi is cooking up stew over a fire, one of the prophets adds some herbs that he has fetched nearby. Turns out they are poisonous, and the whole school of prophets might have died. But Elisha adds some flour, and the stew miraculously becomes edible.

Another food-related miracle occurs sometime later at the school of prophets when Elisha is mingling with the crowd. A traveler arrives with a gift of twenty loaves of barley bread and some apples—enough for him and Gehazi for the next few days. But Elisha tells Gehazi to pass it around for everyone. *Pass it around for one hundred men?* Gehazi is incredulous. It's not nearly enough. But Elisha is insistent. When they are all served, there is food left over.

One day Elisha hears by the grapevine that the king of Israel is terribly upset because the neighboring king of Aram has sent Naaman, his army commander, to be healed of leprosy. The king of Israel has no clue what to do with him and fears this visit might portend an enemy attack. For Elisha, however, healing is part of a day's work. So he sends word that Naaman should come to him, which he does. But Elisha sends Gehazi out to meet Naaman with the message that he should dip seven times in the Jordan River. Naaman is irate.

He had expected some hocus-pocus from the holy man himself; instead he's being told to immerse himself in the dirty water of the Jordan by a mere lackey.

So Naaman storms away, infuriated that he's being treated so disrespectfully, in front of his servants no less. They go after him, begging him to just give it a try. So Naaman, embarrassed and sighing in disgust, agrees to do what the prophet has prescribed. No surprise: he rises out of the Jordan completely healed, his skin as smooth as a baby's.

Naaman then searches out Elisha and confesses that the God of Israel is the only true God. He wants to give Elisha a gift, but Elisha refuses to take anything, and Naaman heads for home. Gehazi, however, slips away and catches up with Naaman, and tells him that he and Elisha just learned of a great need among some other prophets, and thus a gift would be greatly appreciated. Naaman gives him two big sacks of silver as well as clothing. But, led by the Spirit of God, Elisha knows exactly what Gehazi has done. When he innocently returns, having hid the loot, Elisha questions him, and when Gehazi lies, Elisha pronounces a curse on him. He and his family and his descendants will be stricken with the same leprosy of which Naaman has just been cured. A cruel punishment indeed.

As Elijah's successor, Elisha is recognized as the dean of the school of prophets in Israel. They look to him as their leader. One day they come and ask for a more spacious building, proposing to locate it near the Jordan River and build it themselves. Elisha is agreeable and joins them on location. As they are chopping down trees, an ax head flies off the handle, lands in the river, and sinks out of sight to the bottom. These student prophets have little money, and the ax happens to have been borrowed. Elisha to the rescue. He tosses a stick near where the ax head hit the water, and the iron ax head floats to the surface, where it is retrieved.

On a larger scale, Elisha serves as an informer for the king of Israel. Time and again, God reveals to him the military strategy of enemy armies, and he reports to the king, thus giving Israel a military edge. When the king of Aram learns Elisha is the informer and lives in Dothan, he calls out a battalion to surround the town and capture him. When they attack, Elisha calls down blindness upon them, and then he purposely misdirects them away from Dothan into the capital city, Samaria. Elisha restores their sight, and they realize they are trapped. The Israelite king, in disbelief, does not know what to do with these *prisoners*. Elisha says to the king: *Don't kill them; give them a good meal and send them back to Aram.*

Following this incident, the Israelites have several years of peace from the marauding Arameans. But it doesn't last. Some years later enemy forces under King Ben-Hadad devastate the land and lay siege to Samaria, causing a famine so severe that some people resort to cannibalism. The Israelite king blames God, calls for the death of Elisha, and actually shows up himself at Elisha's door. Elisha tells him that God will cause the Arameans to run panic-stricken away from their camp outside the city, leaving everything behind—food, clothing, animals. Furthermore, the famine will end the next day. But the king's personal attendant ignores God's word and taunts Elisha, who angrily pronounces a gruesome death for his unbelief. The next day, following a series of wild and crazy events, the attendant is trampled to death by the starving hordes who rush out and ravage the abandoned camp.

In another instance Elisha predicts Ben-Hadad's death to the very person who will succeed him, the king's confidant, Hazael. Indeed, Elisha is recognized as a reliable holy man, sometimes far beyond the borders of Israel. But in the case of Jehu, Ahab's chief army officer, he does not merely prophesy who will be the new king; he actually determines, with God's leading, that Jehu should be anointed to replace Joram, Ahab's son, and to wreak vengeance on the entire family of Ahab for his (and his wife's) unspeakable wickedness.

Elisha carries on and continues offering his military prophecies to kings. But then he becomes ill and dies of unknown causes. The miracles, however, have not ended. One day some grave diggers, in the process of burying a man, are suddenly interrupted by raiders from across the border. They throw the body in Elisha's grave and get out of there fast. Then the most amazing thing happens. When the body makes contact with Elisha's bones, the dead man suddenly comes to life and walks away—a fitting end to the story for Elijah's successor.

Concluding Observations

Elisha heads up the school of prophets and is active in his profession for some six decades. His miracles are impressive, beginning with his first solo stride across the dry ground of the Jordan River. Like his mentor, he saves a widow from starving and raises the dead. Leprosy is no obstacle, nor is poisoned food. He seems invincible with a double portion of Elijah's spirit—whatever that might have been—and his wonder working continues after his death. What he does not receive from Elijah, however, is a spirit of humility and harmony.

Elisha fearlessly strides around the Northern Kingdom as though no situation is too big for him to handle. *Bring it on!* is his motto. He is the successor of the great Elijah, and now he is surpassing his mentor. No fear of failure. No depression. No anguish over the crippling punishment to his longtime faithful servant.

Elijah, on the other hand, is more human and approachable. He is less than confident of his own abilities and is sometimes unsure about the voice of God. He orders the death of four hundred prophets of Baal—harsh punishment indeed, but they deserved it. However, bringing down the wrath of God on forty-two ill-mannered boys? Elijah would never have been guilty of such a deed.

One E-prophet stands taller than the other—as later biblical references attest. Elijah should never be mistaken for his student Elisha. When Elisha dies, he is dead. His body is buried. Elijah skips that aspect of existence altogether and makes the grandest chariot ride this world has ever known.

Further Reading

Ackerman, Jane. *Elijah: Prophet of Carmel*. Washington, DC: ICS Publications, 2003.

Brueggemann, Walter. *Testimony to Otherwise: The Witness of Elijah and Elisha*. St. Louis: Chalice Press, 2001.

Pritchard, Ray. *Fire and Rain: The Wild-Hearted Faith of Elijah*. Nashville: Broadman & Holman, 2007.

Swindoll, Charles R. *Elijah: Man of Heroism and Humility*. Nashville: Word, 2008.

14

NEHEMIAH, EZRA, ESTHER, AND JOB

Renovation and Salvation

In comparison to building the ark or the Tower of Babel or Solomon's Temple, the work of rebuilding the walls of Jerusalem seemed little more than mundane manual labor. There was no grand design resulting in a spectacular architectural masterpiece. Rather, the work was a renovation project—a dirty, arduous job of making heaps of debris look once again like city walls. There was no romance, no magic or fantasy, in setting stones back in place and slapping on mud to fill the cracks.

The artist's imagination soars as she depicts the Ark, the Tower, and the Temple, but not the walls. All cities had walls; they were part of the dusty Palestinian landscape. How else could a city protect itself against the enemy? If Jerusalem were to be revived, rebuilding the walls was a critical first step.

In many respects Nehemiah and Ezra were eminently suitable for the project at hand. They possessed none of the wealth and brilliance that Solomon exhibited, nor the solitary, ceaseless persistence of Noah. They were good, steady, hardworking men of God who rose to the occasion. They appeared on the scene at a very low point in Judah's history—the

Jeremiah's Lament Over the Fall of Jerusalem

Those who once ate delicacies
are destitute in the streets.
Those brought up in royal purple
now lie on ash heaps.

The punishment of my people
is greater than that of Sodom,
which was overthrown in a moment
without a hand turned to help her.

Lam. 4:5–6 (NIV)

exile and its aftermath. King Josiah had died in a foolhardy attack against the army of Egypt on its way to do battle with the forces of Babylon. Babylon laid siege to Judah and carried away priceless treasures from the Temple and palace, though not without a tug-of-war with Egypt.

Amid this struggle, Judah revolted against Babylon, with the help of Egyptian forces, and King Nebuchadnezzar responded with an all-out military assault. In the process, the Temple, the walls, and many other structures, including private homes, were plundered and destroyed. Thousands of citizens were then carted off to Babylon, including King Zedekiah, who, before his eyes were gouged out, was forced to watch his two sons executed. He was then thrown into prison.

What followed was a traumatic time not only for Judah but for Israel as well. Many years prior to this Babylonian captivity of Judah, Assyrian forces had attacked the northern kingdom and had laid siege to Samaria, the capital city. Thousands of Israelites had been deported and thousands of Assyrians had been forcibly relocated to replace them. Israel and Judah were connected by their joint worship in the holy city of Jerusalem. Thus the destruction of the Temple and the city itself marked a devastating low point for both the Northern and Southern Kingdoms.

In fact, this seventy-year exile is a time when the future of Israel is more uncertain than it had been since the exodus. After King Cyrus of Persia subsequently conquered Babylon, however, the people of Judah, under the leadership of Ezra and Nehemiah, were permitted to return home and rebuild the city—the walls, the Temple, shops, and residential dwellings. The biblical history of this era is confusing, but a simple overview distinguishes among three successive empires to the east, beginning with the centuries-long Assyrian empire, followed by the Babylonian and the Persian empires.

Generations after the reign of King Cyrus, Ahasuerus ascended the throne. Following a serious marital dispute with his wife Vashti, Esther becomes his bride—more than that, the greatest Jewish queen in history. Her story is a favorite for Jews and Christians alike.

The mysterious story of Job is not dated and does not easily fit into the historical chronology of Israel. In the biblical arrangement of narratives, however, the book of Job follows immediately after the book of Esther. That Job has no clear biblical or historical setting or time frame is appropriate. His story, more than that of any other Old Testament figure, is timeless.

Ezra's Courage

In the spring of 458 B.C., Ezra assembled a small group of Jews on the banks of a Babylonian canal. The return of the people seemed less threatening than similar events from the early pages of Jewish history. But for Ezra and those with him, it was no small mission. Ahead stretched nine hundred miles of hostile territory and uncertainty about how the people would receive them. Even so, according to Ezra's journal, he was filled with courage because "the hand of the Lord my God was on me" (Ezra 7:28).

Knute Larson and Kathy Dahlen, *Holman Old Testament Commentary: Ezra, Nehemiah, Esther*, 85

Ezra leading exiles home to Jerusalem

His questions are as applicable today as they were for ancient Israel.

Ezra: Scribe Who Sparks a Revival

Ezra is a scribe and priest living in Babylon, a descendant of Moses' brother Aaron. He is a functionary more than a scholar. True, he knows the law of Moses. But basically he is an archivist, a keeper of past records, including the names and numbers of all the families who had returned from exile some years earlier. They rebuilt the Temple (after many threats and work stoppages), and Ezra's most important role in this situation is to return to Jerusalem, bringing with him all rules and regulations necessary for true worship.

King Artaxerxes of Persia is impressed with him and his God and essentially gives him everything he asks for, including an open account from the royal Persian treasury for miscellaneous expenses. He allows Ezra to return to Jerusalem accompanied by priests and many others associated with temple responsibilities. More than that, he sends a letter of recommendation assigning Ezra and his assistants the high honor of researching all the teachings of

The Memory of Ezra

The memory of Ezra the scribe has scarcely had fair play among Bible-reading people. True, neither his character nor the incidents of his life reach the height of interest or of grandeur belonging to the earlier men and their times. He is no hero, or prophet; only a scribe; and there is a certain narrowness as well as a prosaic turn about his mind, and altogether one feels that he is a smaller man than the Elijahs and Davids of the older days. But the homely garb of the scribe covered a very brave devout heart, and the story of his life deserves to be more familiar to us than it is.

Alexander Maclaren, "Heroic Faith"

God. Beyond that, Ezra is to make judicial appointments, teach the law, and collect taxes. And for all these services he is to be well paid.

True to his assignment, Ezra keeps track of everything, including lists of fellow travelers and men who had married foreign wives, as well as utensils and vessels for temple worship. He's a pencil pusher, some would say—a life with far less flair than that of Joshua, David, or Elijah. But he does rise to the occasion when he hears that there has been reckless intermarriage between the Israelites and their pagan neighbors. His testimony speaks for itself: "When I heard this, I tore my tunic and cloak, pulled hair from my head and beard and sat down appalled."[1] Not until the time of the evening ritual sacrifice does he get up from the ground and call on God for forgiveness: "My dear God, I'm so totally ashamed, I can't bear to face you. . . . We've been stuck in a muck of guilt since the time of our ancestors until right now. . . . Yet here we are, at it again, breaking your commandments by intermarrying with the people who practice all these obscenities!"[2]

His prayer sparks a revival. A vast crowd, confessing sins and weeping tears of great sorrow, gathers around him. After that Ezra fasts and prays until the next morning. Then he returns to the people, demanding that they all abide by a covenant to rid themselves of their pagan wives. They agree and Ezra outlines a procedure for marital separation. It involves some two months of intense negotiation to carry out the plan. When they have completed it, God's wrath is appeased.

After this revival, Ezra summons the priests and Levites to dig deeper into the Book of the Law that God had given to Moses. Again there is much weeping over past infidelities. On hearing these long-forgotten decrees and instructions given by God to Moses, the people confess their sins and dedicate their lives to God. Ezra also

Zerubbabel and the Delayed Rebuilding of the Temple

Five centuries before Jesus was born, the Israelites returned from exile to find Jerusalem in ruins and their beloved temple destroyed. With great enthusiasm they set about rebuilding it. However, Zerubbabel, the governor, got little farther than laying the foundation before opposition set in. Neighbors fought the project tooth and nail, finally succeeding in getting a restraining order to halt construction (Ezra 4). Enemies mocked. Supporters became discouraged. For years the site stood silent. . . . And then one day a man of God, Zechariah, began to speak words that pierced Zerubbabel to the heart and filled him with fresh hope: "This is the word of the Lord to Zerubbabel," came the message. "Not by might nor by power, but by my Spirit, says the Lord Almighty." Zerubbabel could feel his heart pounding as the message continued. "What are you, O mighty mountain? Before Zerubbabel you will become level ground. . . . The hands of Zerubbabel have laid the foundation of this temple, his hands will also complete it" (Zech. 4:6–7).

Ralph Wilson, "Don't Despise the Day of Small Things"

reminds his listeners of the long-forgotten Feast of Tabernacles, an autumn outdoor festival that entails camping outdoors. He sends word to all the surrounding villages and to those who are living in Jerusalem, summoning the people to go out into the countryside and collect leafy branches for the building of booths in the Temple courtyard. The people respond with great delight. It is a seven-day celebration of feasting and listening to Ezra read from God's revelation to Moses. After this, Ezra disappears from the record.

Nehemiah: God's Contractor for Wall Rebuilding

Nehemiah's story is told in his own words. In fact, his writing is the only actual memoir in the Bible. As official cupbearer to Artaxerxes, king of Persia, he holds a most prestigious position, ever on guard against any suspicious activity or plots to poison the monarch. That career is left behind, however, as he travels to Jerusalem to become governor and general contractor for the rebuilding of the walls. His work is critically important, but like Ezra's, not particularly exciting.

As a trusted aide of the king, Nehemiah lives in the large palace at Susa, one of the Persian capitals, known as the Eternal City of the East. Life is good. It would have been tempting to remain in this comfortable situation. Instead he travels to Jerusalem to oversee a massive rebuilding project.

His entry into Jerusalem comes more than a dozen years after Ezra had come to reestablish the law of Moses. A delegation headed by Hanani had arrived in Susa bringing a report: *walls and gates and city in ruins, debris strewn everywhere.* Nehemiah is beside himself, and his weeping extends into days of mourning—prayer and fasting. He confesses the sins of the past and present, his own included, admitting that he and the people have treated God very badly, and he begs forgiveness.

Looking like a wreck—no sleep, red eyes, sad face—he appears as cupbearer before both the king and the queen. The king asks what is wrong. Nehemiah, having prayed that God would open the king's heart, describes in detail a city in ruins—the very place where his ancestors are buried. King Artaxerxes asks him what

Ruins Dearer Than Pomp of Shushan

Ninety years had passed since the returning exiles had arrived at Jerusalem. They had encountered many difficulties which had marred their progress and cooled their enthusiasm. The Temple, indeed, was rebuilt, but Jerusalem lay in ruins, and its walls remained as they had been left, by Nebuchadnezzar's siege, some century and a half before. A little party of pious pilgrims had gone from Persia to the city, and had come back to Shushan with a sad story of weakness and despondency, affliction and hostility. One of the travellers had a brother, a youth named Nehemiah, who was a cup-bearer in the court of the Persian king. Living in a palace, and surrounded with luxury, his heart was with his brethren; and the ruins of Jerusalem were dearer to him than the pomp of Shushan.

Alexander Maclaren, "A Reformer's Schooling"

he desires. Nehemiah is ready. He wishes to return to Jerusalem commissioned by the king himself. That would entail letters of recommendation and authorization, supplies, and a military escort. The king agrees, a gratifying answer to Nehemiah's prayer.

Upon arriving in Jerusalem, Nehemiah surreptitiously inspects the walls and assesses the work ahead of him. Only then does he explain his mission to officials there, emphasizing that both God and the king are behind him. They enthusiastically support the project, eager to get involved themselves. But there are detractors, particularly foreigners residing in the city.

The priests, including the high priest, dig into the work, as do others who are paid for their labor. Nehemiah keeps a detailed record of exactly who repairs what. Every demolished gate, for example, is completely rebuilt: the Sheep Gate, the Fish Gate, the Jeshanah Gate, the Valley Gate, the Dung Gate, the Fountain Gate, the Water Gate, the Horse Gate, the East Gate, and the Inspection Gate. Each one, recorded with workers' names and work accomplished.

The non-Jewish residents, however, oppose the work relentlessly, particularly Sanballat and Tobiah, who spread the word that Nehemiah and his crew are not equipped to do the job: the workmanship is substandard, and the laborers are being overworked. In fact, so threatening is the opposition that Nehemiah stations guards to protect the workers, and he calls on God to bring down the enemies: "Give them over as plunder in a land of captivity. Do not cover up their guilt or blot out their sins from your sight."[3] It is true that Nehemiah is a taskmaster; the wall building goes on day and night. But he expects no more than he gives. Along with the rest, he sleeps in his clothes, ever on the lookout for danger.

Wall construction, however, is not Nehemiah's only responsibility. He must also adjudicate grievances and settle conflicting legal and ethical issues, especially between recently returning exiles and longtime settlers. Furthermore, the Jerusalem officials are demanding high payments from the poor, with taxes and rents on their lands. Wives (as well as their husbands) loudly protest to Nehemiah, complaining that they do not have enough left to even feed their children.

Nehemiah, a man of action, is furious upon hearing of their dire situation. He calls the city fathers and other nobles to a meeting and blasts them: "Each one of

Nehemiah and Sanballat's servant

Nehemiah's Prayer of Retribution

Nehemiah was convinced that the restoration work was the will of God. He had seen it evidenced by Artaxerxes's support and good will and by the rousing support of the Jews. In light of this, those who opposed the Jews were viewed as enemies. Sanballat and his cronies were clearly of this camp.

Many interpreters have trouble with Nehemiah's prayer and his request for retribution on his enemies. The modern Christian often views his prayer as unforgiving and harsh, lacking in the love of Christ which calls us. However, Scripture reminds us that vengeance belongs to God. . . .

Knute Larson and Kathy Dahlen, *Holman Old Testament Commentary: Ezra, Nehemiah, Esther*, 171

you is gouging his brother. . . . What you're doing is wrong." To Nehemiah, this matter is far more than one of fairness and civic duty. It is a religious matter: "Is there no fear of God left in you?" he demands. Then he issues an order: "Give them back their foreclosed fields, vineyards, olive groves, and homes right now. And forgive your claims on their money, grain, new wine, and olive oil."[4]

The wealthy officials and nobles agree to Nehemiah's demands. But he is taking no chances. He summons the priests and requires that this elite gang of Jerusalem landlords promise before them that they will keep their word.

As governor, Nehemiah has the authority to tax the people himself, particularly including a costly food allowance that previous governors had exacted from the citizens. But the fear of God has gotten hold of him, and he is singularly committed to rebuilding the wall.

But the opposition from outsiders continues unabated. Sanballat, Tobiah, and Geshem repeatedly attempt to lure Nehemiah away for a meeting with them. He refuses. So they send a message claiming they know what he's up to. They've heard confirmed reports among Judah's neighbors that he is secretly planning to overthrow King Artaxerxes and set himself up as king, with puppet prophets ready to announce to the people that God has anointed a king in Judah.

The men are lying weasels bent on bringing Nehemiah down. They present their false information to the Jerusalem leaders and nobles. Intimidation is their game. Rumors fly.

Nehemiah is feeling pressured. He agrees to a secret meeting with the prophet Shemaiah, who claims he has a message from God and requests a private audience in the Temple. Nehemiah refuses, sensing Shemaiah has been sent by Tobiah and Sanballat in an effort to trap him. Shemaiah is no more than a prophet-for-hire doing the bidding of his enemies.

Finally, after working night and day for fifty-two days—less than eight weeks—the walls are completed, the product of fine workmanship. It is a stunning accomplishment—enough to cause the opposition to sit up and take notice and to recognize that truly God had been behind the effort. And the dedication ceremony itself is a lavish musical production.

With the walls rebuilt and the new gates all properly hung, Governor Nehemiah sets in place security measures. But Jerusalem is still virtually a ghost town, largely deserted, with most of the homes still in rubble. With the exception of the leaders, those who have returned from the exile as well as those who had never gone into exile are living primarily in small towns in the region. That is where they feel at home and where they feel safest, but Jerusalem needs residents. Those living in towns are informed that one out of every ten families (determined by drawing lots) must relocate to Jerusalem.

For Nehemiah, the rebuilding of Jerusalem is far more than a temporal matter. It is a spiritual rebirth. Revival occurs when Ezra reads from the book of God's revelation to Moses. When the people begin to weep and acknowledge their unfaithfulness, Nehemiah admonishes them to return to their homes and prepare a feast and to celebrate. Social reformer that he is, he makes sure that this day of feasting also includes the poor.

Nehemiah is an effective leader, but when he takes his leave to return to Babylon for consultation with King Artaxerxes, things fall apart. Under his watch—and perhaps outside his purview—the priest Eliashib had been assigned caretaker of the Temple warehouse. Eliashib, a close friend of the troublemaker Tobiah, desecrates the storerooms in Nehemiah's absence. He likewise refuses to dole out the regular provisions for those who are in charge of Temple worship, forcing them to return to the countryside just to have enough to eat.

When Nehemiah returns, he dresses down the Jerusalem leaders, demanding to know why the Temple rebuilding has been forsaken. He takes it upon himself to hire honest, hardworking men to take charge of the storage facility, and he makes sure all workers are paid in full. He also takes the leaders to task for their failure to observe the Sabbath. Indeed, the people are acting as though the Sabbath is just another workday. Such behavior, he knows all too well, will only bring down the wrath of God.

Intermarriage is another very troubling matter. Nehemiah learns that during his absence, men have taken to marrying the women of their foreign neighbors. And to add insult to injury, their children are growing up with no knowledge of the Hebrew tongue. So outraged is Nehemiah that he roughs them up—hitting, punching, and pulling hair. They are following in the evil ways of King Solomon, whose foreign wives contributed to his downfall.

Nehemiah's memoir doubles in many respects as a prayer. He has carried a heavy load of responsibility, and he wants God to recognize that. His purpose is to lay out before God all his efforts to instill in the people the precepts given to Moses for appropriate conduct in everyday life and in divine worship. Nehemiah was a good man. God surely heard with a nod of approval his final prayer: "Remember me, O my God, for good."[5]

Vashti: Queen Who Refuses to Demean Herself

Few queens in history have lived in such wealth and splendor. Vashti is the wife of

King Ahasuerus (Xerxes), who rules a vast empire of more than a hundred provinces from Ethiopia to India. She lives at the plush palace complex in Susa. Her husband is arrogant and utterly self-absorbed, wallowing in his incredible wealth. And he wants the world to know, so he sponsors a six-month fair, during which time his extravagant treasures are on display for others to see. He rightly assumes that his ostentatious wealth impresses his provincial governors and administrative staff, to say nothing of his ordinary subjects.

The culmination of the grand expo is a seven-day feast for everyone living in the city—a garden party of eating and drinking. The courtyard décor is luxurious, the furniture plush, the columns draped in fine woven fabrics, and the gold and silver accessories perfectly arranged. Equally impressive are the culinary delights. The wine flows freely, and it's all you can drink, no questions asked.

In another wing of the palace Queen Vashti is hosting her own feast for the prominent ladies of the empire. They are all dressed in their finery and flattered to be in the very presence of such a dazzling, regal woman.

On the last day of the feast, after six days of indulging heavily in wine and spirits, the king summons Vashti to show herself before all the men. She finds the request demeaning, especially in light of cultural considerations. He is intoxicated, and she is not about to lose her dignity by appearing before a courtyard full of ogling and guffawing men. In defiance of the king, she sends a message back that she will not appear.

Vashti's Womanly Self-Respect

To Vashti, the command of the king—her husband, who alone had the right to gaze upon her beautiful form—was most revolting to her sense of propriety, and knowing what the consequences of her refusal to appear before the half-drunken company would entail, refused in no uncertain terms to comply with the king's demand. She stood strong in womanly self-respect and "refused to come at the king's commandment." Her noble scorn at her threatened indignity deserves finer recognition. What the king sought would have infringed upon her noble, feminine modesty, therefore she had every right to disobey her wine-soaked husband. . . . All praise to the heroic Vashti for her decent disobedience.

Herbert Lockyer, *All the Women of the Bible*, 166

How dare she! She is the wife of the king and legally his property. If he can make a public exhibit of his wealth and splendor, why not of his own wife? He is outraged by her independent frame of mind. He'll show her. So he calls in his counselors—accountants, attorneys, ambulance chasers—anyone who can figure out a way to stick it to Vashti. *What are the legalities of this situation?* he asks. *What laws has she broken?*

One of his toadies speaks, insisting that Vashti has offended not simply the king but the whole population—all the leaders down to the lowliest menial worker. More than that, she will set the whole empire upside down. When other married women get word of what she has done, they all

The Impotent Ahasuerus

The story of Esther is vivid. . . . The absolute authority of Ahasuerus is stressed in different ways. . . . However, the plot makes clear it is also about challenging imperial power. It is Vashti's failure to obey that leads . . . one of the great king's counselors to suggest that no man's authority will survive if Vashti's challenge to Ahasuerus is allowed to go unpunished. . . . In this connection events later take on a comic turn. . . . In chapter 5 Esther arranges a dinner for three with the king and Haman. At last in chapter 7 the dinner takes place. Esther denounces Haman (v. 6) who is terrified, but somehow the all-powerful Ahasuerus goes out to the garden. Meanwhile, to beg for his life "Haman had thrown himself on the couch where Esther was reclining." The king returns to find him lying on top of the queen, and expostulates: *Will he even molest the queen while she is with me in the house?* (Est 7:8) . . . An all-powerful emperor, who makes laws that cannot be repealed, yet cannot control his wife, and leaves his replacement wife alone with his prime minister for a moment, and returns to find an attempted rape.

Tim Bulkeley, "Hebrew Narrative: Humour and Irony"

will think they can defy their husbands. The last thing Persia needs is to be under the thumb of uppity women.

Thus it is concluded by the law of the Medes and Persians that Vashti is banned from the court, never to again come into the presence of the king. The proclamation will be published throughout the land and no household is to be excluded: "All the women will respect their husbands, from the least to the greatest."[6]

After his hangover has worn off and he has sobered up and his seething anger has subsided, the king seems to second-guess his decision. Maybe Vashti is a proper queen after all. Maybe his action the previous night was a thoughtless mistake. But his aides will hear nothing of it. They are hankering to humiliate Vashti by downplaying her beauty in comparison to that of others. They insist she must be replaced by a new queen.

They specify a virgin and propose a Miss Persia Pageant. Each provincial leader is to assemble the most beautiful women and bring them to the palace. There they will be offered creams, lotions, hair-styling, make-up, jewels, fashions—whatever it takes to enhance their appearance before they are presented to the king. He will be the sole judge as to which one will replace Vashti. How Vashti is holding up under such an undignified and demeaning sport is not revealed.

Enter Esther.

Esther: Queen Who Saves Her People

Absolutely stunning, she is the adopted daughter of her cousin Mordecai, a Jew in exile and a high official in the king's court at Susa. Mordecai hears about the beauty pageant and is eager that Esther should compete. He is able to pull strings, and her good looks puts her in the running. Hegai, the palace official who oversees the well-being of the pageant participants, takes

Queen Esther prepares for the king

Esther under his wing. He assigns her several personal assistants to attend to her every need, coach her in proper etiquette, and groom her for her appearance before the king. She is served the finest delicacies and offered the best salon treatments money can buy.

After spending a year in preparation, each young woman takes her turn to present herself before the king, though not on a runway strutting one after another. Rather, each one goes to the king's residence in the evening and stays the night. If she has pleased him, he may call her back for a return engagement. When it is Esther's turn to appear before the king, he immediately falls for her and decides to crown her queen as a replacement for Vashti. To mark the occasion he announces a day of celebrations throughout the kingdom. He bestows lavish gifts and throws an extravagant party. Esther is the center of attention.

Queen Esther assumes the duties once reserved for Vashti. Life in the palace carries on without incident until Esther receives word from Mordecai that he has gotten wind of a conspiracy to assassinate the king. She immediately reports to her husband King Ahasuerus. He tracks down the conspirators and orders them hanged.

Sometime after this, Esther learns of a more far-reaching conspiracy. The target is the entire Jewish population in exile. But in this case the king himself is involved. He has agreed to purge all the Jews in the

Esther: Ordained for God's Purpose

It was a very strange thing that Esther, who was the foster child of Mordecai, a humble Jew, would rise from lowly rank to be queen of Persia. Out of all the women gathered from every province how singular that she should be chosen to be queen! . . . If God has brought Esther to the throne that she may go in unto the king and save her people; go in, good Esther! Fear not the risk. Fast and pray your three days before you go; but be not dismayed. . . . Ahasuerus cannot kill you; you cannot die: he can refuse his golden sceptre to all the princes of the empire, but not to you; for God has placed you where you are, and ordained you for his purpose.

Charles Haddon Spurgeon, "Esther's Exaltation; or, Who Knoweth?"

Living in a Hostile World

Imagine living life teetering on an unstable perch in a hostile world, while trying to perform a difficult task. This is the metaphor that dominates the classic film, *The Fiddler on the Roof*. . . . The image of the fiddler on the roof applies to the Jews in Persia in Esther's time just as much as it does to early-twentieth-century Russian Jews. They were not like those who lived around them, and they knew that their overlords could not be trusted. The Persians held all the power in their hands and the Jews had none. Even though these Jews had been born in Persia, they were exiles far from their homeland, surrounded by strangers. Their property could be seized or their life ended in a moment on the whim of some petty bureaucrat. On the other hand, if fortune smiled on them, they might yet survive to a good old age and make a reasonable living. As Tevye put it, "It isn't easy . . . but it is home." In such a difficult situation, why should the Jews take the risk of living a distinctive lifestyle? Why not just give in to the empire's demands and allow themselves to be assimilated and become invisible? To reverse the old Japanese proverb, "The nail that doesn't stick out is much less likely to get hammered."

Iain M. Duguid, *Esther and Ruth: Reformed Expository Commentary*, 3

kingdom at the behest of his most trusted administrator, Haman. Haman is irritated that Mordecai has refused to properly bow before him. As punishment he decides to vent his anti-Semitic rage on all Jews by circulating vicious rumors of a massive Jewish takeover plot.

Esther is terrified when she hears what has transpired behind her back. The order confirming the slaughter has been posted throughout the provinces. She learns that Jews all over the kingdom are in mourning. Mordecai wants her, the queen, to do something about it. She sends a message back that she would be risking her own life if she did.

She is queen. Why would she drag her feet? Apparently things have not been going so well for her and the king, who no doubt has a very large harem. She reminds Mordecai that anyone who barges in on the king without an invitation is put to death. As for her—the queen herself—she has not been invited to see him for a month.

But Mordecai is not about to let her off the hook. She is the Persian king's wife, to be sure, but as a Jew she bears a grave responsibility for her people. "Don't think that just because you live in the king's house you're the one Jew who will get out of this alive," he tells her, and lays the guilt trip on her. "If you persist in staying silent at a time like this, help and deliverance will arrive for the Jews from someplace else."[7] Deliverance here and now is the very reason, he is convinced, for her being in this royal position.

So she relents and tells him to call for fasting among God's people. She promises she will go to the king even without an invitation. Dressed in her finest, Esther waits outside the door to the chamber where the king is seated on the throne. He sees her and invites her in. He is most pleased with what he sees, and asks her what she wants. He'll give her anything her heart desires.

She does not reveal the reason she has come. First she wants him to be her guest at dinner and to bring Haman along. The king is ready to go right away, and he summons Haman. After he is merry with wine, he asks her again what her request is. He'll give her half the kingdom if that's what she wants. But she puts him off again. Come back tomorrow for dinner, she tells him. Then she will disclose her request.

Haman thinks his dinner invitation from Queen Esther is another mark of his prestige. He tells his friends and is eager for the royal feast. He is on top of the world—except

Everyday *Life*

Anti-Semitism and Assimilation

It is sometimes thought that anti-Semitism began in the Christian era, but hundreds of years earlier it is seen in all its ugly guises in the book of Esther. Jews were ordered exterminated not because of some collective crime they may have committed but for no other reason than that they were Jews. But the degree to exterminate the Jews that the wicked Haman had demanded served to bring a strong sense of unity while at the same time putting the brakes on the assimilation process.

The Feast of Purim is the most festive of the Jewish holidays. This centuries-old tradition recounts Esther's deliverance of her people. The Scroll of Esther is read out loud in the synagogue, sometimes to boisterous cheers and boos as the story unfolds. Children and adults often attend dressed in costume, giving the celebration a carnival air. It is a joyful time that commemorates this stand against anti-Semitism.

The Physical Survival of the Jews

It is to such a setting that we are introduced in the book of Esther. Never before have the Jews experienced anything like it, unless it was in Egypt, a thousand years earlier. Persia is an archetypal Oriental tyranny, in which the peoples live by grace of the despot's wishes, and in which the physical survival of the Jews implicitly remains an open question. . . . Under these circumstances, the narrative of Esther is faithful to the tenor of the times, seeming to bypass issues of theology and religious observance to cope with the more burning issue of the actual physical survival of the Jews. . . . At the same time, [the book of] Esther also moves to assert itself against that other, more subtle opponent. . . . In Persia, as elsewhere, the Jews begin to disappear into the fabric of the empire, some of them changing their names and their dress, and arguing with self-confidence against the possibility and desirability of a continuation to Jewish history.

Yoram Hazony, *The Dawn: Political Teachings of the Book of Esther,* 5 for when he sees Mordecai, who refuses to bow to him. So furious is he that, with encouragement from his wife and friends, he determines to build a high gallows and hang Mordecai the following morning, so that he can be entertained by the queen with no thought of this thorn in his flesh.

Unbeknownst to Esther, the king has been reading some old records and is troubled by the fact that he had never properly rewarded Mordecai for exposing an earlier conspiracy against him. He asks Haman how best to honor someone who has done fine service for the king. Haman, thinking the king is referring to him, suggests the man be paraded around town in the king's very garments. So the King orders Haman to perform that very service for Mordecai. Haman complies but now fears for his own life.

Esther's servants have prepared the feast, and now she is welcoming the king and Haman to sit at her table. The king is impatient. He wants to know Esther's request. So she tells him everything—that she is a Jew and that she and her people have been set up for a slaughter. The king demands to know who the fiend is behind such an order. Then she exposes Haman. The king is livid. Haman's scheme would have meant the death of Queen Esther herself. Inexplicably, the king wanders off to the adjoining garden, perhaps to calm himself. He returns to find Haman prostrate and pleading with Esther for his life. When the king returns, he accuses him of molesting his wife. This, not surprisingly, seals Haman's doom.

One of the king's attendants speaks up with a suggestion. A gallows has already been prepared. Why not use it for Haman? The king agrees. Before he makes any further decisions, the king gives Esther a vast tract of land belonging to Haman, and he rewards Mordecai by promoting him to the position that Haman had held.

But Esther wants to make sure the king will expunge Haman's order to massacre the Jews. The king obliges her, and more than that. He sends word to all the provinces that Jews have the king's authority behind them to respond with force against anyone who might attack them. In every province Jews are celebrating their newfound freedom. "Not only that, but many non-Jews became Jews—now it was dangerous *not* to be a Jew!"[8]

As Esther's adoptive father Mordecai attains more power in the royal court, and anyone who so much as threatens any Jew is put to death. Indeed, some five hundred adversaries are killed in the king's palace alone. The king approves of all of this, and he's eager to grant anything else that Esther desires. She requests that the bodies of Haman's ten sons, who had also been killed, be not hastily buried but rather hanged for public viewing. The king complies. The killing extends far beyond Susa. Out in the provinces, Jews kill seventy-five thousand of their enemies. Then they celebrate with joyful partying—a time of feasting known as Purim.

Job: Talks Back to God amid Testing

The book of Job has all the marks of a grand parable. Unlike other figures in the Bible since the time of Abraham, Job has

Story of Job as Parable

Calvin . . . doubted whether the story of Job were history or fiction. . . . The Book of Job appears to me unhistorical because it begins about a man quite unconnected with all history or even legend, with no genealogy, living in a country of which the Bible elsewhere has hardly anything to say; because, in fact, the author quite obviously writes as a storyteller not as a chronicler.

C. S. Lewis, *Reflections on the Psalms*,109

no chronological place in the span of generations. He rises out of the text with no heritage—no father or grandfather, no ancestry at all. He hails from Uz, a geographical location that perplexes archaeologists. Who then is this man named Job?

He is an incredibly prosperous rancher: a flock of seven thousand sheep, three thousand camels, hundreds of donkeys and teams of oxen. He has all the servants he could ever need to tend his vast holdings. His wife and ten children—seven sons and three daughters—complete his most fortunate life. He is a man of influence—more than anyone else in the known world. More than that, he is a man of integrity—not a dishonest bone in his body, a man who does not tolerate wrongdoing. He is God-fearing and known for decency in everything he does.

Job, Not a Parable

But there were some who held that Job was not someone who was in the nature of things, but that this was a parable made up to serve as a kind of theme to dispute providence, as men frequently invent cases to serve as a model for debate. Although it does not matter much for the intention of the book whether or not such is the case, still it makes a difference for the truth itself. This aforementioned opinion seems to contradict the authority of Scripture.

Thomas Aquinas, *Commentary on the Book of Job*

The same cannot be said for the boys. They are partyers. They're rich kids who know how to have a good time, always including their fun-loving sisters. Job is concerned about their behavior, fearing that amid their good times they might be blaspheming God. So after every party he arises in the morning and prepares a sacrifice of atonement for each child. This, he hopes, will cover transgressions they may have committed the previous night.

Unbeknownst to Job, God and Satan are having a discussion about him. Satan had come along with the angels one day to meet with God. God asks Satan what he has been doing. Satan shrugs and says he's been doing what he usually does—looking down on earth to see what's going on. So God asks him if he has observed his friend Job, a good and righteous man in every sense of the word. Satan has observed, but he is not impressed. The only reason Job behaves so well, he insists, is that he's got everything anyone could ever want. Things would be very different if he were to lose his health and his wealth and his wonderful family.

God disagrees. He dares Satan to test Job. *Do anything to him you want to except kill him*. So Satan is off to do what he does best.

Job's Perfect Family Life

He was a happy man to have had so many children all comfortably settled in life. . . . Not like Abraham's household, where there was an Ishmael who mocked Isaac; nor like Isaac's household, where there was an Esau and a Jacob who sought to supplant him; nor like Jacob's household, where there was a Joseph, and all the rest of his brothers were envious and jealous of him; nor like David's household, where there was perpetual strife and bickering between the one and the other.

C. H. Spurgeon, "A Merry Christmas"

Totally oblivious to this otherworldly conversation, Job carries on with his daily duties. That is, until he is stopped dead in his tracks. A field hand has come racing in from the distance. He has horrific news. An enemy tribe has swept down on him and the others when they were plowing and has killed all the oxen and donkeys as well as the servants. He is the only survivor.

Without even a moment to catch his breath and ask a question, Job sees a shepherd racing toward him to report that an electrical storm has taken out every one of the seven thousand sheep and all the other shepherds. Barely has the shepherd delivered his grim news when another messenger arrives, this time to tell Job that all of his three thousand camels have been stolen by raiders and the drivers have been slaughtered.

Job is too numb to even think straight. But he's jolted out of his stupor when still another messenger races in to bring the most terrible news a father could ever imagine. All ten of his children were together at one of their usual parties when a tornado struck and they all died—they and their servants. The messenger is the only one who survived.

Job's response is almost as stunning as the news. He tears his clothes, shaves off all his hair, and then falls on his face and worships God. His words are memorable:

> Naked I came from my mother's
> womb,
> And naked shall I return.
> The Lord gave, and the Lord has
> taken away;
> Blessed be the name of the Lord.[9]

In many respects the man Job is unfathomable, particularly in comparison to the long train of biblical figures from Genesis onward. They practically flaunt their character flaws. Sin is ever lurking at the door. One after another they anger God. But not Job. He is too good to be true. Adultery, idolatry, murder, theft—these are not uncommon among God's people. Not so with Job. When Chaldean raiders steal his three thousand camels and kill his camel drivers, he does not call on God to strike the raiders dead. There is not a hint of revenge.

Rather, Job carries on with his life, having lost everything but his wife and his integrity. Satan was wrong. Amidst such devastation, Job remains a righteous man. But unbeknownst to him, God and Satan are again conversing. Satan argues that a man can maintain his goodness as long as he has his health, but give him physical afflictions and he will shake his fist at God. God insists this is not true, but he tells

Bankruptcy and More

Job is left bankrupt, homeless, helpless, and childless. He's left standing beside the ten fresh graves of his now-dead children on a windswept hill. His wife is heaving deep sobs of grief as she kneels beside him, having just heard him say, "Whether our God gives to us or takes everything from us, we will follow Him." She leans over and secretly whispers, "Just curse God and die." Pause and ponder their grief—and remember the man had done nothing to deserve such unbearable pain.

Charles Swindoll, *Job: A Man of Heroic Endurance*, 4

Satan he can do what he wants with Job as long as he doesn't kill him.

One day as he is trying to come to terms with his terrible losses, Job notices a rash, then boils on his skin. They itch and he scratches. Spreading quickly, they cover his whole body. Worse yet, the sores are oozing with puss. There's not a square inch of his body that's not infected. He scratches himself with a pottery shard, but it only makes matters worse. It is revolting just to look at him. He goes out and sits on the smoldering ashes of a garbage pile.

If he were still in his right mind, he would want to end it all—perhaps using the pottery shard to slit his wrists. That course seems logical to his wife. *Curse God and die*, she rages. She is in the anger stage of grief and can hardly be faulted for her words. But he will not cave. Indeed, he shows his own righteous indignation: "You're talking like an empty-headed fool. We take the good days from God—why not also the bad days?"[10]

The days must surely drag on for Job. But news gets out, and three friends hear of his misfortune. They travel to visit him, each one coming from a different homeland. Eliphaz, Bildad, and Zophar, who have obviously expended some effort in making the journey, bring neither gifts nor healing remedies for their now destitute and disease-ridden friend.

When they initially arrive (apparently all at the same time), they are shocked. He is not the man they once knew, and they demonstrate their profound sadness. They cry out in grief, tearing their clothes and smudging their heads and faces with dust. Then they join him on his garbage heap for seven long days. Not a word is spoken.

Finally Job clears his throat. His anger has been building up inside him, and now

Job's suffering

he explodes. He curses the day he was born. All the goodness he has enjoyed for so long does not begin to equal the unbearable misery that he has been suffering. If only the calendar could be turned back. If only his parents had not been intimate that night long ago. If only he had never been born. If only, if only, if only . . . How much better it would be if he were nonexistent.

Eliphaz is the first to speak. He's a windbag whose response is much longer than Job's cry of lament. After rambling on about the ways of God, he asks a pointed question and then, without waiting for a response, answers it himself:

> Where were the upright ever destroyed?
> As I have observed, those who plow evil
> and those who sow trouble reap it.
> At the breath of God they perish;
> at the blast of his anger they are no more.[11]

He goes on to admonish Job not to shrink from God's discipline. God is simply meting out the punishment he deserves.

Job is not buying it. Eliphaz has completely missed the point. Job's suffering is beyond what he can bear. "Is it any wonder," he demands, "that I'm screaming like a caged cat?" All he is asking for is that God let him die quickly—"squash me like a bug."[12] Then he turns on Eliphaz and the others, ordering them to point specifically to his sins if they think that is the issue. "Honest words never hurt anyone, but what's the point of all this pious bluster?"[13]

Job goes on to say that they are not going to shut him up—that his grievances are bitter, but at least they are honest, which is more than he can say for them. He hates his life; he wants to die, and they have come to suggest that he's gotten what he deserves. He's outraged.

Bildad then pipes up, scolding Job and suggesting that his words are nothing more than pathetic drivel. How dare he question the ways of God! Rather, he should fall on his face and confess his wretched sinfulness. If he's not guilty as he claims, God will restore everything he's lost. Indeed, Bildad suspects that Job must have offended God. Otherwise God would not be causing him to suffer.

Job is incredulous. Is he supposed to bring his case before God as though God is a judge? God is far beyond our ways. He's in charge of the entire universe. Here on earth he causes earthquakes and controls the tides. Job is aware of God's presence, but he has no recourse when bad things happen: "If he steals you blind, who can stop him?"[14] He could only wish that God were a man:

Job's Friends

In their ministerial anxiety, they are like flies buzzing around him on his dung heap. If they would just shut up . . . They are in his way. They are in God's way. They are trying to insert themselves between the silence of God and the one for whom the silence is intended.

Barbara Brown Taylor, *When God Is Silent*, 69

He is not a mere mortal like me . . . ,
that we might confront each other in court.
If only there were someone to mediate between us,
someone to bring us together,
someone to remove God's rod from me,
so that his terror would frighten me no more.
Then I would speak up without fear of him,
but as it now stands with me, I cannot.[15]

Job concludes that he might as well give up, because even if he is innocent there would be no way to prove it before a judge like God. All he can do is beg for mercy. But at the end of the day, God is essentially aloof from the anguish and pain he is suffering. All Job wants is to die in peace.

Zophar is distressed by Job's cynicism. Job has stepped over the line; no one should be allowed to speak of God the way he does. He is only making his situation worse, and he needs to come clean of all his sin.

Job will have none of it. He comes back to his point that God's ways are so far above ours that there is simply no way to make sense of them. Then he goes on the attack, telling them that if they have nothing helpful to say, they ought to shut up.

With that Job turns to God, begging him first of all to quit torturing him. Secondly, he would like to interact with God directly. If God has things against him, he would simply like to know what they are. But maybe this is not the issue at all. God probably has nothing to do with his troubles—or maybe he does. Job goes back and forth—at times seeming to lose faith altogether. *Is this miserable life all there is?* he wonders. *Or, is there actually life after death?*

The three friends take their turns scolding Job, accusing him of being unspiritual. They keep going back to the same refrain. God's law is that the wicked are punished. Who does he think he is? Should God change the laws of the universe just for him? *Come on, Job, get serious!* They pounce on Job's lack of faith, insisting that all he is interested in is his own well-being.

Job is sick and tired of his three friends, but he understands human nature. Friends often behave in fickle ways. Besides, his real beef is with God. His friends blabber on while God is silent. Where is God in

Where Is God When It Hurts?

God wants us to choose to love him freely, even when that choice involves pain, because we are committed to him, not to our own good feelings and rewards. He wants us to cleave to him, as Job did, even when we have every reason to deny him hotly. That, I believe, is the central message of Job. Satan had taunted God with the accusation that humans are not truly free. Was Job being faithful simply because God had allowed him a prosperous life? Job's fiery trials proved the answer beyond doubt. Job clung to God's justice when he was the best example in history of God's apparent injustice. He did not seek the Giver because of his gifts; when all gifts were removed he still sought the Giver.

Philip Yancey, *Where Is God When It Hurts?*, 98

all of his misery? If he were able to locate God, he would go directly to him. But God seems to be hiding.

For a while Job reminisces, longing for the times past when God was his friend, when he enjoyed laughter with his children and when he walked into the marketplace and was hailed with friendly greetings. It was a time when people showed him respect and when he in turn freely gave to those in need. Now he is held in contempt and bullied by the very ones who had looked up to him. This is the kind of treatment he receives for his upright life of faithfulness to his wife, fairness with his employees, and generosity to the poor.

Job and his three friends are getting nowhere in their arguments when Elihu, a young acquaintance of Job's, enters the discussion, imagining he can set all four of them straight. He promises to teach them wisdom. Some of his words Job has heard before, but he ends his long monologue with a benediction and a plea for wisdom.

After all of this, God finally speaks from the eye of a hurricane. Here God presents a panorama of the incredible marvels of the natural world—stars, oceans, fearsome beasts. As Job contemplates these wonders, God asks him if he had anything to do with any of this. Is he the one who brought the world into being and carried it to fruition? If not, does he really think he has the right to haul God into court and press charges?

Job, after offering several long monologues, is suddenly cowed and regrets his rantings. With Job's regrets proffered, God turns his attention to the friends. To Eliphaz he rages: "I've had it with you and your two friends. I'm fed up! You haven't been honest either with me or about me—not the way my friend Job has."[16] But God goes a step further and tells them to make an offering of seven bulls and seven rams for a burnt sacrifice. Job, who was straight and honest with God, is to oversee this burnt offering and to pray, asking God to spare them the punishment they deserve for all of their opinionated blather and phony righteousness.

God's final act is to bless Job by giving him back twice the flocks and herds he originally possessed, plus seven more sons and three more daughters. Interestingly, there is no further information offered about the sons. The daughters alone receive dazzling publicity. They are the loveliest young women in all the East, and their names capture that beauty: Dove is the oldest; Cinnamon, the middle daughter; and Darkeyes, the youngest. And, along with their brothers, they share in their father's inheritance.

Job lives to be an old man, an additional 140 years. He is again highly respected in the region, and family and friends come bearing gifts to congratulate him on his newfound prosperity. More than that, he enjoys family life, children, and grandchildren on to the fourth generation.

Concluding Observations

Scripture offers many details on the life of Job, but some are noticeably absent. How long is the time span of the conversations? Do they last weeks or months or more? Is the reader to assume that Job and his wife repaired any damage that might have been done to their relationship during the total obliteration of family and property? Did she work through her grief, as Job apparently did? Did she then bear him ten more children? Or are such questions entirely irrelevant to the parable-like account of this ancient righteous man of God?

Perhaps the most stunning aspect of Job's spiritual life is that he talks back to God—at times with a palpable sense of anger and outrage. It is the apologists, his three friends, who are severely taken to task. God does not need their defense. God's answer to the knotty questions of life appears through a display of his natural wonders.

Ezra and Nehemiah leave far fewer questions unanswered and appear almost pallid alongside Job. Not so with Vashti and Esther. They are beautiful and dynamic women—one who suffers for her strength of character, the other who is forever celebrated as the great Jewish queen of Persia who saved her people.

Further Reading

Duguid, Iain M. *Esther and Ruth: Reformed Expository Commentary*. Phillipsburg, NJ: P&R, 2005.

Janzen, J. Gerald. *Job: Interpretation; A Bible Commentary for Teaching and Preaching*. Louisville: Westminster John Knox, 1997.

Larson, Knute, and Kathy Dahlen. *Holman Old Testament Commentary: Ezra, Nehemiah, Esther*. Nashville: B & H Publishing Group, 2005.

Swindoll, Charles. *Job: A Man of Heroic Endurance*. Nashville: Nelson, 2009.

Taylor, Barbara Brown. *When God Is Silent*. New York: Cowley, 1998.

15

ISAIAH, JEREMIAH, EZEKIEL, AND DANIEL

Crying Out for God's People

If they were active in ministry today, the Major Prophets, with the possible exception of Daniel, would be regarded as seriously demented. They were not merely those who appear at outdoor festivals with placards declaring *The End Is Near!* Such activity would have been far too tame. Isaiah walked around naked for three years. The weeping Jeremiah wore a yoke around his neck and broke clay jars and was mocked and ridiculed day and night. Ezekiel lay on his side for more than a year (and that is the least of his apparent antics). Indeed, were they making their rounds today, the prophets would be deemed certifiable.

They hear the voice of God and comply with the directives no matter how bizarre they appear to be. And for all the indignity they endure, their reward is mockery. God in past times had often made strange demands on the patriarchs and judges and kings, but they witnessed the results in military victories and eye-popping miracles. Such was not typically the case with these prophets. Zealous in their faithfulness to God, they fueled their engines on high-octane humiliation.

Isaiah and Ezekiel

Prophets foretell things to come, sometimes in plain Hebrew, other times in religious riddles. Sometimes their words seem to make perfect sense only centuries later in light of subsequent events. Isaiah prophesied words that speak to the military maneuvers and human conditions of his own day and are also fulfilled in the life of Jesus. Jeremiah lamented the destruction of Jerusalem, and today in the Old City, Jews on Fridays read his Lamentations at the Wailing Wall, vowing never to forget the anguish of God's people so many centuries ago.

Ezekiel's bizarre visions are so complex as to confound both seers and ordinary citizens of any generation. Daniel, courageous and uncomplicated, is everyone's favorite prophet, though he too has baffled his readers through the ages, though some zealous present-day Christians confidently use his visions to predict the very day of Christ's return.

The era of the Major Prophets roughly coincides with the events leading up to the exile and the exile itself. Isaiah (whose contemporaries include Amos, Hosea, and Micah) is the most renowned prophet during King Hezekiah's reign over Judah prior to the exile, when the Assyrian forces were conquering Israel and preparing to lay siege to Jerusalem. Isaiah's prophecies relate to the fall of Jerusalem and the subsequent Babylonian captivity, as well as the future return of the Israelites to their land.

How deserted lies the city,
once so full of people!
How like a widow is she,
who once was great
among the nations!
She who was queen
among the provinces
has now become a slave.
Bitterly she weeps at night,
tears are on her cheeks.
Among all her lovers
there is no one to
comfort her.
All her friends have
betrayed her;
they have become
her enemies.
After affliction and
harsh labor,
Judah has gone into exile.

Lamentations 1:1–3 (NIV)

Jeremiah preaches in Judah during the reign of King Josiah. *The word of the Lord*

Saddest Day in the Old Testament

Perhaps the saddest day in Old Testament history was when Jerusalem was breached by the Babylonian army and the Hebrew temple was burned to the ground (586 B.C.). The prophet Jeremiah had foretold these gruesome days, and in his follow-up document, Lamentations, he further pursued the matter.

Wayne Jackson, "Survey of the Major Prophets"

comes to him more than 150 times during his some sixty years of prophesying. Amid the chaos of foreign occupation, he flees to Egypt in his old age.

The setting for Ezekiel is Babylon, where he is relocated as a result of the second deportation of Jews. Daniel, however, is among the first of the Israelites carted off to Babylon, and King Nebuchadnezzar factors significantly in his story.

Isaiah: Reluctant Prophet

He is a prophet, son of Amoz, whose voice was heard during the reigns—or partial reigns—of four kings of Judah: Uzziah, Jotham, Ahaz, and Hezekiah. He also delivers prophetic messages beyond the borders of Judah—to enemy tribes as well as the Northern Kingdom of Israel. His wife is also a prophet, and they have two sons: Shear-jashub and his younger brother Maher-shalal-hash-baz, a name bestowed by God—surely not by his mother.

In the year that King Uzziah dies, Isaiah's prophetic call is confirmed. He sees a grand vision of the Lord high on a throne, dressed in splendor, the train of his robe filling the whole Temple and his shining brightness covering the entire earth. Six-winged angels hover above, singing praises to God. It's almost too spectacular to look at, until suddenly everything is covered in a cloud of smoke.

Here is Isaiah in the midst of God's glory, and in an instant it's gone. The glorious face of God is enveloped in smoke. Isaiah's first words: "Doom! It's Doomsday! I'm as good as dead! Every word I've ever spoken is tainted—blasphemous even!" He is interrupted by an angel who flies down to him and touches his lips with a burning coal. The angel's words explain the significance: "Gone your guilt, your sins wiped out." Then the Lord calls out: "Whom shall I send? Who will go for us?" With no hesitation, Isaiah responds: "Here am I; send me."[1]

Only then does Isaiah learn how filled with doom his message will be. He is to warn the people of Judah that both their towns and their countryside will be devastated because of their evil behavior. Later on, after Jotham is no longer on the throne

The Son of a Prophet

The practice of naming children after one's vocation owes something to Israel's greatest prophet, Isaiah. . . . So critical was repentance to the prophet Isaiah that he named his son *Shear-Yashuv*, "a remnant will return/repent" after judgment (Isa. 7:3). Imagine growing up with that as your handle. . . . Isaiah's action of naming is among the notoriously interesting prophetic actions of the prophets.

Scot McKnight, *Turning to Jesus: The Sociology of Conversion in the Gospels*, 32 and his son Ahaz is ruling, God speaks to Isaiah again, telling him that he is to meet with Ahaz, accompanied only by his son Shear-jashub. Isaiah conveys to Ahaz he should not be threatened by what he is hearing about planned attacks from his enemies, the Arameans, allied with Israel, the Northern Kingdom.

Ahaz is less than convinced by these prophetic words from Isaiah. He's preparing for a counterattack and is not about to just sit back and do nothing. Isaiah tells Ahaz to ask for a sign from God to confirm his prophecy. Ahaz demurs. How dare he demand a sign from God? So Isaiah tells him that God will give him a sign anyway, whether he wants one or not. Here is the sign:

> A girl who is presently a virgin will get pregnant. She'll bear a son and name him Immanuel (God-With-Us). By the time the child is twelve years old, able to make moral decisions, the threat of war will be over. Relax, those two kings that have you so worried will be out of the picture. But also be warned: God will bring on you and your people and your government a judgment worse than anything since the time the kingdom split, when Ephraim left Judah. The king of Assyria is coming!"[2]

Here Isaiah has prophesied that the lands of Aram and Israel will be destroyed by the mighty Assyrians, but the king and the people of Judah largely ignore him, while at the same time they worry about trivial matters. Isaiah himself might be tempted to dismiss his own words but for God's continual prodding. "God spoke strongly to me," he testifies, "grabbed me with both hands and warned me not to go along with this people."[3] Yet there is also a word from God concerning the impending destruction of those same Assyrians.

Isaiah receives another message from God in the year King Ahaz dies—this time, however, not the glorious vision of the Almighty on a throne. Rather, it appears to be a warning to the Philistines not to celebrate too soon the end of their own oppression. There will be a terrible famine, and the population will be decimated. And neither will Moab be spared, nor Damascus (Syria).

In the end Judah will emerge victorious, with a new government that harks back to the time of David. The new leader (possibly King Hezekiah) will be known for compassion and justice. A time of peace will follow.

"Isaiah" in West Michigan

A Hastings man attracted attention of horn-honking motorists as he disrobed on an afternoon stroll. By the time he got to Hastings Library, he was naked. Police received several calls just before 4 p.m. Monday about a naked man walking on East State Street. "When Hastings police officers arrived, there were several cars behind him honking their horns since he was, indeed, naked," Police Chief Jerry Sarver said. The explanation: "He told police . . . God wanted us all to be peaceful and that this world was an evil place." Police arrested the 42-year-old man for indecent exposure.

John Agar, "Naked Man Tells Hastings Police: God Wants All to Be 'Peaceful'"

But before then, times will be hard, not for Judah only but also its neighbors Ethiopia and Egypt. Indeed, Isaiah is an international prophet, for he speaks God's judgment on entire peoples across a vast region.

Isaiah is not one to talk back to God as Job did. He takes God's orders seriously even when he would no doubt rather run away and hide like Elijah. So when God instructs him to strip naked and go out about town prophesying, that's exactly what he does—for three years no less. This is God's way of warning Ethiopia and Egypt of their coming enslavement by

Everyday *Life*

Ailments and Remedies

When Hezekiah is sick unto death with a boil, the remedy of choice is a lump of figs. The Israelites utilized a variety of herbs and roots and other folk medicines. The most frequently referenced healing substance in the Old Testament is the balm of Gilead, used for a variety of ailments. This balm, or balsam, is a gum resin that is found in a thorny flowering shrub native to the Near East. It was used as a healing salve as well as in the making of perfume. Jeremiah uses the term metaphorically: "Is there no balm in Gilead? Is there no physician there? Why then is there no healing for the wound of my people?" (Jer. 8:22 NIV).

Few illnesses mentioned in the Old Testament are clearly identified. For example, King Asa suffered from a disease of his feet. His ailment is often presumed to be gout, but it could have been no more than a bad case of athlete's foot. Nor are Job's dreadful boils diagnosed apart from the burning itch. Leprosy was a common biblical malady—a most frightful skin disease with no cure, often viewed as a curse from God. And indeed it was so in the case of Moses' sister Miriam, Elisha's servant Gehazi and his family, and King Uzziah and his family and descendants.

Natural Roots and Remedies

Since the ancient peoples knew so little about the causes of disease and death, their medicine and healing depended largely on the use of natural roots and plants that had proven useful in the past for certain symptoms. For wounds and external sores, they had many useful remedies, including the famed balm of Gilead that Jeremiah mentions in his oracles (Jer 8:22). But for fevers and viral diseases, there was little that they could do since they did not even guess the causes. For these dangerous and often fatal illnesses, the ancient world either tried fantastic cures, using strange and exotic animal parts almost as though one could stop the strange disease by an even stranger medicine, or else they resorted to prayer, begging the gods for mercy and healing.

Lawrence Boadt, *Reading the Old Testament: An Introduction*, 248 the Assyrians. But to people around town it no doubt seems ridiculous—or worse. Indeed, it is amazing he was not arrested for indecent exposure.

Sometime later, in the fourteenth year of King Hezekiah's reign, Judah faces a dire political situation due to Assyria's attack and the capture of Judah's fortified cities. At one point, Assyrian king Sennacherib sends his top military general to warn Hezekiah not to depend on Egypt for protection. Even with such an ally Judah doesn't stand a chance against the mighty Assyrian army. The general tries to influence the people to simply give up and make peace with Assyria.

Hezekiah hears the news, and he tears his clothes in anguish, thinking this is Judah's darkest day. He sends for Isaiah, who brings him a message from God: *Calm down. The news isn't bad after all.* Indeed, it is not. God sends his angel of death to decimate the Assyrian camp. Nearly two hundred thousand soldiers die in one day, and the king, after fleeing home to Nineveh, is murdered by his sons.

But no sooner does Hezekiah think things are going his way than he becomes seriously ill. Isaiah shows up with a message from God that this is a terminal illness and Hezekiah should get his affairs in order. As Isaiah leaves, Hezekiah turns to face the wall, and he weeps and prays, begging God to spare his life. While he is still praying, God is speaking to Isaiah, telling him to go back to Hezekiah, for he has heard Hezekiah's prayer and will give him fifteen more years. In addition he will save Judah from the grip of Assyria. As a sign of God's promise, the shadow of the sundial moves backward as the sun sets.

Later, when Hezekiah gives the son of the king of Babylon a tour of the palace complex with all its royal treasures, Isaiah reproves him for showing off and prophesies dire consequences. Everything Hezekiah has proudly displayed to the Babylonian delegation will one day be confiscated by the Babylonians themselves.

Isaiah's prophecies are not all doom and gloom and judgment. He is a good-news prophet with a message of hope and salvation who foretells a glorious Messianic age when God's Kingdom will rule upon the earth.

> Arise, shine, for your light has
> come,
> and the glory of the LORD rises
> upon you.
> See, darkness covers the earth
> and thick darkness is over the
> peoples,
> but the LORD rises upon you
> and his glory appears over you.
> Nations will come to your light,
> and kings to the brightness of
> your dawn.[4]

And he reminds his hearers of God's constant faithfulness toward his chosen people despite their betrayal of him.

> Can a mother forget the baby at her
> breast
> and have no compassion on the
> child she has borne?
> Though she may forget,
> I will not forget you![5]

Jeremiah: Weeping Prophet

Born into a priestly family in the Benjamite town of Anathoth, Jeremiah first hears and delivers God's word in the thirteenth year of the reign of Josiah, king of Judah. His prophetic ministry lasts through the reigns of Judah's two succeeding kings, Jehoiakim and Zedekiah. In addition, God briefly sends him to the northern kingdom as well. He is the son of Hilkiah, who found the lost copy of the Book of the Law and encouraged King Josiah to have it read before the people.

More than any other prophet, he is the one remembered for prophesying the exile. The first message Jeremiah hears from God is very personal: he had been tagged for ministry even before he was born. His response is reminiscent of that of Moses, though in this case, the excuse is youth: "I don't know anything. I'm only a boy!"[6]

God is tender with him, telling him not to be afraid. Then going a step further, he touches his mouth and says: "Look! I've just put my words in your mouth—hand-delivered!"[7] The words Jeremiah is to deliver are declarations of doom on Israel. His assignment is not easy. Among other things, he is to compare Israel with an unfaithful wife who runs off with another man—maybe more than one. "And isn't that what you've done—'whored' your way with god after god? And now you want to come back as if nothing had happened."[8]

Calling out this message of doom sometimes really gets to Jeremiah. Nobody is listening: "It's hopeless! Their ears are stuffed with wax—deaf as a post, blind as a bat."[9] He is convinced the message is all too true and becomes depressed and wishes he could get away from it all. He laments,

> I wish my head were a well of water
> and my eyes fountains of tears,
> So I could weep day and night
> for casualties among my dear,
> dear people.
> At times I wish I had a wilderness
> hut,
> a backwoods cabin,
> Where I could get away from my
> people
> and never see them again.[10]

Yet Jeremiah is told not to pray for his dear, dear people. Later on Jeremiah is less inclined to think of his audience as dear people. He realizes that they are out to get him. Indeed, God confirms to him that conspirators in his hometown of Anathoth are plotting his murder.

In this context, Jeremiah raises the fairness issue with God. He lives with death threats while the wicked prosper. *Why?* he wonders. And much more personally, it seems God doesn't overlook any of his flaws. God essentially tells him not to be so impatient. Their time is coming. In the meantime he must continue preaching. He hasn't seen the worst of it. As for Jeremiah himself, he must keep his wits about him and remain calm.

Sometimes God gives Jeremiah object lessons to prove his point. On one occasion Jeremiah is instructed to purchase a pair of linen undershorts and to wear them, not removing them for washing. Later he is told to take the shorts to Parath and hide them between two rocks and after a period of time go and fetch them. They are nearly decomposed. So it will also be, God tells him, with Judah—a one-time proud nation that will become as soiled and decayed as his underpants.

Things will be so bad that God warns Jeremiah not to get married, not to even think of having a family. The doom is deserved—so much so that Jeremiah is told not to attend burials or grieve with those who have lost loved ones. In fact, he is to abandon any social get-togethers. No feasting or celebrations. Rather, he should stand out in the marketplace and preach the necessity of Sabbath keeping.

Again on God's orders, Jeremiah goes to a potter's shop. As he observes, he notices a piece turning on the wheel that has flaws, so the potter starts over with the same hunk of clay. This is how it is, God tells him. If the people repent, he won't cast them out; rather, he will mold them into a fine piece of pottery. But God is not done with his pottery object lesson. He tells Jeremiah to go back and purchase a clay pot. Then he is to gather together some of the leaders and preach God's call to repent, culminating with a warning of what will happen if they do not. He smashes the pot right before their eyes. That is their doom.

Jeremiah in deep contemplation

The leaders—priests included—are not amused by such dire threats. They blame the messenger. The chief Temple priest, after listening to one of Jeremiah's sermons, lashes him and locks him in stocks at one of the Temple gates. But even when locked up, Jeremiah keeps preaching God's doom on the priest and his family and all of Judah. They will all be hauled off into exile.

Jeremiah's outward confidence contrasts with his private humiliation. It's awful. Why does God do this to him?

> You pushed me into this, GOD, and I
> let you do it.
> You were too much for me.
> And now I'm a public joke.
> They all poke fun at me.
> Every time I open my mouth
> I'm shouting, "Murder!" or
> "Rape!"
> And all I get for my GOD-warnings
> are insults and contempt.[11]

Jeremiah wants to give up. He's exhausted. It's painful being a prophet. Friends from

Sorrow, Pain, Ending My Days in Shame

The voice of Jeremiah is compelling, often on an overwhelmingly personal level. One morning, I was so worn out by the emotional roller coaster of chapter 20 that after prayers I walked to my apartment and went back to bed. This passionate soliloquy, which begins with a bitter outburst on the nature of the prophet's calling ("You enticed me, O Lord, and I was enticed"), moves quickly into denial ("I say to myself, I will not mention him, I will speak his name no more. But then it becomes like fire burning in my heart, imprisoned in my bones"). Jeremiah's anger at the way his enemies deride him rears up, and also fear and sorrow ("All my close friends are watching for me to stumble"). His statement of confidence in God ("The Lord is with me like a dread warrior") seems forced under the circumstances, and a brief doxology ("Sing to the Lord, praise the Lord, for he has delivered the life of the needy from the hands of evildoers") feels more ironic than not, being followed by a bitter cry: "Cursed be the day that I was born." The chapter concludes with an anguished question: "Why did I come forth from the womb, to see sorrow and pain, to end my days in shame?"

Kathleen Norris, *Cloister Walk*, 36

long ago are scorning him. Yet he is of two minds. God is powerful and is on his side. Praise God! But then again, life is grim. Like Job, he curses the day he was born. No, rather it would have been better if his mother had miscarried and he would have had the good fortune of having died in the womb.

Like Nehemiah and others before him, Jeremiah speaks God's message of justice. To Zedekiah, the king of Judah, he declares: "Attend to matters of justice. . . . Rescue victims from their exploiters. Don't take advantage of the homeless, the orphans, the widows. Stop the murdering!"[12] Only then will Zedekiah follow in the line of King David. And later Jeremiah rails against Zedekiah and the residents of Jerusalem for reneging on their covenant promise to free their slaves.

On another occasion God gives Jeremiah an object lesson, showing him two baskets of figs, one filled with the best available on the market, the other with spoiled figs. The first is God's assurance of good treatment to those in exile in Babylon; the second is how God will treat the king, his henchmen, and all the rest who have stayed behind in Judah.

Everywhere Jeremiah goes he faces opposition. Later he is preaching a sermon of doom in the Temple. Hardly has he given the benediction when he is attacked by the crowd—priests, prophets, and ordinary people. They charge him with blaspheming the Temple because he is saying it will become a pile of ruins. They have no other choice. He must die. But in the end he is spared by officials who take him at his word, convinced that he is preaching God's message.

Jeremiah is certainly not the only prophet in the land. Time and again he faces off with them, each claiming the other is preaching a false message. Hananiah is one such opponent. When Jeremiah is going around wearing a harness and yoke to show how the king and the people will be under the yoke of Babylon, Hananiah yanks it off Jeremiah's shoulders and shatters it on the ground—telling the crowd that the yoke of Babylon will be smashed in the same way. But God, through Jeremiah, has the last word. Within a year Hananiah will be dead.

While warning of doom to fall on the king and others who have remained behind, Jeremiah sends words of hope to those in exile. They are to settle in and establish homes and gardens and families—and be loyal to Babylon. They should look forward to coming back home, but not before the prophesied seventy years in exile.

At one point in his prophetic ministry, Jeremiah travels from Jerusalem to a region in the tribe of Benjamin for personal matters. There his political loyalties are questioned, and he is hauled in by law enforcement and incarcerated in an underground dungeon. After a lengthy imprisonment, King Zedekiah, fearing Jeremiah may actually have a pipeline to God, frees him from the dungeon and places him under palace house arrest.

But Jeremiah is surely not yet out of the woods. The king's highest officials want him put to death for prophesying the imminent destruction of Jerusalem. The king gives in to their demands and turns Jeremiah over to them. They are not satisfied with merely killing him. Torture is their aim. They take him out to an old cistern no longer in use. With ropes they lower him deep down into the mud, which will serve as his tomb.

A Prophet Torn between Faith and Doubt

Although it is not an easy task simply to read the Book of Jeremiah, given the form in which its subject matter has survived, nevertheless it is an indisputable fact that, taken at face value, a partial but striking picture of the prophet emerges from the pages of the book named after him. Unlike many of the biblical prophets, who remain perpetually as figures in the shadows of history, Jeremiah stands out as a truly human figure. He is torn between faith and doubt, he is deeply involved in the contemporary affairs of his time, and, in the pages of his book, he passes from youth to old age against the backdrop of the history of the era.

Peter C. Craigie et al., *Jeremiah 1–25*, xxxvii

When the king learns of this plot to torture him, however, he orders his Ethiopian palace officer to procure a small team of men to rescue Jeremiah and bring him back to the palace. Taking Jeremiah aside in private, the king questions him about his prophecies. Jeremiah pointedly tells him to surrender to the forces of Babylon in order to prevent his own destruction and that of his family and the entire city.

The king ignores his counsel and suffers the consequences. King Nebuchadnezzar of Babylon attacks Jerusalem, overrunning the city. Zedekiah, his sons, and his top officials escape but all are hunted down and killed, except the king, who is tortured and taken captive to Babylon. Before the carnage is over, Jerusalem is in ruins and its citizens are taken into exile. Jeremiah, however, is given special treatment.

In addition to his prophecies against Judah and her kings, Jeremiah preaches destruction and doom against nearly every other nation and people in the region—even the Babylonians, their captors.

When given the opportunity to go with the exiles to Babylon or to remain in Judah, Jeremiah decides to remain. Jerusalem had met its destruction, but the towns and countryside are largely unaffected. He is free to reside wherever he wishes. He speaks, with God's authority, informing the leaders remaining in Judah that they and the people should not make an exodus to Egypt.

But, par for the course, they ignore Jeremiah's prophecy, and many make their way to Egypt, taking Jeremiah with them. There he sets up stones and declares God's word: "I'm sending for and bringing Nebuchadnezzar the king of Babylon—my servant, mind you!—and he'll set up his throne on these very stones that I've had buried here and he'll spread out his canopy over them. He'll come and absolutely smash Egypt."[13]

Jeremiah goes on to prophesy that those who had come to Egypt against God's command would be slaughtered or die of starvation. At the same time, those in exile will soon be able to return home safely and rebuild all that is in ruins. This is good news, and Jeremiah does remind them that God still is their covenant Lord despite their ruined cities and their own exile. But most of what Jeremiah has prophesied is bad news—particularly the destruction of Jerusalem. For this terrible series of events, he writes his Lamentations, the words of the "weeping prophet," the name by which he has become most well known. But more than *weeping*, Jeremiah should be remembered as the *suffering* prophet. There is no record of his death, but it is presumed that he died while in Egypt.

Ezekiel: Visions of Wheels and Dry Bones

Ezekiel's fantastic visions are what distinguish him from the other prophets. At the age of thirty, the heavens open up and he sees God. Not the magnificent,

Ezekiel's Task

The task that was assigned to Ezekiel was to prophesy to the exiles of Judah, who had been carried away into captivity in distant Babylonia. It was an audience close to despair, asking why this disaster had come on them and where God was in the middle of their personal holocaust. Their assessment of their own conditions was: "Our bones are dried up and our hope is gone; we are cut off" (Ezek. 37:11). What use was a God who seemed unable or unwilling to protect his own land? What use was a God who allowed his own temple in Jerusalem to be defiled? What use was a God who allowed his own people to be carried away from the land he had promised to the patriarchs? Even if he were to intervene now on behalf of his land, how would that help those who were far away in exile? These were the questions with which the exiles struggled.

The answers to these questions permeate the book.

Iain M. Duguid, *The NIV Application Commentary: Ezekiel*, 35 anthropomorphic God of Michelangelo's paintings. Rather, an undomesticated, electrifying God of a special-effects action film. Ezekiel is not necessarily the kind of person one would associate with such visionary spectacles. He is no wild and crazy prophet living in desert caves. Ezekiel is a priest, the son of Buzi. His waterfront residence is on the Kebar River in the beautiful city of Babylon, where many of his fellow Jews are in exile.

The vision God sets before him is spectacular, if not scary. He looks up and sees a fireball within a tornado, and inside the fire are four figures with columned legs, each creature with four wings and four faces, part human and part animal. Fire and lightning are everywhere, and beside these figures are wheels—and more wheels flashing and spinning like helicopter blades. And above all this there is a huge, skylike dome. The flapping wings of the creatures are deafening, like the roar of a waterfall and the booming of battlefield cannons.

Ezekiel falls on his face and hears a voice calling him to preach to the rebellious house of Israel. God tells him he will be treated very badly, making him feel as though he is being attacked by scorpions. Then he is told to open his mouth and eat what is handed to him. No tasty food for Ezekiel to inaugurate his ministry. Rather, a scroll with a message of doomsday. But amazingly enough, the book tastes like a honeycomb.

God gives Ezekiel, whom he calls *Son of man*, the message. But Ezekiel is to make the words his own as though he is carried away by the spirit. Such a condition might have filled him with the joy of the Lord. It doesn't; he's outraged and distraught. Why couldn't God have picked on someone else? His life is routine and peaceful. The last thing he wants is controversy and conflict. He goes out along the Kebar River and sits there for a week. Then God speaks to him again. More than that, he yanks him up by the shoulder and tells him to get out into the country on the plain, where God can talk to him again.

Again he sees God's glory like he had seen before. He falls before God, and the Spirit comes on him and tells him to go home, where he will be bound with ropes and will be tongue-tied. When God unties the ropes and his tongue, he will be ready to preach. Then God tells him to do something truly bizarre. He is to lie on his side for 390 days, representing the same number in years that the Israelite exiles have been living in sin. By this enactment God is telling him that he must bear the sin of Israel and that he is responsible for their salvation.

God goes on to give him instructions on preparing his food during this more-than-yearlong confinement. Ezekiel protests. God relents on one issue, agreeing that he will not be forced to bake his bread over human dung. All this is done in preparation for God's warning of an impending famine.

Sometimes Ezekiel prophesies terrifying events that make the people shudder, as when he declares: "I'm going to do something to you that I've never done before and will never do again: turn families into cannibals—parents eating children, children eating parents!"[14] After that God decrees that all but a few of the people will die one way or another. Only then will God's wrath be assuaged.

Again Ezekiel is swept into the heavens by the Spirit. There he sees more visions, including pornographic images of Asherah, the sex goddess. More visions appear of people worshiping false gods, and still more of angels and people being slaughtered. All the while the Spirit of God is sweeping him off his feet and taking him from one place to another in Jerusalem and then back to Babylon.

Ezekiel receives more visions and pursues his thankless task, but the people are unmoved. In their mind he is no more than a crank, and his message a broken record, *same old, same old*. But God does not let up on him. He is to preach whether the people listen or not. To complicate matters, there are competing prophets—both men and women—with popular appeal. Ezekiel is commanded to oppose them to their face.

Poor Ezekiel. God continues to make severe demands of him. He is told to endure the death of his dearly beloved wife, but not to mourn. What an awful sacrifice this is. For the Jewish people, mourning is not simply the shedding of tears. It is a long-established, ritualized custom. He is to use this shocking cultural *faux pas* as an illustration of how God regards Israel's spiritual death.

Sometimes Ezekiel's prophecies are parables, as in the case of the two sisters, Oholah and Oholibah, representing Samaria and Jerusalem, capitals of Israel and Judah. The sisters became "whores from a young age. Their breasts were fondled, their young bosoms caressed." Oholibah, the youngest, is looser than her sister, "crazy with lust" and "incredibly filthy," going "public with her fornication" and displaying "her sex to the world." All this

Ezekiel preaching and prophesying

Preaching Dry Bones in the Rain

We had an attentive congregation at Gloucester in the evening. In the morning . . . I preached to about five thousand there. . . . It rained violently at five in the evening; notwithstanding which two or three thousand people stayed, to whom I expounded the glorious vision of Ezekiel, of the resurrection of dry bones.

John Wesley, *The Journal of Rev. John Wesley*, 202

"whetted her appetite for more virile, vulgar, and violent lovers—stallions obsessive in their lust." In the end both sisters are "worn-out whores," having been abused by their Assyrian and Babylonian lovers.[15]

At other times Ezekiel soars into poetic ecstasy:

> A great eagle
> with a huge wingspan and long feathers
> . . . took a cutting from the land
> and planted it in good, well-watered soil,
> like a willow on a riverbank.[16]

Again, he writes:

> Your mother was like a vine in a vineyard,
> transplanted alongside streams of water,
> Luxurious in branches and grapes . . .
> fit to be carved into a royal scepter.
> It grew high, reaching into the clouds.[17]

Clearly the most colorful of the prophets, Ezekiel is not only a priest but also a preacher and an actor. The images he sees in the heavens are displays of spectacular wonder, but it is his own creative genius that allows him to transmit God's message to the people in such multilayered richness. His pleas and accusations are filled with metaphors and glittering images of emeralds, diamonds, sapphires, and costly silks. Perfume, incense, and oil serve as aroma therapy. But then with no warning, the listeners gag over an image of a bloody infant, and they cringe as he spews forth invective on whores, fornication, brothels, and pornography.

Ezekiel's most memorable vision calls forth the valley of dry bones. Imagine peering into a valley—once a city—whose only residents are bones. God instructs him to prophesy to these bones. Bones? They are the remains of dead people. How could bones possibly hear his voice? But the bones are a metaphor for the people. They have no life left in them. They have simply dried out. Now Ezekiel is telling them that they can live again—a message for God's backslidden people of any time or place.

Daniel: Surviving a Furnace, a Lion Den, and Bad Dreams

An Israelite in exile, he might have gone unnoticed and blended in with all the other young men of the city. But King Nebuchadnezzar is looking for the cream of the crop—young men who meet the qualifications for leadership positions. They will receive the best Babylonian training—and propaganda—money can buy. Daniel is one such young man. He is from a blue-blood family in Judah with ties to nobility. Possessing a brilliant mind and the recipient of a rigorous education, he is athletic, good-looking, and brimming with health.

Transformation is what the king has in mind. A Babylonian name change is a requisite. From that point on he will be known as Belteshazzar. Also necessary is language and cultural immersion—no more confining himself to the Jewish ghetto. He needs to become part of Babylonian society, and, in particular, he must develop a deep familiarity with the magic arts. Finally, a special diet. The menu will be the same as that of the king—the most delectable dishes and the most expensive wines.

It is an opportunity of a lifetime. Daniel, along with Shadrach, Meshach, and Abednego, is chosen out of all the young male Israelite exiles. But he balks—particularly over the required diet. The cultural immersion program he can deal with—so also the name change. But he is determined not to eat the king's food, heavy on meat and sweets. It simply is not the proper diet for a Jewish youth devoted to God.

Defying the king, however, does not seem to be in his own best interest. But he has found favor with the palace director, who is willing to comply with Daniel's dietary preferences. He is concerned, however, that such a diet might make him weak and pale in comparison to those who eat the king's food. Daniel talks to the head of food services and arranges for a plain and simple vegetarian fare for him and his three friends.

At the end of ten days these four young men look healthier than those eating from the king's menu. So they carry on with their diet. But they do not only stand out in matters of health. They learn quickly and pass all the tests with flying colors. In fact, Daniel and his friends rank highest in everything. Moreover, they excel in knowledge of visions and dream interpretation. The king finds them far more capable than his own magicians and seers.

Daniel's reputation catches the attention of King Nebuchadnezzar, who is having nightmares so troubling that he can hardly sleep at all and cannot remember in the morning what he had dreamt. His own magicians are at their wit's end. The king is furious. If they are truly fortunetellers, why can't they tell him what his dreams were and what they mean? He is so outraged that he orders the execution of all so-called diviners, including Daniel and his three friends.

Daniel immediately sends a message to the king that he wants a shot at interpreting his dreams. When the king questions Daniel's competency, wondering why he thinks he can do what the royal diviners cannot, Daniel tells him that no human being possesses such psychic powers. Only God. He then proceeds to tell the king that his vision was of a giant statue of a man made from head to toe of various metals—gold, silver,

A Tale of Two Cities

One of the most influential books on theology ever written is *The City of God*, by Saint Augustine of Hippo (written between AD 412 and 426). Its theme concerns the existence of two societies, which Augustine calls "cities." One is God's society. The other is the society of this world. Augustine described them, saying, "Two cities have been formed by two loves: the earthly by the love of self, even to the contempt of God; the heavenly by the love of God, even to the contempt of self." . . . Much of his discussion concerns the contrast between Babylon, which he sees as a spectacular embodiment of the earthly city, and earthly Jerusalem which he sees as a symbol of the city of God.

James Montgomery Boice, *Daniel: An Expositional Commentary*, 16 bronze, iron. In the dream a boulder hits the statue and crumbles it to bits, while the boulder becomes a massive mountain.

The interpretation, Daniel informs the king, is that the statue stands for a series of empires, including his own, which will be overcome by other kingdoms. Eventually the realm will deteriorate and crumble altogether. In the end, however, God's kingdom will rule forever. Amazingly, Nebuchadnezzar not only accepts Daniel's words as true but falls before him and worships Daniel's God.

Now in the king's favor, Daniel is put in charge of the palace complex, with his three friends in lesser positions. Things go well until the king decides to have his sculptors erect a ninety-foot gold statue. It is a sight to behold, but it has more than aesthetic qualities. On the day of its dedication the people are expected to fall on their knees and worship it. The penalty for defying the order is *time-out* in a furnace.

Not surprisingly, Daniel and his three friends do not comply. Shadrach, Meshach, and Abednego are reported and brought before the king. When threatened, they stand their ground, insisting that God will keep them safe—even in a furnace.

The king is upset with their defiance and orders that the furnace be stoked up much hotter than usual and that the men be tied up. But getting the three young men inside turns out to be such an ordeal that the guards commissioned to carry out the dastardly deed are scorched to death. Daniel's three friends, however, are not even singed.

But what happens next is most stunning. The king looks into the fire and declares that he sees four men walking around in the fire unharmed, one of whom has the appearance of a god. The king orders them to come out of the furnace, recognizing that their God has saved them. In fact, he makes a proclamation forbidding any abuse of their God.

More than that, Nebuchadnezzar becomes a short-term evangelist, telling people what God has done for him. He praises God for his miracles and for his kingdom, which will last forever. But the king soon realizes that his commitment to God doesn't mean that he will have no more nightmares. Hardly has his praise of God spread over the land before he endures another frightful night of dreaming. Again he summons his diviners. None can interpret his dream. So he calls for Daniel.

In the dream a magnificent fruit tree is growing toward the sky, with limbs stretching across the world, giving shelter to birds and animals of all kinds. A man is coming down from heaven, ordering that the tree be cut down and denuded. The birds and animals are to be scattered. All that is to remain is a stump along with the roots. And something else: there's a man in the dream acting and looking like an animal.

Daniel interprets it. Immediately he knows this dream is not about foreign empires and kings. It is about Nebuchadnezzar himself. The tree, Daniel tells the king, represents his rule over his vast realm. God, however, has put judgment on him. Not only will his realm be chopped down, but he himself will essentially be driven insane, living with wild animals and grazing on the grass of the field. This will continue for seven years.

Daniel is bold in delivering God's message and advises the king to turn from his wicked ways and look after the needs of the poor. Nebuchadnezzar is indeed punished. He does lose his mind, eat grass, and look less than human with his disheveled hair of feathers and his clawlike feet. Once his seven-year sentence is over, however, he is a reformed man, back to ruling his expanded kingdom, but now again singing praises to God.

Visions and dreams are not the stuff of royalty alone. Daniel is a dreamer himself—though hardly of what might be described as *sweet dreams*. The first dream he records is a night terror. Four beasts rise out of the sea—a winged lion, a bear, a panther with four wings and four heads, and a ferocious ten-horned dragon. As the dream progresses, flaming thrones come into view, and also an *Old One* dressed in white with a vast multitude of servants. Then there is a trial of sorts, with the monster thrown into the fire. Finally, a man descends from the clouds, and the Old One bestows on him the power to reign eternally.

So troubled is Daniel that he asks a passerby what his dream means. The fellow offers an elaborate interpretation without any prodding. One ruler will displace another until finally the people of God will reign forever. The interpretation terrifies Daniel as much as did the dream itself, but he tells no one about it.

Two years later Daniel records another dream. This time he sees a ram with large, uneven horns. It charges in all directions, defeating every foe. Then Daniel sees a single-horned, flying billy goat charge and overcome the ram. After that the billy goat increases to a massive size, all the while sprouting new horns, one of which reaches to heaven and throws stars down and tramples them in defiance of God. Daniel learns from an angel that this desecration will last twenty-three hundred evenings and mornings.

Daniel is befuddled. This vision, he learns, relates to the end times, but he cannot make sense of it. He is very much troubled as he fasts and prays and repents, not for himself only but for all of God's people. He is in the midst of his intense devotional time when suddenly the angel Gabriel comes flying in. Gabriel's mission is to visit Daniel and clarify the future, particularly the seventy sevens of time (sixty-two of which the people will be spending rebuilding Jerusalem and getting right with God). This vision will intrigue end-time preachers into the twenty-first century.

When Nebuchadnezzar dies he is succeeded by his son Belshazzar, who continues the worship of false gods. During a lavish banquet, when he and his guests are more than merry with wine, he sees a ghostly hand writing on the wall. Terrified, he recognizes this immediately as an evil omen. Remembering his father's troubles, announced by visionary warnings, he summons all the court magicians. They come up dry—no clue as to what the writing portends. When the queen hears of the king's alarm, she hurries to the ballroom to remind him of Daniel.

Belshazzar seems to have forgotten all about him. When Daniel is summoned, the king inquires if he is the same Daniel who had interpreted his father's dreams. If so, Belshazzar is confident the mystery will be solved. He requests a repeat performance and offers generous compensation—a royal robe, complete with a gold necklace. Daniel will also be restored to his high position of power.

Daniel eagerly accepts the challenge, but he tells the king that he desires no remuneration. Then he begins dressing down the king, pointing out that he is just as bad as, maybe even worse than, his father had been. Indeed, his guests are drinking from chalices pillaged from the Temple in Jerusalem, offering toasts to their false gods.

So what is the meaning of the writing on the wall? First of all, God is saying that King Belshazzar's days are numbered. Secondly, when his worth is weighed on the balancing scale, it is not impressive. Thirdly, his realm is now to be divided between the Medes and Persians.

Daniel's Glorious Night

What a splendid night he must have spent with those lions! I do not wonder that in after days he saw visions of lions and wild beasts; it seems most natural that he should; and he must have been fitted by that night passed among these grim monsters to see grand sights. In any case he must have had a glorious night. What with the lions, and with angels all night to keep him company, he was spending the night-watches in grander style than Darius.

C. H. Spurgeon, "Daniel Facing the Lions' Den"

Another king might have locked Daniel in prison. Not Belshazzar. He carries out his promises of remuneration to Daniel, who backs down and accepts. Now donned in a royal robe and a gold chain necklace, he steps into his high court position. But he wakes the next morning to learn that the king has been murdered. The Medes are now in control, and Darius is king.

With the changing of the guard, Daniel might have easily found himself on the losing end. But he is one of three top administrators who supervise regional governors. So resourceful and competent is he that Darius promotes him to second in command. The other administrators and governors resent him and vow to undermine his efforts. They know where Daniel is vulnerable. He is unconventional, insisting on worshiping his God and none other.

So they plot together and request an audience with the king. They praise him as though he is a god and then suggest that he issue a proclamation dedicating thirty days of prayer to one god only. The god they have in mind is Darius himself. Defiance of the decree, they propose, will mean *time-out* not in a fiery furnace, but something more interesting—a lions' den. Darius snaps at the proposal, and marks it with his irreversible stamp of approval.

No sooner has Darius stamped the decree than Daniel is reported for defying the king's irreversible proclamation—praying to his own God publicly no less than three times a day. The king is beside himself and seeks to weasel out of his irreversible decree. Surely he can figure out some way to exempt his most trusted advisor. But the conniving administrators hold him to the law—his own law. So Daniel is unceremoniously ushered into a dungeonlike cave occupied by hungry lions, heavily secured on all sides. There is no way of escape.

Daniel realizes that his friend Darius is guilty of gross arrogance, but surely not malice. Unbeknownst to Daniel, the king is so upset he refuses any food in order to fast and pray through the night. At dawn he rushes to the lions' den, fearing the worst. Instead he hears Daniel's greeting and his story of how an angel of the Lord entered the den and clamped shut the mouth of each and every lion.

Darius celebrates the occasion by ordering all those involved in the scheme against Daniel to try their own hands at taming lions—the administrators, their wives, and their children. Within a matter of minutes they are all ripped apart and eaten by the ravenous beasts. With that accomplished, he decrees that everyone in the realm is required to worship Daniel's God. Life continues to go well for Daniel in the years that follow, even on through the reign of Cyrus.

Daniel continues to have visions, the interpretation of which comes by special revelation from God. Daniel spends three weeks mourning over Jerusalem's sin, depriving himself of tasty food and taking no baths. As this period comes to an end, he is with some companions on the bank of the Tigris River. Suddenly a larger-than-life human figure with a deep voice appears in front of him, his legs straddling the river. His companions see nothing, but they scatter in great fright.

On hearing the voice, Daniel faints dead away. The angelic man then pulls him up and tells him he has been sent with a message that there are wars to be fought—apparently both in heaven and on earth, where kingdoms rise and fall. The angel continues on and on about specific future

Daniel and the Latter Days

So when you see standing in the holy place "the abomination that causes desolation," spoken of through the prophet Daniel—let the reader understand—then let those who are in Judea flee to the mountains. Let no one on the housetop go down to take anything out of the house. Let no one in the field go back to get their cloak. How dreadful it will be in those days for pregnant women and nursing mothers! Pray that your flight will not take place in winter or on the Sabbath. For then there will be great distress, unequaled from the beginning of the world until now—and never to be equaled again. . . .

Immediately after the distress of those days
the sun will be darkened,
and the moon will not give its light;
the stars will fall from the sky,
and the heavenly bodies will be shaken.

Then will appear the sign of the Son of Man in heaven. And then all the peoples of the earth will mourn when they see the Son of Man coming on the clouds of heaven, with power and great glory. And he will send his angels with a loud trumpet call, and they will gather his elect from the four winds, from one end of the heavens to the other.

Jesus, Matt. 24:15–21, 29–31 (NIV)

events. Daniel is dumbstruck. His mind is numb.

Then suddenly two more men appear, one on each side of the river, wondering about the time span for all the events. The angelic figure straddling the river answers that it will be three and a half times. Daniel doesn't get it. When he asks for an explanation, he is told not to concern himself with it. He doesn't. Nevertheless, the angelic riddle has captured end-times speculators ever since.

There is no record of the remainder of Daniel's life or of his death. He is simply left standing along the bank of the Tigris River.

Concluding Observations

It might be natural to imagine that Old Testament prophecy is irrelevant and utterly boring. But a glimpse into the lives of Isaiah, Jeremiah, Ezekiel, and Daniel proves otherwise. They were in many respects ordinary men. What sets them apart, more than anything else, is their absolute belief in God—or nearly absolute. They seem to almost blindly follow God's orders. They do not question the voice of God—even when that voice is telling them to do utterly outlandish things.

Isaiah spends three years preaching *au naturel*. Jeremiah preaches to constant scoffing. Ezekiel tells of jaw-dropping visions that make the hearers' heads spin. Daniel (as do the other three) boldly transmits God's bad news to powerful kings.

They were prophets for their own time as well as for times to come. Jesus freely quoted from them, as did other New Testament figures. Indeed, one might ask how the Gospel of Matthew would stand up without Isaiah's prophetic voice.

Further Reading

Baldwin, Joyce G. *Daniel*. Tyndale Old Testament Commentaries. D. J. Wiseman, General Editor. Downers Grove, IL: InterVarsity, 1978.

Beckwith, Carl, ed. *Ezekiel, Daniel*. Reformation Commentary on Scripture, vol. 12. Downers Grove, IL: InterVarsity, 2012.

Brueggemann, Walter. *A Commentary on Jeremiah: Exile and Homecoming*. Grand Rapids: Eerdmans, 1998.

Motyer, J. Alec. *The Prophecy of Isaiah: An Introduction & Commentary*. Downers Grove, IL: InterVarsity, 1993.

16

JONAH AND THE MINOR PROPHETS

A Warning, a Whale, and a Whore

The just shall live by faith. These words heralded the Reformation—Martin Luther quoting the apostle Paul, who himself was quoting the obscure Minor Prophet Habakkuk of centuries earlier.[1] When Herod inquired of the chief priests and scribes as to where the Christ would be born, they answered by quoting another of the Minor Prophets, Micah: "In Bethlehem in Judea."[2]

In Matthew's Gospel, Jesus' death (and resurrection) is prefigured by Jonah: "For as Jonah was three days and three nights in the belly of a huge fish, so the Son of Man will be three days and three nights in the heart of the earth."[3] The prophet Joel pointed to a day when sons and daughters would prophesy, and Peter repeated his prophecy on the day of Pentecost:

> In the last days, God says,
>   I will pour out my Spirit on all people. . . .
> Your sons and daughters will prophesy,
>   . . . both men and women. . . .

I will show wonders in the heavens
above
and signs on the earth below,
blood and fire and billows of
smoke.
The sun will be turned to darkness
and the moon to blood
before the coming of the great
and glorious day of the Lord.
And everyone who calls
on the name of the Lord will be
saved."[4]

The Minor Prophets should not be regarded as lesser than the Major Prophets—farm-team prophets in the minor leagues waiting for a break to make it into big-league prophecy. Their writings were shorter than those of the Major Prophets, but what they said was no less significant or insightful. Nor were their lives less colorful. Jonah flees the face of God and gets stuck in the belly of a fish. Hosea marries a prostitute. Amos has visions of swarming locusts and devouring fire, and compares rich, highborn ladies to a herd of heifers.

Definition of Minor Prophets

They are called minor prophets not because their message is less weighty than that of the major prophets, but because it is briefer. The combined writings of the minor prophets make a smaller volume than the book of Isaiah. . . . The arrangement of the minor prophets in our Bibles does not follow a chronological order. Amos, whose career dates from the middle of the eighth century before our era, is undoubtedly the oldest of all the prophetical writers.

Franklin V. N. Painter, *Introduction to Bible Study: The Old Testament*, 214

Prophets, whether Major or Minor, were not part of any clerical hierarchy (with the possible exception of Ezekiel, who was a priest). They did not have official titles or ranking, as did the king and those in his court, or as did judges or priests. Prophets were independent—no popes or bishops or denominational leaders among them. Their authority was derived directly from God, a tradition that has a long lineage throughout church history and to the present day.

Not all of the Minor Prophets emerge from the text with fascinating personal lives. In fact most of them are obscure characters with few biographical details attached to their writing. Men like Joel, Obadiah, Micah, Nahum, Habakkuk, Zephaniah, and Zechariah almost seem to hide behind their words. This is not entirely true, however, with Jonah, Hosea, Amos, and Haggai.

Obadiah is in the shadows but for a very short prophetic work (the shortest Old Testament book). His focus is the punishment of the Edomites, descendants of Esau. Micah is a contemporary of Isaiah, and his writings are similar. His most memorable lines are: "What does the LORD require of you? To act justly and to love mercy and to walk humbly with your God."[5] Nahum prophesies the downfall of Assyria's capital city, Nineveh. Habakkuk wonders aloud about God's justice, especially when God seems to turn a blind eye to evildoers, letting them get off scot-free.

God's judgment on all people is the theme of Zephaniah's prophecy. Zechariah, through visions and divine messages,

Timeless Minor Prophets

The corpus of biblical books we call the Minor Prophets has not enjoyed great prominence in the history of biblical interpretation. It is not difficult to understand why this is so. Where is the edification for a modern Christian in a dirge celebrating the downfall of an ancient city? How can the gloomy forecasts of captivity for Israel and Judah lift the heart today? . . . A careful study of these prophets, however, reveals that . . . they speak of the love of God as well as his justice. Their prophecies are not all doom, but are often rich with hope. Hosea based his hope on God's compassion, while Joel envisioned a new era for the people of God. Amos spoke of the restoration of David's collapsing monarchy, and Micah foresaw the coming ruler whose birthplace would be the insignificant town of Bethlehem. . . . The Minor Prophets are not as time-bound as we may think.

Thomas Edward McComiskey, *The Minor Prophets: An Exegetical and Expository Commentary*, ix

preaches repentance and justice to the postexilic Jews. He encourages them and their governor Zerubbabel to continue the rebuilding of the Temple, despite intense opposition. Malachi, whose prophecy brings a finale to the Old Testament, speaks against corruption among religious leaders and the spiritual malaise among the people in general. Although the people weep and wail, they do not demonstrate the zeal for God they once had. But there is hope. The day of the Lord is coming: "I will send the prophet Elijah to you before that great and dreadful day of the LORD comes."[6]

Jonah is everyone's favorite prophet. He doesn't rant and rave. He is not the voice of righteousness railing at sinners. Far from it. Rather, he is the sinner himself, running from God. Through the ages, those feeling the weight of the call of God have identified with him. He is a prophet that even young children understand and appreciate. That he is swallowed by a great fish has only added to his superstar status.

Jonah: A Runaway Prophet

He is a singular biblical character. From Moses to Jeremiah, others have resisted God's call and insisted they were not up to the task. Job angrily argued with God, demanding to know why and where God was hiding. But Jonah alone runs away and hides from God.

Jonah, the son of Amittai, hails from the small town of Gath Hepher, near Nazareth. He boldly takes God's message to Jereboam II, the king of Israel, who then "restored the boundaries of Israel from Lebo Hamath to the Dead Sea."[7] That he could go up against a powerful king speaks to his effectiveness as a servant of God.

But on another occasion he is simply minding his own business when, from out of the blue, he hears God telling him to go and preach to the people of Nineveh. Nineveh, of all places—the capital city of Assyria, Israel's archenemy. Why would God want him to expend any energy on a preaching assignment to such wicked foreigners?

He might have stayed put, imagining the command is merely a figment of his imagination. But he is so sure of this demand on his life that he flees his home in an effort to escape God. He heads for the seaport of Joppa and boards a ship for Tarshish, way across the Mediterranean in Spain, as far away from God as he thinks he can get. On board ship he is mingling among the rowdy sailors, somehow thinking that God would never bother to look for him there.

Everything is going as planned. He hides himself away below deck. After a nerve-wracking flight, he is exhausted and needs some shut-eye. Indeed, so soundly does he sleep that he is entirely oblivious to the swelling sea and the storm clouds gathering in the distance. Nor does he awaken when the wind picks up and the waves begin pummeling the ship. Before long the breakers are pitching over the entire vessel as the storm surges. The helpless craft is about to capsize in the raging waters. This is more than your ordinary storm—so say the sailors. It's the vengeance of the gods. The crew is frantically pleading with their deities to spare their ship, while at the same time attempting to save themselves by throwing the cargo overboard.

And Jonah sleeps on. He awakens abruptly as he is shaken to his senses by the rough grip of the ship's captain, more than a little agitated by Jonah's absence of alarm. The captain screams at him to get up and do something—do anything—to try to save the ship. What's wrong with him? Doesn't he care? Everyone else is on deck. *Pray to your god!* the captain bellows. Tell him to call off the storm.

When Jonah is hauled up on deck, he faces a scene almost reminiscent of *Survivor*. The ship is about to sink, and the deckhands are in a panic trying to save it, all the while imploring their deities and trying to figure out which one of them is guilty of enraging his god. Jonah himself is accused, and—no surprise—he comes up short when they resort to the ancient practice of casting lots. He is responsible, they determine, for their predicament, and it is up to him to get them out of this fix. They pound him with questions: *What crime has he committed? Where does he live? What are his family connections?*

Jonah's only response is: "I am a Hebrew and I worship the LORD, the God of heaven, who made the sea and the dry land."[8] The crew panics. They have heard about the Hebrew God. They demand to know how Jonah has so offended him. When they learn he is running away from God, they are beside themselves, trying to figure out a way to appease this supernatural being.

Then Jonah speaks again. In the midst of the howling wind and towering waves, he offers a solution. He wants them to throw him overboard because his sin has caused the storm. That is the only way to calm the sea.

To throw someone overboard because they are running from God just doesn't seem right. Surely the sailors must have thought of their own lives in comparison. They are reluctant to do it, but the

Jonah and the great fish

violent winds and waves are battering the boat so badly they cannot even row. They are doomed. They try praying to Jonah's God, but the storm only gets worse. So after a most hasty conference, they take his advice and hurl him into the swirling dark waters.

The moment he hits the water, the seas become calm. It is eerie. Jonah surely senses the change as well, convinced that God has obviously tracked him down. What he does not know is that the sailors are so much in awe of his God that they begin offering sacrifices to him.

As for Jonah, he is suddenly engulfed in utter blackness. Here he is paddling around on the calm Mediterranean, and suddenly his world goes dark and squishy—and gross. He's struggling to free himself, only to discover he is trapped. There is no escape. He is engulfed in slime. Indeed, for three long days and nights he is encased in a digestive system that isn't digesting him. He desperately flails about, but to no avail. He is in his grave, entombed and awaiting an agonizing death, never expecting to see the light of day.

But in this intestinal tomb, Jonah, in utter desperation, remembers God. Of all things. If all else fails, maybe God could come to his rescue. He cries from "out of the belly of hell,"[9] pleading with God to give him one more chance. And then the drama ends as quickly as it began. God hears him and causes the fish to vomit—to hurl him up on the shore. In an instant Jonah finds himself covered with sand and slime, crawling on the beach, getting to his feet none the worse for his harrowing experience.

How had this happened so suddenly? What moved God to rescue him? Jonah shakes himself off, remembers what has happened, and gives thanks to God:

> From deep in the realm of the dead I
> called for help,
> and you listened to my cry.
> You hurled me into the depths,
> into the very heart of the seas,
> and the currents swirled about
> me;
> all your waves and breakers
> swept over me. . . .
> To the roots of the mountains I
> sank down;
> the earth beneath barred me in
> forever.
> But you, LORD my God,
> brought my life up from the pit.
>
> When my life was ebbing away,
> I remembered you, LORD,

and my prayer rose to you,
to your holy temple.[10]

But hardly has he finished his song of praise and gotten his bearings when he hears the voice of God again. He is ordered for the second time to go to Nineveh and call the people to repentance. This time he obeys. Greatly preferring the big-city life of Nineveh to the belly of a big fish, he goes there straightaway. His message, though lacking fiery rhetoric, is forthright: "In forty days Nineveh will be smashed."[11] It's not the kind of message he likes to deliver; he's heard it before from prophet after prophet. These types are not popular. People ridicule them and worse.

To Jonah's astonishment, however, these foreigners are attentive. They actually believe what he is saying. Indeed, the whole population takes part in a revival—confessing their sins, fasting and praying. Even the king publicly repents of his sins. In fact, he issues an edict that requires everyone to worship Jonah's God. Through Jonah's preaching, Nineveh is spared.

Is Jonah ecstatic with the results? No other preacher has ever seen such success. He will be the headliner on the preaching circuit. No. This is hardly his reaction. In fact, he pouts and is downright depressed. More than that, he spouts off to God, sneering that he knew all along that God would back down and not exterminate Nineveh. That's exactly why he didn't want to go there in the first place—precisely why he ended up tangled in the entrails of a fish. God, he rails, is way too easygoing with his mercy and grace.

Jonah preaching to the Ninevites

Jonah is so upset that he won't even listen to God's point of view. Rather, he heads out to the edge of town in a major funk. He refuses to join in the revival that is still on fire in the city, hoping it will quickly fizzle. He is wandering around in the heat of a sizzling day, wishing he could get his old life back. He sits down to rest under a small, primitive shelter. But as he is sitting there, a wonderful, shady vine springs up almost before his eyes. Not realizing this is an object lesson from God, he sits back and relaxes, imagining his good fortune is just a wonder of nature.

But just as quickly as the vine grows and leafs out, it shrivels into almost nothing—the work of a voracious worm. By morning the tree is of no use, and the blistering sun sucks the energy right out of him. He begs God to simply let him shrivel up and die. God is not done with Jonah, however. God has provided this object lesson to make Jonah recognize his misplaced anger. God clarifies to Jonah that he has no right to get angry about a tree that he had no part in upkeeping. It is God's call whether it lives or dies, even as it is for Nineveh, with its "hundred and twenty thousand people who cannot tell their right hand from their left," plus all the animals.[12] *So there, Jonah!* God is in control.

Here in the scorching desert is where the recorded life of Jonah ends.

Why Tarshish?

When Jonah received his prophetic call to preach in Nineveh, he headed the other direction to Tarshish. . . . Why Tarshish? For one thing, it is a lot more exciting than Nineveh. Nineveh was an ancient site, with layer after layer of ruined and unhappy history. Going to Nineveh to preach was not a coveted assignment for a Hebrew prophet with good references. But Tarshish was something else. Tarshish was adventure, the exotic appeal of the unknown. . . . Scholar C. H. Gordon says that in the popular imagination it became a distant paradise. Shangrila.

Eugene Peterson, "The Jonah Syndrome"

Hosea: A Cuckolded Prophet

There is a first time for everything. The first time a prophet hears the voice of God is no doubt memorable. For Hosea the message is astonishing—not the kind of message he would expect if he were anticipating a word from God. But from out of the blue, as sure as the sun rises in the morning dawn, the command comes loud and clear: "Find a whore and marry her." Huh? That's the only response Hosea could have offered. But the voice continues: "Make this whore the mother of your children."[13]

This is no prank. Israel had long been whoring after other gods, and Hosea is chosen to act out the metaphorical object lesson. God has utilized object lessons before, as when Isaiah was told to walk naked through the streets for three years. Now God wants to demonstrate the distress of marrying a trashy woman and then continuing to live with her when she becomes an unfaithful *wife* (as Israel is). Hosea is the man for the job.

The son of Beeri, Hosea prophesies during the reigns of Judah's kings Uzziah, Jotham, Ahaz, and Hezekiah; but his message is aimed primarily at the Northern Kingdom (often referred to as Ephraim)

Gaudy Gomer

She was always good company—a little heavy with the lipstick maybe, a little less than choosy about men and booze, a little loud, but great at a party and always good for a laugh. Then the prophet Hosea came along wearing a sandwich board that read "The End Is at Hand." . . . The first time he asked her to marry him, she thought he was kidding. The second time she knew he was serious but thought he was crazy. The third time she said yes.

Frederick Buechner, *Peculiar Treasures: A Biblical Who's Who*, 47 under King Jereboam II, son of Joash. He wastes no time in carrying out God's marching orders. He chooses for his wife Diblaim's daughter Gomer, a harlot. Soon she is pregnant and bears a son, whom God names *Jezreel*. Pregnant again, she gives birth to a daughter, who, at God's instruction, is named *No-Mercy*. Her third child, a boy, is named *Nobody*.

As God's object lesson, Hosea is the cuckolded husband. Speaking for God and Israel, he laments about Gomer, who is "dressing like a whore, displaying her breasts for sale . . . bringing bastard children into the world." Amid his anger with his wife and her bastard children, Hosea hears another message from God: "Start all over: Love your wife again, your wife

Everyday *Life*

Prostitution

God instructs Hosea to marry a prostitute. Rahab, who gave refuge in Jericho to Israelite spies and who was among those honored as ancestors of Jesus, was a prostitute. Judah, thinking the veiled woman was a prostitute, had sex with Tamar, his daughter-in-law. Had she not been his daughter-in-law, the incident would have gone unnoticed. Samson, a judge in Israel, traveled to Gaza, where he utilized the services of a prostitute.

Prostitution was obviously not unknown among the Hebrews of the Old Testament. Yahweh did not sanction prostitution, however. Indeed, *harlotry* was the negative concept most often used for Israel's unfaithfulness to the Lord. And Hosea's marriage to a harlot illustrated that very sin.

Yet there was a guarded acceptance of prostitution among the Israelites. When two prostitutes came to King Solomon seeking justice, he gave his verdict without passing judgment on their profession—and lifestyle. Prostitution was taken for granted, while at the same time it warranted Yahweh's disapproval.

The Depravity of Prostitution

God adamantly opposes the practice of harlotry, both in the literal and metaphorical senses of the term. This opposition is primarily rooted in the damage caused by prostitution to God's purpose of creating a holy people for Himself. Certainly, the prohibitions regarding the practice in the Mosaic Law aim towards this goal, as do the vivid and alarming judgments of the prophets. Harlotry always serves to drag people away from God. . . . The depravity of this disposition is matched only by the selfishness, lewdness, and spiritual bankruptcy of her male clientele, whom the Scriptures also thoroughly condemn. Moreover, the end results of such corrupt lifestyles are horrifying to behold—an increasing slavery to one's passions, personal degradation, poverty, and ultimately death.

Andrew Buelow, "Towards an Old Testament Theology of Prostitution," 37–38

The Madness of Love

But poor Gomer passed from man to man, until at last she fell into the hands of a man who was unable to pay for her food and her clothing. Her first lover had given her a mink stole, but this one made her clothe herself from the Goodwill store. News of her miserable state came to the prophet and he sought out the man she was living with. He knew where he would find him, down at the local tavern, and when he met this man, the conversation may have gone something like this. "Are you the man who is living with Gomer, daughter of Diblaim?" The man must have said, "If it's any of your business, I am." Hosea said, "Well, I am Hosea, her husband." A tense moment followed. But the man said, "What do you want? I haven't done anything wrong." Hosea said, "Listen, I'm not interested in causing any trouble. But I know that you are having difficulty making ends meet. I want you to take this money and buy Gomer some clothing and see that she has plenty of food. If you need any more I will give it to you." The man probably must have thought, "There's no fool like an old fool. If this sucker wants to help pay her expenses, that's all right with me." So he took the money and bought her some groceries and went home.

Now you may say, "That's a foolish thing for a man to do." But who can explain the madness of love?

Ray Stedman, "Hosea: The Prophet and the Prostitute"

who's in bed with her latest boyfriend, your cheating wife. Love her the way I, God, love the Israelite people, even as they flirt and party with every god that takes their fancy."[14]

Hosea actually has to make a purchase—the cost of a slave—in order to ransom her from her lover. He insists that from now on she must be faithful to him alone, but if she is like God's people, give her time and she will be whoring around again. Such are the messages that Hosea offers the people: "No one is faithful." They're all guilty of every sin imaginable, including "loose sex"—"a life of rutting with whores." Israel is a land of debauchery—"a bunch of overheated adulterers . . . red-hot with lust," trying to bring Judah down as well.[15]

As God's object lesson, Hosea pleads for God's people even as he pleads for his harlot wife, begging them to return to God. God loves them and is willing to start all over with them, even as Hosea will make a fresh start with his wife.

The Ultimate Victory of Love

Out of his own heart agony Hosea learned the nature of the sin of his people. They were playing the harlot, spending God's gifts in lewd traffic with other lovers. Out of that agony he has learned how God suffers over the sin of His people, because of His undying love. Out of God's love Hosea's new care for Gomer was born, and in the method God ordained for her, he discovered God's method with Israel. Out of all this process of pain, there came full confidence in the ultimate victory of love. Thus equipped he delivers his messages and all through them will sound those deep notes of Sin, Love, Hope.

G. Campbell Morgan, *The Minor Prophets*, cited in Herbert Lockyer, *All the Women of the Bible*, 61

Amos: A Sheep-Herding Prophet

Like many of the other prophets, Amos served as God's mouthpiece prior to the time of the exile. He is a contemporary of Isaiah, and he hears God's call during the reign of Uzziah, king of Judah, and Jeroboam II, king of Israel. He is not a professional prophet—not counted among the guild of prophets.

Amos is first introduced as a shepherd from Tekoa, a dozen miles south of Jerusalem. His ministry might have lasted a few days or a week—probably no longer than a year or two.

His testimony is straightforward: "I never set up to be a preacher, never had plans to be a preacher. I raised cattle and I pruned trees. Then God took me off the farm and said, 'Go preach to my people Israel.'"[16] Though he does not consider himself to be a career prophet, he is secure in his vocation and will not be silenced. God, he declares, does not send out prophets willy-nilly.

The message God gives Amos is a thundering judgment—in poetic form, no less—against the surrounding nations. But the primary focus is on the Northern Kingdom. Despite one warning after another, the people have paid no attention. God has sent famine, indeed, to the point that people are lined up for bread. God has stopped the rain and so severely parched the land that the people are dying of thirst. But amid all this suffering they have never hungered or thirsted after God.

Although Amos hails from Judah, God calls him to leave and go to the shrine at Bethel, a center of idolatry, and there to prophesy against Israel—most notably against King Jeroboam II. Indeed, rumor has it that Amos is plotting the king's downfall. When the resident priest, Amaziah, warns the king, and then orders Amos to get out of Israel, Amos pays no heed. Rather, he slaps him in the face with a message directly from God:

Amos: An Impolite Prophet

Tekoa was not a place famous for wealth; and as I have said, it was a small town, and of no opulence. I do not then doubt, but that Amos, by saying that he was a shepherd, pours contempt on the pride of the king of Israel, and of the whole people; for as they had not deigned to hear the Prophets of God, a keeper of sheep was sent to them. . . . But there was a special reason as to the Prophet Amos; for he was sent on purpose severely to reprove the ten tribes: and, as we shall see, he handled them with great asperity. For he was not polite, but proved that he had to do with those who were not to be treated as men, but as brute beasts; yea, worse in obstinacy than brute beasts; for there is some docility in oxen and cows, and especially in sheep, for they hear the voice of their shepherd, and follow where he leads them. The Israelites were all stubbornness, and wholly untamable. It was then necessary to set over them a teacher who would not treat them courteously, but exercise towards them his native rusticity.

John Calvin, *Commentary on Joel, Amos, Obadiah*, Vol. 2, Amos 1:1

> Your wife will become a whore in
> town.
> Your children will get killed.
> Your land will be auctioned off.
> You will die homeless and
> friendless.
> And Israel will be hauled off to
> exile, far from *home*.[17]

Amaziah is surely no friend of Amos, who, in a flurry of sarcasm, targets the phony religiosity of the people of that region. Bethel is merely a showplace that beneath the surface is rotten to the core.

These are surely not the only harsh words Amos preaches. He castigates the people for their taking bribes and for failing to care for the poor. In fact, his tone is downright nasty at times, avoiding any attempt at political correctness. To the rich ladies, he does not mince words:

> Listen to this, you cows of Bashan
> grazing on the slopes of Samaria.
> You women! Mean to the poor,
> cruel to the down-and-out!
> Indolent and pampered, you de-
> mand of your husbands,
> "Bring us a tall, cool drink!"[18]

Some of his direction from God comes in the form of object-lesson visions. One such vision is a massive swarm of locusts that eats all the crops before they can be harvested. Another vision is of a firestorm so hot that it burns up the ocean. Still another is of God standing by a wall with a plumb line, signifying that Israel does not stand straight according to a true measure of righteousness.

His summary of creation is picturesque: "Look who's here: Mountain-Shaper! Wind-Maker! He laid out the whole plot before Adam. He brings everything out of nothing, like dawn out of darkness. He strides across the alpine ridges. His name is GOD . . ."[19]

Yet for all the judgment and doom and gloom heaped upon the wayward Israelites, Amos also prophesies God's restoration of David's line, the rebuilding of the nation, and the blessings to be poured out from God's bounty.

How Amos meets his end is not recorded, but two years after he prophesies the exile of Israel to a faraway land, there is a great earthquake—so serious and frightening that entire populations flee their hometowns.

The Prophet Amos for Today

> I can't stand your religious meetings.
> I'm fed up with your conferences and
> conventions.
> I want nothing to do with your religion
> projects,
> your pretentious slogans and goals.
> I'm sick of your fund-raising schemes,
> your public relations and image
> making.
> I've had all I can take of your noisy
> ego-music.
> When was the last time you sang to
> *me?*
> Do you know what I want?
> I want justice—oceans of it.
> I want fairness—rivers of it.
> That's what I want. That's *all* I want.

Amos 5:21–24 (emphasis original)

Haggai: A Prophetic Plea for Temple Rebuilding

He appears on the scene and then vanishes, with no record of his ancestry or hometown.

He preaches in Jerusalem some seventy years after the exile began, but his ministry spans only four months. He had apparently stayed behind in Jerusalem, because his name is not listed among those who returned from Babylon. His message is terse and focused—two chapters of biblical text. One theme only: rebuild the Temple.

Unlike many other prophets, who preached out in the streets for all the people to hear, Haggai delivers his first prophecy to Zerubbabel, governor of Judah, and Joshua, the high priest. His first words from God comprise no more than two sentences, pointing out that the people are slackers. They keep putting off the rebuilding of the Temple.

The governor and the priest are not very enthusiastic about this construction job, but they apparently transmit Haggai's message to the people, who make the classic excuse—something like: *Sure we'll rebuild the Temple, but the time is just not right*. Haggai's rejoinder is biting. He accuses them of being more concerned about fixing up their homes than about repairing God's Temple, which lies in ruins.

The people continue to make excuses, so Haggai presses harder, telling them to look at their own lives and ask themselves what they have accomplished. They have all the money and food and drink and clothing they could want, but they have little to show for it. So, he prods them to get busy—to go out into the hills and cut timber for the Temple.

The Temple is not for show, he insists. It is a house for God, and rebuilding it is the least the people should be doing for God, who has been faithful to them. But instead they spend their time building equity in their own homes. As a result God's Temple is no more than a pile of debris. They ought to be ashamed of themselves. And by the way, he sneers, if they are wondering why they have been suffering so long without rain, he has the answer from God. No rains will come until they get back to work on the Temple.

That gets their attention. Now the matter is hitting their pocketbooks, where it hurts. So Zerubbabel and Joshua gather all the people, determined to hear exactly what Haggai has to say. Indeed, they actually pay attention to a prophet for once. They honor both God and his prophet. He asks them if anyone was around to see the Temple back in the days of its glory—perhaps a rhetorical question.

In fact, he may have been one of the few in the crowd who had actually seen and remembered the magnificence of the Temple some seventy years earlier. He wants them to build a structure even more glorious, and now is the time to do it. Within three weeks, the people get to work, and the rain comes. Haggai is there to prod them on with encouragement. The people continue working, and the Temple is rebuilt, but Haggai's ministry is over. His singular message has been heeded. There is nothing more to say.

The message of Haggai may seem entirely irrelevant to a modern-day audience, but ministers through the centuries have laid claim to his message when a church building project needs to be pushed through.

Concluding Observations

The neglect of the Minor Prophets is unfortunate. Their words were meant primarily for their contemporaries, but they are words that echo through the centuries, spoken by individuals whose issues often parallel our own.

Haggai's message is loud and clear for every generation. Self-centered greed is not the way of the Lord. But his message is not the only one of the Minor Prophets that is relevant today. Amos's brusqueness is applicable in an era when political correctness rules. He calls it like it is, without concern for the tender feelings of the rich and powerful. He is sick and tired of one seminar after another; he wants action.

Hosea's prophecy is also relevant, though marrying a wayward prostitute may not be the best means of conveying a warning in today's culture. The object lesson, however, powerfully communicates a vital message. In a contemporary situation, that may mean being vulnerable about one's own failures in seeking to minister to others with similar issues. In Hosea's case, he was showing people how God's heart aches when his bride is unfaithful.

Jonah's relevance for today goes without saying. How easy it is in an era of tempting alternatives to avoid God's work and flee to the greener pastures of Tarshish. And what an apt image of humankind he portrays: sulking alone in the blazing sun when things do not go his way.

The lives and the messages of the Minor Prophets easily make us uncomfortable. That is the way it should be. We often imagine God to be a conveyor of comfort only. But God also conveys discomfort, as is seen in the words and actions of these men. Their messages also pave the way for New Testament events. Micah's words flow seamlessly to the occasion of Mary's childbirth: "But thou, Bethlehem Ephratah, though thou be little among the thousands of Judah, yet out of thee shall he come forth unto me that is to be ruler in Israel; whose goings forth have been from of old, from everlasting."[20] Zechariah and Haggai call for the rebuilding of the Temple, a worship center that would have profound significance in the new faith of the first century.

Further Reading

Feinberg, Charles L. *The Minor Prophets*. Chicago: Moody Press, 1990.

McComiskey, Thomas Edward. *The Minor Prophets: An Exegetical and Expository Commentary*. Grand Rapids: Baker, 2009.

Morgan, G. Campbell. *The Minor Prophets: The Men and Their Messages*. Fleming Revell, 1955.

PART 3

A *Messiah* AND HIS *Mission*

17

MARY, JOSEPH, AND JOHN THE BAPTIST

Down Home in Palestine

The most celebrated *saint* of all time, hands down, is Mary. Her *saintly* status, however, was not clearly recognized during her lifetime, and Paul, in his writings, makes no mention of her. Indeed, the Gospel accounts that relate Mary's activities offer no indication that she behaved in a recognizably saintly manner or was regarded as an unusually holy woman by others.

The New Testament begins with the story of Mary. True, the seventeen opening verses of Matthew are devoted to Jesus' genealogy through his adoptive father Joseph. But to anyone reading or hearing the story for the first time, nothing makes sense until Mary suddenly steps out of the pages, albeit without reference to a single ancestor.

Joseph's genealogy is presented twice in the Gospels, but Joseph plays only a secondary role. He is the recipient of angelic visitations and is the father of Mary's other children, but he disappears from the narrative only a dozen years after he is introduced. After that Mary is presented alone or joined by her sons or other women, though not as a distinctly remarkable person. More than any other biblical figure,

Gospels, "Nothing Less Than Biographies"

Recognizing the differences between the Gospels and ancient biographies, as well as the diversity in the different types of biographies of the ancient Greco-Roman and Semitic worlds, a growing number of scholars maintain that biography is the only generic text type with which the gospel genre can be compared. . . . Although the Gospels fall short in literary style and language usage, they are nothing less than biographies.

Willem Vorster, "Gospel, Genre," *Anchor Bible Dictionary*, 3:1079

however, Mary is singled out by God for special blessing, that of giving birth to the very Son of God.

But if Mary is the most blessed, John the Baptist is surely the sorriest saint in all Scripture. His birth brings tidings of great joy to his aged parents—especially his no-longer *barren* mother. But in the blink of an eye, his childhood has slipped by and he is taking residence in the desert, wearing camel's hair, and eating honey and grasshoppers.

Next we find him on the Jordan River baptizing. The privilege of lowering his cousin Jesus into the water is offset by Jesus' comment that whoever is least in the kingdom of God is greater than John. If he heard that comment, it surely must have taken the wind out of his sails.

Hardly has he dried himself off when he sees his own disciples following after Jesus. But he nevertheless soldiers on, railing out against Herod and his sordid affair with Herodias. Herod's disdain for the truth, however, lands John in jail—a dungeon with no celebrity quarters. With time on his hands, he begins to think and to doubt. Is Jesus really the promised messiah? He sends his remaining disciples to find out.

Sometime later John is put to death, after Herodias demands his head on a platter. John actually fares better in death than in life. The Catholic Church considers him a genuine saint and commemorates him on two separate feast days. Eastern Orthodoxy commemorates him on six feast days. At least one British pub has recognized him, though sardonically, in its name—the *Baptist's Head*.

Apart from the life of Jesus, the life of John is the only one in the New Testament that is recorded from birth to death. John is featured in all four Gospels, and his words are well documented. Indeed, with the exception of Peter he speaks more than any of the twelve disciples.

Mary: Mother of Jesus

A teenage girl, Mary enters the biblical narrative as a key character, but with no recorded lineage. Why she is singled out by God is not clearly spelled out. Surely not for any claim to social status. Indeed, she appears from seemingly out of nowhere. Nazareth is a small hamlet, hardly a place of recognition. Her parents and ancestry are absent from the text. She stands alone. Her role requires no genealogical line or societal connections.

How familiar she may have been with messianic prophecies is unclear. King Herod asks the critical question: *Where is the Messiah supposed to be born?* Without missing a beat, the high priests respond. It was a no-brainer. Micah, the prophet, was very specific:

> But you, Bethlehem, in the land of Judah,
> are by no means least among the rulers of Judah;
> for out of you will come a ruler
> who will shepherd my people Israel.[1]

Though it may have been common knowledge among religious scholars *where* Jesus would be born, no one knew *when*. Like her friends and relatives, Mary had grown up awaiting the coming Messiah,

Everyday *Life*

A Town Called Nazareth

Nazareth! Can anything good come from Nazareth? This is the memorable question Nathaniel posed when he heard about Jesus for the first time. Nazareth was certainly not the Palestinian tourist town of the first century. The settlement was a drab outpost—a Galilean village lacking bustling commerce, political significance, or exciting night life. Most of the several hundred residents were peasant farmers who worked the surrounding fields in the Galilean hills.

The one-room houses in the village were packed cheek by jowl, facing narrow, crooked streets that typically allowed for no more than one-way oxcart traffic. These alleys were either dusty or muddy, depending on the season. But with thick walls, the dwellings were not uncomfortable. Warm in the winter and cool in the summer, they efficiently served family needs. Rooftop accommodations, sometimes joined to another house by a platform bridge, afforded social interaction and space for sleeping in the cool of the evening.

Shops (often attached to houses) and a common courtyard spawned a lively community atmosphere in what might have otherwise seemed like the end of the world. Indeed, in many ways Nazareth provided the best of small-town life—a perfect place to raise a family.

Low-Class Mary

She belonged to the peasant class, which eked out its living through agriculture and small commercial ventures like carpentry, the profession of both Joseph and Jesus. This group made up 90 percent of the population and bore the burden of supporting the state and the small privileged class. Their life was grinding, with a triple tax burden: to Rome, to Herod the Great and to the temple (to which, traditionally, they owed 10 percent of the harvest). Artisans, who made up about 5 percent of the population, had an even lower median income than those who worked the land full time. Consequently, in order to have a steady supply of food, they usually combined their craft with farming.

Robert P. Maloney, "The Historical Mary"

but she could not have supposed it would be in her own lifetime or that she, in her wildest imagination, would play a key role as mother. Nor could she have realized when she looked out into the night sky that the brightest star was pointing to the place where her little one would be found. She had no notion of the shenanigans that would be carried out behind the scenes and that astrologers from the East were on a trajectory that would align with her own—the destination being the little town of Bethlehem.

Though unaware of this global positioning system and the evil schemes of Herod, Mary does have her own insider information, which comes from the angel Gabriel. After bidding her a *good morning* on one otherwise ordinary day, he tells her she is a most fortunate young woman—favored by God. This is astounding. She had never before had such an encounter. Rather than being flattered, however, she is thoroughly frightened. But Gabriel quickly puts her at ease. Then he drops the bombshell. She will become pregnant and give birth to a boy. She is to name him Jesus.

To say that Mary is shocked is an understatement. She is absolutely dumbfounded. This is impossible. Sure, she is betrothed to Joseph, but they had never engaged in sexual intimacies, nor had she been with any other man. How could this possibly be so? Gabriel informs her that this will be a one-of-a-kind pregnancy. The Holy Spirit will come over her, and she will become pregnant and give birth to the very Son of God.

Before Mary can respond, Gabriel adds that Elizabeth, her cousin, has conceived a son. Elizabeth? She is the last person Mary could imagine being pregnant. She is old, long past childbearing years, always pitied for the B-word—barren. Only then does Mary realize she is not the only one for whom God is working a miracle. As dazed as she is, she accepts the verdict calmly, telling the angel she is the Lord's handmaid and is up to this incredible responsibility.

The angel leaves. Mary's heart is pounding. Does it enter her mind to rush out and find her fiancé and tell him the news? Does she dance a little jig on the rooftop? Does she bid her family and neighbors *goodbye*? The text reports only that she departs in a hurry, heading for the hill country in Judah, where Elizabeth lives. When she arrives, she greets her cousin with excitement. But before Mary can even tell her about Gabriel's message, Elizabeth, filled with the Holy Spirit, sings out the joyful news that Mary is blessed, as is the baby she is carrying. Does Mary even know that she is already pregnant? Had this supernatural conception occurred while she was on the road to the hill country?

She has little time to ponder such matters. Elizabeth confirms the good news of her own pregnancy. In fact, the moment she hears Mary's cheery greeting, the baby in her womb leaps for joy. Elizabeth continues her song of praise to God as Mary listens. Oh to have been a fly on the wall listening to their conversation that followed. Two expectant mothers, filled with excitement as well as trepidation. Mary stays on with Elizabeth for three months, then bids farewell to her beloved cousin

Mary visits Elizabeth

and returns home, walking alone on the dusty road back to Nazareth.

Mary still does not say a word to Joseph about the visitation from Gabriel or her pregnancy. She knows that she can't keep this a secret forever, and it must be tempting to obsess about how to broach the topic. Will he believe her bizarre story? But, as it turns out, any fretting is for naught. One day, perhaps after what might have appeared to be a season of uneasiness between them, Joseph simply informs Mary that the time has come for them to marry.

And then when Mary is in her ninth month of pregnancy, she learns that she must pack up and prepare for a trip to Bethlehem, accompanying Joseph, who must report there for an imperial census for tax purposes. When they arrive they find the village teeming with people who have also come to register. These common folk already are paying too much of their income in taxes, and the general mood is probably less than celebratory.

Mary and Joseph inquire about a place to spend the night, only to learn that every room is taken, every bed is full. What they do find is a sheltered lean-to for cattle. Here in these shabby surroundings, Mary gives birth. Do women learn of her plight and quickly come to her aid? Or is this a private affair for Mary and Joseph alone?

If so, their solitary world is suddenly shattered by the rough voices of shepherds, initially from a distance but now poking around, invading her space. Mary's initial reaction to their discovering her and the baby may have been less than welcoming. She is, after all, recovering from the exhausting labor of childbirth, while coaching her little one to take her nipple. And now she is confronted by a delegation of strangers, smelly shepherds no less.

She may have been distressed, but she is taken with their amazing story. They tell her how they were minding their own business, tending the sheep as they typically do, when suddenly standing in their midst was an angel, lit up like a giant sparkler. The shepherds testify that the angel announced the Messiah had been born nearby in Bethlehem that very night. They were instructed to search for him—a baby bundled in swaddling clothes and lying in a cattle trough.

So here they are, excited, all talking at once. Theirs is indeed a remarkable story. Mary listens intently, and after they leave she ponders in her heart everything the shepherds had said. Their words confirm what she has already begun to grasp. But the family does not linger in Bethlehem. There is a road trip ahead of them and religious rites to be conducted: circumcision on the eighth day and then a sacrifice to God at the Jerusalem Temple. At least for now, Mary's infant must be treated like any other Jewish infant boy.

Potty training and weaning are all part of the early childhood routine—all uneventful, until one day strangers appear at the door, having been guided astonishingly to the very spot by a star. These colorfully clad foreigners stand out like exotic aliens among the locals. Turns out they are scholars from the East.

When they see Mary holding Jesus, they instinctively know their long journey has been successful; their search is over. They fall to their knees, worship the boy, and offer gifts. Mary's eyes must have almost popped out. She lives in the most humble surroundings, and these are not the kinds of trinkets one buys at the town market. Now right here in front of her are wealthy Bedouins bearing gold, frankincense, and myrrh. Did she even know what these substances were? What does she do with them? And what are the neighbors saying about these unusual visitors? But they leave, going back in the direction from which they came, and life for Mary goes back to normal.

Since the angelic visitation a few years earlier, informing her she would bear a son, Mary had been living a very public life. Her *secret* had been confirmed in four separate settings, first by Elizabeth and then by shepherds and scholars, and in between by clerics in Jerusalem. Here her baby had been all the buzz when they arrived at the Temple. Now in Nazareth, the attention has dwindled and she settles into the daily routine. That is, until Joseph suddenly tells her that he has had an angelic visitation, and they must flee to Egypt under the cover of darkness to elude King Herod's murderous henchmen.

Away from Palestine, they escape the terrible *slaughter of the innocents* that their neighbors and fellow countrymen endure. They must surely have heard of the anguish after the fact, but for now they are safe in a foreign land.

When word comes that things have calmed down, Mary returns with Joseph

A fresco of a black Madonna and Jesus in Axum Cathedral, Ethiopia

and Jesus to Galilee and settles down in Nazareth, where she had grown up. But every year she goes to Jerusalem for the Passover with Joseph, Jesus, and her growing family. During one such holiday, when Jesus is twelve, Mary and Joseph are on their return trip, a full day's journey out of Jerusalem. Only then does she realize Jesus is not with the company of returning pilgrims.

Mary had assumed he was part of the crowd, perhaps having a good time with boys his own age. But she is distraught when she learns no one has seen him. So they turn around and head back to Jerusalem. When they find him in the Temple, taking part in a discourse with religious elders, Mary is not amused. "Young man," she abruptly addresses him, "why have you done this to us? Your father and I have been half out of our minds looking for you."[2] His response about doing his Father's business bewilders her, but she lets it go for the moment. Back in Nazareth, however, she often contemplates his words, wondering about their deeper meaning.

Mary had received no instructions about rearing Jesus or becoming involved in ministry herself. She might have carried out her duty and faded from the scene. But Mary is a strong-minded woman who captures the attention of the Gospel writers. Jesus is not her only responsibility. Although he is certainly the most celebrated of her children, the others must have been equally dear to her heart—her daughters (whose names are lost in the annals of time) and her sons: James, Justus, Jude, and Simon. Joseph is absent from the story after their twelfth year of marriage, perhaps having died.

Now moving on in years—likely approaching fifty—Mary attends a wedding in Cana, a small hamlet some nine miles north of Nazareth. Jesus, who had already begun to gather disciples, also attends and brings them along. At some point, perhaps well into the festivities, Mary notices that the wine is running low. She is concerned and relays the problem to Jesus. Is she hoping for a miracle? Probably not. Jesus is her oldest son, and she no doubt has depended on him for many things. She apparently thinks he can come up with a solution and only wants to spare the host embarrassment.

Maybe she actually does believe he has special powers. His response to her is telling: "Is that any of our business,

On the Road with Mary

Mary [as many Bible teachers have claimed] may well have been retiring and home-loving, but with the possible exception of the angel's announcement of the coming conception, the scriptural record never shows us Mary at home. She is hurrying off to Elizabeth, then going to Bethlehem for the census, then to Jerusalem for purification rites, down to Egypt, back to Nazareth, then to Jerusalem again for the Passover, to Cana for the wedding, to Capernaum, to a city near the Sea of Galilee with her other sons to persuade Jesus to come home, and finally to Jerusalem again. It therefore requires an exercise of imagination to learn from her lessons "mostly related to home."

Dorothy Pape, *In Search of God's Ideal Woman*, 53

Mother—yours or mine? This isn't my time. Don't push me."[3] But she doesn't cower before her strong son. She goes to the servants and tells them to do whatever Jesus asks them to do. She must be truly taken aback, however, when she hears him tell the servants to fill the jugs with water. Is this some sort of practical joke?

But when the water is poured out for the guests, she quickly realizes it is actually wine. In fact, the guests are commenting on its delicate taste—what fine wine it is. They simply think the best has been saved for last. She and the servants, as well as his disciples, know differently. But there is no discussion—no questions about how this could have happened.

This is an incredible first miracle—enough to stir loyalty and *belief* among his disciples. But does Mary actually believe in him in the same way? She still seems to be on the fence. Yet she is ever close by, going with him and her other sons and his disciples to Capernaum, staying there for a short time.

After Jesus' ministry gathers momentum, Mary cannot keep track of him. But she hears by the grapevine things that concern her. He has been out on the road preaching and appointing apostles. Religious leaders from Jerusalem are claiming he's in league with the devil. Hometown friends fear that he may be losing it. So when he gets to the outskirts of Nazareth and is preaching to a crowd, Mary and her other sons arrive, hoping to take him aside and maybe talk some sense into him.

When someone passes the word on to Jesus that they have come and want a private audience with him, Jesus repeats the request to his listeners and turns this little domestic matter into a teaching moment. He asks the crowd, *Who are my mother and brothers?* Most of them obviously know. But he turns his own question upside down and answers that anyone who obeys God is a mother and a brother to him.

Family is foundational among this hometown Jewish crowd. Do the people show surprise and whisper among themselves? Does anyone call out for further explanation? The only response from Mary is the sound of silence.

Soon after this Jesus again returns home. Mary's presence is not mentioned, but *home* is not merely Nazareth. It is Mary's home. She is somewhere in the background.

Mary is not named among those who are with Jesus at the Triumphal Entry into Jerusalem on the first day of the week just before his crucifixion and resurrection. But she is present at the crucifixion itself. What terrible anguish it must have been for Jesus' disciples and brothers and sisters. But for Mary, the pain permeates every particle of her being. He is her firstborn son—the infant, the boy, the young adult; and now this horrific death on a cross.

That Jesus, so near death, compassionately acknowledges his mother is a selfless act that she can treasure the remainder of her life. Through her sobs, she hears him appoint his disciple John (and her nephew) as her son and in turn appoint her as his mother. It's a tender moment that eases the raw evil of the nightmare she is enduring.

Mary's Sister Salome

From Matthew's account we know that James and John were the sons of Zebedee. By comparing Matthew and Mark we discover that Salome was the name of the wife of Zebedee and the mother of James and John. From John we see that Salome was Mary's sister.

I first thought that there could be other women in the account as well, but the order of the names and the similarity of the language in the accounts leads me to be almost certain that Jesus' mother's sister is Salome, the wife of Zebedee and the mother of James and John. Therefore, James and John were Jesus' first cousins.

The implications of this are enormous when we consider how the various books of the New Testament were compiled and the roles that James and John, and also the "brothers of the Lord" James and Jude, had in writing and compiling the New Testament canon.

Jay Rogers, "Jesus' Cousins Were the Apostles James and John"

But tragedy turns to triumph. Mary hears the incredible news that Jesus has risen from the dead. How does she process this information? Her grief was beyond anything she had ever known, and now suddenly she's wild with excitement. There is no report of their postresurrection reunion, but Mary knows that her son now lives.

Sometime later Mary is in the upper room in Jerusalem with the disciples. Pentecost is ahead of them. She is now officially part of Jesus' following, but she is never again mentioned in the biblical narrative. She simply disappears.

Joseph: Husband of Mary

Not just a name to be appended to that of Mary, Joseph is an important biblical figure in his own right. In fact, the New Testament opens with his genealogy. The family tree begins with Abraham and continues for forty-one generations to Joseph (preceded by his father Jacob), ending with his adopted son Jesus. Joseph is a builder engaged to be married to Mary. But he hears by the grapevine that she's pregnant. Who could the father possibly be? This is an absolutely awful turn of events. Sheer torment. Mary, of all people. No one could have guessed. She's the least likely person to be running around—when betrothed to another, no less.

He is in shock. But he cares deeply for her and is determined not to make a public spectacle. The marriage is off, but he will handle the matter privately with her and her family. A dream, however, prompts him to reverse course. An angel appears with a message that Mary is pregnant by the Holy Spirit; she will give birth to a son; he is to be named Jesus—*God saves*—because he will save God's people from their sin.

Joseph surely must have wondered how such a pregnancy without a human father could occur. But like all faithful Jews, he is not unaware of angel messengers from God, and he is not about to put up an argument. So Joseph takes the message to heart and carries on with his plans to marry. At this point Joseph knows more about the expected birth of Jesus than does Mary.

The biblical text reveals nothing of the actual marriage celebration. The parable of the ten virgins details an elaborate affair with food and festivities.[4] But for Joseph and Mary, the marriage may have been very low key. Both the circumstances and their own social status would have been factors.

Hardly has the groom settled into married life when he learns he must prepare for a journey to Bethlehem to register for an imperial census. In Bethlehem, consigned to a cattle shelter for the night, he must have felt helpless when Mary began labor. His bride is in agony, and she doesn't even have a decent bed in a warm inn to lie on. Does he question his decision making? What if he had looked for lodging before arriving in town?

The hours that follow are shrouded in privacy and pain. Every contraction and tortured cry cuts to the bone. If only he could relieve her agony. Then she's pushing and at last he hears the healthy cry of a baby boy—his son. He stands by, the proud father, as shepherds come and go. And he's the one who takes charge of circumcision and the Temple sacrifice. But life goes on. He has work to do in the shop, and Mary is responsible for domestic chores and child care.

Before he disappears from the biblical record, Joseph has another angelic visitation. This time the angel warns him to flee the wrath of King Herod, who is about to issue a death warrant for all the little boys of the land. Herod is convinced one of them (per the report of the wise men) will one day usurp his throne. Joseph, Mary, and Jesus hastily leave town and travel to Egypt.

How Joseph secured money for travel and for the family's extended stay in Egypt is not recorded. Perhaps he traded carpentry work for food and lodging. Joseph's decision to return to Nazareth after King Herod dies is prompted by an angel.

It is natural to imagine Joseph a quiet man. He is not the one who takes charge when the twelve-year-old Jesus appears to have gone missing after the Passover in Jerusalem. Mary does. To what extent he communicates with Mary is not disclosed. That he communicates with an angel—more than most people do—is not disputed.

John the Baptist: Desert Prophet

At first glance someone might dub him *the wild man from the wilderness*. The

Gabriel, a Catholic Saint

The name Gabriel means "man of God," or "God has shown himself mighty." It appears first in the prophesies [*sic*] of Daniel in the Old Testament. The angel announced to Daniel the prophecy of the seventy weeks. . . . He was the angel who appeared to Zachariah to announce the birth of St. John the Baptizer. Finally, he announced to Mary that she would bear a Son Who would be conceived of the Holy Spirit, Son of the Most High, and Saviour of the world. The feast day is September 29th. St. Gabriel is the patron of communications workers.

Catholic.org, "St. Gabriel, the Archangel"

desert is his home, and he eats what he can scavenge, mainly locusts and wild honey. In fact, long before drawing public attention, he seems to have been living an ascetic lifestyle. To those who initially come out to hear him, he is no more than another stump preacher, perhaps more than a little peculiar, but so it is with desert prophets. That he hasn't had a recent bath and wears a covering made of camel's hair is beside the point. His words are fiery, and he is a good diversion on an otherwise dreary day.

John is the son of the elderly priest Zachariah and his wife Elizabeth, who live in the hill country of Judea. They observe the commandments and live blameless lives. Elizabeth and Mary are cousins, thus making John and Jesus second cousins. John's birth had been foretold by the angel Gabriel while his father was participating in a once-in-a-lifetime opportunity to burn incense in the Temple. As would be true of Mary and Joseph, Zachariah is initially frightened, but he seems to take the angelic visitation in stride, more stunned by the message than the messenger. What a jolt it was for this elderly priest! True, it is an answer to prayer, but does he really imagine he will be changing diapers at his advanced age? Indeed, he is so shocked that he questions Gabriel as to the veracity of the message, and for that he is stricken mute.

He returns home to share the good news with Elizabeth, but he cannot speak. One can only imagine how he might have conveyed her prophesied pregnancy without words.

Elizabeth will in turn share the good news when Mary comes to visit. The two of them bond as never before—women chosen by God to bear sons destined for greatness. Elizabeth, however, has clearly recognized their different roles. "Why am I so favored," she asks Mary, "that the mother of my Lord should come to me?"[5]

After her baby is born, Elizabeth announces at the circumcision ceremony that his name will be John. The officiants and guests are shocked. There is not one in the family so named, and the baby, after all, is the firstborn and only son of Zachariah in his old age. What an insult not to name him after his father. But Zachariah signals that Elizabeth has gotten it right. So they name him John, and at that moment Zachariah opens his mouth and sings a song of praise to God.

From Gabriel he had learned that this baby will be filled with the Holy Spirit from the time of his birth. He will be set apart for ministry, expected to follow a Nazirite code of conduct, forbidding him to touch even one drop of alcohol. More than that, he will become a great prophet, like Elijah of old. Whether the parents would ever live to see this fulfilled is not recorded. But they carry out their end of the bargain by giving their infant a solid start.

Fast-forward thirty years, and people actually are speaking of John and Elijah in the same breath. It's as though Elijah, the prophet who did not die, is back in the person of John. John's message is delivered in anything but well-crafted sermons. Rather, he feeds off the crowds with spontaneous and straightforward exhortations. Bottom

A Prophet Leaping Out of the Gospel Pages

John the Baptist cuts an imposing figure in the opening pages of the New Testament. Wearing coarse camel's hair and leather, eating locusts and wild honey, shouting a the top of his lungs in a wilderness place to the penitents and curious, John leaps out of the Gospel pages as the frightening first figure of a new age. He rants of the coming judgment when the unjust will be destroyed, he demands conversion, he washes those who've begun to change their lives, and he is ultimately beheaded by a ruler who would not repent. . . . John the Baptist inaugurates the good news of God's kingdom like a champagne bottle shattered against the hull of a new ship.

Catherine M. Murphy, *John the Baptist: Prophet of Purity for a New Age*, 1

line, he's a colorful, attention-grabbing street evangelist. Preaching repentance is his strong suit. Although people had heard the message before, John's style is captivating, and his words hold more than just a ring of truth. Soon there are pilgrims coming from great distances to hear his preaching. He fearlessly summons the people to confess their sins. As they do, he baptizes them in the Jordan River.

But some of the people are coming with false motives, seeking to discredit his preaching. When they demand to know who sent him and why he baptizes, he identifies himself with unforgettable words. Quoting from Isaiah, he tells them, "I am the voice of one crying in the wilderness, 'Make straight the way of the Lord.'"[6]

Still other individuals are imposters wanting to make a show of their public baptism. John sniffs them out in a heartbeat. He is livid. "You brood of snakes!" he hisses. "Who warned you to flee God's coming wrath? Prove by the way you live that you have repented of your sins and turned to God. Don't just say to each other, 'We're safe, for we are descendants of Abraham.' That means nothing, for I tell you, God can create children of Abraham from these very stones."[7] Had anyone ever dared to stick it to the religious elite in this manner? They are stunned. How dare this two-bit preacher demean them in front of the crowds? But they bide their time.

John the Baptist in the desert

John goes on to explain his practice of water baptism. It is only the initiation. The one who comes after him will baptize with the Holy Spirit and fire. As for John himself, he is not worthy to even stoop down and loosen the sandals of this one who follows.

Then, almost on cue, Jesus appears, requesting his own baptism. John's spontaneous salutation rings through the ages: *Behold the Lamb of God!* What transpires next is shocking. Jesus asks John to baptize him. Jesus? To John and to alert bystanders, such an act seems entirely upside down. John protests, insisting that it should be the reverse—that he is not worthy of such an honor—to baptize the *Lamb of God*. But Jesus holds his ground, and John baptizes him.

That John attracts large crowds and delivers captivating messages makes him stand out among the many wandering prophets and preachers of the day. More than that, however, his calling is unique, since he has been directly commissioned by God to pave the way for Jesus' ministry. Perhaps he has mixed emotions, then, when two of his loyal disciples, one of them Andrew, leave him to follow Jesus.

But John carries on in ministry even after he baptizes Jesus, calling on his listeners to repent and live righteous lives. He specifically piles it on the Pharisees and Sadducees—and even on King Herod. It is well known that Herod is involved in an adulterous affair with his brother's wife Herodias. Most people are simply looking the other way. Not John. He does not mince words.

King Herod

Herod Antipas, the son of Herod the Great (who slaughtered the infants in attempting to eliminate baby Jesus) was a wicked and egotistical ruler. Known as the "tetrarch" (Luke 3:19), he had inherited certain portions of his father's kingdom in Galilee and in Peraea (west of the Jordan). The major mention of him in the New Testament is with reference to his imprisonment and execution of John the Baptist. That is a tragic way to "make history."

Herod was married to the daughter of Aretas IV, a Nabatean king (SE of the Jordan), but on a certain trip to Rome he stopped to visit his half-brother, Philip, and was "smitten" with Philip's wife, Herodias. He influenced her to leave his brother, and then he himself divorced his own wife. The two, Antipas and Herodias, thus entered an "unlawful" live-together relationship (though it was accommodatively called "marriage"). It was inevitable, therefore, that John (who denounced sin) and Herod (who reveled in it) would clash.

Wayne Jackson, "Who Was John the Baptist?"

In the mind of Herod, the death penalty is what John deserves. He has stepped over the line. It's one thing to rail against the religious leaders; it's another to find fault with the king—and in personal, private matters, no less. The king is not oblivious to John's popularity with the people, and he fears an uprising. Perhaps more than that, he is convinced John is truly a man of God. But prophet or not, Herod is fed up with John's insults. So he throws the nettlesome prophet in jail.

There John has time to reflect on what is going on outside the dungeon walls and what is likely to happen to him. Has he been on the right track? Is his cousin Jesus actually the Messiah? Maybe not. Maybe such claims are just pie in the sky. He is unsure and begins to doubt. He ponders his own role in Jesus' messianic ministry—how at one point he had been so certain of his cousin being the very Son of God. Didn't the Spirit descend like a dove from heaven the moment he baptized him? Didn't he hear the very voice of God? *Here is my beloved Son in whom I am well pleased.*

But that was then; this is now. He's in prison, and he has doubts. That his cousin is actually the Son of God, now that he has had time to really think about it, seems far-fetched. So he sends his remaining disciples to find out for sure what is really going on. They go and find Jesus and ask him directly if he is the One they are waiting for. Jesus simply tells them to look at his track record.

After John's disciples leave, Jesus turns to the crowd and sings John's praises. True, he looks like a desert caveman. But the fact remains: he is the Elijah, prophesied to reappear and pave the way for the Messiah.

Sometime after this, King Herod is hosting a birthday celebration for himself with food and live entertainment on a grand scale. Among the dancers is Salome, a nubile lass, the daughter of Herodias. Herod is completely charmed by her—more so as the wine flows and the night wears on. Feeling altogether mellow and magnanimous, he tells the young beauty that he will give her anything she asks for. Her mother, overhearing the vow, secretly prompts her daughter. So when Herod asks the girl to specify her wish, she is ready with an answer: the head of John the Baptist—not just chopped off, but displayed on a platter for all at the feast to see. Thus it was that decapitation ended the ministry of this seemingly crazy prophet from the desert. John's disciples, loyal to the end, give his body a proper burial and mourn his passing.

Concluding Observations

From a human perspective, John's is a sad story—altogether different from the story of his cousin Jesus. Jesus is actively involved in the Jewish cultural life of his time. He has close friends and relatives, he enjoys good meals, he outwits the Pharisees, and he tantalizes his listeners with parables. None of this *good life* applies to John. From the time of his youth he has eked out a subsistence in the desert. His initiation to the public is not as a rabbi who is calling disciples and performing miracles. Rather, he is consigned to the hard life of a street preacher, railing out about sin and repentance. His baptism and introduction of Jesus lead to the desertion of most of his own followers. He doubts and he dies an ignominious death.

Joseph, husband of Mary, is an all-around decent fellow. Without Mary, his story would be swept away by the winds of time. She, on the other hand, did not need him in order to fulfill her role and complete her story as the most celebrated woman ever. Another descendant of David might have served as well.

As for Mary, she is God's first choice. Indeed, never before or after would God pick out an ordinary human being to carry out such an intimate and earth-shattering assignment. Did it even occur to her to argue with the angel Gabriel when he came with the message? Moses argued, so also Jeremiah. Does Mary, nourished on the Law and the Prophets, realize she is the virgin of ancient prophecy? Whatever the case, she hurries to celebrate with Elizabeth. Her story that follows is that of a young woman who matures into motherhood. She is a strong, independent Jewish woman—a role model whose true identity is blurred in Renaissance paintings and mute garden statues.

In some segments of Christianity and during certain eras of church history, Mary has been raised to a position above all other biblical figures—even Jesus himself. What is most strange in the biblical text is her disappearance after Pentecost. One wonders if she died shortly thereafter. Paul never mentions her, though he had close ties with some of the disciples, including her sons. It is safe to assume that she did not live on to be the grand matriarch of the infant church.

Further Reading

McKnight, Scot. *The Real Mary: Why Evangelical Christians Can Embrace the Mother of Jesus.* Brewster, MA: Paraclete Press, 2007.

Murphy, Catherine M. *John the Baptist: Prophet of Purity for a New Age.* Collegeville, MN: Liturgical Press, 2003.

Perry, Tim. *Mary for Evangelicals: Toward an Understanding of the Mother of Our Lord.* Downers Grove, IL: InterVarsity, 2006.

18

JESUS OF NAZARETH

An Unlikely and Unflappable Savior

> I am the vine, ye are the branches: He that abideth in me, and I in him, the same bringeth forth much fruit: for without me ye can do nothing.
>
> John 15:5 (KJV)

Here is a sermon in song. Jesus was a poet. His words easily vibrate in the vocal chords and realize their rhyme and rhythm in all languages and cultures. A man for all seasons, he speaks to both kings and commoners. Complex concepts are unraveled and rendered approachable even as simple notions soar on literary wings. For English speakers his poetry is seamlessly captured in the King James tongue. "Consider the lilies of the field, how they grow; they toil not, neither do they spin: And yet I say unto you, That even Solomon in all his glory was not arrayed like one of these."[1]

Who else besides Jesus could call our attention to a simple wildflower and remind us of its most exquisite beauty, while at the same time downplaying all the wealth that money can buy? Jesus, the poet, was not impressed with the Solomons of this world. He recognized beauty in ordinary objects. But beauty is often offset by worldly cares and hardship. Jesus understood and offered solace: "Come unto me, all ye that labour and are heavy laden, and I will give you rest. Take my yoke upon you, and learn of me; for I am meek and lowly in heart: and ye shall find rest unto your souls. For my yoke is easy, and my burden is light."[2] Here Jesus is down-to-earth—labor, laden, yoke, burden. His parables, a form of his poetry, were also earthy. One single sheep out of the large flock has gone missing. Jesus turns his attention from the ninety-nine to the one that is lost—a parable that easily finds its way into song lyrics.

Even the mundane fact that Jesus had no earthly home was transformed into poetic lines: "Foxes have holes and birds of the air have nests, but the Son of Man has nowhere to lay His head."[3] At the same time, a notion so lofty as heaven is brought down to earth: a dwelling place filled with mansions—not, however, mansions to be equated with Solomon's lavish living quarters, but dwelling places for Jesus and his followers.

> Let not your heart be troubled: ye believe in God, believe also in me. In my Father's house are many mansions: if it were not so, I would have told you. I go to prepare a place for you. And if I go and prepare a place for you, I will come again, and receive you unto myself; that where I am, there ye may be also.[4]

The poetic phrases are not all words of comfort. In fact, in describing hell Jesus rivals the great poet John Milton: "Where their worm dieth not, and the fire is not quenched." In fact, that phrase is repeated three times in the King James Version.[5]

Though spare with words, Jesus is not afraid of repetition. For him, rhythm and repetition are an essential means of communication. *Blessed are the . . . Blessed are the . . .* serve as a foundation for the Sermon on the Mount. But Jesus does not offer only blessings in repetitive form. In addressing the Pharisees he uses repetition for seven curses: *Woe unto you . . .* Other repetitive phrases are: *You have heard it said . . . but I say unto you . . .* and *The kingdom of heaven is like . . .*

Much of Jesus' poetic language is drawn from Old Testament stories and the Psalms. In fact, in some respects Jesus steps straight out of the Old Testament. His family tree, beginning with Abraham, presents a litany of household names: patriarchs, prophets, priests, and kings. Also featured in the family tree are unforgettable Old Testament women: Tamar, Rahab, Ruth, and Bathsheba. Jesus matter-of-factly references the Hebrew Bible to make analogies with his own life and ministry: Moses lifting the serpent in the wilderness, Elijah and the widow of Zarephath, Elisha and the healing of Naaman, Jonah and his three days in the belly of a big fish. These were more than historical figures. They were the very ones who, like John the Baptist, paved the way for his ministry.

Indeed, the words of the Hebrew Bible easily flow from the tongue of Jesus. Drawing from the poetry of Isaiah, Jesus inaugurates his ministry with a short, crisp mission statement.

> The Spirit of the Lord is on me,
> because he has anointed me

to proclaim good news to the
poor.
He has sent me to proclaim freedom
for the prisoners
and recovery of sight for the
blind,
to set the oppressed free,
to proclaim the year of the Lord's
favor.[6]

Perhaps even more significant are his words on the cross, taken from the psalmist: "My God, my God, why hast Thou forsaken me?"[7]

Who is this Jesus? John the Baptist, Mary, and the disciples themselves pondered this question more than once. Theologians continue to dispute the matter to the present day. The biblical text itself does not offer easy answers. Indeed, the Jesus of the Gospels comes across as much more human than divine, an ordinary Palestinian first-century Jew. A man of miracles, to be sure; but he appears to be anything but a mystical god whose habitation is an ethereal, heavenly realm. He eats and sleeps and weeps like ordinary individuals. Even the accounts of his incredible miracles and astounding resurrection exhibit ordinary humanity.

Throughout his ministry Jesus is approachable, hardly a stuffy holy man. In fact, he would not necessarily have resonated with those who have longed in the generations since to be *so Christlike*. He had a common touch and a lively personality—a natural way with people that is not easily associated with God. For people who encountered him, Jesus was simply Jesus. Most of the time he was not consumed with feeding five thousand or walking on water or being transfigured. He never boasted of his virgin birth or being the second person in the Trinity.

His reputation, rather, was that of a rabble-rouser—a religious lawbreaker. He dined with sinners; he broke the Sabbath; he railed against Pharisees; he championed the poor; he chided male chauvinists. He was edgy—not always *really nice*, as we might expect the Son of God to be. The words *gentle*, *meek*, and *mild* in many instances simply do not apply. He cursed a barren fig tree. He deliberately provoked the gushing hometown crowd in the Nazareth synagogue—indeed, so much so that they ran him out of the village. He appeared to be a less-than-adoring son when his mother showed up at the edge of a crowd, and his reference to dogs might have easily been taken as a rude insult by the Syrophoenician woman. Likewise, he spoke harsh and unnerving words about bringing to earth a sword instead of peace.

A Mister Rogers Jesus

Recently I read a book that the elderly Charles Dickens had written to sum up the life of Jesus for his children. In it, the portrait emerges of a sweet Victorian nanny who pats the heads of boys and girls and offers such advice as, "Now, children, you must be nice to your mummy and daddy." With a start I recalled the Sunday school image of Jesus that I grew up with: someone kind and reassuring, with no sharp edges at all—a Mister Rogers before the age of children's television. As a child I felt comforted by such a person.

Philip Yancey, *The Jesus I Never Knew*, 14

Jesus was not politically correct. He called the shots as he saw them, with no apologies. His followers through the centuries, however, have too often sought to apologize for him by making excuses for his actions or weakening his words. Jesus needs no apologies. A virgin-born Galilean, he was crucified, dead, buried, and resurrected from the grave. Along the way, he lived a uniquely authentic and inspiring life.

Jesus of Nazareth: Son of Mary, Son of God

In his short life of little more than thirty years, he changed the course of history, though his profound influence would not be recognized until long after his death. His divine identity disguised, he lived and died and went about his daily routine, appearing most of the time to be altogether ordinary. Walking the dusty roads of Galilee, he would easily have been mistaken for just another first-century rabbi. There was nothing about him that initially made him stand out in a crowd. In Nazareth he had been one of the boys, a carpenter's son. That he had been conceived of a virgin was something of which he and others seemed oblivious. Indeed, at no point did he speak of his auspicious beginning. Nor did he tout his miracles. Unlike many *divine healers* then and now, he often admonished the cured individual to tell no one. When he fed five thousand, there was surely no chest beating on his part.

Yet his three-year ministry—and the aftermath—would make a larger footprint on the planet than that of anyone else in history. What is so different about Jesus? That question is answered at his baptism. He is the very Son of God.

That the Son of God would be born in a stable (or cave) where animals are sheltered sets the stage for the years to follow. He essentially lives a life of obscurity for three decades, from infancy until the time his ministry begins. After his circumcision and presentation at the Temple, the only details specified about him relate to brief episodes involving his parents. The first is the flight to Egypt, a relocation meant to protect him from the evil designs of King Herod.

The second incident occurs a decade later. Jesus is with his parents in Jerusalem for the Passover. As teeming crowds are milling around in the streets, he becomes absorbed with the discourse of the religious leaders in the Temple. This episode is most telling. At twelve he is coming into his own. He does not have to hold hands with his mother any longer. While other boys his age are sneaking around behind the market stalls or eyeing the girls, he heads for the Temple. So self-assured is he that he sits among the rabbis and asks questions.

But when the fullness
of the time was come,
God sent forth his Son,
made of a woman,
made under the law.
Galatians 4:4 (KJV)

The rabbis, for their part, are impressed with the youngster. He has an amazing grasp of concepts they themselves contemplate and debate. What an incredible scene this is. A youth, long before the bar mitzvah will become a Jewish tradition, is conversing with scholars and challenging their thinking.

His parents, when they finally find him after having been a day's journey out of Jerusalem, are not amused. In fact, his mother is downright annoyed. They have been worried sick about him, and he is not even apologizing. Rather, he acts bewildered: "Why were you looking for me?

Everyday *Life*

Roman Power and Puppet Rulers

Jesus lived in momentous times. The Mediterranean world seemed then like the center of the universe. Only decades before his birth, Mark Antony and Cleopatra flaunted a very public romance and reigned in glory over their respective realms. The wealth of Egypt under Cleopatra was the envy of the known world. Only a few years earlier the famed Julius Caesar reigned supreme over the Roman Empire, which stretched from northern Italy to the Black Sea. For the rich and famous, it was a magnificent time to be alive—unless life was cut short by scheming adversaries.

Of all the rulers of this era, King Herod the Great, however, wielded the most direct influence over the Jews of Palestine. He was loyal to Rome and Mark Antony, but after Antony's downfall, he easily changed loyalties. A onetime practicing Jew, he was despised by most Jews for his concessions to Rome and his evil ways. Indeed, his tag *the Great* was a label Jews deeply resented. He was both a murderer and a madman—a madman who ordered the execution of rabbis and his own relatives.

The most infamous execution order associated with Herod was that which singled out baby boys. Always fearful of rivals, Herod was willing to stoop to pure evil to prevent the possibility of a Messianic king who would threaten his rule. The birth of Jesus coincided with a terrifying political time in history.

Herod's Obituary

During the last few years, Herod was troubled by family intrigues, making the succession a matter of constant concern. Just last week his oldest son, Antipater, was executed in Jericho for plotting Herod's death, thus removing the strongest and most obvious successor. Three years ago two promising but disappointing sons, Alexander and Aristobulus, were tried and executed for plotting a coup and suborning the military. The great Augustus, a keen judge of character and sympathetic to Herod's troubles, was heard to say one evening at that time: "Gentlemen, it is better to be Herod's pig than to be his son."

Peter Richardson, *Herod: King of the Jews and Friend of the Romans*, 2–3

Didn't you know that I had to be here, dealing with the things of my Father?"[8]

How Jesus spends most of the next two decades is not disclosed. He no doubt studies the Torah and travels to Jerusalem every year for the Passover. On a day-to-day basis, however, he may have worked as a builder alongside his father—though it is noteworthy that few of his later parables are drawn from the building trades.

The first public event of Jesus' life is his baptism. He simply shows up one day with no fanfare at the Jordan River, where John is baptizing. At that time John was drawing large crowds. Did Jesus just get in line to wait his turn? When John sees him, he is taken aback. How can he baptize Jesus? That would suggest some sort of preeminence. Moreover, John's baptism connotes repentance. But Jesus insists.

So John immerses him in the waters of the Jordan River. In this moment, Jesus is both baptized and anointed by God for ministry. As he comes out of the water, he sees and hears God's confirmation. The Spirit in the form of a dove alights upon him, and God speaks: "This is my beloved Son, in whom I am well pleased."[9]

A baptism is a special day, to be marked on a calendar or on a certificate. For Jesus the day is far more than just baptism, however. He now understands that God the Father is behind everything that is happening. The Holy Spirit is empowering him. But before he even opens his mouth to preach, he comes to grips with a feeling of utter abandonment.

He is led by the Spirit into the untamed wilderness. This might seem like a normal way of life for John, but surely not for Jesus. *Where is the Father in this desolate desert?* he must have asked. He is alone but for wild animals, fasting for forty days and forty long, dreary, dark nights. He is desperately hungry, his stomach hollow. While he is in this famished state, the devil toys with him. If he is really the Son of God, he ought to be able to turn the rocks into loaves of bread. The devil is right. Jesus could do just that, but he doesn't bite. *There is a lot more to living than mere bread*, he retorts.

So the devil pursues another tactic. He leads Jesus to a high overlook and points to the many political realms spread out before them. They are all ruled in splendor,

Jesus in the Wilderness

Wildernesses come in so many shapes and sizes that the only way you can really tell you are in one is to look around for what you normally count on to save your life and come up empty. No food. No earthly power. No special protection—just a Bible-quoting devil and a whole bunch of sand. . . . What did that long, famishing stretch in the wilderness do to him? It *freed* him—from all devilish attempts to distract him from his true purpose, from hungry craving for things with no power to give him life, from any illusion he might have had that God would make his choices for him. After forty days in the wilderness, Jesus had not only learned to manage his appetites; he had also learned to trust the Spirit that had led him there to lead him out again, with the kind of clarity and grit he could not have found anywhere else.

Barbara Brown Taylor, "The Wilderness Exam"

and Jesus could be the one reigning over all of them. All he would have to do to enjoy this kind of power and prestige is to bow down and worship the devil. Jesus responds by quoting Scripture: *One must worship God alone*.

Finally, the devil leads Jesus out of the wilderness into Jerusalem, to the very peak of the Temple. The devil tells him to jump off in order to prove he's God's Son. It's no risk. Surely angels would catch him. Jesus responds forcefully, staring the devil down: "Don't you dare tempt the Lord your God."[10] With that the ordeal has ended. Jesus returns to Galilee, now prepared to enter his ministry, fully empowered by the Spirit.

Soon Jesus is back along the bank of the Jordan River, where John continues his ministry of preaching and baptizing. John, true to his calling, points people to Jesus—even his own disciples. Among those is Andrew, who switches teams and follows Jesus. He and another disciple go to where Jesus lives and stay on for a day, no doubt talking things over. They are facing a big decision. Andrew is convinced, and he leaves to find his brother Simon, telling him, "We've found the Messiah."[11] So Simon Peter also joins this tiny band.

If Peter and Andrew have any misgivings about their decisions to follow Jesus, their commitment is soon confirmed. They go with Jesus to a wedding in Cana, where they witness his first miracle. For Jesus this miracle, at least from a human standpoint, is a matter of testing the waters. Does he experience any fear or sense of uncertainty when he instructs the servants to fill the wine jugs with water? And then he tells them, without so much as tasting it, to offer it first to the wedding host. This is truly astounding. Water? If this miracle had gone wrong, what a humiliating episode it would have been—far worse than no attempted miracle at all.

As it turns out, the host raves about the delightful taste, surprised that the best wine has been left until last. Having been convinced by the miracle, "his disciples believed in him."[12] That factor for Jesus is no doubt of far greater consequence than saving a household from embarrassment.

From Cana, Jesus goes to Capernaum, his mother, brothers, and disciples still with him. Then he moves on to Jerusalem for the Passover feast. Here he encounters Nicodemus, a Pharisee who sits on the Jewish

Jesus at the Wedding in Cana

ruling council. He is a secret believer who seeks out Jesus in the dead of night, whose questioning prompts Jesus to respond with his most memorable minisermon—John 3:16 (KJV): "For God so loved the world, that he gave his only begotten Son, that whosoever believeth in him should not perish, but have everlasting life."

Jesus then returns to the Jordan with his newly acquired disciples and begins a ministry of baptism himself, though his disciples do the actual baptizing. But then rumors start flying that Jesus is competing with John and that he is now surpassing John in the number of baptisms. This is not at all what Jesus has in mind, so he leaves the region and returns to Galilee.

On the way, he is traveling through Samaria with some of his disciples. They stop at a well just outside the town of Sychar at noon. The disciples go into town to purchase lunch while Jesus remains at the well. As he waits, a woman approaches. Jesus asks her for water. His request leads to a prolonged conversation. When the disciples return, they are mortified that Jesus is talking to a stranger—a woman, no less. And not just a woman, but *that kind* of woman. They don't say anything, but they surely think it odd that he would carry on in such an inappropriate manner, little realizing that this encounter will lead to a revival in Sychar.

After this episode the disciples seem to just wander off and go back to their daily routine. Then one day Jesus is walking along the Sea of Galilee. He sees Simon Peter and Andrew busy with their fishing business. He watches as they cast their nets into the lake. They're good at what they do. But there is more important work to be done. Without small talk, Jesus tells them to come along with him. He will show them how to fish for people. They make no excuses nor even take time to tend to their nets. They know he means business, and they follow.

Not until sometime later does Jesus officially name the ones who will become known as the Twelve Apostles. In the meantime he moves from place to place in Galilee with his disciples and many more hangers-on. His most public ministry involves healing people physically, emotionally, and spiritually. Among those healed are Simon Peter's mother-in-law, a leper, and a paralytic man. He casts a demon out of a man, and he transforms the tax collector Matthew (also known as Levi) into a disciple.

A Taxman Comes to Jesus

After this, Jesus went out and saw a tax collector by the name of Levi sitting at his tax booth. "Follow me," Jesus said to him, and Levi got up, left everything and followed him.

Then Levi held a great banquet for Jesus at his house, and a large crowd of tax collectors and others were eating with them. But the Pharisees and the teachers of the law who belonged to their sect complained to his disciples, "Why do you eat and drink with tax collectors and sinners?"

Jesus answered them, "It is not the healthy who need a doctor, but the sick. I have not come to call the righteous, but sinners to repentance."

Luke 5:27–32 (NIV)

At this point Jesus is keeping a low profile. When he cures the leper, he specifically tells him not to go around telling everyone. He instructs the leper to present himself to the priest just for the record and to thank God for the healing, but otherwise to keep it to himself. But word gets out. More come to be healed, and the curious and the paparazzi are eager to get in on the action.

Like all practicing Jews, Jesus makes the annual pilgrimage to Jerusalem for Passover. Here the critics are more numerous. When he heals a paralyzed man on the Sabbath at the pool of Bethesda, he quickly slips into the crowd. He knows the keepers of the law will be on his case. When they do find him and try to nail him for Sabbath breaking, he for the first time declares to them that he is the Son of God. Now he's really stepped over the line. Sabbath breaking is one thing, but this is blasphemy. They are now conspiring to kill him.

But Jesus continues his public ministry, ever aware that he is under the watchful eyes of the Pharisees. As the crowds grow larger, the verbal attacks increase. Yet there are those who are willing to join him in ministry, going out on their own in pairs to work the same miracles he is known for. Escaping the crowds, Jesus goes to a mountain to pray and then calls the Twelve to join him and appoints them his apostles.

When he descends the mountain, he is joined by many more disciples who have for some time been in his company. Word quickly spreads that he is about to begin teaching. Indeed, without any form of social media other than word of mouth, flash crowds materialize almost spontaneously. People are coming from Jerusalem and all over Judea, and even as far away as the coastal towns of Tyre and Sidon. They are mostly curiosity seekers and those seeking a cure.

They crowd around, pushing in from all sides, and listen to the longest address he will ever deliver—what becomes known as the Sermon on the Mount. What he preaches is no less than radical. He is offering them a revolutionary way of living that emphasizes love over rigid observance of the law.

Amid the pushing and shoving and crying babies, the onlookers may not have heard all he had to say. But even if they catch only a few sentences, they know that his words are like nothing they have heard before:

> Love your enemies. Let them bring out the best in you, not the worst. When someone gives you a hard time, respond with the energies of prayer for that person. If someone slaps you in the face, stand there and take it. If someone grabs your shirt, giftwrap your best coat and

A Rabbi Talks with Jesus

In this book I explain in a very straightforward and unapologetic way why, if I had been in the Land of Israel in the first century, I would not have joined the circle of Jesus's disciples. I would have dissented, I hope courteously, I am sure with solid reason and argument and fact. If I heard what he said in the Sermon on the Mount, for good and substantive reasons I would not have followed him.

Jacob Neusner, *A Rabbi Talks with Jesus*, 3

> make a present of it. If someone takes unfair advantage of you, use the occasion to practice the servant life. No more tit-for-tat stuff. Live generously.
>
> Here is a simple rule of thumb for behavior: Ask yourself what you want people to do for you; then grab the initiative and do it for *them*! If you only love the lovable, do you expect a pat on the back? Run-of-the-mill sinners do that. If you only help those who help you, do you expect a medal? Garden-variety sinners do that. If you only give for what you hope to get out of it, do you think that's charity? The stingiest of pawnbrokers does that.
>
> I tell you, love your enemies. Help and give without expecting a return.[13]

After delivering this most profound sermon, Jesus is on the road again, throngs of people following along. On his way into Capernaum, some Jewish leaders rush out to meet him, pleading for him to come immediately. A young man is critically ill. He is the faithful servant to the local Roman captain, a man who has bent over backwards to help the Jews. Now, with a miracle, they want to repay his kindness.

Jesus is glad to accommodate them, but before he arrives, friends of the captain approach, saying he need not come any farther. The captain, they say, is embarrassed to be in the company of a holy man like Jesus. He knows that Jesus can heal if he just gives the command. Why not? If the captain's orders to his soldiers are heeded without question, why wouldn't Jesus' words have the same effect? Jesus gives the command, and the young man is healed. Then turning to the crowd, he acknowledges the captain's faith as greater than anything he's ever witnessed among the Jews.

Jesus and his disciples move on to the hamlet of Nain. As they are coming into town, they hear the loud weeping of mourners who are carrying a coffin outside the city gates for burial. When Jesus learns that the young man who has just died is the only son of a widow, he feels great compassion. Then he performs his most spectacular miracle to date. After comforting the mother, he puts his hand on the coffin, and the son springs back to life.

Soon after this, Jesus visits Capernaum again. Here he is entertained at the home of a Pharisee. He and the invited guests have

A Jesus Minus Miracles

A study of the life of Jesus that excludes the miraculous is destined from the start to produce a Jesus who is an aberration. He will be a stranger both to his opponents, who acknowledged his miracles . . . and to his followers, who will no longer be able to identify him as the object of their faith. There is a certain wholeness about the Jesus who preached the arrival of the kingdom of God, who ate with tax collectors and sinners, who healed the sick and raised the dead, who died sacrificially on the cross and rose triumphantly from the dead. This wholeness produces an overall portrayal of Jesus of Nazareth that is convincing to a sympathetic reader of the Gospels. Attempts to strip the supernatural from Jesus' life can only produce a Jesus so radically different that he is unrecognizable and his impact on history unexplainable.

Robert H. Stein, *Jesus the Messiah: A Survey of the Life of Christ*, 24 just begun to eat when a local prostitute barges in, goes straight to Jesus, and spills expensive perfume on his feet. Jesus takes it in stride, but the host is shocked—even more by what happens next. The woman lets her hair down and kneels before Jesus. Weeping, she kisses his feet and dries them with her hair. What a low-down circus this is, the Pharisee is thinking. How could Jesus possibly be a prophet and not know that this sleazy woman is embarrassing everyone in the room.

Jesus, however, regards the incident very differently. After affirming what the woman has done, he forgives her sins, telling her that her faith has saved her and that she can go in peace. Those words surely do not ease the tension. But so it is with Jesus' ministry—always drawing controversy with the prevailing orthodoxy.

Word of Jesus' teaching spreads, and the crowds increase, often numbering in the thousands. Miracles draw the multitudes. But are they sincere disciples or merely fickle curiosity seekers? Only time will tell. At this point, Jesus' teaching begins to shift and takes the form of parables. Even the Twelve, however, have trouble comprehending their hidden meanings, though with prodding Jesus unravels the mysteries. But straight talk is Jesus' forte. He does not mince words on moral values regarding money, divorce, honesty, hard work, loving one's enemies, caring for the poor, and healing the sick.

Most of Jesus' miracles have involved individuals who have suffered some sort of malady. But when he is in a boat with his disciples on the Sea of Galilee, he takes on nature itself. A sudden squall comes up while he is napping in the stern. The disciples fear the boat will capsize out in the middle of the lake. They awaken Jesus, pleading for help. He rebukes them—and also the wind and the waves.

Again the disciples are out in a boat when a storm arises, this time late at night. Struggling amid the waves, they see a mysterious figure walking toward them on the water. They are terrified, thinking they've seen a ghost. It turns out to be none other than Jesus himself, who tells them not to fear. When Peter attempts to walk out and meet him, he sinks and Jesus rescues him, chiding him for his lack of faith. When they are back in the boat, the rolling waves are calmed.

Another encounter with nature occurs when Jesus casts demons out of two severely disturbed men—casts them directly into a herd of swine. The pigs run pell-mell over a cliff into the sea and drown. The owners and their neighbors are upset about the loss and order Jesus out of the region.

The focus of Jesus' ministry, however, is less on making the winds and waves and pigs obey than on ministering to those who are marginalized. He heals the blind and mute and even an *unclean* woman with severe menstrual bleeding. To serve the needs of more people, he commissions his disciples and gives them authority to cast out demons and heal the sick.

At certain times Jesus manages to escape from everyone just to be alone. One such occasion is when he hears John the Baptist has been beheaded. Poor John. What a terrifying moment this must have been for him—the very anguish and dread that Jesus himself is facing. He is alone for these moments of privacy to process his grief and pray. But someone has spotted him. Word quickly gets out, and soon whole villages are vacated as people trek off to find him.

He might have cursed at the sight of them. But he doesn't. He has compassion. He spends the next hours healing the sick. Both he and the people lose track of time—though not the disciples. They are fully cognizant of being out in the middle of nowhere, and they want Jesus to send the people home for their evening meals. Jesus responds to their irritation by telling them to feed the crowd. What? He can't be serious. There are some five thousand people milling around, and there's nowhere to purchase food even if they had the money. There is a boy, however, with a bag lunch—five little loaves and two dinky fish.

This is obviously not a major setback for Jesus. Whether making wine from water or calming waves or curing cancer, he is onto it. He blesses the bag lunch and gives the contents to the disciples. As they distribute the meager meal, it miraculously multiplies—enough to feed a crowd of more than five thousand.

As the popularity of Jesus soars and his fame spreads, opposition becomes more hardened. Conspiracies are afoot, and rumors fly: this man must be taken out. He is deemed a threat in both political and religious sectors. But ordinary people are captivated by him, perhaps a miracle-working Elijah come back to life.

When Jesus asks the disciples who he is, Peter nails it—he is the Messiah, the Son of God. Jesus blesses Peter for the answer, but tells the disciples to keep it quiet. The disciples assume that Jesus as Messiah will soon be reigning over Israel, and they along with him. But he soundly puts that pipe dream to rest. His reign will not be as an earthly king. He will reign in heaven. Before then he will be killed. That will not be the end, however. He will rise from the dead on the third day and be with them again. Peter is incredulous. He insists that this must not happen. Jesus, however, is ruthless in his response: *Get behind me, Satan.*

On another occasion Jesus invites his inner circle—Peter, James, and John—to join him on a hike up a mountain. Perhaps thinking they will be sitting down for an intimate conversation, the disciples are treated to something far more spectacular. Before their very eyes, Jesus is transfigured, becoming translucent, with light filling his entire being. Then he is joined by

A Reluctant Miracle Worker

The Gospels record about three dozen miracles, some of them group healings. (Many other miracles performed by Jesus, John tells us, are not recorded.) Although very impressive to eyewitnesses, the miracles affected a relatively small number of people who lived in one tiny corner of the world. No Europeans or Chinese felt Jesus' healing touch. Clearly, he did not come to solve "the problem of pain" while on earth. Augustine and other church fathers were as impressed with the miracles Jesus did *not* perform as with those he did.

Philip Yancey, "Jesus, the Reluctant Miracle Worker"

Moses and Elijah, and the three of them begin talking. Hardly does Peter blurt out a proposal to build them shelters when the three figures are engulfed in a cloud. God speaks from heaven signifying Jesus as his Son. The disciples fall down and worship, and it's all over as suddenly as it has begun.

As they are descending the mountain, Jesus tells them to keep this experience to themselves—at least until he has risen from the dead. After this eye-popping incident, Jesus carries on with his teaching ministry.

Next to the Sermon on the Mount, the parables of the good Samaritan and the prodigal son are Jesus' grandest moments of teaching. As he is speaking about loving one's neighbor, someone in the crowd asks him to define the term *neighbor*. So Jesus tells a story of a man traveling from Jerusalem to Jericho who is attacked by thugs who steal his clothes. A priest happens by, but he ignores the severely injured, naked man. A Levite does the same. But a Samaritan simply does what comes naturally. He helps the man onto his own donkey, takes him to an inn, and pays for his care. *Which one*, Jesus asks, *is a neighbor?* If the answer seems like a no-brainer to a modern-day reader, it was not to his Jewish listeners, who despised Samaritans.

The story of the prodigal son is equally provocative. A man has two sons. The younger demands his inheritance so that he can leave home and make a life for himself. The father gives him his share, and the boy heads off to a faraway land. But rather than buying a home or investing his money in the market, he squanders it. In fact, he goes broke—in the midst of a famine, no less. His only means of survival is hiring himself out to feed hogs, a filthy and demeaning job that pays so little he is forced to sleep and eat with the very creatures he feeds. How he wishes he had never left home. Then it occurs to him to return home and ask for menial work as a mere field hand, which would offer him a much better lifestyle than he now has.

As he approaches his father's estate, he sees his father, wild with excitement, coming to welcome him home with open arms. No fieldwork for him; rather a homecoming bash. It is a time for celebration. A lost son has been found. The older brother, however, is not joining in the festivities. Why should he? He did the wise and honorable thing. He stayed put and didn't squander his money. And for that, why doesn't his father throw him a party? This, Jesus explains, is how God welcomes home a lost sinner.

These stories are classics in the making. Is it any wonder the crowds are captivated?

Jesus is a people person. He loves telling stories and engaging his audience. He

Zacchaeus sees Jesus

needs downtime, however, and for that he slips away to pray or to talk with his disciples alone. On other occasions he visits friends, most notably Mary and Martha of Bethany and their brother Lazarus, whom Jesus later miraculously brings back to life after a fatal illness.

In some instances, Jesus singles out individuals for special treatment. Zacchaeus is a case in point. Jesus is surrounded by a large crowd as he is making his way through Jericho. People are begging to be healed, and religious leaders are clamoring to have their questions answered. In the midst of all the commotion, Jesus looks up and sees a man perched on a branch in a sycamore tree.

Jesus intuitively knows that this man, short of stature, has run ahead trying to get a spot in front of the crowd, but with no success. So he climbs up in a tree just to get a look. He's an important man about town—in charge of collecting taxes for the Romans—and it probably seems odd to ordinary citizens that he's up in a tree, considering his status. Most of them, however, would not even have noticed amid all the commotion.

But Jesus looks him straight in the eye, calls him by name, and tells him to climb out of the tree because he's coming to his house for the afternoon meal. Zacchaeus is thrilled. The locals are not. Why would Jesus give special recognition to a big-time cheat—a tax collector? But Jesus has his reasons. He sees right through the man. In fact, Zacchaeus's first words are an admission of his guilt, with the promise to give away half his income to the poor and to pay four times over to those he has cheated. Jesus recognizes his sincerity and affirms his commitment.

For other individuals with whom Jesus interacts along the way, the outcome is not so affirming. Such is the case with a young man—a wealthy government official—who seeks Jesus out. He asks what he must do to gain eternal life. Jesus points to the commandments. He counters that he keeps all of them. But Jesus goes on to the matter of discipleship. Is the young man willing to follow him? That will mean disposing of his wealth and giving it to the poor. The cost of discipleship is too high. The young man leaves, sober and sad.

Jesus does not warn the rich young ruler of the fires of hell, as he might have done when asked about gaining eternal life. On other occasions he does not mince words.

Jesus Gives Life to a Little Girl and Her Mother and Father

It was not just the child's life that had been given back, of course, but the lives of the mother and father, who stood there with no words they knew how to say. The worst thing that had ever happened to them had suddenly become the best thing that had ever happened to them, and you can imagine their hardly daring so much as to breathe for the fear of breaking the spell. You can imagine her walking around the room touching familiar things—a chair, a comb, a flower somebody had left, a chipped plate—trying to get the world back, trying to get her self back.

Frederick Buechner, *Secrets in the Dark: A Life of Sermons*, 272–79

> As it was in the days of Noah, so it will be at the coming of the Son of Man. . . . Two men will be in the field; one will be taken and the other left. Two women will be grinding with a hand mill; one will be taken and the other left. . . . He will cut him to pieces and assign him a place with the hypocrites, where there will be weeping and gnashing of teeth. . . . Then he will say to those on his left, "Depart from me, you who are cursed, into the eternal fire prepared for the devil and his angels."[14]

The cost of discipleship is more than giving all one's possessions to the poor. That will become very clear to Jesus' disciples in the weeks that follow, when their commitment to him will be severely tested.

Having moved from one town to another, Jesus heads back to Jerusalem for the upcoming Passover feast. As usual, the streets are teeming with people. The disciples, on Jesus' instructions, have arranged for him to ride on a colt, and as he enters the city, the people on the parade route wave palm branches and throw down a carpet of coats in front of him. They shout *hosanna* and hail him as their Messiah, Son of David.

The Pharisees are in a dither, demanding that the disciples organize some kind of crowd control. But for all those close to Jesus this is a glorious day. They ignore the words he had spoken concerning his death. They are in denial.

This scene of joyous acclamation is quickly reversed when Jesus arrives at the Temple. There he observes merchants and money changers, their booths and tables set up for business. People are milling around, dickering for bargains. Jesus sees what is going on and is livid. He barges through the crowd, knocks over the tables, scatters the merchandise, and shouts out that God's house must not be turned into a *den of thieves*. The onlookers are too stunned to react.

The religious leaders, however, are up in arms. How dare Jesus stride in from Galilee and take over the Temple. From their perspective, he is a devious and dangerous man who must be eliminated. They are plotting against him even as he carries on with his teaching. He well knows that his days and his very words are numbered.

On the day of the Passover feast, the disciples prepare the meal at a home in Jerusalem. Late in the day, when Jesus and the disciples are eating and talking together around the table, Jesus gets up, fills

Washing Feet, More Than a Symbolic Gesture

Looking back over the whole chapter [John 13] on the washing of the feet, we may say that in this humble gesture, expressing the entire ministry of Jesus' life and death, the Lord stands before us as the servant of God. . . . Indeed, Saint John's whole Passion narrative is built on this connection between humble service and glory (*dóxa*): it is in Jesus' downward path, in his abasement even to the Cross, that God's glory is seen, that the Father and, in him, Jesus is glorified. . . . The hour of the Cross is the hour of the Father's true glory, the hour of Jesus' true glory.

Joseph Ratzinger (Pope Benedict XVI), *Jesus of Nazareth: Holy Week; From the Entrance into Jerusalem to the Resurrection*, 74–75 a basin with water, and begins washing his disciples' feet. It is a fitting demonstration of servant ministry.

At this point Jesus drops the bombshell. *One of you*, he tells them, *will betray me—hand me over to the enemy*. The disciples are flabbergasted. They know each other; they've traveled and eaten and lived together. How can this be true? The whole thing is preposterous. They wonder aloud if one of them is *that one*. Jesus responds that he will signify who it is by giving that person a piece of bread dipped in wine. All of them but Judas remain bewildered. Judas takes the bread and goes out into the night.

In the hours that follow, Jesus continues to teach his disciples, offering them his final testament. His words are specifically for them, but they will ring in the ears of believers down through the centuries:

> Let not your heart be troubled; you believe in God, believe also in Me. . . . I am the way, the truth, and the life. No one comes to the Father except through me. . . .These things I have spoken to you while being present with you. But the Helper, the Holy Spirit, whom the Father will send in My name, He will teach you all things, and bring to your remembrance all things that I said to you. Peace I leave with you, My peace I give to you; not as the world gives do I give to you. Let not your heart be troubled, neither let it be afraid.[15]

After the Passover meal ends and his teaching has come to a conclusion, Jesus offers a prayer for his followers—that they might fully realize a spirit of unity among each other. They sing a hymn, and then he goes out into the Garden of Gethsemane to pray. He knows his time is very short. One day hence, it will be all over. He loves life and doesn't want to die—surely not an agonizing, shameful death of a criminal. He pleads with God to spare him the terrible suffering. He is weeping now—even as his three closest disciples fall asleep. How can they be so indifferent? They sleep on.

Then out of the blackness of the night Judas appears. With him are religious leaders, some of them with swords. Jesus knows exactly what Judas is up to. As Jesus is about to be arrested, Peter wakes up in a panic, pulls out a sword, and cuts off the ear of the high priest's servant. Jesus, with little ado, reattaches it.

The disciples scatter as Jesus is taken to stand before the chief priest, Caiaphas, where he is roughed up and accused of blasphemy—claiming to be the Messiah and the Son of Man, who will soon be seated at the right hand of God. This creates an uproar. How dare he make such claims? By the Jewish leaders' calculations, he has condemned himself. They have no choice but to sentence him to death.

The next morning Jesus is brought before Pilate, the Roman governor. Pilate wants nothing to do with this religious dispute. He tells the Jewish leaders to deal with him under their own law. The fact is they had already done that by condemning him to death, but they did not have the authority to execute him, and that is precisely what they want.

So Pilate grudgingly summons Jesus to stand before him. He questions Jesus

The Real Pilate

The Bible is rather kind to Pilate, presenting him as a reasonable man who was forced by the crowd into condemning Jesus despite his belief in Jesus' innocence. . . . However, everything we know of Pilate from non-biblical sources indicates that he was a brutal, vicious, and completely unfeeling monster.

Richard R. Losch, *All the People in the Bible*, 347

about claiming to be the king of the Jews. Jesus tells him that his kingship is not of this world, but rather a heavenly one. Pilate doesn't get it. So he asks the question again. He wants to know if Jesus is claiming to be the king of the Jews. Jesus responds in the affirmative, adding that he has been sent as a witness to the truth and that anyone who is concerned about truth will recognize who he is.

Whether sincere or cynical, Pilate then asks the ultimate question: *What is truth?*

But above all else, Pilate is pragmatic. He is convinced that Jesus has committed no crime and suggests that he be the one given the customary Passover pardon.

The religious leaders, however, insist that Barabbas, not Jesus, be granted the pardon. So Pilate orders that Jesus be whipped. Then soldiers dress him in a purple robe and a crown of thorns, mocking him all the while as *King of the Jews*. Pilate appears again and reiterates his earlier position—that Jesus is not guilty of any criminal activities. But in the end Pilate washes his hands before all the people, symbolically demonstrating that he will have no blood on his conscience.

When Jesus is brought outside, a roar goes up from the mob, *Crucify him!* This is the crowd—the same fickle crowd—that sang *hosanna* and hailed him king only days earlier. So, with no legal recourse, Jesus is taken away to face the most scornful and cruel death—crucifixion. He is forced to carry his own cross to Golgotha, also called Skull Hill. At one point he stumbles beneath the weight, and Simon of Cyrene is ordered to lug it the rest of the way.

When they arrive at the destination, the place of the skull, he is crucified between two thieves; one thief rebukes the other for mocking Jesus and is rewarded with the promise of immediate paradise with Jesus. Roman soldiers wager on his coat, winner takes all. Jesus looks at them in pity amid his agony and then says "Father, forgive them; for they know not what they do."[16]

Jesus on the road to Calvary

At the foot of the cross, blinded by grief, are loved ones, including Jesus' mother, Mary Magdalene, and John, whom Jesus commissions to be a son to his mother. When Jesus tells them he is thirsty, they bring him vinegar wine. All the while soldiers and passersby are mocking, saying that if he is truly the Son of God and can save others, he ought to be able to save himself.

By noon the sky has become as black as midnight and remains that way until midafternoon. Then Jesus groans from the depths of his being, calling out, "My God, my God, why hast thou forsaken me?"[17]

Soon thereafter Jesus cries out again very loudly, and then in a horrifying moment he is dead. At the very same time the curtain in the Temple splits down the middle into two pieces. There is also an earthquake, at which time the graves are opened and people—some of whom have been long dead—begin walking out of their tombs. What a stunning turn of events this is. Surely this, more than the crucifixion of Jesus, should have grabbed the headlines of the Jerusalem *Daily News*.

In the meantime, Jesus is taken off the cross. Joseph of Arimathea, an undercover disciple, asks if he can bury the body in his garden tomb, where no one previously had been buried. The body is wrapped in linen with spices added, as was the custom of the day. The tomb is tightly sealed and placed under heavy guard. Jesus is now in Paradise.

But two days later, on the first day of the week, he is just outside the tomb, mistaken for a gardener by Mary Magdalene. He asks her why she is weeping, and she

The Empty Tomb Is Not the Point

That is all the disciples saw when they got to the tomb on that first morning—two piles of old clothes. Mary didn't even see that much. . . . She ran to tell Simon Peter and the other disciples that Jesus' body had been stolen. . . . Only why would grave robbers have bothered to undress him first? . . . None of it was making any sense to them, John says, because no one who was there that morning understood the scripture, that Jesus must rise from the dead. Still, when the beloved disciple followed Peter inside the tomb and saw the clothes lying there, he believed. Believed what? John does not say. He simply believed, and without another word to each other he and Peter returned to their homes. . . . Peter and the beloved disciple . . . saw nothing but a vacant tomb with two piles of clothes in it. They saw nothing but emptiness and absence. . . . Any way you look at it, that is a mighty fragile beginning for a religion that has lasted almost 2000 years now, and yet that is where so many of us continue to focus our energy: on that tomb, on that morning, on what did or did not happen there and how to explain it. . . . But as it turned out that did not matter because the empty tomb was not the point. . . .The appearances cinch the resurrection for me, not what happened in the tomb. What happened in the tomb was entirely between Jesus and God. For the rest of us, Easter began the moment the gardener said, "Mary!" and she knew who he was. That is where the miracle happened and goes on happening—not in the tomb but in the encounter with the living Lord.

Barbara Brown Taylor, "Escape from the Tomb"

does not even recognize him. But when he says her name—*Mary*—she knows in an instant it is he. *Teacher*, she cries, starting to embrace him. He asks her not to cling to him because he has not yet ascended into heaven.

Several hours later as Jesus' frightened disciples and some of his followers are meeting clandestinely in a private, dimly lit, locked room, Jesus suddenly enters right through the closed door. He stands around engaging in small talk for a short time, showing them the scars on his hands and side. Then he blesses them and leaves.

Later in the day two of Jesus' followers are walking to the little hamlet of Emmaus several miles outside of Jerusalem. They are deep in discussion about the events that have just taken place when all of a sudden Jesus begins walking beside them. He asks them what they are so solemnly talking about. They are surprised that he doesn't know. Hasn't he heard all the goings-on about Jesus in the past few days?

At their request Jesus joins them for a meal. When he breaks the bread and blesses it, they recognize him. But in that instant he is gone. They return to Jerusalem and find the other disciples to inform them. While they are narrating the story, Jesus appears to the whole group. He again shows his scars, and this time eats some fish.

After this Jesus appears to a crowd of more than one hundred people. That Jesus had performed mighty miracles during his lifetime should have been enough to clarify his identity. But his postresurrection appearances are the clincher, and this would not be the last. Sometime later, Peter and some of the other disciples are back on the Sea of Galilee fishing. They have been out all night but have caught nothing. Now it's morning and they are nearing shore. With no warning, Jesus walks by, asking if they have caught anything. Knowing it has not been a profitable night for them, he instructs them to throw the net out on the other side of the boat. They do, and they can hardly haul in the heavy net full of fish. When they realize it is Jesus, they join him for breakfast on the beach.

Later Jesus appears again to the apostles. This time in Galilee, on a mountain where he promised to meet them. Even though they have seen him before, they can hardly contain themselves, some falling down in worship before him. Here he commissions them all to go out and carry the gospel to all nations. "Go ye therefore, and teach all nations, baptizing them in the name of the Father, and of the Son, and of the Holy Ghost: Teaching them to observe all things whatsoever I have commanded you: and, lo, I am with you always, even unto the end of the world."[18]

Jesus appears one last time to his disciples. On this occasion they interact with him, asking him questions, particularly about setting up his kingdom on earth. *When will this happen?* they want to know. He tells them the timing is something they cannot know. What they do need to know is that soon the Holy Spirit will come upon them and that they will be witnesses in Jerusalem, Judea, Samaria, and to the ends of the earth.

With that final commission, he is carried up into heaven. They are looking up when two angels appear, offering a final tribute to Jesus—one that would ring in their ears as they set out to live by the words he had taught them. "You Galileans!—why do you just stand here looking up at an empty sky? This very Jesus who was taken up from among you to heaven will come as certainly—and mysteriously—as he left."[19]

Concluding Observations

The only way to conclude an abbreviated biography of Jesus such as this is to quote the apostle John: "Jesus did many other things as well. If every one of them were written down, I suppose that even the whole world would not have room for the books that would be written."[20] John, of course, was speaking of all the things Jesus did that were not included in his own Gospel account.

John, who knew Jesus so well as boyhood cousin and friend and as his closest confidant among the apostles, surely could have filled up books of his own. But did John or anybody really know Jesus? His mother and Mary Magdalene no doubt had insights the male disciples missed, but did they really know him? The apostle Paul's deep longing was to *know* Christ. New Testament scholars and mystics all profess to know Jesus even as those closest to him must have thought they did. But at the end of the day he remains most elusive.

On a surface level our knowledge of Jesus is perhaps best summed up in an old Fanny Crosby hymn I often sang in my childhood. But this skeleton summary of mere words is only transformed into *knowing* when sung by a choir of voices stretching across time.

> Tell me the story of Jesus,
> Write on my heart every word.
> Tell me the story most precious,
> Sweetest that ever was heard.
> Tell how the angels in chorus,
> Sang as they welcomed His birth.
> "Glory to God in the highest!
> Peace and good tidings to earth."
>
> Fasting alone in the desert,
> Tell of the days that are past.
> How for our sins He was tempted,
> Yet was triumphant at last.
> Tell of the years of His labor,
> Tell of the sorrow He bore.
> He was despised and afflicted,
> Homeless, rejected and poor.
>
> Tell of the cross where they nailed
> Him,
> Writhing in anguish and pain.
> Tell of the grave where they laid
> Him,
> Tell how He liveth again.
> Love in that story so tender,
> Clearer than ever I see.
> Stay, let me weep while you whisper,
> Love paid the ransom for me.

Further Reading

Johnson, Paul. *Jesus: A Biography from a Believer*. New York: Viking, 2010.

Neusner, Jacob. *A Rabbi Talks with Jesus*. Montreal: McGill-Queen's University Press, 2000.

Stein, Robert H. *Jesus the Messiah: A Survey of the Life of Christ*. Downers Grove, IL: InterVarsity, 1996.

Yancey, Philip. *The Jesus I Never Knew*. Grand Rapids: Zondervan, 2002.

19

MARY MAGDALENE AND THE SCANDAL OF SYCHAR

Women Disciples of Christ

She is ritually unclean—a woman not merely in her monthly menstrual cycle, but hemorrhaging profusely, a condition that has afflicted her for more than a decade. Such a woman should be confined to the home, surely not mingling in a crowd, contaminating others—particularly Jewish men. Indeed, the men in the multitude, if they had been aware of her presence, would have been alarmed. But she takes the risk, pushing her way through the throng in order to touch the hem of Jesus' garment. She is instantaneously healed. Now she can slip away unnoticed and make her way out of the mass of people.

But not so fast. Jesus turns around and demands to know who touched him. What kind of a question is that? *There are people pressing in from all sides*, the disciples point out. But Jesus is adamant. He demands to know who it was.

Unclean! Unclean! The words are ringing in her ears. There is no escape. She knows he knows. Terrified, she steps forward. Then, falling down at his feet, she confesses that she is the guilty one. She pours out her heart, telling him how she has found no relief from physicians with their dubious remedies. Jesus simply does what he does best. He looks with compassion on her. "Daughter," he says matter-of-factly, "your faith has healed you. Go in peace and be freed from your suffering."[1]

Women are an important part of Jesus' ministry. He is at ease with them and naturally reaches out to them—even to those with sullied reputations. He engages in an animated conversation with the woman of Sychar, and he serves as a spontaneous defense attorney for a woman caught in an adulterous relationship. Forever nameless, she is the woman *taken in adultery*, caught in the very act. The Bible leaves little to the imagination. How utterly embarrassing! But the matter quickly moves far beyond that of mere disgrace. She is hauled before a group of men, who intend to stone her.

Such is the legal code that holds the woman responsible while letting the guilty man go scot-free. Jesus will have none of it. He takes his time, kneeling down and writing something in the sand. The men, however, are not about to be put off. This floozy has transgressed the law, and she must pay. Jesus stands up, looks them directly in the eye, and dares any one of them who claims to be without sin to throw the first stone. He goes back to writing in the sand while her accusers, one by one, walk away speechless and humiliated.

But Jesus isn't finished. He turns to the woman and asks if anyone has condemned her. She says that no one has. "Then neither do I condemn you," he responds. "Go now and leave your life of sin."[2]

On another occasion, when Jesus is being wined and dined in the home of a Pharisee, a town harlot interrupts the meal and anoints him with perfume. The Pharisee, mumbling under his breath, wonders why, if Jesus is a prophet, he doesn't know that this woman with perfume is actually a prostitute. He should have sent her away before she started making a scene. Jesus is entirely at ease—and grateful for her lavish gift. True, she's a sinner, but through her expression of love she repents, and Jesus forgives her.

Women—whether sick or widowed, poor or prostitutes—are on Jesus' radar screen. And he is anything but condescending. Unlike the typical wags of the day, he does not perceive women as weak or helpless or deficient. Rather, he acknowledges their full personhood and recognizes their strength and independence. Among them are the Samaritan woman, Mary and Martha of Bethany, and Mary Magdalene.

Jesus Was a Feminist is the title of a book by Leonard Swidler. The use of the term *feminist* is offensive to many people, but the author's point is that Jesus stood out among teachers and thinkers of his day. A well-known rabbi of the time spoke for many Jews when he wrote that it is better that the Torah be burned than be entrusted to a woman. Likewise, Jewish men often in their prayers thanked God for not making them female.

Such gender bias was simply not part of Jesus' makeup. Rather than barring women from studying Scripture, he expected them to hear and understand the gospel message and to reach out with that message to others.

Jesus and Women

Perhaps it is no wonder that women were first at the cradle and last at the cross. They had never known a man like this Man—there never had been such another. A prophet and teacher who never nagged at them, never flattered or coaxed or patronized; who never made arch jokes about them, never treated them either as "The women, God help us!" or "The ladies, God bless them!"; who rebuked without querulousness and praised without condescension; who took their questions and arguments seriously; who never mapped out their sphere for them, never urged them to be feminine or jeered at them for being female; who had no axe to grind and no uneasy male dignity to defend; who took them as he found them and was completely unselfconscious. There is no act, no sermon, no parable in the whole Gospel that borrows its pungency from female perversity; nobody could possibly guess from the words and deeds of Jesus that there was anything "funny" about women's nature.

Dorothy Sayers, *Are Women Human?*, 47

Woman of Sychar: Meeting Jesus at the Well

She carries the good news of Jesus to her hometown neighbors and thus becomes one of the New Testament's first and most effective evangelists. With no more than a lunch-hour session, she is ready to hit the streets. Her lack of structured discipleship training, however, is not the only strike against her. Other barriers include her ethnic background, her gender, her questionable reputation, and her marginalized status.

In the biblical account there is yet another strike against her. She has no name. Yet she is a very interesting and approachable Bible character: a lively conversationalist who becomes a believer only after she dares to challenge Jesus.

Nevertheless, she has not always had good press. In fact, one biblical commentator characterized her as ignorant and uncouth and gullible. She was anything but that. Indeed, in comparison to Nicodemus, who also encounters Jesus (one chapter earlier in the Gospel of John), her questions and interaction with Jesus indicate intelligence and clarity of thought. She stands her ground, but when she becomes convinced Jesus is the Messiah, she immediately acts on that truth. Hers is a rare conversion story in Scripture.

Known as *the woman at the well*, the account of her story opens right after she has encountered a group of men—strangers—as she is heading just outside the small town of Sychar to fetch water. She would not have recognized them as Jesus' disciples. Had she been a typical woman of the era, she would have looked down and avoided making eye contact. But she isn't typical. She appears to be anything but a properly cowering woman. She passes on by and arrives at the well, surprised to encounter one lone man.

It's high noon, and it's very unusual to find anyone at the well in the blistering heat. By going at this time of day herself, she avoids the stares and glares and gossip of the local women. But now she is alone with a stranger. It's an awkward moment, but then he breaks the silence and asks for a drink of water.

She's shocked. Of course she will give him a drink. But how is it this man is breaking custom and engaging a woman in conversation—a *Samaritan* woman at that? It is a serious breach of protocol. Even she knows that. And she's bold enough to call him on it: "How come you, a Jew, are asking me, a Samaritan woman, for a drink?"[3] Seriously.

Jesus jumps on her question and turns it around. He tells her that if she only knew

Everyday *Life*

Water and Wells

Jesus told the Samaritan woman that he would have given her living water if she had only asked for it. She is bewildered. The concept of water—*living water*, whatever that may be—free for the asking is startling. Water is a most precious commodity in arid regions of the world, and the very thought of being in possession of some sort of mysterious *living* water is intriguing.

Springs and wells were the center of everyday life in biblical times. Shepherds would bring their flocks to drink at wells while they themselves engaged in social interaction, unless rivalry prevailed and fighting ensued. Village women often transformed the arduous work of carrying water into a neighborly activity that marked the hours of the day.

The patriarchs and the generations that followed built wells and struggled with their enemies over wells. The Psalms repeatedly refer to water. Psalm 1 opens with a description of an upright person who is "like a tree planted by the rivers of water." In Psalm 23, the Lord is described as one who "leadeth me beside the still waters" (KJV). Water is a symbol that relates to both the fear and the grace of God. Indeed, God (as depicted in Psalm 107) is not only the one who "turned rivers into a desert, flowing springs into thirsty ground," but also the one who "turned the desert into pools of water and the parched ground into flowing springs" (Ps. 107:33, 35 NIV).

Wells of the Ancient, Arid World

The wells of these semi-desert regions must not be thought of as like our modern wells which are narrow and deep with a raised curb. The wells of the Near East have a diameter at their opening of eight to twelve feet, thus enabling a fair number of shepherds to draw water at the same time. Obviously, the depth depends on the underground water level. Usually the well is surrounded by large rough stones to a height of between one and a half to two and a half feet above the ground to prevent the caving in of the sides. Over the centuries these stones have been worn into a series of parallel ridges by the rubbing of the cords pulling up the filled buckets.

David Roberts, "On the Road from Ur to Haran"

who he was, she would not just be asking, but pleading with *him* for a drink. He has her attention. Then he adds that the water he is offering her is *living* water.

She is used to men toying with her. Is Jesus one such man? Or is he just talking nonsense in this midday desert heat? (Does she roll her eyes?) While addressing him respectfully, she points out that he does not even have a bucket. The well is deep. How could he possibly offer her water? With that she could have simply taken her bucket and headed home. But she is eager to pursue the conversation and perhaps taunt him a bit.

She asks if he is a greater man than their mutual ancestor Jacob, who not only was responsible for having the well dug, but also drank from it and watered his livestock. This very same well, after so many generations, belongs to her and all the people in Sychar. So why is he offering *her* water? She thinks she has him cornered. How dare any man think himself greater than Father Jacob? He was God's man, after all. He had issues, to be sure, but God had blessed him with a new name—Israel—that would be forever honored by his descendants. And she, with all her own baggage, was one of them—a proud one of them at that.

Jesus talks right past her, going back to the matter of *living* water. Jacob's well water, he explains, or that from any other well, is ordinary water. Anyone who draws from this well for a drink will soon be thirsty again. The water he is offering her, on the other hand, is an entirely different kind of water—water that will quench her thirst once and for all so that she will never be thirsty again.

She is now beginning to realize that he is speaking metaphorically, about the spiritual realm. Indeed, there is every indication by her next words that she is a seeker—someone who knows there is something beyond—far beyond—her mundane life. She asks Jesus to give her this water that will prevent her from ever thirsting again. In response, Jesus probes her on a personal level. He asks her to summon her husband and then return. She's suspicious. What's he getting at? She tells him she has no husband. *Nice try* is essentially how Jesus responds. What she has said, strictly speaking, may be true. But Jesus knows the whole truth—that she has had five husbands and the man she is currently living with is not her husband.

How could he possibly know that? But she doesn't ask. She quickly moves the conversation away from her and back to him. Acknowledging him to be a prophet, she asks why, since their mutual ancestors worshiped God on the nearby mountain, do Jews worship exclusively in Jerusalem?

Jesus replies that Samaritans are not on the right track when it comes to worshiping God—that salvation comes through the Jews. But the time will come and is actually now here when people can worship anywhere—*in Spirit and in truth*. The woman is catching on and asks if the Messiah, when he comes, will clearly explain all of this. Jesus then identifies himself as the very Messiah. This is one of his early and no-less-than-astonishing self-revelations.

At that point the disciples—the same group of men whom she had encountered on the way out to the well—show up. They do not greet her and appear to be put off that Jesus would be talking in such a familiar way with a Samaritan woman. She realizes it is time to absent herself and does so in such haste she leaves her water jug at the well. But she doesn't forget the eye-opening conversation. Jesus' words have cut through to the core of her being.

As soon as she gets back to the village, she tells everyone she meets about the stranger who knew all about her personal life. She does not make any doctrinaire assertions. Rather, she invites the people to go out to the well and see for themselves. Her follow-up question piques their curiosity: *Do you think he might be the Messiah?* Her neighbors wonder if she is on to something. They hurriedly make their way to the well to see Jesus for themselves.

As a result of her enthusiastic witness, many of the Samaritans from Sychar believe in Jesus as Messiah. In fact, they are so convinced that they beg Jesus to come into their village and teach them. After his brief, two-day visit, the people know for certain that this woman has pointed them to the Messiah. Now with deep conviction they can say to her: "We no longer believe just because of what you said; now we have heard for ourselves, and we know that this man really is the Savior of the world."[4]

Martha, Mary, and Lazarus: Dear Friends from Bethany

They live together in Bethany with their brother Lazarus. Martha, initially named first, is likely the older of the two sisters, and perhaps the head of the home. All three appear to be unmarried, and they are good friends of Jesus. How this friendship

The Three Marys

Once the conflation of Mary Magdalene with the unnamed sinful woman of Luke's gospel has been gently disentangled, the more gnarly question remains: how about Mary Magdalene and Mary of Bethany? If the woman who performed the anointing ceremony has been traditionally remembered as Mary Magdalene—except in the Gospel of John, where she is specifically identified as Mary of Bethany—could the solution to this puzzle lie in the fact that the two Marys are actually the same person? . . . Arguing against this interpretation are two significant difficulties. First, the Gospel of John itself clearly distinguishes between these two characters. There is no conflation in the author's mind. Mary of Bethany is the one who performs the anointing, named as such. And Mary Magdalene, named as such, is the one who stands watch at the foot of the cross and engages in the resurrection drama. . . . Second, as we meet these women in the gospels, it is difficult to make the case that they are the same person because their energies seem so vastly different. Mary Magdalene is bold and brash, "out there," witnessing and proclaiming. Mary of Bethany's role is more "yin": inward, passive, gentle, and softer.

Cynthia Bourgeault, *The Meaning of Mary Magdalene: Discovering the Woman at the Heart of Christianity*, 23–24 developed is not recorded, but they are the only ones identified in the Bible as being simply *friends* of Jesus—very dear friends. There is no evidence that they were related to him, nor were they ones who followed after him. Unlike most of his other associates, they are not Galileans. Bethany is a small village just a short distance from Jerusalem.

He stays with them in their home, perhaps every time he travels to Jerusalem for Passover. Their connection with him is singular. They provide not only accommodations, but also warmth and easygoing camaraderie, allowing him to feel very much at home. In fact, their relationship with him in some respects seems more that of equals than of master and disciple. Perhaps he had visited them on many occasions in the years before his ministry began.

On one occasion when they welcomed him into their home, he is surrounded by others eager to listen to his teachings. Martha, ever conscious of customary hospitality, is busy trying to prepare a meal. She feels pressured and indeed is overwhelmed by the amount of work to do. Word has quickly gotten out that Jesus is paying them a visit, and people seem to appear out of nowhere, some no doubt slipping in without an invitation. What can she do? It's Bethany, after all, and neighbors are neighbors.

She is outside cooking and tending the fire and cannot hear a word Jesus is saying, though she is as eager as any of the men are to listen to his teachings. But she knows well the role of women—unless they happen to be out on the road, following along with the crowd. It's unfair, but she does not challenge custom. What does irritate her is Mary's front-row seat at Jesus' feet. Mary, in fact, is so intent on hearing every word Jesus says that she ignores Martha's signals to come out and help prepare the meal. Martha seethes. *Mary is so selfish and inconsiderate.*

Martha simply cannot do it all alone. Finally, she's had enough. She marches into the sitting room and interrupts the teaching, thinking that Jesus surely must be aware that she needs Mary to come and help her. Jesus knows the plight of women. He'll be sympathetic to her cause. She addresses him as *Master*, and asks if he does not care—or hasn't he even noticed?—that Mary has left all the meal preparation to her. *Would you please tell her to come out and help?*

The response is vintage Jesus. He uses a mundane problem to teach a far-reaching truth: "Martha, dear Martha, you're fussing far too much and getting yourself

Mary and Martha

worked up over nothing. One thing only is essential, and Mary has chosen it—it's the main course, and won't be taken from her."[5]

Preparing a meal is part of the normal workday. Hospitality is an essential ingredient in community living. But Mary, Jesus tells Martha and all the other listeners, has her priorities right in this instance. The refreshments can wait. She is more than just a friend. She is a disciple of Jesus, learning all she can absorb from his teachings.

Sometime after this, Lazarus falls ill. Mary and Martha, well aware of Jesus' miraculous healings, send word, asking him to come quickly and heal their brother. As the hours drag, their brother's condition worsens. They very impatiently wait for Jesus to come, pacing back and forth, walking out to the road to see any sign of him coming. Lazarus is deteriorating rapidly, and they are more anxious and upset with every passing minute. Then they realize it's too late. He is dying. There's nothing anyone can do for him. He takes his last breath. Friends and neighbors gather to comfort and help prepare his body for burial.

Passive-Aggressive Martha

A friend of mine recalls that her mother always sat sideways in her chair during meals. Whether the table was surrounded by family members or invited guests, she was poised for action. She'd jump up if she'd forgotten something in the kitchen, if someone wanted steak sauce rather than the ketchup that was on the table, or if it was time to pass the serving dishes around again. . . . There is biblical precedent for that instinct and posture in the account of Jesus' visit to the home of two sisters, Mary and Martha. . . . One can imagine how the clatter of dishes in the kitchen grows steadily louder until Martha's exasperation at working alone is audible to Mary, who is engrossed in what Jesus is saying. Who is to say that passive-aggressive behavior didn't exist in New Testament households?

Stephanie Frey, "Living with Martha"

Four days later Jesus comes walking into town as though nothing is wrong. His disciples are with him. He has already learned that Lazarus has been dead for four days. He seems to shrug it off. When Martha hears that he is coming, she goes out to meet him. She is in deep mourning. Her brother meant everything to her. Why couldn't Jesus have come right away? She is more than a little perturbed. Her first words are a rebuke. *Master, if you had come sooner, my brother would not have died*. She does, however, add a caveat, suggesting that even at this point he might be able to perform a miracle.

Jesus tells her that her brother will be raised up. She responds that she knows that—that of course he'll be raised at the end, when all are resurrected. But Jesus insists that she doesn't have to wait that long. He tells her that he himself is *the resurrection and the life* and that those who believe in him will not die. He asks if she believes that. Martha no doubt does a double take. But then she makes a profound profession of faith. She knows exactly who Jesus is—that he is the promised Messiah, the Christ, who has come into the world.

Then Martha goes back to the house and tells Mary that Jesus is asking for her. Mary hurries out of the house to meet him and falls at his feet, crying out in anguish and repeating Martha's words. If he had only come earlier—if he had only dropped everything and hurried—Lazarus would not have died. Jesus feels her pain and is deeply moved. He inquires where they have laid her brother. By this time everyone, including Jesus, is weeping. Lazarus was a close friend, whom he dearly loved.

When they arrive at the tomb, Jesus asks onlookers to roll away the boulder. Martha protests. He's now been dead for days, and even with the cave covered, she smells the foul odor. But Jesus persists. They roll away the boulder, and Jesus calls for Lazarus to come out. When Lazarus appears, bound in grave clothes, Jesus tells the onlookers to unwrap the linens so that he can walk. Martha and Mary are as astounded as everyone else. Their brother four days dead—so dead that his body is decaying—is now alive and well.

Jesus takes the miracle in stride, and the three siblings bid farewell, with Jesus promising to return soon. When he does return, there are big crowds—those who have come to see Lazarus, the dead man walking, and those who want to see the holy man who performed the incredible miracle. Religious leaders are also there, many of whom want Jesus and his *cult following* to just go away. Jesus makes his way through the crowds and gets inside the house, where Martha is hosting a feast in his honor. Lazarus joins the lively conversation and enjoys the meal as well.

As they are eating Mary comes in with a very expensive container of perfume and pours it on the feet of Jesus. She then kneels down and wipes his feet with her hair. The fragrance fills the entire house. *What a waste of money*, Judas complains, adding that it would have been far better if she had sold it and given the money to the poor. Jesus defends her, saying that what she had done was an act of love intended for his burial.

Debunking the Prostitute Myth

Modern scholarship has tended to soften up the prostitute aspect. . . . But the memory of a broken person whose conversion was synonymous with her healing remains front and center in the portrait of Mary Magdalene. She is the "type" of the recovering sinner. . . . It may be surprising, then, to discover that this theoretically "scriptural" portrait actually hangs on the very slimmest of scriptural threads. It is almost entirely a concoction of patristic and medieval Western piety. . . . It's "real" to the degree that it actually came to life within the church and both did and continues to exert a huge influence on Christian spirituality. But it's not "true," if by true you mean faithful to what actually happened or to what the scriptural accounts themselves actually say or imply. What scripture actually says about Mary Magdalene is a lot more positive—and for exactly this reason, a lot more unsettling.

Cynthia Bourgeault, *The Meaning of Mary Magdalene*, 4

Walking Ten Hard Miles Demon Possessed

Mary appears for the first time in the chronology of Jesus' life in this brief passage from Luke's Gospel (8:2–3). Luke indicates when she entered Jesus' life and why she sought him out. Jesus' reputation must have drawn her the ten hard miles from her home in Magdala to Capernaum. . . . She probably came to him alone, on foot, over rock roads and rough paths, possessed by demons, her clothing in tatters. . . . Given Mary's demonic possession, there is little mystery about her being single. Possession carried the stigma of impurity, not the natural impurity of childbirth (for example), but the contagion of an unclean spirit. She had no doubt been ostracized in Magdala in view of her many demons.

Bruce Chilton, *Mary Magdalene: A Biography*, 1, 4

Mary could not have known how fast the events of the coming week would unravel—that she had anointed him barely a week before his death.

Mary Magdalene: Bringing News of the Resurrection

Mary Magdalene is an enigma. One learns right up front that she has had seven demons cast out of her—almost as a badge of honor. Whether all at once or one demon at a time over the course of months or years is not recorded. Nor is there any hint of how those demons manifested themselves in her life. Perhaps she suffered from severe depression or bipolar disorder or some other affliction. Whatever the symptoms and the duration of her difficulties, Jesus healed her and she was one of his closest disciples—always the first named among his women followers.

Mary hails from Magdala, a fishing village lying on the northwest shore of the Sea of Galilee. Unlike most women in the Bible, she appears not to be dependent on a husband or father. Did she come from a moneyed family—with money enough to cover her traveling expenses as she follows Jesus? She is likely one of his earliest followers, since she is named along with other women who ministered to Jesus by supplying provisions. Like the Twelve, she and the other women traveled with Jesus from town to town, listening to his teachings.

She was perhaps the single most important person in the new faith's most crucial three days. Yet she is not mentioned again—not in Acts, not in the various epistles. . . . Magdalene disappeared from the official record Easter afternoon.

James T. Baker, "The Red-Haired Saint"

It is during Passion Week, however, that Mary Magdalene comes to the fore. She is among the women (and John) who do not flee for fear of persecution when Jesus is arrested and crucified. Indeed, she not

"Apostle to the Apostles"

The text [Mark 16] also provides an opportunity to lift up the importance of women in the ministry and mission of Jesus. Because we are so familiar with the story, we are prone to forget what a startling thing it is that the apostolic commission is entrusted to women. History's most important message is given to those who could not give legal testimony in court in their own culture. Here is a Markan irony with an important message for those who still question the legitimacy of women's ministry in the church. In the Orthodox tradition, Mary Magdalene is called "apostle to the apostles," an apt designation.

Bonnie Bowman Thurston, *Preaching Mark*, 188

only holds vigil from a respectful distance but also comes close and stands at the very foot of the cross, seeking consolation and offering comfort to Jesus.

Indeed, Mary is the first mentioned of several women who are at the crucifixion, painfully standing by Jesus to the very end. She, along with Mary the mother of James and Joseph, stays behind at the tomb after Joseph of Arimathea departs. They leave and prepare the spices for burial. Then before dawn on the first day of the week they return to the tomb with their spices. This is the least they can do for their beloved Master. But now they find the tomb barred by a boulder and guarded by Roman soldiers.

The sky is still dark, and there is no place to go. What should they do with the spices? Even their smallest deeds of reverence are thwarted. Mary is weeping. It is so depressing. How can she contemplate anything but the awfulness of the crucifixion? Amid their sadness and the spooky half-light of daybreak, the women are suddenly jolted by an earthquake. More than that, the soldiers are struck down as though dead. At that moment the women are stunned to encounter a brilliant angel right in front of them, who proceeds to roll back the boulder from the entrance to the tomb.

Shafts of light are blazing from the angel as they walk inside, but the most startling detail is that Jesus' body is no longer there. The angel tells them that Jesus is risen and that they must hurry and give the news to the other disciples. The angel adds a final comment—Jesus is going on ahead to Galilee, where they will find him.

Jesus and Mary Magdalene

So the women, gathering their skirts, run to tell the disciples the joyful news. But before they can get to them, they are stopped dead in their tracks by Jesus himself. When Jesus calls her by name, Mary recognizes him. She gasps as she addresses him—her dear teacher—and then falls down to worship him. He pushes her back, insisting that she not cling to him, because he has not yet ascended into heaven. He tells the two women to hurry on and inform the other disciples. When they arrive, out of breath, Mary tells the eleven apostles that she has seen the Master. What on earth is she talking about? How could the tomb be empty and the recently dead Jesus be walking around and talking to her? It's impossible.

Whether the men believed her or not, Mary knew exactly what she had seen at the tomb. Her spices had been of no use. Jesus was alive and well, and she would always treasure that awesome moment when she recognized him risen from the dead—when he called her by name.

Concluding Observations

If Mary the mother of Jesus is the *first lady* of the Gospels, Mary Magdalene is surely the second—one who in many ways plays a more enviable role. She does not carry the load of demure perfection that the mother of Jesus has been saddled with. Rather, she is a friend and colleague, working alongside Jesus in the rough-and-tumble work of discipleship. She is the spirited redhead (as some artists have depicted her), complete with a questionable past. Tormented by demons, the girl with so much promise has no hope of recovery—until she comes face-to-face with a man who was himself severely tempted by demonic forces. He harbors no scorn for her as others have. He simply heals her, and her life is transformed. One can almost hear her joyful squeal of freedom, her laughter ringing out while Jesus looks on, beaming with pleasure.

From seminary scholars and preachers to neighborhood Bible study facilitators, people wrestle with Mary and Martha, making application to contemporary living. How would they have felt if they had known that down through the centuries their differences would be magnified and serve as talking points for proper Christian conduct? Mary is the one who is praised, though not without a loyal opposition taking the side of Martha. They are us, and we so easily resonate with their issues. But we do them a disservice if we see them only as sisters with opposing personalities.

The woman of Sychar, like Mary Magdalene, is an enigma. How on earth, living in the hamlet of Sychar, could she have been married to five different men? But basically it's none of our business. With the exception of one memorable day in her life, this nameless woman is lost in the annals of time. Her ministry, therefore, stands out as a monument to nameless evangelists through the ages—a monument and a reminder to Christians worldwide: the expansion of the faith is largely due to nameless, untrained, ordinary individuals, some with serious skeletons in their closets.

Further Reading

Bourgeault, Cynthia. *The Meaning of Mary Magdalene: Discovering the Woman at the Heart of Christianity*. Boston: Shambhala, 2010.

Chilton, Bruce. *Mary Magdalene: A Biography*. New York: Doubleday, 2005.

Spencer, F. Scott. *Dancing Girls, Loose Ladies, and Women of the Cloth: The Women in Jesus' Life*. London: Continuum, 2004.

20

ANDREW, THOMAS, JUDAS, AND STEPHEN

Disciples on the Fringe

Twelve run-of-the-mill men. They were not ones likely to be chosen to sit on a board of directors. Yet it would be difficult to imagine Jesus' earthly ministry without the twelve disciples. Except for rare occasions, they were all present whenever he was engaged in ministry. He needed them. He could not have carried out his mission without them, unfaithful and fickle as they sometimes were.

Despite their flaws and failures, the disciples apparently get along well. This is remarkable considering their close, almost-daily contact and their bare-bones lifestyle. In fact, only once, when James and John are trying to weasel thrones next to Jesus in heaven, is there any indication of dissension among the twelve disciples. Such harmony is truly remarkable.

The twelve disciples are most often depicted dining with Jesus during the last Passover meal or following him as he travels from town to town. But, after having singled them out for ministry, Jesus calls them all together and commissions them to go out and conduct the work themselves, giving them the power to heal and to exorcise demons. There are strict rules: preach that the kingdom of heaven is coming soon; concentrate only on fellow Jews; take no money; secure lodging with friendly locals; be prepared for persecution.

Such instructions might seem normal enough. But then Jesus concludes with words that must have been very difficult for the disciples to digest. In this Jewish culture, family relationships reign supreme. Sons revere their fathers. But Jesus turns this familial bond on its head: "For I have come to turn a man against his father. . . . Anyone who loves their father or mother more than me is not worthy of me."[1]

Is it any wonder the disciples struggle in their commitment? How could any one of the Twelve fit this job description? They were being sent out like *sheep among wolves.* At the same time, they were to act *wise as serpents and harmless as doves.* A tall order. On a very practical level, they were to go out without a shekel in their pockets—not even a change of clothes. And if that were not enough, family ties were to be forsaken for the sake of the kingdom. There was to be no halfheartedness. *Take up your cross*, Jesus said, *and follow me.* Needless to say, many of Jesus' followers did not make the cut.

The same is true after the resurrection. The community of believers is expected to give all its money and property to a common fund, but in the midst of these high ideals some widows receive less support than others, some people lie about their giving, and others are no more than shysters, looking for a quick buck.

Peter and John each merit attention as major biblical figures in their own right. Indeed, they tower over the rest, particularly Peter. If the other ten disciples played lead roles in the drama of the first-century Jesus movement, the biblical narrative does not record it. Some of the twelve disciples have small, walk-on roles that give the reader a mere glimpse of their personalities and relationships. Others are even more obscure, including Bartholomew (also known as Nathanael), Matthew (a tax collector, also known as Levi), James (the less, son of Alphaeus), Thaddeus (also known as Judas, son of James), and Simon (the Zealot).

Those of the Twelve who make cameo appearances do not necessarily have high profiles, but they play important roles nonetheless. Among them are Andrew (brother of Peter), Thomas (the doubter), and Judas Iscariot (the traitor). During the days after Pentecost, other disciples come to the fore, including Stephen, Ananias and

Twelve Ordinary Men

I have always been fascinated with the lives of the twelve apostles. Who isn't? The personality types of these men are familiar to us. They are just like us, and they are the people we know. They are approachable. . . . They were ordinary men in every way. Not one of them was renowned for scholarship or great erudition. They had no track record as orators or theologians. In fact, they were outsiders as far as the religious establishment of Jesus' day was concerned. They were not outstanding because of any natural talents or intellectual abilities. On the contrary, they were all too prone to mistakes, misstatements, wrong attitudes, lapses of faith and bitter failure.

John MacArthur, *Twelve Ordinary Men: How the Master Shaped His Disciples for Greatness*, xii

Sapphira, and Philip. They are key players alongside Peter and the other apostles.

Andrew: Behind-the-Scenes Disciple

In the list of the Twelve, Andrew is second, always following his brother Peter. His name is indelibly recorded in all four Gospels. That makes him the most publicized invisible disciple of Jesus. One could say that his chief contribution is that of simply *showing up*. He's always there with the other disciples, but unlike Peter, he rarely does anything extraordinary. Indeed, not one miracle is attributed to Andrew.

Yet this behind-the-scenes disciple carried out one of the most far-reaching religious coups in all history. He convinced his hotheaded, independent, domineering brother Simon to follow Jesus. Had it not been for Andrew, the history of Christianity might have taken a very different path. It is difficult to contemplate this centuries-old faith without the larger-than-life Simon—Andrew ever in the background.

Andrew, son of Jonas, works alongside his brother helping their father manage a prosperous fishing business. He is from Bethsaida, on the northeast coast of the Sea of Galilee. Also involved in the fishing business are James and John and their father Zebedee. But Andrew has additional interests. Like many other Jews, he is eagerly awaiting the Messiah's coming. He becomes a disciple of John the Baptist, the fiery desert prophet who preaches repentance. But when John points to Jesus as the Lamb of God, Andrew is stirred. Could this man really be the Promised One—the Messiah?

With John's ringing endorsement of Jesus, it is not surprising that the next time Andrew sees Jesus, he leaves the company of John and begins to follow this new rabbi. With him is another of the Baptist's disciples. In response to their question about where he is residing, Jesus invites them to come and see. They remain with him a day,

The Real St. Andrew

When I was a child, our family attended a church at the end of our street named for St. Andrew. It featured a statue that represented exactly what you would think of a saint. The man wore sandals and long, flowing robes. His hands were folded and he bore the face of a determined, yet gentle leader. I couldn't resist touching the statue and, in my little mind, thinking *Wow! Saint Andrew!* He seemed larger than life.

As I matured, I learned that the biblical account of Andrew does not portray anyone particularly remarkable. In fact, if you were hiring someone to lead your company, you probably would not hire Andrew. He was timid. Unimpressive. A follower. A man standing in the shadow of his more charismatic brother, Simon. Andrew, like all of the disciples, was anything but heroic, and certainly not saintly. They were far from the flawless specimens of perfection we tend to imagine. Instead, they were like us. Confused, called to fulfill roles far beyond their abilities, weighed down by all sorts of flaws, and hindered by individual quirks. Candidly, they were saints just like you and me!

Charles Swindoll, "Saints like Me"

no doubt relishing their private audience with him. Andrew is convinced he is in the company of at least a very great teacher. Indeed, more than that. He excuses himself and rushes to find his brother Simon Peter, excitedly telling him, *We have found the Messiah*. Without further explanation, he brings Simon to Jesus. This is truly Andrew's shining moment.

At this point, the fishing business is down to only half its manpower, though the men will return to it periodically, taking breaks from their ministry with Jesus.

A fascinating footnote is that these men may very well have known Jesus from their youth—surely Jesus' cousins, the sons of Zebedee and his wife Salome, sister of Mary and Jesus' aunt. Mary had traveled some sixty miles to visit her cousin Elizabeth, and thus it is not difficult to imagine that she would have visited her sister, who lived much closer, in Bethsaida. Perhaps they rendezvoused each year for the journey to Jerusalem for Passover. John the Baptist, having spent many years in the desert, would have likely been a stranger to the fishermen. Not so Jesus.

Icon of St. Andrew

Andrew is a loyal disciple who is often overshadowed by his domineering, exuberant brother Peter. He does play his role well, however, in a bit part in the feeding of the five thousand. The people are hungry, and Jesus asks Philip where they could go to buy bread. Philip says the idea of buying bread is preposterous. They don't begin to have enough money for that (and he might have added that it is doubtful there would be a bakery open that time of day anyway). Then Andrew steps up, telling Jesus that he has found a young boy who has a bag lunch with two fish and five barley loaves, though he concedes that such a small amount is hardly worth bothering about. But as he quickly discovers, it is just the amount Jesus needs to get things going and feed the whole crowd.

Andrew, more than the other disciples, brings people to Jesus. First his brother, then the boy with the bag lunch, and finally at the Passover dinner, when he escorts a delegation of Gentiles to meet his master, prompting Jesus to say something that might have troubled his Jewish disciples, had they gotten it: "And I, when I am lifted up from the earth, will draw all people to myself."[2] Andrew is faithful to his calling, the quiet man in the back pew who does little more than simply bring people to Jesus.

Thomas: Remembered for His Doubts

He is known as the doubting disciple, but he was much more than that—most significantly, a believing disciple. But Thomas, perhaps more than any of the others, possesses a melancholy personality. When he hears that Lazarus, Jesus' good friend, has died, he is the pessimistic one. Jesus has said he is glad because this will inspire people to believe. In fact, Jesus seems to have a skip in his gait as he heads

Everyday *Life*

Food and Mealtime

Little children often eat with their fingers in their food. So also did people of all ages in biblical times. Thus the practical custom of hand washing before meals, which became more ceremonial under rabbinic law. Food was typically spread out on a mat, though low tables were also utilized. The diners squatted around the mat, where they ate from common baskets or copper dishes. Leonardo da Vinci's iconic artistic depiction of Jesus and his disciples eating the Last Supper at a high table simply does not correspond to custom in ancient Palestine.

Special banquets to celebrate a wedding or birthday or Passover were often grand events. Invitations came by word of mouth through a servant, who would usually return to remind the guests just before the event was to start.

The consumption of wine was an important aspect of any meal—especially celebratory meals. It would have been a major etiquette *faux pas* had the hosts actually run out of wine at the wedding Jesus attended in Cana. When guests dined around low tables or mats, the most renowned of them was positioned next to the host.

An Invitation to Dine

In biblical times, an invitation to dine, whether with family and friends or with complete strangers, was taken most seriously. The Middle Eastern code of ethics held strongly to a belief that good hospitality was the command of The Divine, and the offer to partake of a meal was sacred. In deference to and respect for God the Jews of the biblical era began all meals with a ritual washing of hands. . . . Strangers at a meal were a *mitzvah* (Hebrew for "blessing"), as acknowledged by the author of the Letter to the Hebrews, who imparts (13:2), "Be not forgetful to entertain strangers, for thereby some have entertained angels unawares." Often, as at the Passover meal, an extra place was set at table and a portion set aside in anticipation of the arrival of one more for dinner.

Anthony F. Chiffolo and Rayner W. Hesse Jr., *Cooking with the Bible: Recipes for Biblical Meals*, xiii for Bethany. But Thomas is ready to give it all up, for he fears the evil intentions of the religious leaders, many of whom have come down from Jerusalem to Bethany. Though he urges the other disciples to hustle along, his gloom is palpable. *We might just as well go and die with him.*

Thomas is a twin, though no sibling is mentioned in the Bible. Like the other disciples (with the exception of Judas), he is a Galilean. At the Last Supper, when Jesus is spending his final moments teaching and giving them last-minute instructions, he tells the disciples that he is leaving them and that he is preparing a place for them where they can join him. The disciples—or at least Thomas—imagine that this is some sort of hideout where they can stay until things calm down. But then Jesus seems to make an unwarranted assumption by saying that they already know the place where he is going.

What are you talking about! Thomas is shaking his head in dismay. The political situation is getting tense. *We need a plan. And the fact is, Lord, we do not know where you are going. So how can we find you! We need directions if we are going to find our way.* Thomas does not realize that Jesus is speaking of the spiritual realm and that Jesus himself is the way. In fact, Jesus' response to Thomas has become the age-old treasured summation of his identity: "I am the way and the truth and the life. No one comes to the Father except through me."[3]

After Jesus is crucified, Thomas is again ready to give up. Jesus has been his beloved teacher, rabbi, master. Now he's dead. He had feared this was exactly what would happen. Now the dream—the grand vision—has died as surely as has Jesus. Thomas is not with the other disciples in the Upper Room when Jesus first appears to them on the evening of his resurrection. That fact is telling in itself. What was he doing during that absence? Merely moping around in plain sight, or was he hiding? Wherever he was, the other disciples track him down and tell him that Jesus came right through a locked door and they saw him with their own eyes. They are ecstatic as they exclaim that they have seen the Lord.

Thomas, however, is more than a little bit skeptical. He knows that people can be fooled by their imagination. Jesus is dead and buried. How can he possibly be out and about, alive and well? Is there someone out there impersonating Jesus? Thomas is adamant. Unless he sees the scars from the nails pounded through Jesus' hands, and unless he can actually touch the sword wound in his side, he will not be convinced. Here Thomas plays a critical role. In his capacity as doubter, he stands in for all skeptics ever since.

Later that same week, the disciples are in the same room—this time Thomas among them. Again the doors are locked, but Jesus suddenly appears. The first thing Jesus does is turn to Thomas and tell him to touch the nail prints in his hands and put his hand on his side where he has been speared. As Thomas does so his astonishment is forever sealed and sanctified in his short exclamation: *My Lord and my God!*

Thomas then hears Jesus offer a blessing that excludes him: "Because you have seen me, you have believed; blessed are those who have not seen and yet have believed."[4] Thomas, ever quick to question and talk back, has no response. His story ends with his silence.

Judas: Betrayer Who Commits Suicide

Judas Iscariot. His name is indelibly imprinted on the mind of anyone who has heard even an abbreviated version of the gospel story. He always comes in dead last in the lists of disciples. The son of Simon, he alone among the disciples is from Judea, the rest hailing from Galilee. His story comes to light during the events surrounding Passion Week.

Just seven days before the crucifixion, Judas is with the other disciples and Jesus enjoying a dinner at the home of Martha, Mary, and Lazarus, the last having recently been raised from the dead by Jesus. They are all sitting around enjoying this feast in honor of Jesus. Martha is serving. Then Mary comes into the room and pours very expensive perfume on Jesus' feet. Judas is appalled. What kind of a charade is this? Why is she wasting such a valuable substance on Jesus' feet? Far better given to the poor, though Judas had apparently never before demonstrated any concern about those in poverty.

Jesus tells Judas to leave Mary alone, emphasizing that there would always be opportunity to give to the poor, but time is running out for anointing him. Judas no doubt imagines this is a highly improper way to anoint a ruler, assuming that Jesus is waiting for the right time to initiate a political coup. Then there will be no shortage of funds. But for now he serves as the self-appointed fiscal watchdog.

In fact, Judas is in charge of the finances for Jesus and the disciples, and it is later learned that he had been stealing from the treasury. But his real aim is to personally profit from this growing mass movement that features miracle displays and Palm Sunday parades. Like the other disciples, he assumes Jesus is going to set up a kingdom and that he, Judas, will play an important role—perhaps one that will make him rich. But in the meantime, he pilfers from the money bag.

Within days after Mary's anointing, Judas, prompted by Satan, arranges to have a back-alley meeting with religious rulers in Jerusalem. Perhaps he is coming to realize that Jesus' kingdom is not an earthly realm. If not, then what good would it do him? Knowing that Jesus is in the crosshairs of the big guns in Jerusalem, Judas asks how he can be of assistance. He offers to hand him over to them if they will reward him for his efforts. They agree to give him a fair price—thirty pieces of silver, valued at more than ten thousand dollars in today's currency.

On the evening of the Last Supper, after he washes the disciples' feet, Jesus offers some final instructions and blesses them, though he pointedly says that he's not including all of them. One of them who is eating this very meal will betray him. The disciples are taken aback, not knowing what he is talking about. They have come to know each other well, even Judas from Judea, whom they have entrusted with the treasury. Who could Jesus possibly be referring to? Jesus responds, perhaps as an aside, that it's the one who takes the dipped crust of bread.

Still the disciples don't get it. Judas, however, does. He takes the bread and leaves. Still the other disciples don't suspect him. They assume that Jesus had asked him to purchase more food or make a charitable donation with the money that had been collected.

Judas goes out into the night and meets with the religious leaders to finalize their plans. They might have gone directly to where Jesus and the disciples are partaking of the Last Supper. Instead, they bide their time and wait until it's late at night and Jesus is in the Garden of Gethsemane with only his closest disciples. It's dark when they come upon Jesus. Judas, as planned, identifies him with a kiss. The religious leaders and their cronies are wielding clubs and swords.

Judas has earned the money he was promised, and now he can take life easy. Perhaps he's thinking that if he hadn't pointed out Jesus, someone else would have. Besides, this whole kingdom thing didn't seem to be going anywhere anyway. So, no harm done.

But Judas has a restless night. The next morning, when he has fully comprehended what he has done and that the plot to kill Jesus is actually being carried out, he is remorseful. Why did he do such a terrible thing? Why did he put the temptation of riches ahead of his loyalty to Jesus? Thirty pieces of silver. Could such money actually buy him happiness? He has done a deed so terrible that he will never be able to live with himself. And it can't be undone. It's way too late.

So he goes back to the religious leaders and wants to return the blood money. He tells them he has sinned by betraying an innocent man. They couldn't care less. He can wallow in his guilt if he wants to, but it's none of their concern. So Judas throws the money down inside the door of the Temple. He leaves, and it is later learned that he has committed suicide by hanging, his body then falling and *bursting asunder*.

The religious leaders pick up the coins, but they think twice about what to do with

Confusion over Judas's Death

Through the years, the description of Judas Iscariot's death has been one of the most popular alleged Bible contradictions. . . . Whereas Matthew records that Judas "went and hanged himself" after betraying Jesus for 30 pieces of silver (27:5), Luke records that "falling headlong, he burst open in the middle and all his entrails gushed out" (Acts 1:18). . . . According to ancient tradition, Judas hanged himself above the Valley of Hinnom on the edge of a cliff. Eventually the rope snapped (or was cut or untied), thus causing his body to fall headfirst into the field below, as Luke described. Matthew does not deny that Judas fell and had his entrails gush out, and Luke does not deny that Judas hanged himself. In short, Matthew records the method in which Judas attempted his death. Luke reports the end result.

Eric Lyons, "Did Judas Die Twice?"

Judas: Betrayer or Friend of Jesus?

One point of vulnerability to every position that assumes Judas either betrayed or surreptitiously handed over Jesus is the strong self-confidence of Jesus that is communicated by the Gospels themselves. Jesus is clearly depicted as being in charge of his own destiny. Not Peter, not his mother, not his brothers or sisters, and certainly not any "betrayal" by Judas, takes that aura of confidence and clarity of purpose away from Jesus. It is consistently affirmed that his "handing over" was "according to the scriptures," the will of God. . . . But what if Jesus was "betrayed" by Judas and caught off guard? Again, the Gospel accounts are unanimous in telling us that Jesus predicted the action Judas would take. Indeed, they indicate that he selected Judas to do it, or pointed out that he would. . . . What is clear from the evidence, however, is that Judas is consistently a disciple of Jesus and that he did only what Jesus asked him to do—and that, only when Jesus was ready for it.

William Klassen, *Judas: Betrayer or Friend of Jesus?*, 44–45

them. How can they take the money as a Temple offering? This is blood money, which has been the price of a conspiracy to kill. So they purchase land that will be used as a burial ground for indigents—a fitting end to the story of this most unforgettable disciple of Jesus.

Ananias and Sapphira: Death Sentence for Lying

The followers of Jesus are expected to leave worldly goods behind. They go out two by two without even taking a satchel with pocket change. Similar expectations are continued after Pentecost, as the infant community is growing by the thousands. There is a consensus that all goods and property are to be shared and used in the ministry. Indeed, new converts are selling their property and giving the proceeds for the poor, so that no one goes without necessities. It's an idealistic system, and one open to fraud.

This landowning married couple, Ananias and Sapphira, like many others who hear the news of the resurrection of Jesus, join the faith community. But their names are forever linked as liars—liars of biblical proportions. They lie to Peter and to the Holy Spirit. But surely their lives entail far more than this one incident would suggest. Apart from this duplicity, they may have been good, hardworking citizens, friendly neighbors, doting parents and grandparents—and even faithful followers of the resurrected Jesus.

Together, however, they hatch a dishonest scheme. They sell their property and tell the apostles they are contributing the entire proceeds to the general fund, while actually keeping a portion for themselves. They do this publicly for all to see, laying the money at the apostles' feet. Others may have been awed by their generosity. Perhaps it was a large piece of property.

Peter approaches Ananias when Sapphira is elsewhere, asking him how it is that he has allowed Satan to so tempt

Ananias and Achan

The story of Ananias is to the book of Acts what the story of Achan is to the book of Joshua. In both narratives an act of deceit interrupts the victorious progress of the people of God. It may be that the author of Acts himself wished to point to this comparison: when he says that Ananias "kept back" part of the price (v. 2), he uses the same Greek word as is used in the Greek version of Josh. 7:1 where it is said that the Israelites (represented by Achan) "broke faith" by retaining for private use property that had been devoted to God.

F. F. Bruce, *The Book of Acts*, 102–3

him. "Before you sold it," Peter points out, "it was all yours, and after you sold it, the money was yours to do with as you wished." In other words, no one was holding a gun to his head demanding the money. "So what got into you," Peter continues, "to pull a trick like this?"[5]

Ananias drops like a rock. Dead. Not even an opportunity to offer an excuse like owing back taxes or medical bills. Those who witness the sudden death are terrified. Honesty is not merely an option for this budding faith community; it is a core ingredient. The younger men put his body on a board and take him out to be buried. No questions asked.

Some three hours later, Sapphira happens by, totally unaware of the calamity. She actually is given the opportunity to tell the truth. Peter specifies the amount of money they donated and asks her if that is the amount they received for the sale of the field. That amount precisely, she says. Peter asks her why she conspired with her husband to lie to the Holy Spirit, and then he tells her that the same men who just buried Ananias are prepared to do likewise for her. Before she can comprehend what has happened to her husband, she herself drops dead.

The young men who have just buried her husband return, no doubt stunned to realize they must now take her body to the same burial plot. Indeed, this has been a most terrifying incident for the entire faith community. They must know that Abraham and Isaac and many other Hebrew saints lied and lived—though perhaps to regret it. But to the early Christians such a punishment as sudden death must surely seem like overkill.

Stephen: First Martyr of the New Faith

A man full of faith and the Holy Spirit, Stephen is exactly the kind of person needed for a difficult task in the early days of the Jesus movement, now expanding rapidly. Some of these new followers are poor widows with children. Their needs are great. But it turns out that Hebrew-speaking Jews are given a distinct advantage. They are served first, and the Hellenistic Jewish widows receive what, if any, is left over. It's an unfair system, and someone needs to take charge to ensure equality. Stephen is that man. He and six others are chosen as deacons.

The role of deacon, which involved food distribution, was different from that of apostle, but no less important. And Stephen is far more than a one-man

Raised from the Dead and Doing Good Deeds

She is a disciple from Joppa by the name of Dorcas, also known as Tabitha. Skilled in dressmaking and tailoring, she devotes her time to helping the poor, particularly by designing and sewing clothing for them. She has many friends, some of them widows like herself. On one occasion when she becomes ill her condition deteriorates to the point of death. Friends had served her in her illness, and they are now there to prepare her body for burial. Word reaches Peter who is ministering nearby. He comes immediately and goes alone into the room where her body is lying. He prays and then orders her to get up. With his help she does. They then go out to greet the mourners. It is a stunning miracle, and when word gets out many people in Joppa join the community of believers.

meals-on-wheels. He performs miracles—great signs and wonders—as he goes about his ministry. But such mighty works are exactly what incite conspiracies against him. His enemies initially try to talk him down, but his God-given wisdom deflates all their arguments. So they start rumors that he has been blaspheming not only Moses but also God.

They gather false witnesses, and with their charges they stir up ordinary citizens and the Jewish leaders. Stephen is then brought to face the Sanhedrin. Before he even has a chance to speak, his face lights up like that of a neon angel. He is asked if the blasphemy charges are true. He might have simply said no. But this affords him an opportunity to preach before this august body and the onlookers. It turns out that Stephen knows his Hebrew Bible.

He grounds his very detailed sermon in the call of Abraham to the Promised Land and the covenant of circumcision. From there he proceeds to Isaac, Jacob, and Joseph, sold by his brothers as a slave to be taken to Egypt, where later his famine-stricken family comes for food. With that setup he launches into the generations of slavery under the Pharaohs in Egypt and God's incredible work of salvation through his servant Moses, who heard God's voice in a burning bush. But the children of Israel complained against not only Moses but all the prophets who followed him.

Then Stephen comes to a powerful and stunning conclusion—before the Sanhedrin, no less: "Was there ever a prophet your ancestors did not persecute? They even killed those who predicted the coming of the Righteous One. And now you have betrayed and murdered him—you who have received the law that was given through angels but have not obeyed it."[6]

The religious leaders are visibly enraged by Stephen's words. Pandemonium ensues. But Stephen calmly looks up into the sky and says aloud for all to hear that he sees heaven opening and there beholds the Son of Man at the right hand of God. By now, the members of the Sanhedrin, like a bunch of elementary school boys, are plugging their ears and screaming and rushing to attack him. Helpless to defend himself, he is dragged outside the city, where people begin throwing stones at him.

With each rock that hits him, he knows he is closer to death. He cries out for Jesus

Feast of St. Stephen

St. Stephen was one of the first "social workers" in the Church, and it was his task to organize meals to feed the poor. In remembrance of Stephen's work for the needy, the British people used to collect money throughout the year in little clay boxes. On the feast of St. Stephen or "Boxing day" as it is called in Britain, these boxes were broken and the money was distributed to the poor. . . . In some homes and communities a box is labeled and set beside the Christmas tree. Members of the family, in gratitude for their Christmas blessings, choose one of their gifts for the "St. Stephen's Box"—clothing and other useful articles which are sent abroad to the poor or to a mission country.

As the family gathers around the lighted Christmas tree in the evening to eat minced meat pie dessert, the mother or father reads the story of Good King Wenceslaus who "looked out on the Feast of Stephen" and who enjoyed eating his minced meat pie after sharing his meal with a poor peasant family.

CatholicCulture.org, "Feast of St. Stephen"

to receive his spirit. Then he prays the prayer of Jesus on the cross, asking God not to hold this sin of murder against them. With that he collapses dead on the ground. Saul (later to become the apostle Paul) is in the crowd, observing with approval this murderous mayhem.

Philip: Deacon and Evangelist

The list of deacons chosen to distribute offerings to the poor includes Philip. Like Stephen, he assumes a much broader role. After Stephen's death by stoning, many in the community of believers get out of town, Philip included. But everywhere they go, they spread the word of the risen Messiah. Philip draws large crowds as he preaches and casts out demons and heals the sick.

On one occasion, an angel tells Philip to head south on the desert road that leads out of Jerusalem to Gaza. Along the way he meets a man who is sitting in his chariot reading. The Spirit tells Philip to go up and introduce himself to the man. Turns out he's a financial administrator in charge of the Ethiopian treasury—a eunuch working closely with the Queen of Ethiopia.

Philip asks him what he's reading. Perhaps he shouldn't have been surprised that it would be the perfect launching pad for a witness—the written words of the prophet Isaiah. He asks the man if he understands it. The man says it is impossible to understand unless someone explains it to him. The passage that is stumping him is no less than Isaiah 53.

> He was led like a sheep to the slaughter,
> and as a lamb before its shearer is silent,
> so he did not open his mouth.
> In his humiliation he was deprived of justice.
> Who can speak of his descendants?
> For his life was taken from the earth.[7]

The man wonders if Isaiah the prophet is speaking of himself or someone else. So Philip joins him in the chariot and explains the passage, telling him it points to the good news of Jesus. They continue their way south, as Philip shares the whole story of Jesus' death and resurrection. When they arrive at an oasis, where there is water, the man asks if there is anything that would prevent him from being baptized. Philip says there is not. So the man orders the driver to stop, and Philip baptizes him then and there.

Simon the Sorcerer

Philip is not the only evangelist who preaches in and around Palestine and Samaria. Indeed, Simon arrives in Samaria before Philip and is spicing his message with magic. The people are bowled over by him, thinking him to be a great worker of miracles. But when they hear Philip they recognize his authenticity and the truth he is preaching. Large numbers are baptized, including Simon himself. He comes across as a sincere believer, following close wherever Philip goes. But his motives are more than a little questionable.

Later when Peter and John join with Philip to lay hands on the new believers so that they might receive the Holy Spirit, Simon wants to know their secret. He wants them to show him how to do the same thing—not for nothing, of course. He'll pay good money for their magic trick.

Peter is livid. "To hell with your money!" he thunders. "Why, that's unthinkable—trying to buy God's gift!" (Acts 8:20). He tells Simon to ask God for forgiveness immediately. Simon begs him to pray for him so as to avoid God's wrath.

What happens next is most strange. Philip doesn't stand around and make small talk. The chariot driver is apparently ready to get going. So without any ado, the Holy Spirit snatches Philip away, and he is never seen again by the Ethiopian man. This does not signal the end of Philip's preaching, however. He continues evangelizing in towns along the route, all the way to his home in Caesarea.

Unlike any of the other New Testament evangelists, Philip has a common ministry bond with his children. His four daughters, all virgins, minister as prophets.

Concluding Observations

Jesus is the focal point of the disciples' ministry, both before and after the resurrection. That's a given. But the spotlight also turns on the disciples, sometimes for only brief episodes. Dorcas is devoted to charitable ministry, and the reader yearns to learn more about her. Alas, Luke in Acts has space only for an account of her death and Peter's miraculous restoration of her life. Nor does Luke devote descriptive details to Simon the Sorcerer or Ananias and Sapphira. In each instance the whole of their life is contained in one shameful episode.

Stephen and Philip merit fuller coverage but their stories are also episodic. Stephen experiences fifteen minutes of fame that stretches into millennia. His dreadful martyrdom is a memorial to all martyred Christians in every time and place. He did not have an opportunity to meet the soon-to-be-converted Saul who was lurking on the edge of the crowd. Philip, also an early church deacon and evangelist, however, did. Paul stayed in his home while engaged in his own evangelistic outreach in Caesarea.

In the Gospels, the spotlight occasionally turns to otherwise obscure disciples. Andrew, Thomas, and Judas are among them. The reader suspects that there are so many more fascinating accounts of both Thomas and Judas that are not recorded. Nothing in the biblical narrative suggests that either of them is an ordinary, run-of-the-mill guy. Whatever the writers of the Gospels knew, however, they kept it to themselves.

Andrew's claim to fame is his bringing his brother Peter to Jesus. That is enough. Throughout the ministry of Jesus Peter is there—except when he heads home to fish. His story, more than that of any other disciple, is fleshed out and given substantial treatment by the Gospel writers.

Further Reading

Bruce, F. F. *The Book of Acts*. Rev. ed. Grand Rapids: Eerdmans, 1988.

Klassen, William. *Judas: Betrayer or Friend of Jesus?* Minneapolis: Fortress, 1996.

MacArthur, John. *Twelve Ordinary Men: How the Master Shaped His Disciples for Greatness*. Nashville: Thomas Nelson, 2002.

21

PETER

Fisherman with a Foot in His Mouth

Peter is impulsive and domineering, short tempered and stubborn. Subtlety is not his strong suit. Neither *wise* nor *winsome* is a term that applies. He simply does not have the traits one would immediately look for in choosing a leader. If permitted to enroll in seminary at all, he would no doubt be sent to group therapy. Jesus, however, does not require a personality makeover for his disciples. His demands on Peter will be far greater than anything group therapy can offer.

Anyone other than Peter might have gone back to his fishing business for good after Jesus makes plain what discipleship entails. But Peter, the *rock*, manages to stumble along a rocky road of discipleship. He takes one misstep after another, only to find his footing after Pentecost as he leads the followers of Jesus into a new era.

In fact, after Pentecost, when Jesus is no longer with him in person, he demonstrates maturity and self-assurance that had not been evident earlier. As brash as he was, his actions had often shown him weak and tentative. Jesus had expected more of him.

On one occasion, a man comes up to Jesus. He's beside himself. His beloved son is afflicted with a dreadful malady. He has severe seizures, losing consciousness and control of his limbs, sometimes falling into the fire and even into the river. Is there anything at all that Jesus can do for him? The man is pleading for help. He tells Jesus that he has already brought his son to the disciples, but this case was too hard for them.

Jesus is exasperated. Why? Why? Why don't his disciples get it? He's gone over this time and again with them. They aren't like generations of old—Moses, Joshua, Elijah. No, his disciples are a different breed: "You unbelieving and perverse generation," Jesus laments, "how long shall I stay with you? How long shall I put up with you?"[1] He then turns to the stricken boy and orders the demon to come out of him. In an instant the boy is entirely normal.

When they are alone with him, the disciples ask Jesus why they could not do the very same thing he had done. Jesus lays into them, telling them they don't have sufficient faith. Indeed, if they had even a tiny seed of faith—a mustard seed, for example—they could move a mountain, perhaps even a mountain of problems these people are enduring.

This seems like a tall order. Will any of them ever meet the criteria? And how can thinking, rational people submit themselves to this kind of extraordinary faith? Peter does, and apart from Jesus, he ranks alongside Paul as the most astounding miracle worker in the New Testament, both of them equaling the great prophets of old.

A significant difference between Peter and Paul, however, is that Paul is introduced to Jesus by way of a miracle (smitten with blindness and hearing a voice from heaven), whereas Peter joins the fold with a simple name change. Peter's miracles do not begin until after Pentecost.

In many respects the miracles of Peter and Paul, as recorded in Acts, are very similar. Both performed *many signs and wonders*: Peter, primarily before Jewish audiences; Paul, before Gentiles. They both heal men who have been lame from birth,

Miracles in the Gospels and Acts

Practically all the types of phenomena narrated in the Gospels are duplicated in the Acts of the Apostles: the lame walk, the blind see, paralytics are cured, and the dead are restored to life. . . . But the most striking difference is the number of punitive miracles in the Acts, of which there is not a single clear example in the Gospels. Ananias and Sapphira are suddenly struck dead for having lied to the Holy Ghost; Saul is struck blind on his way to Damascus in search of Christians; Herod is suddenly killed by an angel for arrogating to himself the honors due to God; Paul curses the false prophet Elymas who tried to turn the pro-consul Sergius Paulus from the faith, and immediately "there fell upon him a mist of darkness" (13:10–11). . . . More significant than the number or type of miracles is the manner in which they were performed in the Acts of the Apostles. All the miracles of Christ were wrought by His own power and in His own name. . . . But in the Acts, whenever the Apostles performed a miraculous sign and the full details are given, they invoked the name of Jesus as a regular prelude to the occurrence.

John A. Hardon, SJ, "The Miracle Narratives in the Acts of the Apostles" and both preside over punitive miracles (the deaths of Ananias and Sapphira and the blinding of Elymas). Both are able to perform miracles without being personally cognizant of what is going on. Some people are apparently healed merely by walking in Peter's shadow; others through contact with aprons and handkerchiefs presumably touched by Paul. Both men restore to life one who has died (Dorcas and Eutychus), and both are miraculously freed from jail when their chains are loosened.

Though often given short shrift by Protestants (who typically favor Paul), Peter is in many ways Paul's equal. Paul, of course, is the prolific writer. The uneducated Peter

Everyday *Life*

The Fishing Business

"I'm going fishing"—three little words from the most celebrated fisherman of all time. History and literature offer a vast array of fishermen, but none whose fame is as far-reaching as that of the apostle Peter—ever associated with his vocation.

Fishing was hard work—no lazy-day sitting on a shady riverbank with a cane pole and a can of worms. Only muscular men with their calloused hands were suited for the long days of arduous labor. With little education and few social skills, their manners were rough, their speech crude. The job involved lifting heavy nets and hoisting the catch into the vessel. But that was only the beginning. There were dangerous squalls and crashing waves. Then too there were the fierce negotiations involving transport and marketing and, at the end of the day, there were always nets to mend and boats to repair.

Days were long, with few opportunities for relaxation apart from the banter and coarse humor that came with the work. But fishing was very serious business. Jewish religious regulations and Roman laws of trade and commerce combined to place stringent controls on the industry. Only those with at least modest wealth owned boats and were able to hire laborers. In fact, the majority of fishermen barely eked out a living.

Huge Freshwater Fish Pond

Capernaum, according to Josephus, was the site of a fertile spring which enabled perch especially to thrive there. This made the village an integral part of the Galilean fishing industry which was rapidly expanding in the first century. Apart from the Passover lamb, meat is never mentioned in the Gospels. It was fish that formed the protein in most people's diet. . . . Fresh fish could command high prices and it was usually beyond the means of the poor; they ate cheaper dried and salted fish, usually broiled to make it taste better. . . . Lake Galilee was and still is a huge freshwater fish pond, and fishing was big business in the first century.

Richard Cooke, *New Testament*, 11

is not. But Peter walked and talked with Jesus for three years. After Pentecost he is the main speaker at mass evangelistic rallies and the one who presides over the infant Jewish church. Paul will focus on Gentiles, and bitter differences will arise between them. Paul will set the stage for a worldwide church, but never without building on Peter's *rock* foundation.

Simon Peter: Leader of the Disciples

Neither educated nor sophisticated, Simon Peter is the de facto vice president of the Jesus band. He shoots from the hip—a personality trait that gets him in trouble more than once. A rugged fisherman, he pushes others around when they get in his way.

Born in the town of Bethsaida (a town that will later factor into Jesus'—and his own—ministry), Peter and his brother Andrew may have grown up with Philip, who also resided there. At a later date Peter and Andrew relocate in the nearby fishing town of Capernaum. Peter hears about Jesus through his brother Andrew, a disciple of John the Baptist. He and Andrew, along with Zebedee and his sons James and John, have been working together in a prosperous fishing business along the Sea of Galilee. The work is hard, but he is determined to make a go of it, and he returns to this family business even after Jesus has called him to be a disciple.

In Capernaum Peter resides with his wife and mother-in-law. Indeed, Peter's wife is apparently active alongside him in the ministry. The apostle Paul slips this fact in while defending his own ministry to the Corinthians, implying that fellow Christians are gladly supporting both Peter and his wife (as well as other disciples and their wives), while at the same time being stingy with him and Barnabas.[2] Peter is the only one of the Twelve who is known to be married.

When Andrew introduces Peter to Jesus, it is unlikely they are strangers. Rather, it is an introduction to the now recognized Messiah, as John the Baptist had announced. Almost nothing is recorded of this meeting except that, with no fanfare, Jesus gives Peter a new name. He is now Cephas (meaning "rock")—in the Greek, *Petros*. At this point, however, he and Andrew do not immediately follow after Jesus. They return to their nets.

Sometime later, when they are casting their nets close to shore, they see Jesus coming. He approaches and tells them to come with him—that he will teach them how to fish for people. There is no indication that

Peter and Friends

Peter and Andrew lived in Capernaum and were business partners with Zebedee and his sons James and John at the time that the four were called to become followers of Jesus. There is some evidence that Zebedee's wife Salome was Jesus' aunt. Since Capernaum was only about a day's journey from Nazareth, it is entirely possible that Jesus knew Zebedee, his sons James and John, and their friends Peter and Andrew for many years before Jesus called them to be his disciples. Jesus and Peter may have played together when they were boys.

Richard R. Losch, *All the People in the Bible*, 339

Peter with keys to the kingdom

they were expecting him to stop by. They might have said they needed time to think about the proposition. Or they might have volunteered to give him only a few hours a week. But to just pick up and leave their business behind? That would seem to be out of the question. But they drop their nets and follow Jesus. That same day, farther down the shore, Jesus offers the same opportunity to James and John.

Their training begins immediately, as they follow Jesus throughout Galilee, listening to him teach in the synagogues. They go with Jesus to Cana when he turns water into wine and later when he begins healing the sick, and they have front-row seats for his Sermon on the Mount. After that they are on the road again. When they arrive in Capernaum at Peter's house, they find his mother-in-law sick in bed with a high fever. With a touch from Jesus, the fever is gone and she is up and about waiting on him. All the while Peter is being slowly transformed from fisherman to apostle.

A natural-born boss, Peter quickly becomes the titular head of the Jesus band. His name always comes first on the list of disciples. Indeed, any consideration of the other eleven seems to make Peter the obvious choice. But his foibles are just as evident as his force of personality.

On one occasion, when the disciples are crossing the Sea of Galilee to meet Jesus on the other side, a sudden storm threatens to capsize their boat. As they are struggling to keep the craft upright against the waves, they fear for their very lives. Then, amid all the commotion, they glimpse someone walking toward them on the rough seas. Now they are more frightened by this *ghost* than by the gale-force winds.

Even though Jesus identifies himself, doubt remains. Peter then calls out, *Lord, if it's actually you, let me walk to you on the water.* Jesus bids him come, but he no more steps in the water than he begins to sink like a rock. Jesus pulls him out, chiding him for his lack of faith.

Not long after this the disciples are alone with Jesus, and he asks them what the word is on the street regarding his identity. They chime in saying they've heard people suggest he is John the Baptist or Elijah—even Jeremiah or another prophet returned from the dead. Then Jesus asks them pointedly who they think he is. Is there a long pause as they all sit on their hands, afraid to answer? Peter is the spokesman. He answers for himself, perhaps for the other disciples as well. His memorable lines indicate the progress in discipleship that he has already made: *You are Christ, the Messiah, the Son of the living God.*

Peter could not have known that this would be his most defining moment. Jesus singles him out and sets him apart from the others. In front of the other disciples, he blesses him and again reminds him of his new name *Peter*—a name that signifies his future ministry as foundational to the infant church.

> Blessed are you, Simon son of Jonah, for this was not revealed to you by flesh and blood, but by my Father in heaven. And I tell you that you are Peter, and on this rock I will build my church, and the gates of Hades will not overcome it. I will give you the keys of the kingdom of heaven; whatever you bind on earth will be bound in heaven, and whatever you loose on earth will be loosed in heaven.[3]

But hardly have these words been uttered when this same Peter is being rebuked by the very one he had called the Son of God. Jesus discloses to the disciples that he must go to Jerusalem, where he will be put to death and on the third day rise again. Peter comprehends only the first half of the sentence. He's horrified. Jesus suffer a torturous death? *No way*, he cries. If Jesus can calm the sea and work other incredible miracles, surely he can prevent this from happening. Peter's head is spinning. Does Jesus have a martyr complex? What's going on?

Peter's Shelters and Shekhinah Glory

During the Transfiguration of Jesus, which the gospels portray as a spectacular, visually dazzling event, Peter responds with the words, "Lord, it is good for us to be here; if You wish, I will make three tabernacles here, one for You, and one for Moses, and one for Elijah" (NASB). Given the nature of the setting, Peter's statement appears irrelevant, even foolish. What on earth was he thinking, to offer to build three shelters at a time such as this? . . . From childhood, I was always puzzled by Peter's strange response, and simply concluded he firmly placed both feet in his mouth. Several commentators concur. Some suggest Peter was so awed by the occasion that he did not know how to respond. Others believe his ineptitude was the result of being only half-awake. . . . Yet explanations based on ineptitude or semi-consciousness appear inadequate. . . . It is while he is confronted with this majestic Christ that Peter immediately offers to build three tabernacles (Gk. *skēnē*, meaning tabernacle, or booth). This is far from a blundering fool making an irrelevant statement. After the Exodus, the Mosaic Law details how the Jews were instructed to build the Tabernacle. (In fact, we know from the book of Hebrews that the Tabernacle is a type of heaven, see 9:1–6, 11–14). When it was finally completed and pitched for the first time, the glory of God filled the Tabernacle (Exod. 40:32–35). Jews refer to this glory, the presence of God, as the shekhinah, the "dwelling of God."

Calvin L. Smith, "What on Earth Was Peter Thinking?"

But Jesus doesn't mince words: "Get behind me, Satan! You are a stumbling block to me; you do not have in mind the concerns of God, but merely human concerns."[4] Peter is jolted. This time he has no response. Does he realize that he has become the tempter—that he is *tempting* Jesus no less than Satan himself had tempted him?

Less than a week later Jesus invites Peter, along with James and John, to go with him up a mountain. Peter and the others are stunned when they see Jesus become almost translucent, shining with a bright, supernatural glow. They have no idea what is happening and are nearly bowled over when Moses and Elijah suddenly appear. Peter is utterly awestruck by the event and wants to capture the moment by constructing three shelters, one for each of them: Jesus, Moses, and Elijah.

Jesus ignores him. All Peter can see is a cloud enveloping Jesus and the heavenly visitors. Then he hears the voice of God declaring that Jesus is truly his Son. Peter and the other two disciples fall flat on the ground, but Jesus tells them to get back up. When they do, they see only Jesus in his normal state. They return with him down the mountain, utterly mystified. Jesus orders them to tell no one until he has risen from the dead.

Peter continues to follow after Jesus, and it just seems that one crazy thing happens after another. Peter and the others are given power to heal, but they're impotent. They simply can't do it—weak faith, Jesus tells them. Perhaps that is to be expected, but what happens next is truly bizarre. Officials had inquired of Peter whether Jesus had paid the required Temple tax. Peter said he did, but when he is behind closed doors Jesus asks him what seems to be an easy question about who really owes taxes. When Peter answers correctly, Jesus tells him to go out and catch a fish, open its mouth, pull out a coin, and pay the taxes for them all. What's this all about? Peter's head must be spinning.

It is time for the annual Passover celebration, and Jesus with his disciples travels from Galilee to Jerusalem. Peter and John are instructed to secure a room and prepare the ritual Passover meal. At this Last Supper, as Peter is seated with the other

Peter holding coin from fish's mouth

Peter's Extended Conversion Process

If we take a full account from the pages of the New Testament, we begin with Peter being led to converse with Jesus by his brother (John 1:35–42), and then, after his return to Galilee, we find Peter embarrassingly converted by learning from a nonfisherman, Jesus, how to fish and be wildly successful (Luke 5:1–11)—Peter confesses his sinfulness, drops his nets, and follows Jesus. But Peter's faith was not all smooth sailing: only later does he confess Jesus as Messiah (Mark 8:27–30), but he does so with less than a clear understanding of who Jesus is. In fact, here we see Peter squaring off with Jesus, looking him straight in the eyes, and asking to be taught by the master—but with his ears corked! Later he abandons Jesus in his most important hour (Mark 14:66–72).

Scot McKnight, *Turning to Jesus: The Sociology of Conversion in the Gospels*, 16

disciples, Jesus, without warning or explanation, kneels down to wash their feet, hardly a routine occurrence. The disciples are mute—but for Peter. No way is Jesus going to wash his feet. Jesus is the Master. It should be the other way around. Peter is adamant about this. Jesus responds that if he doesn't relent, he will have no part of the ministry. Always quick on the draw, Peter responds, *Well, then go ahead and wash my whole body!*

As the Supper is coming to a conclusion, Jesus is again talking about his death and how he will be betrayed. Peter is incensed by the thought. He insists that even if everyone else in the room were to betray him, he would not. Not a chance. Never. Jesus responds that he ought not to be so cocksure of himself, for this very night, before the rooster crows at dawn, he, Peter, will deny him, not once but three times. Peter responds that such talk is ridiculous—that he would die with Jesus rather than deny him.

In the ensuing hours, Peter, James, and John follow Jesus into the Garden of Gethsemane. They wait while he goes alone to pray. It's a terrible time of anguish for Jesus, but Peter and the other two are exhausted and fall asleep. Suddenly Peter is awakened. Jesus is staring down at him with a look of utter disappointment. *Can't you stay awake with me*, he pleads, *even for a single hour?*

After having fallen asleep a second time, Peter is jolted awake and hears the sound of scuffling feet and tense voices. Up in a flash, he is in a frenzy when he realizes that a band of armed thugs, religious leaders among them, are rough-handling Jesus. He jumps into the fray, sword in hand, and slices off the ear of the servant of the high priest. Jesus mends the ear and tells Peter to put his sword away. Chastened and frightened, Peter then flees with the other disciples.

All Peter knows is that Jesus has been arrested and taken away. He's numb with fear. What will happen next? Has it all been for nothing? It's pitch dark, and he goes into the courtyard and sits down, warming his hands by a fire. Among those crowded around, a young female servant spots him and accuses him of being one of Jesus' followers. Peter acts insulted by this servant's claim and insists he doesn't have a clue what she's talking about. Minutes later a man makes the same accusation. Again

Henri Nouwen: A Holy Week Prayer

Dear Lord, your disciple Peter wanted to know who would betray you. You pointed to Judas but a little later also to him. Judas betrayed, Peter denied you. Judas hanged himself, Peter became the apostle whom you made the first among equals. Lord, give me faith, faith in your endless mercy, your boundless forgiveness, your unfathomable goodness. Let me not be tempted to think that my sins are too great to be forgiven, too abominable to be touched by your mercy. Let me never run away from you but return to you again and again, asking you to be my Lord, my Shepherd, my Stronghold, and my Refuge. Take me under your wing, O Lord, and let me know that you do not reject me as long as I keep asking you to forgive me. Perhaps my doubt in your forgiveness is a greater sin than the sins I consider too great to be forgiven. Perhaps I make myself too important, too great when I think that I cannot be embraced by you anymore. Lord, look at me, accept my prayer as you accepted Peter's prayer, and let me not run away from you in the night as Judas did.

Bless me, Lord, in this Holy Week, and give me the grace to know your loving presence more intimately. Amen.

Henri J. M. Nouwen, *A Cry for Mercy*, 61

Peter denies being with Jesus, cursing and swearing that he's had nothing to do with the man of whom they speak. But still another makes a similar charge: *Aren't you one of his followers? You speak just like a Galilean.* Peter is adamant that he does not know Jesus. Only then does he hear the rooster crow. He gets up and makes a hasty exit, bowed over in sobs of despair.

Events now move very quickly, all of the disciples having fled, perhaps realizing they are powerless to prevent the crucifixion of Jesus. The whereabouts of Peter during this time are unknown. Like the other disciples, he is hiding from authorities. Surely he and the others are aware of all of the gory details of the crucifixion. John was right there. How is Peter dealing with the tragedy—and his own guilt? In part by hiding out with his closest friends.

That is exactly where he is when Mary Magdalene comes running in, out of breath, telling them that Jesus is no longer in the tomb—that he's risen from the dead. To Peter and the others it seems like utter nonsense. But he and John nevertheless race to the tomb. When Peter arrives, he finds it empty. He bends down and sees the linen burial clothes, and then he leaves, completely mystified.

Others soon confirm that Jesus has indeed risen from the dead, and twice Peter is present when Jesus comes right through the locked door of the Upper Room.

Peter's most personal encounter with Jesus during this time occurs at the Sea of Galilee. He is out in his boat with several other disciples. They had been out all night fishing, but with no luck. A man comes walking along the shore—someone they don't recognize in the predawn darkness. He greets them and asks if they've caught anything. They haven't. He tells them to throw the net on the other side of the boat. They do and the net fills up with fish, loaded to the breaking point.

Peter: Magnified and Misrepresented

No character of the Bible, we may say, no personage in all history, has been so much magnified, misrepresented and misused for doctrinal and hierarchical ends as the plain fisherman of Galilee who stands at the head of the apostolic college. . . . He was the strongest and the weakest of the Twelve. . . . He had all the excellences and all the defects of a sanguine temperament. He was kind-hearted, quick, ardent, hopeful, impulsive, changeable, and apt to run from one extreme to another. He received from Christ the highest praise and the severest censure. . . . With all his weakness he was a noble, generous soul, and of the greatest service to the church.

Philip Schaff, *History of the Christian Church*, Vol. 1, *AD 1–100*, 256–57

When Peter realizes the man on the shore is Jesus, he dives in the water and swims to greet him. By the time the other disciples arrive—pulling the net full of fish behind them—a breakfast of fish and bread is already on the fire.

After they have eaten, Jesus asks Peter if he loves him *more than these*—perhaps referring to the fish and his fishing venture. Three times he asks the same question. (Three times Peter had denied him.) But Peter expresses his love as tender affection (*philia*) rather than responding with love as sacrificial devotion (*agape*) as Jesus asks and wants to hear.

Later on Jesus again appears to Peter and the disciples as well as other close followers—this time on the Mount of Olives. He gives them a final commission to spread the good news and then ascends into heaven. Peter and the others immediately make the fifteen-minute walk back to Jerusalem, where Peter presides over the naming of a replacement for Judas. From a short list of two, Matthias is chosen.

Sometime later the disciples are all together on the Feast of Pentecost. Without warning they are suddenly caught up in the sound of a fierce wind accompanied by slashes of fire streaking down and settling upon them. Before they can even begin to comprehend what is happening, the Holy Spirit descends on them and they all start speaking at once in strange tongues—actual languages understood by foreigners who happen to be in town. People are stunned, and some wonder if these Galileans are drunk.

Peter now takes the stage and preaches up a storm. *These men are not drunk*, he insists, and begins quoting from the prophet Joel. *These are the Last Days, and what you see is God pouring out his spirit on both sons and daughters.* He then focuses on Jesus, whose ministry was authenticated by miracles—how he was betrayed, crucified, and raised from the dead.

He accuses his listeners of killing this very Messiah sent from God. But it's not too late for them to turn their lives around, be baptized, and follow him. It's a long sermon, and by the time it's over some three thousand people have signed up and are being baptized into the Way, this new fellowship of Jesus. In fact, the new followers share their wealth and live together in community even as their numbers continue to grow.

Having previously been unable to work miracles like Jesus and having been chided for lack of faith, Peter now ministers to others with strength and authority. He's on his way to the Temple one day, accompanied by John. They see a disabled man who from birth has been unable to walk. He's been there year after year begging for handouts. When he looks over to Peter, hoping to get some coins, Peter says to him: "I don't have a nickel to my name, but what I do have, I give you: In the name of Jesus Christ of Nazareth, walk!"[5] He pulls the man off his pallet, and the man starts walking. More than that, he dances around the Temple, singing and praising God.

People are awestruck. This man was paralyzed. How can he now walk? Peter has their attention, so he launches into another powerful sermon. Again he accuses the crowd of putting Jesus to death. But, he concedes, they didn't realize what they were doing, even though his coming had been foretold by the prophets. It's not too late, however, to repent and partake in his blessings. This is truly one of the most remarkable sermons ever delivered. Some five thousand embrace his message and unite with the other believers.

The religious leaders are not taking this lying down. They are distressed by the rapid expansion of this *cult of Jesus*. They take Peter and John into custody, and the next morning they summon them from their jail cell to answer questions. For Peter this is a grand opportunity before a captive audience. When they begin to question him, he seizes the opportunity to deliver another masterful sermon. The authorities are amazed by his speaking ability as well as his ease and confidence. They confer privately, concluding that this man and his sidekicks have to be stopped, but they fear taking drastic measures.

Peter and John are sent back to jail, only to be summoned again and ordered not to preach. The apostles respond with boldness, saying that, in the name of God, they cannot stop witnessing to what they have seen and heard. The authorities are not amused by their answer, but they reluctantly let them go.

So once again Peter is drawing large crowds, preaching and healing people. In fact, Peter is regarded as almost a god. People with infirmities believe they will be healed if they can only get close enough so that his shadow falls on them. Again he is arrested, along with the other disciples who are ministering with him. But they miraculously walk right out of the locked jail past the guards and resume their preaching the following morning. Peter and the others continue to be harassed by the religious leaders, but they take it all in stride.

Up to this point, Peter's audience is primarily Jewish—his own people, with whom he is most comfortable. But Jesus' last instructions to the disciples were explicit: *Take the gospel into all the world.* Peter will need an extraordinary reminder for those words to sink in.

He is on his rooftop praying before the noonday meal. He's hungry, but he carries on with his daily devotions. Without realizing it, he falls into a trance. He has a vision of a huge tarp filled with animals being lowered from heaven. A voice tells him to kill the animals and eat them. But these are unclean animals—reptiles, birds,

Peter and Ethnocentrism

A critical moment in the gospel's initial movement from the domain of ethnic Judaism into the Gentile arena comes in the story of Cornelius and Peter. . . . Without this forward leap in the life of the church the translation of the gospel into new cultures and milieus would not be possible. . . .

For Jewish Christians like Peter, the problem focused on how they could maintain their purity and distinctiveness and at the same time eat with unclean Gentiles. Luke painstakingly describes each step in the process of breaking down social and ritual walls. Peter has a vision of a "nonkosher picnic" that announces the divine decontaminating of unclean foods. . . .

It is striking that at each stage of the story the primary adjustment needed for the gospel to bridge social and religious boundaries comes not from the Gentile "outsiders" but from Jewish "insiders," who must let go of their ethnocentric attitudes and practices.

Dean E. Flemming, *Contextualization in the New Testament: Patterns for Theology and Mission*, 35–36, 38

pigs, and wild rodents of all kinds. As a good Jew, he can't possibly eat something so unclean as these alien creatures. But the voice from God insists otherwise.

He comes out of the trance just as the tarp has retreated to heaven. *What on earth does this mean?* he thinks to himself. But even as he is puzzling over his vision, the Holy Spirit tells him there are strangers at the door and that he is to do what they ask of him. When he greets them, the men explain their mission, and the next day they take him to Joppa to meet Cornelius, a devout, God-fearing man and a centurion of an Italian regiment, a commander in the Roman military.

Here at the home of Cornelius, Peter's life is transformed. He realizes the gospel is good news not only for Jews but for Gentiles as well. Before he leaves, Peter baptizes everyone in the household.

Upon his return, he finds that word had already found its way to some of the disciples who are now leaders in Jerusalem. They are not pleased that Peter has baptized anyone who is not circumcised. But Peter repeats the whole story to them, beginning with the trance and ending with how the Holy Spirit had descended on Cornelius and his household. With that, the Jerusalem leaders agree that this was certainly the work of God.

Until now Peter and the disciples have endured little more than harassment. Suddenly that changes when King Herod orders the execution of James, son of Zebedee, brother of John. Peter is then incarcerated and placed under heavy guard. It is Passover season, and the Jewish leaders decide to deal with Peter after Passover to avoid inciting the crowds. Peter is shackled and guarded by four armed soldiers. There is no way he can possibly escape. But in the dead of the night he is awakened by an angel, who unshackles him and leads him right past the sleeping guards through the now miraculously unlocked doors.

He goes straightaway to a residence where the other disciples are waiting in fear. There is a cloud of terror hanging

Leaving Peter with the Papacy

Despite his prominence in the New Testament story, the Apostle Peter has been whisked away from the center of Christian reflection. He's become one of the "Lost Boys," orphaned by turns in ecclesiastical history, the pen of the critics, and the popular consciousness of Christians. Protestants were separated from Peter by no less a figure than Martin Luther who discovered the true Gospel in the writings of Paul. . . . In recounting the biblical narrative, Luther had his eye on Rome. The Reformation put Paul in Protestant hands, gladly leaving Peter with the papacy. "Good riddance to you, Peter, and your successors!" was the cry. While Roman Catholics inherit Peter and the Holy See, Protestants end up with Paul and the true gospel. . . . Peter gets at best a few lines in our books where he is portrayed as the confused theologian who serves as the perfect foil for our beloved Paul.

Gene L. Green, "Peter: Apostolic Foundation," 32

over them. Are they all going to be killed? They mull things over in tense whispers. Then there's a knock at the door. They send the servant Rhoda to see who is there while they hover in the back room. When she excitedly reports that it is Peter, they don't believe her, imagining she has seen a ghost. But it is Peter all right. From that point on he is on the run until the death of Herod, not long hence.

Sometime later, Peter finds himself in the midst of a heated meeting in Jerusalem, where leaders of the Jesus movement are debating matters of the law. Must Gentile converts be required to undergo circumcision? Peter stands up and makes a case for cross-cultural evangelism, insisting that new converts not be forced to live by the letter of Jewish law. In the end, the council sides with Peter, and they determine that no unnecessary demands should be placed on new converts who are not Jewish.

But the matter does not end here. Peter and Paul will butt heads as Paul makes large numbers of converts among uncircumcised Gentiles. When Peter was residing in Antioch, he enjoyed fellowship with uncircumcised Gentiles—that is, until Jewish Christians from Jerusalem pay a visit. In order to impress them he avoided the uncircumcised like a plague. Peter even influenced Barnabas to keep his distance from Gentiles.

Although there is no clear scriptural evidence, it is assumed that Peter returns to his previous position of fellowshiping with Gentiles. In fact, the Jerusalem church would clarify the matter by tearing down religious and legal barriers between Jews and non-Jews, although tensions would linger and become more explosive with every passing generation.

Peter and Paul

The Gospels and Paul's writings are all silent about Peter's later years. Where he traveled, with whom he associated, and how he died are pure speculation.

Concluding Observations

Peter is the *rock* on which Jesus will build his church. But is he the founder and head of the church at Rome? Indeed, did he ever even visit Rome?

In his letter to the Romans, Paul emphasizes how much he has been longing to visit them and promises to do so soon. He ends his letter with a lengthy series of personal greetings, making no mention of Peter. Indeed, there is no biblical evidence at all that Peter ever visited Rome, much less was the founder of that church. Whether he visited Rome or not, it is safe to say that as a Jewish fisherman, he, far more than Paul, would have felt out of place in that cosmopolitan, imperial city.

Paul further emphasizes in his letter to the Galatians, "It was soon evident that God had entrusted me with the same message to the non-Jews as Peter had been preaching to the Jews."[6]

Nevertheless, it is no exaggeration to say that Peter played an unprecedented role in the early church. His tenure lasts for years, stretching all the way from his fishing nets in Galilee to his leadership in Jerusalem and Antioch. Except for his failure to stand by Jesus at the sham trial and the terrible agony of the cross, Peter was front and center for every important event.

According to tradition, Peter was martyred in Rome during Emperor Nero's reign. He, to use Paul's words, had "fought the good fight" and "finished the race."[7] Writing in the third century, Clement of Rome spoke of Peter's hardships in life and his martyrdom that launched him into "the glory due to him."

Whether Peter was the first pope has been hotly debated, especially since the Protestant Reformation. But that he holds the keys to heaven is a given. No joke about heaven is complete without Peter guarding the gates.

Further Reading

Card, Michael. *A Fragile Stone: The Emotional Life of Simon Peter*. Downers Grove, IL: InterVarsity, 2006.

Hengel, Martin. *Saint Peter: The Underestimated Apostle*. Translated by Thomas Trapp. Grand Rapids: Eerdmans, 2010.

Perkins, Pheme. *Peter: Apostle for the Whole Church*. Minneapolis: Fortress, 2000.

22

THE APOSTLE PAUL

From Persecutor to Preacher

Paul is God-intoxicated. More than Jacob, more than David, more than any other biblical figure, he strives to serve God and gives himself wholly to that cause. He is God's bodyguard and bouncer and chief apologist all bound up in one—a Pharisee of the Pharisees who will go to any extreme to defend God. But then in a blaze of light, he answers a voice from heaven that inspires even more zeal. Now he willingly offers everything—his very life—to be crucified with Christ, who is the very God of the universe.

In the years that follow, his life will take many twists and turns. He wrestles with God and his own demons even as he testifies to God's supreme greatness—God, who is three in one as expressed in his classic benediction: "May the grace of the Lord Jesus Christ, and the love of God, and the fellowship of the Holy Spirit be with you all."[1] He is the Bible's foremost theologian, one who easily entwines theology with spiritual formation—*that I may know Christ and the power of his resurrection.*[2] Indeed, his personal life is thoroughly integrated with his theology. His *magnum opus*, the Epistle to the Romans, emerges out of turmoil and inward strife.

Paul's Christology

Who, being in the form of God, thought it not robbery to be equal with God: But made himself of no reputation, and took upon him the form of a servant, and was made in the likeness of men: And being found in fashion as a man, he humbled himself, and became obedient unto death, even the death of the cross. Wherefore God also hath highly exalted him, and given him a name which is above every name: That at the name of Jesus every knee should bow, of things in heaven, and things in earth, and things under the earth; And that every tongue should confess that Jesus Christ is Lord, to the glory of God the Father.

Phil. 2:6–11 (KJV)

Perhaps only Paul, out of all the writers in the New Testament, could write as he did. Having never physically encountered Christ, much less grown up with this Son of Man, he has an advantage in being able to perceive him very clearly as God. His longing to know Christ is the yearning of one who has not known him in person as the others had, thus setting an example for all those in generations to follow who would seek to know Christ.

His coming late on the scene clearly sets him apart from the other disciples, as do his hailing from Tarsus in Asia Minor and his stellar Jewish education. Having never spent time walking and talking with Jesus, he must seek to grasp every single parable and every sermon secondhand, if at all. The miracles, the transfiguration, the triumphal entry, the Last Supper, the postresurrection appearances, and the ascension have all happened without involving him. How he must often have wished that he had come to know Jesus earlier.

That he actually did find Jesus at all, however, is most startling. He is the least likely individual to lay out the pros and cons and on that basis decide to follow Jesus. He was no Simon Magnus looking for clever tricks or easy money. There was nothing in this new *cult of Jesus* that offered him anything remotely bordering on prestige or prosperity. To make the switch is incomprehensible apart from his miraculous conversion.

No individual conversion in the history of Christianity rivals Paul's. No one has been so adamantly opposed to the faith only to become its most ardent and effective advocate. He was an outstanding preacher and evangelist, never imagining the two roles could be separated. But even more foundational for the infant church and its eventual worldwide reach was his writing. It is well-nigh impossible to imagine the Christian faith without Paul and his written words.

Paul, a Diaspora Jew

By the middle of the first century, there are probably more Jews living outside of the homeland, than actually live back in Judah proper. This is what we call the Diaspora, that is, the dispersion of Jewish population throughout the Empire, and we know that there are major Jewish communities in most of the large cities of the Empire, all the way from the Persian Gulf on the east to Spain on the west.

L. Michael White, "The Jewish Diaspora"

And yet he is such an utterly ordinary man. He refuses to hide his feelings and pretend he has no issues and has gotten his life together now that he is a big-time mover and shaker in the church. Leaders are not supposed to spill their guts to their followers or associates. No leadership manual would countenance such conduct. But Paul's leadership philosophy belongs to him alone—and it worked. Few people in recorded history have made such an indelible mark on the world as he has.

Today, however, the dusty roads that Paul traveled and the cities he visited are no longer locales where he would meet his converts. In fact, for all practical purposes, Christianity has entirely died out in most of the places he knew so well. The land is essentially devoid of the Christian faith—like it was when he arrived on the scene.

Were he alive today, would he see that dismal situation as an obstacle or an opportunity?

Paul of Tarsus: Missionary Motivator

On the sidelines when Stephen is stoned to death, Saul is thinking, *Good riddance!* Stephen is no more than a two-bit troublemaker, and his execution will serve as a deterrent to the rest of those ragtag followers of Jesus. Saul has no qualms about this being the right thing to do. He had listened to the man's entire sermon—actually a well-developed overview of God's work among the often-rebellious Jewish people. But the ending was outrageous. How dare he pollute the message of the prophets by comparing their ministries to that of Jesus—and, to compare the rebellious Jewish ancestors with those who now deny Jesus as the Messiah? Rubbish! Utter, unadulterated blasphemy!

Saul is an Israelite from Tarsus and a Roman citizen by birthright. (He will take his roman name, Paul, after he is converted and begins his missionary outreach.) He has studied under the noted teacher

The Three Worlds of Paul

The first world . . . was of course Judaism. . . . Second-Temple Judaism was a many sided and vibrant mixture of what we would now call (though they would not have recognized these distinctions) religion, faith, culture and politics. . . . This was the world from which Paul came, and in which he remained even though he said things which nobody within that world had thought of saying before and which many in that world found shocking, even destructive. The second world was that of the Greek, or Hellenistic, culture which by Paul's day had permeated most of the recesses of the Eastern Mediterranean world and a good deal beyond. Ever since Alexander the Great three hundred and more years earlier, Greek had become not only everybody's second language, like English today, but in many parts everybody's assumed framework of thought. . . . And it was the world rulers of Paul's day, and the world which they were bent on creating, that formed the third sphere which Paul inhabited . . . the Roman empire, with its ideology and burgeoning emperor-cult.

N. T. Wright, *Paul: In Fresh Perspective*, 3–5

Tarsus: A City Framed by Snow-Capped Mountains

Tarsus was the principal city of the lush plain of Cilicia in the southwest corner of Asia Minor. The sea lay out of sight a dozen miles south. The Taurus mountains curved in a great arc some twenty-five miles inland, coming nearly to the sea on the west and marked to the north by gorges and cliffs which stood like rock fortresses before the snows; a magnificent background for childhood, especially in winter when the snow showed smooth on cloudless peaks.

The river Cydnus, narrow and swift, and usually superlatively clear, ran through the city. It flowed into the artificial harbor, an engineering masterpiece of the ancient world, where Cleopatra had stepped ashore some forty years before Paul's birth to meet Antony, while all Tarsus marveled at silver oars, a poop of beaten gold, and purple sails.

John Pollock, *The Apostle: A Life of Paul*, 14–15

Gamaliel and is a strict Pharisee. From his perspective, this cult of Jesus must be stopped. Stoning Stephen will send a signal: *You follow the Way at the peril of your life*. He is aware that many of Jesus' disciples have the crazy idea they too must suffer even as their Master did; so if that is what they want, he will gladly accommodate them.

Thus he devotes his energy as a self-appointed commando, breaking down the doors of those known to be followers of Jesus. He tortures and kills as though it were a sport. He is obsessed with his mission, dragging people out of their houses in the dead of night to be locked in jail. It's a God-honoring purge, he reasons, of those who promulgate blasphemous teachings. He is essentially a self-appointed, independent, lone terrorist. However, he does need official sanction from the religious leaders, so he meets with the high priest to obtain authorized arrest warrants for anyone who has anything to do with the Way.

Considering Saul's reputation, it is most shocking when rumors surface that he is now a convert himself. Is he faking it, so as to get on the inside and do even more damage? How can this claim possibly be true?

Saul, it turns out, is indeed a brand-new convert. In fact, as he testifies, he was heading to Damascus to carry out more arrests when he was suddenly stricken by what might be described as lightning or an electrical current. So intense was the light that it blinded him. Then he distinctly heard a voice saying, "Saul, Saul, why are you out to get me?" Saul was utterly dumbfounded. "Who are you, Master?" he asked. The voice continued: "I am Jesus, the One you're hunting down."[3] The voice told him to go into town and await further instructions.

Those traveling with him neither saw nor heard a thing. They were totally bewildered by what had just happened, but they picked up their blind companion and led him into Damascus. There Ananias met Saul, having been summoned in a dream to search him out. Ananias laid his hands on him and prayed as Saul was filled with the Holy Spirit and his eyes were opened.

Without so much as taking a catechism class, Saul was baptized. He stayed for a time in Damascus with the community of believers there. But then, according to his letter to the Galatians, he went to Arabia to live—perhaps as long as three years.

Now that he has returned to Damascus, he has begun preaching. His message is simple—that Jesus is truly the Son of God. Both enemies and followers of Jesus are taken aback. But his words are convincing—so much so that the Jewish leaders of Damascus hatch a plot to kill him. He escapes the guards stationed at the city gates by having friends lower him in a basket over the city wall. Now out of town, he's on the road heading south.

Arriving in Jerusalem, he spends some two weeks with Peter, but he is viewed with

Everyday *Life*

A Good Jewish Education

Education for first-century Jewish boys like Paul was based on the Torah. The school building was the synagogue, where law and history and ethics were woven into a structured system of learning. Unlike the Greek system, which focused on science, linguistics, the arts, and athletics, a Jewish education aimed at moral living.

Boys began their education at five, learning how to read and write. By age ten they were studying the law. While the boys studied in the synagogue, girls were at home learning the skills of homemaking from their mothers. On completing their formal education, Jewish boys typically followed the occupation of their fathers. Some, however, continued their studies in rabbinic law with a scholar. Paul studied under Gamaliel, a renowned educator and popular Pharisee of his day.

Paul was obviously influenced by the Hellenistic culture around him, particularly by the Septuagint (the Greek translation of the Hebrew Bible) and his use of Greek for all his written works. Some scholars believe that he was also influenced significantly by Greek rhetoric, which emphasized the art of oral persuasion. His frequent appeal to the emotions and his use of irony and forceful figures of speech may have come naturally, or were perhaps drawn from the skills of rhetoricians of his day.

Paul Defying the Categories

There are many astonishing things about him. For example, in modern scholarship, we have tended to divide various categories. There are gentiles, and there are Jews. There are Greek speaking people and there are Hebrew speaking people. There's Palestinian Judaism, which includes *apocalypticism*. There's Rabbinic Judaism and there's Hellenistic Judaism, which has derived deeply from the Greek world. Paul seems to fall into several of these categories, therefore confounding our modern divisions. So he's an intriguing and puzzling character in some respects.

Wayne A. Meeks, "Paul's Mission and Letters"

Paul let down in the basket

skepticism by the other disciples. They simply don't think he's for real. Barnabas, however, sees in him confirmation of the very message he himself has been preaching. Indeed, if the gospel cannot transform a terrorist, why sacrifice so much for it? Barnabas spends time with Paul, personally introducing him to each of the apostles. Paul wins them over with his story of conversion and his fearless preaching.

Jewish leaders, however, are out to get him. They understand that his conversion is a significant shot in the arm for this new movement. They desire nothing other than to be rid of him. Word of their conspiracies surfaces, and Paul is spirited off to Caesarea, and from there returns to his hometown of Tarsus, where Barnabas fetches him and brings him to Antioch to begin a yearlong teaching and preaching ministry.

Here the believers learn that the church at Jerusalem is facing dire financial straits. They take up a collection and send it with Paul and Barnabas to Jerusalem. Upon their return to Antioch, accompanied by John Mark, they continue their ministry. Here the community of believers is growing and is now self-sufficient. The leaders are thus eager that these two evangelists spread the good news elsewhere. So they commission them as missionaries to go to Cyprus, traveling by way of Seleucia. Here Paul and Barnabas, with John Mark, preach throughout the island. Impressed by their message, the governor invites them to preach to him.

Their work, however, is hindered by Barjesus, a shaman, who is threatened by their presence. He has magical tricks galore up his sleeve—so many that he ingratiates himself with the governor. Annoyed by the game he is playing, Paul, prompted by the Holy Spirit, takes him on: "You bag of wind, you parody of a devil," he sneers, "now you've come up against God himself."[4] With that the shaman goes blind and begins to stumble around. The governor is impressed by the display of God's power and becomes a believer.

From Cyprus the three missionaries sail back to the mainland and travel elsewhere to preach, often facing opposition. It's not an easy life being an itinerant evangelist, and John Mark finds the pressure too much. He abandons the team and returns home. Paul and Barnabas carry on,

Martin Luther, Paul, and Adam

Paul, good man that he was, longed to be without sin, but to it he was chained. I too, in common with many others, long to stand outside it, but this cannot be. We belch forth the vapours of sin; we fall into it, rise up again, buffet and torment ourselves night and day; but, since we are confined in this flesh, since we have to bear about with us everywhere this stinking sack, we cannot rid ourselves completely of it, or even knock it senseless. We make vigorous attempts to do so, but the old Adam retains his power until he is deposited in the grave.

Martin Luther, cited in Karl Barth, *The Epistle to the Romans*, 263

preaching primarily on Sabbath days in local synagogues. In the style of Stephen, Paul begins his message deep in the drama of the Hebrew Scriptures.

Paul proves to be a very effective communicator, and many are converted under his preaching. But as the numbers grow, so does the opposition from Jewish leaders. He and Barnabas are preaching not only that Jesus is the Son of God, but that the salvation Christ offers is open to anyone, Jew and Gentile alike. With this open invitation, the "Message of salvation spread like wildfire all through the region."[5]

Paul and Barnabas are continually on the move, ever fleeing the opposition of local authorities and thugs. In Lystra, they meet a disabled man who had never been able to walk. When Paul heals him, the man jumps to his feet and walks, with no ill effects. Never before having witnessed such a miracle, people in the crowd conclude that Paul and Barnabas are gods—Hermes and Zeus. *Of course not*, they insist; *We are just ordinary people*. The friendly atmosphere, however, does not last. Zealous Jews arrive from neighboring towns and stir up the crowds against them. Paul is attacked by the mob and beaten to death—or so they think. They drag him outside the gate and leave him for dead, but he regains consciousness and, with the aid of a small band of believers, dusts himself off and goes right back into town.

The next day he and Barnabas, realizing they have overstayed their welcome, leave for Derbe. Wherever they go they leave behind new converts, and before winding up this first missionary journey, they revisit all the towns they had previously passed through, encouraging new believers and appointing leaders. When they return to Antioch, the elders there are eager to hear the report of all their achievements as well as setbacks and opposition.

After staying in Antioch for a time, Paul and Barnabas go to Jerusalem to present a report of their itinerant mission work to the leaders there. On the way they meet with communities of believers and report to them about the incredible breakthrough they had seen among Gentiles.

The purpose of their trip to Jerusalem, however, involves more than merely reporting on their cross-cultural evangelism. Their very success is creating dissension in the church. Devout Jews who have become followers of Jesus have come to Antioch to meet Paul and Barnabas and find out more about their ministry. They are pleased to welcome Gentiles into the faith community, but, they insist, only after they become circumcised. Paul and Barnabas are adamant. No way! Such a regulation would have devastating effects on the gospel, not just among their own converts but for all times. So they are determined to get things settled once and for all.

After much discussion and after a strong case is made by Peter, James, the brother of Jesus, takes the floor and pronounces a verdict in favor of not requiring circumcision of male Gentile converts. Then Paul and Barnabas and others leave for Antioch to inform the church there of the momentous decision.

They stay for a time in Antioch, but soon make preparations to return to some of the towns they had previously visited to encourage the communities of believers. It's a great idea. They are itching to get back out on the trail. But there's one critical roadblock—John Mark. Barnabas wants to take him along; Paul is adamantly opposed. John Mark is simply not trustworthy. He bailed out on them last time, and they don't need the likes of him along with them again. He's a worthy young man, Barnabas argues, and should be given another chance.

Now the fight is on—two strong-willed individuals, both claiming the side of right. Both are infuriated by the other's lack of insight and understanding. Neither will back down. Indeed, so angry are they that they part company and go off in different directions. Paul, accompanied by Silas, journeys to towns in Syria and Cilicia to work with the new congregations there, while Barnabas and John Mark ship off to Cyprus.

In Lystra, Paul is introduced to a young man, son of a Greek father and Jewish mother. He is a new convert whom Paul wishes to groom for ministry. So what does Paul do? It would be only natural to take him aside for personal instruction, but for circumcision? What on earth is going on? Paul, the very one who took a strong stand on not requiring circumcision, has now flip-flopped and is expecting Timothy to

Paul Confronts Peter

Later, when Peter came to Antioch, I had a face-to-face confrontation with him because he was clearly out of line. Here's the situation. Earlier, before certain persons had come from James, Peter regularly ate with the non-Jews. But when that conservative group came from Jerusalem, he cautiously pulled back and put as much distance as he could manage between himself and his non-Jewish friends. . . . Unfortunately, the rest of the Jews in the Antioch church joined in that hypocrisy so that even Barnabas was swept along in the charade. . . . I spoke up to Peter in front of them all: "If you, a Jew, live like a non-Jew when you're not being observed by the watchdogs from Jerusalem, what right do you have to require non-Jews to conform to Jewish customs just to make a favorable impression on your old Jerusalem cronies?" . . . We know very well that we are not set right with God by rule-keeping but only through personal faith in Jesus Christ.

Galatians 2:11–16

be circumcised. Here we see the pragmatic Paul, who does not wish to offend Jews.

Moving on, they continue to preach and encourage the disciples in towns along the way, though their travel plans are sometimes blocked by the Spirit. After arriving in the coastal town of Troas, Paul has a dream about a man from Macedonia standing on a faraway shore, calling for him to come and help. Convinced that this is the voice of God calling him to Macedonia, Paul, never one to dilly-dally around, makes arrangements to sail there the next day with Silas, Timothy—and now Luke, who has joined them at Troas.

Upon arriving in Macedonia, they walk the distance to Philippi, the major metropolis in the region. Here they settle in for several days. From the locals, they learn that an outdoor service along the riverbank is about to begin. When they arrive they discover a group of God-fearing women. Paul and Silas join in and soon begin explaining the gospel message to those gathered.

One of those at the riverbank service is Lydia, a businesswoman who buys and sells purple, a high-quality fabric for dressmaking. She hangs on every word they say and becomes a true believer before the meeting is over. She wastes no time in being baptized, and after that invites the traveling preachers to her home.

Paul is haunted with the sense of his own sin. In some ways the most profound thing he contributed to the history of Christian thought was his analysis of the nature of human evil. He says the fundamental problem we face is that, in our attempt to be righteous, pride sets in.

Richard Wood, cited in Bruce Feiler, *Abraham: A Journey to the Heart of Three Faiths*

On one occasion while they are out preaching, Paul and Silas encounter a young woman who appears to be mentally deranged. They learn that she is a slave and also a certified psychic, whose fortune-telling is making her owners a small fortune. She has become mesmerized by the traveling evangelists and begins following them around, yelling out to everyone along the way: *These are God's men, bringing the message of salvation.*

On the surface, it might appear that she is just another *John the Baptist*, paving the way for Paul and Silas. But her yelling is a distraction, turning people off. She's hindering the ministry. Day after day she keeps it up. Paul's patience wears thin. Finally, he's had enough. He turns around and orders the demon to come out of her. A minor miracle in itself, but her owners are furious. Without the demon she has no psychic powers. Now she's just another fortune-teller who can't tell fortunes.

So outraged are the owners that they attack Paul and Silas and have them arrested and taken before the civil authorities. The local judge sentences them to be publicly beaten and incarcerated. Guards are posted at the entrance of the jail, and both men are held in chains in the most secure cell to prevent any possibility of escape.

First-Century Church Planter

In little more than ten years St. Paul established the Church in four provinces of the [Roman] Empire, Galatia, Macedonia, Achaia and Asia. Before AD 47 there were no churches in these provinces; in AD 57 St Paul could speak as if his work there was done.

Roland Allen, *Missionary Methods: St. Paul's or Ours?*, 3

Despite their pain and discomfort, Paul and Silas sing hymns and pray. But their singing is suddenly interrupted. A massive earthquake shakes the foundations of the jailhouse so violently that the doors fly open, as do the locked chains on the prisoners' legs. The jailer is panic stricken. He is responsible for the prisoners. If they escape, his own life is on the line. In fact, he's better off dead. Just as he's about to fall on his sword, Paul screams for him to stop. Nobody has so far escaped, and nobody intends to do so.

So taken aback is the jailer that he rushes into their cell and asks them what he must do to be saved. They explain the way of Jesus to him while he escorts them to his home to wash and tend their wounds. After a meal, the jailer and his household are baptized.

The next morning word comes to the jailer that he should let Paul and Silas go free. Paul might have been grateful, but he is not about to forget the injustice of the previous day. He's still irate about being manhandled like a criminal. A Roman citizen, he was beaten and thrown in jail without a trial, and now the officials are expecting him and Silas to just get out of town. He informs the messenger that if they want to be rid of him, they will have to give him an official escort out of town. Not wanting to further alienate a Roman citizen, the officials do just that, though not before Paul makes an important visit to the home of Lydia, where he and his companions meet with the new believers.

Again on the road, Paul and Silas soon arrive in Thessalonica. Here they are, as is becoming all too common, berated and threatened by angry crowds. The town leaders make wild accusations, telling the townspeople that the visitors are seeking to tear down the town's treasured traditions with their new religious ideas. Paul and Silas escape to Berea, where they are welcomed by people who listen intently to their preaching and ask serious questions. But even in this town troublemakers incite mobs against Paul. He escapes to Athens, where he is later joined by Silas and Timothy.

In Athens, Paul is shocked by what could be described as a cesspool of idolatry, a veritable museum of idols. But he sees the city as a mission field, and he begins interacting with people on the street, particularly the intellectual elites—philosophers of every stripe. A delegation of them comes to Paul, asking him to give a public address on his religious beliefs at the Areopagus. He eagerly agrees, beginning with a gripping illustration that grabs their attention:

> It is plain to see that you Athenians take your religion seriously. When I arrived here the other day, I was fascinated with all the shrines I came across. And then

> I found one inscribed, TO THE GOD NOBODY KNOWS. I'm here to introduce you to this God so you can worship intelligently, know who you're dealing with.[6]

Look around you, he admonishes them, *at a world created by God*—a God who is surely no idol. *God has created us; we don't create him as you have created these idols.* Paul is a brilliant apologist who quotes their own cherished literary figures to make a point for the God of Scripture. But his preaching is very personal as well. God, he tells them, is running out of patience. They must turn their lives around and come to God—a God who has already named a judge who has risen from the dead.

At this point he is heckled by loud scoffers as they storm out of the meeting. Others urge him to continue, but he leaves them hanging. Another day for the *rest of the story*.

From Athens Paul heads to Corinth, where he realizes he is running out of funds. With no other alternative, he returns to his earlier, arduous vocation, working alongside Priscilla and Aquila in their tent-making business. But he remains in ministry, going to the synagogue every Sabbath to preach and teach. Many believe, though not without harsh Jewish opposition. Later, accompanied by Silas and Timothy, he is able to devote all of his time to ministry. But most of the Jews remain adamantly opposed to his ministry.

> *These were more noble than those in Thessalonica, in that they received the word with all readiness of mind, and searched the scriptures daily, whether those things were so.*
>
> Acts 17:11 (KJV)

At this point he makes his stand: Enough of Jewish evangelism; from now on the focus will be Gentiles. "Your blood be on your own heads! I am innocent of it. From now on I will go to the Gentiles."[7]

Determined to Know Nothing but Jesus Crucified

Let's imagine Paul going up the main street of Corinth through the monumental Roman archway into the forum, the center of city life, the place where all the business and most of the political activities are done in the public life of this Roman city. Here are the shops. Here are the offices of the city magistrates, and we're standing literally in the shadow of the great temple of Apollo. It's among these artisans, among the shopkeepers, among the bustle of activity of a Greek city that we must imagine Paul beginning to talk about his message of Jesus and so when we hear Paul say "I've determined to know nothing among you but Jesus Christ, Jesus the Messiah and him crucified," that must have struck an interesting chord among these cosmopolitan Greeks who would have inhabited Corinth at that time.

L. Michael White, "Paul in Corinth"

He decides to leave town and be done with these hardheaded Corinthians. But, maybe not so fast. He has a dream, a voice from heaven is speaking: "Keep it up, and don't let anyone intimidate or silence you. . . . You have no idea how many people I have on my side in this city."[8] So irritated has Paul been with the naysayers that he has been almost oblivious to those who do listen attentively. In fact, many Corinthians are hearing the message gladly, and some are requesting baptism—here in Corinth of all places. Crispus, who has stepped up to organize the meetings, has turned out to be a true gem. He and his whole family believe.

So Paul stays on for more than a year, despite official persecution. He then sails for Ephesus (in present-day Turkey), accompanied by Priscilla and Aquila. Here, though having said he is done with the Jews, he goes to the synagogue and reasons with Jewish leaders there. Before boarding the ship, however, he has his head shaved—apparently to fulfill a vow, a strange and unexplained episode. His companions stay in Ephesus while he goes on to Caesarea and back to Jerusalem, then on to Antioch, where he stays for some time before heading back on the road. This third missionary journey takes him to Galatia and other places where he has been before, ever conscious of building up the faith of the believers in each community.

In Ephesus, where he stays for some three months, Paul encounters believers who have been converted through the teachings of Apollos, well meaning but not fully trained for ministry himself. Indeed, he is still essentially preaching the message of John the Baptist. So Paul preaches to them of Jesus' death and resurrection and baptizes them, at which time the Holy Spirit comes on them and they speak in tongues. For three months after that, Paul preaches boldly in the synagogue. Again opposition flares up. Enough already. So Paul moves to another venue in the city, where he continues his teaching and preaching for some two years.

Opposition and persecution follow Paul wherever he goes, but so do new converts. Word gets out that he is on his way, and believers and curiosity seekers hurry to meet him, crowding around him with anticipation. Some think his spiritual power stems from magic. They imagine that they can attain the power themselves if they touch him with a handkerchief. And indeed, in some cases their touch actually heals them. With the excitement of miracles comes conversions—and more persecution, particularly

Paul and Corinthian Scandal

A member of the Corinthian church had begun to cohabit with his father's wife. . . . That was bad enough, but even worse was the fact that many members of the church were disposed to be proud of this situation, looking on it as a rather fine assertion of Christian Liberty, setting at naught the inhibitions of Jewish law and pagan convention alike. Such conduct, if tolerated within the church, would corrupt the whole fellowship, said Paul. . . . The offender must be disowned, excluded from the membership of the church, for the church's health and also for his own ultimate salvation.

F. F. Bruce, *Paul: Apostle of the Heart Set Free*, 262

from those who are in the businesses of making and selling idols.

Ephesus, in fact, is the home of the goddess Artemis. She is the driving force in pilgrimage tourism and generates business for craftsmen who fashion images in her honor. Demetrius is one such skilled craftsman—a silversmith by trade—whose business has suffered on account of Paul. He sends out word to his competitors, both workers and management, calling for a meeting to make a formal protest against this outside interference. He has his speech prepared (a rare quotation in Scripture of a speech in opposition to the gospel):

> You know, my friends, that we receive a good income from this business. And you see and hear how this fellow Paul has convinced and led astray large numbers of people here in Ephesus and in practically the whole province of Asia. He says that gods made by human hands are no gods at all. There is danger not only that our trade will lose its good name, but also that the temple of the great goddess Artemis will be discredited; and the goddess herself, who is worshiped throughout the province of Asia and the world, will be robbed of her divine majesty.[9]

The gathered crowd makes its protest by shouting slogans of praise to the goddess. Their actions are contagious, and soon the whole city is in an uproar over the idea that anyone would dare discredit their own Artemis. The mob seizes two of Paul's coworkers and then begins searching for Paul himself. When Paul is apprised of the danger, he insists on speaking to the raging crowd. But his supporters, including certain local officials, are adamant that he lie low.

Paul's Vision and Thorn in the Flesh

I know a man in Christ who fourteen years ago was caught up to the third heaven. Whether it was in the body or out of the body I do not know—God knows. And I know that this man—whether in the body or apart from the body I do not know, but God knows—was caught up to paradise and heard inexpressible things, things that no one is permitted to tell. . . . these surpassingly great revelations. Therefore, in order to keep me from becoming conceited, I was given a thorn in my flesh, a messenger of Satan, to torment me. Three times I pleaded with the Lord to take it away from me. But he said to me, "My grace is sufficient for you, for my power is made perfect in weakness." Therefore I will boast all the more gladly about my weaknesses, so that Christ's power may rest on me.

2 Corinthians 12:2–9 (NIV)

What follows is a most interesting reflection on first-century civic life. As is often true in similar situations, the crowd is fickle, not sure what is going on and what side to support. Finally the city clerk takes the floor, reminding the people that the preeminence of Artemis is a given. She is not threatened by words, and nobody has trashed her temples.

So just calm down! Demetrius and others have every right to make their case in court, but this is no place for mob justice. *So just go home, all of you.*

And so the commotion in Ephesus ends, and Paul leaves town for Greece, visiting new church-plants along the way. In Troas, he gets so carried away that his sermon lasts well into the night. The meeting room is on the third floor, where a young man named Eutychus finds a place to sit on an open windowsill. It's a great spot to catch the fresh evening air, but he falls asleep before the benediction and tumbles out the window down to the ground. People rush outside to his aid, only to discover he is dead. Paul deals with the unfortunate turn of events by restoring his life, almost as though such is a routine activity for him. He returns to the third-floor meeting room, grabs a bite to eat, and carries on with his message until dawn, then leaves town. He is truly a driven man.

From there Paul is determined to go to Jerusalem. Believers warn him this would be foolhardy. The Jews are out to get him. He concedes that even the Holy Spirit has warned him that such a move will only lead to imprisonment. But Paul is bullheaded. He is bound and determined to go there despite the danger. He delivers an ominous farewell to the elders from Ephesus, essentially telling them that they will never see him again. Now they are on their own. He warns them about deceivers who will try to steer them away from the true gospel. He reminds them that he's never expected them to keep supporting him in a high lifestyle, that he has earned his keep by doing manual labor. Then they all kneel to pray, some trying to hang on to him amid their sobs.

Paul as Missionary to Unreached People

It has always been my ambition to preach the gospel where Christ was not known, so that I would not be building on someone else's foundation. . . . I will go to Spain and visit you on the way.

Romans 15:20, 28 (NIV)

Next, Paul heads for Rome, stopping along the way at the seaport of Tyre. Here again disciples, prompted by the Spirit, beg him not to go to Jerusalem. He is dearly beloved, and when he leaves, whole families come out to see him off, bidding their fond farewells amid great fear for his well-being.

When Paul arrives in Caesarea, a Judean prophet named Agabus searches Paul out, telling him he has a message from the Holy Spirit. Assuming words are not enough to get Paul's attention, he grabs Paul's belt and wraps it around his own feet and hands, demonstrating to him exactly what the Jews in Jerusalem will do to him.

Others join in the effort to persuade Paul not to go to Jerusalem. The whole idea is insane. He's just asking for trouble. But Paul will not be dissuaded. For the sake of Jesus, it is Jerusalem at any cost.

In Jerusalem, Paul receives a warm welcome. So far so good. He gives a full report of his work. The believers are most pleased to learn how well his message has been received and that as a result the number of disciples has increased daily. They offer positive reinforcement, but at the same time they are concerned about the content of his messages. Word has gotten back to the Jerusalem church that he is instructing the Jewish followers of Jesus to disregard Moses, particularly on the matter of circumcising their children.

Jewish believers in Jerusalem are making converts as well. But those living in

Jerusalem and those out in the provinces are getting mixed messages, a situation that has potential to do great harm. The Jerusalem church wants this matter settled now. So the Jewish leaders of the church, headed by James the brother of Jesus, put Paul to the test, insisting that he participate in Jewish vows with four other men—not only that, but that he foot the bill himself. This ritual involves a seven-day purification rite. He agrees, and the next day, like a good Jew, he goes to the Temple to formalize the rite with the necessary sacrifice.

While he is at the Temple, some Jews from out of town spot him. They are in a furor, accusing him of defiling the sacrifice by bringing non-Jewish men into the Temple, which he hadn't actually done. A riot ensues, and thugs begin attacking him. Soldiers come to his aid, thus preventing the mob from killing him. And before they haul him away, Paul receives permission to speak to the people.

Speaking in Aramaic, one of the three languages in which he is conversant, he

Paul arrested

captivates the crowd with his Damascus Road conversion story in his own inimitable style. But even more graphically, he recounts his preconversion story of the good Jew studying under Rabbi Gamaliel and later making it his mission to track down and torture followers of Jesus. His listeners stay with him until he comes to the climax, telling them he has been sent to evangelize Gentiles. The crowd explodes in rage. Paul is hastily taken away for his own protection—and to be whipped by civil authorities.

At this point, Paul pulls the citizenship card. How dare they whip a Roman citizen? This is a stunning twist. Not knowing what else to do, the officials send him on to stand before Jewish religious authorities. Aware that the council is made up

Paul and Caregivers

As you know, it was because of an illness that I first preached the gospel to you, and even though my illness was a trial to you, you did not treat me with contempt or scorn. Instead, you welcomed me as if I were an angel of God, as if I were Christ Jesus himself. Where, then, is your blessing of me now? I can testify that, if you could have done so, you would have torn out your eyes and given them to me. Have I now become your enemy by telling you the truth?

Galatians 4:13–16 (NIV)

of both Pharisees and Sadducees, he cleverly exploits their differences on the issue of the validity of a resurrection and gets them arguing among themselves. But he's not out of the woods yet. From Paul's own nephew, stationed in the nearby military garrison, word comes that conspirators are plotting to kill him.

So in the dark of night Paul is transported under armed guard to the palace of Governor Felix in Caesarea. Here he is accused of disturbing the peace. Paul serves as his own defense, claiming that he had come to Jerusalem to worship God as his ancestors had done, and in so doing had done no wrong. Felix postpones a decision, fearing that whatever decision he makes will upset one side or the other. So he drags his feet—for more than two years, while Paul languishes in prison.

When Festus succeeds Felix, things start moving. To please the Jewish leaders, he suggests a trial be conducted in Jerusalem. Knowing full well that a trial in this venue will seal his doom, Paul appeals to Caesar. He's a Roman citizen, and he demands Roman justice. If that's what he wants, Festus reasons, that's what he'll get. In the meantime, he brings up the subject of Paul's case to King Agrippa, who has come to town with his wife Bernice. Both ask for an opportunity to talk with Paul.

So Paul is brought before the king, and once again he gives his testimony. The king listens intently until Paul, basing his claims on Moses and the Prophets, says that the promised Messiah had been prophesied to be born and die and be raised again. Festus interrupts him, sarcastically suggesting he's insane. Paul shoots right back, implying that King Agrippa knows very well he's not insane. He's been listening way too intently to believe that Paul is out of his mind. Indeed, the king admits as much. "Keep this up much longer," he says, "and you'll make a Christian out of me!"[10]

Then the three of them—King Agrippa, Bernice, and Festus—and their counselors leave to talk things over. They all agree that Paul has committed no crime, and justice requires that he be set free, except for the fact that he's appealed to Rome. They have no other choice. Paul, well guarded and in the company of other prisoners, is now on his way to Rome.

The sea voyage to Rome turns into a harrowing ordeal. After being delayed on the island of Crete, they set sail again. Soon they are facing heavy winds and waves crashing over the deck. The captain steers for an island, only to discover the shore is way too rock strewn for the ship to make landfall. Dumping cargo along the way, he sails on, the ship now seriously damaged. Eventually all onboard give up hope—except for Paul. An angel has told him that they will be shipwrecked but that the crew and passengers will be saved.

And so it is. Amid shipwreck, all 276 crew and passengers are saved. They have landed on the island of Malta. There the natives perceive Paul to be a god because he survives a venomous snakebite. His reputation soars further when he heals the father of the island's highest official—as well as many more who had heard the news and come for healing.

The Apostle Paul: Fanatic, Compulsive, A Little Crazy

I doubt very much whether Paul impressed sophisticated people as an appealing character. To say the least, he must have embarrassed them. He was obsessed with his mission, unbending and endlessly aggressive in his religious views, absolutist and authoritarian in his dealings with others. We may reconstruct the adjectives and phrases used to describe him both at the cocktail parties of the Corinthian elite . . . and in the pubs:

"fundamentalist,"
"simplistic,"
"compulsive,"
"asking too much of sensible people,"
"never listening to the other side of an argument,"
"perhaps a little crazy"—

in sum, something of a disagreeable fanatic.

Peter Berger, *A Far Glory*, 14

Finally, Paul arrives in Rome with many stories to tell the believers who come to welcome him. There he is placed under house arrest and has opportunity to carry out his ministry as people meet with him and converse about the Jesus way. He also writes letters, a body of literature that has come to be known as the prison epistles: Colossians, Philemon, Ephesians, and Philippians.

According to tradition, he is martyred during the intense persecution by Nero in the year 64. A Roman citizen, he is marched through the walls of the city along the Ostian Way, where he is beheaded. It's all over in an instant, with one slash of a sword.

Concluding Observations

Though Paul has been designated a *saint* by Catholic, Orthodox, and Protestant churches alike, he would not have emphasized that point himself. In fact, as pertains to his own faults and failures, Paul is consistently the most open and honest of all biblical figures. Such should not be interpreted to suggest that Paul, any more than others, encountered personality conflicts and struggled with inner demons. Rather, Paul, without the aid of a therapist, was able to assess his own issues—though not necessarily overcome them.

What is most remarkable is that he is so open about such matters. He has a pastoral heart and is fully aware that his own struggles are universal struggles, and that by being transparent he will best serve those who are also seeking to faithfully serve in gospel ministry. No other biblical figure is so self-revealing as Paul. Indeed, his writings are a treasure trove of emotions. From ecstasy and serenity to anger, resentment, and guilt, he spills his guts for all to scrutinize. He is a biographer's dream. For anyone seeking to truly understand the personality of a biblical figure, Paul is the biggest prize. Nor does his life conclude with the tying up of loose ends. We never learn, for example, whether Paul and Peter ever worked through their differences or how Paul and Barnabas settled their issues.

Unlike most successful preachers today, Paul was not afraid of disclosing his setbacks and failures. In fact, he almost seemed to revel in them, enumerating a long list to the church at Corinth that included not only shipwreck and beatings but also lack of support and even opposition from fellow Christians. Someone reading his résumé might imagine him quite unqualified for ministry. Paul reversed the standard qualifications for leadership: weakness is strength, dying is gain.

It is difficult to overstate the influence of this ordinary man on religion and culture in general. From Augustine to Luther and Calvin and the Puritans, his footprint has been enormous. Yet it is not surprising when people say they do not like Paul—or perhaps even hate him. He held strong positions and did not mince words. That being said, however, Paul, perhaps more than any other man in history, has been misinterpreted—and overinterpreted. What would he think if he knew how many books and articles were being written about him today? Might he say *Enough already*?

It is interesting to speculate where Paul's pilgrimage might have led him had he not been struck down on the road to Damascus. How long can a terrorist make a career out of killing people? Might he have left off tormenting people and gone back to his books? Perhaps a nondescript first-century Jewish scholar forever lost in history.

Further Reading

Bird, Michael, ed. *Four Views on the Apostle Paul*. Grand Rapids: Zondervan, 2012.

Bruce, F. F. *Paul: Apostle of the Heart Set Free*. Grand Rapids: Eerdmans, 2000.

Picirilli, Robert E. *Paul: The Apostle*. Chicago: Moody Press, 1986.

Pollock, John. *The Apostle: A Life of Paul*. David C. Cook, 1994.

Wright, N. T. *Paul: In Fresh Perspective*. Minneapolis: Fortress, 2009.

23

BARNABAS, SILAS, AND PRISCILLA AND AQUILA

Paul's Coworkers

"God knows how much I love you and long for you." Paul is not sparing in his expressions of love for his coworkers. His emotions are spilling onto the pages as he writes to the Philippians from his house arrest in Rome: "So it is right that I should feel as I do about all of you, for you have a special place in my heart." Who are these people to whom he is writing? "You have been my partners in spreading the Good News about Christ from the time you first heard it until now."[1]

Paul is a demanding team leader who not only engenders love and loyalty but also provokes dissension. In some cases his coworkers defy his authoritarian nature and protest his religious perspectives, and they abandon him in fits of anger. Paul writes to Timothy of one such situation: "You know that everyone in the province of Asia has deserted me, including Phygelus and Hermogenes."[2] Some Bible scholars imply that this desertion was due to widespread persecution, but Paul, in this instance and others, sees it as a very personal affront. He goes on, however, to give Timothy some good news: "But God bless Onesiphorus and his family! Many's the time I've been refreshed in that house."[3]

Paul adds that Onesiphorus was not humiliated by Paul's being locked in jail, as other coworkers presumably were. It is interesting that Paul speaks of shame rather than fear. Fear of state persecution is typically assumed to be the reason early Christians would desert the faith. Although in this case they seem to be deserting Paul, but not necessarily the faith.

In another instance Paul writes that "Demas, having loved this present world, has deserted me."[4] Certainly this was a painful ordeal for Paul, but what about Demas? What is his side of the story?

Paul, in fact, does not hesitate to censure those who are not advancing the cause of the true gospel. In his greeting to the Galatians, he speaks even more forcefully about those who are deserting. Indeed, he extends grace and peace—though noticeably no love—and then proceeds directly to the topic at hand:

> I am astonished that you are so quickly deserting the one who called you to live in the grace of Christ and are turning to a different gospel—which is really no gospel at all. . . . Am I now trying to win the approval of human beings, or of God? Or am I trying to please people? If I were still trying to please people, I would not be a servant of Christ.[5]

Elsewhere Paul laments his struggles with *false brothers*, again referring to those who have deserted him. He oversees a large network of people who have been part of his ministry, but perhaps fewer than half of them remain faithful to him and the gospel he preaches.

Anything but a loner, Paul works closely with dozens of men and women, whom he refers to in a variety of ways: apostles, brothers and sisters, partners, coworkers, and even children (if they were his converts), as well as relatives. Indeed, a mark of Paul's credibility is his influence with family members. Several of them served in the gospel ministry, including Andronicus and Junia, Lucius, Jason, and the unnamed son of his sister.

Among his converts—or "sons"—who work alongside him are Timothy and Titus. Onesimus is also one of his "sons." Brothers and sisters in the ministry include Apollos, Philemon, and Phoebe. Counted as well among Paul's long list of coworkers (sometimes referred to as "fellow soldiers" or "fellow prisoners") are many whose conversions either predated his or are associated with someone other than himself. In some cases he had close interaction with them, as with Peter, Barnabas, Silas, and Priscilla and Aquila. With others the relationship is more distant, as in the case of John, James (brother of Jesus), and other leaders in Jerusalem.

It is noteworthy that women are so significantly represented among Paul's close associates. In addition to Phoebe, Priscilla, and Lydia, whose names are well known, he points to Damaris, Apphia, Euodia, Syntyche, Nympha, Junia, Mary, Julia, the mother of Rufus, and others.

Paul is effusive in commending his co-workers, and his expressions of gratitude are models for today. "I thank my God every time I remember you," he writes to the Philippians. "In all my prayers for all of you, I always pray with joy because of your partnership in the gospel from the first day until now."[6] More than any other biblical writer, Paul expresses love and appreciation for those involved in the ministry. Nearly one full chapter in his grand epistle to the Romans is devoted to praise for his partners in the gospel.

Barnabas: Encouragement and Partnership

His name is Joseph, but they call this man—known for his good cheer and for rallying the troops—Barnabas, meaning "Son of Encouragement." Perhaps he is one of those who encouraged others to give their money and possessions to the general fund in the early days of the new *Jesus Way* so that no one would be in want. For his part, he sells his own field and brings the money to the apostles.

It's an exciting time to be alive. Generosity is overflowing. Everyone is taking a cue from Barnabas and donating their estates—however meager—to the cause. Then, without a hint of warning, Ananias drops dead, and shortly afterward, Sapphira. There is sin in the camp that sucks the air right out of the excitement. Barnabas is there. How desperately his encouragement and comfort must have been needed at that moment.

A Levite from Cyprus, Barnabas is a leader in the Jerusalem congregation who takes a stand at a critical moment in the life of the emerging church when the apostles in Jerusalem appear to be overly cautious about outsiders. Word has come to them that Saul, the great persecutor, has suddenly been converted. It's all a ruse, some are saying. He's an opportunist seeking to infiltrate the ranks. He's simply not trustworthy. But Barnabas steps forward to stand by this new convert. He is convinced that Paul is for real, and he is eager to encourage him and introduce him to other believers.

The early faith community does not immediately reach out to the Greek, or Gentile, world—even after Peter's dream of unclean animals and the baptism of Cornelius and his family. Nevertheless, the young movement experiences considerable growth following the general persecution in the terrifying time after the stoning of Stephen. As believers flee, they share their faith and their numbers increase, though most specifically among God-fearing Jews.

But then some lay evangelists from Cyprus and Cyrene come to Antioch and share the testimony of Jesus with Gentiles, many of whom believe. This stirs up a commotion among the believers in Jerusalem. So they send Barnabas to Antioch to check things out for himself. There he finds a growing community of faith. True to his character, he encourages the new believers and appears to be not in the least threatened by the influx of non-Jews into the Way.

A Term of Derision

Ancient Antioch was famous for its humor, especially the coining of jesting nicknames. When an organized brigade of chanting devotees of Nero led crowds in adulation, this band of imperial cheerleaders with their ludicrous homage was quickly dubbed *Augustiani*. And earlier, when the devotees of the one called Christ came to public attention, they were named *Christianoi*, partisans of Christ (11:26). What may have been first coined by outsiders as a term of derision (see Acts 26:28 and 1 Pet. 4:16, the only two other New Testament occurrences of the term—both on the lips of hostile unbelievers), the followers of the Way embraced it as a fitting label.

William J. Larkin Jr., *Acts*, 175

More than that, Barnabas is looking optimistically to the future and the need for strong leadership and teaching. So he goes to Tarsus seeking out Paul, who had fled to his hometown after his life was threatened. Paul may have been discouraged, but Barnabas encourages him to come to Antioch with him, where they can work together as a team with the new believers. They spend a year there building up the infant church, and it is here in this town where the followers of Jesus are first called Christians.

From Jerusalem comes word, by way of the prophet Agabus, that in Judea there are hard times. Drought and crop failures have had devastating effects on the lives of the believers. So the *Christians* up there in Antioch take a collection, perhaps prompted by Barnabas. He and Paul travel down to Jerusalem to present the funds to the leaders in the congregation there. Then Barnabas and Paul return to Antioch, accompanied by John Mark, nephew of Barnabas.

Sometime after this, the Holy Spirit gives instructions to the church in Antioch: "Set apart for me Barnabas and Saul for the work to which I have called them."[7] The prophetic word might have seemed altogether vague, but it does not take long for the local leaders to spell out the specifics. The *work* for which they are commissioned entails what will become known as Paul's first missionary journey.

No surprise, they sail for Cyprus on their first assignment—Cyprus, home base of Barnabas (and perhaps John Mark also). The governor invites them to his residence to talk about their message. But they are drawing interference from a local psychic charlatan. Paul strikes him blind, and that incredible display of supernatural power turns the governor into a believer. From this point on, Paul takes over as leader of the missionary journey. The team, except for rare occasions, is referred to as *Paul and Barnabas*.

No doubt Paul is the more commanding preacher of the two. Converts are plentiful. But wherever he goes he stirs up controversy and opposition. When they arrive in Lystra, Paul heals a lame man and the crowd goes wild, thinking he and Barnabas are gods. So they identify Barnabas as Zeus and Paul as Hermes. Indeed, Barnabas becomes a bit of a celebrity when a priest of Zeus calls for a parade honoring these two gods. Now Barnabas apparently takes the lead. He and Paul insist that the celebration be halted because—plain and simple—they are not gods: "We also are men of like passions with you."[8]

Now stirred up by Jews from neighboring towns, the tide turns and the people rage against the preachers. Their vicious attacks are aimed not so much at Barnabas but at Paul, whom they consider to be the chief speaker. They beat him senseless and leave him for dead. The next day, having recovered sufficiently to get out of town, Paul leaves with Barnabas and heads for Derbe. After spending time there, they retrace their route and follow up on their preaching, encouraging believers all along the way. On arriving back in Antioch, they give an account of their good fortune as well as their struggles and setbacks.

The harrowing stories of mob attacks capture the attention of their supporters in Antioch. But there is another matter that perhaps is not so publicly discussed. John Mark, nephew of Barnabas, had abandoned the team in Pamphylia for reasons unknown.

While Barnabas is in Antioch, the church there receives a delegation of believers from Jerusalem who insist circumcision is a requirement of all male believers—Jew and Gentile alike. As a result Barnabas and Paul, as well as Silas and Barsabbas, are commissioned to go to Jerusalem to settle the matter once and for all. Barnabas is one of those who speaks at the Jerusalem Council, emphasizing the necessity of welcoming those outside the Jewish fold into the community of faith, without requiring circumcision. His position prevails.

After the meeting, Barnabas and the others return with the decision, much to the pleasure of the church in Antioch. They stay on in Antioch for a time, but it quickly becomes apparent that the church there is sufficiently supplied with teachers. So Paul, chomping at the bit to get out on the road, suggests to Barnabas that they go on a second missionary journey, in part to encourage the believers in the various towns in which they had previously planted churches.

Barnabas is also eager to get back on the road, but not without his nephew John Mark. He is the encourager, and his opinion is that they should give him another chance. Paul is uncompromising. He will not even countenance the possibility of taking back on the team this unreliable young man, nephew of Barnabas or not. A bitter argument ensues, resulting in their separation. Barnabas and John Mark head back to their home territory on the island of Cyprus, while Paul and Silas go to Syria.

Needing a Second Chance?

Many of us may be a bit drawn to Barnabas when we reflect upon the fact that we too occasionally have needed a second chance. Over the long haul, the decision of Barnabas may have proved best—at least for John Mark. Years later, Paul finds the formerly useless Mark "useful," as revealed in the apostle's concluding epistle. "Get Mark and bring him with you, for he is useful to me for ministering" (2 Tim. 4:11). And in Colossians 4:10, one observes that the once-rejected young worker was commended, and the Colossian saints were asked to be receptive to him.

Wayne Jackson, "The Separation of Paul and Barnabas"

How the return mission of Barnabas and John Mark to Cyprus played out is not recorded, nor is anything further known about this *good man* who served so faithfully as a missionary and church leader. Indeed, he alone in the book of Acts is described as good. Antioch becomes his home base, and he is identified as one of five in that congregation who serve as prophet-preacher and teacher.

It is assumed that he and Paul were able to get beyond the matter that split them as a team. Sometime later Paul, writing from jail to the Colossians, commends John Mark to them. And Paul also mentions Barnabas in his first letter to the Corinthians, where he is chastising the church in Corinth for lack of support. His reference to Barnabas is most interesting, since it comes after their fractious split. The grievance is vintage Paul. One wonders if Barnabas would have been so bold as to demand the financial support he deserved.

> We who are on missionary assignments for God have a right to decent accommodations, and we have a right to support for us and our families. You don't seem to have raised questions with the other apostles and our Master's brothers and Peter in these matters. So, why me? Is it just Barnabas and I who have to go it alone and pay our own way?[9]

Silas: Playing Second Fiddle to Paul

He "looked death in the face time and again for the sake of our master Jesus Christ."[10] Thus the apostles in Jerusalem commend Silas in a letter sent to Antioch. The larger issue is whether circumcision must be required of non-Jewish converts. Silas accompanies Paul and Barnabas (and Judas Barsabbas) to deliver the letter. As a Jewish convert himself and a leader of the Jerusalem Council, Silas is a key player in this most controversial matter that plagues the infant faith community. Acts also describes him as a prophet.

But Silas, no matter how much he might want to be regarded as a preacher and prophet in his own right, cannot escape the reality of being a sidekick ever in the shadow of Paul. His name is always preceded by *Paul and*. When Paul travels to another city without him, Silas simply fades away. A Hellenistic Jew, Silas (also known as Silvanus) is mentioned in close connection with many of the major players in the early faith community, but never standing alone. Indeed, he effectively illustrates the concepts of partnership and collaboration that were so very foundational to the early church.

Silas and Judas, having arrived in Antioch with Paul and Barnabas, speak words of encouragement to the believers there, and then Judas returns to Jerusalem. Silas, perhaps planning to return to Jerusalem as well, is instead singled out for an unexpected ministry assignment. He may have been present when Paul and Barnabas were locked in a bitter dispute over whether or not to take John Mark on their missionary journey.

Paul, still smarting from John Mark's desertion during the previous journey, refuses to give him a second chance. So they split, Paul choosing Silas as a partner in building up the congregations in Syria and Cilicia. In the months that follow, Silas is with Paul when he visits Lystra and spends time with a young man named Timothy, whom Paul circumcises. He is also with Paul at the seaport of Troas, where Paul dreams of a Macedonian man calling out for him to come and help.

In Macedonia (present-day Greece), he accompanies Paul to Philippi, the largest city in the region. While there, they spend time with Lydia, a God-fearing woman who is holding a Sabbath-day riverside service. They preach the gospel to the group, she believes, and she and her entire household are baptized—most likely by Silas.

Following the baptism, Silas and Paul remain in the region and continue their preaching ministry. As they move around from place to place, they are followed by a psychic who loudly proclaims their presence to those they meet. Annoyed, Paul casts an evil spirit out of her. She loses her psychic powers, and with that all hell breaks loose. The young woman happens to be a slave, and her psychic capabilities provide income for her owners, who are furious with the preachers. They pummel both Paul and Silas, bring them before local magistrates, and have them arrested, whipped, and thrown in jail.

The jailer takes no chances. He chains them up and bolts the door. The prisoners offer no resistance. Though their wounds are smarting, they take advantage of the downtime for prayer and hymn singing. But devotions are interrupted by an earthquake. Their chains fall off and the doors fly open. They might have escaped, but they purposely remain in their cell. So shocked and inspired is the jailer by their decency that he asks them how to be saved. Silas and Paul explain the gospel, and after washing their wounds, he and his entire household are baptized—again most likely by Silas.

On learning that Paul and Silas are Roman citizens, the local officials bend over backwards in offering apologies for the beatings and incarceration; and the local police fetch them and escort them out of the prison. With the ordeal behind them, they return to the home of Lydia.

After leaving Philippi, Silas and Paul pass through towns on their way to Thessalonica, where they preach for three successive Sabbath days in the synagogue and spend time in small group discussion. Many believe, including women of

Lydia: Leader of the European Band

I half envy Lydia that she should be the leader of the European band; yet I feel right glad that a woman led the van, and that her household followed so closely in the rear. . . . Not only, however, was Lydia a sort of first-fruit for Europe, but she probably also became a witness in her own city of Thyatira, in Asia. We do not know how the gospel was introduced into that city; but we are informed of the existence of a church there by the message of the ascended Christ, through his servant John, to "the angel of the church in Thyatira." Very likely Lydia became the herald of the gospel in her native place. Let the women who know the truth proclaim it; for why should their influence be lost?

C. H. Spurgeon, "Lydia, the First European Convert"

A Jailer's Leap of Faith

We have here and in the context an account of the conversion of the jailer, which is one of the most remarkable instances of the kind in the Scriptures. . . . Before, he was quiet and secure in his natural state. But now his eyes are opened. He is in the utmost haste. If the house had been on fire over his head, he could not have asked more earnestly, or as being in greater haste. He could soon have come to Paul and Silas, to ask them what he must do, if he had only walked. But he was in too great haste to walk only, or to run; for he sprang in. He leaped into the place where they were. He fled from wrath. He fled from the fire of divine justice, and so hastened, as one that fled for his life.

Jonathan Edwards, "Natural Men in a Dreadful Condition"

high status. But as interest and commitment grow, so does the opposition. Jewish leaders incite mobs to attack the traveling preachers, but the believers there manage to surreptitiously help them.

When they arrive in Berea, the situation is much better. The people are willing to study the Scripture to see for themselves whether the message Paul and Silas are presenting adds up. But soon word comes to the Berean citizens that these preachers are troublemakers. So Paul gets out of town again, this time leaving Silas and Timothy behind. They remain in Berea while Paul goes on to Athens, but later rejoin him in Corinth.

After this, Silas fades from the record, although he is mentioned in Paul's letters as one who sends greetings to various churches. He has also worked with Peter, who speaks of him as a brother in the ministry and who holds him in very high regard. This affirmation is included in Peter's first epistle, which Silas may have helped to write.

Priscilla and Aquila: Marriage and Ministry Partnership

Aptly described as the *power couple* of Paul's ministry network, Priscilla and Aquila are converts who have settled in Corinth, having been forced out of Rome. (In AD 49 Emperor Claudius had ordered an expulsion of all Jews from that city, including Jewish followers of Jesus.) Theirs is a *mixed* marriage, Aquila being a Jew from Pontus and Priscilla (or Prisca, her Roman name) a Gentile. Paul, running low on funds, seeks them out and works with them for more than a year in their tentmaking business in Corinth. Together they plant the church in that city.

Then they pull up stakes and accompany Paul to Ephesus, where he leaves them on their own to continue in the ministry. Like many of the early apostles and evangelists, they do not establish permanent residences anywhere. From Pontus (in Asia Minor), Aquila initially moves to Rome; from there he and Priscilla move to Corinth, then to Ephesus, back to Rome, and to Ephesus again—and perhaps they make many more moves not mentioned in the text.

While preaching the gospel in Ephesus, they meet Apollos, an evangelist who is also preaching about Jesus in the local synagogue. What a coincidence! He seems

Tentmakers Priscilla and Aquila

They were both tentmakers by trade, but it is not clear in what way. The term "tentmaker" meant anything from the actual sewing of the tents to the weaving of the cloth or tanning of the leather from which they were made. Since the Roman army was by far the biggest market for tents and used leather tents almost exclusively, it is suggested that Aquila and Prisca were leatherworkers. Since by Jewish Law Jews could not tan leather that did not come from a ritually slaughtered animal (and never pigskin, a common Roman leather), it is likely that Priscilla, as a Gentile, did not feel bound by Jewish Law, or that they were involved only with cloth tents.

Richard R. Losch, *All the People in the Bible*, 41

like a nice fellow, and he has great enthusiasm for the message of Jesus, but he is still baptizing people according to John's Jewish ritual of baptism—a baptism of repentance but apparently not one of commitment to the Christian faith.

So Priscilla and her husband Aquila take him aside and explain more fully the message of Jesus and the true meaning of baptism. It is interesting that here and elsewhere in the text, Priscilla's name most frequently precedes that of Aquila. There is no indication that her teaching Apollos, accompanied by her husband, would have been a controversial matter in the early Christian church, as it likely would have been in either a Jewish or Roman context.

When Emperor Claudius dies in 54, Jews are permitted to return to Rome. Among those who do are Priscilla and Aquila, who establish a church in their home. When Paul writes to the Roman Christians, he makes personal mention of them with heartfelt gratitude: "Greet Priscilla and Aquila, my co-workers in Christ Jesus. They risked their lives for me. Not only I but all the churches of the Gentiles are grateful to them."[11]

Later Priscilla and Aquila move back to Ephesus and again minister there, as Paul notes in his greeting to them when writing his second letter to Timothy, that being his final letter. In all probability, Priscilla and Aquila continued in ministry after Paul's death.

Timothy: Paul's Son in the Faith

The apostle Paul arrives in Lystra, where he meets a young disciple whose mother and grandmother had played an important role in his faith—"sincere faith, which first lived in your grandmother Lois and in your mother Eunice."[12] So impressed is Paul with Timothy that he wants to train him personally by having him come along on the missionary journey. First, however, Paul circumcises him.

Timothy's father, who may have been deceased, is Greek. So it stands to reason that Timothy would not have been circumcised. But why Paul would have performed this rite, after having previously insisted that Gentiles need not be circumcised, is a mystery—unless perhaps Timothy's Jewish mother was advocating for such. It is true that Jews lived in the region, and they might have become offended had he not been circumcised. Furthermore, Paul is grooming him for leadership in his own right—so he represents much more than just another convert.

Timothy bids his mother and grandmother farewell and begins his life on the road with Paul. It could not have been an easy family decision, because Paul makes no secret of the life-threatening persecution he had earlier faced along the way. But as they visit churches, their teaching is eagerly devoured by the believers, and new converts are received into the faith. When Paul and Timothy arrive in Berea, Timothy

Everyday *Life*

Family and Women's Roles

Eunice and Lois. Mother and grandmother of Timothy, Paul's closest associate. Paul commends them for their sincere faith, but otherwise they are shrouded in obscurity. Who were they, and how did they spend their days in first-century Palestine?

The everyday life of women was as varied as were the women themselves, especially when factoring in matters of personality, family size, social status, and religious inclinations. Some women traveled about in ministry or on business. Others maintained a large household filled with three generations of family members. Still others were impoverished widows supported by the church.

Paul, writing to Timothy, shows concern for the everyday life of women (1 Tim. 5). He offers specific guidelines regarding the support of widows, insisting that such matters are first and foremost the responsibility of the immediate family. In the case of a younger widow, he challenges her to marry and *manage* her home. Here Paul employs a strong Greek word, *oikodespotein* (from which the word *despot* is derived).

The women with whom he worked and interacted were anything but Victorian ladies who fanned and fainted. They were robust and resilient Mediterranean women who bargained their way through market day and stood their ground on the home front, sometimes virtually as *despots.* Yet they faced restrictions—both Jewish and Roman—in every aspect of life.

Gender Roles in First-Century Palestine

The results of ancient forms of gender division were heightened expectations that males and females would function differently. Household management was for females, field management for males. Public representation of the family in negotiations, making contracts, and in court was for males. Informal familial connections to other families was for females (marriage plans, for example). Sacrificing at the temple was for males. Childrearing was for females. Only males functioned as priests. Only females functioned as midwives. Formal education was limited to males. Male and female clothing had to be carefully distinguished. These are all generalizations, and they are affected by status as well as gender.

K. C. Hanson and Douglas E. Oakman, *Palestine in the Time of Jesus: Social Structures and Social Conflicts*, 26

Timothy, an Extension of Paul

In time, Paul came to see Timothy as an extension of himself, sending his "true child in the faith" to solve problems he normally would have undertaken. On his second missionary journey, when Paul worried that the churches in Macedonia—Thessalonica in particular—might have succumbed to Jewish persecution, he sent Timothy into the unknown to "strengthen and encourage" the members of the church (1 Thess. 3:1–2). During his third missionary journey, he sent ahead Timothy (and Erastus) from Ephesus to prepare the churches in Macedonia and Greece for his visit (Acts 19:21–22). Then, in final preparation for his long-anticipated journey to Spain—he never expected to see most of his pupils again—Paul placed Timothy in charge of the church in Ephesus, the most strategically important congregation in Asia and the church most susceptible to corruption.

Charles R. Swindoll, *Insights on 1 and 2 Timothy, Titus,* 16

remains while Paul goes on to Athens, and they team up again in Corinth.

On Paul's third missionary journey, they again travel together. Timothy is sometimes sent on ahead, however, while Paul stays behind, and on other occasions Paul goes on ahead, later to be joined by his younger colleague. Their separations offer opportunity for Paul to contact Timothy in letters—writings that demonstrate Paul's devotion: "I write this to you, Timothy, the son I love so much."[13] Paul emphasizes that Timothy should teach the Scripture and never let anyone intimidate him because of his youth. Rather, he must remember how he was commissioned with the laying on of hands for ministry—bold ministry that does not back down in the face of influence from the rich and famous. Indeed, he should avoid any temptation for wealth and fame.

Paul shows tenderness for the young man who has worked so tirelessly and faithfully alongside him: "Every time I say your name in prayer—which is practically all the time—I thank God for you. . . . I miss you a lot, especially when I remember that last tearful good-bye, and I look forward to a joy-packed reunion."[14] The tenderness is balanced by confidence that Timothy is the most trustworthy of Paul's

Timothy and his grandmother

Paul's Counsel to Timothy

Repeat these basic essentials over and over to God's people. Warn them before God against pious nitpicking, which chips away at the faith. It just wears everyone out. Concentrate on doing your best for God, work you won't be ashamed of, laying out the truth plain and simple. Stay clear of pious talk that is only talk. Words are not mere words, you know. If they're not backed by a godly life, they accumulate as poison in the soul.

2 Timothy 2:14–17

closest associates. Indeed, Paul passes the mantle on to him near the end of his life when he is facing certain death.

When Paul writes these words, he is in prison, and he wants Timothy to come to be with him as soon as possible—and not to come empty-handed: "Bring the winter coat I left in Troas with Carpus; also the books and parchment notebooks. . . . Try hard to get here before winter."[15] Timothy does come to Rome to spend time with his dear mentor. Together they write letters, including that most memorable letter to the Philippians: "Paul and Timothy, servants of Christ Jesus . . . Grace and peace to you from God our Father and the Lord Jesus Christ."[16]

Apollos: African Evangelist

A Jewish believer hailing from the cosmopolitan African city of Alexandria, he is both eloquent and erudite as a preacher

Onesimus, Slave and Coworker

A most unlikely candidate as an apostolic associate was a slave from Colossae whose name was Onesimus. Onesimus had abandoned his master, Philemon, and fled to Rome, probably hoping to lose himself in that crowded metropolis, perhaps stealing money from his owner in the process (Philemon 18). In the providential scheme of things—note that "perhaps" (v. 15)—he encountered Paul and was led to the Lord (v. 10). Eventually, Onesimus (whose name means "useful") made himself so "useful" (NASB) that Paul was loath to part with him. But the apostle would not retain his services under these circumstances (Roman law required returning a slave to his owner), especially without the permission of Philemon (vv. 11–14).

And so Paul was sending Onesimus home (in the company of Tychicus) with high praise; he was a "faithful and beloved" kinsman in the Lord (Col. 4:9). Moreover, Paul urged Philemon to receive Onesimus "no longer as a servant, but more than a servant"—as "a beloved brother" (v. 16). Indeed, he is encouraged to embrace his servant with the same spirit he would have extended to Paul himself (v. 17). If this disposition was adopted, then Onesimus would have remained a slave no longer—at least practically speaking. This is virtually a "proclamation of emancipation" without the specific words, "free him," being spoken. There may be no document in all history that has done more to remedy the evil of slavery than has Paul's letter to Philemon.

Wayne Jackson, "Paul's Two-Year Roman Imprisonment"

and missionary in Paul's wider network. But his initial teaching in the synagogue is surely not the Pauline line. Here is Apollos, more than a decade after the death and resurrection of Jesus, boldly preaching about Jesus while at the same time hanging on to the teachings of John the Baptist. Had he, while living in Alexandria, taken to heart the words of John: "Behold the Lamb of God, which taketh away the sin of the world"?[17] Had he traveled from Alexandria directly to Ephesus without earnestly interacting with Christians along the way?

Whatever the circumstances, he is teaching publicly about Jesus, perhaps never having fully comprehended that this very Jesus, God, very God, is risen from the dead—and is seated at the right hand of God the Father Almighty. In Alexandria he may have studied under the renowned Jewish philosopher Philo and may have availed himself of the writings in the city's very prestigious library of more than a half million scrolls. But with all his knowledge, he is more deficient than fishermen and tentmakers as an evangelist.

So Priscilla and Aquila take Apollos aside and fill in the missing details. They are patient teachers to this most eager learner, who now becomes even more ardent as an evangelist and teacher. He is not satisfied staying put, so, with a character reference from the local leaders, he travels to Achaia. "When he arrived there, he proved to be of great benefit to those who, by God's grace, had believed."[18]

Apollos also becomes known as a brilliant apologist, "vigorously refut[ing] his Jewish opponents in public debate, proving from the scriptures that Jesus was the Messiah."[19] Ephesus is his home base, but from there he is again on the road, this time to Corinth, where again he is highly regarded. Indeed, he is so popular with some of the local Christians that they are taking sides with him against Paul (though there is no evidence that Apollos himself was divisive). Soon, there are four groups staking their claims, not only for him and Paul but also for Peter—and Christ.

Paul is distressed when he learns that there are these divisions—particularly regarding Apollos. Both of them, he insists, are "ministers of Christ, and stewards of the mysteries of God."[20] They are two very different individuals, whose personalities and gifts are complementary. They work together for the kingdom: "I have planted," Paul writes to the Corinthians, "Apollos watered; but God gave the increase."[21]

Apollos is last mentioned in Scripture in the letter to Titus, where Paul again affirms

Apollos Compared with Timothy

Apollos was not recruited by Paul to join his social network as was the case with Timothy. . . . Apollos was embedded in the Pauline social network through his interaction with Paul's coworkers, Priscilla and Aquila, as well as with the Jesus group of Corinth that Paul had founded. But, Apollos' association with Paul and his assistants never reached the same level as Timothy shared with Paul. Timothy traveled with Paul on his numerous journeys and collaborated with him in the writing of a number of letters.

Patrick J. Hartin, *Apollos: Paul's Partner or Rival?*, 108–9

Phoebe as Servant Leader

There is a compelling but often-overlooked example of servant leadership in Romans 16:1–2. Here Paul commends "our sister, Phoebe, a deacon (minister) of the church at Cenchrea" and Paul asks the Romans to welcome her, and help her in whatever she requires. Why? Because, Paul states, "Phoebe has been a benefactor of many and of myself as well." Although most English translations do not do these verses justice, this is a remarkable passage in the original Greek. Paul is not only commending a woman who was in an ordained post, a *diakanos*, but a woman who was a *prostatis*. The English word benefactor does not give the full range of meaning, but Phoebe was someone in a position of trust, leadership, and even authority. Furthermore, Phoebe had been a prostatis in relation to Paul! Paul was being served by the leadership gifts of Phoebe, and Paul as himself a true servant leader was free enough, relaxed enough, and secure enough to share ministry at every level. Paul as a true servant leader rejoiced when another, like Phoebe, was empowered to lead in her own sphere of ministry. I don't think it is stretching the text to think that Paul received significant aid in ministry from Phoebe. Would Paul have felt diminished to be under a woman's ministry? Not according to this text. Why? Because the servant leader is not someone whose title denotes "I'm in charge and you are under me." Gifted people are not empowered to be *over* others, but empowered to serve others by offering up their gifts for the good of the entire faith community.

Gretchen Gaebelein Hull, "Empowered to Serve"

him as his partner in ministry: "Give Zenas the lawyer and Apollos a hearty send-off. Take good care of them."[22]

Concluding Observations

Paul's partners in the gospel all play a secondary role to the great apostle, none of them known for their writings or for taking over the ministry after his death, as was the case with Peter and John after the death of Jesus. With the writings of Paul, Peter, and John, the New Testament canon will become complete.

Paul, however, could not have accomplished what he did without the considerable help of others. Barnabas was critical in Paul's early years of ministry and first missionary journey. Silas stepped in to take his place for the second evangelistic tour. Priscilla and Aquila were business and ministry partners as well as friends. One can only imagine their deep sense of camaraderie and the joy of being reunited after their frequent separations. Apollos would forever be remembered as the one who *watered* that which Paul had planted. Timothy was a *son*, the one who would take over after Paul died. But he knew as well as anyone that no one would ever rise to the stature of this singular apostle and father in the faith.

But Paul's coworkers were certainly not all equally loyal to him. He was pained by this realization, though he sought to make the best of it, as he so pointedly wrote from Rome to the church in Philippi:

> It is true that some preach Christ out of envy and rivalry, but others out of goodwill. The latter do so out of love, knowing that I am put here for the defense of the gospel. The former preach Christ out of selfish ambition, not sincerely, supposing that they can stir up trouble for me while I am in chains. But what does it matter? The important thing is that in every way, whether from false motives or true, Christ is preached. And because of this I rejoice.[23]

Some of Paul's partners, though barely mentioned in the biblical narrative, nevertheless play a significant role in ministry. Titus, who is not mentioned in Acts but is referred to more than a dozen times in Paul's letters, is one such individual. An uncircumcised Greek, he serves in Corinth and later on the island of Crete. Other individuals referenced, though only in passing, include Euodia and Syntyche, who, Paul writes, "have contended at my side in the cause of the gospel."[24] Unfortunately, they are at odds with each other, and Paul pleads with them to get along and for others to help them do so. Phoebe is another woman who played a key role in Paul's ministry network.

Expressions of appreciation for coworkers fall easily from Paul's lips, and the reader feels fortunate when he includes context for the person he is praising, as in the case of Epaphroditus:

> But I think it is necessary to send back to you Epaphroditus, my brother, co-worker and fellow soldier, who is also your messenger, whom you sent to take care of my needs. For he longs for all of you and is distressed because you heard he was ill. Indeed he was ill, and almost died. But God had mercy on him, and not on him only but also on me, to spare me sorrow upon sorrow. Therefore I am all the more eager to send him, so that when you see him again you may be glad and I may have less anxiety. So then, welcome him in the Lord with great joy, and honor people like him, because he almost died for the work of Christ. He risked his life to make up for the help you yourselves could not give me.[25]

As is typical, Paul's warm commendation of Epaphroditus, included in his letter to the Philippians, is followed by a warning. "Watch out for those dogs," he writes.[26] The term *dogs* illustrates Paul's contempt for those supposed coworkers who were preaching another gospel—in this case, the necessity of circumcision. For every Epaphroditus there was a *dog*, as much a thorn in the flesh as any physical ailment he ever endured.

Further Reading

Hartin, Patrick J. *Apollos: Paul's Partner or Rival?* Collegeville, MN: Liturgical Press, 2009.

Hiebert, D. Edmond. *In Paul's Shadow: Friends and Foes of the Great Apostle*. Greenville, SC: BJU Press, 2001.

Keller, Marie Noel. *Priscilla and Aquila: Paul's Coworkers in Christ Jesus*. Collegeville, MN: Liturgical Press, 2010.

24

JOHN OF PATMOS

The Ultimate Visionary *Leader*

John is the old man of the New Testament. Probably only in his twenties when he becomes a disciple of Jesus, he is in his nineties when he dies of natural causes in Ephesus—or perhaps on the island of Patmos. Indeed, if one assumes (as do the *NIV Study Bible* and most evangelical scholars today) that John the fisherman and John the apostle were one and the same with John the evangelist and John the author of Revelation, he is active in ministry longer than any other individual featured in the New Testament. John is the only one of Jesus' immediate disciples and followers believed to have had a direct connection with the second-generation, postapostolic period. John's most notable disciple was Polycarp, the second-century bishop of Smyrna.

John survived by more than fifty years his brother James, the first apostle to be martyred. Yet despite his long life, details are obscure, particularly in comparison to the lives of Peter and Paul. Whereas Paul often focused on himself and his own issues, John seeks to avoid any personal identity. In fact, in his Gospel he repeatedly refers to himself in the third person, *the disciple whom Jesus loved*.

Of all the New Testament writers, John, had he been so inclined, had the best opportunity to write a biographical history of the first-century faith. He was the most knowledgeable about the early life and later ministry of Jesus as well as the development of the church to the end of the first century. By his own testimony he is very close to Jesus and other disciples and thus would have been a perfect candidate for such a task. But alas, he chose not to write personally and fill in biographical details that the present-day reader so longs to know.

John is the *apostle of love*. *Love* is the word that identifies him, not only in his writing but also in his relationship with Jesus. He and Jesus model the mutual love of disciple and master. But more than that, he writes of God's love and of each Christian's love for one another. The most quoted verse of the New Testament comes from the pen of John, the familiar John 3:16: "For God so loved the world, that he gave his only begotten Son, that whosoever believeth on him should not perish, but have everlasting life" (KJV).

John also quotes Jesus on love in his Gospel: "A new command I give you: Love one another. As I have loved you, so you must love one another. By this everyone will know that you are my disciples, if you love one another."[1] John's first epistle, his most concentrated writing on love, is as pointed and applicable today as it was when it was written two thousand years ago.

> This is how we know what love is: Jesus Christ laid down his life for us. And we ought to lay down our lives for our brothers and sisters. If anyone has material possessions and sees a brother or sister in need but has no pity on them, how can the love of God be in that person? Dear children, let us not love with words or speech but with actions and in truth.[2]

John ends his first epistle with a powerful challenge that makes demands on those who dare call themselves Christians:

Who Wrote the Gospel of John?

The Fourth Gospel does not bear its author's name: like the Synoptics, it is formally anonymous. . . . The fact remains that, despite support for Johannine authorship by a few front-rank scholars in this century, and by many popular writers, a large majority of contemporary scholars reject this view. As we shall see, much of their argumentation turns on their reading of the *internal* evidence. It also requires their virtual dismissal of the external evidence. This is particularly regrettable. . . . In short, the internal evidence is very strong, though not beyond dispute, that the beloved disciple is John the apostle, the son of Zebedee. Who, then, is the Evangelist? . . . The traditional answer is that they are one and the same. . . . If, then, we tentatively affirm that the beloved disciple is both John the son of Zebedee and the fourth Evangelist, what difference does it make to our interpretation of the Fourth Gospel? At one level, very little. . . . At another level . . . [we] are driven to listen more acutely to what the Evangelist says about Jesus.

D. A. Carson, *The Gospel according to John*, 68, 75, 81

> Whoever claims to love God yet hates a brother or sister is a liar. For whoever does not love their brother and sister, whom they have seen, cannot love God, whom they have not seen. And he has given us this command: Anyone who loves God must also love their brother and sister.[3]

John: Apostle, Evangelist, and Writer of the Revelation

Who could have ever imagined that John, a no-nonsense fisherman on the Sea of Galilee, would one day in his old age be transported into such a lofty and vivid and altogether spectacular visionary world as is recorded in that most colorful book of Revelation? John recounts fascinating stories in his Gospel, and his epistles are rich in metaphor and symbolism. But his Apocalypse is in a category by itself. Nothing rises to its beauty—and horror—in the annals of literature.

John is ready to become a disciple when Jesus shows up walking along the shore of the Sea of Galilee. He may have observed Jesus interrupting Peter and Andrew as they were casting their net into the water. They simply leave their nets and follow, and it's perhaps only a few dozen paces down the shore when the three of them now approach John and James, the sons of Zebedee. Simon Peter and Andrew are in partnership with Zebedee and his sons—perhaps a sizable fishing operation that is able to spare the men for ministry. Still, one wonders who picked up the slack when these four burly fishermen simply walked off the job. And later, with no apparent reapplication process, they return to their nets as though they had never left.

John is the more prominent of the two brothers in Jesus' ministry, though James is named first, probably indicating that he is the older one. Jesus refers to them as Boanerges, meaning "sons of thunder." This may indicate that they were fiery, intense, demanding, something Jesus might have been cognizant of since childhood. Indeed, the three of them may have been youthful buddies.

Zebedee is frequently mentioned as the father of John and James. Their mother, however, is not specifically named, even though she is apparently part of a small inner circle of women who surround Jesus. She is variously referred to as Salome, as the mother of the sons of Zebedee, and as Mary's sister. If Salome is indeed the mother of the brothers and if she is the sister of Mary, John and Jesus are first cousins and thus would have undoubtedly known each other long before their relationship as disciple and master.

Part of Jesus' inner circle, which also includes Peter and James, John is privileged to be present when Jesus raises Jairus's daughter from the dead. He is also present at the transfiguration of Jesus, though he remains silent during these and other tension-filled moments.

John, unlike Peter, is not outspoken or aggressive and is not easily identified as a naturally gifted leader. He is, however, concerned about rank and status, threatened by anyone who might challenge his position. On one occasion he reports to

Jesus: "We saw someone driving out demons in your name and we told him to stop, because he was not one of us."[4] Jesus does not agree with John and the other disciples. He tells John not to dissuade such individuals, but he does not rebuke him as he does Peter on several other occasions.

Sometime after this the disciples, John included, ask Jesus who is the greatest in the kingdom of heaven. Jesus responds by pointing to a child, saying that this youngster, who has essentially no status at all, represents the one who is greatest. Still another conversation arises when Peter observes that he and the other disciples have left everything behind to follow Jesus, no doubt hoping that Jesus would assure them of great reward for their sacrifice. Jesus responds by saying that the Son of Man will sit on a magnificent throne and that the twelve disciples will also have thrones in their capacity as judges of the twelve tribes of Israel.

Such a claim coming from the Master is heady stuff. It is not surprising then that the sons of Zebedee might talk privately with their mother, Jesus' aunt, and ask if she would put in a good word for them. The three approach Jesus together and kneel down to ask him a favor. Their mother requests that James and John be given thrones next to Jesus, on his right and left sides.

John the Apostle

Without sarcasm or rebuke, Jesus puts her and her sons in their place: "You don't know what you are asking! Are you able to drink from the bitter cup of suffering I am about to drink?" They answer that they are able, and he responds with less than good news: "You will indeed drink from my bitter cup. But I have no right to say who will sit on my right or my left. My Father has prepared those places for the ones he has chosen."[5] They are obviously contemplating a temporal realm while Jesus is focusing on the spiritual.

When the other disciples hear of the audacity of John and James—and their mother, no less—they are furious. Who do they think they are to make a claim on such seats of power, setting themselves above the rest? Now Jesus addresses all of them, and, in words that confound and confuse, tells them that they should not be grasping for authority and flaunting their status in front of others. Rather, each must assume the position of a lowly servant—actually a slave.

A slave? Such a radical turnabout surely leaves John's head spinning. Having just spoken of twelve thrones for the disciples, now Jesus is telling them their place is that of slaves. That would put them at a level lower than the hired hands of his father's fishing business. But Jesus has made what seem like bizarre statements before.

Now events begin to move quickly as Passion Week approaches. Again John must surely be confused by what appear to be conflicting messages. Jesus has been talking about his death, but then there is the Triumphal Entry into Jerusalem. With no benefit from hindsight, John must feel the rush of victory. This kingdom thing may be coming together in a matter of days after all.

Until this time John has not been in the forefront. But that changes, and he becomes noticeably more involved. He alone is sent with Peter to make preparations for the Passover. Are they quizzing each other about the mixed signals they have been getting? By now they must both realize that this will be more than the usual ritual meal, but still they have no real comprehension of how momentous the occasion is.

Then comes the moment. The Supper is in progress. Conversation is interrupted. Jesus now has the floor. He almost casually reveals that one of them—one of his very disciples—will betray him. John (the disciple whom Jesus loved) is sitting next to him, his head on Jesus' shoulder. This is a shocking disclosure, and the disciples don't know what to make of it. They are stunned. Then, with Peter's prompting, perhaps a nudge and a whisper, John with some hesitation asks to whom Jesus is referring. In fear and trepidation he then inquires: *Lord, is it I?* Jesus responds very indirectly. In fact, none of them, including John himself, suspects Jesus is referring to Judas.

Following the supper, John, with James and Peter, goes to the Garden of Gethsemane to offer solace to Jesus, who is now in deep anguish over his impending death. Still, they don't get it. Exhausted, all three of them fall asleep, but are twice awakened and rebuked by Jesus. When Jesus is arrested by the Temple authorities and their thugs, John, frightened to death and confused beyond measure, flees. But he returns to be with Jesus during his agony on the cross. He is the only one of the Twelve who is there in Jesus' final hours. When Jesus looks down and sees John, who is no doubt comforting his own mother, he says to Mary, *here is your son*, and to John he says, *here is your mother*. John's own mother, Mary's sister, is also at the cross. It seems strange that Jesus would make John Mary's titular son, since Jesus has brothers who would supposedly step into this role. But Jesus is closer to John than he is to his own brothers. And this was no doubt perceived as a spiritual relationship as much as a physical one.

John is with the other disciples after the body of Jesus had been laid in the tomb, and they remain together through the predawn hours of the first day of the week. It is then that Mary Magdalene comes running from the tomb, out of breath, telling the disciples that Jesus' body is no longer there. Peter and John race to the tomb, John getting there first. But he waits outside until Peter arrives and goes inside. Then he joins him, and on seeing the graveclothes all lying in place, he believes that Jesus has truly risen from the dead.

From Rascally Thunderbolt to Apostle of Love

One word comes to mind when we think of the apostle John: love. But John's own "story of love" is not pretty. Love, for John, didn't come easy. . . . For someone who spends his last days writing about love-love-love, John sure fails when his love is tested. John may learn about love, but as a young man, he is crusty and cranky. . . . The young apostle who wanted to turn Samaritans into ash and who thought gifts of exorcism were limited to one small group of disciples comes full circle. . . . This is the story of John: the rascally thunderbolt becomes a tender apostle of love.

Scot McKnight, *The Jesus Creed: Loving God, Loving Others*, 104–10

Following the resurrection, John is with the other disciples as they see Jesus ascend into heaven, and he is there at Pentecost to witness the spectacular tongues of fire. But after this the disciples are no longer a customary group of twelve as they often had been during Jesus' ministry. Now Peter and John come to the fore. On one occasion they go to the Temple for prayer. Here a disabled man requests money from them. Peter tells the man they have none, but he commands him to get up and walk, which the man does. This is the first miracle performed in Jesus' name after his resurrection.

Peter takes the opportunity to preach to the onlookers, and John joins in. The Jewish leaders are upset with any talk of the resurrection of Jesus, so they lock them up in jail. So powerful is the apostles' message, however, that many of the listeners join with the company of believers.

The next day the officials order both John and Peter to come before the high priest. He could have simply kept them locked up, but he does not want to risk an uprising. So the two evangelists are ordered to do no more preaching. Say what? *We must obey God rather than man.* With a final threat, the officials let them go. Later, as a result of more miraculous healings, John and Peter are again brought before the Sanhedrin, and this time they are jailed and shackled. At night an angel appears and releases them, and the next day they are right back in the Temple preaching. No civil or religious authority can quench their zeal.

Later word comes to Jerusalem that there is a revival going on in Samaria as a result of Philip's preaching. John and Peter are sent to check things out. They discover that the Holy Spirit had "not yet come on any of them."[6] With John and Peter's laying on of hands, the matter is dealt with, apparently in such a show of power that Simon the Sorcerer offers to pay for their spiritual secret. What a sacrilege! It's an outrageous offer. But John remains silent as Peter scorches Simon with a blistering reprimand.

After this John fades into the background. Peter takes the lead, and other disciples become more prominent, including Barnabas, Silas, James (the brother of Jesus), and Paul. John remains in Jerusalem for some time and is recognized by Paul as one of the pillars of the church there.

John would live to witness terrible tragedies during the remainder of his long life,

John's Old Age—Another View

Just before the final passion prediction of Jesus . . . we find the story of the Zebedee boys' request for the box seats in the Kingdom. . . . Jesus tells them that it is not for him to grant them such seats, but he predicts the following: "You will drink the cup I drink and be baptized with the baptism I am baptized with." . . . In [Acts] 12.1–3 we hear about the seizing of "James the brother of John" who is executed by King Herod (Agrippa presumably). This event transpires sometime in the 40s. James Zebedee is put to death by the sword, thus fulfilling the prediction of Jesus, and it is noteworthy that John Zebedee is mentioned briefly in the company of Peter in Acts 8.14 as going down to Samaria to check out Philip's work, but after that we hear nothing of the man, except his return to Jerusalem (v. 25). It is like he fell off the planet after that. . . . John had been one of the inner circle of three within the Twelve. Where was he, if neither Acts nor Paul mentions him at all after Acts 8.14, 25 which surely refers to an event in the late 30s? In my view it is likely that he was already martyred before the 50s, just as Jesus had predicted, and as had happened to his brother James.

Ben Witherington, "The Martyrdom of the Zebedee Brothers"

including the execution of his brother James. In fact, James is the first of the apostles martyred, cut down by a sword on orders of King Herod. Who the next of the Twelve Apostles would be to wear the martyr's crown is not recorded. But John surely would have received the terrible news from Rome probably in the year 64, that Peter, his longtime friend and coworker, had been brutally slain, reportedly on orders of Emperor Nero.

Sometime later, Jews in Jerusalem, suffering under the high-handed tactics of the Roman governor, stage a revolt—a revolution that would end with what would become known as the fall of Jerusalem in the year 70. Before "the Jewish War" (as Josephus titled his book) had even heated up, many Christians, including John, had fled to Ephesus and other towns in Asia Minor.

Here John continues in ministry as the elder statesman in the entire region, much

John writing his Revelation

John's Midlife Vision

We hold, then, as the most probable view, that John was exiled to Patmos under Nero, wrote the Apocalypse soon after Nero's death, AD 68 or 69, returned to Ephesus, completed his Gospel and Epistles several (perhaps twenty) years later, and fell asleep in peace during the year of Trajan, after AD 98.

Philip Schaff, *A History of Christianity*, 1:429

revered for his apostolic role and close relationship with Jesus. He likely served as an overseer of the seven churches in Asia to whom he would later write. But his bold testimony of Jesus, Son of God, risen from the dead, brings down the wrath of civil authorities. He is exiled to the Island of Patmos by Emperor Domitian, who ruled from the year 81 to 96. Or, perhaps, he was exiled much earlier than that.

The text offers no biographical data on John in his later years, but many scholars believe that he returned from exile on Patmos and lived out his final years in Ephesus. It is in this setting, as an old man, that the boy Polycarp, who later becomes Bishop of Smyrna, remembers him.

From this unexpected exile some fifteen miles southwest of Ephesus on a small, barren, rocky island in the Aegean Sea comes a writing that John testifies is not his own words. He is a fisherman, after all, hardly capable of inventing such soaring rhetoric. Here is the great apostle, perhaps confined in a cave, writing words that would fill a most remarkable scroll—a scroll that would for the next two millennia inspire theological discourse, commentaries, hymns, fiction, film, and more. Indeed, while on the Island of Patmos, John receives a vision and is told to write it down—a vision that will form the final book of the Bible: the book of Revelation.

John opens by greeting the seven churches in the province of Asia—a greeting that also comes from his onetime close companion and Master, "Jesus Christ, who is the faithful witness, the firstborn from the dead, and the ruler of the kings of the earth."[7]

Then John goes on to explain the background of this vision. He is suffering because of his witness for Jesus; thus his confinement on Patmos. How long or what his circumstances are, he does not say. But then something incredible happens. It is the *Lord's Day*, and he is *in the Spirit*. Suddenly he hears what he identifies as a loud voice, but the sound is that of a trumpet.

Polycarp: Disciple of the Apostle John

While I was still a boy I saw . . . the place where blessed Polycarp sat and talked, his goings out and comings in, the character of his life, his personal appearance, his addresses to crowded congregations. I remember how he spoke of his intercourse with John and with the others who had seen the Lord; how he repeated their words from memory; and how the things that he had heard them say about the Lord, His miracles and His teaching, things that he had heard direct from the eye-witnesses of the Word of Life, were proclaimed by Polycarp in complete harmony with Scripture.

Irenaeus, cited in Eusebius, *Ecclesiastical History*, bk. 5

The voice summons him to action: "Write on a scroll what you see and send it to the seven churches: to Ephesus, Smyrna, Pergamum, Thyatira, Sardis, Philadelphia and Laodicea."[8] Only then does he see the image of Christ, who tells him not to be afraid—that he is the "Living One." And the voice of the risen Jesus assures him: "I was dead, and now look, I am alive for ever and ever! And I hold the keys of death and Hades."[9]

So John writes the words that the Lord gives him to each of the seven churches to whom he himself had given pastoral care. Though he is technically speaking for God, these messages clearly come from John

Everyday *Life*

Visionary Experiences

That Scripture would conclude with John's great Revelation is fitting. Spectacular visions and dreams are part and parcel of the biblical narrative. In fact, some scholars insist that fully one-third of the Bible relates to dreams or visions.

The mind-set of the ancient world viewed as normal what would today be regarded as *paranormal* and downright kooky. That Saul, through the witch of Endor, was able to call back the spirit of Samuel (1 Sam. 28) does not fit well with a post-Enlightenment mentality. Nor does the incident involving the servant girl Rhoda (Acts 12). In the midst of a prayer meeting for Peter, who had been locked in jail, she answers the door and then tells those praying that Peter is at the door. They insist it couldn't be Peter, rather his angel. That an angel would more likely be knocking at the door than a jail escapee says something about the outlook of the times. Indeed, angel appearances are almost ordinary events in the Bible.

Other notable biblical figures besides John are associated with dreams and visionary experiences: Joseph and Daniel can interpret dreams, Moses meets God at the burning bush, Ezekiel sees spectacular visions of wheels and dry bones, Peter dreams of unclean animals, and Paul takes flight to the third heaven. Such experiences are not necessarily perceived to be extraordinary.

The Bible and Divination

In Ancient Near Eastern culture dreams and visions were a practice associated with the whole area of divination. . . . The Ancient Near East had elaborate dream books they used to help interpret dreams. . . . Daniel and Joseph stand out as featured interpreters of dreams in the Scriptures and both strongly state that interpretation of dreams is from God (Gen. 41:16 and Dan. 2:28). Daniel is in a similar position to the diviners of the day yet the narrative clearly demonstrates that he receives interpretation through his relationship with God and not through the Ancient Near Eastern practices of divination.

Tina Brown, "Dreams and Visions in the Old Testament"

John the Evangelist on Patmos

also. He knows them well—particularly Ephesus, where he resided and ministered for many years. All seven of these messages are direct, matter-of-fact, and personal, except for the figurative salutations—greetings to the *angel* of each church.

To Ephesus he emphasizes its good deeds, perseverance, and discernment. But this church so dear to his heart has "forsaken the love you had at first."[10] Early on, this church had been known for its love of God and others, but no longer. John reminds those at Smyrna that they are rich despite their hard times. He also warns them of suffering and persecution to come. To those barely hanging on to the truth in Pergamum he says in no uncertain terms that they must repent for straying into immorality and heresy.

The church in Thyatira is recognized for its faith and charity but lambasted for putting up with a false prophetess, who is blatantly preaching an antinomian gospel involving sexual immorality. John challenges the once-vibrant church of Sardis to wake up from its slumber—a church now dead as a doornail. The church in Philadelphia is weak, but he commends it for staying true to the faith, promising security "from the hour of trial that is going to come on the whole world."[11]

Finally, John aims both barrels at the church in Laodicea. "I know your deeds, that you are neither cold nor hot. I wish you were either one or the other! So, because you are lukewarm . . . I am about to spit you out of my mouth."[12] Yet he holds out victory and hope that applies to all the churches:

> Those whom I love I rebuke and discipline. So be earnest and repent. Here I am! I stand at the door and knock. If anyone hears my voice and opens the door, I will come in and eat with that person, and they with me. To the one who is victorious, I will give the right to sit with me on my throne, just as I was victorious and sat down with my Father on his throne. Whoever has ears, let them hear what the Spirit says to the churches.[13]

John's Revelation is far more than a spectacular panoramic vision of which he

John's Strange Visionary World

When we open up a Bible to the book of Revelation, if we open up a Bible to that book at all, we open ourselves up to a strange world indeed. We are greeted by a fiery, glowing Jesus who looks nothing like the man we knew from the stories in the Gospels (even the shining Jesus of the transfiguration is tame by comparison). . . . We enter into scenes of heavenly worship involving fantastic heavenly hybrid creatures and stretching out through hosts of angels to all of the creation, all surrounding a seven-eyed Lamb, slaughtered but standing, and all this to-do over some sealed scroll.

And that's the *easy* part of the book. Then come the devastations of the seals, the army of white-robed martyrs, seven trumpets unleashing unnatural disasters and armies of unnatural creatures. When we encounter a colossus with pillars of fire for legs, we actually breathe a sigh of relief before being plunged again into a world where a dragon has it in for some star-crowned woman and her offspring. . . . The dragon is bound in the abyss while the dead followers of the Lamb enjoy a thousand-year reign with him, after which the dragon is teased with having one last crack at overthrowing God and God's Anointed, which lands him in the fiery lake as well. Then comes the final judgment, sorting out humanity into their eternal destinies, and the bride appears at last—as a city, the new Jerusalem, descending from a new heaven to the new earth, where God's kingdom is realized at last in an urbanized garden of Eden.

David deSilva, *Seeing Things John's Way: The Rhetoric of the Book of Revelation*, 1–2

is an observer only. He actually becomes an active participant. True, he is standing on the sidelines as the elders are casting their crowns before the throne. And he remains a bystander as a formidable angel shouts out in a thunderous voice: "Who is worthy to break the seals and open the scroll?" The silence is deafening. Not even one voice ventures an answer. There is "no one in heaven or on earth or under the earth [who] could open the scroll or even look inside it."[14]

At this, John weeps uncontrollably. And suddenly, he is no longer merely a spectator. One of the elders approaches him and says, "Do not weep! See, the Lion of the tribe of Judah, the Root of David, has triumphed. He is able to open the scroll and its seven seals."[15]

In an instant John sees not a lion but a lamb that appears to have been slain. The twenty-four elders fall down and worship

John and the Old Testament

Of the 404 verses that comprise the 22 chapters of the book of Revelation, 278 verses contain one or more allusions to an Old Testament passage. John had so thoroughly pondered the Old Testament that when it came to recording the import of his visions of God and of heaven, he expressed himself by using phrases borrowed from the prophets of Israel. Therefore, in attempting to understand John's symbolism, we must consider not only the book itself, but also his use of the Old Testament.

Bruce Metzger, *Breaking the Code: Understanding the Book of Revelation*, 13 the lamb, and they sing a triumphal song: "You are worthy to take the scroll and to open its seals, because you were slain, and with your blood you purchased for God persons from every tribe and language and people and nation."[16]

If that is not enough to convince him, John then sees hundreds of thousands of angels encircling the throne, singing out in unison, "Worthy is the Lamb, who was slain, to receive power and wealth and wisdom and strength and honor and glory and praise!"[17]

Here is John secluded on the Island of Patmos, enthralled by a most magnificent vision that brings him right back to the day he, the lone apostle, was at the foot of the cross. So far he appears to comprehend the message of this incredible visual schoolroom. All of the elders and creatures are worshiping the Lamb. But now things become more complicated and mysterious.

The Lamb has taken an extraordinary scroll, tightly bound with seven seals. When he opens each of the first four seals, the four creatures around the throne in unison bid John to come. And as each seal is opened, a horse of a different color appears, the meaning of each briefly explained. Then the remaining three seals are opened—all seven of them, when opened, revealing what will happen at the end of time.

But the end of time relates as well to the beginning of time. The world created by God, John learns, will be destroyed by God. John's vision draws from his own study of the Torah. The number of those who are sealed by God is 144,000, twelve thousand from each tribe: Judah, Reuben, Gad, Asher, Naphtali, Manasseh, Simeon, Levi, Issachar, Zebulun, Joseph, and Benjamin.

Again John is brought into the vision personally when an elder asks him outright to identify those who are parading around in white robes. Is this a trick question? John dares not venture an answer. Trembling in fear and awe, not wanting to be wrong at this critical moment, his response is classic: *Sir, surely you know.* And, indeed, the elder does. Those in white robes have come through the great tribulation. "They have washed their robes and made them white in the blood of the Lamb."[18]

After many more breathtaking events, John is again approached—this time by a voice from heaven: "Go, take the scroll that lies open in the hand of the angel who is standing on the sea and on the land."[19] John is now an active participant, no longer on the sidelines. He must enter the arena and approach a massive and most formidable creature. So he goes up to the angel and asks for the small scroll. The angel tells him to eat it. It will taste sweet while at the same time making him feel like throwing up. "I took the little scroll from the angel's hand and ate it," John testifies. "It tasted as sweet as honey in my mouth, but when I had eaten it, my stomach turned sour."[20]

With an upset stomach, John sits back and watches the war in heaven between Michael with his angels and the dragon with his army. The dragon, who is thrown out of heaven and lands on earth, is the devil, who then gives his power to a beast,

Dragons Within, Dragons Without

Throughout John's Apocalypse, as the frightening images unfold, all the angels and the figures of Christ himself continually tell John: "Do not fear." I find the angels of Revelation refreshingly terrifying—calmly they stand at the four corners of the earth, holding the four winds; they plant one foot on land, one on the sea and, roaring like lions, invoke seven thunders. No warm, fuzzy gift-shop angels, nothing for the New Age or "personal spirituality" markets. I love the story of the red dragon with seven heads and ten horns, and his defeat at the hands of the archangel Michael. . . . Dragons within, dragons without. Evil so pervasive that only the poetry of apocalypse can imagine its defeat. And to do that it takes us to the limits of metaphor, of human sense, the limits of imagining and understanding. It pushes us against all our boundaries and suggests that the end of our control—our ideologies, our plans, our competence, our expertise, our professionalism, our power—is the beginning of God's reign. It asks us to believe that only the good remains, at the end, and directs us toward carefully tending it here and now. We will sing a new song. Singing and praise will be all that remains. As a poet, that's a vision, and a promise, I can live with.

Kathleen Norris, *The Cloister Walk*, 213–14

identified by the number 666, who arises out of the sea. The beast deceives the inhabitants of earth, luring them away from God into lives of unspeakable degradation. God is merciless and continues to pour his wrath out in the form of biological warfare and environmental destruction. This devastation is carried out in part by seven angels who pour out seven bowls of God's wrath in the form of seven plagues.

Now John is suddenly transported by an angel into the desert. Here he sees Babylon, with whom the kings of earth have all committed adultery. She is depicted as a great harlot sitting on a seven-headed, ten-horned beast, clad in red and purple, and "glittering with gold, precious stones and pearls."[21] At this point John is absolutely flabbergasted, but an angel explains to him that when Babylon (the great harlot) falls there is great rejoicing because now "the wedding of the Lamb has come, and his bride has made herself ready."[22]

The angel dictates to John God's very words: "Blessed are those who are invited to the wedding supper of the Lamb!"[23] John is so carried away that he falls down

Seven bowls of God's wrath

before the angel and worships him. But the angel tells him to worship God alone.

Now all the stops are out, and the narrative in this action-filled visionary production races forward. A rider on a white horse leading a white-robed army comes down from heaven and engages in battle with the beast and his armies from all the nations of the world. In fact, an angel cries out to the birds flying overhead to come to a great supper featuring the flesh of all the followers of the beast who will be slain.

The beast is thrown alive into the lake of fire. The kings and their armies are all killed by a sword that comes out of the mouth of the rider on the white horse, "and all the birds gorged themselves on their flesh."[24]

The dragon is bound for a thousand years, during which time the 144,000 martyrs come to life and reign with Christ. After that, the final judgment. Then from heaven comes down "the Holy City, the new Jerusalem . . . prepared as a bride beautifully dressed for her husband."[25] Then one of the angels bids John come:

> And he carried me away in the Spirit to a mountain great and high, and showed me the Holy City, Jerusalem, coming down out of heaven from God. It shone with the glory of God, and its brilliance was like that of a very precious jewel, like a jasper, clear as crystal. It had a great, high wall with twelve gates, and with twelve angels at the gates. On the gates were written the names of the twelve tribes of Israel.[26]

John continues his vivid description. The angel gives him a guided tour of this fantastic city, which is lighted not from the sun or moon but from the glory of God. The only ones who will ever enter its gates are "those whose names are written in the Lamb's book of life."[27] The angel then shows John the crystal river, bordered by fruit trees and flowing from the throne of God. John is so awestricken that again he falls prostrate in worship before the angel.

Now the grand apocalyptic vision is over. Jesus announces the finale, telling John, "I am coming soon. . . . I am the Alpha and the Omega, the First and the Last, the Beginning and the End. . . . I am the Root and the Offspring of David, and the bright Morning Star. . . . Let the one who is thirsty come. . . . Yes, I am coming soon."[28]

John then offers the benediction: "Amen. Come, Lord Jesus. The grace of the Lord Jesus be with God's people. Amen."[29]

Concluding Observations

It is fitting that John, the intimate disciple of Jesus, should live to be a gray-haired old man and carry the gospel right into the era that now becomes *church history*. One could only wish that he had been as open as Paul was with his personal struggles and relationships—though Paul, unlike John, was tight lipped about his visionary experience.

John refers to himself in the third person throughout his Gospel narrative and gives the reader no personal details in his letters, while identifying himself very clearly as the author of Revelation. Paul is the opposite, relating many personal stories and freely revealing his emotions in his letters, while referring to himself in the third person when he tells of his heavenly experience: "I know a man in Christ who fourteen years ago was caught up to the third heaven. Whether it was in the body or out of the body I do not know—God knows."[30]

Paul sets his experience in the distant past, while John writes his on the very Lord's Day it begins. John goes into great detail on his heavenly experiences and repeatedly puts himself right in the middle of the action. Paul is very reserved in his descriptions. His third heaven is an experience to which others might easily relate. John's is a one-of-a-kind experience so striking that it stands alone and as such forms the final book of the Bible.

In the end John returns to Ephesus with his almost-too-hot-to-handle scroll. Here he continues in his pastoral ministry. His scroll, however, was probably not circulated until after his death.

"Little Children, Love One Another"

There is a church tradition, which says, that when John was evidently an old man in Ephesus, he had to be carried to the church in the arms of his disciples. At these meetings, he was accustomed to say no more than, "Little children, love one another!" After a time, the disciples wearied at always hearing the same words, asked, "Master, why do you always say this?" "It is the Lord's command," was his reply. "And if this alone be done, it is enough!"

William Selkirk, *The Jerusalem Conspiracy*, 39–40

Further Reading

Carson, D. A. *The Gospel according to John*. Grand Rapids: Eerdmans, 1990.

deSilva, David. *Seeing Things John's Way: The Rhetoric of the Book of Revelation*. Louisville: Westminster John Knox, 2009.

Metzger, Bruce. *Breaking the Code: Understanding the Book of Revelation*. Nashville: Abingdon, 2008.

EPILOGUE

> The Bible stands though the hills may tumble,
> It will firmly stand when the earth shall crumble;
> I will plant my feet on its firm foundation,
> For the Bible stands.

These are the words to the chorus of a rousing hymn by Haldor Lillenas that I often sang in decades past when I was actively involved in three different Bible churches. All else could be wiped away, we were firmly convinced, but the Bible would stand forever.

Nearly two millennia have passed since John's grand psychedelic vision. For Christians the end is always near. Signs seem to be everywhere. The hills tumble and the earth crumbles. Yet here we are in the twenty-first century, and the Bible is still standing.

And so shall it ever be.

NOTES

Introduction

1. Neh. 5:9, 11.
2. Beloit College, 2012, http://www.beloit.edu/mindset/2016/.

Chapter 1 Adam, Eve, and the Boys

1. Rom. 5:12 KJV.
2. 2 Cor. 11:3 NIV.
3. Apart from passing mentions in Isaiah 54:9 and Ezekiel 14:20.
4. Matt. 24:37 and Luke 17:26, NIV; 1 Pet. 3:20; 2 Pet. 2:5; Heb. 11:7.
5. Gen. 3:1.
6. Gen. 3:4–5.
7. Gen. 3:11.
8. Gen. 3:12 NIV.
9. Gen. 3:19.
10. Gen. 3:22.
11. Gen. 4:1.
12. Gen. 4:6–7.
13. Gen. 4:9 NIV.
14. Gen. 5:29 NIV.
15. 2 Pet. 2:5 NIV.
16. Gen. 6:4.
17. Gen. 6:1–3 NIV.
18. Gen. 6:7 NIV.
19. Gen. 6:20.
20. Gen. 9:13 NIV.
21. Gen. 11:4.

Chapter 2 Abraham and Sarah

1. Stott, "The Living God Is a Missionary God," 2, 3.
2. Gen. 12:2–3 NIV.
3. Gen. 12:11–13.
4. Gen. 12:14–15.
5. Gen. 12:19.
6. Gen. 13:10.
7. Gen. 15:4–5.
8. Gen. 15:18–21.
9. Gen. 17:10–11.
10. Gen. 20:13 NIV.
11. Gal. 4:30 NIV.
12. Gen. 16:5 NIV.
13. Gen. 16:8 NIV.
14. Gen. 16:8–10 NIV.
15. Gen. 16:12 NIV.
16. Gen. 16:13 NIV.
17. Gen. 21:12 NIV.
18. Gen. 21:14 NIV.
19. Heb. 11:12 NIV.
20. Luke 17:28–32 NIV.

Chapter 3 Isaac and Rebekah

1. Gen. 16:11–12.
2. Gen. 16:10 NIV.
3. Gen. 17:20.
4. Gen. 21:13.
5. Gen. 21:17.
6. Gen. 21:20–21.
7. Gen. 25:13–15 NIV.
8. Gen. 24:50–51.
9. Gen. 25:23.

Chapter 4 Jacob and Esau

1. Rom. 9:13 KJV.
2. Obad. 10, 18.
3. Heb. 12:16–17.
4. Rom. 9:13 KJV.
5. Rom. 9:13.
6. Matt. 2:18.
7. Gen. 28:20.
8. Gen. 29:21.
9. Gen. 29:26–27.
10. Gen. 30:25–26.
11. Gen. 31:34–35.
12. Gen. 31:40–41.
13. Gen. 27:39–40.
14. Gen. 30:15.
15. Gen. 49:29–32 NIV.

Chapter 5 Joseph and His Siblings

1. Heb. 11:22 NIV.
2. Gen. 41:41–43.
3. Rom. 8:28.
4. Gen. 47:21.
5. Gen. 49:22–25.
6. Gen. 34:11–12.
7. Gen. 34:31.
8. Gen. 35:22.

9. Gen. 42:22 NIV.
10. Gen. 49:3–4.
11. Gen. 49:5–7.
12. Matt. 1:2.
13. Gen. 49:8–10.

Chapter 6 Moses

1. Exod. 2:14.
2. Exod. 3:4.
3. Exod. 3:10.
4. Exod. 3:14 NIV.
5. Exod. 3:19.
6. Exod. 3:22.
7. Exod. 4:24–25.
8. Exod. 12:38.
9. Exod. 14:14.
10. Exod. 18:11 NIV.
11. Exod. 18:17.
12. Exod. 19:4–5 NIV.
13. Exod. 21:7, 17.
14. Exod. 22:21–22.
15. Num. 11:11–15.
16. Num. 21:8.
17. Num. 20:26 NIV.
18. Deut. 34:10–12 NIV.
19. Num. 22:18.
20. Num. 22:30.
21. Num. 23:8.
22. Num. 31:16 NIV.
23. Exod. 15:21.
24. Mic. 6:4 NIV.
25. Heb. 11:24–27 NIV.

Chapter 7 Joshua and Caleb

1. 2 Chron. 8:7–8 NIV.
2. Num. 11:28–29.
3. Deut. 31:23 KJV.
4. Josh. 1:2–3.
5. Josh. 3:7–8.
6. Josh. 3:16.
7. Josh. 4:6–7.
8. Josh. 10:11.
9. Josh. 10:14.
10. Josh. 23:2–3, 6.
11. Josh. 24:15 KJV.
12. Josh. 24:25–26.
13. Num. 13:27–28.
14. Num. 13:30.
15. Num. 14:11–12.
16. Josh. 14:11.
17. Josh. 2:5.
18. Josh. 2:9–10.

Chapter 8 Deborah, Gideon, and Samson

1. Judg. 1:2 NIV.
2. Judg. 17:6 KJV.
3. Judg. 3:21–22.
4. Judg. 4:7 NIV.
5. Judg. 4:8–9.
6. Judg. 5:7–8.
7. Judg. 6:15.
8. Judg. 7:20.
9. Judg. 8:27 NIV.
10. Judg. 11:35.
11. Judg. 14:14.
12. Judg. 14:18.
13. Judg. 19:30.

Chapter 9 Naomi, Ruth, and Hannah

1. Ruth 1:8–9.
2. Ruth 1:15.
3. Ruth 4:16–17.
4. Ruth 1:16–17 KJV.
5. Ruth 2:7.
6. Ruth 2:10.
7. Ruth 2:12.
8. 1 Sam. 1:14.
9. 1 Sam. 1:15 NIV.
10. 1 Sam. 2:1.

Chapter 10 Samuel and King Saul

1. 1 Sam.15:22 NIV.
2. 1 Sam. 7:12 KJV.
3. 1 Sam. 9:20.
4. 1 Sam. 12:2–3.
5. 1 Sam. 15:33 NIV.
6. 1 Sam. 16:1.
7. 1 Sam. 11:7.
8. 1 Sam. 19:23–24.
9. 1 Sam. 24:16–17.
10. 1 Sam. 28:19.

Chapter 11 King David

1. Ps. 23:1–4 KJV.
2. 1 Sam. 17:34–35 NIV.
3. 1 Sam. 17:28 NIV.
4. 1 Sam. 18:7.
5. 2 Sam. 1:26 NIV.
6. 2 Sam. 15:13–14.
7. 2 Sam. 18:33 KJV.
8. 2 Sam. 19:5–7 NIV.
9. 1 Kings 2:1–2.
10. Ps. 24 KJV.

Chapter 12 Solomon and a Succession of Kings

1. 1 Kings 3:12–13 NIV.
2. 1 Kings 11:4 NIV.
3. Eccles. 1:1–2 NIV.
4. 1 Kings 3:8.
5. 1 Kings 9:21 NIV.
6. 1 Kings 6:22.
7. 2 Chron. 6:32–33.
8. 1 Kings 9:13.
9. 1 Kings 11:11–13.
10. 2 Chron. 15:9.
11. 1 Kings 18:17.

Chapter 13 Elijah and Elisha

1. 2 Kings 2:12 KJV.
2. Mal. 4:5 NIV.
3. Luke 1:17 NIV.
4. Matt. 17:11–12 NIV.
5. 1 Kings 17:3 KJV.
6. 1 Kings 17:4 KJV.
7. 1 Kings 17:18.
8. 1 Kings 18:23–24.
9. 1 Kings 21:19, 23.
10. 2 Kings 3:13.

Chapter 14 Nehemiah, Ezra, Esther, and Job

1. Ezra 9:3 NIV.
2. Ezra 9:6–7, 14.
3. Neh. 4:4–5 NIV.
4. Neh. 5:7, 9, 11.
5. Neh. 5:19 NASB.
6. Esther 1:20 NIV.
7. Esther 4:12–14.
8. Esther 8:17.
9. Job 1:21 ESV.
10. Job 2:10.
11. Job 4:7–9 NIV.
12. Job 6:3, 9.

13. Job 6:25.
14. Job 9:12.
15. Job 9:32–35 NIV.
16. Job 42:7.

Chapter 15 Isaiah, Jeremiah, Ezekiel, and Daniel

1. Isa. 6:5–8; Isa. 6:8 KJV.
2. Isa. 7:14–17.
3. Isa. 8:11.
4. Isa. 60:1–3 NIV.
5. Isa. 49:15 NIV.
6. Jer. 1:6.
7. Jer. 1:9.
8. Jer. 3:1.
9. Jer. 6:10.
10. Jer. 9:1.
11. Jer. 20:7–8.
12. Jer. 22:3.
13. Jer. 43:10–11.
14. Ezek. 5:9.
15. Ezek. 23:3, 12–13, 18, 44.
16. Ezek. 17:3, 5.
17. Ezek. 19:10–11.

Chapter 16 Jonah and the Minor Prophets

1. Hab. 2:4.
2. Matt. 2:5 NIV.
3. Matt. 12:40 NIV.
4. Acts 2:17–21 NIV, quoting Joel 2:28–32.
5. Mic. 6:8 NIV.
6. Mal. 4:5 NIV.
7. 2 Kings 14:25 NIV.
8. Jon. 1:9 NIV.
9. Jon. 2:2 KJV.
10. Jon. 2:2–7 NIV.
11. Jon. 3:4.
12. Jon. 4:11 NIV.
13. Hosea 1:2.
14. Hosea 2:2, 5; 3:1.
15. Hosea 4:1, 2, 10; 7:4, 6.
16. Amos 7:14–15.
17. Amos 7:17; emphasis original.
18. Amos 4:1.
19. Amos 4:13.
20. Mic. 5:2 KJV.

Chapter 17 Mary, Joseph, and John the Baptist

1. Matt. 2:6 NIV.
2. Luke 2:48.
3. John 2:4.
4. Matt. 25:1–13.
5. Luke 1:43 NIV.
6. John 1:23 KJV.
7. Matt. 3:7–9 NLT.

Chapter 18 Jesus of Nazareth

1. Matt. 6:28–29 KJV.
2. Matt. 11:28–30 KJV.
3. Matt. 8:20 NKJV.
4. John 14:1–3 KJV.
5. Mark 9:44, 46, 48.
6. Luke 4:18–19 NIV, quoting Isa. 61:1–2.
7. Matt. 27:46 KJV, quoting Ps. 22:1.
8. Luke 2:49.
9. Matt. 3:17 KJV.
10. Luke 4:12.
11. John 1:41.
12. John 2:11 NIV.
13. Luke 6:27–35.
14. Matt. 24:37, 40–41, 51; 25:41 NIV.
15. John 14:1, 6, 25–27 NKJV.
16. Luke 23:34 KJV.
17. Matt. 27:46 KJV.
18. Matt. 28:19–20 KJV.
19. Acts 1:11.
20. John 21:25 NIV.

Chapter 19 Mary Magdalene and the Scandal of Sychar

1. Mark 5:34 NIV.
2. John 8:11 NIV.
3. John 4:9.
4. John 4:42 NIV.
5. Luke 10:41–42.

Chapter 20 Andrew, Thomas, Judas, and Stephen

1. Matt. 10:35, 37 NIV.
2. John 12:32 NIV.
3. John 14:6 NIV.
4. John 20:29 NIV.
5. Acts 5:3–4.
6. Acts 7:52–53 NIV.
7. Acts 8:32–33 NIV.

Chapter 21 Peter

1. Matt. 17:17 NIV.
2. 1 Cor. 9:5.
3. Matt. 16:17–19 NIV.
4. Matt. 16:23 NIV.
5. Acts 3:6.
6. Gal. 2:7.
7. 2 Tim. 4:7 NIV.

Chapter 22 The Apostle Paul

1. 2 Cor. 13:14 NIV.
2. Phil. 3:10 NRSV.
3. Acts 9:4–5.
4. Acts 13:10.
5. Acts 13:49.
6. Acts 17:22–23.
7. Acts 18:6 NIV.
8. Acts 18:9–10.
9. Acts 19:25–27 NIV.
10. Acts 26:28.

Chapter 23 Barnabas, Silas, and Priscilla and Aquila

1. Phil. 1:5–8 NLT.
2. 2 Tim. 1:15 NIV.
3. 2 Tim. 1:16.
4. 2 Tim. 4:10 NASB.
5. Gal. 1:6–7, 10 NIV.
6. Phil. 1:3–5 NIV.
7. Acts 13:2 NIV.
8. Acts 14:15 KJV.
9. 1 Cor. 9:4–8.
10. Acts 15:26.
11. Rom. 16:3–4 NIV.
12. 2 Tim. 1:5 NIV.
13. 2 Tim. 1:2 NIV.
14. 2 Tim. 1:3–4.
15. 2 Tim. 4:13, 21.
16. Phil. 1:1–2 NIV.
17. John 1:29 KJV.
18. Acts 18:27 NLT.
19. Acts 18:28 NIV.
20. 1 Cor. 4:1 KJV.
21. 1 Cor. 3:6 KJV.

22. Titus 3:13.
23. Phil. 1:15–18 NIV.
24. Phil. 4:3 NIV.
25. Phil. 2:25–30 NIV.
26. Phil. 3:2 NIV.

Chapter 24 John of Patmos

1. John 13:34–35 NIV.
2. 1 John 3:16–18 NIV.
3. 1 John 4:20–21 NIV.
4. Mark 9:38 NIV.
5. Matt. 20:22–23 NLT.
6. Acts 8:16 NIV.
7. Rev. 1:5 NIV.
8. Rev. 1:11 NIV.
9. Rev. 1:18 NIV.
10. Rev. 2:4 NIV.
11. Rev. 3:10 NIV.
12. Rev. 3:15–16 NIV.
13. Rev. 3:19–22 NIV.
14. Rev. 5:2–3 NIV.
15. Rev. 5:5 NIV.
16. Rev. 5:9 NIV.
17. Rev. 5:12 NIV.
18. Rev. 7:14 NIV.
19. Rev. 10:8.
20. Rev. 10:10 NIV.
21. Rev. 17:4 NIV.
22. Rev. 19:7 NIV.
23. Rev. 19:9 NIV.
24. Rev. 19:21 NIV.
25. Rev. 21:2 NIV.
26. Rev. 21:10–12 NIV.
27. Rev. 21:27 NIV.
28. Rev. 22:12–13, 16–17, 20 NIV.
29. Rev. 22:20–21 NIV.
30. 2 Cor. 12:2 NIV.

REFERENCE LIST

Ackerman, Jane. *Elijah: Prophet of Carmel*. Washington, DC: ICS Publications, 2003.

Ackerman, Susan. *Warrior, Dancer, Seductress, Queen: Women in Judges and Biblical Israel*. New York: Doubleday, 1998.

Adeney, Miriam. *A Time for Risking: Priorities for Women*. Vancouver, BC: Regent College Publishing, 1987.

Agar, John. "Naked Man Tells Hastings Police: God Wants All to Be Peaceful." MLive.com. Published September 27, 2011. http://www.mlive.com/news/grand-rapids/index.ssf/2011/09/naked_man_tells_hastings_polic.html.

Allen, Roland. *Missionary Methods: St. Paul's or Ours?* Grand Rapids: Eerdmans, 1962.

Apples of Gold in Pictures of Silver. "Abraham—Father of Believing." Last modified January 1, 2012. http://www.picturesofsilver.com/Teachings/02genAbe1.htm.

Aquinas, Thomas. *Commentary on the Book of Job*. Translated by Brian Mulladay. http://dhspriory.org/thomas/SSJob.htm#0.

Baker, Donald. *Joshua: The Power of God's Promises*. Downers Grove, IL: InterVarsity, 1999.

Bakhos, Carol. *Ishmael on the Border*. Albany, NY: SUNY Press, 2006.

Bankson, Marjory Zoet. *Seasons of Friendship: Naomi and Ruth as a Pattern*. Philadelphia: Innisfree Press, 1987.

Barth, Karl. *The Epistle to the Romans*. Translated by Edwyn C. Hoskyns. London: Oxford University Press, 1933.

Batuman, Elif. "The Sanctuary: The World's Oldest Temple and the Dawn of Civilization." *New Yorker*, Dec. 19 & 26, 2011, http://www.newyorker.com/reporting/2011/12/19/111219fa_fact_batuman#.

Baxter, J. Sidlow. *Explore the Book*. Grand Rapids: Zondervan, 1960.

Bell, Rob. *Velvet Elvis: Repainting the Christian Faith*. Grand Rapids: Zondervan, 2006.

Bellis, Alice Ogden. *Helpmates, Harlots, and Heroes: Women's Stories in the Hebrew Bible*. Louisville: John Knox, 1994.

Beloit College. *The Mindset List*. 2016 ed. Beloit, WI: Beloit College, 2016. http://www.beloit.edu/mindset/2016/.

Berger, Peter. *A Far Glory*. New York: Macmillan, 1992.

Berlin, Adele. "Bathsheba: Bible." In *Jewish Women: A Comprehensive Historical Encyclopedia*. N.p.: Jewish Women's Archive, 2009. http://jwa.org/encyclopedia/article/bathsheba-bible.

Berry, Wendell. *Jayber Crow*. Washington, DC: Counterpoint, 2000.

Biale, David. *Eros and the Jews: From Biblical Israel to Contemporary America*. Berkeley: University of California Press, 1997.

Birnbaum, Toby H., and Paul J. Herskovitz. "The Biblical Story of Joseph: Lessons in Servant Leadership." http://aa.utpb.edu/media/leadership-journal-files/2009-archives/The%20Biblical%20Story%20of%20Joseph.pdf.

Boadt, Lawrence. *Reading the Old Testament: An Introduction*. Mahwah, NJ: Paulist Press, 1984.

Boice, James Montgomery. *Daniel: An Expositional Commentary*. Grand Rapids: Baker Books, 2006.

Booth, Robert. "Did Jephthah Kill His Daughter? An Examination of Judges 11:29–40." April 15, 2008. http://rwbooth.files.wordpress.com/2009/05/did-jephthah-kill-his-daughter-final-pdf.pdf.

Borgman, Paul. *David, Saul, and God: Rediscovering an Ancient Story*. New York: Oxford University Press, 2008.

———. *Genesis: The Story We Haven't Heard*. Downers Grove, IL: InterVarsity, 2001.

Borowski, Oded. *Agriculture in Ancient Israel*. Winona Lake, IN: Eisenbrauns, 1987.

Bourgeault, Cynthia. *The Meaning of Mary Magdalene: Discovering the Woman at the Heart of Christianity*. Boston: Shambhala, 2010.

Bratcher, Dennis. "Ba'al Worship in the Old Testament." The Voice: Biblical and Theological Resources for Growing Christians. Last modified November 11, 2011. http://www.crivoice.org/baal.html.

Brown, Tina. "Dreams and Visions in the Old Testament." webjournals.ac.edu.au. http://webjournals.ac.edu.au/journals/PCBC/200801/04-dreams-and-visions-in-the-old-testament/.

Bruce, F. F. *The Book of Acts*. Rev. ed. Grand Rapids: Eerdmans, 1988.

———. *Paul: Apostle of the Heart Set Free*. Grand Rapids: Eerdmans, 2000.

Buechner, Frederick. *Peculiar Treasures: A Biblical Who's Who*. San Francisco: HarperCollins, 1979.

———. *Secrets in the Dark: A Life of Sermons*. San Francisco: HarperOne, 2007.

Buelow, Andrew. "Towards an Old Testament Theology of Prostitution." Course paper, Phoenix Seminary, submitted March 22, 2010. http://streetlighttucson.com/streetlight/Prostitution%20in%20OT.pdf.

Bulkeley, Tim. "Hebrew Narrative: Humour and Irony." http://www.bible.gen.nz/0/humour.htm.

Calvin, John. *Commentary on Genesis*. Vol. 1. Christian Classics Ethereal Library. http://www.ccel.org/ccel/calvin/calcom01.

———. *Commentary on Joel, Amos, Obadiah*. Vol. 2. Christian Classics Ethereal Library. http://www.ccel.org/ccel/calvin/calcom27.iv.ii.i.html.

———. *Commentary on Joshua*. Christian Classics Ethereal Library. http://www.ccel.org/ccel/calvin/calcom07.xiii.i.html.

———. Commentary on Numbers 22:28. Christian Classics Ethereal Library. http://m.ccel.org/study/Bible:Num.22.28?device=mobile.

———. *Institutes of the Christian Religion*. Translated by Henry Beveridge. Peabody, MA: Hendrickson, 2008.

Carson, D. A. *The Gospel according to John*. Grand Rapids: Eerdmans, 1990.

CatholicCulture.org. "Catholic Activity: Day Two ~ Activities for the Feast of St. Stephen." http://www.catholicculture.org/culture/liturgicalyear/activities/view.cfm?id=988.

Catholic Online. "St. Gabriel, the Archangel." http://www.catholic.org/saints/saint.php?saint_id=279.

Chiffolo, Anthony F., and Rayner W. Hesse Jr. *Cooking with the Bible: Recipes for Biblical Meals*. Westport, CT: Greenwood, 2009.

Chilton, Bruce. *Mary Magdalene: A Biography*. New York: Doubleday, 2005.

Constable, Thomas L. "Notes on 1 Samuel." 2012 ed. http://www.soniclight.com/constable/notes/pdf/1samuel.pdf.

Cooke, Richard. *New Testament*. London: SCM, 2009.

Craigie, Peter C., et al. *Jeremiah 1–25*. Word Biblical Commentary 26. Dallas: Word, 1991.

Deffinbaugh, Bob. "The Life and Times of Elisha the Prophet." Bible.org. http://bible.org/seriespage/life-and-times-elisha-prophet%E2%80%

94-elisha%E2%80%99s-accreditation-2-kings-2198211327.

deSilva, David. *Seeing Things John's Way: The Rhetoric of the Book of Revelation*. Louisville: Westminster John Knox, 2009.

Diamond, Jared M. *Guns, Germs, and Steel: The Fates of Human Societies*. New York: Norton, 2005.

Duguid, Iain M. *Esther and Ruth: Reformed Expository Commentary*. Phillipsburg, NJ: P&R, 2005.

———. *The NIV Application Commentary: Ezekiel*. Grand Rapids: Zondervan, 1999.

Edwards, Jonathan. "Natural Men in a Dreadful Condition." Sermon delivered to Native Americans in Stockbridge, MA, February, 1753. http://www.sermonindex.net/modules/articles/index.php?view=article&aid=3378.

Elazar, Daniel J. "Jacob and Esau and the Emergence of the Jewish People." Jerusalem Center for Public Affairs. http://www.jcpa.org/dje/articles/jacob-esau.htm.

Eusebius. *Ecclesiastical History*. Translated by Frederick Cruse. Grand Rapids: Baker, 1955.

Exum, Baxter T. "King Uzziah." Sermon (no. 1110) delivered at Four Lakes Church of Christ, Madison, WI, April 10, 2011. Madison, WI: Four Lakes Church of Christ, 2011. http://www.fourlakescoc.org/Sermons/websermonupdates/1110_web.pdf.

Feiler, Bruce. *Abraham: A Journey to the Heart of Three Faiths*. New York: William Morrow, 2002.

———. *America's Prophet: Moses and the American Story*. New York: William Morrow, 2009.

Finkelstein, Israel, and Neil Asher Silberman. *David and Solomon: In Search of the Bible's Sacred Kings*. New York: Simon and Schuster, 2006.

Finney, Charles G. "Forfeiting Birth-Right Blessing." Sermon delivered May 13, 1846. Online edition 1999. http://www.gospeltruth.net/1846OE/460513_birth_right.htm.

Flemming, Dean E. *Contextualization in the New Testament: Patterns for Theology and Mission*. Downers Grove, IL: InterVarsity, 2005.

Fletcher, Elizabeth. "Clothes." Bible Archaeology. http://www.bible-archaeology.info/clothes.

Frey, Stephanie. "Living with Martha." *Christian Century*, July 13, 2004, 16.

Gaubert, Henri. *Isaac and Jacob: God's Chosen Ones*. Translated by Lancelot Sheppard. New York: Hastings House, 1969.

Gold, Nora. "Rachel and Leah: A Jewish Model of Sisterhood." *Kerem: Creative Explorations in Judaism* 12 (2010): 96–105. http://www.noragold.com/publisher/articleview/frmArticleID/25/.

Gordon, Charlotte. *The Woman Who Named God: Abraham's Dilemma and the Birth of Three Faiths*. New York: Little, Brown, 2009.

Gow, Murray D. "Ruth." In *Theological Interpretation of the Old Testament*, edited by Kevin J. Vanhoozer, 102–10. Grand Rapids: Baker Academic, 2005.

Green, Gene L. "Peter: Apostolic Foundation." Unpublished paper, Wheaton College, 2010. Quoted with permission.

Halpern, Baruch. *David's Secret Demons: Messiah, Murderer, Traitor, King*. Grand Rapids: Eerdmans, 2003.

Hanson, K. C., and Douglas E. Oakman. *Palestine in the Time of Jesus: Social Structures and Social Conflicts*. Minneapolis: Augsburg, 1998.

Hardon, John A., SJ. "The Miracle Narratives in the Acts of the Apostles." http://www.therealpresence.org/archives/Miracles/Miracles_004.htm.

Hartin, Patrick J. *Apollos: Paul's Partner or Rival?* Collegeville, MN: Liturgical Press, 2009.

Hayes, John Haralson. *Introduction to the Bible*. Philadelphia: Westminster Press, 1971.

Hazony, Yoram. *The Dawn: Political Teachings of the Book of Esther*. Shalem Press, 2000.

Hobbins, John. "Breathing New Life into the Doctrine of Inerrancy." March 10, 2009. http://ancienthebrewpoetry.typepad.com/ancient_hebrew_poetry/2009/03/breathing-new-life-into-the-doctrine-of-inerrancy.html.

Hull, Gretchen Gaebelein. "Empowered to Serve." http://www.cbeinternational.org/?q=content/empowered-serve.

Hunter, David G. "Sex, Sin and Salvation: What Augustine Really Said." National Institute for the

Renewal of the Priesthood. http://www.jknirp.com/aug3.htm.

Jackson, Wayne. "Paul's Two-Year Roman Imprisonment." ChristianCourier.com. http://www.christiancourier.com/articles/144-pauls-two-year-roman-imprisonment.

———. "The Separation of Paul and Barnabas." ChristianCourier.com. http://www.christiancourier.com/articles/813-the-separation-of-paul-and-barnabas.

———. "Survey of the Major Prophets." ChristianCourier.com. http://www.christiancourier.com/articles/143–a-survey-of-the-major-prophets.

———. "Who Was John the Baptist?" ChristianCourier.com. http://www.christiancourier.com/articles/266-who-was-john-the-baptist.

Johnson, Rajkumar Boaz. "The Bible's Answer to Human Trafficking, Part 2." *Arise*, December 8, 2011. http://www2.cbeinternational.org/ARISE/bible-answer-human-trafficking_120811.htm.

Johnson, S. Lewis, Jr. "David and Jonathan." Sermon on 1 Sam. 18:1–20, 42 http://www.sljinstitute.net/sermons/topical_studies/pages/life_david3.html.

Katz, John. *The Dogs of Bedlam Farm*. New York: Random House, 2004.

Keathley, Hampton, IV. "Jacob." http://bible.org/article.

Keck, Chad. *Ordinarily Faithful: Life Lessons from the Judges*. Bloomington, IN: LifeWay, 2011.

Kirsch, Jonathan. *The Harlot by the Side of the Road*. New York: Random House, 1998.

———. *King David: The Real Life of the Man Who Ruled Israel*. New York: Ballantine, 2001.

———. *Moses: A Life*. New York: Random House Ballantine, 1998.

Klassen, William. *Judas: Betrayer or Friend of Jesus?* Minneapolis: Fortress, 1996.

Klein, Lillian R. *Deborah to Esther: Sexual Politics in the Hebrew Bible*. Minneapolis: Fortress, 2003.

Larkin, William J., Jr. *Acts*. IVP New Testament Commentary Series. Downers Grove, IL: InterVarsity, 1995.

Larson, Knute, and Kathy Dahlen. *Holman Old Testament Commentary: Ezra, Nehemiah, Esther*. Nashville: B & H Publishing Group, 2005.

Lewis, C. S. *Reflections on the Psalms*. New York: Harcourt, 1986.

Lockyer, Herbert. *All the Women of the Bible*. Grand Rapids: Zondervan, 1991.

Losch, Richard R. *All the People in the Bible*. Grand Rapids: Eerdmans, 2008.

Luther, Martin. *Lectures on Genesis 1–5*. Translated by George V. Schick. Vol. 1 of *Luther's Works*. St. Louis: Concordia, 1958.

Lyons, Eric. "Did Judas Die Twice?" Apologetics Press. http://www.apologeticspress.org/apcontent.aspx?category=6&article=1761.

MacArthur, John. *Twelve Ordinary Men: How the Master Shaped His Disciples for Greatness*. Nashville: Nelson, 2002.

Maclaren, Alexander. "Heroic Faith." Sermon on Ezra 8:22, 23, 31, 32. http://www.preceptaustin.org/maclaren_on_ezra.htm#hf.

———. "A Reformer's Schooling." Sermon on Nehemiah 1:1–11. http://www.preceptaustin.org/nehemiah_exposition_-_maclaren.htm#ARS.

Maloney, Robert P. "The Historical Mary." *America: The National Catholic Weekly*, December 19, 2005. http://www.americamagazine.org/content/article.cfm?article_id=4546.

Mariottini, Claude. "Deborah: A Judge in Israel." Blog entry. Dr. Claude Mariottini, Professor of Old Testament. April 2, 2009. http://doctor.claudemariottini.com/2009/04/deborah-judge-in-israel.html.

———. "Ur and Abraham." Blog entry. Dr. Claude Mariottini, Professor of Old Testament. February 28, 2006. http://doctor.claudemariottini.com/2006/02/ur-and-abraham-rejoinder-to-tim.html.

Martin, Malachi. "Footsteps of Abraham." *New York Times*, March 13, 1983. http://www.nytimes.com/1983/03/13/travel/footsteps-of-abraham-by-malachi-martin.html?pagewanted=all.

McCann, J. Clinton. *Judges: A Bible Commentary for Teaching and Preaching*. Louisville: Westminster John Knox, 2011.

McComiskey, Thomas Edward. *The Minor Prophets: An Exegetical and Expository Commentary*. Grand Rapids: Baker Academic, 2009.

McGrath, Alister. *The Journey: A Pilgrim in the Lands of the Spirit*. New York: G. K. Hall, 2000.

McKenzie, Steven L. *King David: A Biography*. New York: Oxford University Press, 2002.

McKnight, Scot. *The Jesus Creed: Loving God, Loving Others*. Brewster, MA: Paraclete Press, 2004.

———. *Turning to Jesus: The Sociology of Conversion in the Gospels*. Louisville: Westminster John Knox, 2002.

Meeks, Wayne A. "Paul's Mission and Letters." *Frontline*. April 1998. http://www.pbs.org/wgbh/pages/frontline/shows/religion/first/missions.html.

Meyer, F. B. *Great Men of the Bible*. Vol. 1. Grand Rapids: Zondervan, 1981.

Minnicks, Margaret. "Why Solomon Had 700 Wives and 300 Concubines." *Richmond Christian Education Examiner*, April 16, 2011. http://www.examiner.com/article/why-solomon-had-700-wives-and-300-concubines.

Moyers, Bill, ed. *Genesis: A Living Conversation*. New York: Doubleday, 1996.

Murphy, Catherine M. *John the Baptist: Prophet of Purity for a New Age*. Collegeville, MN: Liturgical Press, 2003.

Neusner, Jacob. *A Rabbi Talks with Jesus*. Montreal: McGill-Queen's University Press, 2000.

Norris, Kathleen. *Cloister Walk*. New York: Riverhead, 1996.

Nouwen, Henri J. M. *A Cry for Mercy*. New York: Doubleday, 1981.

Oursler, Fulton. *The Greatest Book Ever Written*. New York: Doubleday, 1951.

Painter, Franklin V. N. *Introduction to Bible Study: The Old Testament*. New York: Sibley & Co., 1911.

Pape, Dorothy. *In Search of God's Ideal Woman*. Downers Grove, IL: InterVarsity, 1976.

Peterson, Eugene. Interview. *Image* 62 (Summer 2009): 66–75.

———. *The Jesus Way*. Grand Rapids: Eerdmans, 2011.

———. "The Jonah Syndrome." *Leadership Journal*, Summer 1990. http://www.christianitytoday.com/le/1990/summer/9013038.html?start=2.

Piper, John. "Ruth: Sweet and Bitter Providence." Sermon on Ruth 1 delivered July 1, 1984. http://www.desiringgod.org/resource-library/sermons/ruth-sweet-and-bitter-providence.

Plotz, David. "Blogging the Bible." *Christianity Today*, April 2009, http://www.christianitytoday.com/ct/2009/april/2.64.html.

Pollock, John. *The Apostle: A Life of Paul*. Colorado Springs: David C. Cook, 1994.

Pritchard, Ray. *Fire and Rain: The Wild-Hearted Faith of Elijah*. Nashville: Broadman & Holman, 2007.

Ratzinger, Joseph (Pope Benedict XVI). *Jesus of Nazareth: Holy Week; From the Entrance into Jerusalem to the Resurrection*. San Francisco: Ignatius Press, 2011.

Reiss, Moshe. "Rebekah and Isaac and Their Children." *Bible Commentator*. http://www.moshereiss.org/messenger/03_rebekahandisaac/03_rebekahandisaac.html.

Remnick, David. "We Are Alive: Bruce Springsteen at Sixty-Two." *New Yorker*, July 30, 2012, http://www.newyorker.com/reporting/2012/07/30/120730fa_fact_remnick.

Rendsburg, Gary A. "The Fate of Slaves in Ancient Israel." *The Jewish Daily Forward*, February 4, 2005. http://www.forward.com/articles/2888/.

Richardson, Peter. *Herod: King of the Jews and Friend of the Romans*. Minneapolis: Fortress, 1999.

Roberts, David. "On the Road from Ur to Haran." Yahweh's Sword. http://www.yahwehsword.org/s-abraham/05_on_the_road_from_ur_to_haran.htm.

Robinson, Marilynne. *Housekeeping*. New York: Picador, 1980.

Rogers, Jay. "Jesus' Cousins Were the Apostles James and John." The Forerunner. August 28, 2007. http://www.forerunner.com/blog/jesus-cousins-were-the-apostles-james-and-john.

Roper, David. *Elijah: A Man like Us*. Grand Rapids: Discovery House, 1998.

Russell, Letty. "Women Quilting a Biblical Pattern." http://gbgm-umc.org/response/articles/quilting.html.

Saake, Jennifer. *Hannah's Hope: Seeking God's Heart in the Midst of Infertility*. Colorado Springs: NavPress, 2005.

Sayers, Dorothy. *Are Women Human?* Grand Rapids: Eerdmans, 2005.

Schaeffer, Francis A. *Joshua and the Flow of Biblical History*. Wheaton: Crossway, 1975.

Schaff, Philip. *A History of Christianity*. Vol. 1. Grand Rapids: Eerdmans, 1979.

———. *History of the Christian Church*. Vol. 1, *AD 1–100*. New York: Charles Scribner's Sons, 1910.

Schauss, Hayyim. *The Lifetime of a Jew throughout the Ages of Jewish History*. New York: Union of American Hebrew Congregations Press, 1950.

Selkirk, William. *The Jerusalem Conspiracy*. Victoria, BC: Trafford Publishing, 2004.

Smith, Calvin L. "What on Earth Was Peter Thinking?" King's Evangelical Divinity School. http://www.kingsdivinity.org/theological-articles?id=107.

Spiro, Rabbi Ken. "History Crash Course #18: David, the King." March 24, 2007. http://www.aish.com/jl/h/cc/48936837.html.

———. "History Crash Course #19: King Solomon." March 7, 2001. http://www.aish.com/jl/h/cc/48937102.html.

Spurgeon, C. H. "Caleb—The Man for the Times." Sermon delivered at the Metropolitan Tabernacle, Newington (London), November 1, 1863. http://www.spurgeon.org/sermons/0538.htm.

———. "Daniel Facing the Lions' Den." Sermon (no. 1154) delivered at the Metropolitan Tabernacle, Newington (London). http://www.spurgeon.org/sermons/1154.htm.

———. "Esther's Exaltation; or, Who Knoweth?" In Sermons of Rev. C. H. Spurgeon of London, 73–94. New York: Robert Carter and Brothers, 1885. http://books.google.com/books?id=HY9mm1SWAKQC&pg=PA73&lpg=PA73&dq=%22Esther's+Exaltation%22+spurgeon&source=bl&ots=jUh4M-WRrL&sig=ysBl7LTioHjN9L_7vxRI1s9wN7o&hl=en&ei=lxirSqmfN5OKsgP3mrDtBA&sa=X&oi=book_result&ct=result&resnum=1#v=onepage&q&f=false.

———. "Joseph Attacked by the Archers." http://www.reformedsermonarchives.com/sp16.htm.

———. "Lydia, the First European Convert." Sermon (no. 2222) delivered at the Metropolitan Tabernacle, Newington (London), September 20, 1891. http://www.spurgeon.org/sermons/2222.htm.

———. "A Merry Christmas." Sermon delivered at Exeter Hall, December 23, 1860. http://www.spurgeongems.org/vols7-9/chs352.pdf.

———. "Hannah: A Woman of a Sorrowful Spirit." In *Spurgeon's Sermons on Old Testament Women*, 57–70. Grand Rapids: Kregel Publications, 1994.

Stedman, Ray. "Hosea: The Prophet and the Prostitute." http://www.raystedman.org/bible-overview/adventuring/hosea-the-prophet-and-the-prostitute.

———. *Man of Faith: Learning from the Life of Abraham*. Portland, OR: Multnomah, 1986.

Stein, Robert H. *Jesus the Messiah: A Survey of the Life of Christ*. Downers Grove, IL: InterVarsity, 1996.

Stott, John R. W. "The Living God Is a Missionary God." In *Perspectives on the World Christian Movement*, edited by Ralph D. Winter and Steven Hawthorne, 3–9. Pasadena: William Carey Library, 2004.

Swindoll, Charles R. *Elijah: Man of Heroism and Humility*. Nashville: Word, 2008.

———. *Insights on 1 and 2 Timothy, Titus*. Grand Rapids: Zondervan, 2009.

———. *Job: A Man of Heroic Endurance*. Nashville: Nelson, 2009.

———. *Moses: A Man of Selfless Dedication*. Nashville: Nelson, 1999.

———. "Scriptural Insights with Chuck Swindoll—Saints like Me." *Zondervan Blog*. July 26, 2010. http://zondervan.typepad.com/zondervan/2010/07/scriptural-insights-with-chuck-swindoll-saints-like-me.html.

Taylor, Barbara Brown. "Escape from the Tomb." *Christian Century*, April 1, 1998, 339.

———. *When God Is Silent*. Boston: Rowman and Littlefield, 1998.

———. "The Wilderness Exam." February 21, 2010. http://day1.org/1756-the_wilderness_exam.

Thurston, Bonnie Bowman. *Preaching Mark*. Minneapolis: Augsburg Fortress, 2002.

Tucker, Ruth A. *Multiple Choices: Making Wise Decisions in a Complicated World*. Grand Rapids: Zondervan, 1992.

Twain, Mark. *The Adventures of Huckleberry Finn*. In *Tom Sawyer and Huckleberry Finn*. Wordsworth Classics. London: Wordsworth, 1992.

———. *Eve's Diary*. Reprint of the 1906 Harper & Brothers edition, Project Gutenberg, 2004. http://ww.gutenberg.org/files/8525/8525-h/8525-h.htm.

Vander Laan, Ray. *That the World May Know*. Teacher's Guide. Colorado Springs: Focus on the Family, 1995.

Visotzky, Burton L. *The Genesis of Ethics: How the Tormented Family of Genesis Leads Us to Moral Development*. New York: Crown, 1996.

Vorster, Willem. "Gospel, Genre." In *The Anchor Bible Dictionary*, ed. David Noel Freedman, 2:1077–79. New York: Doubleday, 1992.

Vreeland, G. D. *The Darker Side of Samuel, Saul and David*. XulonPress, 2007.

Walk Thru the Bible. *A Walk Thru the Life of Solomon: Pursuing a Heart of Integrity*. Grand Rapids: Baker Books, 2009.

Weitzman, Steven. *Solomon: The Lure of Wisdom*. New Haven: Yale University Press, 2011.

Wesley, John. The Journal of Rev. John Wesley. Sunday, July 15, 1739. London: J. Kershaw, 1827. http://books.google.com/books?id=s__4_HHCedgC&pg=PA202&lpg=PA202&dq=john+wesley+sermon+ezekiel+dry+bones&source=bl&ots=hFMWJaBeHk&sig=d71aHFc9Ht3lkf07QshQGA2WvnY&hl=en&ei=u_TcTp7tG6mLsQLYkZz7DQ&sa=X&oi=book_result&ct=result&resnum=5&sqi=2&ved=0CD4Q6AEwBA#v=onepage&q&f=false.

White, L. Michael. "The Jewish Diaspora." *Frontline*. April 1998. http://www.pbs.org/wgbh/pages/frontline/shows/religion/portrait/diaspora.html.

———. "Paul in Corinth," Frontline. April 1998. http://www.pbs.org/wgbh/pages/frontline/shows/religion/first/missions.html.

Whitefield, George. "Abraham's Offering Up His Son Isaac." http://www.reformedsermonarchives.com/whit3.htm.

Wiesel, Elie. *Messengers of God: Biblical Portraits and Legends*. New York: Random House, 1976.

Wikipedia. "Wine Bottle." Wikipedia. Accessed February 27, 2013. http://en.wikipedia.org/wiki/Wine_bottle.

Williams, Sandra S. "David and Abigail: A Non-Traditional View." http://www.sandrawilliams.org/David/david.html.

Wilson, Ralph. "Don't Despise the Day of Small Things." Joyful Heart Renewal Ministries. http://www.joyfulheart.com/encourag/small-tg.htm.

Wink, Walter. "Wrestling with God: Psychological Insights in Bible Study." In *Psychology and the Bible: From Genesis to Apocalyptic Vision*, edited by J. Harold Ellens and Wayne G. Rollins, 2:9–22. Westport, CT: Praeger, 2004.

Witherington, Ben. "The Martyrdom of the Zebedee Brothers." Ben Witherington (blog), February 4, 2007. http://benwitherington.blogspot.com/2007/02/martyrdom-of-zebedee-brothers.html.

Wood, John A. "War in the Old Testament." In *Peace and War*, 11–17, edited by Robert B. Kruschwitz. Christian Reflection: A Series in Faith and Ethics. Waco, TX: Center for Christian Ethics at Baylor University, 2004. http://www.baylor.edu/christianethics/peaceandwararticlewood.pdf.

Wright, N. T. *Paul: In Fresh Perspective*. Minneapolis: Fortress, 2009.

Yancey, Philip. *Disappointment with God*. Grand Rapids: Zondervan, 1988.

———. *The Jesus I Never Knew*. Grand Rapids: Zondervan, 2002.

———. "Jesus, the Reluctant Miracle Worker." *Christianity Today*, May 19, 1997. http://www.christianitytoday.com/ct/1997/may19/7t6080.html?start=2.

———. *Where Is God When It Hurts?* Grand Rapids: Zondervan, 1990.

IMAGE CREDITS

The maps on pages x and xi (×2) © Baker Photo Archive.

Photo on page 168 © Alexey Goral / Wikimedia Commons, CC-by-sa-3.0.

Photo on page 218 © deror avi / Wikimedia Commons.

Photo on page 49 © Ed Brambley / Wikimedia Commons, CC-by-sa-3.0.

Photo on page 288 © Miko Stavrev / Wikimedia Commons, CC-by-sa-3.0.

Photo on page 334 © MrPanyGoff / Wikimedia Commons, CC-by-sa-3.0.

Photos on pages 55, 84, 93, 106, 139, 387, 395, 398 © The Yorck Project / Wikimedia Commons.

INDEX